TO SAVE THE UNION

Volunteers in the Civil War from

Centerville, Hume and Granger Townships

Allegany County

New York

Robert N. Colombo

HERITAGE BOOKS
2007

HERITAGE BOOKS
AN IMPRINT OF HERITAGE BOOKS, INC.

Books, CDs, and more—Worldwide

For our listing of thousands of titles see our website
at
www.HeritageBooks.com

Published 2007 by
HERITAGE BOOKS, INC.
Publishing Division
65 East Main Street
Westminster, Maryland 21157-5026

International Standard Book Number: 978-0-7884-4394-7

TABLE OF CONTENTS

ABBREVIATIONS

AC   - Army Corps
AWOL   - Absent Without Leave
B   - Born
Capt   - Captain
Cav.   - Cavalry
C.H.   - Court House
C-H-G   - Centerville-Hume-Granger Townships
Co.   - Company
Cos.   - Companies
Corp.   - Corporal
DC   - District of Columbia
DD   - Died of Disease
Fed.   - Federal
Ft.   - Fort
G.A.R.   - Grand Army of the Republic
G.H.   - General Hospital
HA   - Heavy Artillery
INA   - Information Not Available or not researched
INF   - Infantry
INJ.   - Injured
KIA   - Killed in Action
LA   - Light Artillery
Lt   - Lieutenant
MIA   - Missing in Action
MR   - Mounted Rifles
NYC   - New York City
NYS   - New York State
N/A   - Not Applicable
POW   - Prisoner of war
Pvt   - Private
QM   - Quarter Master
RR   - Railroad
Sgt   - Sergeant
SS   - Sharp Shooters
Twp.   - Township
US States   - Standard abbreviations are used for all States in the USA
Unk.   - Unknown
USGH   - United States General Hospital
VRC   - Veteran's Reserve Corps
Yrs   - Years

ACKNOWLEDGMENTS

Much of the information for this study was obtained from the Military and Pension Files of the Centerville-Hume-Granger soldiers, and other source documents, located in the National Archives in Washington, DC. All of the employees at the Archives were enormously helpful, courteous, knowledgeable, and competent in assisting me in my research. I am very grateful to them for their assistance. I am also very grateful to Edward S. Milligan LTC USA (ret). Without his thoughtful recommendations, there would have been no book. I also owe Ed and his friend Andrew Johnson, Past Commander in Chief, Sons of Union Veterans of the Civil War, a special thanks for reviewing a draft of the book.

Many other people were also extremely helpful. I especially want to thank all of those who took the time to locate and let me use pictures of their ancestors. They are identified by name below each relevant picture. Others provided me with family stories and history. They are recognized as a source following the appropriate soldier's summary. Thanks also go to Canadians Thomas Brooks and Joseph O'Neil for their information regarding Canadians who fought in the Civil War and for information on American Civil War soldier George Pitt, who settled in Canada after the war.

Finally, I want to thank those who constantly provided whatever support I needed at any particular time, and who constantly allowed me to bother them with none too bright questions. They include: Virginia Colombo Schroeder, Donald and Janet Thomas, R. Craig Mills, Bernard & Lousie Mills, Calvin & Arleen Carmer, William Smith, Loretta Blencowe, Jean Bailey Colombo, Merrill Nevinger; Hume Township Historian Rondus Miller, Allegany County Historian Craig Braak, Sharon Myers, Mary Colombo, Gary Nevinger, Ronald and Nancy Gillette, Betty Luckey, W. Richard Miller, Judy Fraser Hodnett, the Nunda Historical Society, and James Mowers and Darlene Williams Mowers. Jim graciously accompanied me on several research trips, helping me to both find my way and to find important information.

INTRODUCTION

This study is about volunteers, mostly from the Townships of Centerville, Hume, and Granger (C-H-G), Allegany County, New York, who participated in the War Between the States. It is not about the war. The war is addressed as necessary to put into historical context events impacting C-H-G soldiers. The study does attempt to identify all the C-H-G men who fought in the war. It identifies their families, where possible, where they fought, and what happened to them during and after the war. Numerous sources were used to identify the men. This study also looks at the Centerville - Hume - Granger area just prior to the war, based on the 1860 Federal Census, and just at the end of the war, based on the 1865 New York State Census.

A variety of sources identify a total of 689 men from the C-H-G area who served in the war. Of this number 27 turned out to be duplicates, or men who did not serve despite the source documents. Duplicates were primarily the result of significant different spellings of the last name or confusion regarding the man's first name. It appears that middle names were commonly used in lieu of actual first names in local documents, including censuses. However, in almost all cases, the military used the given first name. Forty names turned out to be soldiers who were not from the Centerville, Hume, Granger area. These men appeared in a source document because their enlistment was credited to one of the townships. The township paid the bounty the men received for enlisting or re-enlisting. Most likely the bounty (bonus) was paid by the township as a way of meeting the township's enlistment quota. For 42 other men, to date, no military files have been located. These men may or may not have served. Of the remaining 580, 507 have, through various documents, been proven to have lived in the townships of Centerville, Hume, or Granger area at some point during their lifetime. To date no documents have been identified directly showing that the other 73 men ever lived in those townships. There are documents that establish a connection to the C-H-G areas for these 73, such as military muster cards showing place of enlistment. Most, if not all, of these men were from areas adjacent to C-H-G and quite likely did live in one of the townships sometime during their lives.

The number of men serving in the various regiments, 606, exceeds the total number of men who served. This is because many men served in more than one regiment and are, therefore, included in the count for each regiment.

In the narrative, C-H-G refers to the townships unless otherwise noted. While many of the men's names are spelled differently in different source documents, I have tried to be consistent in the spelling throughout the narrative when discussing the same person. One regiment, the 1st New York Dragoons, started life as the 130th New York Infantry. For a short period of time it was also the 19th New York Cavalry. Its final designation was 1st New York Dragoons. I use 19th New York Cavalry when referring to the men of this regiment because, except for a handful of men, all of the men's personnel files (military and pension) at the National Archives are listed as 19th New York Cavalry. I also use volunteered, enrolled, and enlisted interchangeably. In many cases, the same date appears for enlisted/enrolled/volunteered and mustered although, in fact, most men enlisted/enrolled/volunteered on one date and then on a different later date were mustered. However, many of the military records have these events occurring the same day. Most men volunteered for service, although beginning in mid-1863 a few were drafted. A state is listed for all towns, cities, villages, counties, etc., except for those in New York State, and major U.S. cities.

Where there is contradictory information, and there is a lot, I have used the information that is most consistent, or that appears to make the most sense.

In most cases, the information is organized chronologically, year by year, with relevant battles organized by year. This approach is not for the purpose of discussing the progress of the war, but to sequence C-H-G soldiers' participation, and what happened to them.

It also permits one to see the cumulative effect of the war on the men and families of the C-H-G area. The battles are those in which the men participated, and in which they died, were captured or were wounded. Other C-H-G men died of diseases, with their units or as prisoners of war. Many others suffered various non-combat injuries, some quite serious. This approach allows one to view these men not only in the context of the war and its horrors and impact, but also in relationship to historical events in which they played a part. They were not only there when history was being made, they were helping to make it. Finally, the study points out how the lives of some men were effected by the actions of famous historical figures, both directly and indirectly. For instance, the famous Southern spy, Rose Greenhow negatively impacted the lives of C-H-G men, and others, of the 27th New York Infantry when she managed to get news to the South of the North's plans to attack at 1st Bull Run. The men also met some historic figures. At least two shook hands with Lincoln. Others attended his funeral. Many were present at the climax of the war, both at Appomattox Court House and at Bennett's House, at the surrenders of Generals Lee and Johnston respectively. The impact on the home front is also pointed out. Many wives became widows and many children lost their fathers. In a couple of cases widows married other soldiers, only to see their second husbands also die in the war.

Very little, if anything, of note happened during the war which did not involve at least one C-H-G soldier. They volunteered and were drafted, furnished substitutes, paid commutations, were killed in action, wounded in action, injured, died of disease, became prisoners of war, escaped from captivity, deserted, were court-martialed, were honorably and dishonorably discharged, were sick, fought in most major and minor battles, kept diaries and journals, visited historic places, went insane, served in experimental units such as the Balloon Corps, were present at the final surrenders, and marched in the grand parades in Washington, DC when it was over. Later they applied for the pensions awarded to veterans. Their history is the history of the war.

PREFACE

At 4:30 in the morning of April 12, 1861, Confederate batteries opened fire on the federal garrison, Fort Sumter, located in the harbor of Charleston, South Carolina. The War Between the States had officially begun.

Thirteen days later Stephen H. Draper became the first resident, in this case future resident, from the Centerville-Hume-Granger (C-H-G) area to volunteer and be mustered into a New York State (NYS) regiment. (The 1865 NYS Census for Centerville indicates that Milton S. Weaver volunteered April 19, 1861, for the 11th Illinois Infantry. However, the 11th Illinois was not organized until July 30, 1861. His military records show he joined the 11th Illinois July 30. He probably did volunteer prior to the 30th.) Draper enlisted in Company B of the 13th New York Infantry April 25, 1861. He was born in Gainesville and was a carpenter in civilian life. His grandparents were born in Scotland. He enlisted at Dansville, New York and was mustered as a private at Elmira on May 14, 1861. On January 1, 1862, he was promoted to corporal. During the March - April 1862 period he was detached as a hospital nurse, returning to Company B April 26, 1862. During May he was again on duty as a nurse. Draper was wounded in the head, spine and right hand on August 30, 1862 during the Second Battle of Bull Run at Manassas, Virginia. This was just one of the five times he was wounded or injured. He also served as a scout, guide and sharpshooter and was credited with running two locomotives out from enemy lines during the war according to the book, *Allegany & Its People*. The book also says that he is the scout mentioned in a history of the first battle of Bull Run. The history indicates that the scout brought in a "colored man" who was able to provide General Sherman with important information. Draper was discharged from the 13th Infantry May 13, 1863.

He then served with Co. K of the 21st Cavalry, apparently using the name Henry H. Draper. His military files for the 21st are listed under that name. He received his commission as a 2nd lieutenant while with the 21st. He was at, but apparently did not participate in, the Grand Review in Washington, D.C. on May 23, 1865. Special Order No. 288 issued by the Adjutant General Office, War Department at Washington on May 18, 1865, provides the following: "61. Under the provisions of General Orders No. 82, May 6, 1865, from this Office, 2nd Lieutenant Stephen H. Draper, 21st New York Cavalry, is hereby mustered out and honorably discharged from the service of the United States, to take effect May 15, 1865, on account of his service being no longer required. He will receive no final payments, until he has satisfied the Pay Department that he is not indebted to the Government. The vacancy created by this discharge will not be filled. By Order of the Secretary of War: E.D. Townsend, Assistant Adjutant General." Some documents indicate a later discharge.

In later life Draper worked as a day laborer, merchant, and pension attorney. On March 26, 1867, he married Ellen Burke. They had a son Frank. Draper lived in Rossburg and died there August 12, 1917. He is buried in Wiscoy.

(According to the book *Allegany & Its People*, the railroad community Rossburg was named after Mahlon L. Ross. Some sources indicate that Mahlon served in the Civil War. However, no military file for him has been found. The Federal Census indicates that Mahlon was 53 in 1860.)

Draper would be followed by at least 506 then current or future residents of the Centerville-Hume- Granger area. In addition, another 73 soldiers appear in some records as having been from the C-H-G area, but no evidence has been found that conclusively shows their direct attachment for at least some period of time to the area. (Some of the 73 men lived in townships that may have been part of Granger or Hume at the time the men enlisted. This includes, in particular, men from Portageville, Pike, and Allen.) Some appear to have belonged to the Granger Army of the Republic Post after the war, despite not living in Granger proper. Including these men, the total for the C-H-G area comes to 580. The enlistments of another 40 men from non C-H-G areas were credited to C-H-G. Most likely this was due to the C-H-G area paying the bounty these men received for enlisting or reenlisting in the military. Finally, there are some 42 names of individuals, with ties to the C-H-G area, which appear in at least one source document as having served in the war, but for whom no military or pension files have been located.

Of the 507 certain C-H-G soldiers, 121 lived in Centerville, 226 lived in Hume and 160 lived in Granger. In reality many of these men lived in more than one of the townships during their lives. The above numbers represent the jurisdiction they were associated with during the Civil War. There are census cites for 464 of these men. For 13 more there is documentation showing they were born in the area, and for another 21 there is documentation showing that they are buried in the area. (Many of the 464 were also born and/or buried in C-H-G.) For nine, information in their pension records shows that they lived for at least some period of their lives in the C-H-G area. Additional research may adjust the above numbers slightly.

The total of 580 known volunteers, including the 73 from near C-H-G areas, would serve in sixty-three New York State Army regiments and twenty-two non-New York State army regiments. One volunteer, Barzillia Weeks, served in the United States Navy on several ships including the *USS Tawah*, *USS Potomac*, *USS Kittatinny*, the *USS Great Western*, and the *USS Cincinnati*. Twenty-four of the volunteers would serve in 22 regiments from seven other states. Two served with regular Army regiments, James Bradshaw with the 2nd United States Cavalry and Edward Bezant with the 5th United States Artillery. The total number of "men" serving in these regiments comes to 606. This includes 26 men who served in more than one regiment, such as Draper, and are counted twice because this book contains information from both regiments in which they served. Several more men served in more than one regiment but data from these additional regiments has not been obtained for various reasons. Many men also served in the Veteran's Reserve Corps (VRC) after being wounded or suffering health problems. VRC regiments are also not included in the above figures.

Collectively these men participated in almost all of the major battles and campaigns and a significant number of the skirmishes of the war, especially those in the East. Most would participate in battles in Maryland and Virginia. Several men would serve in the Army of the West under General William T. Sherman, and would participate in his march to the sea. One would win the Medal of Honor.

The overwhelming majority of the men, 474, would serve in just 12 regiments. These included: the 4th New Heavy Artillery - 113; 1st New York Dragoons - 117 (originally the 130th New York Infantry, then the 19th New York Infantry, and finally the 1st New York Dragoons); 104th New York Infantry - 68; and the 85th New York Infantry - 53. The other units with 10 or more volunteers from the C-H-G area were: the 2nd New York Mounted Rifles - 20; the 5th New York Cavalry - 17; the 136th New York Infantry - 23; the 64th New York Infantry - 17; the 33rd New York Infantry - 12; the 160th New York Infantry - 10; the 184th New York Infantry - 12; and the 194th New York Infantry - 12.

THE HOME FRONT PRIOR TO THE WAR

The Federal Census of 1860 records 2,142 residents in the town of Hume, 1281 in Granger, and 1403 in Centerville. The village of Fillmore (part of Hume Township) was still known to many by its original name, Mouth of the Creek. The name had been officially changed in 1850 when the town fathers renamed the community Fillmore in honor of Millard Fillmore, 13th President of the United States, for the purpose of getting a post office located in the village. The effort had been successful and the first Fillmore Postmaster was Asgill S. Dudley. The village of Hume, part of Hume Township, and once known as Cold Creek, contained two churches, a saw mill, a grist mill, and some three hundred residents.

Interestingly, the military records of Joel William Bardwell indicate that he enlisted at Cold Creek (rather than Hume) in Company E of the 85th New York Infantry on September 1, 1861, as a private. Bardwell, the son of Harrison and Anna Smith Bardwell, was born October 20, 1829 in Granger. His grandfather and namesake, Joel Bardwell, was a famous lawman in the area and for years served as a deputy sheriff. Prior to the war young Joel was a day laborer. During the war he fought in, among others, the battles of Williamsville and Fair Oaks, where he was captured. After spending six months in Libby Prison in Richmond he was paroled. He was discharged November 13, 1862, suffering from diarrhea and diseases of the kidneys and bladder. He left the service as a third sergeant.

The 1860 Census lists 74 different occupations and 1,319 "employed" people in the C-H-G area. Both these numbers are slightly overstated in one sense and understated in another. The Centerville census taker, H. Darling, included occupational titles for elderly unemployed people calling them gentlemen and ladies. Additionally, both Darling and Philip D. Atwood, who was the census enumerator for both Hume and Granger, listed ministers by denominations as different occupations. The fact that Atwood did the census in both Hume and Granger, however, provides for a consistent comparison between those two jurisdictions. There are slight differences between Hume/Granger and Centerville. Besides the inclusion of gentlemen and ladies, Darling has a category called common laborer, which is most likely the same as Atwood's day laborer. Both listed law student as an occupation. Since many students became lawyers by working for another lawyer, it likely was their occupation. These, and two or three other possible exceptions, reduce the number of actual occupations in the three jurisdictions to about 65, and the total "employed" by about ten or fifteen. At the same time, occupations are not listed for everyone. Some of those people were clearly employed, most likely as either farmers or farm laborers. By including those for whom no occupation is listed, the number of employed would increase by one hundred or more.

Darling also listed six women as housekeepers. This is obviously a very low number. Atwood didn't list this category at all. Both listed domestic as an occupation, and it was a major occupation in the area with 39 domestics in Centerville, 35 in Hume, and nine in Granger. Almost all of the domestics were men.

Number of Occupations and Employed Workers

The census lists 23 different occupations, including house keepers, gentlemen and ladies, for

Centerville. This is the smallest number of total occupations among the three townships. Of the 327 people listed as employed in those occupations, 215 were farmers and 15 more were farm laborers. Another 12 were common laborers and 34 were domestics. Thus, 84% of the people in Centerville Township in 1860 were employed in only four different occupations.

For Granger, 38 different occupations are listed employing 320 people. Sixty-four of these were farm laborers, 158 were farmers, nine were domestics and eight were day laborers. Seventy-four percent of the employed workers in Granger were in those four occupations.

The data for Hume show 66 different occupations employing 671 people. Of those, 265 were farmers, 81 farm laborers, 39 day laborers, and 35 were domestics. Those four occupations accounted for 63% of the employed workers in Hume Township. Hume Township included the villages of Hume, Fillmore, and Wiscoy, plus balance of township.

Types of Occupations

Outside of farming, the Genesee Valley Canal almost surely provided the most jobs. This is reflected in job titles such as canal boatman, lock tender, and raftsman. It is also likely that many of the day/common laborers worked for the canal. Those types of workers are distinguished from farm laborers in the census, although many day laborers likely worked on the many farms in the area.

The day laborers may have also worked for the lumber industry, although there doesn't seem to be as many employees in that industry as one might expect, based on the history of the area. The census shows one lumber dealer, V.P. Peet of Fillmore (originally from Connecticut), one lumberman, and one lumber lawyer, Nelson Cook of Granger. There were also some eight sawyers. There may have been a few more. The penmanship in the Census is such that it is hard to distinguish between sawyers and lawyers.

Other titles such as blacksmith and harness maker, reflect ties to the farm industry. Most other jobs are the types that would exist in most communities - cooper, mason, machinist, millwright, dressmaker, basketmaker, shingle maker, seamstress, stone cutter, wheel wright, tailor, tailoress, molder, wagon maker, and shoemaker. Except for farmers, domestics, farm laborers, common/day laborers and teachers, shoemaker was the occupation with the most employees. There were also grocers, one each in Fillmore, Wiscoy, Centerville, and Granger. There were eight landlords, two lawyers, and two pedlars. Nellie Huckly of Fillmore, who was born in Ireland, listed herself as a washer woman.

Unique Occupations/Workers

Finally, there are some unique occupations or circumstances about occupations that one might not expect. Watch repairer is one. There was only one watch repairer in the area and it was a woman, Hariette Hunter of Wiscoy. Engineer is another. There were three, James Hensworth of Granger who worked for a sawmill, Joseph Hildreth of Mills Mills who worked for the railroad, and Hiram Palmer of Fillmore. Hensworth was born in Canada and Hildreth in Vermont.

There was only one gunsmith, I.M. Benson of Hume. There were three basket makers: Rufus Morse of Granger, age 48; Benjamin Mach, 60, of Fillmore; and 15 year old L.L. Hamilton of Fillmore, a woman. Basket making was not a lucrative job.

Two men are listed as proprietors of factories. William Mills, 62 of Wiscoy, was the proprietor of a wool factory. Joel Sherman, 63, was the proprietor of a stocking factory. Mills was born in New York and Sherman in Connecticut. The census also shows eleven factory operatives living in the hamlet of Mills Mills, most likely working in the stocking factory. Four of the eleven are living with Joel Sherman, including his 26-year-old daughter M.F. Sherman. Eight of the eleven are females. One of the males was 16 year old George E. Meach who was destined to win the Medal of Honor. Another was 26-year-old Mary Hart, born in Ireland, who became the great great-grandmother of Robert N. Colombo of Fillmore, the author of this study. Meach and Hart, among others, were living with blacksmith James Kearns, and Kearns was a next door neighbor of Sherman. Kearns volunteered for the military and would die during the war under unusual circumstances. The other women ranged in age from 15 to 18.

Only one operative is listed for Wiscoy, a Mr. Whitney, age 26. He listed himself as a furnace operative and probably worked in William Mill's wool factory.

There are three traders listed in the census. One, Alexander S. Dudley, 58, who was also a postmaster in Fillmore, listed real estate valued at $1000 and a personal estate valued at $300. Dudley was born in Connecticut. The other traders were William Keeler, 71, of Wiscoy and Samuel Burnell, 66, of Hume. Keeler had real estate valued at $1,000 and a personal estate valued at $2,000. The figures for Burnell were $1,500 and $1,000 respectively.

Wagon makers are worth mentioning. There are three listed. None of the three showed any real estate and only one, John Bullock, 24, of Granger listed personal estate valued at $200. Bullock served nine months with Co. A of the 184th New York Infantry and was honorably discharged on June 29, 1865. He fought in the battle of Cedar Creek and in operations against Peterburg and Richmond. His brother Eber died in the war. His father was David Bullock.

Alexander Kelsey Thorp, another of the wagon makers, served with, and helped to organize Co. F of the 130th New York Infantry (the 130th became the 19th New York Cavalry and later the 1st New York Dragoons). Alexander entered the service September 3, 1862, as a lieutenant. He was promoted to captain December 22, 1862, and died September 19, 1864, after being wounded at the battle of Winchester, VA He was born June 21, 1828, in Amherst, NY. On February 16, 1851, he was married to Mary E. Stewart, probably in Allen, by Justice of the Peace Luson Van Nostrand. J. W. Stewart and Louisa Daggett were witnesses. Their wedding certificate was a standard certificate which had been created, and apparently licensed according to an Act of Congress, by Mr. N. Currier of New York City. On the same day that Thorp was killed in action, George Meach captured the enemy's flag which earned him the Medal of Honor.

Francis Palmer of Hume, age 34, is listed as a publisher's agent. No additional information is available describing exactly what he was doing.

One of the most unique occupations was ambrotype artist. Five men: George W. Pitt, 25, and

Edmund Daggett, 32, of Granger; Edgar Snyder, 25, of Fillmore; D.B. Granger, 24, of Wiscoy; and Martin A. Bree, 33, of Hume Village were engaged in this occupation. Ambrotype was an early form of photography. The occupation does not appear to have been profitable with only Bree showing real estate of value and only Bree and Snyder showing any personal estate of value.

George W. Pitt would serve in the war. After the war he returned to Granger and worked as an artist for a short period before entering the watchmaking and jewelry business, first in Friendship and later in Cuba. In the early 1870's Pitt moved to New York City to work as a traveling jewelry salesman for H. Davis & Company. In 1876 the Company located him in London, Ontario Province, Canada. Two years later he opened his own watchmaking and jewelry business in London.

He became a leading citizen of the town helping to found London's Grand Army of the Potomac Post 652, "Hannibal Hamlin." He was also a member of the Independent Order of Foresters. While initially he lived in a poorer section of London, as his income grew he was able to move into the more prosperous areas of the town. He eventually lived a short distance from the family of movie actor Hume Cronyn. George had married Mary Lena Grant of Wellsville on May 18, 1869, and they had two daughters, Mamie and Maude. One of the daughters married into the locally well known and wealthy Darch family of London. George died April 21, 1921, at Victoria Hospital in London, just eight days after his 91st birthday. He was buried in the Darch family plot without a headstone. This was discovered by London residents planning a town celebration. Working with Civil War researchers and veteran organizations in the United States, in 2003 they managed to get the U.S. government to purchase a headstone for him.

Following is more detailed information on selected occupations.

Farmers and Farm Laborers

The occupation with the largest number of employees was "farmer", with 215 farmers in Centerville, 265 in Hume, and 158 in Granger. (Many men for whom no occupation is listed were likely farmers or farm laborers.) Farm laborer was the next largest group with 15 in Centerville, 81 in Hume and 64 in Granger. The most well-off farmer was Alanson Elmer of Wiscoy with real estate valued at $20,000 and a personal estate valued at $25,000.

School Teachers

The Census lists 34 school teachers (four in Centerville, 23 in Hume, and seven in Granger) and one school "professor" in Granger. All of the teachers except one, G.S. Alber who taught mathematics, were young females. The only other male was the professor, William H. Pitt of Granger. (William's two brothers, George and John, served in the War.)

Of the 23 teachers in Hume Township, seven taught in Fillmore including G.S. Alber. All but two, Sarah Palmer (21) of Michigan and Ruthan Smith of Vermont, were born in New York. Among the women, Lorette Calkins, Alvira Clark, and Clarinda Wilson were the oldest at 26. William Pitt was 28. Julie Benton was the youngest at 16. None of the teachers made much money. Only one, Delvina Claus, had real estate valued at $500, and a personal estate valued at $200. This most likely was because Delvina was also the head of house. G.S. Alber also listed a personal estate valued at $300.

Physicians/Surgeons

There were four physicians and seven physician-surgeons in the area. Centerville had one physician, Hume one physician and five physician-surgeons, and Granger, two physicians and two physician-surgeons. All of these men had personal estates valued from $200 to $7000. All but three had real estate valued from $200 to $1800. Their backgrounds varied. Of the 11, five were born in New York, four in Massachusetts, one in New Jersey, and one in England.

The book *History of Allegany County 1879* lists several other physicians for Hume over the years, but none of the men listed in the *History* appear in the 1860 Census as physicians or under any other occupation.

The two physicians in Granger were R.H. Smith, age 64, originally from Massachusetts, and William H. Ferns, age 30, born in New York. The physician-surgeons were William M. Smith, age 34, and Charles G. Anderson, age 26. Both were born in New York. Then as now, being a doctor was much more lucrative then being a school teacher, although age was, and is, a factor. Both Ferns and Anderson had no real estate, but had personal estates valued at $300 and $200 respectively. R. H. Smith had real estate valued at $1325 and a personal estate valued at $1000. The same figures for William M. Smith were $2000 and $1000.

William Mervale Smith had a distinguished Civil War career. He served from October 29, 1861, to June 17, 1863, as a physician-surgeon with the 85th and 103rd Infantries. Smith was born July 18, 1825, in Patterson, New Jersey, the son of Rueben and Orpha E. Van Blarcom Smith. His father was also a physician. He was active politically prior to the war and was a delegate to the 1860 Republican convention. He cast a vote for Lincoln to be the Republican nominee for President. Post war he eventually moved to Redlands, California and died there in 1902. The book *Swamp Doctor* is based on his Civil War diary. In the diary, among other things, he reflects on his frustration with the medical treatment, or non-treatment, of Civil War soldiers. He believed that poor treatment resulted in many unnecessary deaths.

For instance, Smith notes in his Monday, November 17, 1861, entry that, "I fear the conveniences for & management of the sick in that regiment (that regiment being the 130 NY Infantry, later the 19 NY Cavalry & still later the 1st NY Dragoons) is not what it should or might be . . ." Smith's entry was prompted by his visit to a neighbor and friend from back home, Aaron Van Nostrand, at the 130th Infantry's camp hospital. Van Nostrand died the night of November 20 per Smith's diary. (Van Nostrand's military records say he died November 19 of a fever.) Smith later tried to get the 130th's physician removed for incompetence but was unsuccessful. He believed that Van Nostrand's death was due to poor treatment.

Aaron Van Nostrand was born to Isaac & Grace Hatch Van Nostrand May 30, 1825, in Granger. He was 37 when he enlisted in the 130 NY Infantry on August 13, 1862. His wife Almira applied for his pension after his death. His brother Isaac also served with the 130th. Some source documents indicate that his brother William served, but no military file of William's service has

8

been located. Dr. Smith notes in his diary that Isaac was ill in the same hospital as Aaron at the time of Aaron's death.

Dentists

There were two dentists in the area, Darwin Barrows in Fillmore and Myron Miller in Granger. Both were young, 24 and 26 respectively, and both were born in New York. Neither reported any real estate. Barrow valued his personal estate at $60, and Miller valued his at $200. Millers' wife, Henrietta, was a school teacher. They were almost surely the first married "professional" couple in the area, although women teachers were not likely considered professionals at that time. Darwin served with Co. F, 4th New York Heavy Artillery and Myron served with Cos. E and G and as staff with the 85th New York Infantry. Darwin was killed in action at Petersburg, VA on October 4, 1864. He died one day after being shot. He is buried in Popular Grove National Cemetery at Petersburg, VA.

Myron, the son of Robert Miller and Jane Daggett, was born August 27, 1832 in Andover and enlisted September 1, 1861. His military file indicates he served as a hospital steward and was discharged April 6, 1862. He died June 6, 1873, of war related causes. He is buried in Short Tract.

Merchants

Ten merchants served the C-H-G area, three in Centerville, six in Hume (three in the Village of Fillmore, two in the Village of Hume, one in the balance of Hume Township), and one in Granger. Three of the merchants were Skiffs, Milton (age 49) and E.C. (age 38) in the Village of Hume and Alanson (age 52) in the Town of Hume. The most successful merchant was P.B. Whitbeck (age 44) of Fillmore, with real estate valued at $7,950 and a personal estate valued at $9,385. Milton Skiff was not far behind with real estate valued at $5,000 and a personal estate valued at $7,000. The least well off was S.A. Dorman of Fillmore who at the age of 24 listed a personal estate valued at $200. The other merchant was Charles Balcom (age 37) of Fillmore. All of the merchants were born in the state of New York except Richard Groves of Granger. Richard (age 45) was born in England and served in the war. His son and namesake died in the war. Centerville was served by Franklin Williams (age 25), Peter Cole (age 39), and Jeremiah Lamberson (age 35).

Ministers

The Census shows that the C-H-G area was served by five different churches, Baptist, Wesleyan, Presbyterian, Universal, and Methodist. Hume Village had four ministers, Granger three, Centerville two, and Wiscoy one. There was no Catholic Church in the area despite the presence of numerous Irish who had moved into the area to help build the Genesee Valley Canal. Catholics at this time traveled to Belfast for services, although upon occasion mass was also celebrated in private homes. Interestingly, John Whiteside, who had been born in Ireland, was a Methodist minister in Centerville.

It appears that ministers were paid modestly. All of them, except Willard Beardsley, a Baptist minister in Hume Village, claimed personal estates valued from $300 (John Trowbridge - a

Baptist minister in Hume Village whose son John, also a minister, served in the war), to $2,000, (James Bills, a Methodist minister in Wiscoy.)

Despite their personal estate holding, only five of the ten (Trowbridge; Alanson Bixby, a Wesleyan minister from Granger; John Whiteside; J.W. Lane, a Methodist minister from Centerville; and I. B. Sharp, a Universal minister from Hume Village) claimed any real estate holdings. The value of real estate holdings ranged from $200 (Bixby) to $1000 (Trowbridge).

Trowbridge's son John died during the war. When applying for his son's pension, Trowbridge claimed little real or personal estate of any value. He further claimed that his son had contributed to his support. He was supported in his claim by many members of his church. Documents in the pension file also appear to support his contention that his profession provided little income.

I. B. Sharp, according to the *History of Allegany County 1879*, organized the First Universalist Church of Hume on January 25, 1842. He would have been 30 at that time.

THE WAR - 1861 - EXCITEMENT & ENTHUSIASM

In July of 1861, Stephen Draper, the first man from the C-H-G area to volunteer, also became the first man "injured." The injury was minor, a bayonet cut of the wrist, and it was accidently self-inflicted. Draper would become a casualty four more times, twice with wounds and twice more with injuries.

Manassas, Virginia, First Battle of Bull Run, July 1861
(Also referred to as Centerville, Manassas and Manassas Junction.)

The battle of Manassas, the first major battle of the Civil War, took place July 21, 1861. Manassas was the site of two of the most important battles of the war. Only 30 miles from Washington, D.C., Manassas was located on one of the two key roads south out of Washington. One was the Washington - Richmond Road. The other was the Warrenton Turnpike. What really made Manassas so important, however, was the fact that two railroads, the Manassas Gap and the Orange and Alexandria, ran through the town. Both the North and the South placed the highest priority on controlling this junction. Bull Run was the river that ran through the area. The Confederacy won a decisive victory at 1st Bull Run.

Confederate Women Spies

The person who may have been most responsible for the Union defeat at 1st Bull Run was the Confederate spy, Rose O'Neal Greenhow, a prominent Washington hostess and confident, especially of South Carolina Senator John Caldwell Calhoun. Greenhow, who lived just across Lafayette Park from the White House, learned of the pending Union attack and managed to get the message, "Order issued for McDowell to move on Manassas tonight," to Confederate General P.G.T. Beauregard. Greenhow was eventually exposed and imprisoned in the Old Capitol Prison in D.C. She was subsequently deported to Richmond. Confederate President Jefferson Davis used her as a courier to Europe. There she continued to spy for the South, but when she returned in 1864 the ship she was on was captured near Cape Fear River, NC by Union forces. She escaped in a lifeboat just before the capture, but the boat overturned in heavy seas and she drowned, largely due to the $2,000 in gold she had hidden in her dress. Greenhow was just one of many women who spied for the Confederacy. Another famous Southern spy was Belle Boyd.

First Manassas is also famous for the comment made by Brigadier General Barnard Elliott Bee, who was mortally wounded during the battle. Just prior to being wounded he uttered the phrase "stood like a stone wall" that would immortalize Confederate General Thomas Jonathan Jackson. The problem is that historians still debate whether Bee meant Jackson was courageously standing like a stone wall against the advancing Union troops, or whether he was standing like a stone wall blocking Bee's troops desire to advance on the Union troops.

Presaging the future, hoards of noncombatants from Washington, DC and the surrounding areas traveled to the Manassas area to watch the battle live. Almost all expected a quick Union victory, bringing the entire war to an end. One Congressman, Alfred Ely of New York, managed to get himself captured by Confederate troops. The Congressman, elected originally in 1858, was not reelected for a third term in 1862. Today, via television, American citizens once again watch soldiers fight wars live.

At least six men from the C-H-G (Centerville-Hume-Granger) area participated in the first battle of Bull Run. All served with the 27th New York Infantry, also known as the "Union Regiment." At the time the 27th was part of the Army of Northeast Virginia.

The men included Jacob Darling Weaver, son of Ira Ransom and Cheney White Smith Weaver. He was born July 28, 1842, in Granger. Jacob served with I Company. After completing his service with the 27th, Jacob enlisted in the 1st New York Veteran Cavalry. He was captured March 14, 1864, at Snickers Gap, VA. He died in Andersonville Prison, Georgia on September 21, 1864.

Willis James Kendall, son of Clark and Roxanna Gilman Kendall, was born October 22, 1840 in Centerville. He enlisted May 13, 1861, in Company I at Angelica, entering as a first corporal. When he was honorably discharged two years later on May 31, 1863, he had risen to the rank of second lieutenant. He was sick in the White House, VA hospital during May and June of 1862. Kendall eventually moved to Denver and is buried there in Riverside Cemetery.

Justin Bingham, Jr. enlisted in Company I on May 13, 1861. His records indicate he was 43 years old, but actually was considerably older. In 1850 he was working in Eaton County, Michigan, although his wife was living in Hume. His age was given as 41. He also appears in the 1870 Census and his age is shown as 68. That is probably close to correct, making him 59 when he enlisted in 1861. When he received a disability discharge, less than a year after enlisting on March 18, 1862, his Doctor called him an old man. Nevertheless, Bingham was able to enlist in Company F, 9th Iowa Infantry on October 26, 1863, again giving his age as 43. He served until at least October 26, 1865, although some of his records indicate he deserted from a hospital in Little Rock, Arkansas on November 28, 1865. Justin died April 3, 1871, in Centerville. Bingham also has the unfortunate distinction of being the first C-H-G man wounded in battle. In his case it was a slight wound but given his age was probably quite painful! He was butted in the ribs with a rifle on July 21, 1861, at 1st Bull Run.

Also serving at 1st Bull Run were Everett Van Nostrand and Rawson Hultz. Rawson was the son of Richard and Mandana Hultz. He was born January of 1841 in Steuben County. He served in both the 27th New York Infantry and the 21st New York Cavalry. He was killed in action March 22, 1865, at White Post, Virginia while on a scouting mission. Several of his letters to his mother still exist. On December 22, 1862, he wrote his mother from White Oak Church, VA. He advised her that he intended to send her $30.00 and enclosed $15.00 in that letter. He was afraid to send it all at one time. He also reflected on the recent battle of Fredericksburg. He wrote, "We Mother are not in as good a condition as 's could wish. Our defeat at Fredericksburg was shameful to the credit of our generals but it is what we deserve for our own punishment & to open the eyes of the people & learn them to let the soldiers have there own officers." He went on to say that he was busy building shelters for the horses and that he was now driving a two horse ambulance, which was a lot easier than carrying a knapsack. He expressed concern for his mother's financial condition but went on to ask her to send him some things, or at least as much as she could. The "things" included butter, tea and chocolate cake. He ended by telling her his fingers were so cold he couldn't continue writing. Another letter in January expressed concern that he had not heard from her and that he had sent the other $15.00 in a letter dated 12/26/62. He also said he hadn't heard from his father. He asked her to send him postage stamps as he was unable to get any locally. The last letter is dated January 29, 1865. He warns his mother that he had little money, having not been paid. He had heard from his father who was working some but was unable to do a lot. He informed her that he was now in charge of his ninety man company; telling her, "I am doing the same work that the Government pays three commissioned officers for doing." He also asked her to thank Louise Thayer for sending him her picture. He told her not to worry because the Rebs "wont get me as long as I can fight" and if they do "you will heare of it soon enough." He finished by telling her that the band was playing, and it was the best band in the valley and keeps the men's spirits up. He was killed less than two months after writing that letter.

His father Richard was also a Civil War soldier. He served with Company H of the 50th New York Engineers. Born in Seneca County, he was 44 when he enlisted August 22, 1862, and was a carpenter and minister in civilian life. Richard received a disability discharge January 31, 1863, and died April 8, 1883, probably at Millport, Chemung County. The 1860 Federal Census shows him living in Hume Township with his wife and several children, but not Rawson. However, the Allegany County Town Clerk Register for Hume shows Rawson enlisting at Hume.

Everett Van Nostrand was born in Granger on January 15, 1840, to Luzon and Harriet Gilchrist Van Nostrand. He joined the 27th New York Infantry May 13, 1861, (he was attending school at Rushford) at the age of 21. He is reputed to be the first man from Granger to volunteer. Actually, he and Jacob Darling Weaver, also from Granger, volunteered the same day, and were mustered the same day, May 21, 1861. He spent most of the war as an attendant and nurse at Regimental Hospital. He was discharged May 31, 1863. In 1869 he married Prudence M. Smith. Post war, he became a druggist in Wellsville and died there January 24, 1935, one of Wellsville's most colorful and beloved figures according to his obituary. According to his obituary in the January 24, 1935 *Wellsville Daily Reporter*, Everett spoke of meeting President Lincoln following the 1st Battle of Bull Run. The obituary reported that Lincoln visited the "torn brigade" accompanied by his wife. Mrs. Lincoln was stirred by the long lines of tired men under a blazing sun with only small skull caps for protection. Van Nostrand told of how Mrs. Lincoln made the men hooded sun shades to wear over the caps. While the obituary does not indicate where the men met Lincoln, it is likely that it took place at Franklin Square, only a few blocks from the White House and the bivouac location for the 27th Infantry following 1st Bull Run. Franklin Square is discussed below.

It is also likely that Aaron H. Wright or Wight participated in 1st Bull Run. While his military records show "not stated" for roll call for the time period of the battle, he almost surely was present and fought in the battle. Aaron was 28 when he enlisted on May 13, 1861. The son of Lowell and Catherine Wright, he and his wife Julia Ann were the parents of at least two children. Aaron served the entire two years for which he volunteered, being mustered out July 31, 1863. During that time he was never wounded, captured, or sick. He was the company cook, which may have contributed to his health.

Frederick H. Dyer's *A Compendium of the War of the Rebellion - Part 3* provides the following information on the 27th New York Infantry:

Organized at Elmira, N. Y., May 21, 1861. Mustered in June 15, 1861, and left State for

Washington, D.C., July 10. Attached to Porter's Brigade, Hunter's Division, McDowell's Army of Northeast Virginia, to August, 1861. Heintzelman's Brigade, Division of the Potomac, to October, 1861. Slocum's Brigade, Franklin's Division, Army of the Potomac, to March, 1862. Slocum's 2nd Brigade, Franklin's 1st Division, 1st Army Corps, Army of the Potomac, to May, 1862. 2nd Brigade, 1st Division, 6th Army Corps, to May, 1863.

SERVICE.--Advance on Manassas, Va., July 16-21,1861. Battle of Bull Run, Va., July 21. Duty in the Defenses of Washington, D.C., till March, 1862. Expedition to Pohick Church October 3, 1861. Advance on Manassas, Va. , March 10-15, 1862. McDowell's advance on Fredricksburg April 4-12. Ordered to the Peninsula, Virginia, April 22. Siege of Yorktown, Va., April 24-May 4, <dy-1415> on transports. West Point May 7-8. Near Mechanicsville May 20. Seven days before Richmond June 25-July 1. Gaines' Mill and Chickahominy June 27. White Oak Swamp and Glendale June 30. Malvern Hill July 1. At Harrison's Landing till August 16. Movement to Fortress Monroe, thence to Centreville August 16-28. In works at Centreville August 28-31, and cover Pope's retreat to Fairfax Court House September 1. Maryland Campaign September 6-22. Crampton's Gap, South Mountain, September 14. Battle of Antietam September 16-17. Duty in Maryland till October 29. Movement to Falmouth, Va., October 29-November 19. Battle of Fredericksburg, Va., December 12-15. "Mud March" January 20-24, 1863. At Falmouth till April. Chancellorsville Canpaign April 27-May 6. Operations about Franklin's Crossing April 29-May 2. Maryes Heights, Fredericksburg, May 3. Salem Heights May 3-4. Banks' Ford May 4. Mustered out May 31, 1863, expiration of term. Three years' men transferred to 121st Regiment New York Infantry. Regiment lost during service 2 Officers and 72 Enlisted men killed and mortally wounded and 2 Officers and 70 Enlisted men by disease. Total 146.

At least six men from the C-H-G area served with the 27th Infantry at some time during the War. They were Justin Bingham, Jr., Rawsom B. Hultz, Willis James Kendall, Everett Van Nostrand, Jacob Darling Weaver, and Aaron H. Wright. One of the five men was WIA and sick and received a disability discharge. Two others were also sick during their service.

After 1st Bull Run, the battered "healthy" men of the 27th Infantry encamped at Franklin Square in DC The square is still prominent today, serving as, among other things, a pleasant park in which workers can relax on a nice spring, fall or summer day and enjoy their paper bag lunches.

Franklin Square

Franklin Square started life as a fresh water spring and a source of water for the White House. In 1898, during the Spanish-American War, fears that Spanish sympathizers would poison the waters caused the government to close down the spring. During the Civil War, in addition to being used by the 27 New York Infantry to regroup after 1st Bull Run, it was used as a camp ground by the 12th New York Infantry, and likely by others. The square is bordered by 13th Street on the east and 14th Street on the west. K Street is north of the square and I Street is on the south.

Pension Building

A little south and east of Franklin Square stands the Pension Building (bordered by 4th and 5th, and E and F Streets) which was completed in 1887 (although President Grover Cleveland held an inaugural ball there in 1885) and is the largest all brick building in the world. The dead, dying, and wounded from 1st Bull Run were brought to this site that was an open field at the time. After 1885 the 1st Bull Run survivors, as well as thousands of others, would apply here in person or through the mail to collect their Civil War pensions. To this day, rumors abound that many important Civil

War papers are inside the giant columns in the building. One rumor is that the missing pages of Edwin Booth's "diary," that was in the custody of Secretary of War Edwin McMasters Stanton after Booth's death, are inside one of the columns. Some believe that these missing pages contain information about the Lincoln assassination. One myth around Lincoln's death is that Stanton was involved in the assassination plot. To add to the intrigue, the Smithsonian Institution, which now owns the building, did drill a hole in one of the smaller columns and sent a camera inside for a look. There are papers in there, however, that was expected since the architect of the building, General Montgomery C. Meigs, believed that the columns would be excellent preservation spaces for important documents. It is known that a collection of maps, War Department records and a copper facsimile of the Declaration of Independence were enclosed in the columns. It is believed that Meigs filled more than twenty columns with important documents and newspapers of the time. Who knows what else is there. There are dozens of columns. (Most historians, however, believe that Booth himself tore the missing pages out of his "diary," which was actually more a note book than diary. There is no real evidence at all that Stanton was involved in the assassination plot.)

Following the debacle of first Manassas (1st Bull Run), the balance of 1861 was taken up primarily with organization and reassignment issues. President Lincoln removed General George B. McClellan from command of the Army of the West and put him in charge of the federal troops around Washington, D.C., which included organizing and equipping a major army in the DC area. In November of 1861, upon the retirement of General Winfield Scott, McClellan was appointed General-in-Chief of the Union Armies. However, due to his failure to act (he made no move to fight), in March of 1862 President Lincoln relieved him as Commander-in-Chief. He was left as head of the Department of the Potomac. Lincoln was not the only one to notice McClellan's reluctance to fight. In his diary (later the book *Swamp Doctor*), Dr. William M. Smith of Granger refers to McClellan several times, never favorably. His Monday, July 14, 1862, entry mentions that delays on the part of McClellan had enabled the Rebels to bring a large part of Stonewall Jackson's and Beauregard's forces to Richmond, and to sweep the Union army's right flank. It is interesting that Smith refers to Jackson as Stonewall Jackson. Jackson had only received his nickname a year earlier at 1st Bull Run, and yet it was already apparently common knowledge, not only among Southern forces, but Northern ones as well.

Plans for the war were being developed and discarded during this period. In December of 1861 and January of 1862 there were some minor military operations in Eastern Tennessee. In February of 1862 the battles of Forts Henry and Donelson took place. It does not appear that men from the C-H-G area participated in these battles, but the battles do mark the first major appearance in the war of General U.S. Grant. His actual name was Hiram Ulysses Grant, but he did not like the name Hiram and went by Ulysses. When he was nominated for West Point, the Congressman who recommending him couldn't remember his first name and thus nominated him as Ulysses Simpson (U.S.) Grant, Simpson being his Mother's maiden name.

The First To Die

Milton S. Weaver, the first C-H-G man to die in the war, died of typhoid fever on September 20, 1861. Weaver, the son of William Weaver and Rachael Lyon of Centerville, enlisted July 30, 1861, in Company A of the 11th Illinois Infantry at Freeport, Illinois. He was 21 years old and had been in the service only two months when he died in City Point, Virginia. Despite the fact that he was most likely born in Centerville (his brother James who also served was born in Centerville) and that his parents lived there, he was buried in Freeport, Illinois.

Irwin Vanbrunt was the second C-H-G volunteer to die in the war, and the first serving with a New York regiment, Company F of the 33rd New York Infantry. He died at Fort Ethan Allen of a "service related disease" on October 16, 1861. Irwin was the son of David Vanbrunt and Harriet Johnson. The 1860 Census shows him working for a James W. Fisk as a domestic. He was born in Centerville and was only 18 at the time of his death.

Frederick H. Dyer's *A Compendium of the War of the Rebellion - Part 3* provides the following information on the 33rd New York Infantry:

> 33rd Regiment Infantry - Ontario Regiment. Organized at Elmira, N. Y, and mustered in July 3, 1861, to date May 22, 1861. Moved to Washington, D. C., July 8. Attached to W. F. Smith's Brigade, Division of the Potomac, to October, 1861. 2nd Brigade, W. F. Smith's Division, Army of the Potomac, to March, 1862. 3rd Brigade, 2nd Division, 4th Army Corps, Army of the Potomac, to May, 1862. 3rd Brigade, 2nd Division, 6th Army Corps, to June, 1863.
> SERVICE.--Duty in the Defenses of Washington, D. C., till March, 1862. Advance on Manassas, Va., March 10-15, 1862. Embarked for the Peninsula, Va., March 23. Near Lee's Mills April 15. Siege of Yorktown April 5-May 4. Lee' Mills near Burnt Chimneys April 16. Battle of Williamsburg May 5. Storming of Fort Magruder. Mechanicsville May 23-24. Seven days before Richmond June 25-July 1. Gaines' Mill, Garnett's Farm, June 27. Garnett's and Golding's Farms June 28. Savage Station June 29. Wllite Oak Swamp and Glendale June 30. Malvern Hill.' July 1. At Harrison's Landing till August 16. Movement to Fortress Monroe, thence to Centreville August 16-28. In works at Centreville August 28-31, and cover Pope's retreat to Fairfax Court House September 1. Maryland Campaign September 6-22. Crampton's Pass, South Mountain, September 14. Battle of Antietam September 16-17. Duty in Maryland till October 29. Movement to Falmouth, Va., October 29-November 19. Battle of Fredericksburg, Va., December 12-15. "Mud March" January 20-24, 1863. At Falmouth till April 27 . Chancellorsville Campaign April 27-May 6. Operations about Franklin's Crossing April 29-May 2. Maryes Heights, Fredericksburg, May 3. Salem Heights May 3-4. Banks' Ford May 4. Three year men transferred to 49th Regiment, New York Infantry May 14. Mustered out June 2, 1863, expiration of term. Regiment lost during service 3 Officers and 44 Enlisted men killed and mortally wounded and 105 Enlisted men by disease. Total 152.

At least 12 C-H-G men served with the 33rd New York Infantry during the war. They were: Edwin Buchanan, Willard Eddy Calkins, Daniel Chillson, William Decordus Dodge, John Curdin Franklin, John Lafoy, George Morel Poole, Charles Wesley Poole, Hiram Robbins, Irwin Vanbrunt, Albert Watson, and Marvin Wilson. Of the 12 C-H-G men three were WIA, one was injured, four became POWs, and two died of disease. Two others were sick. Two received disability discharges. There is some overlap in these figures. For instance, Willard Calkins was WIA, injured, and a POW.

The last C-H-G casualty of 1861 was Wilmot E. Robbins, who died December 20, 1861, of congestion of the lungs caused by measles. Wilmot was born in 1842 in Centerville to Asa Robbins and Louisa C. Dow and enlisted August 30, 1861, in Company F of the 85th New York Infantry at Black Creek. He was home on furlough when he died and was buried in his uniform with his furlough and other military papers. He was 19 and had served a little less than four months. His brother Hiram O. Robbins also served.

By the end of 1861 the battle toll for C-H-G men was modest. No one had been killed in action and no one had been captured. Three men had died of diseases. One man, Justin Bingham, Jr. of Company I, 27 New York Infantry, had been wounded in action, and one man, Stephen Draper, had been accidently injured.

THE WAR - 1862 - MOSTLY CONFIDENCE, SOME REALITY

Eighteen sixty-two was not a day old when the first C-H-G soldier was injured. William H. Parks was thrown from his horse at Poolesville, MD Parks was born in Bradford, Pennsylvania around 1820. Actually no evidence has been located that he ever lived in C-H-G, although one source document claims he enlisted at Granger. His military records say he enlisted at Oramel. The 1860 Federal Census shows him living in Caneadea with his wife Mary. In March, William McHill (or Hill) of the 50th New York Engineers, injured his spine while helping to construct a bridge

In April Francis Gibbs Dodge was injured when he fell on his hip in Washington, DC Dodge, the son of Francis W. and Emily Scott Dodge, was born in Hume September 26, 1841. He first served with Company C, 104th New York Infantry enlisting October 21, 1861, at Genesee. Later he served with Company B, 2nd New York Mounted Rifles, enlisting December 17, 1863, at Hume.

Shiloh (Pittsburg Landing), Tennessee - April 1862

Shiloh was the first major battle in the state of Tennessee. The Federal troops, the Army of Tennessee, were headed by General Ulysses Grant, fresh from his initial triumphs at Forts Henry and Donelson. The battle and battlefield were named for a small log meeting house known as Shiloh Church. The Southern troops were led by General A.S. Johnston who was killed during the fighting. The Confederate troops held the higher ground above the Shiloh battlefield. While the Union "won" the battle, Shiloh is more famous for the poor generalship exhibited by commanders on both sides.

Non-New York State Regiments

At least twenty-four men from the C-H-G area served in 22 different regiments from seven states other than New York. One of these men was John Milton Skiff. John was born May 26, 1840 in Hume. He was the son of Joseph and Lidia Fitch Skiff. Prior to the war he had been a school teacher in Iowa. It is not certain why John was in Iowa, however, an ancestor of John's had fought in the War of 1812. Following that war the U.S. Government made land grants in Iowa and Illinois to veterans of the war. It is possible that John was in Iowa with relatives who received such a grant of land. The 1860 Federal Census shows him living with his parents in Hume. His parents were still living in Hume in 1865, according to the 1865 New York State Census. The census also shows a William Skiff, age 50, living in Newton, IA with his wife Abigail and son Vernon. William was possibly the brother of John's Father Joseph.

On May 22, 1861, Skiff enlisted in Company E of the 3rd Iowa Infantry as a corporal at Newton, Iowa. He was 21. On April 6, 1862, he was killed in the battle of Shiloh, and thus became the first C-H-G man to be killed in action. Originally he was buried on the Shiloh battlefield. Today he is buried in Section RG, grave number 394 at the Shiloh National Military Park.

In addition to John M. Skiff, C-H-G men who served in regiments from other states included, Justin Bingham, Jr. - Company F, 9th Iowa Infantry; John H. Boss, Jr. - Company E, 55th Ohio Infantry; William H. Cary - Co. I, 1st Wisconsin Infantry; John C. Crocker - Co. K, 82nd

Pennsylvania Infantry; John Daggett - Co. G, 4th Michigan Cavalry; Henry C. Doolittle - Co. K, 19th Ohio Infantry; Edwin S. Drury - Co. C, 4th Michigan Infantry; John C. Franklin - Cos. A and E, 1st Michigan Cavalry; Peter V. Granger - Co. D, 3rd Michigan Infantry; Jared A. Gorton, 4th Michigan Cavalry; David Grover - Co. A, 84th Ohio Infantry; Oscar R. Hildreth - Company D, 76th Pennsylvania Infantry; George H. Hotchkiss - Co. G, 7th Michigan Infantry; Arthur L. Ingham - Co. H, 94th Illinois Infantry; Joseph N. Ingham - Battery C, 1st Michigan Light Artillery; Charles Keeber - Co. C, 1st Michigan Sharp Shooters; Joseph Morris - 23rd Kentucky Infantry; Samuel B. Myers - Co. B, 154th Illinois Infantry; David Ratchford - Co. I, 108th Illinois Infantry; Augustus Sartar - Co. I, 147th Pennsylvania Infantry; Charles Van Nostrand - Co. D, 1st Michigan Engineers; Milton S. Weaver - Co. A, 11th Illinois Infantry; and John H. Welstead - Battery F, 1st Illinois Light Artillery.

Oliver J. Hopkins is not included in the above totals. He primarily served with the 19th New York Cavalry (1st Dragoons), but also served for short periods with Cos. E and C of the 16th Michigan Infantry and Co. I of the 1st Michigan Engineers and Mechanics.

Williamsburg, Virginia - May 5, 1862

The two-day battle of Williamsburg is significant to the Civil War history of C-H-G because it was the first time that a local volunteer was captured during the war. He was also the first C-H-G man wounded by gunfire, a shot to his right arm. According to descendants, Willard Calkins was with an advance group consisting of several companies who were chasing the Southern army as it voluntarily retreated from Yorktown. The purpose of the retreat was to form a defensive line around Richmond, but due to conditions created by a driving rain, the Northern army caught them at Williamsburg. It may have been during this period when Calkins, out front with the advance party, was captured. If so, it was a very short period of captivity. There is no evidence that he was ever in a Southern prison, and no personal documents of Calkins mention his capture. Documents in his service file however, one as late as October 3, 1878, report that he was captured.

Lt. Henry A. Hills of Co. F, in an affidavit 30 years later, when supporting Calkins application for a pension, wrote that the battle (in which Calkins was wounded) took place between three and four o'clock in the morning, "A brigade of rebs came out of Fort Magruder near Williamsburg, Va. and made an attack upon our line . . . " He went on to say that Calkins was the first man he had ever seen wounded by gunfire and that when Calkins saw the blood rushing down his arm he dropped his rifle.

Willard Eddy Calkins was born in Hume on September 13, 1835, to Hiram and Rhoda King Calkins. Hiram was born in Massachusetts per most contemporary documents, but descendants believe he was born in Painted Post, NY. Rhoda was born in Rhode Island. Prior to his enlistment Willard had been a raftsman, most likely working on the Genesee Valley Canal. He had enlisted May 13, 1861, at Nunda and had been mustered May 22, 1861, at Elmira into Company F of the 33rd New York Infantry. Following his wound, Calkins was absent from his regiment for about two months. However, by July he was back with his regiment and engaged in several more crucial battles. In January of 1863 he was injured. While cutting wood in the snow for his camp, he slipped on a snow covered, downed tree, fell against the tree and injured his back. This injury led to kidney problems which plagued him the rest of his life. He was discharged at the completion of his enlistment on June 2, 1863.

He returned to Hume Township and became a farmer. On March 26, 1865, he married Frances Ellen Smith in Castile. For a while they lived in Hume, but eventually he moved his family to Hansen, Idaho where he died April 25, 1914, and is buried in Twin Falls Cemetery, Twin Falls, ID.

Calkins was a crusty guy who engaged in some spirited exchanges with the pension bureau. In one letter he wrote that he suspected that the bureau thought he was a crank. He told them, "well I am a crank and the pension department needs a crank to turn them." Calling it presumptuous on his part, he nevertheless wrote to President Theodore Roosevelt complaining about the pension bureau. Roosevelt never knew how presumptuous. In another letter to the bureau, he had called Roosevelt "Ceasar." He also questioned the manhood of the Commissioner of the pension bureau.

C-H-G Prisoners of War (POW)

Calkins was the first of some 95 different men from the C-H-G area who were to be captured. Since three men were captured twice each, the total number of captures was 98. A little more than 65 percent of the 98, 65, were captured in 1864 and 27 of the 98, about 27 percent, were captured on one day, April 20, 1864, at Plymouth, North Carolina. All but one of the men captured at Plymouth were members of the 85th New York Infantry and most of those were from Company E. In addition to the 85th, there were eight other regiments that had more than one soldier from the C-H-G area captured during the war. They were the 104th New York Infantry - 15; the 4th New York Heavy Artillery - 11; the 19th New York Cavalry (1st New York Dragoons) - 9; the 5th New York Cavalry - 9; the 64th New York Infantry - 3; the 33rd New York Infantry - 4; the 2nd New York Mounted Rifles - 3; and the 1st New York Veteran Cavalry - 2.

In no other place, and in no other battle, were there anywhere near the number of men captured as occurred at Plymouth. The closest was the battle of Ream's Station on August 25, 1864. Eight C-H-G men were captured that day, all members of Company F of the 4th New York Heavy Artillery. During July 1- 3, 1863, seven local men were captured at Gettysburg. All of those captured at Gettysburg served with Company E of the 104th New York Infantry.

Deaths of POWs, Where and Why

Of the 95 C-H-G individual volunteers who ended up as prisoners of war (POW), 35 died in prison. Over half of those (18) died at Andersonville, Georgia. Six more died at Richmond, Virginia prisons - (Libby & Belle Island), seven at Salisbury, North Carolina, three at Florence, South Carolina and one at Charleston, South Carolina. Due to poor, destroyed, and lost records there is some question as to whether some of these men actually died at the prison listed in their military records. This is true especially for Florence, Charleston, and Salisbury prisons.

Of the 35 men who died in prison (one actually died while in transport between prisons), 23 died of just four diseases; sixteen died of diarrhea and dysentery, four died of starvation, and three died of scorbutus. The others died of debility, pneumonia, bronchitis, and typhoid fever. Despite the various causes cited it is likely that starvation, poor food, and unclean water were the root causes of many of the deaths. For seven men no cause of death appears in the records.

One man, Daniel Wight of Company F of the 5th New York Cavalry, died July 20, 1864, of wounds received at the Battle of Ream's Station on June 30, 1864. While he died in prison, for purposes of this study he is treated as killed in action. Sadly, Edwin Wight of Company F of the 19th New York Cavalry and Daniel's brother, also died in the war. He was killed near Centerville, Virginia on October 17, 1864.

Paroles

At the start of the war, neither the North nor the South had facilities for a large number of prisoners. Further, it is likely that neither side foresaw the massive numbers of captives with which they eventually had to deal. As a result, they quickly adopted the European system of parole, or prisoner exchange. Under this system, prisoners were exchanged for someone of equal rank. There were exceptions to this rule, however. It was determined that 60 privates were equal to one general. The captives were generally set free within ten days after giving their word that they would not take up arms against their captors until a formal exchange had been completed. Initially, freed prisoners waited near their commands for the necessary paperwork to be completed. Later, some went home.

The system became unworkable rather quickly, primarily because of the numbers. The paper work involved became enormous, expensive and time consuming. Less ethical soldiers allowed themselves to be captured so that they could go home while awaiting the official exchange. Some just never returned to their units once they were released. Both sides were concerned that paroled prisoners were being used for non-combative duties, which freed up other soldiers to fight. Engaging in combat before the official exchange was not "legally" permitted under this "honor" system. When the North set up detention camps for parolees, there was extreme anger among the troops. The camps were hot beds for dishonest soldiers and were not properly maintained, lacking nutritious and sufficient food and clean facilities.

It also became apparent to Northern authorities that for the South, by 1863, paroled soldiers were the primary source of maintaining troop strengths, manpower being more plentiful in the North than in the South. General Grant strongly opposed the system. In April of 1863 Grant ordered the exchanges stopped, although the exchange of sick prisoners was re-instituted in early 1865. From the records it appears that some exchanges continued even after Grant's order.

Deaths, Killed in Action and Died of Disease

Disease was a major factor in this war. More men died of diseases than died in battle. Many more were incapacitated for extended periods of time due to various diseases. For the 15 regiments containing the most C-H-G men, total casualties for the regiments (not just C-H-G men) were 1,547 killed in action and 2,026 died of diseases. One interesting thing is that 81 officers and 1,466 men were killed in action. That appears to be a reasonable ratio. However, for men who died of diseases, only 25 were officers versus 2,001 enlisted men.

For volunteers from the C-H-G area, a total of 49 died in battle either immediately or shortly thereafter from wounds received in battle. One died in prison from his battle wounds. This compares to a total of 99 who died of diseases. In addition one man drowned and another died of an overdose of morphine. The military claimed it was self administered, which is at least debatable. In addition to those who died of diseases, there were at least 199 other cases of reported sicknesses. A few men spent their entire service in hospitals. Twenty-seven of the 99, (which includes POWs) died of diarrhea and dysentery, twenty-nine from typhoid fever and remittent fever, four from scurvy, and three from small pox. The others died of many different diseases. (The records for 14 men do not indicate the actual disease. Those records simply say "service related disease," so the numbers for at least some of the specific diseases listed above are not complete. Half of the men for whom no specific disease is listed died in prison. More than 35 percent of the men who died of diseases died in prison.

An additional 21 men died within ten years after returning home from the war. A minimum of eleven of them died of service related causes. Four of the eleven had received disability discharges.

Looked at another way, a total of 580 men from the C-H-G area or nearby area served. Of these, 49 died in battle, or shortly thereafter, from wounds received in battle, including one man who died of battle wounds in prison. Another 99 died of various diseases. One man drowned, another died of morphine. That means that 150 of the 580 men, or close to 30 percent of the men from the area, died during their service. An even larger number were wounded, or injured, or had health problems. Many of these received disability discharges. And this is without even considering the mental impact the war had on these men. While no data exists with respect to men who suffered mental problems, the lives of some men indicate they may have suffered from such problems. Those who survived the war intact, mentally and physically, were few and far between.

Chandler W. Warn of Company D, 4th New York Heavy Artillery drowned in the Potomac River. Chandler was the son of David H. Warn and Clarissa A. Robbins. He was born February 28, 1844, in Hume. Prior to enlisting in Company D, 4th New York Heavy Artillery on August 13, 1862, at Rochester, he was a farmer according to his military records. More then likely, he was a farm laborer, probably working for his father. He drowned while bathing in the Potomac River near Chain Bridge, a bridge (though rebuilt) that still exists. The Potomac River is famous for its strong undercurrent and Chandler is just one of many who have been caught in that current over the years.

The spot near Chain Bridge is especially interesting as it is the location of the curse of the Three Sisters. The sisters were Indian maidens who attempted to cross the Potomac on a raft to avenge the slaughter of their beaus, who had been murdered by another tribe. The bodies of the beaus, according to the legend, were thrown into the Potomac River near Chain Bridge. The sisters, caught in the dangerous currents near Chain Bridge, were unable to make it across. They decided to jump to their deaths to join their boyfriends in the river. But before doing so, they pronounced a curse. No one would ever be able to cross the Potomac at the point where they had failed. The next morning three rocks appeared at the spot where the sisters jumped into the river. The rocks have been there ever since. The "curse" continues to this day and anyone foolish enough to challenge the currents in that area merely adds to the legend of the sisters.

Chandler's parents applied for a pension, but were denied on the basis of his death not being in the line of duty. The pension board, in making this decision, apparently ignored the position of Warn's Commanding Officer, Captain G.M. Ingalls. Ingalls wrote a nice letter to Warn's parents following the drowning. He explained what had happened, the efforts they had made to save Chandler, and finished by saying that "he had died in service to his country." The Captain also advised that the date of death was September 6. Warn's military files show September 7. His body was never found. He was 18 years old and had only been in the service 24 days.

Warrenton, Virginia

On May 24, 1862, Flavel Ruthvan Palmer (some records say Ruthvan Flavel) was severely injured near Warrenton, Virginia. Palmer was on picket duty when a tree fell on him, hitting him in the left shoulder and breaking his clavicle. He was born December 15, 1831, in Centerville to William Palmer and Elaine Knickerbocker. Prior to the war he had attended Leland Seminary in Vermont, the birthplace of his father. His mother was born in Connecticut. He volunteered October 9, 1861, and was assigned to Company C, 104th New York Infantry. Due to his injury, he received a disability discharge from Carver General Hospital in Washington, DC on September 25, 1862. Palmer was first married on August 5, 1854, to Cynthia Angeline Kellogg in Warsaw, New York. Cynthia died March 31, 1893, and Flavel married Salinda Mason Frye March 30, 1895. After Salinda died in 1913, he married Jane Kate Phillips in 1914. He died December 11, 1919 in Oramel.

Hanover Court House, Hanover, Virginia, May 27, 1862

This battle took place just prior to the major confrontation at Fair Oaks. Two local men were wounded at Hanover, George V. Hill and Horatio A. Smith, both members of the 44th New York Infantry. Hill was born in Hornell, March 1843, to Franklin Hill and Louisa Goltia. He enlisted August 20, 1861, probably at Hume (file doesn't say where). A letter in his pension file says he was living in Wiscoy at the time. At Hanover he suffered a flesh wound to the head from an exploding shell. He was also wounded July 1, 1862, in a skirmish at Malvern Hill, Virginia. Despite his combat record his pension request was denied. The military carried him as a deserter.

Horatio Smith was wounded by a gunshot to his left arm at Hanover on the 27th. He would be killed in action three months later at the 2nd Battle of Bull Run.

Frederick H. Dyer's *A Compendium of the War of the Rebellion - Part 3* provides the following information on the 44th New York Infantry:

44th Regiment Infantry - "People's Ellsworth Regiment." Organized at Albany, N. Y., and mustered in August 30, 1861. Moved to Washington, D.C., October 21,1861. Attached to Butterfield's Brigade, Fitz-John Porter's Division, Army of the Potomac, to March, 1862. Butterfield's 3rd Brigade, Porter's 1st Division, 3rd Army Corps, Army of the Potomac, to May, 1862. 3rd Brigade, 1st Division, 5th Army Corps, to October,1864.
SERVICE.--Duty in the Defenses of Washington, D. C., till March, 1862. Advance on Manassas, Va., March 10-15. Moved to the Peninsula, Va., March 22-24. Reconnaissance to Big Bethel March 30. Warwick Road April15. Siege of Yorktown April5-May 4. Reconnaissance up the Pamunkey May 10. New Bridge May 24. Battle of Hanover Court House May 27. Operations near Hanover Court House May 27-29. Seven days before Richmond June 25-July 1. Battles of Mechanicsville June 26. Gaines' Mill June 27. White Oak Swamp and Turkey Bend June 30. Malvern Hill July 1. At Harrison's Landing till August 16. .,

Movement to Fortress Monroe, thence to Centreville August 16-28. Pope's Campaign in Northern Virginia August 28-September 2. Battle of Bull Run August 30. Maryland Campaign September 6-22. Battle of Antietam September 16-17. Shepherdstown September 19. At Sharpsburg, Md., till October 30. Movement to Falmouth, Va., October 30-November 19. Battle of Fredericksburg, Va., December 12-15. Expedition to Richards and Ellis Fords, Rappahannock River, December 29-30."Mud March" January 20-24, 1863. At Falmouth till April27 . Chancellorsville Campaign April27-May 6. Battle of Chancellorsville May 1-5. Aldie June 17. Middleburg and Upperville June 21. Battle of Gettysburg, Pa. , July 1-4. Pursuit of Lee July 5-24. Duty at Warrenton, Beverly Ford and Culpepper till October. Bristoe Campaign October 9-22. Advance to line of the Rappahannock November 7-8. Rappahannock Station November 7. Mine Run Campaign November 26- December 2. At Beverly Ford till May, 1864. Campaign from the Rapidan to the James May 3-June 15. Battles of the Wilderness May 5-7; Laurel Hill May 8; Spottsylvania May 8-12; Spottsylvania Court House May 12-21. Assault on the Salient May 12. North Anna River May 23-26. Jericho Ford May 23. On line of the Pamunkey May 26-28. Totopotomoy May 28-31. Cold Harbor June 1-12. Bethesda Ch~cp June 1-3. Before Petersburg June 16-18. Siege of Petersburg June 16 to October 11, 1864. Six Mile House, Weldon Railroad August 18-21. Poplar Springs Church, Peeble's Farm, September 29-October 2. Mustered out October 11,1864. Recruits transferred to 140th and 146th Regiments New York Infantry. Regiment lost during service 4 Officers and 178 Enlisted men killed and mortally wounded and 2 Officers and 145. Enlisted men by disease. Total329.

At least five C-H-G men served with the 44th New York Infantry. They were: James Andrew Boardman, Hugh Gallagher, John Madison Hammond, Jr., George V. Hill, and Horatio Augustus Smith.

Two of the five C-H-G men who served with the 44th were killed in action, another died of disease, five were wounded in action, and one became a prisoner of war. Obviously, some men suffered more than one casualty, but each man was a casualty at least once during his service.

Fair Oaks (Seven Pines), Virginia, May 31, 1862

In this battle, a Union victory, Confederate forces lost some 5,000 men while the Union lost 4,000. It is hard to feel victorious after losing 4,000 men. The battle produced no strategic victory for the North. It actually had a more long lasting and, most would say, positive effect for the South. The Southern Commander, General Joseph E. Johnston, was seriously wounded, and was replaced by General Robert E. Lee as the Commander of Northern Virginia.

Five men from C-H-G were killed in action. Four of them died on the battlefield on May 31 - June 1. One died on June 3 from wounds received May 31. The five men were: John Edmonds, Richard Groves, Ezra H. Kendall, Jefferson Osborn, and Myron Standish. All, except Richard Groves, were members of Company D of the 64th New York Infantry. In addition to those killed in action, seven C-H-G men were wounded and three were captured.

John Edmonds , born in January of 1840, was the son of Rowland Edmonds and Elizabeth Jones of Centerville. He enlisted September 13, 1861, at Rushford in Company D. He was killed May 31, 1862, at age 22, and was buried at Fair Oaks, Virginia.

Richard David Groves, born 1841 in England, was the son of Richard and Olivia Groves of Granger. While no occupation is listed for him in the 1860 Census, his father was a merchant and it is likely he was working for his father. He enlisted September 1, 1861, at Granger in Company E of the 85th New York Infantry. Several of Richard's letters survive. On January 2, 1862, he wrote both his mother and his sister from Washington. His letters were optimistic. Everything was fine and he expected the war to be over by April. He expressed sorrow at missing Christmas and not seeing the Christmas tree. The weather was very warm and he had been sunning himself on Meriden Hill (still a famous DC location) just prior to writing. He asked his sister how come their father had allowed her to go to a dance. He also mentioned that they were required to wear "leather collars." (This is interesting in that Groves was Army Infantry. The military branch famous for leather collars is the Marines. In fact, it is why the Marines are nicknamed Leathernecks.) His letters reflect great fondness for his family. In a footnote to a sister in the letter to his mother he told her to, "Give my love to Rebeca and Grace. Tell them to carry a pocket handkerchief in their pockets and wipe their noses when they get dirty." He jokingly told his mother to tell his father to be a good boy, and drew two funny faces above his signature.

On May 8 Richard wrote what may have been his final letter. The letter, written at a camp near Williamsburg, perfectly reflects both the confidence that the soldiers still had and the growing reality of the horrors of war. It reads:

Dear Mother. I fancy I can see you anxiously enquireing for a letter after what stiring news you must have heard. You must not blame your boy for want of affection in not writing to his parents before. I did write to you the day before York town was evacuated. The morning of the following day. We were called in hot pursuit of the rebles and have been on forced marches ever since with the exception of the time we have been drawn up in the line of battle. We were called out one evening before the enemy fled, and marched through the woods untill we passed the last of our pickets. We advanced a few rods farther when crack, crack, crack, went the rebels rifles. Our Colonel gave the order to cover ourselves behind trees, and fier as fast as we could see a man to aim at. The guns cracked lively for a few moments but the rebles soon fell back under cover of their rifle pits, where we dared not follow them. None of our regiment were injured for the reason that we were on much the lower ground which caused them to shoot several feet over our heads. One of 56th N.Y. Reg't. had one poor soldier caried back to camp mortally wounded. This is the first day we have had to rest for sometime. I took a walk this afternoon over the battle field of last Monday. They are burying our dead and bringing in the wounded now. Though they have been doing thier best meny poor fellows have had to lay on the ground untill today. The rebles are not buried yet. They lay scattered all over the ground blackening and bloated in the sun. I saw one who was shot in the back with a cannon ball. It passed through his vitles and came through his breast. His heart was thrown in his face. So they lay all over the field and through the woods shot and torn in every shape. There was sickening stench in the air. The most of the dead rebles are young, but large good looking men. I could not help but pitty them. No one to give them a burial of any kind untill they become black and offensive. They have lain over tow days and nights on the field exposed to the flies and sun of a southern clime. They are meny of our own men in the same condition though they are burying them as fast as possible. 35 of our own soldiers were put in one pile ready for one burial to day and there are graves on row of graves to be seen in every direction. There are 160 wounded rebles in a couple of barns here. Our doctors have been waiting on them. Many of them have had thier legs taken off. I went there this morning. Outside of the door there was a pile of bloody legs were they were thrown by the doctors as they were cut off. Our doctors use them well. You must not be uneasy about me. I do not know why it is, but I have always had a presentment that I should live to see the close of this war uninjured, and I think I shall. But let that be as it may, the sight I have seen to day showed me how nessay it is that a soldier should be prepared to die; and I shall endeavor to live accordingly. Remember we are in the hands of God; and though dangers are thick in our path, none of us can die unless it is his will. And the will of God, though it should afflict us, we should respect and bare without a mumer. We are looking for a speedy close to the war. I think in one month more all the heavy fighting will be over. When it does close then the soldiers will have a mery mery time. None but the soldier can realize the meaning of the word peace. In the one word when spoken in the United States what joy it will be for thousands. You must write to me often, for I am often disappointed when the mail is brought for our company. That was my picture in with the blankets. I had it taken in Elmira to send to Father, but it was so poor that scarcely eny of the boys knew who it was. So I did not send it home on that account. Tell Father he will find 30 dollars in Angelica at C Dutremonts from me. Give him my love also the girls. I do not know when I shall be able to send this letter. It will take a long time for it to go through. Our mail has to be caried so far before it gets to eny office. I cannot tell where we will go from here, but I think it will be toward Richmond. It is likely we shall follow the reble army wherever it goes we shall go. I am very tough now. There is scersely a man in the regiment who has been sick as little has myself. Each of us have a little tent of our own which we have to cary on our backs, besides our blankets, cloths, rations, gun and 40 rounds of catrizes. This through Virginia mud a foot and ofter two feet deep, sometimes in a drenching rain makes a pretty good load. It is generally after a days march of this kind that soldiers are called into action. My paper is almost full. I must close soon. Tell Father i would be thankfull if he would be so kind as to send me a paper once a week. Remember me to all enquirening friends of old Allegany. Tell them I hope to be with them soon. Your Most Affect Son R.D. Groves.

Richard was killed May 31, 1862. Dr. William M. Smith mentioned Richard's funeral, which he attended on June 29, 1863, in his diary (book - *Swamp Doctor*). He wrote that, "Richard fell near the close of the struggle at the front of Casey's Line, just as the 85th was compelled to fall back before the overwhelming numbers of the rebels ---- he was always a willing soldier in the discharge of his duties and proved himself in this terrible battle a cool, brave man."

George Washington Pitt, who was with Groves at Fair Oaks and was wounded, wrote two letters to Grove's father telling him what had happened. He promised to do all he could to return the body home. He was successful, as indicated by the remarks in Dr. Smith diary. Pitt was the son of Professor William Pitt of Dorchester, England (who was also the son of a William Pitt) and Elizabeth Vincent, and is discussed in the 1860 Federal Census section above. In addition to his wounds at Fair Oaks (gunshot to left foot and knee), he was captured at Plymouth, North Carolina on April 20, 1864, which was his birthday.

Ezra Hiram Kendall, age 26 at the time of his death, was born in Centerville to Clark Rufus Kendall and Roxanna Gilman. On October 13, 1859, he married Eliza Rachael Pratt and they had a daughter Eliza Freemont Kendall. Prior to the war he was a farmer. He enlisted September 14, 1861, at Rushford. He was killed in action on June 1, 1862, at Fair Oaks. While this battle was fought May 31, and June 1, 1862, all five men from the C-H-G area were killed or wounded in the battle on June 1. Kendall was originally buried at Fair Oaks, however, there is now a headstone for him in Centerville, indicating that his body was shipped home at some point. His brother, Ferris Enoch Kendall, also died in the war. Ferris was born November 30, 1837, in Centerville. He enlisted August 9, 1862, at Centerville in Company F of the 130th New York Infantry (19th New York Cavalry - 1st New York Dragoons) and was mustered at Portage, August 19, 1862. He entered the service as a third sergeant and was a 2nd lieutenant at the time of his death. He was captured October 25, 1863, at Morristown, Virginia , and died in Rushford of service related typhoid fever on March 26, 1865.

Ezra and Ferris Kendall were one of nine pairs of brothers from the C-H-G area who died in the war. The others were Andrew and Elias Andrews, Augustus A. and Sidney Chase, David and Robert T. Lockwood, Emerson M. and Jefferson M. Parker, David and Elisha Prior, John M. and Stephen M. Skiff, Aaron and Issac Van Nostrand, and Daniel and Edwin Wight.

Jefferson Osborn enlisted September 13, 1861, at Rushford. He was mustered September 24,

1861, at Elmira into Company D. He had been born in 1838 in Centerville to Oramel and Caroline Osborn, according to the Allegany County Town Clerk Register. However, the 1850 Census shows his parents as Oramel and Lydia Ann Osborn. His name is recorded as Thomas J. Assuming the 1850 Federal Census is correct, his name was most likely Thomas Jefferson Osborn. This would have been consistent with the practice of the day of naming children after Presidents of the United States. For some reason, however, his military records are under the name Jefferson. It was common practice to call children by their middle names. Nevertheless, when they entered the service the military usually used their correct first names, which in this case would have been Thomas. The name Thomas is not found in either his military or pension file. On December 28, 1858, he married Sarah E. Hagg in Rushford. The 1860 Census lists his occupation as farmer. He was killed in action June 1, 1862, at Fair Oaks and is buried there, according to his military file.

Myron M. Standish was born November 17, 1837, to Ira Standish and Laura Berman. On October 2, 1861, he enlisted in Company D, 64 New York Infantry at Rushford. Prior to the war he was a gunsmith, according to the Allegany County Town Clerk Register. On August 18, 1860, he married Eunice M. Isted. Standish was wounded by gunshot on June 1, 1862, at Fair Oaks and died June 3, 1862, in White House, Virginia. He was 25.

In addition to the five men killed in action, as mentioned above, three C-H-G men were captured and six others, in addition to Standish, were wounded. Joel William Bardwell, Josiah L. Keith, and Jefferson Myron Parker were all captured on May 31. Michael Collins, David Prior, Orin N. Standish, Edwin R. Meabon, George Washington Pitt, and Thomas J. Thorp were wounded on June 1. Pitt and Prior are discussed elsewhere in this study. Bardwell, also discussed elsewhere, was imprisoned at Libby Prison in Richmond, Virginia and survived the war. Post war he worked as a laborer, a bartender, and in a hardware store. He died November 16, 1923, in Elmira, the city where he had been mustered into the service on October 26, 1861.

Keith was in three prisons - Florence and Charleston, South Carolina and Andersonville, Georgia. He too survived the war but suffered from scurvy and was partially deaf. He became an oil driller after the war and died in Holgate, Ohio on February 23, 1914. Jefferson Myron Parker was in Libby Prison. He had been born September 24, 1837, in Granger to Ira Parker and Polly Rosina Smith. His brother Erland also served. He was a boatman on the canal prior to the war. He died in prison on July 23, 1862.

Michael Collins was born in Mallin Town, County Donegal, Ireland most likely around 1815. He married Catherine Gallagher January 12, 1834, and their first child Elizabeth was born in 1835. On October 16, 1861, he enlisted in Company F, 85th New York Infantry at Granger and was wounded in the left hip by a shell at Fair Oaks on June 1, 1862. He died December 17, 1882.

Edwin P. Meabon was born in Erie County, Pennsylvania in 1840. He enlisted in Company E, 85th New York Infantry October 10, 1861. He was wounded in the left leg by gunfire at Fair Oaks. He died October 18, 1906, at the Hospital for the Insane in Spencer, West Virginia.

Orin Nelson Standish was wounded by a gunshot to the left hand at Fair Oaks. Born May 8, 1834, in South Bristol, New York; he was the son of Ira Standish and Laura Berman. He enlisted

October 5, 1861, at Rushford in Company D, 64th New York Infantry. His brothers Gideon and Myron also served, with Myron dying at the Battle of Five Forks, Virginia. Orin died August 5, 1897.

Thomas James Thorp was one of the organizers of Company E, 85th New York Infantry. He enlisted September 1, 1861, and was discharged August 20, 1862. On August 27, 1862, he joined Company C of the 19th New York Cavalry (1st NY Dragoons). On May 31, 1862, at Fair Oaks he was wounded in both the left thigh and below the left knee. Entering the service as a captain on September 1, 1861, he was ultimately discharged as a colonel. On October 14, 1865, Thorp was promoted to brevet brigadier general. Brevet is an honorary rank and is generally awarded for gallant and meritorious service. He was born in May of 1837 to Montgomery and Bethiah Thorp. On September 9, 1862, he married Mandana C. Major in Portage. After the war they moved to Corvallis, Oregon where he died August 25, 1915.

Thorp is mentioned several times in Dr. William M. Smith's diary (book - *Swamp Doctor*). Some comments indicate that Smith did not think highly of Thorp. On Thursday, November 27, 1862, he wrote that he dined with Thorp at a "sumptuous" Thanksgiving day dinner at the 85th Infantry officer's mess. At that time the 85th was at a camp somewhere north of Franklin, Virginia. On April 3, 1863, Smith attended the theater in Norfolk where he ran into Thorp and his wife. Earlier that day he had met a friend, James Cook of Granger, and Thorp had been a topic of their conversation. In his diary he wrote that Cook, "tells me that Thorp continues to indulge very freely in strong drink – on one occasion --- he was so intoxicated that he could not get from the town (Suffolk) to his camp, his horse came into camp without him, and he returned the next morning, though his wife was waiting him at the camp." By this time Thorp was with the 19th New York Cavalry. (First Dragoons). There is some confusion about this diary entry. The James Cook he mentions appears to be James C. Cook of Company I, 19th New York Cavalry (1st Dragoons). There is no other James Cook with the 19th who would have been in a position to relate the story about Thorp to Smith. The problem is, that James C. Cook died of chronic diarrhea in Baltimore on January 30, 1863, and could not have been in Norfolk on April 3. Maybe there was another James Cook, or maybe Smith remembered his conversation with the 19th Regiment Cook when making his April 3 entries, and simply recorded the conversation then, rather than when it had actually taken place. There were other James Cooks in the war, but James C. is the only one who served with the 19th. James C. Cook was not from Granger, but from Burns, a little way from Granger. Since the Burns Cook was a pedlar, he most likely was frequently in Granger.

On the other hand, Colonel Alfred Gibbs, in a letter dated August 28, 1864, described Thorp as "one of the best officers in the service." Gibbs also claimed that Thorp was wounded four times. Thorp's files only document two wounds. Thorp was captured at Trevillian Station on June 11, 1864.

Famous Names

Numerous C-H-G Civil War soldiers were named after Presidents or other famous persons. Soldiers so named included George Washington Babcock, Martin Van Buren Babcock, Daniel Webster Blake, Thomas Jefferson Curtis, Henry Clay Dresser, William Henry Harrison Keyes, DeWitt Clinton Nye, Andrew Jackson Oakley, Walter Scott Parsons, and others. By far the most popular name was George Washington, but Andrew Jackson and William Henry Harrison were also popular.

Frederick H. Dyer's *A Compendium of the War of the Rebellion - Part 3* provides the following information on the 64th New York Infantry:

64th Regiment Infantry (Cattaraugus Regiment). Organized at Elmira, N. Y., September 10 to December 10, 1861. Left State for Washington, D.C., December 10, 1861. Attached to Casey's Provisional Division, Army of the Potomac, to January, 1862. Howard's Brigade, Sumner's Division. Army of the Potomac, to March 1862. 1st Brigade, 1st Division 2nd Army Corps, Army of the Potomac, to June, 1862. 3rd Brigade, 1st Division, 2nd Anrmy Corps, to August, 1862. 1st Brigade, 1st Division, 2nd Army Corps, to April, 1863. 4th Brigade, 1st Division, 2nd Army Corps, to July, 1865.
SERVICE.--Duty in the Defenses of Washington, D.C., till March. 1865. Advance on Manassas, Va., March 10-15. Ordered to the Peninsula, Virginia, March. Siege of Yorktown April 16-May 4. Battle of Fair Oaks or Seven Pines May 31-June 1. Seven days before Richmond June 25-July 1. Battles of Gaines' Mill June 27. Peach Orchard and Savage Station June 29. White Oak Swamp Bridge and Glendale June 30. Malvern Hill July 1. At Harrison's Landing till ~ August 16. Moved to Fort Monroe, thence to Alexandria and Centreville August 16-30. Cover retreat of Pope's army to Washington, D.C., August 31-September 2. Maryland Campaign September 6-22. Battle of Antietam September 16-17. At Harper's Ferry, W. Va., September 22 to October 29. Reconnaissance to Charlestown October 16-17. Advance up Loudoun Valley and movement to Falmouth, Va., October 29-November 17. Battle of Fredericksburg, Va., December 12-15. Duty at Falmouth till April 27, 1863. "Mud March" January 20-24. Chancellorsville Campaign April 27- May 6. Battle of Chancellorsville May 1-5. Gettysburg (Pa.) Campaign June 11-July 24. Battle of Gettysburg, Pa., July 1-4. Pursuit of Lee July 5-24. Duty on line of the Rappahannock till October. Advance from the Rappahannock to the Rapidan September 13-17. Bristoe Campaign October 9-22. Auburn and Bristoe October 14. Advance to line of the Rappahannock November 7-8. Mine Run Campaign November 26-December 2. At and near Stevensburg, Va. till May, 1864. Demonstration on the Rapidan February 6- 7. Campaign from the Rapidan to the James May 3-June 15. Battles of the Wilderness May 5-7. Spottsylvania May 8-12. Po River May 10. Spottsylvania Court House May 12-21. Assault on the Salient, or "Bloody Angle," May 12. North Anna River May 23-26. On line of the Pamunkey May 26-28. Totopotomoy May 28-31. Cold Harbor June 1-12. Before Petersburg June 16-18. Siege of Petersburg June 16, 1864, to April 2, 1865. Jerusalem Plank Road June 22-23, 1864. Demonstration north of the James July 27-29. Deep Bottom July 27-28. Demonstration north of the James August 13-20. Strawberry Plains, Deep Bottom, August 14-18. Ream's Station August 25. Reconnaissance to Hatcher's Run December 9-10. Dabney's Mills, Hatcher's Run, February 5-7, 1865. Watkins' House March 25, Appomattox Campaign March 28-April 9. Hatcher's Run or Boydton Road March 29-31. White Oak Road March 31. Sutherland Station and fall of Petersburg April 2. Sailor's Creek April 6. High Bridge and Farmville April 7. Appomattox Court House April 9. Surrender of Lee and his army. Moved to Washington, D.C., May 2-12. Grand Review May 23. Mustered out July 14, 1865. Regiment lost during service 13 Officers and 160 Enlisted men killed and mortally wounded and 5 Officers and 114 Enlisted men by disease. Total 292.

At least 17 C-H-G men served with the 64th Infantry. They were: Daniel Webster Blake, Chauncey Abram Cronk, Chester Boughton Cronk, Stephen S. Davis. Alonzo Almeron Disbrow, John Edmonds, Henry L. Hotchkiss, Ezra Hiram Kendall, Leander Millspaugh, Jefferson Osborn, David Prior, Elisha Prior, Vernon Patrick Smith, Benjamin Swezy Snider, Myron M. Standish, Orin Nelson Standish, and Lewis Wright.

Of the 17 C-H-G men in the 64th, fourteen became casualties: five were killed in action, seven were wounded (one twice), one was injured, three became prisoners of war, and two died of disease. (Some men suffered more than one casualty.) In addition, two who received disability discharges died at home before the end of the war. Four others also received disability discharges. At least eight of the men, other than those who died of disease, were sick at some time during the war.

The Seven Days Battles, Virginia, June-July, 1862

The Peninsula Campaign consisted of a number of significant battles, including the seven days battles. These battles followed the siege of Yorktown (April 4 to May 3) and a major two-day engagement at Williamsburg. They occurred over a period of seven days, but each battle has so many names it would appear they took place over a period of several months. Actually the battles were: June 26 at Mechanicsville (also known as Meadow Bridge, Ellison's Mill, and Beaver Dam Creek); June 27 - 28 at Gaines Mill (also known as First Cold Harbor, and Chickahominy Bluffs); June 27 - 28 at Garnett's Farm (also known as Golding's Farm); June 29 at Savage Station; June 29 at Peach Orchard (also known as Allen's Farm); June 30 at White Oak Swamp (also known as Glendale, Freezers Farm, Nelson's Farm, Turkey Bridge or Bend, Charles City Crossroads, and Newmarket Cross Road), and July 1 at Malvern Hill (also known as Harrison's Landing, Crew's Farm and Poindexter's Farm). The C-H-G area suffered three casualties during the seven days - one dead and two wounded.

Amos Frank Drew was injured just prior to the start of the seven days battles. On June 7, 1862, Drew injured the lumbar region of his back while helping to build a bridge near Catlett's Station, Virginia. Drew would suffer two more injuries prior to the end of the war. The son of Nathaniel Drew and Sally Nichols, Drew was born in Warsaw August 22, 1825. By at least 1860 he was living in Hume. Initially he volunteered for Company F, 4th New York Heavy Artillery. He was with the 4th when he was injured at Catlett's Station. After being discharged January 13, 1863, he volunteered for Company C, 104th New York Infantry. While with the 104th, his hearing was affected during the battle at Spotsylvania on May 16, 1864. A little over a month later, June 18, 1864, at Petersburg he suffered a gunshot wound to his left thigh. Drew married his cousin Hannah A. Drew in Portage June 14, 1853. While they lived in the Hume area for a couple of years following his discharge, they eventually moved to Michigan where Drew died October 16, 1905.

Zenas Bradley, Company F, 104th New York Infantry was also injured at Catlett's Station on July 3. He injured his right side attempting to jump across a small stream. The embankment gave way as he jumped and he fell on his equipment. That same month he suffered a sunstroke. Bradley was primarily from Allen Township, although numerous documents in his pension file indicate that he lived in Granger during the 1870's. His son Charles Nathan Bradley also served and starved to death at Libby Prison in Richmond. Zenas was 44 when he enlisted January 29, 1862. His military file lists him as a mechanic, but more likely he was a farmer. He was born in St. Albans, Franklin County, Vermont about 1818 and married Mary White July 16, 1832, in Bethany, New York. He received a disability discharge from the 104th October 4, 1862. On October 3, 1864, he enlisted in the 16th Veteran's Reserve Corps serving in Companies A and B. Returning from a ten-day leave April 27, 1865, he was on a cow train that was in a severe accident while crossing a bridge that collapsed at Painted Post, New York. His right leg and hip were injured. Zenas was killed May 29, 1880 when a tree fell on him.

Omar W. Fuller, Company F, 4th New York Heavy Artillery, was injured in June or July of 1862. He hurt his back and hip lifting green logs while helping to build a "bomb" proof barracks near the famous Chain Bridge in Washington, DC Fuller was born in Hamburg, Erie county, New York

May 7, 1829, to William H. Fuller and Mary W. Blackmer. He married Eliza G. Guptill September 29, 1852, and in 1860 they were living with Eliza's family in Short Tract. After the war he was a farmer in Granger and died there September 26, 1900.

The C-H-G man killed (died of wounds) during the seven days battle was John Hammond, Jr. Ironically, he was wounded on the last day of these battles, July 1, at Malvern Hill. Hammond, Jr. was the son of John Madison Hammond and Elisa Ann Gillett. He was born June 4, 1842, in Hume. A single man, he enlisted August 19, 1861, at Hume and was mustered August 30, 1861, at Albany, Albany County into Company B of the 44th New York Infantry. He died July 2 of his wounds. He was 20. While John Jr. had no children, there was a John Hammond living in Fillmore for at least 100 years. As late as the 1950's an elderly John Hammond was one of the most colorful people in town.

One of the men wounded during the seven days was George V. Hill of the 44th New York Infantry. Hill was wounded July 1 at Malvern Hill, only a few days after having been wounded at Hanover Court House. In a skirmish during the battle, Hill tripped over a log and ruptured the veins in his right leg. Despite his wounds and his participation in several battles, including Hanover Court House, the siege of Yorktown, Gaines Mill, and Malvern Hill, he was denied a pension. This was because the Army carried him as a deserter. He failed to return from a furlough and was dropped from his regiment's roles as a deserter October 3, 1862.

The other man wounded was Hugh Gallagher, Companies B and C, 44th New York Infantry. Gallagher received a gunshot wound to a knee. He was captured at 2nd Bull Run.

Elisha Prior was captured June 30, 1862, at Savage Station. Born in Pennsylvania, he had enlisted October 11,1861, at Rushford, at age 18, in Company D of the 64th New York Infantry. He died April 6,1864, in Caneadea of service related diseases, including hepatitis. There is no evidence, as yet, showing that Elisa ever lived in the C-H-G area, although his parents were living in Hume in 1865 per the 1865 New York State Census. His brother David also died during the war.

Monitor and Merrimack

During this same seven day period the final epic battle between the *C.S.A. Virginia*, formerly the *USS Merrimack*, and the *USS Monitor* took place. The first engagement between the two ironclads occurred March 9 with the *C.S.A. Virginia* forced to withdraw due to a falling tide. On May 11 the *C.S.A. Virginia* was destroyed by the South when Confederate troops were forced to abandon Norfolk, VA. This opened the James River to Union forces.

It appears that only one man from the C-H-G area served in the Navy. He was, as previously mentioned, Barzillai R.Weeks who enlisted September 1, 1864, at Erie. He was born in New York, was married to Charlotte A. Buck in Hermitage, Wyoming County, and was a farmer prewar. He served on at least four ships, the *USS Tawah*, the *USS Great Western*, the *USS Cincinnati*, and the *USS Potomac*. While aboard the *USS Tawah*, he participated in the battle of Johnson Mills. The *Tawah* was lost during the battle and Barzillai was transferred to the *USS Great Western* and then to the *USS Cincinnati*. The *USS Cincinnati* operated in the Mississippi Sound and Mobile Bay areas for the balance of the war. Barzillai was discharged September 13, 1865, as the Master of Arms, the highest ranking noncommissioned officer aboard a ship. He died in Hume on November 23, 1893.

Orange County Court House, Virginia, August 2, 1862

In early August of 1862 the 5th Cavalry took part in a battle near the Orange County Court House. The basement of the Court House was used as a Southern arsenal. The area is famous historically for more than the Civil War. Just outside of Orange is Montpelier, the home of the fourth president of the United States, James Madison. Both Madison and his equally famous wife, Dolley, are buried there. Dolley lived her later years in the "Dolley Madison House" on the north east corner of Lafayette Park, across from the White House. To this day, there are people who claim that they have seen Dolley in her rocking chair on her front porch during pleasant summer evenings. Montpelier was later owned by the Dupont's who actually built a railroad station there so that the train would stop at the plantation. Dupont left Montpelier to his daughter, who at one time was married to the movie star Randolph Scott. General Robert E. Lee and his troops camped just outside of town during the 1863-64 winter.

Three C-H-G residents, John S. Trowbridge, Eugene M. Pratt, and Henry C. Browne were captured at the Orange County Court House on August 2. Trowbridge would be killed in less than a year at Hanover, Pennsylvania.

Henry C. Browne was born August 29, 1839, in Norfolk, St. Lawrence County. (The name is spelled Brown in many documents, but in documents which he personally signed, he spelled it Browne.) Prior to the war he was a harness maker. He enlisted August 17, 1861, at Cuba at age 22 in Company E of the 5th New York Cavalry. During his service he was a saddler. Post war he was a prominent citizen in Hume where he owned the hotel Ingham House, was a Master of Oriona Lodge, F.A.M., and a charter member and First Commander of Burnside G.A.R. (Grand Army of the Republic) Post 237 of Hume. On April 11, 1866, he married Melinda Price who died in 1890. Browne then married Ruthem T. Smith on November 22, 1892. He died June 7, 1907, in Belfast and is buried at Pine Grove Cemetery in Fillmore.

On August 7, 1862, the battle of Fort Fillmore was fought in New Mexico. No one from the C-H-G area participated in this battle.

In August 1862 Elisha O. Perkins, Company C, 104th New York Infantry, injured his spine by just lying on his back. He had come down with a fistula which caused a partial loss of sight. He was being shipped from Falls Church, Virginia to the District of Columbia on a flat bed railroad car. After he was placed on his back on board the train, it began to rain. The train departure was held up several hours, and all of this time he was on his back on the flat bed car in the rain unable to move. The son of Elisha and Mary Orswell Perkins, he volunteered November 20, 1861. The injury resulted in his discharge less than a year later on October 15, 1862. There is conflicting information about his birth. His military file says he was born in Allegany County. His discharge papers say Barnard, Vermont which is probably correct. By 1860 he was living in Centerville with his wife Clarissa Haskins and their two children. Clarissa died in 1869. He eventually moved to Michigan and there married a divorcee, Caroline Lucinda Humphrey Watrous.

Cedar Mountain and the 2nd Battle of Bull Run, Virginia, June-September, 1862

In late June of 1862 the Army of Virginia was created by President Lincoln. It was this Army that was to fight the battles of Cedar Mountain and 2nd Bull Run.

The battle of Cedar Mountain (also known as Slaughter Mountain, Southwest Mountain, Cedar Run, and Mitchell's Station) took place August 9, 1862. The 2nd battle of Bull Run was fought August 29-30, 1862, and is the first battle in which significant numbers of men from the C-H-G area participated. The 104th New York Infantry fought in this battle. Some 68 men from the C-H-G area served with the 104th. Thirty-nine of the men served in Company C, fifteen in Company F, six in Company E, six in Company A, and two in Company B. The 104th was to participate in many of the most famous battles of the war, including Antietam, Fredericksburg, Gettysburg, and the Wilderness.

Dyer's *Compendium of the War of the Rebellion, Part 3* provides the following information on the 104th Infantry:

104th Regiment Infantry ("Wadsworth guards" "Livingston County Regiment"). Organized in Geneseo, N. Y., October, 1861, to March, 1862. Left State for Washington, D.C., March 22,1862. Attached to Wadsworth's Command, Military District of Washington, to May, 1862. 2nd Brigade, 2nd Division, Dept. of the Rappahannock, to June, 1862. 1st Brigade, 2nd Division, 3rd Corps, Pope's Army of Virginia, to September, 1862. 1st Brigade, 2nd Division, 1st Army Corps, Army of the Potomac, to March, 1864. 1st Brigade, 2nd Division, 5th Army Corps, to June, 1864. 1st Brigade, 3rd Division, 5th Army Corps, to August, 1864. 2nd Brigade, 3rd Division, 5th Army Brigade, 3rd Division, 5th Army Corps, to May, 1865. 2nd Brigade, 3rd Division, 5th Army Corps, to July, 1865.
SERVICE.--Duty in the Defenses of Washington, D.C., till May, 1862., Expedition to Front Royal, Va., to intercept Jackson, May 28-June 1. Picket duty on the Shenandoah and at Front Royal till June 10. Duty at Catlett's Station, Warrenton and Waterloo, Va., till August. Battle of Cedar Creek August 9. Pope's Campaign in Northern Virginia August 16-September 2. Fords of the Rappahannock August 21-23. Thoroughfare Gap August 28. Groveton August 29. Bull Run August 30. Chantilly September 1. Maryland Campaign September 6-22. Battles of South Mountain September 14; Antietam September 16-17. Duty near Sharpsburg till October 30. Movement to Falmouth, Va., October 30-November 19. Battle of Fredericksburg, Va., December 12-15. At Falmouth and Belle Plains till April 27, 1863. "Mud March" January 20-24. Chancellorsville Campaign April 27-May 6. Operations at Fitzhugh's Crossing April 29-May 2. Battle of Chancellorsville May 2-5. Gettysburg (Pa.) Campaign June 11- July 24. Battle of Gettysburg, Pa., July 1-3. Pursuit of Lee July 5-24. Duty on line of the Rappahannock and Rapidan till October. Bristoe Campaign October 9-22. Advance to line of the Rappahannock November 7-8. Mine Run Campaign November 26-December 2. Demonstration on the Rapidan February 6-7, 1864. Campaign from the Rapidan to the James May 3-June 15. Battles of the Wilderness May 5-7; Laurel Hill May 8; Spottsylvania May 8-12; Spottsylvania Court House May 12-21. Assault on the Salient May 12. North Anna River May 23-26. Jericho Ford May 23. On line of the Pamunkey May 26-28. Totopotomoy May 28-31. Cold Harbor June 1-12. Bethesda Church June 1-3. White Oak Swamp June 13. Before Petersburg June 16-18. Siege of Petersburg June 16, 1864, to April 2, 1865. Mine Explosion, Petersburg, July 30, 1864 (Reserve). Weldon Railroad August 18-21. Reconnaissance toward Dinwiddie Court House September 15. Warren's Raid on Weldon Railroad December 7-12. Dabney's Mills, Hatcher's Run, February 5-7,1865. Appomattox Campaign March 28-April 9. Lewis Farm, near Gravelly Run, March 29. White Oak Road March 31. Five Forks April 1. Fall of Petersburg April 2. Pursuit of Lee April 3-9. Appomattox Court House April 9. Surrender of Lee and his army. Moved to Washington, D.C., May 1-12. Grand Review May 23. Duty at Washington till July. Mustered out July 17,1865. Regiment lost during service 5 Officers and 81 Enlisted men killed and mortally wounded and 2 Officers and 145 Enlisted men by disease. Total 233.

At least 68 C-H-G men served with the 104th Infantry. They were: Henry Lyman Abbey, James Harvey Aikin, Rennsalear Allen, Andrew Judson Andrews, Jesse Bennett, Samuel Bennett, Noble Bolton, Thomas W.E. Boss, Zenas Bradley, William H. Brownell, Maurice Buckingham, Rozell, Butterfield, Yost Cain, Andrew Clark, Daniel J. Clark, George Nathan Clark, Andrew W. Cooley, George E. Coolidge, John Henry Crowell, Oliver Theodore Crowell, William Henry Culver, Thomas Jefferson Curtis, Charles Seymour Daley, William Henry Daley, William L. Davis, Francis Gibbs Dodge, Orrin Marshall Dow, Amos Frank Drew, John Drew, Oscar Peter Emery, George W. Flint, Eli Gardner, Jasper M. Griggs, Patrick Haley, John D. Hall, Ira W. Higby, Ephraim Bolivar Higby, Henry C. Hoadley, William Hussong, Festus G. Lafoy, Francis S. Lincoln, Hugh McElroy, John Peck Myers, Flavel Ruthvan Palmer, Francis Palmer, Elisha Ogilvie Perkins, John Samuel Pitt, Edwin Chester Poole, William Henry Rich, Wilson C. Robbins, Marshall James Rogers, Adonirana Judson Rose, Charles Williams Snyder, David E. Tadder, William Wallace Thurston, George Trall, Ralph R. Van Aikin, Alfred Philip Van Dresser, Almon Benton Van Dresser, Lewis Cass Veazey, Strong Warner Veazey, William Wallace, George Westbrook, W. Amarcus Whaley, John Wiederight, Emery M. Wood, David Youngs, and William W. Youngs.

Eight of the C-H-G men serving with the 104th Infantry were killed in action, 27 were wounded in action, 11 died of various diseases, 15 were captured and eight suffered various injuries. These figures represent 46 different men, since some were both wounded and captured, or some other combination. Another 16 men were sick at one time or another. This means that almost 70 percent of the 68 C-H-G men who served with the 104th were casualties of one sort or another. Almost twelve percent of them died in the war. The 104th served from January of 1862 until the war's end and was in many of the major engagements. The toll of combat is evident in the fact that although all but one of the 68 men were with the regiment at the start, only four, William Brownell, Yost Cain, John H. Crowell, and John Pitt, were present with the regiment at Appomattox Court House at Lee's surrender. A total of eight likely marched in the Grand Review. One, Adonirana J. Rose, was court-martialed which is discussed later. A staggering 28 received disability discharges, including one man, George Flint, who died of disease at home prior to the end of the war and is included in the eleven who died of disease. These are in addition to the eight killed in action.

No C-H-G men were killed or captured during the battle of Cedar Mountain. This would not be true for 2nd Bull Run. Three local men were killed in action on August 30, three were wounded, and one was captured. The men killed were John Claus, John Drew, and Horatio Smith. The man captured was Hugh Gallagher. Regiments that fought in this battle, and which contained C-H-G men, included the 104th New York Infantry, the 5th New York Cavalry, and the 44th New York Infantry.

John W. Claus, carried by the military as John W. Closs, was born January 7, 1842, in Hume to William Claus and Lucinda Klock. Prior to the war he was a farm laborer. He enlisted at Hume on September 13, 1861, in Company F, 5th New York Cavalry, also known as the 1st Ira Harris Guard, and was killed in action at 2nd Bull Run on August 29, 1862, at age 20. He was buried on the battlefield, a common practice.

John Drew enlisted in Company C, 104th New York Infantry on December 30, 1861, at Geneseo, New York. At the time of his enlistment he was a farm laborer. He was born in September of 1835 to Hiram Drew and Anna Hopkins in Orangeville, Wyoming County. In 1850 they were living in

Canaedea. He was killed in action on September 30, 1862, and was originally buried on the battlefield. He eventually was moved, and is now buried at Arlington National Cemetery. He was 27 at his death. The Allegany County list of men killed in service that is read on Decoration Day credits Drew to Hume Township. However, no information has yet been found showing that he ever resided in that township.

Horatio Augustus Smith was born to Watson Smith and Betsey Miller in 1837 or 38 in the State of Pennsylvania. He enlisted in Company B, 44th New York Infantry on August 19, 1861. In 1850, at age 12, he was living with Hammond Emmons in Hume Township. He was wounded May 27, 1862 during the battle of Hanover Court House. Three months later, on August 30, 1862, he was killed in action at 2nd Bull Run. He was 25 years old and had been in the army just a little more than one year.

The men wounded at 2nd Bull Run were Stephen H. Draper (discussed earlier), possibly John Townsend (one of the most wounded men in the war), and Festus G. Lafoy. Lafoy was born October 4, 1862, in Castile to John Lafoy and Martha Johnson Decker, and enlisted in Company C, 104th New York infantry on October 9, 1861. His brother John also served. The family lived in Hume. He was shot in the right shoulder and arm at 2nd Bull Run.

Hugh Gallagher, son of John Gallagher, enlisted August 27, 1861 at Hume in Company B, 44th New York Infantry. He was born in Ireland in 1842. A farm laborer prior to the war, he participated in the seven days battles and was wounded at Malvern Hill, July 1, 1862. He was captured August 30, 1862, at 2nd Bull Run. Imprisoned in Richmond, Virginia, he was paroled September 4, 1862, and ultimately discharged on October 11, 1864. On August 25, 1866, he married Bridget Henley and shortly thereafter moved his family to Minnesota. He died September 9, 1870, in Wabasha County, Minnesota of a tumor, which was determined to be service related. His wife received a pension.

South Mountain, Maryland, September 14, 1862

Like Hanover Court House was for Fair Oaks, South Mountain was, what today would be called a warm-up, albeit a deadly serious one, for Antietam. The battle of South Mountain took place just three days prior to, and a few miles away from, Antietam.

Marshall James Rogers of Hume was wounded during this battle. Rogers had enlisted October 9, 1861, at Geneseo in Company F of the 104th New York Infantry at the age of 23. He was born in Wyoming County to Nathaniel and Lucretia Rogers in 1838. He was a distinguished soldier and recognized as such by the military. He was promoted to corporal November 11, 1861, sergeant December 15, 1862, first lieutenant November 8, 1863, and captain May 25, 1865. In addition to being wounded at South Mountain, he was captured at Weldon Railroad (Petersburg) on August 19, 1864. He was paroled February 25, 1865, and resigned his commission July 14, 1865. He married Elizabeth Haynes in Greene, Chenango County and died August 23, 1870, in Franklinville, at the age of 32.

Sharpsburg (Antietam), Maryland, September 17, 1862

As previously mentioned, multiple names for Civil War battles were very common. One reason for this was that the Confederates tended to name the battles after the closest town or city, whereas the Union tended to name the battles after a natural attribute of the area such as a river or a mountain. Antietam was a creek in the Sharpsburg area. This battle was "won" by Union forces, but General Lee escaped with much of his army intact due to what most consider poor Generalship by General McClellan, although some would argue that he handled the battle correctly. Many would call the battle a draw, but with Lee withdrawing, the South's invasion of Maryland ended. One thing everyone does seem to agree on is that this was the bloodiest one day battle in North American history. Over 23,000 Americans were killed and wounded that day - 12,400 from the North and 10,700 from the South. Shortly after the battle, on September 22, 1862, President Lincoln issued his Emancipation Proclamation.

Incredibly, despite the slaughter, and the fact that a significant number of men from the area participated in the battle, no C-H-G men were killed or captured.

At Antietam multiple regiments with more than one or two local men again fought in the same battle. In the next two years of the war this would be a common occurrence. Regiments with multiple C-H-G men that participated at Antietam included the 27th New York Infantry, the 33rd New York Infantry (the Ontario regiment), the 44th New York Infantry, and the 104th New York Infantry.

Antietam did represent another milestone for C-H-G volunteers. More men from the area were wounded in this battle than in any other battle of the war. Altogether 14 men suffered various wounds. Ten of the 14 men wounded served with the 104th New York Infantry Regiment. They were: William H. Brownell, Daniel J. Clark, Oliver T. Crowell, Thomas J. Curtis, Jason M. Griggs, William Hussong, John P. Myers, Francis Palmer, George Westbrook, and William Youngs. There was one each from the 33rd New York Infantry (William Decordus Dodge), 7th Michigan Infantry (George H. Hotchkiss), 89th New York Infantry (William N. Chamberlain), and the 26th New York Infantry (James Wilson). Crowell, Palmer, and Hotchkiss were all born in Centerville, Curtis and Dodge in Hume, and Hussong in Granger. Of the 14 men, two, Thomas J. Curtis and William Hussong, died at Gettysburg less than two months after Antietam. Incredibly, seven lived until well into the 20th Century. Of these seven, Crowell was the first to go, passing away in 1905. Daniel J. Clark lived until 1926.

In addition to a gunshot wound to the head, which caused a partial loss of hearing, William H. Brownell was also injured on the march to Antietam. He fell down a 12-foot embankment and severely damaged his right knee. Brownell was born June 9, 1841, to William Brownell and Phobe Wyman Youngs in Livingston County. His enlistment was recorded by the Allegany County Town Clerk Hume Office, so he must have been living in Hume by 1860. He is living there in 1865 per the 1865 New York State Census. Prewar, he was both a farmer (more likely farm laborer) and a canal driver. On October 9, 1865, he married Adaline Hill in Mount Morris. He died May 4, 1910 in Rochester and is buried there.

Daniel J. Clark was from the C-H-G area, but probably never actually lived in any of the townships. His records indicate two different birthplaces, Allegany and Onondaga Counties. He has an outstanding service record. At Antietam he was wounded in the left thigh by gunshot.

Oliver T. Crowell was born in Centerville May 5, 1834, to Samuel and Lucy Wight Crowell. He received a gunshot wound to his left leg at Antietam. He married Rose Ann Moore November 3, 1875, in Fillmore. He eventually moved to Rockford, Iowa where he died November 14, 1905.

Francis Palmer was born June 25, 1826, in Centerville to Humphrey Palmer and Sally Stacey. Both parents were born in Vermont. At Antietam he was wounded by a musket ball to the left ankle. He was an exemplary soldier, being regularly promoted. He was discharged July 17, 1865, as a first lieutenant. Palmer was married twice, first to Amelia B. Vickery, whom he divorced May 25, 1871. He later married Frances S. Prichard Rockafellow in Alma, Michigan. He died in Alma August 16, 1915.

William Decordus Dodge was born January 19, 1843, in Hume. One record says Nunda, but that may be simply a mistake involving where he enlisted. He volunteered May 13, 1861, in Nunda. A document in his pension file says he was living in Fillmore at the time of his enlistment. His parents were Francis W. Dodge and Emily T. Scott. His brother Francis also served. At Antietam on September 17, 1862, he was wounded by gunshot to his left foot. Dodge married Isadore Rawson in Caneadea on July 14, 1870. He died January 6, 1923, (only 13 days short of his 80 birthday) in Boonville, New York. He is buried in Caneadea.

William Nelson Chamberlain was born in Wyoming County on January 14, 1840, to Luther and Lucy Kendall Chamberlain. He participated in numerous battles. At Antietam he was slightly wounded by gunshot. Near Suffolk in April of 1863, he and three other men captured a Confederate battery. As they neared the battery, a canon was fired, throwing Chamberlain to the ground and causing temporary deafness. He never fully recovered his hearing. He lived in both Centerville and Granger and had two wives. The first, Loana S. Crane, he married December 24, 1866, in Freedom. After Loana died, he married Mary Faulkner August 22, 1872, at a hotel in Wellsville. He died August 10, 1917, in Dalton.

John Peck Myers (whose name may have originally been spelled Maier) survived the war, but mysteriously disappeared in 1895. He led an almost storybook life up to, or close to, the time of his disappearance. He was born in Hume on July 1, 1843, per the Allegany County Town Clerk for Hume, who in 1865 recorded July1 as Myers' birth date; in later years he apparently used July 4 as his birthday. His son-in-law, in a deposition he made when Myers' wife applied for his pension, claims Myers told him he expected to be home from a trip on his birthday, July 4. His parents were William Myers and Lucinda L. Burnell. The 1860 Federal Census shows him working as a farm laborer for a John Reas.

He volunteered for military service on October 30, 1861, at Hume for a three-year term. According to his military file, he was mustered into Company C, 104th New York Infantry that same day at Geneseo. Most likely, he had volunteered some time earlier since the 104th was organized at Geneseo from October 1861 through March of 1862. The 104th participated in many major battles and Myers received a gunshot wound to his left ankle at Antietam on September 14, 1862. His wounds were severe enough that he had to spend some time in the hospital. However, he was back with his regiment for the battle of Gettysburg where he was captured July 3, 1863. He was imprisoned at Andersonville, Georgia, and was one of the few to survive that horror, eventually being released on April 21, 1865. His term of service had actually expired during his capture. Some records indicate that he was discharged May 14, 1865, but he was still in a hospital on June 1, 1865. Further, his regiment was not discharged until June 30, 1865. It is more likely that he was mustered out with his regiment.

On September 28, 1870, he married Florence A. Beebe in Sandusky, New York. They had one daughter Ethel L. and an adopted daughter Ellen. Ellen's husband, and Myers' son-in-law, James Wells, in his deposition mentioned above, also said that Myers was a devoted husband and father.

There is no information available on Myers' education, but he must have had some, since at some point he moved to Buffalo and became a successful commission merchant. In fact, the firm bore his name, Myers, Woodward and Drake. When he disappeared, he had advised that he was going to New York City on business and that he would be meeting with a Chauncey Depew and the Governor of New York. He left his home in Springville on July 1, 1895, promising to be home by July 4, "his birthday." A few days later, his wife received a confusing letter, post marked New Rochelle, New York. He was never heard from again. It was later determined that he was deeply in debt, but according to his son-in-law there were no criminal charges against him. Wells, himself a prominent Buffalo businessman, at the urging of the family, made extensive efforts to locate him. These efforts included visiting New York City, New Rochelle, Bridgeport, Connecticut, and following up leads in Chicago and even Venezuela. He also called upon Chauncey Depew and the Governor. No trace of Myers was ever found.

George Westbrook received a gunshot wound to the head at Antietam. George was born October 21, 1841, in Wyoming County. His parents were born in England. He served honorably with Company A, 104th New York Infantry. On December 9, 1862, he received a disability discharge due to typhoid fever. He married Estella Nichols in Castile December 24, 1860. After the war they owned a hotel in Hunts, New York, but lost it due to poor management. They had a son George who was killed in the Spanish American War. The senior George died at the Soldiers and Sailors Home in Bath, New York July 13, 1917, and is buried in Warsaw.

James Wilson was born February 20, 1843, in Clarendon, Orleans County to Andrew and Elizabeth McConnell Wilson. Andrew and Elizabeth were both born in Scotland. On December 21, 1870, he married Mary L. Raymond in Venango County, Pennsylvania. At Antietam he suffered a gunshot wound to his right arm. Wilson served with Company C, 26th New York Infantry.

William W. Youngs spent most of his life in Granger, although he died March 16, 1912, in Pike and is buried there. His father Simeon was born in Vermont and his mother was born in Rhode Island. He was born January 27, 1829, in Castile, Wyoming County. He married Saphronia Greene at her father's home in Granger September 10, 1846. Serving with Company A, 104th New York Infantry, he suffered a gunshot wound at Antietam.

George H. Hotchkiss suffered a gunshot wound to his left arm at Antietam. Hotchkiss would be wounded again at the Wilderness battle in May of 1864.

Suffolk, Virginia

In early November 1862, on a night march from Suffolk to Black Water, Virginia, Simeon B. Clark injured his right knee when he fell between two pieces of timber. Clark served a little less than two years with Company B, 92nd New York Infantry. Due to his knee injury, which occurred less than two months after his September 23, 1862 enlistment, Clark spent several months at Foster General Hospital in New Bern, North Carolina. Clark was born in 1820 in Roxbury, Vermont. By 1860, Clark's family was living in Hume. Clark was one of the few who did not participate in any battles. He received an honorable disability discharge on June 1, 1864.

Fredericksburg, Virginia, December 12-15, 1862

In addition to the Regiments with multiple C-H-G men that fought at Antietam, both the 64th New York Infantry (known also as the Cattaraugus Regiment) and the 86th New York Infantry (known as Steuben's Rangers), participated in the battle at Fredericksburg, Virginia.

Just prior to this battle, President Lincoln removed General McClellan as head of the Army of the Potomac. He replaced him with General Ambrose E. Burnside who was most likely the worst of the four choices available. Many people considered McClellan a very good general. He was an outstanding organizer, a good strategist, and a fine soldier, but he was not successful in his campaigns and never won a decisive victory. It would appear he was not a risk taker. Lincoln was probably thinking of McClellan when he made his famous statement asking where could he find a general who would fight.

Chauncey Cronk (who lived in both Hume and Centerville at various times) of the 64th Infantry wrote in his journal about Fredericksburg, "We lay in the woods back of the brest works we are ready for a fight any time they are a mind to pich one we I feel very (scart althe) we have lost 8 good brave boys but it may be are turn next, chancey." Chauncey was disappointed because at Fredericksburg, it never became their turn. The Union forces suffered a major defeat.

However, C-H-G volunteers fared somewhat better at Fredericksburg than at Antietam, but did suffer a fatality, Andrew Andrews. Three men, in addition to Andrews, were also wounded on December 13, 1862. All three men were with the 104th New York Infantry, John H. Crowell and Jason Griggs with Company C and David E. Tadder with Company A.

Andrew Judson Andrews was the son of Alanson Andrews (born in Connecticut) and Mineva Fassett (born in Vermont). Andrew was born December 27, 1834, in Rushford. He was wounded by gunshot to the lower leg on December 13, 1862. The wound was so severe that it eventually required the amputation of his leg. He died January 26, 1863, as a result of the amputation. In one of those tragic ironies of war, his brother Elias had been killed just eight days earlier. Elias was with a scouting party near Aldie, Virginia and was killed by guerillas on December 5, 1862. Elias served with Company E of the 5th New York Cavalry. He was born October 5, 1836, in Rushford and enlisted August 29, 1861, at Centerville. Both Andrew and Elias were farmers prior to the war.

On October 3, 1861, Elias wrote his brother Amos from Camp Scott, Staten Island, New York.

The letter is interesting in that it shows that Elias, despite being just a country farmer, had a keen understanding of the events taking place and that, then as now, military contractors may not be the most ethical people on earth. He wrote:

> I rec'd yours of the 23rd & hasten to reply. You wished to know if you could endure the hardship of camp life; I answer not if you had seen the pain, sickness & misery I have, for the last month, (arising not so much from lying on the ground without sufficient clothing as from improperly cooked food) you would have very little desire to enlist, notwithstanding the patriotic feelings now predominant in your section of the country. It is very easy to converse on the topics of the day & arouse ones passions & form an opinion that it is our duty to go & fight to redeem the freedom of our country, & so it is; but it is as much the duty of the country to inform itself of the character of its contractors so to be sure that the soldiers receive what it furnishes for them & not robbed & starved by dishonest contractors. There are at present about 1400 persons in the camp of which near 60 are unable to march the dist. of sixty rods for their meals & are obliged to have them brought to them & we call it healthy at that. I believe no one has died in this regiment yet, but one of our Co. has lain in the hospital since we came to this camp. Last night he was so deranged as to be unable to distinguish me when I brought him his rations. I was sorry to learn that Andrew had enlisted, but should be more so to have you had. Andrew will endure all the hardships he may be called on to endure, but you could not. I am glad you have been able to get the money for Hig. & Pratt, but was sorry to learn you were obliged to sacrifice property to get the money. Tell father to sell no more property unless he is obliged to; put off our creditors & tell them I will send you some money as soon as I get pay which will be soon now. I have a good set of barbers tools & with them I manage to get all the money necessary to me at present. I shall therefore be able to send all of my wages home as fast as I get my pay. I have to perform no guard duty or other drudgery of the camp; yet I am not officer & will not except an office. I might have had the office of corporal if I had desired it but I did not; one only gets two dollars more per month & the trouble is double that of a private. Thirty of our boys are now gone to the city for horses for this Co. so we shall have more to do in the future. We are liable to be called to the seat of war at any moment as our regiment is now full & more coming in daily; but I do not think we shall be ordered to march in some time yet. I have not heard from Andrew yet only by the boys in the Co. from east Pike & not much from them. Address yours to me as before. Truly yours E.N., Andrews

Several of Elias' letters survive. One to his sister Sylvia on November 15, 1861, from Camp Scott, another to Amos on January 22, 1862, from Camp Harris, Annapolis, Maryland, and still another from Annapolis to Amos on March 2, 1862. The last existing letter, to his brother Wiley, was written September 29,1862, at a camp near Fort Blenker, probably in Virginia. He had just witnessed, but had not participated in the battle of Ashby's Gap in the Blue Ridge Mountains, which took place on September 22. He sent his brother some fish hooks and a line that had been lost by "some rebel soldiers," that he found on the battle field.

He also mentioned that he had taken a revolver from a rebel soldier the last time he was at Orange County Court House. He indicated that he and four other men had captured fourteen rebel soldiers and all their arms. While technically they were not allowed to keep captured arms, it was the practice of the day to give the arms of captured soldiers to their captors. Elias sold a "revolver of Colts Navy" for $4.00, but arranged for a mutual friend to give Andrew a revolver he had captured that was worth $20.00. His letter indicates that the regiment had been in a number of battles but doesn't mention any particular ones. The total strength of the regiment had been reduced from about 1,000 to some 300, not just from those killed in action, but those wounded and sent home, and from sickness. He also states that men were lost because of "breaches" caused by hard riding. While Elias doesn't mention it in his letters, his military files indicate that he was a scout for General Windham when he was killed. Elias served with Company F, 5th New York Cavalry, a regiment that participated in numerous battles.

In another twist, a William B. Willey claimed Andrew's pension. Willey testified that he had enrolled under the name Andrew J. Andrews and had been wounded at Fredericksburg. However, since he had both legs, he also claimed his leg had not been amputated and that he had recovered from his wounds. As might be expected, his pension claim was denied. Andrew's mother filed for Elias' pension but her application was also rejected. The reason for this rejection was that she was receiving a pension earned by her husband Alanson, who was a veteran of the War of 1812. Alanson had also been awarded a land grant for his service, in his case 160 acres. However, he sold the rights to the grant to a Goodien S. Gordon.

Not much information is available on David E. Tadder or Tedder. He was born in Livingston County. He enlisted December 4, 1861, at Granger. He received a head wound, resulting in the loss of his left eye at Fredericksburg. On February 28, 1863, he married Charlotte M. Aldrich in Oakland, Livingston County. He died May 27, 1884. Jasper M. Griggs suffered a gunshot wound to his thigh at Fredericksburg. He had received a slight gunshot wound to his hand at Antietam and he would be wounded again at Gettysburg. Crowell would be captured in 1864.

Death from disease began to take a heavy toll in 1862. Some of the men died in prisons where the lack of sanitary conditions and substandard and lack of food created an atmosphere conducive to disease. But many others were infected even when with their own regiments. The first to die of disease in 1862 was Thomas W.E. Boss (Company F, 104th New York Infantry) on April 6 of typhoid fever. The list for the balance of the year is as follows: April 16 David Youngs (Company C, 104 New York Infantry) of pneumonia; April 21 Daniel Chillson (Company F, 33rd New York Infantry) of inflamation of the bowels; April 23 Lewis J. Holbrook (Company E, 85th New York Infantry) of typhoid fever; April 28 James Andrew Boardman (Company G, 44th New York Infantry) of typhoid fever; May 13 Oscar Peter Emery (Company C, 104th New York Infantry) of typhoid fever; May 16 Andrew W. Cooley (Company C,104th New York Infantry) of "service related disease"; June 26 W.A. Marcus Whaley (Company I, 136th New York Infantry) of typhoid fever; July 23 Jefferson Myron Parker (Company E, 85th New York Infantry) as a POW of "service related disease"; September 11 William Henry Daley (Company F, 104th New York Infantry) of typhoid fever; October 3rd Emery M. Wood (Company C, 104th New York Infantry) of "service related disease"; October 19 John L. Myers (Company D, 154th New York Infantry) of congestion of the brain; October 28 Albert Owen Taber (Company E, 85th New York Infantry) of remittent fever; November 5 Addison H. Caldwell (Company F, 19th New York Cavalry) of typhoid fever; November 19 Aaron Van Nostrand (Company F, 19th New York Cavalry) of a fever; Pembroke Berry (Company F, 4th New York Infantry) of typhoid fever; John Peter Bogardus (Company H, th New York Cavalry) of "service related disease"; November 24 Marion C. Plumb (Company D, 154th New York Infantry) of pneumonia; December 3 Robert Vallance (Company F, 19th New York Cavalry) of remittent fever and John Paul Chase (Company F, 19th New York Cavalry) of typhoid fever; and December 4 Norman J. Smith (Company C,136th New York Infantry) of chronic diarrhea.

At the end of 1862, the battle toll for local men was beginning to have a major impact. During the year eleven men had been killed in action and another 21 had died of various diseases. In addition, at least 35 men had been wounded, eleven others had been injured, and nine men had been captured. One man had accidentally drowned. Some of these data represent the same men. One reason for many men suffering more than one casualty was the battlefield practice of both sides.

For example, during the war the losing side would withdraw from the battlefield, many times leaving their wounded and dead on the field. That meant wounded men would also end up as prisoners of war. Some men were wounded more than once and some men were wounded in one battle and killed in another. There were many combinations. George V. Hill was wounded twice in two different battles. Willard Calkins was both wounded and became a POW in the same battle. Andrew Andrews was wounded, but later died and was thus wounded and killed in action. In cases like Andrews, I have tried to be consistent by treating them both as wounded and killed in action. Where wounded men died within a short time of being wounded, usually hours, I have treated them only as killed in action.

THE WAR - 1863 - GRIM REALITY

After the battle of Fredericksburg the troops from both sides of the war in the East essentially went into winter quarters. January of 1863 was like other Januarys during the war. Few, if any, men were killed and/or wounded in battle. However, the month of the year had no effect on those dying of disease. They died in January as they died in every other month of the year. Charles H. Leach of the 19th New York Cavalry was the first to succumb, dying of malaria fever on the first day of 1863. Leach was followed by Anson H. Spensor, also of the 19th New York Cavalry, who died of fever on the 5th. Two more died on February 14, James Bradshaw, 2nd United States Cavalry, of typhoid fever, and Frederick Gillett, 4th New York Heavy Artillery, of small pox. Death took a disease holiday during March, but John L. Shoots, 19th New York Cavalry died April 18 of remittent fever and Harvey B. Osborn, 19th New York Cavalry, died April 27. The specific cause is not listed in his records. Isaac Brewster, 114th New York Infantry, died May 1 of remittent fever. June was another month off, but Michael McDermott, 160th New York Infantry, died July 18 of chronic diarrhea. Reuben W. Madison, 160th New York Infantry, died of chronic dysentery August 16, and Isaac Van Nostrand, 19th New York Cavalry, died of chronic dysentery August 25. Laselle Ellenwood,102nd New York Infantry, died September 28, disease not identified. Death skipped October, but Robert T. Lockwood, 4th New York Heavy Artillery, died November 16 of typhoid fever. Patrick McCabe, 76th New York Infantry, died of chronic diarrhea on December 28.

New Orleans, January 12 - 15, 1863

The 160th New York Infantry was organized at Auburn, Cayuga County and mustered November 21, 1862. It was ordered to New Orleans, Louisiana in December 1862 and attached to General William T. Sherman, Department of the Gulf - 2nd Brigade, 1st Division, 19th Army Corps. On an expedition to Bayou Teche January 12 - 15, 1863, it engaged in a battle with the Confederate Gunboat "Cotton." During this battle, Gardner Robinson, born June 3, 1836, in Hume, was hit in the eye by a gun cap. Despite his wound and some subsequent combat injuries, Robinson soldiered on and was not discharged until May 18, 1865. After the war Gardner married a Lois Ann Moore who died April 1, 1880. He then married a widow, Augusta Delia Catlin Grant, with whom he had two children. The second child, a son, born April 22, 1884, he named Sherman. Gardner died February 22, 1913.

Robinson was the second non-disease casualty of the year. The first had been Willard E. Calkins. Calkins who had been wounded in action May 5, 1862, at the battle of Williamsburg, and had also been, for a very short period, a POW. Calkins was hurt January 15, 1863, while cutting wood for his camp. He slipped, fell on a snow-covered tree, and injured his back. The back injury eventually led to kidney problems which plagued him the rest of his long life.

Deserted House, Blackwater, Virginia, January 30, 1863

In late January the 19th New York Cavalry (1st New York Dragoons) conducted an expedition toward Blackwater, Virginia. On January 30 they engaged in a conflict at a vacant farm that forever after would be known as the battle of Deserted House. George W. Abbott, Company H, and Oliver R. Washburn, Company A, were killed during the engagement. William Morris King of Company F was wounded. Another C-H-G man, Ebenezer Augustus Bean, serving with Company

I, 160th New York Infantry also was wounded.

George W. Abbott was born October 6, 1836, in Granger to Charles Abbott and Lois Chapman. Never married, he volunteered for the war August 13, 1862 at Portage at the age of 27. He is buried in Hampton, Virginia National Cemetery. George was a farmer at the time of his enlistment.

Oliver R. Washburn, the son of Abel S. Washburn and Philanca Morgan was born in Hume in 1844. At the age of 18 he volunteered on August 4, 1862. Six months later he was killed at Deserted House. He is buried in Pine Grove Cemetery in Fillmore. Some source documents indicate that his father Abel also served, however, no military records have been located for him. Since Abel was only 43 in 1860, it is plausible that he served, but unlikely given the lack of records.

Ebenezer Augustus Bean was the son of Orson Bean and Clarinda Van Buren and only 18 when he volunteered August 9, 1862, at Centerville. On January 30, 1863, he was hit by gun fire and lost the thumb on his right hand. After the war Ebenezer lived in both Hume and Knoxville, Pennsylvania. He married three times, twice to women from Hume and once to a woman from Knoxville. His first wife, Flora A. Stacy of Hume, died. He divorced his second wife, Ollie G. Clossen of Knoxville. He married his third wife, Abblie C. Knox in Hume.

William Morris King, the son of Solomon King and Catherine Snider, was born April 24, 1832, in Middletown, Orange County. Prior to the war he was a carriage maker. He volunteered August 9, 1862, at Hume. At Deserted House he was wounded in the left ankle. Prior to the war he married Amy P. Bush, who died in 1872. He later married Jennie Williams. Eventually he moved his family to the state of Washington where he died September 22, 1899, in Centralia in Lewis County.

The 1st New York Dragoons (19th New York Cavalry) saw at least as much action during the war as any other regiment in which C-H-G men served, with the possible exception of the 5th New York Cavalry and the 104th New York Infantry. However, only seventeen local men served with the 5th Cavalry and 68 with the 104th, whereas at least 117 served with the 19th Cavalry (1st Dragoons). Fourteen C-H-G men serving with the 19th died in various battles. The regiment with the next highest number of local men killed in battle was the 104th with eight. Further reflecting the many battles fought by the 19th, the fourteen men died in 12 different engagements. Seven of the eight 104th men died at Gettysburg. This latter fact illustrates the serverity of Gettysburg.

Dyer's *Compendium of the War of the Rebellion, Part 3* provides the following information on the 19th New York Cavalry (1st New York Dragoons):

1st Regimental Dragoons -- 19th Cavalry. Organized at Portage, N.Y., as 130th Infantry and mustered in September 2, 1862. Left State for Suffolk, Va., September 6, 1862. Attached to Provisional Brigade, Peck's Division at Suffolk, 7th Army Corps, Dept. of Virginia, to October, 1862. Spinola's Brigade, Peck's Division at Suffolk, 7th Army Corps, to December, 1862. Gibbs' Brigade, Peck's Division at Suffolk, 7th Army Corps, to January, 1863. Terry's Brigade, Peck's Division at Suffolk, 7th Army Corps, to April, 1863. Terry's Brigade, Corcoran's 1st Division, 7th Army Corps, to June, 1863. 1st Brigade, 1st Division, 7th Army Corps, to July, 1863. Provost Marshal General's Command, Army of the Potomac, to August, 1863. Designation of Regiment changed to 19th Cavalry August 11, 1863, and to 1st Dragoons September 10, 1863. Reserve Cavalry Brigade, 1st Division, Cavalry Corps, Army of the Potomac, to March, 1864. 3rd

(Reserve) Brigade, 1st Division, Cavalry C.orps, Army of the Potomac, and Army of the Shenandoah, to September, 1864. 2nd Brigade, 1st Division, Cavalry Corps, Army of the Shenandoah and Army Potomac, to June, 1865.

SERVICE.--Duty at Suffolk, Va., till May, 1863. Expedition from Suffolk December 1-3, 1862. Action on the Blackwater near Franklin December 2. Reconnaissances from Suffolk to Blackwater December 23 and 28. Near Suffolk and at Providence Church December 28. Expedition toward Blackwater January 8-10,1863. Deserted House January 30, Siege of Suffolk April 12-May 4: South Quay Road, Suffolk, April 17. Suffolk April 19 .Nansemond River May 3. Siege of Suffolk raised May 4. South Quay Road June 12. Franklin June 14. Blackwater June 16-17. Dix's Peninsula Campaign June 24-July 7. Expedition from White House to South Anna River July 1- 7. Baltimore Cross Roads July 4. Ordered to Washington, D.C. Ashby's Gap July 19. Advance from the Rappahannock to the Rapidan September 13-17. Between Centreville and Warrenton September 22. Manassas Junction October 17. Bristoe Station October 18. Buckland Mills October 18-19. Advance to line of the Rappahannock November 7-8. Culpeper Court House November 20. Mine Run Campaign November 26-December 2. Demonstration on the Rapidan February 6-7,1864. Barnett's Ford February 6-7. Rapidan Campaign May-June, 1864. Wilderness May 5-7. Todd's Tavern May 7-8. Spottsylvania May 8. Sheridan's Raid to James River May 9-24. Davenport Bridge, North Anna River, May 10. Yellow Tavern and Ground Squirrel Bridge May 11. Fortifications of Richmond and Meadow Bridge May 12. On line of the Pamunkey May 26-28. Hanovertown May 27. Haw's Shop May 28. Totopotomoy May 28-31. Old Church and Mattadequi Creek May 30. Cold Harbor May 31-June 6. Sheridan's Travillian Raid June 7-24. Trevillian Station June 11-12. Newark or Mallory's Ford Cross Roads June 12. White House or St. Peter's Church June 21. Black Creek or Tunstall's Station June 21. Jones' Bridge June 23. Charles City Court House June 24. Before Petersburg and Richmond June 27-July 30. Demonstration north of the James River July 27-29, Deep Bottom July 27-28. Malvern Hill July 28. Sheridan's Shenandoah Valley Campaign August 7-November 28. Shephardstown August 8. Near Stone Chapel, Berryville Pike, August 10. Tell Gate near White Post and Newton August 11. Cedar Creek August 12. Cedarville August 13 and 16. Summit Point August 21. Near Kearneysville and Shephardstown August 25. Leetown and Smithfield August 28. Smithfield Crossing, Opequan Creek, August 29. Bunker Hill September 13. Sevier's Ford, Opequan Creek, September 15. Battle of Opequan, Winchester, September 19. Middletown and Strasburg September 20. Fisher's Hill September 21. Near Edenburg September 23. Front Royal, Mt. Jackson, September 23-24. New Market September 24. Port Republic September 26-27. McGaugheysville September 28. Mr. Crawford October 2. Tom's Brook, "Woodstock Races ," October 8-9. Hupp's Hill near Strasburb. October 14. Battle of Cedar Creek October 19. Fisher's Hill October 20. Liberty Mills October 22. Berryville October 28. Near White Post November 1. Near Kernstown November 11. Newtown November 12. Cedar Creek November 19. Expedition from Winchester into Fauquier and Loudoun Counties November 28-December 3. Bloomfield November 29. Expedition to Gordonsville December 19-28. Liberty Mills December 21. Jack's Shop December 22. Near Gordonsville December 23. Sheridan's Raid from Winchester February 27-March 25,1865. Occupation of Staunton March 2. Action at Waynesboro March 2. Near Charlottesville March 3. Goochland Court House March 11. Appomattox Campaign March 28-April 9. Dinwiddie Court House March 30-31. Five Forks April 1. Scott's Cross Roads April 2. Deep Creek April 3. Tabernacle Church or Beaver Pond Creek April 4. Sailor's Creek Apri16. Appomattox Station April 8. Appomattox Court House April 9. Surrender of Lee and his army. Expedition to Danville April 23-29. March to Washington, D.C., May. Grand Review May 23. Mustered out June30, 1865, and honorably discharged from service. Regiment lost during service 4 Officers and 126 Enlisted men killed and mortally wounded and 1 Officer and 130 Enlisted men by disease, etc. Total 261.

At least 117 C-H-G men served with the 19th Cavalry. They were: George W. Abbot, Alphonso J. Aldrich, George Washington Babcock, Martin Van Buren Babcock, Orestus Joseph Ball, Oliver Barnard, Ebenezer Augustus Bean, Robert Bennett, Simeon Bennett, Donald Alonzo Blanchard, John S. Blanchard, John Peter Bogardus, Stephen P. Boss, Erwin Morgan Botsford, John M. Botsford, Azem F. Bowen, Nathan C. Bradley, Warren Major Brown, Joseph Butterfield, Addison H. Caldwell, John Paul Chase, Herbert W. Cheney, Joel B. Clark, Jacob T. Clement, David M.

Cox, Ulysses Eugene Crane, Romanzo Crawford, Clarence Lindon Cudebec, George W. Curtis, Charles S. Daniels, William Curtis Daniels, James K. Dole, Smith Dole, John Dorey, John L. Dudley, George Washington Dutton, Darwin Ellis, Alonzo M. Elmer, John Williams Emmons, Samuel Ara Farman, Charles B. Fox, Chauncey Joel Fox, Albert Dan Goodrich, William W. Gray, Henry Griffith, Charles Grover, John M. Hall, Alva Hamlin, John R. Harwood, Cyrus J. Hatch, Jr., William Hawley, Amos Hopkins, Oliver Joseph Hopkins, Sandford L. Horton, Palmer P. Karns. Ferris Enoch Kendall, George Higgins Kimball, Robert W. King, William Morris King, John Kinney, William A. Knowlton, Charles H. Leach, Reuben Learn, Reuben Lee, Solomon Lee, Frank Cashus Luther, Marcus Dana Merchant, William Whitney Merchant, John Moore, George Washington Morse, Delos Myers, Henry Patrick Neilan, Harvey Blackman Osborn, Emerson Madison Parker, Erland S. Parker, Thomas Pendergast, Nelson A. Pettee. William Dunn Phipps, Abijah Randall, Elijah Rhodes, George H. Sheppard, John Lawrence Shoots, William Henry Sibbald, Stephen Morse Skiff, George Washington Smith, Henry W. Smith, John Alexander Smith, Samuel Smith, Charles E. Snell, Edward Green Snyder, John Lewis Snyder, Martin William Snyder, Henry Whitney Spease, Anson Hinman Spencer, John Murray Stickle, Judson Stickle, George Stockweather, Randall Taylor, Alexander Kelsey Thorp, Thomas J. Thorp, George Titus Underhill, Robert Vallance, Bryon Van Name, Richard Henry Van Name, Aaron Van Nostrand, Isaac N. Van Nostrand, Amos Pratt Vaughn, Stewart Austin Vaughn, Oliver R. Washburn, Theodore Washburn, James Henry Weaver, Edwin Wight, Wilbur S. Wight, Sylvester Wilday, James Williams, William Jay Wolsey, and John H. Yager.

Of the 117 C-H-G men who served with the 19th New York Cavalry, 14 were killed in action, 19 died of diseases (two while POWs), 14 were wounded in action, 10 suffered other injuries, and nine were captured. A total of 17, Alphonse Aldrich, Stephen Boss, William Boyd, Joseph Butterfield, Jacob Clement, Charles Fox, William Hawley, Palmer Karns, Robert King, William Knowlton, Reuben Learn, Marcus Merchant, William Phipps, James Weaver, Wilbur Wight, William Wolsey, and John Yeager were at Appomattox Court House when Lee surrendered. A total of 48 marched in the Grand Review in Washington on May 23, 1865. One was discharged as a deserter and eighteen received disability discharges. Some 57 of the 117 soldiers suffered at least one casualty, and at least another 13 were sick at some point during the war.

Falmouth - New Baltimore, Virginia

The 33rd Infantry was stationed at Falmouth in the early part of 1863. At a skirmish at New Baltimore, near Falmouth, William H. Wells of the 5th New York Cavalry was captured on February 13, 1863. Wells would be captured a second time at Ellis Ford on January 22, 1864. He was paroled following his first capture, but in his second captivity, died at Andersonville on February 15, 1864, of scurvy. Wells was born February 4, 1842, in Pike to Nathaniel Wells and Polly Wright. By 1850 the family was living in Hume.

Suffolk, Virginia, February 15 and April 12 - Dumfries, Virginia, March 4, 1863

Almond Duane Robinson was born in Lodi, NY in 1837. According to an affidavit by Doctor Lyman of Fillmore, given at the time Robinson applied for his pension, the family had lived in the Fillmore area for at least 20 years prior to his enlistment in Company F, 8th New York Cavalry.

Robinson was married to Clara Louise Scott February 20, 1860, in Caledonia, and apparently lived there at the time he enlisted at Rochester. He was captured by guerillas March 4, 1863, at Union Church in Dumfries, Virginia and paroled March 8, 1863. He died February 26, 1880, in Hume and is buried at Pine Grove Cemetery.

Suffolk

The continuing struggle in the Suffolk, Virginia area led to four more casualties in early 1863. Romano Crawford was injured on February 15, Ulysses E. Crane was injured in late February or early March, William Sibbald was wounded on April 13, and John Kinney was injured in mid-April. Crawford was born December 7, 1839, (a date to be made famous in another war a century later) in Oramel. On March 23, 1861, he married Mary Jane Torrey in Centerville. He enlisted in Company F, 19th New York Cavalry at Centerville August 7, 1862. He accidently wounded himself in the left ankle while on picket duty. He was discharged May 13, 1863, and died October 31, 1917. He is buried in Hume Township.

Ulysses E. Crane was born April 10, 1840, in Freedom to Berry Crane and Charity E. Sharp. In February or March 1863, while cutting wood for his camp, he sliced off his big toe. He was treated at a Hampton, VA hospital and transferred to the V.R.C. He was not finally discharged until June 30, 1865. Crane led an interesting life. Married twice, there was some confusion at one point over who his wife was, since it appears he never divorced his first wife. He apparently told his second wife that he was never really married to the first one. He claimed he and his brothers had staged a mock wedding when he married her. Eventually, however, he went back to his first wife. He lived in at least four states including New York, dying in 1923 at Vancouver, WA. He also was an artist and apparently sold a number of paintings at high prices for that time period.

John Kinney (his last name has several different spellings including Kenney or McKenney) was born in 1840 in Roscommon, Ireland. He enlisted in Company F, 19th New York Cavalry at Hume on August 13, 1862. He was injured by falling earth when building fortifications at Suffolk, Virginia. Discharged March 12, 1864, he married Bridget Gallagher on November 13, 1866, at St. Bonaventure Church in Allegany, Cattaraugus County. Unfortunately the church indicates it does not have records that go back to 1866. He died July 17, 1893, at Emlenton, Venango County, Pennsylvania.

William Henry Sibbald was born October 11, 1842, in Oswegatchee, St. Lawrence County, New York to William Sibbald and Sarah Eaton. He enlisted in Company F, 19th New York Cavalry at Granger on August 13, 1862. His brother George also served. He was wounded in the abdomen on April 12, 1863, by Southern sharp shooters. After the war he moved to King City, Missouri where he married Emily Alice Millen of King City December 24, 1873. He died in King City November 4, 1904.

Chancellorsville, Virginia - April 28 to May 5, 1863

The first major battle of 1863 took place at Chancellorsville, just a few miles from Fredericksburg. The campaign ran from April 27 to May 6 with the actual fighting taking place May 1-5. Like many earlier battles, this one was marked by a series of major blunders by the Union Commander,

47

in this case, General Joe Hooker who had replaced Burnside. It could have been worse, but the army did affect a successful withdrawal across the Rappahannock River. Although the South won the battle, it could be argued that the greatest loss at Chancellorsville was suffered by the South when General Thomas Jonathan "Stonewall" Jackson was mortally wounded on May 3 by his own troops. He received three wounds, one of which required the amputation of his left arm. He was actually recovering when he contracted pneumonia and died May 10.

Regiments with significant numbers of C-H-G men at Chancellorsville included the 44th New York Infantry, the 64th New York Infantry, 136th New York Infantry, and the 104th New York Infantry. Six men from the area were wounded at Chancellorsville, three were captured, and one was injured. The wounded were: Benjamin S. Snider (64th Infantry), George W. Bemus (78th Infantry), William L. Tooley (1st Light Artillery), Ira Higby (104th Infantry), John Townsend (136th Infantry) and Albert P. Watson (33rd Infantry). The men captured were: Albert P. Watson (33rd Infantry), Marvin Wilson (33rd Infantry), and John C. Franklin (1st Michigan Cavalry). Lewis Wright (64th Infantry) suffered a ruptured abdomen on May 1.

Benjamin Swezy Snider (64th Infantry), was captured a day later, May 4 1863, at U.S. Ford.

George W. Bemus served with Company G of the 78th New York Infantry (the Eagle's Brigade). He was born July 15, 1831, in Hume. Prior to the war he was a mechanic. He enlisted at age 30 on December 3, 1861, at Hume and was promoted to sergeant June 9, 1862. He married Emily A. Powers January 13, 1858, in Pike. Bemus passed away in Pike on February 20, 1906. Emily and George had a son, also named George.

William L. Tooley of Battery D, 1st New York Light Artillery was born in 1839 in Antwerp, Jefferson County to Isreal and Mary Ann Tooley. After the war he lived in Granger. He was married twice, first to Lydia Clark and then to Emma J. Brewer Duel. He died January 2, 1907, in Portageville. He was wounded in the lower jaw at Chancellorsville on May 3, 1863.

Albert P. Watson served with both Company F of the 33rd New York Infantry and Company B of the 2nd New York Mounted Rifles. He was both wounded and captured at Chancellorsville. The wound was very severe, a gunshot through the right ankle, and it may have led to his capture. Many men with wounds, unable to escape the battlefield, were captured by the opposing forces. Watson was imprisoned at Richmond and survived the war. He was born in Ulster, Ireland and died November 14, 1902, in Pike. Like Tooley, Watson was married twice, first to Calista Guild and then Amelia P. Pratt. While Watson apparently lived primarily in Pike, the 1865 New York State Census shows him living in Hume with his wife Calista and his daughter Stella.

Benjamin Swezy Snider, the son of Benjamin Snider and Charity Green, was born June 14, 1821, in Rushford. He received a slight wound on May 3 and was captured May 4 at US Ford, which was in the Chancellorsville area. It most likely was where the Union Army made its escape back across the Rappahannock River. Since his record indicates that he was slightly wounded, his wound might have played a role in his capture. He was imprisoned at Libby Prison in Richmond. He also was married twice, first to Priscilla B. Ver, who died in 1879, and then to Hannah Webster. His pension file indicates that the second marriage took place in a barn and that he was married by an African minister. That would have been most unusual for the time. Snider was mentally disturbed and was in and out of mental institutions a good part of his life. After the war he billed himself as a National Evangelist and appears to have made his living as an itinerant preacher. A number of the handbills announcing his "meetings" are in his pension file. In one handbill he promised, "With the Aid of Divine Providence," to give one hundred million dollars to the Government of the United States for the "faithful performance of " four pledges. However, the "pledges" are all things he was to do, and he must have meant for the government to let him do them. One pledge he made is still promised, in part, by many politician running for office today. He pledged to "relieve the nation of its present debt by reducing its present expenses one-half and causing the rich instead of the poor to support the government." He also vowed, "to expose the priests who are not only robbers of the widow and orphan, but are still devouring the wine and carcases and charging it to Bel. By so doing I will make of what is now a den of thieves and robbers an asylum for the poor and oppressed."

Ira Higby was the son of Ira Higby (Higbee) and Ruth Fuller. He was born October 15, 1828, in Hume. He married Mary J. Babcock May 16, 1849, in Wiscoy. Prior to the war he was a miller and wheel wright. He received a neck wound at Chancellorsville and was sent to the convalescent camp on Bedloes Island in New York Harbor. That island is more famous today as the home of the Statue of Liberty. Later transferred to the Veteran's Reserve Corps on September 1, 1863, he was mustered out with an honorable disability discharge. After the war he moved his family to Red Cloud, Nebraska where he worked as a miller and died July 20, 1877.

John C. Franklin, Company F, 33rd New York Infantry was captured May 4. He also survived the war. Franklin was born in Buffalo, was probably an orphan growing up and eventually settled in Centerville. At 17, he volunteered for the 33rd Infantry. He was honorably discharged May 4, 1863. He also served with the 1st Michigan Cavalry. His history with the 1st Michigan and subsequent to his service is confusing, at best, and is covered later in this study.

Port Hudson, Louisiana, May 27, 1863

While most C-H-G men participated in military activities in Virginia, Maryland, and Pennsylvania, many fought in battles in several other locations. One such battle was over control of the Mississippi River. By May 1863, the North already controlled most of the river, except for the 110 miles between Vicksburg and Port Hudson. The capture of Port Hudson would leave the North in total control of the Mississippi. The first major attack there occurred May 27. Union forces suffered some two thousand casualties, one of whom was C-H-G soldier Felix Weingartner, who was wounded. The failure of the attack on the 27th resulting in a siege. This lasted until July 8, when the Confederate forces at last surrendered.

Felix Weingartner was born in Switzerland in 1834. He probably arrived in the U.S. 9/1/1857 aboard the ship Gebhard. He may have had a brother named, or called Albert, whom he lived with in Buffalo for some time after his arrival. He volunteered for the service on July 3, 1862, and was assigned to Company G, 116th New York Infantry. During the first major battle to capture Fort Hudson on May 27, Weingartner was severely wounded in the left thigh. Following the war he moved around quite a bit. He never married. He was in and out of the National Soldiers and Sailors Home in Bath, NY several times, the first being from February 4, 1894, to December 15, 1897. He lived in Hume for at least fifteen years, and worked for Phenias Morse. He worked as a laborer both before and after the war. The 1890 Federal Census - Special Schedule for Veterans (the only part of the 1890 Census that survived a fire) indicates he was living in Hume in 1890. He died December 7, 1918, near the end of the First World War, and on a date on which the Second World War would begin for the United States just 23 years later. He is buried in Bath.

Franklin, VA, June 17, 1863

While on picket duty near Franklin, VA, Stephen Skiff of Hume was shot and killed. Skiff was a member of the prominent Skiff family of Hume. He had just turned 21. His brother John had been killed in action at Shiloh a year earlier.

Gettysburg, Pennsylvania, July 1-3, 1863

Most wars have a turning point. Few people, if any, are prescient enough to recognize these turning points at the time they occur. In most cases the wars go for extended periods after the turning points. Any realistic chances the South had of winning the Civil War ended at Gettysburg, however, the war went on for two more years.

C-H-G was well represented at Gettysburg. Regiments with multiple C-H-G volunteers included: the 44th New York Infantry, the 64th New York Infantry, the 85th New York Infantry, the 104th New York Infantry, and the 136th New York Infantry. Never before had so many C-H-G men participated in a single battle. Never before, and never again, would so many C-H-G men be so negatively impacted by a single battle, with the exception of the almost 30 men captured at Plymouth, North Carolina in 1864. However, there were no C-H-G men wounded or killed at Plymouth. A total of 23 different men were casualties at Gettysburg. Seven men were killed in action. Thirteen men were wounded, with four of the thirteen dying later. (These four are included in the seven who died.) Seven were captured.

The thirteen men wounded were: Maurice Buckingham, Jasper P. Griggs, John Wiederight, William Hussong, Strong Veazey, and William H. Rich of the 104th New York Infantry; Daniel Webster Blake, Chester B. Cronk, and Leander Millspaugh of the 64th New York Infantry; Samuel Willard, John Townsend and Alonzo Camp of the 136th New York Infantry; William H.H. Keyes, 78th New York Infantry; and Hugh Gallagher of the 44th New York Infantry. Townsend had been wounded at 2nd Bull Run and would be wounded twice more. At Gettysburg he suffered a gunshot wound just below the left knee.

Worst of all, seven men were killed; three died immediately, and four shortly after being wounded. The three who died immediately were Henry L. Abbey, Thomas Jefferson Curtis, and William L. Davis, of the 104th NY Infantry. Those wounded, who died as a result of their wounds included Maurice Buckingham, William Hussong, and Strong Warner Veazey of the 104th New York Infantry, and William Henry Harrison Keyes of the 78th New York Infantry, who died two weeks after being wounded. The seven men from G-H-G killed at Gettysburg were more than in any other battle of the war. Five were killed at Petersburg, but only four at one time. Only at the battle of Antietam on September 17, 1862, were more men wounded. There were only a couple of battles, Plymouth and Petersburg, in which more C-H-G men were captured than occurred at Gettysburg.

Thomas Jefferson Curtis was born in Hume, the son of Joseph Curtis and Adaline Reed. Prior to the war he was a farmer. He enlisted as a private at Granger on October 1, 1861, and quickly rose through the ranks, eventually being promoted to first sergeant January 19, 1863. A member of Company A of the 104th New York Infantry, he had been wounded at Antietam September 17, 1862. He was killed at Gettysburg by a minnie ball on July 1 and is buried there. He was 25.

Curtis was one of three C-H-G men who were wounded in one battle and killed in another. William Hussong, was wounded at Antietam September 17, 1862, and both wounded and killed (died of wounds) at Gettysburg. The third was Horatio Smith, wounded May 27, 1862, at Hanover Court House and killed at 2nd Bull Run on August 30, 1862.

Curtis' brother, George W. (probably Washington) Curtis also fought in the war. George was with Company A, 19th New York Cavalry (1st Dragoons). Like Thomas he was born in Hume. On August 26, 1861, he married Minerva Karns whose brother Palmer also served. George enlisted September 23, 1862, and was in 23 battles and skirmishes according to one account, including the Wilderness, Cold Harbor, Spotsylvania, Trevillian Station and Winchester. He marched in the Grand Review in D.C. on May 23, 1865, and was discharged June 30, 1865. He was never wounded or captured.

William Hussong was born September 18, 1842, in Granger, the son of Christian (John) Hussong and Doris Lincner Smith. He was engaged in farming when he enlisted January 23, 1862, at Granger in Company F of the 104th New York Infantry. At Gettysburg, on July 1, he received a gunshot wound to his left leg. He died July 4, 1863, at the age of 20.

Another man killed at Gettysburg was Maurice Buckingham and his story is the type that they make into movies. He was born in Livingston, England and it appears he arrived in the United States February 6, 1857 aboard the ship *Emerald Isle*. He enlisted in October of 1861, most likely at Centerville, where he worked as a mechanic. He was mustered February 25, 1862, at Geneseo. His name appears in the 1865 New York State Census, most likely put there by the Centerville family for whom he worked or with whom he lived. It is likely he knew, and was probably friends with, Strong Warner Veazey, from Centerville. Veazey also enlisted in October, 1861, and was mustered at Geneseo. Maurice was a good soldier who rose through the ranks to become color sergeant for the regiment. On July 1, he received a severe leg wound. He died July 20. His story would have ended there except for a nurse who treated him. The story she told has been retold many times. It appears in several Civil War books. The following is copied from the book *Lincoln and the Human Interest Stories of The Gettysburg National Cemetery* by James M. Cole and Rev. Roy E. Frampton. - page 67:

It is difficult to discriminate where all are so brave, yet the bravest was a young Englishman, the color bearer of a New York regiment. He came to this country an orphan boy, was educated in our free schools, found friends who assisted him, and became prosperous in business and when this foul rebellion endangered the liberties of our land, and the bells everywhere were calling together the sons of the republic, he felt that for a country which had afforded him home and happiness it was an honor and a privilege to suffer and die. He volunteered with hundreds of thousands of freemen, and carried the colors of his regiment through all the battles fought by the Army of the Potomac until now, unhurt. All this he told me in broken sentences, and added that 'there was one on whom all his hopes centered, who made life precious and desirable to him,' and much more of a similar import too sacred to relate. To her I wrote a letter, telling of his sad state, how he had fallen, bleeding and wounded; and at his request, added that though he had lost his leg, he was proud to tell her he had saved the regimental colors, and his own life, too, was still spared him, which was only made valuable by thoughts of her. This was surely enough to make any true woman feel proud that over so noble a heart she alone held sway. His wound was doing remarkable well, and every day, while attending to his wants, I would ask him pleasantly about the answer to our letter, remarking, that perhaps it was too full of sweet words to be seen by a stranger. At last, I found that all my cheerful words failed to rouse him from the despondent mood into which he had fallen, and I discovered his great anxiety at not receiving an answer to his letter. I begged him to be patient, and explained that the mail had been interrupted by the recent raid, all of which failed to reassure him; and when, going to him the next morning, I saw lying beside him on his pillow a letter, directed by a lady's delicate hand, I felt all would be well. Yes, the letter was delicately directed, delicately written, and delicately worded – but its meaning was not to be misunderstood, it was a cool, calm, regret that she could no longer be his; to which was added the fear that the loss of his limb might affect his prospects in life. He handed me the letter to read. With a look of fixed despair – buried his head in his pillow and wept like a child. To him she had been the embodiment of all that was true and lovely; and while others had mothers, sisters and friends, she was his all. The blow had been sudden, but sure. When he looked up again, his face fore the pallor of marble, and I saw there was no hope. All day long we gave him stimulants, and tried by words of sympathy to rouse him, but in vain; he lingered two days, when the silver cord was loosed and the golden bowl broken. He died, and his last word were, 'tell her I forgive her.'

The article in the book goes on to explain that historian and battlefield guide, Tim Smith, had unearthed the story and had identified the soldier as Maurice Buckingham. Smith explained that during the fighting on Oak Ridge, where the 104th was located, every member of the 104th color guard was either killed or wounded. Sergeant Buckingham was wounded twice, in the shoulder and the right thigh, while carrying one of the regimental colors. He was evacuated to Christ Lutheran Church on Chambersburg Street in Gettysburg where his right leg was amputated. Smith feels a fitting epitaph for Buckingham is the one given him by his commanding officer who called Buckingham, a "Noble Boy." He was 26 years old.

Since the information in the 1865 Census is sequential, it is likely that Buckingham was working for, or living with, one of 14 families in Centerville. One of the families, headed by Samuel Symes appears to be a good prospect since Symes was also born in England. Further, he had an unmarried daughter a couple of years older than Buckingham. However, without further information it is impossible to identify the girl who wrote the letter.

William Henry Harrison Keyes, named for the ninth President of the United States, enlisted in Company G of the 78th New York Infantry (the Eagle's Brigade) on January 4, 1961, at Centerville. Keyes was born in 1840 in New York State to Thomas J. and Emeline Keyes. While the 1860 Census does not list an occupation for him, he most likely was a farm laborer working for his father. He became unhappy with the disorganization he found in the 78th and deserted April 1, 1862. (This unhappiness apparently was widespread since many men from the 78th were transferred to other regiments and two other C-H-G men deserted from the 78th.) Keyes, while a deserter, enlisted in the 154th New York infantry. He was eventually captured and returned to the 78th, February 27, 1863. At Gettysburg he received severe side and back wounds on July 3. He died July 15 at age 23. Two of his letters survive, both apparently written while he was with the 154th Infantry. One is dated September 26, 1862, when he was at Camp J.M. Brown near Jamestown, N.Y. and the other on February 1, 1863, near Falmouth, Virginia. (The 154th history shows they left New York State September 24 and were near Falmouth, Virginia from about December 1862 to April 27, 1863.) The September 26 letter to his father, whom he addresses as "Old Gent," is primarily about money. Keyes relates that, "Uncle Sam uses me first rate." He is talking about the fact that he had been paid twice in just the last couple of days. He also says that all is well and he "expects to leave for Dixie" and then the Rebels "will catch H- - l." His second letter to "Old Gent" begins, "I have a little leisure time and I will improve it by writing to you." This sentence reflects the love and affection for family that many soldiers exhibited in their letters home. Again this letter talks about finances and he tells his father to get his buggy fixed. He also told his father that he was arranging for funds to be automatically deducted from his pay and sent home.

Henry L. Abbey was born April 2, 1841, in Livingston County to Lyman and Emeline Abbey of Granger. He enlisted in 1861. His records say December 26, 1861, at Geneseo, but that was probably his muster date and place. (Almost all of the G-H-G men enlisted locally and then were mustered at a nearby location. Most were mustered at Elmira or Portage Station, while others were mustered in various places including Geneseo. Some did enlist and were mustered on the same day, but most enlisted a short time prior to being mustered. Their military records do not always reflect this. Many times the distinction shows up in their pension records or by the enlistment dates shown on the Allegany County Town Clerk Registers.) Abbey was a farmer prior to the war.

William L. Davis was born in Ontario County to August and Lovina Davis. His prewar occupation is listed as farmer. He enlisted in Company A of the 104th New York Infantry at Granger on October 1, 1861. At age 25, he was killed in action at Gettysburg on July 1, 1863.

Strong Warner Veazey, who may have enlisted with Buckingham, was born July 9, 1845, at Centerville to Lewis and Sarah Ann Veazey. Like his father, he was a farmer, probably more likely a farm laborer working for his father. He served with Company C of the 104th New York Infantry. Severely wounded on July 1, his left leg was amputated. He died July 4, 1863 at the age of 17, five days short of his 18th birthday. Strong's father, Lewis Cass Veazey, also served with Company C, 104th New York Infantry. Lewis enlisted October 11, 1861, and was discharged March 18, 1863, just missing the Battle of Gettysburg. At enlistment he gave his age as 44, but the Allegany Town Clerk Register lists his birth date as May 21, 1811, making him 50 at enlistment.

Families

The Veazey's were one of at least 91 families from the C-H-G area that had more than one family member in the service. They were one of 11 fathers and sons, the others being: Zenas Bradley and his son Nathan; Robert Chamberlain and his sons Joseph and Stephen; Andrew Clark and his son George; Samuel A. Hyde and his son Wallace W.; Richard Hultz and his son Rawsom; John A. Smith and his son George W; Michael McDermott and his son James; Joel W.W. Smith and his sons Alternus and Vernon; Ira Weaver and his son Jacob; and Edward G. Snider and his sons Charles and Darius. Edward G. Snider's brother Benjamin S. also served. Fifty-four families had two sons in the war, and 22 families had three sons in uniform. In four families four sons volunteered. They were: Charles W., Frederick, George, and James H., sons of James Bennett and Frances Carter; Chauncey A., Edward B., Chester, and Lester V., sons of Daniel V. Cronk and Angeline Thayer; Hiram, John, Lycurgus, and William H., sons of Hiram Drew and Anna Hopkins; and Harmon E., Horatio E., John L, and Martin W., sons of John T. Snider/Snyder and Rachael Emmons. Multiple volunteers from the same immediate families accounted for 214 of the total enlistments from the C-H-G area. There were also numerous cousins who served.

Of the seven men captured at Gettysburg, all were captured on July 1, and all were members of the 104th New York Infantry. Those captured were: Daniel J. Clark (who had been wounded at Antietam), Henry Hoadley, John Peck Myer (also wounded at Antietam), Charles Snyder, William Wallace, Francis S. Lincoln, and Adoriana J. Rose.

A Matter of Honor

Adornian Judson Rose was born in Hume, Allegany County, New York in May of 1834. His father, Uriah Rose, born in Rhode Island, was a farmer. His Mother, Sarah Patch, was born in Vermont. Sarah's mother Mary was born in Canada. He was the middle of five children with two older brothers, Delos and Samuel, and two younger sisters, Malissa and Elisa Ann. While his first name was Adornian (there are different spellings in different documents), except for his military service, he almost always went by his middle name, Judson.

By 1860 Judson was working as a clerk for Frank Thing, a merchant in Olean, New York. It is likely that Thing either was from, or related to people in, the Hume area. There were many Things in the C-H-G area and in 1855, Judson's parents had a neighbor named Henry Thing.

Rose volunteered for the Army October 2, 1861, at Geneseo, New York. He was mustered into Company C, 104th New York Infantry October 9, 1861, as a private. He likely was more educated than his fellow volunteers since two days later he was promoted to sergeant. A month later, November 11, 1861, he was promoted to second sergeant. On May 1, 1862, he was promoted to sergeant major and transferred to the noncommissioned officers staff. His records show that he was 5'8" tall, had blue eyes, brown hair and a light complexion.

The 104th Infantry was organized at Geneseo during the period October 1861 to March 1862. On March 22, 1862, the regiment left Geneseo for Washington, D.C. It served in defense of D.C. until May 1862 as part of the Military District of Washington. The regiment was ordered on an expedition to Front Royal, Virginia in late May, served on picket duty on the Shenandoah and at Front Royal until June 10, and duty at Catlett's Station, Warrenton, and Waterloo, Virginia until August. This was a prelude to the establishment of an envious regimental combat record. During the next 11 months (mid-August 1862 to early July 1863) the regiment, and Rose, would participate in seven major battles, three of which were among the most brutal of the entire war. The seven battles were: Cedar Grove, 2nd Bull Run, South Mountain, Antietam, Fredericksburg, Chancellorsville, and Gettysburg. Rose would participate in all of them and would distinguish himself in battle to the point where he was commissioned a second lieutenant on December 5, 1862. The second lieutenant appointment was made retroactive to September 16, 1862. He had been transferred to Company E on that same date.

In between Antietam and Fredericksburg, Rose spent some time in the hospital. He was sick in Kneedsville in late September, following the battle of Antietam, and in October spent some time in the General Hospital in Chester, Pennsylvania.

Rose's final battle was Gettysburg. In the thick of the battle he was captured by Southern forces. (One muster card indicates that he was also wounded, but no other evidence of a wound exists. It may have been that he was wounded at Antietam, rather than Gettysburg. That might explain why he was in the Chester Hospital, following Antietam. There is no specific information as to why he was in that hospital.)

Rose immediately arranged for his own parole. He likely was a prisoner for no more than two or three days. As previously mentioned, General Ulysses S. Grant was opposed to the parole system. He viewed it as a disadvantage to Northern forces. He felt that by 1863 paroled prisoners had become the major source of "new" recruits for the South. As a result, on April 17, 1863, he ordered that exchanges be stopped. However, since Grant was not in charge of all Union forces at the time, it may be that his order did not apply in Rose's case. Nevertheless, given Grant's stature, his decision would almost certainly have influenced others, including the War Department in Washington.

It is not known whether Rose was aware of Grant's decision in April, when he negotiated his own parole at Gettysburg in early July. Subsequent events would tend to indicate that he did not. It is certainly possible that such a change in policy would not have been communicated to the troops in the field in the short period between April 17 and Rose's capture. Given that the exchange system was very popular with the public, the cessation of the system may not even have been announced publicly, and again, it may not have been applicable in Rose's case. The Confederate forces at Gettysburg appear to have been unaware of the policy change. In fact, assuming Grant was correct about the source of "new" recruits, the South had every reason to continue to encourage the exchange of prisoners.

Following his parole, Rose returned to his company, which by this time was located near Rappahannock Station, Virginia. At Rappahannock Rose was given orders to perform military duties. He refused to obey the orders. As a result, he was court-martialed and charged with disobedience of orders with three specifications. Specification I. was that when ordered to do so, he refused to report to his regiment for duty. Specification II. was that when ordered to do so, he refused to go on picket duty. Specification III. was that when ordered to do so, he refused to superintend the issuing of rations to men on picket duty. Rose pleaded not guilty to the charge and all three specifications.

The court-martial took place August 27, 1863, at Headquarters, 1st Division, 1st Army Brigade at Rappahannock Station, Virginia. There was actually no question about whether Rose had disobeyed orders. The real issue was whether he was within his rights to do so. Ironically, neither the prosecution, nor the defense, really addressed this issue by raising the point that exchanges of prisoners were no longer authorized, and thus paroles, that were conditioned upon the parolee not performing any military functions, were not valid. (This again points to the order not applying to Rose.) The prosecution presented evidence and testimony that Rose had, in fact, disobeyed verbal and written orders. It then elicited testimony that Rose had presented his argument regarding the parole he had signed to the War Department and that the War Department had taken the position that the parole was not valid, but apparently did not say why it was not valid. Here again, no reference is made to Grant's decision to discontinue prisoner exchanges, which made paroles based on future prisoner exchanges irrelevant, and clearly not binding.

The prosecution presented several witnesses to prove the disobedience of orders, including the three specifications. One of the prosecution's witnesses, Colonel Gilbert G. Prey, Commander of the 104th Infantry, made somewhat of a joke of himself. Called to testify to Rose's disobedience of his orders, he was asked if Rose had ever previously refused to carry out any orders. He answered yes. When pressed to identify the situation, he replied that Rose had not performed assigned duties on the grounds of being sick. When asked if the Surgeon General had reported him as sick at these times, he also answered yes. With that answer, Colonel Prey was excused.

Another prosecution witness, Captain Alfred P. Van Dresser, is interesting for two reasons. First, because he testified for both the prosecution and the defense. He confirmed for the prosecution that Rose had not obeyed orders that he, Van Dresser, had given to him. In response to the defense, Van Dresser testified that, to his knowledge, Rose had never previously refused to obey an order. The second reason is that Van Dresser was also born in Hume in 1841, three years prior to Rose. Both Van Dresser and Rose were still living in Hume at least as late as 1850. Yet in his testimony, Van Dresser indicated that he had known Rose for only one year. (Some 68 men from the Centerville-Hume-Granger area served with the 104th Infantry during the war.)

Rose made no effort to deny that he had failed to carry out direct orders. Nor did he deny that the War Department had found that his parole was not binding. He did present the parole in evidence, apparently hoping the court would reach a decision different from that of the War Department. The parole read:

"Confederate States Forces Near Gettysburg, PA. July 3, 1863

I, the subscriber, a prisoner of war, captured near Gettysburg, Pa. July 1, 1863, do give my parole of honor, not to take up arms against the Confederate States of America ------ or to do any Military duty whatever, or to give any information prejudicial to the interests of the same, until regularly exchanged. This obligation is unconditional." The parole was signed as follows: " A. J. Rose 2nd Lieut. Comdg Co. E 104th Regt.---- NYS Vols. Witness; Homer Still Adj. 114 Regt. Test Edward Moore A.D. Genl Johnsons Div 2nd Corps A.N. VA."

Rose also made an oral statement at the trial. He said, "The statement which I wish to make is the same which I forwarded to Washington from this place. The circumstances of my parole. I gave my parole at Gettysburg because I deemed it my duty to avoid a march to Richmond if I could do so honorably. But, I did not suppose any officer at Carlisle would receive us as paroled prisoners unless authorized to do so by the War Department. That we were received by the force there, and the flag of truce and escort which accompanied us, was honored by our forces. That they, receiving us as such, the Confederate Government would hold me for my parole. That under these circumstances, I could not conscientiously violate that parole, and made the request that my parole might be recognized, and I should be regularly exchanged as a prisoner of war, or be allowed to return to the rebel lines as such, or granted an honorable discharge from the services."

The statement is somewhat unclear, but it most likely was totally understood by members of the court who would have been familiar with all of the references and internal Army procedures. The lack of clarity may also be the fault of the secretary of the court. He may not have recorded the statement correctly.

The substance, however, is perfectly clear. Rose had given his word and no matter what, he would not, in fact could not, "conscientiously" go back on his word. It was a matter of honor.

His statement further supports that he was unaware, apparently even at this point, of the change of view in the Army regarding paroles. Or maybe he was aware, and he was hoping that his parole would be accepted anyway. If the parole was not to be recognized, he made two other offers, both of which must have seemed honorable and righteous to Rose. One was that he be allowed to surrender to Confederate forces. The other was that he be honorably discharged.

The position of the Court is difficult to understand. It accepted the position of the War Department that the parole was non binding without making any reference to any decisions to cease prisoner exchanges. In fact, no evidence is presented as to why the parole was not acceptable. The defense also failed to question why the parole was non-binding. There does not seem to be any basis, other than Grant's order, for finding the parole non-binding. Maybe it was the War Department's position that prisoners could not negotiate their own paroles. Both the North and the South had, at various times, refused to parole officers, requiring them to wait instead for the official exchange, That would not have been an issue in this case, since the South was not refusing to parole a Northern officer.

All three of Rose's proposals were rejected by the court. Instead, they found him guilty on the charge and all three specifications. The decision of the court was approved and confirmed October 23, 1863, by Major General John Newton, who noted that, "since Rose is persistent in his refusal of duty, in my opinion his case is deserving of no leniency." Rose was dishonorably discharged from the service on October 24, 1863.

Rose married around 1864 or 65. The 1870 Federal Census for Oil City, Venango County, Pennsylvania shows him working as an oil well engineer. He is married to a Susan M and has a son Freeman, age five. The census has his name as Adner J. By 1880 he was living in Perry, New York, about 30 miles from where he was born, and working as a carpenter and joiner. He and wife Susan now had four children, Freeman, Fred, Lolla, and Gilbert. The census lists him as Judson A. Rose. (Interestingly, John Wilkes Booth, in early1864, had invested in the oil business in Venango County. His investments did not turn out well, and before the end of the year he had disposed of his holdings at a considerable loss.)

The question of honor versus duty is a dilemma. When forced to choose, society tends to come down on the side of duty, apparently fearing that if everyone is allowed to behave according to their own sense of honor, society cannot survive. And those that engage in civil disobedience accept that they may, and most likely will, be punished for their violations of society's rules. Yet, in the long term, society generally recognizes those who act in good conscience as honorable citizens. This may be because, in the long run, most of those who practice civil disobedience are proven to have been correct.

Today we punish those who blindly follow orders they know, or should know, to be illegal. This principle was confirmed by the Nuremberg trials where we held German soldiers liable for war crimes even though they were "just following orders." The Constitution of the United States gives citizens the absolute right to peacefully challenge the decisions of their government. United States citizens may openly disagree with their government without fear of reprisal. A time-honored way of doing this is to openly testify before the Congress of the United States. (Incredibly, there are those among us who call people traitors who exercise this Constitutional right, a right deemed essential to a free society by our Founding Fathers.)

Despite the verdict, and the words of General Newton, the Army may have respected Rose's devotion to honor, more than it would first appear. For instance, based on the specifications, it appears that the duties that Rose was ordered to perform became less and less military in nature. In the end, it appears the Army would have been satisfied if Rose had agreed to merely supervise the distribution of rations, a duty which was virtually ceremonial. The punishment handed out, dishonorable discharge, was certainly severe. However, it could have been worse. He could have been sentenced to prison at hard labor. He could have been fined. One or both of these, and the dishonorable discharge, could have been imposed. Instead it appears that the Army choose a middle course which confirmed the need to maintain order in its ranks, but which also may have made a bow to a man's conscience and honor.

According to a marker in the New York section of the Gettysburg Cemetery, 863 New York soldiers are buried there. Individual military records for the seven C-H-G men killed at Gettysburg, indicate that six are buried there. However, the only markers at the cemetery for C-H-G men are for Maurice Buckingham, Strong Veazey, William Keyes, and Thomas Curtis. It does not appear that William L. Davis and William Hussong are buried at Gettysburg. At least there is no record of such burials at the cemetery.

The regiments with C-H-G men were bloodied, but victorious at Gettysburg. The advance of Southern troops to the North was over. From now on, the war would again be fought on Southern soil. The victory at Gettysburg was complimented by Grant's victory at Vicksburg in the West.

On July 6, 1863, there was an encounter at Hagerstown, Maryland in which the 5th Cavalry participated. George Washington Wells of Company F was captured. Wells, born December 16, 1864, was the son of Nathaniel Wells and Polly Wright. He had enlisted September 2, 1861, at Gainesville and was discharged September 21, 1864, at Harpers Ferry, West Virginia. On March 15, 1866, he was married to Flora A. Daine in Gainesville. Pension records indicate that he was previously married to Minerva Butler, probably in 1859. She died in 1863. Oddly, Minevra does not appear in the 1860 Hume Census with George. He eventually moved his family to Minnesota and died there in Farmington, February 15, 1908.

John S. Trowbridge of Company E, 5th New York Cavalry also died July 6, 1863. Trowbridge had received a gunshot wound to his leg, June 30 at Hanover, Pennsylvania. The wound was so severe that the leg was amputated, and as so often happened during the war, wounded men died of the treatment and not the wound. Trowbridge was 25 years, six months old. He was the son of John Trowbridge and Anna Swin or Swain. Like his father, prior to the war he had been a Baptist minister. He enlisted August 26, 1861, at East Rushford. Ironically, he had been captured a year earlier on August 2 at Orange County Court House, but had been paroled and returned to action.

Roswell Byington of the 5th Cavalry was also wounded June 30 at Hanover, although his files do not mention the type of wound, nor how he was wounded. Byington was born in Cattaraugus County in May of 1840 to Richard and Hestor Byington. By 1850 the family was living in Hume. On December 31, 1872, he married Clara Freeman, his second wife. His first wife, Sophia A. Bixby, whom he married May 3, 1868, had died in 1870. Interestingly, the 1900 Census claims that Roswell and Clara had been married 30 years. Roswell was also wounded June 3, 1864, at Luiney's House, Virginia. He accidently shot himself in the calf of his left leg. He participated in numerous battles and was at Appomattox Court House for Lee's surrender. He also marched in the Grand Review in Washington on May 23, 1865. Byington died August 13, 1915, in Centerville and is buried there.

Dyer's Compendium of the War of the Rebellion, Part 3 provides the following information on the 5th New York Cavalry:

5th Regiment Cavalry -"1st Ira Harris' Guard." Regiment recruited at New York City as Ira Harris Cavalry. Designated Ira Harris Guard October 16,1861, <dy-1374> and 5th New York Cavalry November 14, 1861. Companies mustered in as follows: "A" August 15, "B" August 21, "C" September 3, "D" October I, "E" October 7, "F" September 21, "G" October 9, "H" October 28, "I," "K," "L" and "M" October 31, 1861. Left State for Baltimore, Md., November 18, 1861. Attached to Dix's Command to March, 1862. Banks' 5th Corps March and April, 1862. Hatch's Cavalry Brigade, Department Of the Shenandoah, to June, 1862. Cavalry Brigade, 2nd Corps, Army of Virginia, to September, 1862. Wyndham's Cavalry Brigade, Defenses of Washington, to February , 1863. Price's Independent Cavalry Brigade, 22nd Army Corps, Dept. of Washington, to April, 1863. 3rd Brigade, Stahel's Cavalry Division, 22nd Army Corps, to June 28, 1863. 1st Brigade, 3rd Division, Cavalry Corps, Army of the Potomac, and Army of the Shenandoah, Middle Military Division, to March, 1865. Cavalry , Army of the Shenandoah, to July, 1865.
SERVICE.--Duty at Camp Harrs, Baltimore, Md., November 18, 1861, to March 31, 1862. Ordered to join Banks in the field March 31. South Fork, Shenandoah River, April 19 .New Market April 29. Port Republic May 2. Conrad's Store May 2 and 6. Report to Gen. Hatch May 3. Rockingham Furnace May 4. Near Harrisonburg May 6. New Market May 7. Columbia River Bridge May 8. Bowling Green Road near Fredericksburg May II. Operations in the Shenandoah Valley May 15-June 17. Woodstock May 18. Front Royal May 23 (Cos. "B" and "D"). Strasburg, Middletown and Newtown May 24. Winchester May 25. Defense of Harper's Ferry May 28-30 (4 Cos.). Reconnaissance to New Market June 15. Near Culpeper Court House July 12. Liberty Mills July 17. Near Orange Court House August 2. Cedar Mountain August 9-10. Pope's Campaign in Northern Virginia August 16-September 2. Louisa Court House August 17. Kelly's Ford August 20. Warrenton Springs August 23-24. Waterloo Bridge August 24. Centreville August 28. Groveton August 29. Lewis Ford and Bull Run August 30. Chantilly September I. Antietam, Md., September 17-19. Ash by's Gap September 22. Leesburg October 16. Upperville October 17. Thoroughfare Gap and Haymarket October 18. New Baltimore November 5. Cedar Hill November 5.Hopewell Gap November 8. Thoroughfare Gap November II. Middleburg November 12. Upperville November 16. Aldie November 29. Snicker's Gap and Berryville November 30. Aldie December 18. Cub Run December 31. Frying Pan January 5, 1863. Cub Run January 5. Middleburg January 26. New Baltimore February 9. Warrenton February 10. Aldie March 4. Fairfax Court House March 9. Little River Turnpike and Chantilly March 23. Broad Run April 1. White Plains April 128. Warrenton Junction May 3. Flemming and Shannon Cross Roads May 4. Near Fairfax Court House May 8. Marsteller's Place May 14. Greenwich May 30. Snicker's Gap June I. Middleburg June 10. Warrenton June 19. Hanover"Pa., June 30. Hunterstown July 2. Gettysburg, Pa., July 3. Monterey Pass July 4. Smithsburg July 5. Hagerstown and Williamsport July 6. Boonsboro July 8. Hagerstown July 11-13. Falling Waters July 14. Hagerstown July 15. Ashby's Gap July 26. Expedition to Port Conway September 1-3. Lamb's Creek September I. Advance from the Rappahannock to the Rapidan September 13-17. Culpeper Court House September 13. Rapidan Station September 13-14. Somerville Ford September 14.. Raccoon Ford September 14-16. Kelly's Ford September 18. Madison Court House September 21. Reconnaissance across the Rapidan September 21-23. White's Ford September 21-22. Brookin's Ford September 22. Hazel River Bridge September 25. Creigerville October 8. Bristoe Campaign October 9-22. Russell's Ford, James City and Bethesda Church October 10.

Speuyville Pike, Brandy Station and near Culpeper October II. Gainesville October 14. New Market October 16. Groveton October 17-18. Haymarket, Gainesville and Buckland's Mills October 19. Advance to line of the Rappahannock November 7-8. Stevensburg November 8. Germania Ford November 18. Mine Run Campaign November 26-December 2. Morton's Ford November 26. Raccoon Ford November 26-27. Ely's Ford January 19 and 22, 1864. Demonstration on the Rapidan February 6- 7. Kilpatrick's Raid to Richmond February 28-March 4. Ely's Ford February 28. Beaver Dam Station and South Anna Bridge February 29. Defenses of Richmond March I. Hanovertown March 2. Aylett's and Stevensville March 2. King's and Queen's Court House March 3. I; Ely's Ford March 4. Field's Ford March 8. Southard's Cross Roads March II. Rapidan Campaign May-June. Parker's Store May 5. Todd's Tavern May 5-6. Wilderness May 6- 7. Germania Ford, Brock Road and the Furnaces May 7. Todd's Tavern May 7-8. Spottsylvania May 8-18. Downer's Bridge and Milford Station May 20. Mattapony River and Bowling Green May 21. North Anna River May 24. Mt. Carmel Church May 25. On line of the Pamunky May 26-28. Totopotomoy May 28-31. Hanover Court House May 29. Mechump's Creek May 30. Signal Hill May 31. Ashland Station June I. Cold Harbor June 1-12. Gaines' Mill, Totopotomoy and Salem Church June 2. Haw's Shop June 3. Old Church June 10 Shady Grove and Bethesda Church June II. Riddell's Shop and Long Bridge June 12. White Oak Swamp June 13. Malvern Hill June 14. Smith's Store near St. Mary's Church June 15. White House Landing June 19. Wilson's Raid on South Side & Danville Railroad. June 22-30. Black and white and Nottaway Court House June 23. Staunton Bridge June 24.Roanoke Bridge June 25. Sappony Church or Stony Creek June 28. Ream's Station June 29. Before Petersburg till July 30. (A detachment of Regiment left at Dismounted Camp, participated in actions at Maryland Heights July 6-7. Rockville, Md., July 10. Tell Gate July 12. Poolesville July 15. Snicker's Ferry July 18, and Kernstown July 24.) Sheridan's Shenandoah Valley Campaign August 7-November 28. Winchester and Halltown August 17. Opequan August 19. Summit Point August 21. Charlestown August 22. Duffield Station August 23. Near Kearneysville August 25. Berryville Steptember 2-4. Duffield Station September 3. Darkenville September 3. Opequan September 7 -13-15 and 17. Abraham's Creek near Winchester September 13. Battle of Winchester September 19. Near Cedarville and Crooked Run September 20. Front Royal Pike and Fisher's Hill September 21. Milford September 22. New Market September 23-24. Mt. Crawford September 24. Waynesboro September 26. Port Republic September 26-27. Mt. Meridian September 27. Waynesboro and Railroad Bridge September 29. Bridgewater October 2. Brock's Gap October 6. Forestville October 7. Near Columbia Furnace October 7. Tom's Brook, "Woodstock Races," October 8-9. Back Road Cedar Creek October 13. Lebanon Church October 14. Cedar Run October 18. Battle of Cedar Creek October 19.Newtown and Nineyah November 12. Mr. Jackson November 22. Expedition to Lacy Springs December 19-22. Lacy Springs December 21. Woodstock January 10, 1865. Edenburg January 22. Sheridan's Raid February 27-March 3. Waynesboro March 2. Capture of Gen. Early's Command. Detached from Division to guard prisoners from Waynesboro to Winchester. Mr. Sidney and Lacy Springs March 5. New Market March 6 Rood's Hill March 7. (A portion of Regiment at Dinwiddie Court House March 30-31. Five Forks April 1. Fall of Petersburg April 2. Sweet House Creek April3. Harper's Farm April6. Appomattox Station April 8. Appomattox Court House April 9. Surrender of Lee and his army.) Regiment on duty at Headquarters Middle Military Division and in vicinity of Winchester till.' July. Mustered out July 19,1865, and honorably discharged from service. Regiment lost during service 8 Officers and 93 Enlisted men killed and mortally wounded and 3 Officers and 222 Enlisted men by disease. Total 326.

At least 17 C-H-G men served with the 5th New York Cavalry. They were: Elias Neilon Andrews, Henry C. Browne, Roswell Norton Byington, John W. Claus, Clarence Melville Clough, Riley A. Hurlburt, William H. Parks, Eugene M. Pratt, Perrie C. Soule, William W. Sowersby, John S. Trowbridge, James Vreeland, George Washington Wells, Miles W. Wells, William Harrison Wells, Daniel Wight, and Marvin Wight. Twelve of the 17 men suffered the following: four were KIA, five were WIA, two were injured, nine became POWs, and two died of diseases. In addition, two others were sick during their service and three received disability discharges.

Roanoke Island, North Carolina

William H. Bower, Company I, 85th New York Infantry, injured his hand when he fell crossing Pitt's Bridge at Roanoke Island. The 85th conducted a raid on Roanoke Island in August of 1863, and it is likely that Bower's injury occurred at that time. Bower was born December 20, 1840 in Alfred. He apparently lived in Short Tract late in his life. Prior to that he had lived in Ward and Amity. He died in Short Tract March 15, 1925. His first wife was Mary E. Norton. After she died, he married widow Mary Bradley Streeter. Both Streeter's father and brother, Zenas and Nathan Bradley served in the war. Her grandfather served in the war of 1812 and a nephew served in the Philippines, probably during the Spanish American War. Bower was among the many members of the 85th captured at Plymouth, North Carolina April 20, 1864. He managed to escape, and returned to the remnants of his regiment. He was discharged June 3, 1865. Bower is buried in Belmont.

Manassas Junction, Virginia

Palmer Karns, Company A, 19th New York Cavalry, was born May 10, 1840 in Dansville, New York. Karns volunteered August 31, 1862 and was discharged June 30, 1865. During his service he participated in at least 28 battles and skirmishes, all without being wounded or becoming a prisoner of war. His only injury occurred August 15, 1863, at Manassas Junction when he was loading freight and damaged his hip. He was at Appomattox Court House for Lee's surrender and participated in the Grand Review in Washington, DC May 23, 1865. He was not a C-H-G native, but was in the area by at least November 4, 1881, when he became a Charter Member of Burnside Grand Army of the Republic Post 237. His sister Minerva was married to Civil War veteran, George W. Curtis, and that may be what brought him to the area.

Bristoe Station, Virginia, October 14, 1863

This battle took place as the Confederate Army attempted to regroup following Gettysburg. Lee, upon learning that two Northern corps opposing him had been reassigned, decided to make an advance on Washington. However, the attempt failed miserably when, at Bristoe's Station, the Southern troops, under General Hill, stumbled into a trap and were practically destroyed.

During this battle, Ralph Parker of C-H-G was wounded and Patrick McCabe was captured. Parker was born in April of 1830, in Deerfield, Pennsylvania to George Parker and Polly Cloos. He enlisted August 9, 1862, at Caneadea in Company I of the 6th New York Cavalry, the same company and regiment as future Medal of Honor winner George E. Meach. His file does not indicate the exact nature of his wound, but it was severe enough that he was sent to the Ladies Home Hospital in New York City. While there he reenlisted in 145 Company, 2nd Battalion, Veteran's Reserve Corps. Unfortunately, while in the hospital he also caught pneumonia and died April 28, 1865. Parker is buried at Pine Grove Cemetery, Fillmore.

Patrick McCabe was drafted at Hume on July 14, 1863, into Company A, 76th New York Infantry. He was born in Ireland about 1833, and by 1860 he was living in Hume. He was reported as a deserter October 13, 1863. It was later determined that he had been captured. Imprisoned in one of the Richmond, Virginia prisons, he died December 28, 1863, of chronic diarrhea. His name is spelled differently in different documents with McKail, McCall, being just two spellings.

Manassas - September 22, October 14, October 17, October 19, 1863

Azem F. Bowen was born in February of 1840 to Elias Bowen and Lydia Wellington in East Otto, Cattaraugus County, New York. On August 8, 1862, at Arcade, he volunteered for Company C of the 19th New York Cavalry. After the war he lived mostly in Centerville, although he died at Black Creek on October 24, 1907. Like many men, Bowen fought in numerous Civil War battles, including Deserted House, Manassas, Winchester, Cedar Creek, the Wilderness, Spotsylvania, Cold Harbor, Trevillian Station, in the Shenandoah Valley, and at Weldon Railroad. He was a Charter Member of Grand Army of the Republic Post 237. He was captured at Manassas on September 22, 1863, and was imprisoned both at Libby and Belle Island prisons in Richmond.

The C-H-G area would suffer only one more fatality during the balance of 1863. That would occur at Manassas. On October 17, Thomas Pendergast was killed in action and buried on the battlefield. Thomas had been born in Ireland to Patrick and Mary Pendergast. His father Patrick received his pension. Prewar he was a laborer. At the age of 22, he enlisted at Hume on August 9, 1862, in Company F of the 19th New York Cavalry. The 1860 Census shows that he was working for Augustus Hammond as a farm laborer. All the men buried on the battlefield at Manassas were eventually re-interred in the Rose Garden section of Arlington Cemetery. However, almost all are in graves marked "Unknown."

On October 19 Nathan C. Bradley was captured. When his mother applied for Nathan's pension, he claimed the name was actually Charles Nathan Bradley. Bradley had enlisted in Company H, 19th New York Cavalry August 1, 1862, at Oramel. He was born in 1836 or 37 to Zenas Bradley (who also served) and Mary White. He died at Libby Prison in Richmond March 9, 1864, of diarrhea. An unsolved mystery surrounding Bradley is why he took leave in July of 1863 to visit the Irish Mission (then part of the Great Britain delegation to the United States in Washington, DC). He was born in New York (probably Allegany County) and his parents were born in Vermont.

Manassas had turned out to be a deadly place for C-H-G soldiers, and it would claim one more life before the end of the war. Edwin Wight, Company F, 19th New York Cavalry, was killed in action at Manassas October 17, 1864. The son of Benjamin Wight and Jericho Lyon, he was one of three brothers who fought in the war. Another brother, Daniel, also was killed. His brother Marvin survived the war. Edwin was born January 28, 1844, in Centerville and enlisted August 9, 1862, at Hume. He is buried in Centerville (Manassas), Virginia.

Conscription

The Civil War marked the first time in the history of the country that men were drafted into the military. The South passed the first conscription law April 16, 1862. The North followed a year later. Until that time all the men on both sides had been volunteers. The regiments were, in fact, officially titled Volunteer Regiments. Compulsory service received the same response then as it has throughout much of the country's history, although the reaction was much more heated than in later years. The traditional concerns, conscripted men make bad soldiers and it is an infringement on individual liberties, were voiced, but there was also a feeling that it was bad for morale. Volunteer soldiers didn't like or trust conscripts. More importantly, it appeared to many volunteers that it was an act of desperation by the government and an indication that the war was going badly. The reason that may have made it the most distasteful to many, however, was the class discrimination it permitted. The law allowed for substitutes, exemptions, and commutation. That meant the rich could buy a substitute, or simply pay a fee (commutation - $300 in the North, $500 in the South) and avoid the draft. The poor did not have the resources to do likewise. Worse yet, some doctors (who had to examine and determine the qualifications for service of each man drafted) were not averse to finding healthy rich men unfit for service, while qualifying obviously unfit (including mentally deficient) poor men for service. It also resulted in many desertions. Under the Union draft act, men were conscripted in July 1863 and March, July, and December of 1864. (It appears that, although conscripted in those months, they were not necessarily mustered until sometime later.) There were many riots in response to the law, especially in New York City. National data show that of the 249,000 18 to 35-year-old men drafted, only 3 percent served. The rest paid commutation, hired a substitute, or were exempted for some reason.

The "Registers of Draftees July 1863 to October, 1864" for Centerville, Hume and Granger show the following: In Centerville 42 men were called-up. Of these, at least four served, five men paid commutation, and two furnished substitutes. One, Almond Van Dresser, is listed as "failed to report," but, in fact, he was already in the service. Two were transferred to 2nd class and exempted. Gilbert Foot was rejected due to bad feet. However, per the 1865 New York State Census his mother claimed that he served, and that he was hanged for desertion. No military file for Gilbert Foot has been identified and he does not appear on the list of soldiers executed for desertion during the war. Of the remaining 27 men, 15 were rejected for medical reasons such as a short leg, deaf, missing finger, bad leg, insane, three toes missing, splay feet, dislocated right elbow, hernia, and heart problems. Another nine were excused. One of these was an only son, four were too old, and four were aliens or nonresidents. Two were determined to be dead, and the notation for the last man called-up says he didn't exist. One man, Hiram Chamberlain, is shown as drafted, but no military record appears to exist for him.

Fifty-three men in Hume Township were called-up. Of the 53, eight were finally drafted. One other person, Harvey W. Rice, appears to have paid commutation, but in fact, also served. Seven men were excused, five as only sons and two as nonresidents. Twenty men, not counting Harvey Rice, paid commutation, and one furnished a substitute. Two men did not report, and no outcome is listed for one man, Asian Burr. There is no record that he served.

The register for Granger indicates that 26 men were called-up. Of this number two served, five paid commutation, one furnished a substitute, three were only sons, 14 were excused for various medical reasons, and one for being the father of motherless children.

There were four men from the C-H-G area who furnished substitutes. The military records of 12 men from C-H-G who actually served show that they were, or may have been substitutes, for other men. However, material identified, to date, indicates that only one of these men who actually served was a substitute for one of the four C-H-G men who provided substitutes. The 1865 Allegany County Town Clerk Register for Granger shows that a John Adams was a substitute for a Henry Isaman. Isaman (or Iserman) does appear on the Register of Draftees, and is noted as having provided a substitute.

Overall data for Northern draftees shows that only four of every ten men whose names were called were found eligible for military service. Of the four, two paid commutation. This does not include those who furnished substitutes.

Morrisville, Hay Market, Virginia - Opelousa, Louisiana, October 1863

Three more C-H-G men were captured prior to the end of 1863. Ferris E. Kendall was born in Centerville November 30, 1837, to Clark Rufus Kendall and Roxanna Gilman. He enlisted August 9, 1862, at Centerville in Company F, 19th New York Cavalry. He was captured October 25, 1863, at Morrisville, Virginia and imprisoned at Richmond where he contracted typhoid fever. Captured after General Grant's decision to stop the prisoner exchange program (parole), he apparently was exchanged in early 1865 when the program was reinstated for injured and sick prisoners. He died in Centerville March 26, 1865. (His military records say Rushford, but his mother, when applying for his pension, said Centerville, and she certainly knew.) On the other hand, she thought he was imprisoned at Andersonville, but the military said Richmond and, in this case, the military was most likely correct. Kendall is buried in Centerville. Ferris' brother Ezra was killed at Fair Oaks.

Marvin Wight was captured at Hay Market, Virginia October 29, 1863. He was imprisoned at Belle Island in Richmond. Wright, the son of Benjamin Wright and Jerusha Lyon, was born July 11, 1839, in Centerville and enlisted there September 12, 1861, in Company F, 5th New York Cavalry. His two brothers, Daniel and Edwin, also served. On October 17, 1866, he married Louise Bracken in Columbus, Pennsylvania. He died in Cory, Pennsylvania April 16, 1929.

William Bean was born in Sutton, England April 27, 1820, to Richard Bean and Elizabeth Lime. He married Polly Ann Davis in 1861 and enlisted in Company I, 160th New York Infantry on August 28, 1862. His military records indicate his age as 38 when he enlisted, but he was actually 42. He was captured at Opelousa, Louisiana October 31, 1863. He was paroled, but later contracted chronic diarrhea and died at the 12th Maine Infantry Hospital in Lake End, Louisiana. He is buried near New Orleans.

Chattanooga, Tennessee (Lookout Mountain), September - December 1863

The battle of Chattanooga, a major Union victory, followed close upon the heels of the Union loss at Chickamauga. The most noted engagement was the "battle above the clouds" at Lookout Mountain. Only one New York regiment with a significant number of C-H-G men fought in the battle of Chattanooga, the 136th New York Infantry. This same regiment would be with Sherman on his march to the sea and would participate in the siege and occupation of Atlanta.

One local man was wounded at Lookout Mountain. John Townsend of Company H, 136th New York Infantry was wounded for the third time at Lookout Mountain. This time it was a gunshot wound to his right hip. He had been previously wounded at 2nd Bull Run and at Gettysburg. He was to be wounded once more.

Mine Run, Alexandria, Virginia

Orlon Babcock was born September 6, 1842, in Rushford. He later lived in Centerville with his parents, William and Sarah Austin Babcock. His brothers, George Washington Babcock and Martin Van Buren Babcock, also served. Given the names of his brothers, it may be that Orlon was a family name that had to be given to one of the sons. Orlon served with Company A, 108th New York Infantry. He received a furlough to Centerville in February of 1863, after spending time in Finley General Hospital in Washington, DC and Aquia Creek Hospital. When he failed to return at the appointed time, he was charged with desertion. He was arrested September 26, 1863, in Centerville and returned to his regiment. A $17 bounty was paid for his capture. There apparently were no repercussions for his desertion, since he received an honorable discharge and a pension. At the battle of Mine Run, Virginia, December 1863, Babcock was close to an explosion. He later claimed, and the claim was accepted, that the explosion led to bronchitis. Following the explosion, he was at first sent to Harewood General Hospital in DC, then to DeCamp Hospital on David Island in New York Harbor. He was eventually transferred to a Rochester, New York hospital and from there to the Convalescent Camp on Bedloe Island in New York Harbor. He then returned to his regiment and participated in some of the final battles of the war. He was with his regiment at Lee's surrender and marched in the Grand Review in Washington, D.C. on May 23, 1865. After the war he returned to Centerville and married Phenic C. Jones. He eventually moved his family to Morgan County, Tennessee where he died March 3, 1887. His brother George also settled in Tennessee.

David Wilbur Williams was the son of William and Jane Jones Williams. They were born in Wales. He was born October 17, 1836, in Floyd, Oneida County. The family eventually settled in Centerville. In December of 1863, Williams was helping in the construction of a building in Alexandria, Virginia. He slipped and fell astride a hewn log, injuring his back and left testicle.

Edwin S. Drury, Company C, 4th Michigan Cavalry, was severely wounded by gunshot in Cleveland, Tennessee on December 22, 1863. He died of his wounds January 15, 1864.

Despite the increased intensity of the war and the killing fields of Gettysburg, the overall toll on C-H-G men in 1863 was a little less than had been the case in 1862. Thirteen men were killed in action, two more than in 1862, while 37 were wounded or injured, seven less than in 1862. Those captured totaled 21, versus nine for 1862, while those dying of diseases numbered 13, 9 less than 1862.

THE WAR - 1864 - DEATH

While the bloodiest one day battle of the war occurred in 1862 (Antietam, September 17, 1862), and the bloodiest overall battle occurred in 1863 (Gettysburg, July 1-2-3, 1863), 1864 would be for the men of C-H-G, the bloodiest year of the war. War raged throughout the Southern states. And, wherever war waged, C-H-G men died, were wounded, were injured, or were captured.

In 1864, death appeared to be a constant. In January, combat took Edwin Drury and disease claimed Stephen A. Chamberlain. Disease struck again, taking Francis S. Lincoln, Alva Hamlin, William H. Wells, William Wallace, and John W. Emmons in February; Nathan Bradley in March; and Elisha Prior in April. May saw Henry Hotchkiss, Gurdin J. Franklin, William C. Hall, David Lockwood, George Worden, Darwin Ellis, Oliver Barnard, and Martin Babcock killed in action and Augustus Chase, William W. Warner, and David Evans succumb to diseases. In June, William R. Bentley, Samuel Burleson, William Gillett, and Gilbert Moultrop were KIA and Joseph Bentley, Charles R. Rotch, and William Bean lost their lives to disease. In July, both John Stickle and Daniel Wight died of combat wounds received earlier, and disease struck with a vengeance taking James Bennett, Isaac Morse, Horton Chamberlain , Hiram Drew, Luther Moses, and William Gray. August was even more brutal. Icabod Flenagin, Martin W. Snider, and Emerson Parker died in battle, and Noah L. Myers, Carey E. Bingham, Charles D. Williams, Egbert B. Pierson, James E. Holbrook, Oren S. Reynolds, and David M. Cox were taken by diseases. Alexander Kelsey Thorp and William Curtis Daniels lost their lives in combat, and Sidney M. Chase, George Henry Cole, Daniel Finch, Eber Bullock, Henry Vosburgh, William Elwood, Willliam S. Whittle, and Jacob D. Weaver lost their battles with diseases in September. In October, Darwin Barrows and Edwin Wight were the last to die in battle in 1864. That same month saw Isaiah Brockway, Frederick Willard, John Barney and Charles E. Relya lose out to diseases, as did Silas E. Standard, Charles Buckbee, and George H. Shepard in November, and Moses Luther, Randolph Fox, Ira Burroughs, George W. Jones, William S. Smith, David Prior, and George Sibbald in December.

The C-H-G men who were killed in action in 1864 died in big and small battles. While most died in Virginia, where the war was slowly grinding toward its conclusion, a few died elsewhere, including with General William T. Sherman in a major battle at Resaca, Georgia, just outside of Atlanta.

Cleveland, Tennessee, January 15, 1864

The year 1864 was only fifteen days old when Edwin S. Drury died of wounds received in Cleveland, Tennessee. Drury had enlisted August 9, 1863, in Company C, 4th Michigan Infantry at Comstock, Michigan. Per the 1860 Census, Edwin and his brother Eli were living in Kalamazoo, Michigan with a Dr. Babcock, who was also born in New York. Edwin was working as a farm laborer. Their parents, Samuel and Hannah Burgess Drury, were living in Granger and had been since at least 1850. Edwin was born in Cayuga County in 1835. Upon his death, his commanding officer said of him, "The amiable comrade. A brave and patriotic soldier - he never knew fear. He fell a martyr to the cause for which he so nobly fought."

Ironically, Edwin Buchanan of Hume, moved to Cleveland, Tennessee (situated just north of Chattanooga) after the war. He died there July 31, 1913. He is buried in the local Cleveland cemetery. Buchanan served with both the 33rd New York Infantry and the 2nd New York Mounted

Rifles. Before joining the army he was a teacher in Hume. He was born May 10, 1839, in Hume to John Buchanan and Betsey Slusser. Postwar, he resumed his teaching career. He married four times. His first wife was Adaline Corey, whom he married in 1867 in Cattaraugus County. She died in 1868 in Yorkshire. He next married Elizabeth O. Leech in 1870 in Lane Grove, Wisconsin. She died December 4, 1904, in Cleveland, TN. His third wife was Tabitha Elizabeth Timeley whom he married November 22, 1906, and divorced January 13, 1910. His fourth, and last wife, was Martha Malinda Nipper whom he married April 4, 1911. Martha received his Civil War pension. Buchanan is another one of those very lucky soldiers. He served from July 4, 1861, to June 2, 1862, and despite participating in several battles, including Antietam, 2nd Bull Run and Fredericksburg, he was never wounded, injured, or captured.

Wounded Men

Like all combat soldiers, Civil War C-H-G soldiers had to deal with wounds that, in many cases, were so severe they negatively impacted the soldiers the rest of their lives. Further, being wounded did not necessarily mean the end of the war. Five C-H-G men were wounded in more than one battle. Daniel Algeroy Hildreth, 4th Heavy Artillery, was wounded May 12, 1864, at Spottsylvania and May 20 at Richmond;   Alfonse Aldrich, 19th Cavalry, was wounded at New Market on August 1, 1864, and at New Town on November 11, 1864; Jasper M. Griggs, 104th Infantry, was wounded December 13, 1862, at Fredericksburg and July 1, 1863, at Gettysburg; Alonzo Camp, 136th Infantry, was wounded July 2, 1863, at Gettysburg and May 15, 1864, at Resaca, Georgia. The most wounded man was John Townsend of the 136th Infantry. He was wounded four times: August 30(?), 1862, at 2nd Bull Run below the left knee; July 2, 1863, at Gettysburg above the left knee; November 1863 at Lookout Mountain in the right hip (the minnie ball stayed in the hip); and (probably) February 1865 in the right arm at Fort Fisher, North Carolina. Despite the wounds, Townsend soldiered on until the end of the war, being discharged June 13, 1865.

Wounded/Captured - Wounded/Killed

Seventeen men were wounded and also captured. One of these was Jasper M. Griggs who was wounded at both Gettysburg and Richmond. He was captured at Richmond. Four men were wounded in one battle and killed in another. They were: Thomas J. Curtis wounded September 17, 1862 at Antietam and killed in action July 1, 1863, at Gettysburg; William Hussong was also wounded at Antietam on September 17 and killed in action at Gettysburg; Horatio Smith was wounded May 27, 1862, at Hanover Court House and killed in action at 2nd Bull Run on August 30, 1862. John Trowbridge was captured August 2, 1862, at Orange County Court House, wounded June 30, 1863, at Hanover, Pennsylvania, and died July 6, 1863.

The most men wounded in a one day battle was 14, at Antietam, September 17, 1862. Thirteen men were wounded at Gettysburg during the three day (July 1-3, 1863) battle and seven were wounded May 31 - June 1, 1862, at Fair Oaks. Seven were also wounded May 15, 1864, at Resaca, Georgia.

Not surprisingly, the 104th New York Infantry had the most men wounded during the war - 27. The 104th was followed by the 4th New York Heavy Artillery with 17, and the 19th New York Cavalry (1st Dragoons) and 136th New York Infantry with 14 each. Other regiments with significant numbers of wounded, especially considering the total number of C-H-G men in the regiments, were the 64th New York Infantry with ten, and the 44th New York Infantry and 2nd New York Mounted Rifles with six each. There were only five C-H-G men in the 44th. One of the men, George V. Hill, was wounded twice.

Ellis Ford, January 22, 1864

William Harrison Wells (whose name may have been William Henry Harrison Wells after the practice of the day) was born February 4, 1832, in Pike, New York, to Nathaniel Wells and Polly Wright. By 1850 the family lived in Hume, but Wells, nevertheless, enlisted in Company F, 5th New York Cavalry at Pike. Wells was one of the few men to be captured twice. He was initially captured at New Baltimore, Virginia March 11, 1863, and paroled March 31, 1863. He was captured again January 22, 1864, at Ellis Ford, Virginia while on picket duty. Imprisoned at Andersonville, Georgia, he died of variola on August 15, 1864. He is buried in Andersonville.

Snicker's Gap, Virginia, November 2, 1862 and March 4, 1864

Snicker's Gap is somewhat west of Purcellville, Virginia in the Shenandoah Valley. The site of a number of skirmishes, two C-H-G men were captured there, one on November 2, 1862, and one on March 4, 1864.

William Henry Culver was born January 2, 1841, in Victor, Ontario County to John Culver and Mary Glover. He enlisted February 13, 1862, at Geneseo in Company F, 104th New York Infantry. He married Parmelia Smith August 9, 1863. Captured November 2, 1862, at Snickers Gap he was in the Union Hospital in Georgetown, Washington, DC by February 18, 1863. There is nothing in his file to indicate where, if anywhere, he was imprisoned. He may have been paroled immediately. After the war he moved to Doral, Michigan and worked as a mill engineer. Prior to the war he listed his occupation as farmer. He died in Doral February 21, 1914.

Jacob Darling Weaver initially served with Company I, 27th New York Infantry. He later served with Company D, 1st New York Veteran Cavalry. It was while he was with the 1st Veteran Cavalry that he was captured at Snickers Gap on March 4, 1864. He was imprisoned at Andersonville and died there September 27, 1864. Jacob was born July 28, 1842, in Granger to Ira Ramson Weaver and Cheney White Smith. His father Ira also served and was killed in action at Southside RR in 1865. Ira and Jacob are the only father and son from the C-H-G area to both die during the war.

Southard Crossroads, Virginia, March 1864

On March 11, 1864, while on picket duty, Eugene M. Pratt of Company F, 5th New York Cavalry, was involved in a skirmish in which he received eight flesh wounds to his left leg and thigh. His wounds were treated at Armory Square Hospital in Washington, DC. The skirmish was just prior to the start of the Rapidan Campaign. Pratt, who in future years would live in both Hume and Granger, was the son of Otis and Mary Pratt and was born in Eagle, New York in January of 1844. He married twice, but the name of his first wife is not noted in his records. His second wife was Mary A. Battles. Pratt was one of those men to whom multiple things happened. During the war he was also thrown by his horse and smashed his nose. He was also captured at Berrysville,

VA September 1, 1864. Nevertheless, he survived the war, and married Mary October 6, 1870, in Castile. He is buried in Wiscoy, New York.

Hatcher's Run - Near Petersburg, Virginia

John McElroy, Company D, 4th New York Heavy Artillery, was born in Ireland. He enlisted at Hume December 18, 1863. His brother Hugh also served. He also had a brother Thomas living in Fillmore. He was accidently injured by an axe April 1, 1864, chopping wood (some records incorrectly say April 1863, however, he didn't enlist until December 1863). The wound was from his second toe to the phalanx of his right foot. Originally sent to City Point Hospital, he was transferred to Mt. Pleasant Hospital in Washington, DC May 7, 1864. He was then transferred to Lowell General Hospital in Rhode Island. Lowell records indicate that he deserted from the hospital July 6, 1864. There is no record of any trial, and by August 1864, his company reports him as present for duty. In pension documents he claimed several other wounds as a result of a shell explosion at Petersburg. However, there is no information in his files which support these claims. It is likely that he was injured by a shell at Petersburg, but not severely enough to require hospitalization.

After the war, McElroy first married a Mary Ann O'Brien. She died October 7, 1885. He then married a Maria, May 9, 1886. He worked as a laborer and a farmer, dying September 6, 1900. He is buried at Holy Cross Cemetery in Fillmore.

Foreign-born C-H-G Soldiers

McElroy was one of at least 42 C-H-G men who fought in the war, but were not born in the United States. Of the 42, 19 were born in Ireland, 12 in England, five in Germany, three in Canada, two in Scotland, one in Switzerland and one in Wales. It is estimated that more than 500,000 non-United States citizens fought in the war, mostly for the Union.

Plymouth, North Carolina, April 20, 1864

The 85th New York Infantry was caught in the siege of Plymouth, North Carolina by Southern forces. The siege lasted from April 17 to April 20. On the 20th the entire 85th Regiment was forced to surrender. Some 27 C-H-G men were among those captured, all but one, Sylvester Van Buren, were members of the 85th Regiment. The men captured at Plymouth constituted more than 25 percent of all C-H-G men captured during the war. The 85th was reorganized in January of 1865, and did duty in North Carolina until June 27, when the Regiment was mustered out of service.

The men captured were: George W. Barney, John Barney, George W. Benjamin, James Harrison Bennett, William H. Bower, Josiah Booth, Charles Buckbee, Eber Bullock, John Crotty, James E. Holbrook, George W. Jones, John Azeza Jones, Luther Moses, Walter Scott Parsons, George Washington Pitt, Oren Simeon Reynolds, Charles R. Rotch, Martin V.B. Scott, George Sibbald, Varius Quintilus Smith, William Silas Smith, Darius Martin Snider, George Henry Allen Tibbitts, Edward Underhill, Sylvester Van Buren, William Whittle, and Charles R. Williams.

One of the great ironies of the war is that all the 85th C-H-G men captured had only reenlisted on

January 1, 1864. The founder of Company E, Thomas J. Thorp, had been discharged August 27, 1862, and thus was not among the captured. Of the 27 men captured, 13 died in Confederate prisons prior to the end of the war. Another man, George Sibbald, died December 25, 1864, apparently in a Union Hospital in Annapolis, MD. One man, George Washington Pitt, escaped from Darrien Prison, Georgia after 11 months in captivity, and George W. Barney escaped February 22, 1865. Of the 13 men who died in Southern prisons, nine died at Andersonville, Georgia, two at Florence, South Carolina, one at Charleston, South Carolina ,and one in transit to Andersonville.

George W. Barney suffered in four prisons before he managed his escape. Originally sent to Andersonville, he, and others, were soon transferred to Charleston, SC The South hoped that a large contingent of Northern prisoners in Charleston would halt the shelling of the city. The tactic failed. From Charleston he was sent to Florence, SC and then to Wilmington, NC, where prisoners were being loaded on cattle cars. In the middle of the night on February 22, he simply dropped off the car he was on and made his way to the Union lines, which he reached about March first. In an affidavit supporting Barney's application for a pension, John A. Jones, a fellow soldier from the 85th, described the suffering that Barney endured. He wrote, "He was lame and stiff and when he moved his joints would crack and make a sound that could be heard several feet. He had scurvy. His legs and feet were purple and his teeth were loose and his gums were inflamed and swollen. His breath smealt offensive and he would throw out of his mouth chunks of phlegm."

William Henry Bower managed to escape just shortly after being captured, and thus avoided the hell of prison. In January of 1864 Bower was detached to a pioneer unit. Pioneers were men, generally more skilled than others, who were used to clear and build roads, construct bridges and erect fortifications. Their duties were very similar to those performed by the engineer corps. The Pioneer Corps proved to be extremely valuable, and eventually two men from each infantry company in the Army of the Cumberland were detached to form a 3,000 man strong Pioneer Corps. Bower, however, was returned to the 85th just in time to be captured at Plymouth. He had been injured on Pitt's Bridge at Roanoke Island, North Carolina in August of 1863.

Three other C-H-G men served as pioneers for short periods of time: Warren M. Brown, Company A, and William A. Knowlton and Byron Van Name, Company F, 19th NY Cavalry. One Pioneer group (not including C-H-G men) was part of a plan to free Union prisoners, burn the City of Richmond, and capture or kill Confederate President Davis and members of his Cabinet. The plan involved two forces, one under Brigadier General Judson Kilpatrick, and the other under Colonel Ulric Dahlgren, in a coordinated attack. The pioneers were with Dahlgren. Using oakum, turpentine, and torpedoes, they were to burn Richmond. The plan failed when Kilpatrick's group had to retreat.

Dyer's *Compendium of the War of the Rebellion, Part 3* provides the following information on the 85th New York Infantry:

> 85th Regiment Infantry. Organized at Elmira, N.Y., and mustered in December 2, 1861. Left State for Washington, D.C., December 3, 1861. Attached to 3rd Brigade, Casey's Division, Army of the Potomac, to March, 1862. 3rd Brigade, 3rd Division, 4th Army Corps, Army of the Potomac, to June, 1862. 2nd Brigade, 2nd Division, 4th Army Corps, to September, 1862. Wessell's Brigade, Division at Suffolk, 7th Army Corps, Dept. of Virginia, to December, 1862. 1st Brigade, 1st Division, Dept. of North Carolina, to

January, 1863. 1st Brigade, 4th Division., 18th Army Corps, Dept. of North Carolina, to May, 1863. District of the Albemarle, Dept. of North Carolina, August, 1863. Sub-District of the Albemarle, District of North Carolina, Dept. of Virginia and North Carolina, to April, 1864. Plymouth, N. C., District of North Carolina, January to March, 1865. 2nd Brigade, Division District of Beaufort, N . C, Dept. of North Carolina, to April, 1865. Unattached, 23rd Army Corps, Dept. North Carolina, to June, 1865. '" SERVICE,--Duty in the Defenses of Washington, D. C.,till March, 1862. Advance on Manassas, Va., March 10-15. Moved to the Peninsula, Va., March 28. Siege of Yorktown April 5-May 4. Reconnaissance toward Lee's Mills April 29. Battle of Williamsburg May 5. Reconnaissance to Bottom's Bridge May 20-23. Seven Pines, Savage Station and Chickahominy May 24.Reconnaissance to Seven Pines May 24- 27. Battle of Seven Pines or Fair Oaks May 31-June 1. New Market Road June 8. Seven days before Richmond June 25-July 1. Bottom's Bridge June 27-28. White Oak Swamp June 30. Malvern Hill July 1. At Harrison's Landing till August 16. Moved to Fortress Monroe August 16-23, thence to Suffolk, Va., September 18, and duty there till December. Reconnaissance to Franklin October 3. Blackwater October 9, 26, 29 and 30. Franklin October 31. Zuni November 18. Ordered to New Berne, N. C., December 4. Foster's Expedition to Goldsboro, N. C., December 11-20. Actions at Kinston December 14. Whitehall December 16. Goldsboro December 17. Duty at New Berne, N. C., till April, 1863. Expedition to relief of Little Washington April 7 -10. Moved to Plymouth, N. C. , May 2-,. and duty there till July. Expedition to Williamston and Gardiner's Bridge July 5- 7 (Detachment). Expedition from Plymouth to Foster's Mills July 26-29. Expedition to Roanoke Island August 6-13, and to Columbia August 26-27. Duty at Albemarle Sound and Chowan River till November. Expedition <dy-1439> to Winton November 6-9. Regiment veteranize January 1, 1864. Expedition up the Chowan January 6-21. Harrellsville January 20 (Detachment). Siege of Plymouth, N. C., April 17-20. Surrendered at Plymouth April 20. Regiment reorganized January, 1865, and duty in the Dept. of North Carolina till June. Campaign of the Carolinas March l-April26. Advance on Kinston and Goldsboro March 6-21. Battle of Wise's Forks March 8-10. Occupation of Kinston March 14, and of Goldsboro March 21. Occupation of Raleigh April 14. Bennett's House April 26. Surrender of Johnston and his army. Duty in the Dept. of North Carolina till June. Mustered out June 27, 1865. Regiment lost during service 1 Officer and 34 Enlisted men killed and mortally wounded and 2 Officers and 324 Enlisted men by disease. Total 361.

At least 53 C-H-G men served with the 85th New York Infantry. They were: Joel William Bardwell, George W. Barney, John Barney, George W. Benjamin, Charles William Bennett, James Harrison Bennett, John Melvin Bentley, Josiah Booth, William Henry Bower, Charles Buckbee, Eber Bullock, Michael Collins, John Henry Crotty, Lycurgus D. Drew, Eli Warren Drury, George P. Goodale, Richard David Groves, James E. Holbrook, Lewis James Holbrook, George W. Jones, John Azeza Jones, Josiah L. Keith, Edwin R. Meabon, Myron Miller, Luther Moses, James Edgar Palmer, Jefferson Myron Parker, Jackson Andrew Parkes, Walter Scott Parsons, John Henry Parks (Pasko), George Washington Pitt, Nathan Platt, George W. Randall, Oren Simeon Reynolds, Frank Ricketts, Wilmot E. Robbins, Charles R. Rotch, Martin V.B. Scott, George Sibbald, Andrew Washington Smith, Varius Quintilius Smith, William Mervale Smith, William Silas Smith, Darius Martin Snider, Gideon B. Standish, Albert Owen Taber, Thomas James Thorp, George Henry Allen Tibbitts, Edward Underhill, Milton M. Van Antwerp, James Wallace, William C. Whittle, and Charles R. Williams.

Thirty-six percent (20) of the 53 C-H-G men who served with the 85th Infantry died during the war. Nineteen died of various diseases and one, Richard D. Groves, was killed in action. In addition to the 26 men captured at Plymouth, discussed above, three other men, Joel Bardwell Josiah Keith, and Jefferson Parker were captured at Fair Oaks May 31, 1862. Four C-H-G men were wounded at Fair Oaks. Seven men, who were not casualties, were sick during their service. A total of ten men received disability discharges.

Mitchell's Station - Virginia, April 21, 1864

Yost Cain of Company F, 104th New York Infantry, while on picket duty on April 18, 1864, suffered an accidental gunshot wound to his left foot. He had stuck his rifle in the ground using the bayonet at the end of the rifle and when he pulled it from the ground it went off and hit his left big toe. He was admitted to Armory Square Hospital in Washington, DC on April 21, 1864. Cain was the son of John and Cynthia Cain, and was born in 1833 in Wyoming County. His brother Levi also served. His wife was named Sarah. He is buried in Hume Township.

Cumberland, Maryland - April 27, 1864

There were all kinds of hazards during the war, as there are in any war. Hiram King was seriously hurt when an Army wagon ran over him at Cumberland. He suffered head, lung and shoulder injuries.

Stevensburg, Virginia - May 3, 1864

Almond Duane Robinson was born in 1837 in Lodi, Seneca County, New York. On February 20, 1860, he married Clara Louise Scott in Caledonia, Livingston County. Enlisting at Rochester on August 18, 1862, he served with Companies K and F, 8th New York Cavalry, until May 18, 1865. On March 4, 1863, he was captured at Dumfries (Union Church), Virginia by guerillas. He apparently was paroled fairly quickly, since by no later than June he was reported by his regiment as present. On May 3, 1864, at Stephensburg, Virginia, Robinson was on picket duty when Southern forces commenced firing and attacking. Riding at full speed to warn headquarters, his horse stumbled, throwing Robinson. Landing on his pommel, he was severely injured. He suffered a dislocated and fractured neck and lost use of his left arm. He died February 26, 1880, in Hume and is buried at Pine Grove Cemetery in Fillmore.

Picket Duty

At least nine C-H-G men became casualties while on picket duty. There was great, and perhaps justified, skepticism about men who became casualties while on picket duty. Many of the injuries were self inflicted. While the men claimed that such injuries were accidental, it became clear that some were not. Some men appeared quite willing to permanently harm themselves simply to escape the war. That was certainly not the case with Duane Robinson. Nor does it appear to be true of most of the other eight C-H-G men. One of those eight, William Wells, was captured February 15, 1864, while on picket duty. Some may argue that he allowed himself to be captured. This seems doubtful since at this point in the war paroles were no longer being recognized by the Union Army and the horrors of Civil War prison life would have been known to all soldiers. Four men, Edgar A. Benchley, Smith Dole, George W. Flint, and Amos Hopkins, suffered from cold weather. Two had frostbite, not something they likely planned or allowed to happen. Outside of being cold, they may not have even realized anything was wrong. None of these four received an early discharge. Two others, Darwin Barrows and Stephen M. Skiff, were shot to death while on picket duty. The only C-H-G soldier who may have deliberately injured himself to escape further service was Romanzo Crawford. There is no proof that he did so, and no charges were ever brought against him. He did receive a disability discharge May 13, 1863, three months after accidently shooting himself in the left ankle while on picket duty.

The Wilderness, Virginia, May 5-7, 1864

The Battle of the Wilderness was an effort by General Grant to head south by turning the right flank of the Army of Northern Virginia, commanded by General Robert E. Lee. While the battle is considered a tactical draw, strategically Grant succeeded. He headed south with Lee unable to halt him. The Wilderness itself was marshy land and the battle resulted in some 25,000 casualties. Five C-H-G men, George H. Hotchkiss, Henry Green, Daniel A. Hildreth, John C. Franklin, and Erland S. Parker, were wounded; one, George H. Sheppard, was captured; and one, Noah Myers, was wounded and captured.

John Curdin Franklin had, to say the least, a confusing history. He served with both Company F, 33rd New York Infantry and Companies A and E, 1st Michigan Cavalry. He was honorably discharged from the 33rd on June 2, 1863, and volunteered for the 1st Michigan on November 21, 1863. His career up to that point was fairly normal. He was born in Buffalo August 25, 1843, to Edward Franklin and Emily Higgins. He did live three years with his grandmother Franklin. He may also have been an orphan. The 1850 Federal Census for Buffalo lists an 8-year-old John Franklin in an orphanage. However, surviving documents indicate the orphan, John Franklin, was born in Canada, whereas the soldier John Franklin was born in Buffalo. Nevertheless, they could be the same person.

In 1865 Franklin was living in Centerville with his first wife Sarah. While with the 33rd he was captured at Fredericksburg May 4 and paroled May 15, 1863. He also was court-martialed for some offence and paid a fine of $3.00. He received a furlough in April or May of 1862 to return home to Cold Creek, New York. He also returned there after his discharge. He participated in several battles with the 33rd, including the siege of Yorktown, Williamsburg, 2nd Bull Run, Antietam and Fredericksburg.

His history with the 1st Michigan is much more confusing. Within months of joining, he became ill with debility and on May 14, 1864, was admitted to Emory General Hospital in Washington, DC From there he was transferred May 24 to Summit General Hospital in West Philadelphia. At some point during his time in Philadelphia he met Sarah Waters. Incredibly, they were married August 6, 1864, at the Philadelphia Presbyterian Institute, only two and one-half months after his arrival in Philadelphia. Sarah, who was born in West Virginia, was only 16. On August 20, 1864, he was charged with desertion. Some papers indicate he may have been transferred to Company E on August 20. At this point, muster cards in his file contradict each other. Some have him in the hospital in Philadelphia, others in a Detroit Hospital. However, the 1865 New York State Census has him living in Centerville on June 15, 1865. Some documents tend to indicate he was still officially with his regiment, that had been sent west to fight Indians. The regiment was stationed at Fort Laramie, Wyoming and discharged at Salt Lake City. He denied being there and that is surely correct. He received a dishonorable discharge effective August 30,1864, from the 1st Michigan

Cavalry. He received his pension due to an Act of Congress, presumably for his service with the 33rd Infantry. He died before receiving any benefits.

There is no information on what happened to Sarah, but on December 30, 1877, in Bowling Green, Missouri he married again. His second wife was Emma Dell Putnam. He died February 25, 1908, in Jennings, Louisiana.

George H. Hotchkiss, son of John Hotchkiss and Miranda King was born in Centerville on May 8, 1841. He went to Michigan in 1861 and volunteered August 22, 1861, for Company G, 7th Michigan Infantry. He was wounded by gunshot to the right hand on May 6, 1864, at the Wilderness and had been previously wounded at Antietam. He was married twice, first to Amanda Bennett in Louisbourg, Pa., and then to Ida Mae Johnson March 8, 1886 in Fillmore. He died October 8, 1924, in Franklinville and is buried in Caneadea.

Daniel Algeroy Hildreth was born July 27, 1831, at Camilus, Onondaga County, New York. His parents, Lewis Hildreth and Lucretia Kenyon were both born in Vermont. Hildreth appears to have been unlucky in both war and peace. He volunteered for Company F, 4th New York Heavy Artillery December 31, 1863. Prior to the war he was a boatman, presumably on the Genesee Valley Canal. On all official documents, except one, he listed his name as Algeroy Hildreth. Only on the marriage certificate to his second wife does he list his first name as Daniel. In his first battle at the Wilderness (some records say Spotsylvania, which would make it his second battle), he suffered serious gunshot wounds to his right foot and shoulder. He spent the rest of the war being transferred from one hospital to another, finally being discharged June 24, 1865 at Albany, Albany County. Both the 1860 and the 1865 Censuses show Algeroy married to a woman named Alzada. In the 1860 Census they have two children, Electa and Lucretia. In the 1865 Census they also have two, Linda and Franky. Linda is actually Lucretia. By 1870 Alzada is still living in Hume with Linda, but there is no Electa and no Franky. There is also no Algeroy. It does not appear that he is listed anywhere in the 1870 Census. He next appears in the 1880 Census living in Cleveland, Ohio with his wife Catherine or Katherine and children Ethel A. and Algeroy John. He married Catherine Sullivan in 1873 in Cleveland and she received his pension after his death. Neither Alzada, nor any of his children by Alzada are mentioned in his pension file. He told Catherine that he had never been married. His post war occupations included tanner, cooper, and policeman. Alzada and Linda do not appear in the 1880 Census. Linda could certainly have been married by 1880. It is possible that Alzada passed away before 1873, thus making Algeroy's marriage to Catherine legal. Hildreth died September 18, 1884, at the Soldiers and Sailors Home in Ohio.

Henry Green of Company A, 147th New York Infantry was wounded in the knee on May 6, 1864, at the Wilderness. Actually Green served with Company B, 76th New York Infantry. He was transferred to the 147th on December 31, 1864. However, he was in McClellan General Hospital in December 1864 and he was discharged at that hospital July 8, 1865, having never reported to the 147th. Nevertheless, his military records are filed under the 147th Infantry. Green was drafted into the 76th Infantry July 14, 1863. He was born in Saratoga County, New York, possibly in 1837. His age is not consistent document to document except for the 1850 Federal Census for Caneadea, which lists him as age 16, and the 1860 Federal Census for Hume, which lists him as age 26.

Despite the censuses, he listed his age as 26 in 1863 when he was drafted. His parents were Eben and Caroline Green. He is buried in Caneadea. It is possible that this is the wrong Henry Green, but the known facts, especially the fact that the 1865 Allegany County Town Clerk Register indicates that he was drafted into the 76th Infantry, appear to indicate that this is the correct man. Further research may prove otherwise.

Erland S. Parker of Granger received a gunshot wound to his left hand at the Wilderness May 7, 1864. He lost his middle finger. Parker was born in 1836 in Allegany County to Ira Parker and Polly Rosina Smith. He enlisted January 27, 1864 at Burns in Company F, 19th New York Cavalry. There is some question as to whether Erland was a man or woman. The 1840 Federal Census shows no male the right age for Erland in the Parker family. There is a female of the correct age. The 1850 Federal Census lists Erland as a female, Erlindee. He has not been located in the 1860 Federal Census and all future military and other references have Erland as a male. By 1880 Erland was a "prison convict" at the State Penitentiary in Auburn, Cayuga County. By 1890 he was living in Granger.

George H. Sheppard volunteered for Company F, 4th New York Heavy Artillery on December 26, 1863, at Granger. The son of Henry Sheppard and Mary W. Blackman, he was born November 24, 1842, in Granger. Captured May 6, 1864, at the Wilderness he was imprisoned at Florence, South Carolina where he died November 25, 1864, just one day past his 22nd birthday. He was on his second enlistment when captured, having previously served with Company F, 19th New York Cavalry from August 7, 1862, to May 25, 1863.

Noah Larkin Myers, the son of Eliphalet (Lifelet) Myers and Nancy Robinson, was born in 1836 in Machias, Cattaraugus County. He was drafted July 14, 1863, at Hume into Company K, 147th New York Infantry. The Hume 1860 Census lists him as a farm laborer. His brother Delos also served. He was initially wounded at the Wilderness and then captured May 5, 1864. Imprisoned at Andersonville, he died there August 7, 1864 of dysentery. He is buried in Andersonvillle.

Todd's Tavern, Virginia, May 7, 1864

Todd's Tavern was located just south of the Battle of the Wilderness and north of the Battle of Spotsylvania. General Grant is reputed to have slept on the ground near Todd's Tavern the night of May 7. C-H-G men suffered two casualties here. Henry Patrick Neilan was shot in the jaw and David M. Cox was captured. Neilan was the son of James Neilan and Winifred Radigan. Born March 19, 1835, in Oxford, Chenango County, he volunteered for Company F, 19th New York Cavalry August 9, 1862. Todd's Tavern was his last battle. He returned to Hume, married Ella Barry and worked as both a timber hewer and farmer. He was also a Charter Member of Burnside Grand Army of the Republic Post 237. He died March 18, 1932, in Somerset, Pennsylvania and is buried in St. Patrick's Cemetery in Fillmore. Henry had a brother Nicholas, who, according to the 1865 New York State Census for Hume, also served in the war with the 4th New York Heavy Artillery. However, as yet, no military files have been identified for Nicholas. There is no listing for him in the New York State Adjutant General Report in any regiment including the 4th. Yet the 1865 New York State Census shows him as in the army with eighteen months still to be served.

David M. Cox was born September 18, 1843, to George and Susannah Cox. He volunteered August 10, 1862, at Birdsall for Company H, 19th New York Cavalry. Captured at Todd's Tavern on May 7, 1864, he was imprisoned at both Richmond and Andersonville. He died at Andersonville August 28, 1864, of scurvy. He is buried in Andersonville.

Rocky Face Ridge, Georgia, May 8, 1864

During a "demonstration" at Rocky Face Ridge, Georgia, Sidney Moore, a resident of Centerville, was captured May 8, 1864, but managed to escape. The battle of Rocky Face occurred during General Sherman's Atlanta campaign. Moore, the son of Arel and Catherine Moore, was born September 6, 1831, in Cattaraugus County. He enlisted in Company D, 154th New York Infantry on July 25, 1862, at Freedom. He married Sarah Findlay April 26, 1872, and died March 24, 1891.

Yellow Tavern, Virginia, May 12, 1864

Average people are almost always present at moments of historical note, although not necessarily involved in making the moment historical. They never get their names in the history books either way. On May 11-12, the 19th New York Cavalry and other forces under the command of General Philip Sheridan, clashed with troops under the command of legendary Confederate Cavalry hero Jeb Stuart. Both Darwin Ellis and Jeb Stuart were severely wounded in what came to be known as the battle of Yellow Tavern, which was really part of the Spotsylvania campaign. The battle took place about six miles north of Richmond. Ellis, wounded on May 12, was also captured, officially at Mechanicsville, according to his military file, and died May 16. The famous and historic Jeb Stuart died on the 12th. Ellis, the son of (David?) Ellis and Polly Woodward, was born in January of 1839 in Centerville. He enlisted in Company F, 19th New York Cavalry August 8, 1862 at Centerville. While he listed his occupation as farmer, he was working for Peter Cole, according to the 1860 Federal Census, and was most likely a farm laborer.

New Market, Virginia, May 15, 1864

Horton Chamberlain, or Chamberlin, was born in 1845 in China (Arcade), Wyoming County to Luther Chamberlain and Lucy Kendall. As a resident of Centerville, Horton enlisted in Company D, 1st New York Veteran Cavalry September 23, 1863. Captured at New Market, Virginia May 15, 1864, he was imprisoned at Andersonville, Georgia and died there July 12, 1864. He is buried in Andersonville. Two brothers, Henry and William, also fought in the war.

Spotsylvania Campaign, Virginia, May 7 to 19, 1864

Spottsylvania was another battle in which numerous regiments with multiple C-H-G men took part. The regiments included the: 4th New York Heavy Artillery, 5th New York Cavalry, 19th New York Cavalry, 44th New York Infantry, 64th New York Infantry, 86th New York Infantry, and 104th New York Infantry. More C-H-G men served with the 4th Artillery than any other regiment, except the 19th Cavalry. On May 12 Henry Hotchkiss suffered a wound which resulted in his death. Eight other C-H-G men were wounded and/or injured, and two were captured.

Henry L. Hotchkiss, the son of John Hotchkiss and Miranda King, enlisted September 18, 1861, at Rushford. He was born in Centerville and lived there with his parents when he volunteered. Prior to the war he was a farmer. He served with Company D, 64th New York Infantry. His brothers James and George also served. He was wounded May 12 at Spotsylvania and died May 20 at Harewood General Hospital in Washington, DC. He is buried at Arlington National Cemetery.

Civil War Hospitals

Obviously, there were hospitals all over where wounded, injured, and sick soldiers received treatment. One document says that there were at least 56 facilities serving as hospitals just in the District of Columbia. A number of men from C-H-G were treated at Satterlee General Hospital in Philadelphia. Others were treated at hospitals, in New York, Virginia, Maryland, Louisiana, Arkansas, Kentucky, North Carolina, Georgia, and Tennessee. Many received treatment at regimental and corps hospitals set up wherever the regiment or corps was located.

One local man, Carey E. Bingham, died on the hospital transport ship *Connecticut*. Wounded men were transported by horse drawn ambulances, railroads, ships, horses, litters, or were just carried by other men. Many men were assigned as nurses. Delos Myers, Company F, 19th New York Cavalry, and son of Lifelet and Nancy Robinson Myers of Hume, served as both a nurse and with the ambulance corps.

Harewood General Hospital was just one of many hospitals in Washington, DC where wounded , injured, and sick soldiers were treated. Other hospitals in DC were Douglas, St. Elizabeths, Judiciary Square, Campbell General, Emory Square, Mount Pleasant, Carver General, McDougal General, Armory Square, Lincoln General, Kalorama, and Columbia. Many of these hospitals were opened during the war and, in fact, were temporary hospitals. Scores of C-H-G men were treated in these hospitals. In addition to Hotchkiss, at least Harsey Osborn and Frederick Zorn were treated at Harewood. It appears that Osborn was the 15,000 soldier to be treated there. A picture exists showing Osborn at the hospital holding a sign which gives his name, company, and regiment and the number 15000. He received his discharge when he was released from the hospital. Some men were treated in more than one hospital. Frederick Zorn, besides being treated at Harewood, received treatment at Armory Square, as did Enos C. Mack, and Eugene M. Pratt.

The famous American poet, Walt Whitman, worked as a nurse in many of the temporary hospitals throughout the war and could very well have treated C-H-G men wounded in battle. He spent a great deal of time at Armory Square Hospital, which was located where the National Air and Space Museum now stands. Whitman came to Washington to nurse his brother George, who was wounded at the Battle of Fredericksburg. Whitman also worked for the Patent Office and was fired when Secretary of the Interior Harlan searched his desk and found the manuscript for *Leaves of Grass*. Harlan decided the book did not meet his moral standards and fired Whitman. By this action he condemned what most scholars consider to be one of the great works of American literature. According to Whitman's biographer, Justin Kaplan, Harlan also fired two bureau heads, 79 other clerks (Whitman was a clerk), and all the women, whom he declared were "injurious to . . . the 'morale' of the men."

At least 25 C-H-G men were treated in DC hospitals. (There were likely many more. No attempt has been made to systematically collect that information for this study.) Clarence L. Cudebec, Amos Frank Drew, George Elmer, John C. Franklin, and Vernon P. Smith were all treated at Armory Square Hospital. Who knows, some of these men may even have seen or met President Lincoln on one of his trips to local hospitals. Lincoln visited Judiciary Square Hospital many times. At least two C-H-G men, Samuel Bennett and Yost Cain were treated at Judiciary Square. In addition, at least two C-H-G men died at DC hospitals, Andrew Andrews at Douglas Hospital and David Youngs at Mount Pleasant.

While hospital workers did their best, hospitals, then and now, were dangerous places. Men would enter hospitals with minor injuries or diseases, but would die due to the treatment or lack thereof. An example of this was Wilber Elmer. Wilber was born October 11, 1844, in Hume, the son of George Elmer and Caroline Blackman. He volunteered for Company F, 4th New York Heavy Artillery at Hume on September 9, 1862. The 1860 Federal Census does not list an occupation for 16-year-old Wilber, but most likely he was working for his father, a mason. In the fall of 1862 he entered Fort Gaines, Maryland hospital with the mumps. Shortly thereafter, his father received a notice that if he wanted to see his son alive he should hurry to the hospital. His father did visit the hospital, and he nursed Wilber back to health. After his recovery, Wilber served honorably until his discharge with the rest of his company on June 3, 1865. Thanks to his father, he lived a long and fruitful life. He married Ellen Searl on February 12, 1867, and like his father, worked as a stone and brick mason. He died February 13, 1923, in Oramel at the age of 79, and is buried there at Riverside Cemetery.

One local man did meet and get to shake President Lincoln's hand. Adelbert Romain Foster, who served with Companies D and G of the 21st New York Cavalry, was bivouacked just outside of Washington when the President decided to visit the camp. Foster was one of many soldiers with whom Lincoln shook hands. He was born January 8, 1848, to Lewis Foster and Emma Ann Wheeler in Castile. As a youth he worked as a farm laborer, and later on the Genesee Valley Canal. The family was living in Castile in 1850, but by 1860 they were living in Hume Township. They were still there in 1865. Adelbert apparently lived in Fillmore, Perry, and Pike; dying in Perry during a visit in 1941. He is buried in Gainesville. He always told the story that he had enlisted on a dare by another boy named Pennock, and that he had to "lie like a thief" to convince the recruiting officer he was an orphan and homeless. The story, as related in the obituary of his death, is probably mostly correct. The obituary implies that the story related to his enlistment in the 21st Infantry. Actually the dare almost certainly took place when he enlisted in the 104th Infantry on January 3, 1862. He was underage, 14, and there was a Pennock who enlisted at the same time. In fact there were three Pennocks, a father, Oliver, and his sons Nelson and George. Which one dared him to enlist may never be known. His age was quickly discovered, and he was discharged without ever reporting to his company. George Pennock was also discharged almost immediately. He may also have been underage. George's father Oliver died of typhoid fever while in the service and his brother Nelson was killed in action at Gettysburg. Almost two years later, Foster again enlisted on October 10, 1863, at Troy, New York. He was still underage, but this time was not discovered. The family had ties to the Troy, New York area and it is possible that he was there visiting relatives or that he was in the area as part of his job on the canal. When the Civil War ended, the

21st Infantry was sent west to participate in the Indian Wars. Foster was discharged July 7, 1866, at Denver, Colorado Territory, and returned home. On July 4, 1871, he married Florence Streeter of Pike. They lived for a long time in Perry, returning to Pike in 1883 where his wife died shortly after their return, according to his obituary, which appeared in the Perry newspaper *The Herald*.

Adelbert's older brother Theron also served in the war. He was born March 12, 1837, also in Castile, and enlisted August 13, 1862, at Rochester. Theron died in 1902 in Fillmore and is buried in Wiscoy. He served with Company D, 4th New York Heavy Artillery.

Dyer's *Compendium of the War of the Rebellion, Part 3* provides the following information on the 4th New York Heavy Artillery:

4th Regiment Heavy Artillery. Organized at New York November, 1861, to February, 1862. Left State for Washington, D.C., February 10, 1862. Attached to Military District of Washington to May, 1862. Whipple's Command, Military District of Washington, to October, 1862. Abercrombie's Division, Defenses of Washington, to February, 1863. Abercrombie's Division, 22nd Army Corps, Dept. of Washington, to April,. 1st Brigade, DeRussy's Division, 22nd Army Corps, to May, 1863. 4th Brigade, DeRussy's Division, 22nd Army Corps, to December, 1863. (4 Cos. 11th New York Heavy Artillery assigned July 25,1863, as Cos. "I," "K," "L" and "M."). 3rd Brigade, DeRussy's Division, 22nd Army Corps, to March, 1864. Artillery Brigade, 6th Army Corps, Army of the Potomac, to May, 1864 (Cos. "C~" "D," "L" and "M" 1st Battalion). Artillery Brigade, 5th Army Corps, to May, 1864 (Cos. "E," "F," "H" and "K" 2nd Battalion). Artillery Brigade, 2nd Army Corps, to May, .. 1864 (Cos. "A," "B," "G" and "I" 3rd Battalion). Artillery Brigade, 2nd Anny Corps, May 31 to June 25, 1864. Ist Brigade, 3rd Division, 2nd Army Corps (1st Battalion). 2nd Brigade, 3rd Division, 2nd Army Corps (2nd Battalion), June 25 to July 13, 1864. Artillery Reserve to August, 1864. Unattached, 1st Division, 2nd Army Corps, to September, 1864. 4th Brigade, 1st Division, 2nd Army Corps, to March, 1865. 2nd Brigade, 1st Division, 2nd Army Corps, to June, 1865. 3rd Brigade, DeRussy's Division, 22nd Army Corps, to August, 1865. 2nd Brigade, Dept. of Washington, to September, 1865. (Co. "I)" with Artillery Brigade, 2nd Army Corps, July to December, 1864. Co. "L" with Artillery Brigade, 2nd Anny Corps, July, 1864, to March, 1865. Co. "C" with Artillery Brigade, 2nd Army Corps, October, 1864, to May, 1865.)
SERVICE.--Duty in the Defenses of Washington, D. C., till March, 1864. Action at Lewinsville, Va., July 6, 1862, and October 1, 1863 (Detachment). Rapidan Campaign May-June, 1864. Battles of the Wilderness May 5-7; Spottsylvania May 8-12; Piney Branch Church May 8 (2nd Battalion); Laurel Hill May 10 (3rd Battalion); Spottsylvania Court House May 12-21; Landron's Farm May 18 (Ist Battalion); North Anna River May 23-26. On line of the Totopotomoy May 28-31. Cold Harbor June 1-12. Before Petersburg June 16-18. Siege of Petersburg June 16, 1864, to April 2, 1865. Jerusalem Plank Road, Weldon Railroad, June 22-23, 1864. Deep Bottom July 27-28. Mine Explosion, Petersburg, July 30 (Reserve). Strawberry Plains, Deep Bottom, August 14-18. Ream's Station August 25. Poplar Springs Church, Peeble's Farm, September 29-October 2. Boydton Plank Road, Hatcher's Run, October 27-28. Reconnaissance to Hateher's Run December 9-10. Dabney's Mills, Hatcher's Run, February 5-7,1865. Watkin's House March 25. Appomattox Campaign March 28-April 9. Hatcher's Run or Boydton Road and White Oak Road March 31. Sutherland Station and fall of Petersburg April 2. Pursuit of Lee April 3-9. Amelia Springs April5. Sailor's Creek April 6. Farmville April 7. Appomattox Court House April 9. Surrender of Lee and his army. March to Washington, D.C., May 2-12. Grand Review May 23. Duty in the Defenses of Washington till September. Mustered out <dy-1384> September 26, 1865, and honorably discharged from service. Regiment lost during service 8 Officers and 108 Enlisted men killed and mortally wounded and 4 Officers and 334 Enlisted men by disease. Total 454

At least 113 C-H-G men served with the 4th New York Heavy Artillery. They were: John A. Agar, Vernon Golitz Akin, Alonzo Aldrich, Earl Alfred Allen, Albert Andrews, Byron Barrows, Darwin Barrows, Willis W. Beardsley, David Nortin Bentley, William R. Bentley, Lewis Amasa Berry,

Pembroke Berry, Joseph Benjamin Billington, Carey Edward Bingham, George Edgar Blowers, Ira Hyde Burroughs, John Martin Butler, Seymour B. Butler, Lewis Cain, Frank Caryl, Frederick W. Caryl, Augustus Andrew Chase, Sidney M. Chase, Hiram Clark, George Henry Cole, Frank Marion Cook, Harvey L. Cooper, James Randolph Cowing, Edward Belknap Cronk, Charles Rice Daniels, Francis J. Davidson, Thomas Augustus Davidson, William E. Davidson, Lewis Dill, Myron Landon Dodge, David Smith Downey, Amos Frank Drew, Hiram Drew, Loomis H. Eldredge, Mark Smith Eldredge, George Elmer, Wilbur A. Elmer, Levi Emmons, Daniel Finch, John C. Fish, Coroden Fisk, Leander C. Fitch, Icabod Perkins Flenagin, Theron W. Foster, Rodolph Fox, Omar W. Fuller, Frederick A. Gillett, James M. Granger, Willard Walter Green, Samuel Peter Guernsey, Joseph Nathaniel Guptill, Leonard Orlando Hackett, Robert Hall, Orlando F. Hatch, Samuel Hicok, Daniel Algeroy Hildreth, James W. Hildreth, Sherwood D. Hinman, Henry B. Holley, Leander Hubbard, Samuel A. Plinn Hyde, Wallace William Hyde, Charles William Isted, John Strickland Isted, Samuel McArthur Johnson, Michael Laughlin, Charles Lee, Ira Wells Lockwood, Robert W. Lockwood, James McDermott, John McElroy, John Bradford Millard, Ansel L. Minard, Abel Green Morse, Isaac Lemual Morse, Theodore Morse, William Wesley Morse, Gilbert Stephen Moultrop, Daniel Darwin Nye, Dewitt Clinton Nye, Andrew Jackson Oakley, Harsey Sylvester Osborn, Edward Osman, Andrew Jackson Palmer, Marcellus Palmer, Oren Peck, Edwin Jacob Pettys, Egbert Benson Pierson, Augustus F. Purdy, George Washington Shafer, George H. Sheppard, Manning Hardy Smith, Harmon Emmons Snider, Horatio Emerson Snider, George W. Soule, Silas E. Standard, Lawson Alanson Steward, John T. Stewart, Silas Wyman Stone, Sheldon T. Trall, Spencer Trall, David S. Van Guilder, Theodore B. Wait, Chandler W. Warn, Ira Ransom Weaver, Edwin Merchant Whitney, William Graves Whitney, and Aaron H. Wright.

The men wounded and injured at Spotsylvania included: on May 12th, John L. Dudley, 19th New York Cavalry; Henry Hotchkiss and Chauncey Abram Cronk, 64th New York Infantry; Henry N. Preston, 14th New York Heavy Artillery; Leander C. Fitch, 4th New York Heavy Artillery; and on May 16, John Agar, Samuel McArthur Johnson, and Amos Frank Drew, of the 4th New York Heavy Artillery.

Chauncey Cronk was born to Daniel Cronk and Angeline Thayer in Victor, New York on March 13, 1838. He died June 8, 1917, in Houghton and is buried in Pine Grove Cemetery in Fillmore. By at least 1850 the family was living in Centerville. At the time he entered the service he was 5' 7" tall, had blue eyes, brown hair and a light complexion. He served with Company D, 64th New York Infantry and participated in numerous battles, including Chancellorsville, Gettysburg, the Wilderness, Spotsylvania, Reams Station, and the siege of Petersburg. He was wounded charging the Southern defense at Spotsylvania. At the end of the war he marched in the May 23, 1865 Grand Review in Washington, DC.

From the very beginning of the Civil War, the Federal Government provided financial aid to men severely wounded in battle, and to the wives and children of men who died in service to their country. Long after the war ended, as late as September 1918, a law was passed which provided aid to Civil War widows. In between, numerous laws and resolutions were passed that provided financial assistance to veterans, their wives, their parents, and their children.

The pension laws had eligibility requirements. One main requirement for the veteran was that he be able to show that his disability was related to his military service. With respect to mothers and/or fathers, a major requirement was that they be able to show that the son had provided substantial financial support to the parent(s). In addition to initial eligibility, laws provided for increasing the amount of the pension in certain circumstances. For instance, when the soldier reached 70 years of age, or when the war related disability worsened over the years, resulting in the veteran being less able to earn a living or to take care of himself, the pension was increased.

Chauncey Cronk was an example of a man whose disabilities grew worse as he grew older. He petitioned for an increase in his pension several times. Most men needed considerable assistance in obtaining or requesting increases to their pensions. Almost all had to hire lawyers to assist with the paperwork. Local doctors had to provide information on their medical conditions. The officers and men from their regiments and companies had to provide supporting affidavits, especially if the pension was based on a combat injury. Also, in injury or disease situations, military medical records were consulted. It was a trying process and, in many cases, took a considerable amount of time. The burden on wives and parents was even more extreme, and some applications were abandoned due to the time and effort required. In a few cases, widows died before pensions were approved. The requirements and process were necessary, however. Falsely claiming pensions was common. As mentioned earlier, a William B. Wiley tried unsuccessfully to claim the pension of Andrew J. Andrews, even though Andrews was severely wounded at Fredericksburg, had one of his legs amputated, and died following the operation.

Chauncey Cronk was luckier than most. His quest for an increase in his pension in the early 1910's was aided and abetted by Mrs. V. Ingersoll Butler of Belfast. The 1910 Census shows a Milford and Viola Butler living in Belfast, so most likely Mrs. V. was Viola, which makes the way she signed her name interesting. A first instinct would be to read V. Ingersoll as her husband's name. Further, using only an initial for a first name gives an image of importance and authority to a name, and creates an impression that it is a male. It is likely that Viola understood this and signed her name in such a manner to make it more impressive, to the men she knew would be reading her letters. However, the joke was on them since it is likely the V stood for Viola and Ingersoll was Viola's maiden name. She was a woman who did not take "no" for an answer and almost surely was an early suffragette. Letters detailing her assistance still exist, the first one from 1912 and others from 1916. Her "take no prisoners" approach is evidenced by a paragraph in a 1916 letter. In it she informs the Commissioner of Pensions that, "In regard to the above-mentioned claim, (Cronk's application for an increase) I beg to inform you that I secured the Medical Affidavit of the attending Physician of Chauncey A. Cronk, believing this to be more expeditious way of reaching quick results."

In another 1916 letter, she wrote to Joseph P. Tumulty, secretary to President Wilson, advising that, "I am addressing this letter to you personally because if conditions should be different than what I suspect, then it would be better not to disturb Our President, who is carrying heavy burdens." She must have felt the burdens were not as large in 1912, because in that year she wrote directly to President Taft stating, "As I read from the newspapers almost daily references to 'Federal Officer Holders' and 'their apparent disloyalty to yourself' - I am moved to tell you of a certain instance in connection with an Old Soldier that happened recently----." She was certain that these "Federal Office Holders" were not treating Chauncey Cronk any fairer than they were treating Taft. She advised him that Cronk's pension of $30 per month was a "beggarly sum" and that Cronk's request for an increase had been rejected. He was entitled to "decent remuneration" from "Our Government." In detail she then explained how Cronk had been mistreated by government representatives and how she, and everyone else in town, agreed that he was entitled to a higher pension for the service he had rendered the country. She strongly suggested that Cronk be switched to the Olean agency, which, apparently she felt, would treat him better. She then assured Taft that, "Our Postmaster can vouch for my reliability as he knows me very well." My guess is, that the latter was a very true statement.

In the 1916 letter to secretary Tumulty she also suggested that, "Our government is too busy looking after Old England to have any time for Pensioners." Another part of the problem (in pensioners getting a fair treatment) was "an element in the country whose war cry is anything to beat Wilson." She suspected one of the government doctors who had examined Cronk was part of that group. Her opinions, of course, could be trusted because, as she stated, "I being a woman who has no vote, my party affiliations are not in this case." Being a woman who has no vote, was a recurring theme in her letters. She ended the letter to Tumulty by suggesting that he determine if the present Commissioner of Pensions, Mr. G.M. Saltzgaber, is a hold over from the Roosevelt - Taft administrations, and that his efforts to poison the minds of the pensioners be stopped. To emphasize her objectivity she advised, "I think so as a Jeffersonian Democrat who has no vote." While it is clear that Mrs. Butler assisted a number of men with their pension efforts (she mentions in one letter that she is working on two others while helping Cronk) she may have had a special interest in Chauncey Cronk. Cronk's first wife Mary S. Butler, whom he married December 25, 1868, in Hume, was most likely the sister of Milford Butler, V. Ingersoll Butler's husband. The 1860 Federal Census for Caneadea shows a Milford and Mary living with their parents Robert K. and Polly Butler. Their ages are consistent with ages shown in future censuses for both Mary Cronk and Mrs. V's husband Milford. Mary Butler and Milford, assuming he was Mary's brother, were the great great grandchildren of Colonel Zebulon Butler, a Revolutionary War hero. Milford and Viola were likely well-off. According to the 1880 Census he was a landlord and she was a lane lady. They had two servants. The 1900 Census indicates that they never had any children, which gave her the time to assist so many other people.

Leander C. Fitch was injured in combat at Spotsylvania. His gun prematurely fired, catching him by surprise, injuring his back and causing a partial loss of hearing. Leander was born in Hume February 11, 1844, to Seth Fitch and Caroline Keller. After the war he married Minnie C. Detour in Michigan. He died July 8, 1924, and is buried in Alger Cemetery, Hume. Fitch was lucky to live to such a old age. On August 25, 1864, he was captured at Ream's Station and imprisoned, first at Libby in Richmond, and later at Salisbury, N.C. When he was captured, he weighed 150 pounds. When he was paroled February 28, 1865, six months later, he weighed only 70 pounds.

Henry Preston was born in 1838 in Fowlerville, Wyoming County to Henry N. and Louisa B. Preston. He received a gunshot wound to the right thigh at Spotsylvania. Married twice, first to a Carrie, then to Adell Kinney, he died in 1902 and is buried at Holy Cross Cemetery in Fillmore.

John A. Agar was born in Hume on August 26, 1843. His parents were Absolom Agar and Mary Madison. Absolom was born in England. At Spotsylvania, he suffered a gunshot wound to his right hand. He recovered from his wound and served the remainder of his enlistment, not being discharged until September 26, 1865. He married a woman named Helen. No pension file has been located for Agar.

Samuel Johnson was born to Woodbury Johnson and Matilda Foot March 3, 1839, in Warsaw. By at least 1860 the family was living in Granger. He was wounded by a minnie ball to the abdomen. He died October 25, 1901, in Wiscoy and is buried at Pine Grove Cemetery, Fillmore.

John L. Dudley spent almost his entire service in the hospital. He suffered an injury to his left knee joint, probably at Spotsylvania, about five months after his entrance into the army. Despite writing a number of letters requesting a discharge, he was retained until July 19, 1865, when he received a disability discharge. Dudley was born in Allegany County in September of 1833. His father Elon was born in Connecticut and his mother Fanney, was born in Rhode Island. He married twice and died May 14, 1919, in Granger. He is buried in Short Tract.

The two C-H-G men captured at Spotsylvania were brothers, Augustus and Sidney Chase. Both were captured on May 19, 1864. Augustus Andrew Chase, the son of Jacob M. Chase and Emeline Tucker, was born March 2, 1848, in Castile. When he enlisted in Company D, 4th New York Heavy Artillery on December 28, 1863, at Hume he claimed he was 18. Based on his birth date he was only 15. He was reported missing after the battle of Spotsylvania. Some reports have him as a prisoner of war, imprisoned at Salisbury, North Carolina. He was never found, and most likely died in prison at only 16 years of age. His brother Sidney M. was born in 1844 at Warsaw. He enlisted January 12, 1864, at Centerville. After his capture he was imprisoned at Andersonville, Georgia where he died of hunger and exposure September 1, 1864. He had been in the service less than nine months. Prior to the war Augustus was a laborer and Sidney was a pedlar.

Resaca, Georgia, May 15, 1864

Resaca, Georgia ranks fifth in terms of C-H-G men wounded and killed in a particular location or battle, with eleven. The four most deadly battles: were Gettysburg, with 20; Petersburg, 17; Antietam, 14; and Fair Oaks, 12. It probably should be ranked third, since all 14 at Antietam were wounded and the wounded and killed at Petersburg took place over a period of several months.

All of the C-H-G killed and wounded at Resaca served with the 136th New York Infantry. An indication of the breath of this battle, however, is that the eleven killed and wounded men served in six different companies.

Gurdin J. Franklin was born November 4, 1837, in Brookfield, Madison County to John Franklin and Betsey Miller. Prior to the war he was a farmer. He enlisted in Company E, 136th New York Infantry August 12, 1862, at Allen. He was killed in action May 15. He had a twin sister Gertrude. His brother Julius served, and survived the war. Julius also had a twin sister, Julia.

Lieutenant William C. Hall was born in 1836 to John and Elizabeth Hall. In civilian life he was a teacher. He enlisted August 31, 1862, at Portage. Wounded severely by gunshot to his left foot on May 15 at Resaca, he died in Nashville, Tennessee May 27, 1864. Incredibly, just prior to his death he wrote a letter to the daughter of George Worden, telling her that her father had been killed in action at Resaca. William died just 58 days after his March 30, 1864, marriage to Helen C. Carpenter, and only 11 days after writing Mary Worden about her father. Hall and Worden were both wounded the same day, May 15.

David Lockwood enlisted August 31, 1862, at Granger. He was born in Allegany County in 1827 and married Mary Jane Utter September 12, 1848. Mary died in 1859. David was a farm laborer. When he entered the service, he left his three minor children (Ellen, William, and Eugene) with his father-in-law. The three children eventually received his pension.

Like David Lockwood, George T. Worden, a farmer, was a widower when he enlisted in the Army August 29, 1862, at age 40. He married Mary C. Anderson, November 27, 1850, in Leroy. She died in 1853 during the birth of their son George. David died May 16, 1864, from May 15 wounds. Lieutenant G. C. Parker, like Lt Hall, wrote George's daughter Mary from Cassville, Georgia on May 21. In his letter he mentions that she probably had already heard from Lieutenant Hall. He told Mary that her father, "was nobly fighting in the great cause of his beloved country and died a noble and brave soldier." He went on to say that Worden, "was a firm tried and true soldier very exemplary in his conduct . . . " He closed by telling her that he would, "remain ever the friend of children who have lost fathers in this great and noble cause."

The five men who were wounded and survived at Resaca were: Alonzo Camp, William Clutchey, William D. Harrington, George W. Jones, and Jackson L. Wallace.

Alonzo Camp was born in 1844 in Yorkshire to George and Eliza Camp. He originally enlisted in the 104th New York Infantry, but deserted almost immediately. He then enlisted in Company D, 136th New York Infantry on August 28, 1862. He claimed to be 18, but more likely he was 17. He was wounded twice, first in the head, on July 7, 1863, at Gettysburg and then on May 15, 1864, at Resaca, Georgia. The Resaca wound to his right wrist was severe and it ended his violin playing days. On September 6, 1868, he married Lucy Vreeland in Fillmore. He died June 16, 1893, and is buried in Wiscoy.

William Cluchey was born in Holley, Orleans County in 1846 to Lewis and Jane Cluchey. His parents were most likely born in Ireland. He enlisted August 28, 1862, in Company D, 136th New York Infantry at Pike, claiming to be 21. In fact, he was about 16. He had previously enlisted in the 104th New York Infantry and then, according to his file, deserted. Given his age, it may not have been desertion, he may have just been sent home. His father Lewis also served with the 104th. At Resaca he was wounded by a minnie ball to the thigh. In August of 1867 he married Amelia? E. Elmer in Hume. He was a Charter Member of Burnside Grand Army of the Republic Post 237.

William D. Harrington was born August 9, 1842, in Geneseo. His connection to C-H-G is unclear. The Matteson book has him as a Granger soldier. On August 9, 1862, he enlisted in Company I,

136th New York Infantry at Springwater, Livingston County. He received a gunshot wound to his right side at Resaca on May 15, 1864. He also received injuries to his shoulder, breast, and ankle during his service when he was struck by a tree, cut down by a fellow soldier without warning. On March 8, 1866, he married Cebelia F. Mares in Dansville. He died November 22, 1920, in Canaseraga.

George W. Jones, one of two George W. Joneses from the C-H-G area who served in the war, was born November 27, 1839, in Pike to John and Betsey Jones. He enlisted in company D, 136th New York Infantry August 27, 1862, at Pike, and received a leg wound at Resaca on May 15, 1864. By at least 1880 he was a resident of Hume and a Charter Member of Post 237. On January 27, 1866, he married Ellen Van Dyke Lincoln, the widow of Civil War soldier Francis S. Lincoln, who had died as a prisoner of war at Richmond, Virginia on February 3, 1864. Jones died August 15, 1918, in Hume.

Jackson L. Wallace was born January 13, 1843, in Charleroi, Pennsylvania to William and Harriett Wallace. He enlisted in August 26, 1862, at Portage in Company H of the 136th New York Infantry. His brothers James and William also served. Some source documents indicate his father William served, but there is no military file for him. There is census data showing that William lived in Granger, but it appears that Jackson and James lived in Grove. Jackson married Ellen Texas Gibbs in Portage on October 25, 1866. He died December 7, 1926, in Livonia, New York.

Dyer's *Compendium of the War of the Rebellion, Part 3* provides the following information on the 136th New York Infantry:

136th Regiment Infantry ("Iron Clads"). Organized at Portage, N. Y., and mustered in September 25, 1862. Left State for Washington, D.C., October 3, 1862. Attached to 1st Brigade, 3rd Division, 11th Army Corps, Army of the Potomac, to November, 1862. 2nd Brigade, 2nd Division, 11th Army Corps, Army of the Potomac, to October, 1863, and Army of the Cumberland to April, 1864. 3rd Brigade, 3rd Division, 20th Army Corps, Army of the Cumberland, to June, 1865.
SERVICE.--Moved to Fairfax Station, Va., October 10, 1862; thence to Fairfax Court House, and duty there till November 1. Movement to Warrenton, thence to Germantown, Va., November 1-20. March to Fredericksburg December 10-15. At Falmouth, Va., till April 27 , 1863. "Mud March" January 20-24. Chancellorsville Campaign April 27-May 6. Battle of Chancellorsville May 1-5. Gettysburg (Pa.) Campaign June 11-July 24. Battle of Gettysburg, Pa., July 1-3. Pursuit of Lee July ~ 5-24. Camp at Bristoe Station August I to September 24. Movement to Bridgeport, Ala., September 24-October 3. March along line of Nashville & Chattanooga Railroad to Lookout Valley, Tenn., October 25-28. Reopening Tennessee River October 26-29. Battle of Wauhatchie, Tenn., October 28-29. Ringold-Chattanooga Campaign November 23-27. Orchard Knob November 23. Tunnel Hill November 24-25. Mission Ridge November 25. March to relief of Knoxville, Tenn. , November 28- December 17. Duty in Lookout Valley till May, 1864. Atlanta (Ga.) Campaign May 1 to September 8. Demonstration on Rocky F aced Ridge May 8-11. Buzzard's Roost Gap May 8-9. Battle of Resaca May 14-15. Near Cassville May 19. Advance on Dallas May 22-25. New Hope Church May 25. Battles about Dallas, New Hope Church and Allatoona Hills May 26-June 5. Operations about Marietta and against Kenesaw Mountain June 10-July 2. Pine Hill June 11-14. Lost Mountain June 15-17. Gilgal or Golgotha Church June 15. Muddy Creek June 17. Noyes' Creek June 19. Kolb's Farm June 22. Assault on Kenesaw June 27. Ruffs Station, Smyrna Camp Ground, July 4. Chattahoochie River July 6-17. Peach Tree Creek July 11-20. Siege of Atlanta July 22 August 25. Operations at Chattahoochie River Bridge August 26-September 2. Occupation of Atlanta September 2- November 15. March to the sea November 15-December 10. Campaign of the Carolinas January to April,

1865. Lawtonville, S.C., February 2. Skinnish of Goldsboro Road, near Fayetteville, N. C., March 14. Averysboro March 16. Battle of Bentonville March 19-21. Occupation of Goldsboro March 24. Advance on Raleigh April 9-13. Occupation of Raleigh April 14. Bennett's House April26. Surrender of Johnston and his army. March to Washington, D.C., via Richmond, Va., April 29-May 30. Grand Review May 24. Mustered out June 13, 1865. Veterans and Recruits transferred to 60th New York Infantry. Regiment lost during service 2 Officers and 71 Enlisted men killed and mortally wounded and 1 Officer and 91 Enlisted men by disease. Total 165.

At least 23 C-H-G men served with the 136th. They were: Samuel Bowen, Alonzo Camp, Henry Chamberlain, Daniel Clark, William Cluchey, George Davis, William Elwood, Francis Fox, Gurdin Franklin, William C. Hall, George W. Jones, David Lockwood, John Sears, Alturnia Smith (source documents list him as Altorney or Attorney Smith, but no such person served in the war so it must have been Alturnia, or likely Alternus), Joel Smith, Norman Smith, John Townsend, Jackson Wallace, William Warner, James Welstead, Samuel Willard, and George Worden.

Of the 23 C-H-G men who served in the 136th Infantry, 14 were either killed in action, died of disease, wounded, or captured. Some suffered more than one of the above fates. The total count was four killed in action, one prisoner of war, three died of disease, and eleven wounded in battle. Five others were sick during their service and seven of the 23 received disability discharges. It is likely that four men were at Bennett's House for the surrender of General Johnston and his army. Six of the men marched in the Grand Review in Washington on May 23, 1865.

North Anna River, Virginia, May 23, 1864

While this battle took place near the North Anna River, it was really an attempt by General Grant to capture or destroy the Virginia Central Railroad at Hanover Junction. The battle ended as a stalemate and Grant moved on to Cold Harbor. Two C-H-G men were wounded during the battle, Michael Laughlin of Company F, 4th New York Heavy Artillery and John Samuel Pitt of the 104th New York Infantry. Laughlin, (the name may have been McLaughlin), was born in Ireland in September of 1832, and emigrated to the United States in 1849. He lost two fingers on his right hand in the battle. Laughlin married twice, first to Lucy S. Ralph, and then to Anna Lila Bailey. He died October 4, 1915, in Rossburg.

John Samuel Pitt was from an accomplished family. His brother George Washington Pitt, also a soldier, was an artist. His father William was a Professor. Both his father and his mother Elizabeth were born in England. The father was the son of William Pitt of Dorchester. John was to become a bridge builder for the St. Louis railroad. He was born October 2, 1842, in Granger. Enlisting January 28, 1862, at Granger he served honorably with Company F of the 104th New York Infantry. The book, *Allegany and Its People* says he was in 43 different battles. At North Anna, when chasing the enemy at night, he tripped over something and fell down a bank into a river badly damaging his knee. He was captured August 9, 1863, at Rappahannock and paroled February 27, 1864. The date of parole is interesting because it is after Grant stopped the practice of parole and before it was re-instituted for sick and injured prisoners in early1865. According to *Allegany and Its People* Pitt was at Appomattox Court House for Lee's surrender. On January 29, 1869, he married Lucinda Jane Alston in Allen. He died October 21, 1929, in Fillmore, and is buried in

Short Tract. Pitt was a musician during the war. The March 1926 edition of the *Northern Allegany Observer* reported that he had recently won a prize in a fiddler's contest in Rochester.

Another C-H-G man, Hiram Drew, Company F, 4th New York Heavy Artillery, was captured at the North Anna River on March 25, 1864. Drew was imprisoned at Andersonville and died there July 24, 1864, of typhoid fever. Drew was born in Orangeville, Wyoming County in 1837 to Hiram Drew and Anna Hopkins. A resident of Granger, he married Elizabeth A. Williams on April 13, 1860, in Genesee Falls, Livingston County.

Cold Harbor, Virginia, May 31 - June 3, 1864

The battle of Cold Harbor, Virginia on May 31- June 3, 1864, has been called murder, not war. Cold Harbor was a crucial location commanding roads running north and south. Both sides wanted this strategic point and it was eventually controlled by troops under the command of General Phil Sheridan. With Cold Harbor under control, Grant, who was in overall command of the battlefield, now attacked Lee's entrenched forces. It is this attack that historians debate. It was a straight line attack, poorly planned and poorly executed. In one hour, Grant lost 6,000 men killed and wounded. There is still debate over whether Grant ordered a second attack that the men refused to carry out. Two Generals who were present, Alexander and Titus, gave differing accounts. Alexander denies that it happened, whereas Titus is quoted by General Wheeler as saying the story is true. Things were further clouded by General Burnside. He ordered a man named Swinton, whom Grant called a historian, and who was the source for the story about the second attack, to be shot for a "great offence." Grant ordered Swinton to be released, but did not speak highly of him.

It was in the context of these events that two C-H-G men, Oliver Barnard and Martin Van Buren Babcock, were killed on May 31. It is unlikely that either man knew anything about the intrigue surrounding the battle, and they were dead before any refusal to advance could have taken place, if such did occur. Men in battle, not knowing anything other than what directly concerns them until the battle is over, is not uncommon. It is only afterward they learn what happened, and what the outcome was. Barnard and Babcock were even denied the knowledge that their side won.

Oliver Barnard was born in 1844 in Hume to Charles and Martha Barnard. He enlisted August 9, 1862, at Hume in Company F, 19th New York Cavalry. He was originally buried on the Cold Harbor battlefield, but is now interned at the Cold Harbor National Cemetery. Martin Babcock was born January 31, 1838, in Rushford to William Babcock and Sarah Austin. He married Cornelia R. Allen August 16, 1862, in Centerville. Martin enlisted at Hume August 11,1862, and was shot through the head near a place called Bottom's Ridge at Cold Harbor on May 31. Both Babcock and Barnard were farmers in civilian life.

In addition to Barnard and Babcock being killed, four local men were wounded. Harsey S. Osborn of Company D, 4th New York Heavy Artillery was shot in the left thigh on June 1, 1864. As mentioned earlier, there is a picture of Osborn recovering from his wounds at Harewood General Hospital in DC. The picture had to have been taken sometime between June 1, when he was shot, and June 20, when he went home on furlough. Given that the wound looks well healed, it is likely the picture was taken close to June 20, 1864. Osborn was born July 6, 1839, in Centerville to Charles and Sarah Osborn.

Charles W. Isted, Company F, 4th New York Heavy Artillery, suffered a gunshot wound to the ring finger of his left hand. Isted was born in Hume April 8, 1845, to Thomas Isted and Henrietta Trumbell. He died March 24, 1914, in Spooner, Minnesota.

Orrin Marshall Dow of Company B, 2nd Mounted Rifles, received a gunshot wound just above the heart on June 6. The son of Jacob Dow and Elizabeth Conger, he was born May 14, 1826, in Addison County, Vermont. The family was living in Centerville by at least 1860. Dow had previously served with Company C, 104th New York Infantry before enlisting in the 2nd Mounted Rifles.

Roswell Norton Byington, Company E, 5th New York Cavalry, accidently shot himself in the calf of his left leg on June 3, 1864. Byington had previously been wounded at Hanover, Pennsylvania on June 30, 1863. As pointed out earlier, self inflicted wounds were often means for an individual to get out of the service. This was not true for Byington. He remained with his regiment until he was discharged on July 19, 1865. He participated in other battles, and was with his regiment at Appomattox Court House for Lee's surrender. It is likely that he also marched in the Grand Review May 23, 1865.

Regiments with multiple C-H-G men that fought at Cold Harbor included the 2nd New York Mounted Rifles, the 19th New York Cavalry, the 5th New York Cavalry, and the 104th New York Infantry.

Trevellian Station, Virginia, June 11-12, 1864

The Trevellian Station battle, part of the Cold Harbor campaign, was another unsuccessful attempt by Union forces, under General Philip Sheridan, to destroy the Virginia Central Railroad and the James River Canal. Three C-H-G men were wounded and two were captured on June 12. One of the wounded, John Murray Stickle, would die of his wounds. The two other men wounded at Trevellian Station were George Stockweather and George Titus Underhill. The Granger American Legion list shows an Underhill from Granger as having served in the Civil War. It does not provide a first name. Several Underhill's from the areas around C-H-G served during the war. However, none of the military records for these men definitively identify any one of them as being from Granger. George Underhill's hospital records show that his closest relative was a Phebe Cox of Short Tract, so is likely that he is the Underhill listed, by last name only, by the Granger Legion.

The wounded man who died, John Murray Stickle, served with Company F, 19th New York Cavalry. Stickle was born October 16, 1838, in Centerville to Morris Stickle and Susannah Wight. Prior to the war he was a farm laborer. On August 12, 1862, he enlisted at Hume and on August 19 he was mustered into Company F at Portage. In September 1863 he was promoted to corporal. He was wounded June 12, 1864, at Trevellian Station and died at Gordonsville, Virginia on July 4,

1864, "in the hands of the enemy." He was apparently left wounded on the battlefield and became a POW. William J. Stickle, grandson of Civil War soldier Judson, who likely was John's cousin, was killed 78 years later during World War II when his bomber crashed on December 16, 1942, in the Territory of Hawaii.

George Stockweather was born to George Stockweather and Mahitable Wells in Granger on April 15, 1847. He enlisted December 16, 1863, in Buffalo. His military records list his age as 18, but he most likely was 16. He was both wounded and captured at Trevellian Station. A gunshot wound left him deaf in his left ear. He was imprisoned at Richmond. Subsequent to the war he married Mary A. Vincent in Allen, September 29, 1870. They lived in Granger. He died March 5, 1936, in Hunt and is buried in Short Tract.

George T. Underhill was the son of Livingston and Esther Underhill. He was wounded by a minnie ball to his left leg at Trevillian Station. After the war he married and moved to Michigan. He died in 1909. While Census records tend to indicate he was from Allen, the *History of Allegany County - 1879* indicates he was from Oramel. At some point he was associated with Granger, since he appears on the Granger list of Civil War soldiers.

On June 11 Thomas Thorp was captured at Trevillian Station. Thorp would be imprisoned at Richmond, Macon, GA, and Charleston, SC He arrived at Macon in the latter part of June, according to a Captain H.H. Todd of the 8th N.J. Infantry. Todd submitted an affidavit supporting Thorp's application for a pension. In the affidavit Todd related how he had a "miniature stars and stripes" hidden in his clothes. He suspected it was the only one in the "heart of the Confederacy." Camp morale was low, so he and others decided to celebrate the Fourth of July "whether permitted or not - by the rebels." He would hoist his flag, but they needed an orator for the occasion. One of the "Celebration Committee" had heard of the recent arrival at the camp of the "dashing Col. Tom Thorp." They decided he was just the orator they needed. When first approached however, Thorp was reluctant. He was concerned that such a ceremony might lead to the "ruthless slaughter of his companions." According to Todd, Thorp agreed to proceed with the ceremony when he showed him his miniature flag. (Thorp was the highest ranking prisoner and thus in charge of all of the other prisoners.) Todd related that Thorp, with his crippled leg and inflamed eye, made a "spirited and patriotic oration in behalf of sweet liberty," which made him the "Lion of the Day." Thorp's leg was injured at Fair Oaks, and it must have still been bothering him. There is no evidence he was wounded at Trevillian Station, nor does Todd claim such an injury for him. He also, apparently had an infected eye. Todd also mentions Thorp's escape and recapture, and the fact that they were reunited at a prison in Charleston, SC where Thorp was again suffering from "inflammation of the eyes." Todd eventually successfully escaped and returned to his regiment.

Petersburg, Virginia, June 1864 - April 1865

Except for Gettysburg, and the 27 men captured at Plymouth, more C-H-G (22) men were killed, wounded and captured at Petersburg than anywhere else. Twelve of the 22 were wounded during the siege. This was the third most for any one location, behind the 14 at Antietam and the 13 at Gettysburg. Only Gettysburg with seven killed exceeded the five killed at Petersburg, although there were also five killed at Fair Oaks. However, while those at Gettysburg, Fair Oaks, Plymouth, and other locations such as Spotsylvania, had been killed, wounded, or captured on the same day, or within days of each other, those killed, wounded, or captured at Petersburg were over an extended period of time. All casualties occurred during the siege of Petersburg which took place from the middle of June 1864 until virtually the end of the war. The single worst day for C-H-G men at Petersburg was June 18, 1864. Three men were killed in action that day, and one died later from wounds received on the 18th. A total of eleven men were also wounded on the 18th. (It should be noted that there were several other casualties that could also be ascribed to Petersburg, since the battles in which they became casualties were really part of the Petersburg campaign. However, the military files of only these 28 men specifically list Petersburg as the place where they suffered a casualty.)

The carnage started on June 17. Joseph Nathaniel Guptill received a gunshot wound to his arm on the 17th. The bullet came to rest in his canteen. When he went to the rear for treatment, he left his rifle on the battlefield. After being treated, he realized that he would be charged for the loss of his rifle. That night he returned to the battlefield, and took a rifle from a dead soldier. Guptill was born in Granger May 28, 1842. His parents were William Guptill and Susan Ruth Fox. He died July 11, 1905, in Warsaw and is buried in Granger.

The three men who were killed in action on the 18th were: William R. Bentley, Company F, 4th New York Heavy Artillery; Samuel T, Burleson, Company B, 2nd New York Mounted Rifles; and Gilbert Moultrop, Company F, 4th New York Heavy Artillery. A fourth, William R. Gilbert, Company B, 2nd New York Mounted Rifles, was so severely wounded he was not treatable. He was sent home on furlough and died in Centerville.

Very little information is available on William R. Bentley of Granger. He was born in 1844 according to the 1860 census which shows his age as 16. The son of Ira Bentley and Mary Butler, he was a farmer prior to the war. His military file indicates that he was 21 when he enlisted September 28, 1862, probably at Granger. Most likely he was 18. Since he was of legal age to enlist, the age fibbing was not necessary. He was mustered into the 4th Heavy Artillery at New York City on October 20, 1862.

Granger Civil War Monument

Bentley's name appears on the "Soldier's Monument" erected by Brevet General Thomas J. Thorp at Short Tract. One side of the monument is dedicated to "The brave soldiers of Granger who fell for the Union." The monument lists many of the men from Granger who served in the war and stands today in the middle of the Short Tract Cemetery. The names listed are: "G.H. Cole, F.M. Cook, Wm. Hall, C.P. Emery, Wm. Davis, Wm. Huson (Hussong), E.S. Drury, N.J. Smith, M.W. Snider, G.T. Warden (Worden), G.W. Abbott, M.D. Luther, J.D. Weaver, I.R. Weaver, J.M. Parker, Wm. Wallace, Wm. Whittle, John Parks, J.H. Bennett, Wm. Bentley, Geo. Sheppard, John Emmons, Geo. Sibbald, Jos. Bentley, Eber Bullock, Richard Grove, Daniel Chilson, Luther Moses, Pembroke Berry, Charles Williams, Darius Snider, Robert T. Lockwood, David Lockwood, Attorney Smith, I.N. Van Nostrand, and Aaron Van Nostrand."

There is some mystery about two of the names on the monument. One is a John H. Parks. The office of the New York State Adjutant General, which compiled a listing of all Civil War veterans from the state of New York, showing the regiments in which they served, does list a John H. Parks as having served with the 85ᵗʰ New York Infantry. However, a review of military and pension files indicates that his name was actually John H. Pasko. The Adjutant General information compiled by the state, matches exactly the information contained in the Pasko military file. The 1901 Adjutant General Report, Volume 30, page 1073 indicates that Parks was also "borne as Pasko." Actually, his name was probably Pasco. The 1860 Federal Census for New Hudson Township shows a John Pasco living with his parents. After the war, Pasco returned to Black Creek in New Hudson Township. He eventually moved to Groton, South Dakota where he married Mary Craig on October 21, 1891. He was 50 and she was 18.

The Civil War Monument in Granger also lists an Attorney (also spelled Altorney in some records) Smith. No Attorney Smith served in the Civil War in the 85ᵗʰ New York Infantry or any other New York state regiment according to the Adjutant General reports. The closest is an Alturna C. Smith who served with the 136ᵗʰ New York Infantry. The Town Clerk lists an Attorney Smith as having served in the 136ᵗʰ NY Infantry. It is likely Alturna, also spelled Alturnia and Attorney, are the same person. However, there is nothing in his file to tie Alturna directly to the C-H-G area. He enlisted August 30, 1862, at Genesee Falls and was mustered August 31, 1862, at Portage. Since Portage was considered part of Granger at this time, it may be that this is the connection. According to hospital records, Alturna's father was W. W. Smith of Nunda. It is possible that the hospital made a mistake and his father was actually Joel M.W. Smith, who also served with the 136ᵗʰ. If M.W. was the father, then Alturna was clearly a C-H-G soldier. He died May 30, 1864, from the administration of chloroform being used to prepare him for the amputation of a finger. While it appears that he must be the individual referred to on the Short Tract Monument, other possibilities do exist. Attorney could be a middle name by which he was known in Granger, but the military would have listed him under his actual first name. If so, he would be difficult to find, given a last name of Smith. It is most likely that the monument name does refer to Alturna Smith and that his name was added to the monument list by someone, who only casually knew him, or simply didn't know how to spell the name. Alturna Smith is buried in Nashville, Tennessee.

Gilbert Stephen Moultrop enlisted September 21, 1862, at Hume in Company F, 4ᵗʰ New York Heavy Artillery. He was born to Arila Moultrop and Susan Town June 20, 1835. Prior to the war he was a farmer. He participated in several battles including the Wilderness, Spotsylvania, and Cold Harbor before being killed in action at Petersburg June 18, 1864.

Samuel T. Burleson, a farmer, was born 1829 in Howard, Steuben County. He enlisted January 1, 1864, at Allen in Company B, 2ⁿᵈ New York Mounted Rifles. He was married to Mary M. Kirchbaum on February 28, 1854, in Carson Town, Pennsylvania. He was missing in action and presumed dead at Petersburg on June 18, 1864. However, a note in his file appears to indicate that he returned to his regiment headquarters, but not to his company, on February 20, 1865. There is no further record. His wife applied for, and received, his pension. The note was probably incorrect.

William R. Gilbert, the son of Hiram Gilbert and Anna Holcomb, was born August 22, 1846, in

Yorkshire, Cattaraugus County. A farmer prior to the war, he was severely wounded at Petersburg where he suffered a fractured femur caused by a shell. He was given a furlough starting August 17, 1864, and scheduled to end October 16, 1864. He died September 12, 1864, at the home of his parents in Centerville and is buried there. The family had lived in the Centerville area since at least 1850. He enlisted December 19, 1863, at Centerville in Company B, 2nd New York Mounted Rifles. He was 19 when he died.

The other C-H-G man killed on October 4, 1864, during the long siege, was Darwin Barrows. Barrows, both a printer and a farmer prewar, was drafted into Company F, 4th New York Heavy Artillery, August 24, 1864, at Hume. Born December 24, 1831, he was the son of David L. Barrows and Irena Parmila. He had been only a month and a half in the service, when he was killed by gunshot while on picket duty at Petersburg. His brother Byron also served in the war.

Dyer's *Compendium of the War of the Rebellion, Part 3* provides the following information on the 2nd New York Mounted Rifles:

> 2nd Regiment Mounted Rifles. Organized at Lockport and Buffalo, N. Y., and mustered in by Companies as follows "A" October 31, "I" November 2, 1863; "B" January 12, "C" January 26, "D" January 27, "E" January 29, "L" January 29, "F" and "G" February 5, "H" February 4, "K" February 6 and "M" February 13, 1864. Moved to Washington, D.C., March 4, 1864, thence to Belle Plains, Va. Attached to 22nd Army Corps, Dept. of Washington, D.C., to May 15, 1864. Provisional Brigade, 1st Division, 9th Army Corps, Army of the Potomac, to June 1, 1864. 3rd Brigade, 1st Division, 9th Army Corps, June, 1864. Ist Brigade, 2nd Division, 9th Army Corps, to September, 1864. 2nd Brigade, 2nd Division, 9th Army Corps, to November 16, 1864. 3rd Brigade, 2nd Division, Cavalry Corps, Army of the Potomac, to May, 1865. Dept. of Virginia to August, 1865.
> SERVICE.--Rapidan Campaign May 15-June 12, 1864. Spottsylvania Court House May 15-21. North Anna River May 23-26. On line of the Pamunkey May 26-28. Totopotomoy May 28-31. Hanover Court House May 31. Cold Harbor June 1-12. Bethesda Church June 3. Before Petersburg June 16-18. Siege of Petersburg June 16, 1864, to April 2, 1865. Mine Explosion, Petersburg, July 30, 1864. Weldon Railroad August 18-21. Poplar Springs Church September 29-October 2. Pegram's Farm October 4. Boydton Plank Road, Hatcher's Run, October 27-28. Regiment mounted November 16, 1864. Stony Creek Station December 1. Raid on Weldon Railroad, known as Warren's Hicksford Raid. December 7-12. Bellefield, Hatcher's Run, December 9-10. Dabney's Mills, Hatcher's Run, February- 5- 7, 1865. Appomattox Campaign March 28-April 9. Dinwiddie Court House March 30-31. Five Forks April 1. Namozine Church April 3. Jettersville April 4. Amelia Springs and Jarrett's Station April 5. Sailor's Creek, Harper's Farm, Gravelly Run and Deatonville Road April 6. Farmville April 7. Pamplin Station April 8. Appomattox Court House April 9. Surrender of Lee and his army. Expedition to Danville to cooperate with Gen. Sherman April 23-29. Provost duty in Sub-District of the Appomattox, District of the Nottaway, Dept. of Virginia, till August. Mustered out August 10, 1865. Regiment lost during service 8 Officers and 94 Enlisted men killed and mortally wounded and 1 Officer and 112 Enlisted men by disease. Total 215.

At least 20 C-H-G men served in the 2nd Mounted Rifles regiment. They included: George Benjamin Anstee, Edwin Buchanan, Samuel T. Burleson, Ira Frank Crane, Francis Gibbs Dodge, Orrin Marshall Dow, David Smith Downey, William R. Gilbert, Lamont John Gloden, Cassius C. Granger, Samuel Harvey Morgan, George Madison Mosher, George Morel Poole, Alonzo Smith Powell, Wilson C. Robbins, Charles Dudley Van Dresser, George Van Duzen, Henry Vosbourgh, Albert P.Watson, and Jerome Woodworth.

Nine of the 20 men were KIA, WIA, DD, or were captured. Two men, Samuel Burleson and William Gilbert, were killed in action and one, Henry Vosburgh, died of a disease. Four men were wounded, one twice, and two became prisoners of war. Four others were sick, and only one received a disability discharge. A total of seven, George B. Anstee, Francis D. Dodge, David Downey, George Mosher, George Poole, Alonzo Powell, and Wilson Robbins, were at Appomattox Court House when Lee surrendered. It appears that 13 of the men marched in the Grand Review in Washington, DC.

Almost half of the C-H-G men who served with the 2nd Mounted Rifles had multiple wives. For the most part, this likely reflected the times, especially the fact that a lot of women died in child birth. Nevertheless, it does appear somewhat high for a random group of 20 men. One man, Edwin Buchanan, had four wives. The first two died and he divorced the third.

Another man, George Mosher, had at least three wives, probably four, and possibly five. Mosher, the son of William Mosher and Ann Louise Shaw, was born in Canadice, Ontario County, New York. His father owned a stage coach. At his second enlistment in Company E of the 2nd New York Mounted Rifles on December 23, 1863, at Castile, under the name Edwin G. Mosher, he listed his occupation as carpenter. He had previously enlisted under the name George H. Mosher in the 104th New York Infantry and deserted June 6, 1862, at Catlett's Station, Virginia. He apparently was a good soldier, since he was made company wagoner on August 31, 1864, and was promoted to sergeant November 1, 1864. He was acting sergeant major during July 1865, just prior to his discharge on August 10, 1865.

Despite the fact that his legal name was George Madison Mosher, he never used it. One of his sisters advised, when supporting his application for a pension, that he always liked the name Edwin, and called himself by that name even as he was growing up. He needed his sister's input because the Pension Board was somewhat skeptical about his application. Not only had he served twice under different names, George H in the 104th Infantry and Edwin G. in the 2nd Mounted Rifles, when his actual name was George Madsion Mosher, but he also admitted that post war he used the name Edwin Watson.

While there was no explanation for the name Watson (his sister had explained the Edwin) it may have been related to the fact that an E. Lovejoy had put out a wanted poster on him for stealing $1,100 dollars, a not inconsiderable amount of money in 1868. The reward for his capture was $200. The poster advised that "perspiration starts on forehead at exercise or excitement." A picture apparently was attached to the poster, but unfortunately was not in his pension file. There is also no information in the file as to whether anyone collected the reward, but the pension board did deny his application.

Two dates also stick out with respect to these men of the 2nd Mounted Rifles. Jerome Woodworth enlisted on December 7, which would become a "Day of Infamy" in the 20th Century and Orrin Dow was wounded on June 6, a date and a day (D-Day) that, eighty years later, was to change the world. It also was a date on which thousands of men were wounded and killed in battle.

In addition to William R. Gilbert, five other C-H-G men were wounded at Petersburg on June 18. Four of the men, David Nortin Bentley (gunshot to right breast), Frederick W. Caryl (gunshot to right elbow and shoulder), Amos Frank Drew (gunshot to left thigh), and James W. Hildreth (gunshot to right hand) served with Company F, 4th New York Heavy Artillery. Renanaslear Allen (gunshot lower jaw and right shoulder) served with Company F, 104th New York Infantry. Wilson C. Robbins (gunshot to left knee) served with Company B, 2nd New York Mounted Rifles. Another five men were wounded on other dates during the Petersburg siege. They were: Jerome B. Woodworth - May 16, 1864 (gunshot to a thigh); David Prior - June 22, 1864 (gunshot to head) (Prior had also been wounded in the head in Fair Oaks in 1862.); Francis Henretty - October 4, 1864 (minnie ball to calf of left leg); Andrew Jackson Palmer - November 1, 1864 (a shell burst above his head causing neurological problems); and Omar W. Fuller - February 15, 1865 (a tree fell on him when he was in his tent, hitting him in the head and causing partial paralysis). Frank Caryl was injured on November 16. He and other soldiers were building a breast work when one soldier fell. The fall caused other soldiers to drop heavy logs which landed on Caryl's back. Frank and Frederick Caryl were brothers.

Of the men not wounded on June 18, only David Prior, died before the end of the war. Prior was born in Pennsylvania to Ormand Prior and Elizabeth Wolf. His brother Elisha was also killed in the war. Ironically, Prior may have been wounded twice at Petersburg, once in the head on June 1, 1864, and again to the head June 22. His records are not clear as to whether there were two head wounds or one. One or two, they must have been slight. He recovered, but was captured August 25, 1864, at Ream's Station and died in Salisbury Prison, North Carolina on December 21, 1864.

Eight C-H-G men were captured at Petersburg. They were: Noble Bolton: Company K, 111th New York Infantry, October 30, 1864; Ira Frank Crane, Company B, 2nd New York Mounted Rifles, September 30, 1864; John Henry Crowell, Company C, 104th New York Infantry, August 19, 1864; Owen E. Hinkley, Company B, 14th New York Heavy Artillery, March 25, 1865; Charles E. Relya, Company F, 179th New York Infantry, mid-1864; Albert P. Watson, Company B, 2nd New York Mounted Rifles, October 14, 1864; Charles Keeber, Company C, 1st Michigan Sharp Shooters, June 17, 1864; and William Wallace Thurston, Company C, 104th New York Infantry August 19, 1864. Of these eight, only Noble Bolton and Charles Relyea died in prison. Bolton had previously served with Company E, 104th New York Infantry. It is likely that his re-enlistment in the 111th was as a substitute. While he claimed to be 42 years old when he re-enlisted in 1864, the 1860 Census showed his age as 48 making his age 52 in 1864. He died February 25, 1865, in one of the Richmond, Virginia prisons.

Similarities

These eight men are interesting because they represent many of the characteristics of all the C-H-G men who served. For instance, place of birth, ages, where died and buried, volunteers and substitutes, marriage status, regiments served in, battles fought, and prewar occupations. Thurston was born in Hume, Crane nearby in Freedom, Crowell somewhere in Allegany County and three different locations are listed in various documents for where Noble Bolton was born. Watson and Relya were born in downstate counties, Hinkley was born in another state, Vermont, and Keeber was born in Germany. Crowell died in 1898 and is buried in Centerville, Crane died in 1919 and is buried in Hume Township. Hinkley died in 1906 in Hunt, New York. His place of burial is unknown, as is that of Noble Bolton who died as indicated above in 1865 in Richmond, Virginia. Relya died of disease in the infamous Andersonville. Their ages were mostly very young, Crane was born in 1843, but Bolton was born no later than 1812. While all of them were volunteers, it is likely that Bolton was a substitute in his second enlistment. Watson volunteered twice and served in two different regiments. Four were both married when they volunteered. Most of them were in regiments that contained many C-H-G men, but one served in an out-of-state-regiment, and one was the only C-H-G man in his regiment. They fought in many of the major battles and skirmishes of the war. Prior to the war five of the eight were farmers or farm laborers.

There were also differences, aside from the fact they were all captured and most soldiers were not. Only one of the eight, Albert Watson was wounded in action compared to about one in every six of all C-H-G soldiers. And finally, only one of them, or 17 percent, died in the war. Overall, about 26 percent of C-H-G soldiers died in action, in prisons, of wounds, or of disease.

On June 30, 1864, Robert Bennett, Company H, 19th New York Cavalry, was injured when thrown by a mule he was riding. The wagon the mule was pulling ran over Bennett causing partial blindness. Bennett was the son of Joseph Bennett, born in England, and Eliza Jemmison, born in Ireland. He was born July 5, 1839, in Granger. After the war he married Jane McAllister and moved to Moscow, Pennsylvania. In a twist of fate, after surviving many battles including, Cedar Mountain, 2nd. Bull Run, South Mountain, Antietam, Fredericksburg, Chancellorsville, Gettysburg and the Wilderness, Bennett was killed September 19, 1899, by a railroad locomotive. The government denied his daughter Flora's request that his funeral expenses be reimbursed.

Also, on June 30 Daniel Wight was captured at Ream's Station. He was participating in a raid on the station led by General Wilson. It is likely that he was also wounded that day. His file indicates that he "died in the hands of the enemy" (in prison) in August of 1864. One document in his file indicates he may have died of disease. However, given the date of capture and the fact that the latest date listed for his death is July 25, 1864, it appears more likely that he died of wounds. His mother applied for his pension and claimed he died in Columbia, South Carolina, but that is not certain, nor is the date of his death.

New Town - New Market, Virginia, August 11, 1864

Alphonzo J. Aldrich, Company F, 19th New York Cavalry, was born to Robert Aldrich of Vermont and Sarah Smith of New York in Granger on November 29, 1839. He enlisted at Oramel on August 13, 1862, and rose quickly through the ranks, being promoted to corporal October 24, 1862, sergeant January 1, 1863 and first sergeant January 1, 1864. On January 20, 1865, he was promoted to 2nd lieutenant. Aldrich participated in a number of battles and was wounded in action on August 11, 1864, at either New Town or New Market, Virginia. (Some records say New Town, others say New Market.) He suffered a gunshot to his lower right thigh. He was with his regiment at Appomattox Court House for Lee's surrender and marched in the Grand Review in Washington, DC on May 23, 1865. On April 8, 1865, while at Appomattox, he suffered an annoying injury. He was on forage detail when his horse stumbled, forcing him forward onto the saddle pommel, and injuring his testicles. After the war he married Mary Anna Beach, eventually moving to Canisteo, Steuben County. He died in Canisteo March 28, 1913.

Weldon Railroad (Globe Tavern), Virginia, June 22 - August 21, 1864

The Weldon Railroad battles were part of the battle for, and the siege of, Petersburg. The initial attacks in mid-June failed to sever this vital Southern supply line. On August 18 a major confrontation occurred. When the battle was over, Union forces had captured Globe Tavern on the railroad and permanently cut off the railroad as a source of supply for the South. There would be other battles at Weldon Station, however. On August 19, 1864, four C-H-G men were captured there. On December 15, 1864, John P. Smith was wounded at the railroad station.

The four men captured were: Jesse Bennett, Jasper M. Griggs, Henry C. Hoadley, and Marshall James Rodgers. Griggs (Company C, 104th New York Infantry) had been wounded both at Fredericksburg and Gettysburg before being captured at Weldon. He was imprisoned at Richmond. He survived the war and died in 1920 in Sugar Grove, Pennsylvania. Rodgers (Staff, 104th New York Infantry) also survived the war, but died shortly thereafter on August 23, 1870, in Franklinville. He had survived Salisbury Prison, but it is possible that his health was impaired by his experience and led to his early death. He had risen from private to captain during his service.

Jesse Bennett was born in Granger December 14, 1844, to John Bennett and Sarah Marsh. He served with Company C, 104th New York Infantry. He was imprisoned at Belle Island and Libby Prisons, Richmond, Virginia and Salisbury, North Carolina. Jesse married Carrie Snyder November 5, 1865, in Short Tract. He died July 16, 1911, in Elgin, IL.

Henry C. Hoadley was born in Oneida County in 1828. He married Laurinda Willy Eastman of Hume, December 25, 1858. Prior to the war he was a boatman on the Genesee Valley Canal. He died February 23, 1865, at Salisbury Prison, North Carolina.

Berryville, Virginia, August 24, 1864

William Jay Wolsey was wounded August 24, 1864, at Berryville, one of a number of engagements which took place in the Berryville area. While there is information to tie Wolsey to the C-H-G area, it is not conclusive. He enlisted at Oramel on August 8, 1862, in Company F, 19th New York Infantry. He was an excellent soldier; entering as a private, but being promoted to corporal on June 1, 1863, to sergeant February 1, 1864 and to quarter master sergeant January 20, 1865. He was badly wounded by gunshot to the abdomen and upper third of his right arm on August 24. At first he was treated at the regiment's field hospital. He was transferred and treated at Fredericksburg hospital, later at Patterson General Hospital in Baltimore, and still later at Chestnut Hill Hospital in Philadelphia. While it may seem strange, as mentioned earlier, many soldiers were treated at multiple hospitals during the war. He was discharged June 30, 1865, with his regiment. Post war, he lived in Warren County, Pennsylvania where he died November 5, 1883. He was buried by the

Warren GAR Post. His parents, William and Hester Wolsey, were living in Sullivan County, New York in 1870.

Ream's Station, Virginia, August 25, 1864

The Battle of Ream's Station was another part of the long effort to take Petersburg. Union troops were engaged in destroying railroad tracks that could be used to supply Petersburg. While generally successful in their efforts, when attacked by Confederate troops near Ream's Station the middle part of the Union defenses, primarily held by inexperience troops, gave in, resulting in many killed and captured.

During the one day battle on the 25th eight C-H-G men were captured, one was killed, and one was wounded. The only one day battle in which more C-H-G men were captured was Plymouth, North Carolina. In addition to Plymouth and Ream's Station, the only other one day battle in which more than one or two were captured was Fair Oaks where three were captured. The three-day battle at Gettysburg, saw eight captured, while four were captured during the battles at Manassas, and six during the long siege of Petersburg. Two other men were captured at Ream's Station during the war, Daniel Wight on June 30, 1864, and George E. Coolidge on October 20, 1864.

The C-H-G men captured August 25, were not new recruits. They were seasoned veterans. All, except one, Rodolph Fox, had been in the service since 1861 or 62. Except for David Prior, Company D, 64th New York Infantry, all were members of Company F, 4th New York Heavy Artillery. George E. Coolidge, who was wounded, served with Company E, 104th New York Infantry. David Prior had been wounded previously, on June 22 during a Petersburg engagement.

Of the total of ten men captured at various times at Ream's Station, six died during the war. Four, Ira Hyde Burroughs, Frank Marion Cook, Rodolph Fox, and David Prior died at Salisbury Prison, North Carolina. One, Daniel Wight, died in a prison hospital in Columbia, South Carolina. The other, George E. Coolidge, was paroled February 5, 1865, apparently as a result of the re-institution of the parole system for wounded and sick men. However, he died in a Union hospital in Annapolis on May 10, 1865, and is buried in Annapolis National Cemetery. Four men survived their imprisonment and returned home. They were: Harvey L. Cooper, Lewis Dill, Levi Emmons, and Leander Fitch.

George E. Coolidge, who was wounded in the right ankle at Ream's Station, actually died of meningitis in Annapolis. He clearly contracted the disease while in prison. Coolidge was a substitute for Eli Pratt Sweet of Pike. Born in Hume to Erasmus Coolidge and Mary Elizabeth Curtis on February 9, 1847, he was only 17 when he entered the service on August 11, 1864, and only 18 when he died, less than a year later.

One C-H-G man, Ichabod Flenagin, was killed at Ream's Station. Flenagin, a farmer, was born in Hume on the Ides of March 1834 to James Flenigan and Julia Ann Perkins. On August 22, 1862, he enlisted in Company F, 4th New York Heavy Artillery. He was obviously a good soldier, rising from a private at enlistment to a second lieutenant by the time he was killed in action at Ream's

Station. In another one of those twists of fate, like the men captured at Plymouth, North Carolina, Ichabod had re-enlisted in the 4th New York Infantry on August 3, 1864, less than three weeks before he was killed. While the spelling of his name appears to be correct, based on a number of documents, it is possible that it was, or became, Flanagan, maybe related to the family for whom Flanagan's Pond in Hume is named.

Shepherdstown, West Virginia, August 25, 1864

The same day that Flenagin was killed at Ream's Station, Martin W. Snyder was killed in a skirmish at Shepherdstown, West Virginia. Martin William Snyder was born to John Snyder and Rachael Emmons January 1, 1842, in Hume. He lived most of his life in Granger and worked as a farm laborer prior to the war. On August 4, 1862, he enlisted in Company G, 19th New York Cavalry at Allen. He is buried in Short Tract.

Smithfield, Virginia, August 29, 1864

Just four days after Martin W. Snyder was killed in action at Shepherdstown, another C-H-G man was killed at Smithfield, Virginia. Emerson Madison Parker was born November 24, 1838, in Granger to Ira Parker and Rosina Smith. Prior to the war he was a farm laborer. He enlisted August 13, 1862, at Oramel in Company F, 19th New York Cavalry. He was killed in action August 29, 1864, at Smithfield and is buried in Granger. As mentioned earlier, a lot of men from the area were named after famous people, such as George Washington. While it is impossible to know whether they were actually named after a historical figure, there were a number of other men like Parker, who were given a middle name of a famous man, in this case Madison, again the name of a President. However, since there is only a single name, one cannot be sure that Parker was actually given the name to honor the historical figure. There were many others with middle names that may have been intended to honor someone famous.

Winchester, Virginia (Opequon Creek), September 19, 1864

The Battle of Winchester on September 19, 1864, was the third battle of Winchester, and one of many battles for the Shenandoah Valley. Battle number one had occurred on May 25, 1862, while battle number two took place June 14-15, 1863. The Union won the September 19 battle, but at a heavy cost in casualties.

One C-H-G man was killed and two more were wounded at Winchester.

Alexander Kelsey Thorp was one of the organizers of Company F, 19th New York Cavalry. Born June 21, 1828, in Amherst, Erie County, New York, he was the son of Montgomery Thorp and Bethiah Jones. He was a wagon maker and a leading citizen of Granger, and it was his brother Thomas who established the monument to the Civil War heroes of Granger. Mustered as a 2nd lieutenant, he had enlisted on September 3, 1862, at Granger. He married his first wife, Mary E. Stewart, February 16, 1851. Mary died in 1856, whereupon he married Harriet A. Swain April 29,

1858. Interestingly, he had a daughter by Harriet named Mary E., apparently after his first wife. His military records indicate that he was killed in battle at Winchester on the 19th. His pension records appear to indicate that he was severely wounded on the 19th and died on the 26th. He is buried in Granger.

Thorp's brother Thomas also served in the war. Another brother Simon H. was murdered during the massacre at Lawrence, Kansas carried out by William Quantrill and his men. The slaughter lasted three hours and more than 150 men, women, and children were killed. The Kansas Governor at the time of the Lawrence massacre, stated that, "No fiend in human shape could have acted with more savage barbarity," Quantrill held a captain's commission in the Confederate Army. Despite his atrocities, he was promoted to colonel. Thorp received a telegram from his brother Thomas on August 31, 1863, advising him of the death of their brother. (Thomas was home at the time, apparently dealing with men who had been drafted. Records indicate that the first draft occurred around July 14, 1863, in the Granger area.). The telegram read, "Father can live but short time. Our Brother was killed at Lawrence Kansas. His body will come Thursday. Come home if possible." Thorp received ten days leave.

The two C-H-G men wounded at Winchester were Frank Cashus Luther and George Washington Morse. Luther was born in Wurtenburg, Germany June 5, 1840, and arrived in the United States in 1852. He married Joanna Chamberlain and had a daughter Mary who married Edmond W. Common of Fillmore. He suffered a severe gunshot wound to his right arm, eventually resulted in an inability to use that arm. His pension provided for a two-thirds disability designation. This may be why he became a farmer post war. He had been a wagon maker prior to the war. His daughter was appointed his guardian in later life. He died September 14, 1904, and is buried in Belfast. Morse was born March 21, 1839, in Caneadea to Rufus Morse and Anna Tenyke. As a result of his gunshot wound on September 19 he lost two toes on his right foot. He married Martha Maria Wood on December 5, 1860. He died August 4, 1901, and is buried in Arenac, Mason Township, Michigan.

Despite these casualties, the major significance of the Battle of Winchester on September 19, was the heroism of a C-H-G soldier who lived through the battle.

The Medal of Honor

On September 19, 1864, George Ebenezer Meach of Hume won the Medal of Honor for heroism in battle at Winchester, Virginia.

The September 19 encounter at Winchester was a major battle. Union forces suffered some five thousand casualties and Confederate forces, three thousand five hundred, out of a 12,000 man army.

THE MEDAL

The opening sentence of the book, _The Medal of Honor_ reads, "He who possesses the Medal of Honor is the holder of the highest military award for bravery that can be given to any individual in the United States of America."

The Army Medal of Honor was not conceived, but rather evolved as an idea. A Navy Medal of Honor was actually established first. The Army Medal was finally created in 1862 to honor Union Civil War soldiers, initially only noncommissioned offices and privates. Commissioned officers became eligible in 1863 when the original resolution was amended. The 1863 amendment also allowed the medal to be awarded to men whose actions met the established standards for receiving the award, even where such actions occurred prior to the passage of the original resolution.

The resolution creating the medal was introduced by Senator Henry Wilson of Massachusetts on February 17, 1862. It was passed by both the House and the Senate, with President of the Senate pro tempore Soloman Foot of Vermont signing for the Senate and Speaker Galusha A. Grow of Pennsylvania signing for the House of Representatives. The approved joint resolution was then forwarded to the White House where it became law (Public Resolution 43) when it was approved by President Lincoln on July 12, 1862.

The resolution provided that the medal was to be presented, in the name of Congress, to such noncommissioned officers and privates as shall most distinguish themselves by their gallantry in action and other soldier-like qualities. The inclusion of "in the name of Congress" is why some call it the Congressional Medal of Honor, whereas, in fact, it is officially the "Medal of Honor." This standard for awarding the medal stood until 1918, when Congress enacted a new law. The new standard called for gallantry "above and beyond the call of duty." It applies to all branches of the armed forces.

Ironically, the retroactive provisions of the 1863 amendment resulted in a situation where the earliest action for which the medal was awarded was performed by an officer for a non-Civil War act of gallantry. The action occurred February 14, 1861, in what is now the State of Arizona, although the medal was not actually awarded until January 21, 1894. The gallantry involved rescuing a kidnaped boy and soldiers of the Seventh U. S. Infantry from the Indian Chief Cochise.

The first medals actually presented went to six enlisted men who along with 15 other men had carried out a dangerous mission behind enemy lines during the Civil War. The 21 men, and their leader James Andrews, had attempted to cut off the entire state of Tennessee from the war by sabotaging the Western and Atlantic Railroad. They almost succeeded. However, all the men were captured and eight of them, including James Andrews, the man who had conceived the mission, were tried by court-martial, convicted, and executed. Eight other men later escaped. The last six were finally paroled (exchanged for Southern prisoners held by the North) on March 17, 1863. These six men were each awarded a Medal of Honor. They were the first to actually receive the medal.

Among the acts of gallantry recognized as deserving of the medal during the Civil War was the capture of a flag. This was true even though there was no law or regulation that established such a deed as an act of gallantry deserving of the medal. Soldiers on both sides of the war treasured their flags and considered them worth dying for.

Militarily flags were of some importance in battle. This was pre-radio communication times, and flags were used to establish rallying points for controlling the movement of troops. Nevertheless, it was the immense daring and personal danger involved in the capture of a flag that qualified this act as gallantry in action, and deserving of the medal. Soldiers were loath to see their flags captured, and went to great lengths to protect them. A man capturing a flag put himself in the thick of the battle and became a special target to be stopped at all costs.

THE MAN

George Ebenezer Meach was born March 31, 1845, in Hume to Arlington and Fanny Ayer Meach. The father's name is listed as Arlington in the 1850 Census. Fanny listed his name as George when she applied for her son's Civil War pension. In the pension application she states that her husband George drowned June 9, 1892, age 72. However, the 1865 census indicates that George was her second husband. Other information indicates that her first husband Arlington was killed by a log in 1859, and thus, Fanny's husband George (who most likely was related to Arlington) was a stepfather, and possibly uncle to Fanny's son George. Young George was living with James Kearns in 1860 and worked as a factory operative, probably in the stocking factory of Joel Sherman, Kearns' next door neighbor. According to a map of the period, and long time Hume resident Don Thomas, the Meach family lived in the village of Hume, in a home just a little way up the hill from the bridge over Cold Creek, and the former home and law office of E.E. Harding.

According to his military file, George volunteered November 9, 1861, for Company I, 6th New York Cavalry (2nd New York Harris Guard), at Fort Scott in New York City (NYC). No information is available that explains why he was in the City in 1861. It is likely that he enlisted at Hume November 9 and was sent to New York City to be mustered at Fort Scott November 19. The regimental history shows that the regiment was organized at NYC during the period September 12 to December 19, 1861. It was turned over to the state of New York as the 6th New York Cavalry on November 29, 1861. The companies were mustered on different dates. Company I, to which George was assigned, was mustered November 2, and George was mustered into the company November 19, a couple of weeks after its official formation. The 6th Cavalry Regiment left for York, Pennsylvania on December 23, 1861, and served there until March 1862. It was then ordered to Washington, DC where it was attached to the Military District of Washington, DC and served in defense of that city until July 23, 1862.

The regiment was then assigned to the Cavalry Corps, 1st Division, 2nd Brigade, first with the Army of the Potomac and later with the Army of the Shenandoah. It was with the Army of the Shenandoah, under General Philip Sheridan, that George would distinguish himself in combat.

George's military file indicates that he was 5 feet 8 inches tall, had a dark complexion, black eyes, and black hair. At enlistment he was a private, but was promoted to his final rank of duty sergeant on February 1, 1865. According to his military file he was 21 when he enlisted. Both his birth date and the 1860 Federal Census indicate that he was, in fact, only 18.

As a member of a cavalry regiment he participated in many battles, both on and off a horse, as did other members of the regiment. However, his duty assignment was blacksmith/farrier. His dad Arlington had been a farmer, and it is possible that he had horses. George may have learned to ride on his dad's farm. He may also have learned blacksmith skills on the farm, or he may have learned such skills from local blacksmith, James Kearns, with whom he was living in 1860. If so, he may also have learned to ride there. Certainly, he would have been exposed to many horses, if he did any work for Kearns.

His original enlistment was for a three-year period. Nevertheless, he re-enlisted in the 6th Cavalry for an additional three years on December 16, 1863, at Culpeper, Virginia.

His muster cards show him present for duty at all times from his enlistment until November 1864. For November and December 1864 and January 1865 the muster cards do not indicate whether he was present or absent. He may have been on leave at that time, but most likely was present and it simply was not recorded. Since he was promoted to duty sergeant in February 1865, he certainly was not away without leave, and clearly was not ill at that time.

His combat record is exemplary. It is amazing that he managed to emerge unharmed from all of the combat engagements in which he participated. Along with other members of his regiment, he took part in at least the following battles and skirmishes: Malvern Hill, Warrenton, Orange County Court House, Culpeper, Williamsburg, South Mountain, Antietam, Kearnesville, Snickersville, Ashby's Gap, Waterloo Bridge, Ellis Ford, Fredericksburg, Spotsylvania Court House, Chancellorsville, Gettysburg, the Wilderness, Todd's Tavern, North Anna River, Yellow Tavern, Cold Harbor, Trevillian Station, Charleston Court House, Berryville, Cedar Creek, Winchester, New Market, Port Republic, New Town, and Dinwiddie Court House.

Ironically, with the war won and about to end, he became sick for the first time. On April 4, 1865, he entered Judiciary Square Hospital in Washington, DC with typhoid fever. On June 20, 1865, he was transferred to Douglas General Hospital. This illness caused him to miss the final battles in which his regiment participated. It also meant he was not with his regiment at Appomattox Court House for Lee's surrender. He missed marching with his regiment in the Grand Review in Washington on May 23, 1865. On August 14, 1865, he was transferred to New York City, probably Fort Scott. He was discharged August 16, 1865, a week after the rest of his regiment.

He was discharged from the 2nd Regiment Provisional Cavalry that was organized June 17, 1865, by consolidation of the 6th and 15th New York Cavalry Regiments. The 2nd Provisional was discharged at Louisville, Kentucky, but Meach, as indicated above, was discharged at New York City. It was common practice during the Civil War for Union soldiers to be transferred for discharge to the location where they were mustered into the service, although this did not happen in all cases. Meach had been assigned to the 2nd Provisional Cavalry, for administrative purposes only, and never served with that organization.

THE ACTION

On September 19, 1864, Sheridan's Army of the Shenandoah engaged Southern General Jubal Early's army at Winchester, Virginia. This third battle of Winchester was one of the decisive battles of Sheridan's Shenandoah campaign. Many historians consider it the most important battle of the Shenandoah campaign. It led directly to the October 19, 1864, Battle of Cedar Creek where Sheridan, in effect, destroyed Early's army and permanently secured the Shenandoah Valley for the North.

Sheridan had a large army available to him at Winchester. He had two Infantry Corps, the VI and XIX, an Artillery Corps, and a Cavalry Corps of some 6,000 men. As mentioned earlier, Meach's regiment was part of the Cavalry Corps, First Division, Second Brigade. It was commanded by Brevet Brigadier General Thomas C. Devin, and included the 4th New York Cavalry, the 6th New York Cavalry (Meach's regiment), the 9th New York Cavalry, the 19th New York Cavalry, (1st Dragoons), and the 17th Pennsylvania Cavalry. Since 119 men from the Centerville - Hume - Granger (C-H-G) area of Allegany County, New York served with the 19th Cavalry during the war (although all were not present at Winchester), Meach was certainly among friends September 19. Two other men from the C-H-G area, James Bradshaw and Ralph Parker, served with Meach in the 6th Cavalry. However by September 19, 1864, Bradshaw was dead and Parker was in a hospital in New York City.

A number of men of historical importance participated in this battle besides the opposing generals. The Deputy Commander of the Second Division of Artillery, and Commander of the First Brigade, Second Division, was Colonel Rutherford B. Hayes. Hayes, of course, became President of the United States. The commander of the Southern forces, attacked by George Meach and his fellow cavalrymen, was John Cabell Breckinridge. Breckinridge was Vice President of the United States from 1857 to 1861, and was the youngest Vice President in United States history. And just to Meach's left in the line of battle was the Second Cavalry Division whose Deputy Commander was Brigadier General George A. Custer. (Custer's brother Thomas received two Medals of Honor during the Civil War, both for capturing flags.)

The Battle of Winchester raged all day, starting at about three o'clock in the morning and lasting until after sunset. Losses were heavy on both sides. Initially Union forces advanced rapidly, but then there was a counter attack by the Confederate forces which penetrated the Union center. At this point, Sheridan adjusted his plan of attack and brought in reserve forces on the right flank that he had originally planned to use on the left. The changes made by Sheridan resulted in the North regaining control of the battlefield. Southern General Jubal Early was also making adjustments to his line and one adjustment was to place General Breckinridge's forces in reserve. However, the Northern Cavalry had followed Breckinridge as he repositioned his forces, and was successful in driving Breckinridge's cavalry forces into their own infantry regiments. The first Northern cavalry charge, at this point, was led by General Devin's Second Brigade, which included the 6th New York Cavalry. The battle report notes that Devin's Brigade returned to rally with three battle flags and 300 prisoners.

Following the charge by Devin's Cavalry, there was a second charge by Colonel Charles R. Lowell Jr.'s Reserve Cavalry Brigade, and then a third charge by the entire 1st Cavalry Division. It was during this charge that George Meach captured his battle flag. This is confirmed by the records of the 6th New York Cavalry contained in the *History of the Sixth New York Cavalry* The Blanchard Press, Worcester, Mass. 1908. It provides the following:

Sept.19th. — Saddled up at 1:30 a.m. and at 2:30 moved out of camp, Lowell's brigade in advance, the Sixth of New York taking the advance of Devin's brigade. Lowell's brigade crossed the Opequon at Steven' Ford, capturing about forty prisoners. Custer crossed at Locke's Ford, with McGilvey's section (Second Brigade Battery) and had considerable fighting. About 2 p.m. Devin's brigade was ordered across at Steven's Ford to press the enemy, who had been startled by Averill on the Martinsburg pike; the Seventeenth Pennsylvania had the advance and went in at a trot, the brigade following, soon coming up with the flying enemy, when Devin and Custer, following closely, soon disposed of their cavalry, routing them completely; then turned its attention to the enemy's infantry, which was being engaged by a part of the Eighth Corps. A grand charge was made by the entire First Division, . . . three of the flags, over a hundred of the prisoners, and the gun and cannon were being taken by the Sixth New York ....Captain Thorp, First New York Dragoons, was killed . . . . One of the flags was captured by George E. Meach, Company I, Sixth New York . . . .

At this point, the Southern forces retreated in disorder and were only saved by the night. In describing this action in his report, Sheridan said that the cavalry, "could be distinctly seen sweeping up the Martinsburg Pike, driving the enemy's cavalry before them, in a confused mass through the broken infantry."

At least five flags, including Meach's, were captured by Devin's cavalry that day. Two contained identifying information. A Virginia State Flag was captured by George Reynolds of Company M, 9th New York Cavalry and a 36th Virginia Infantry Flag was captured by Patrick Enroe of Company D, 6th New York Cavalry. In addition, Corporal Chester B. Bowen of Company I, 19th New York Cavalry (not from the C-H-G area) and Private Jeremiah Parks of Company A, 9th New York Cavalry each captured a flag.

A diary kept by Private Francis W. Ackerman, who also served with Company I, 6th New York Cavalry, mentions Meach's actions at Winchester. Ackerman's diary is in the Rare Book's Division at the Library of Congress in Washington, DC.

THE FLAG

The flag captured by George Meach was an Army of Northern Virginia regimental battle flag, red with a white fringe. It belonged to one of the Virginia infantry regiments under the command of General Gabriel C. Wharton. Flags were produced by the Confederate Army and then sent to regiments where the logos and/or other regimental information were added. Apparently the

Virginia infantry regiment had not had time to add the identifying information before this flag was captured. For that reason it is unlikely that the regiment from which the flag was captured will ever be known. In the heat of battle, it was impossible for the soldiers capturing flags to make identifications.

Meach's gallantry in action, demonstrated by his fearlessness in battle in capturing the enemy's battle flag, earned him the Medal of Honor.

The medal was officially issued to Meach on September 24, 1864. It is not known whether Meach actually received the medal at that time. In fact, it is not known if he ever received the medal.

Some 545 Confederate flags were captured by Union soldiers during the war. Most were donated to the Museum of the Confederacy in Richmond, Virginia in 1906. Some were turned over to governors in 1905. There had been attempts prior to 1905 to return the flags to units and/or Southern states. These attempts had been met with anger and protest from Union veterans and their supporters. By 1905 feelings had changed enough that many Union veterans now supported donating the flags to the governors and the museum.

The flag George Meach captured is now maintained by the Museum of the Confederacy in Richmond, Virginia. It was restored to its original condition in 2003, and is exhibited from time to time. When it is not being exhibited, it can be seen by making an appointment in advance by calling 804-649-1861, ext. 24 or by e-mail: flags@moc.org. One can also write to, The Museum of the Confederacy, 1201 East Clay Street, Richmond, Virginia 23219. Reservations must be made two weeks in advance.

This flag, like all the others in the museum, is an artifact of the saddest, most destructive, devastating, and deadly war ever fought on American soil.

THE AFTERMATH

The 6th Cavalry was at the surrender of General Lee at Appomattox April 9, 1865, but Meach was in a hospital in Washington, D.C. He had typhoid fever. He was discharged August 16, 1865.

Meach returned to Hume following his discharge. By 1873, for some as yet undetermined reason, Meach was in Meriden, Mississippi. He was shot to death there on March 21, 1873. He is buried at Pine Grove Cemetery in Fillmore.

Meach and all of his comrades in arms earned another medal. In 1907 the War Department authorized the Army Civil War Medal. That medal was awarded for military service during April 15, 1861 to April 9, 1865, and for service in Texas to August 20, 1866. The obverse side of the medal contains a bust of President Lincoln surrounded by the legend, "With Malice toward None With Charity for All."

The Battle of Winchester, along with General Sherman's successes in Atlanta during the same time period, had a profound impact on American history. Most historians believe that these two major victories, just prior to the 1864 presidential elections, paved the way for the re-election of Abraham Lincoln. Up to the time of these victories, even Lincoln did not believe he would be reelected.

Port Republic, September 22, 1864

William Curtis Daniels, a farmer prior to the war, was born in Allen Township in 1844. His parents were Timothy Spaulding Daniels and Betsey Atherton. Daniels was shot through the heart while on horseback on September 22. He enlisted at Oramel August 2, 1862, and participated in more than 20 battles before being killed at Port Republic. His brother Charles Rice Daniels also served.

Peeble's Farm (Poplar Spring Church), September 30 - October 2, 1864

During the period September 30 to October 2, 1864, federal forces managed to capture and hold Peeble's Farm, tightening the noose around the encircled troops at Petersburg. Charles Dudley Van Dresser of Hume was captured during this battle on September 30. He was imprisoned at both Libby Prison, Richmond, Virginia and Salisbury, North Carolina. Van Dresser was born October 13, 1847, in Hume to Jeremiah Van Dresser and Phebe Ann Slocum. He married Mary E. Butler October 2, 1868. After Mary's death he married Rose Elizabeth Buchanan. At one time he owned Ingham House (a hotel) in Hume. He died March 8, 1909.

Cedar's Creek, Virginia, October 17, 1864

Cedar Creek in the Shenandoah Valley was a camp site for Union troops. With victory in the Shenandoah Valley Campaign apparently in hand, the Union forces grew complacent and were surprised by an early morning attack by General Jubal Early's troops. General Sheridan had been away planning future operations. When he heard about the rout, he rushed back, organized his men, and led a counterattack, which succeeded in destroying Early's army which was celebrating its early morning triumph. By the end of the day the Union victory was assured, but again at a horrendous price. Union casualties totaled 5,665. Among that number was Daniel Steih of Granger who was wounded by gunshot to the right leg. Steih was born November 7, 1844, in Bavaria, Germany to Godfrey and Catherine Steih. He enlisted February 22, 1865, at Canandaigua in Company F, 9th New York Heavy Artillery. It appears that he actually lived in Grove, but was a member of the Granger Grand Army of the Republic (GAR) Post in Short Tract.

Hatcher's Run (Burgess' Mill), Virginia, October 27, 1864

On October 27, 1864, Hiram Eells was wounded at Hatcher's Run (also known as Burgess' Mill). This engagement was part of the seemingly never ending clashes around Petersburg, Virginia. Like others, it was designed to cut off supplies to Lee's beleaguered troops. However, the Confederate troops, after back and forth encounters, were able to hold their positions at the end of the day.

Eells was born in 1845 in Steuben County to Pitkin and Isyphena(?) Eells. At Hatcher's Run he received a gunshot wound to the jaw and was treated at Carver General Hospital in DC He was able to rejoin his regiment and participated in a number of other battles prior to the end of the war. His regiment, and likely Eells, was at Appomattox Court House for Lee's surrender. He moved to Granger after the war. He died April 26, 1921, and is buried in Short Tract.

Mount Jackson, Virginia, November 22, 1864

Perrie C. Soule (military records are under the name Peter) came from a distinguished family. The son of Absalom Soule and Sarah Clement, his father was a doctor. According to the book *Allegany & Its People - A Centennial Memorial History 1795-1895*, his mother was a lineal descendant of Popes Clements XIII and XIV. A Quaker, she was with a group of Quaker women who in 1862 met with President Lincoln and urged him to abolish slavery.

Perrie was born September 16, 1844, in Schenectady, New York. According to *Allegany and Its People*, he was in some 170 engagements. He served in both Company I, 5th New York Cavalry and Company B, 18th New York Infantry. The book indicates he was wounded nine times, including once at Mount Jackson. (Only the Mount Jackson wound is mentioned in his military records.) The book indicates that he carried shot, bayonet, and saber scars for the rest of his life. He was stabbed by a bayonet while charging up South Mountain in Maryland. He also fought in the seven days battles. He suffered a crippling leg injury and his right arm was paralyzed from his wounds. Despite this, he became a successful doctor. He was also involved in manufacturing, and the patent business. He enlisted September 1, 1861, in the 18th Infantry, and re-enlisted January 14, 1864, in the 5th Cavalry. Soule died August 24, 1924, in Rochester. He left all of his records to the University of Rochester. Information about his records may be accessed at www.library.rochester.edu/rbk/soule.stm

Franklin, Tennessee, November 20 - December 1, 1864

Bad tactics by Southern generals resulted in a huge victory for the North and led to the capture of Nashville. Confederate casualties totaled 6,200 including six generals dead, five wounded, and one captured. C-H-G casualties were one man captured. The man was Joseph Morris. Morris was born in South Wales in 1844. His Mother, Hannah, a widow, married John Roberts and they were living in Centerville in 1860. For some unknown reason, Joseph was in Kentucky in 1864 when he volunteered for Company G, 23rd Kentucky Infantry on September 27, 1864. It is especially ironic, that Morris, in Kentucky, was a substitute for John Roberts' son, W.W., who was living in Centerville. John and Hannah Roberts were still living in Centerville in 1865. Captured December 1, Morris was imprisoned at Andersonville. Subsequent to the war Morris married Mercy Louise Holland, March 2, 1876, in Lima, Ohio. He became a lumber merchant, died in Lima April 27, 1903, and is buried in Woodland Cemetery, in Lima.

December 1864

Sometime in December at Smithfield, West Virginia, Stephen Draper, the first C-H-G volunteer, was wounded for the third time. The horse he was riding bolted and hit a tree. He suffered injuries to his spine, right ear, and a thumb.

On December 5, 1864, John P. Smith was injured when he and others were burning Weldon Railroad ties. The pile was high and one of the burning ties fell on him, injuring his back and kidneys.

On December 5, 1864 at Kearneytown, Virginia, James Dole was injured when his horse fell and the pommel injured his testicles, a very common accident. Dole, the son of Summer Dole (born Vermont) and Hannah Griffin (born New York), was born July 31, 1845, in Pike. By 1865 he was living in Hume and by 1890 in Granger. In 1865 he married Catherine McNulty in Hume. They were divorced in 1878, and remarried in 1897 in Cleveland, Ohio. He died January 19, 1916, in Wiscoy.

Gordonsville, Virginia, December 19, 1864

Ironically, during the same time period, James Dole's brother, Smith, was injured at Gordonsville, Virginia. Smith was born August 12, 1844, in Pike. He became a Charter Member of Grand Army of the Potomac Post 237 in Wiscoy. Married twice, first to Hannah J. Luther, and then to Julie I. Hill, he died in 1895 in Wiscoy and is buried there. Smith Dole was the last C-H-G man injured in 1864, although three more men, William Silas Smith (Company E, 85th New York Infantry), David Prior (Company D, 64th New York Infantry), and George Sibbald (Company E, 85th New York Infantry, died of disease prior to the end of the year.

The battle, which lasted several days, was another of Grant's never ending attempts to destroy the Virginia Central Railroad, which would cripple the South's ability to move troops and, more important, supplies. Destruction of an enemy's ability to wage war by destroying its means of production and supply would become more and more important as wars became more and more complicated. The battle at Gordonsville took place on the ground in freezing weather.

In future wars, air power would become a major method of destroying an enemy's means of production and supply. It too would take place in freezing weather, but this time miles high in the sky.

"Air Power" in the Civil War

By World War II, air power had become a part of the strategic battle plan and was reflected in the enormous air effort by the 8th Air Force in Europe to destroy German production facilities. Some would argue that it reached its zenith in the Pacific, when the 20th Air Force completely destroyed the Japanese ability to wage effective war.

While mentioning air power in a discussion of the Civil War may seem inappropriate, such is not the case. For the use of the air to gain tactical and strategic advantage was very much a part of that war. The air "weapon" was the balloon. F. Stansbury Haydon in his book *Military Ballooning during the Early Civil War* covers in detail the development and use of balloons during the early years of the war. This included, in particular, the use of balloons for spying. The men who flew the balloons were called aeronauts. The aeronauts were all civilians. However, regular military men were used in a number of capacities, although few were permanently assigned to the Balloon Corps. Most were detached for specific periods of time. As a rule, regular personnel served as ground crews and in general utility groups. Specialists included telegraphers and draftsmen. The draftsmen were taken aloft by the aeronauts to make aerial maps and panoramic sketches, including sketches of enemy encampments. The number of tents in a camp could give an approximation of the enemy's strength.

While a number of regiments from New York provided detachments to the Balloon Corps during the war, no regiments with C-H-G men were mentioned in Haydon's book. That, however, is wrong. The 85th New York Infantry did provide at least two C-H-G man to the Corps. George Henry Allen Tibbitts of Granger was detached to the Balloon Corps as of May 2, 1862. His file does not provide information on how long he was detached, nor what he did, but his civilian occupation prior to the war was artist. George Pitt was also detached to the Corps.

Tibbitts was born June 12, 1840, in Perry to Charles and Mary Tibbitts. He enlisted September 21, 1861, at Granger. On July 24, 1865, he married Frances J. Bertholf in Whiteford, Monroe County, Michigan. He died December 8, 1929, in Detroit.

George W. Pitt, another member of the 85th Infantry, was detached to the Balloon Corps during May and June of 1862. Pitt also had special skills that may have been useful to the corps. Prewar, as mentioned earlier, he had been an ambrotype artist (an early photographer).

Other C-H-G men were certainly aware of, and saw, the balloons in action. For instance, the balloon *Washington* was used for observation at the Battle of Mechanicsville and the balloon *Intrepid* was used at the Battle of Fair Oaks. C-G-G men participated in both of those battles.

Following the standoff at Gordonsville, most of the troops went into winter quarters. Pickets were set up and it was while on picket duty that Smith Dole was injured. His feet were frozen, sometime in late December. Smith Dole was born August 12, 1844, to Summer Dole and Hannah Griffin. He enlisted September 7, 1864, at Pike in Company D, 19th New York Cavalry. His brother James K. also served in the war. Subsequent to the war Smith lived in Hume Township, probably Wiscoy. He was a charter member and officer of Burnside G.A.R. Post 237. He died in 1895 and is buried in Wiscoy.

This fourth year of war was brutal for C-H-G soldiers. The final totals showed 22 men killed in action, 65 captured, 50 died of diseases, 50 wounded, and 14 injured. The 22 killed were just two less than the total number killed in the first three years of the war combined. The 65 captured were more than double the combined totals for 1861, 1862, and 1863. The fifty men who died of disease were one more than the total for the four other years of the war. The 64 who were wounded and injured were a third of all wounded and injured for the entire war.

THE WAR - 1865 - RELIEF AND HOPE

The most deadly war in United States history was slowly grinding to an end. By early April it would be officially over, although the dying would continue for many months following Lee's surrender at Appomattox Court House, April 9, 1865. (In fact, General Johnston's army would not surrender until May.)

January 1865

Like the last to die in 1864, the first to die in 1865 was a man who fell to disease. On January 11, 1865, Sylvester Wilday died of severe diarrhea, or pneumonia, or both, at Jarvis Hospital in Baltimore, Maryland. Wilday, a resident of Granger, was born April 27, 1826, in Schoharie County. He was married to Roxana Lee, August 13, 1848, in Portage. Volunteering September 9, 1864, at Genesee Falls, he served with Company D, 19th New York Cavalry. He is buried at Loudon Park National Cemetery in Baltimore. He had been in the service only three months.

Frank Marion Cook of Company F, 4th New York Heavy Artillery was born in Allegany County in 1843. A resident of Granger, he enlisted August 27, 1862, at Hume at the age of 19. Captured at Ream's Station on August 15, 1864, he died in Salisbury Prison, North Carolina February 15, 1865, of diarrhea. He is buried in Salisbury National Cemetery.

On January 7, 1865, James Randolph Cowing, Company F, 4th New York Heavy Artillery, was charged with desertion. He was late reporting back from a furlough. Cowing, the son of Warren Cowing and Julia Nye was born October 20, 1835, in Hume. He married Margarite Isted July 2, 1857, in Oramel and he died February 28, 1892, in Monomomie, Wisconsin. His desertion charge apparently didn't amount to much, since no further mention is made of it, and he was determined eligible for a pension. Nevertheless, desertion was a major problem.

Desertions

According to the *Historical Times Illustrated Encyclopedia of the Civil War*, desertion was a serious problem for both the North and the South. By the end of 1864 half of the Southern forces were absent. The Union rate was about one-third. The principal causes were homesickness, boredom, disillusionment, infrequent pay, and depression. Poor record keeping also resulted in some men being charged with desertion. Henry Fetterley, Company I, 81st New York Infantry, was charged with desertion on August 7, 1865. It was later determined that he had already been discharged. While the deserters crossed all groups, the higher risk groups included foreign-born soldiers from the East, recruits who received bonuses, and substitutes (men paid to enlist).

Northern desertions decreased as the punishment became more severe, but still close to 5,500 men deserted each month between 1863 and 1865. Initially, a reward of $5.00 was established for those returning deserters. The reward was later increased to $30.00. Those caught were subject to court-martial. They received punishment ranging from fines, to being flogged, imprisoned, thrown into solitary confinement, or sentenced to make up lost time. A very few were executed. During the war, some 278,000 Union soldiers were recorded as deserters. The figure for the South was 105,000, but the Southern base was much smaller, making the percentage much higher. Henry W. Spease, Company H, 19th New York Cavalry, deserted October 6, 1864. He was arrested the same day, was court-martialed, and fined $10.00.

At least 45 C-H-G men, including those mentioned above, were charged with desertion at some time during the war. Out of the 45, fourteen (Edward Bezent, Justin Bingham, Jr., John M. Butler, Myron L. Dodge, Richard Ellis, George P. Goodale, Henry Griffith, Asa Hawley, Leland Higgins, George V. Hill, John Isted, John A. Johnson, Edwin C. Poole, and Frank Ricketts) were eventually dropped as deserters according to their military files. However, in subsequent years the charges against Dodge and Higgins were removed from their records. Frank Ricketts, dropped as a deserter with the 85th New York Infantry, enlisted in the 184th Infantry and received an honorable discharge. Justin Bingham also had an honorable discharge as a result of previous service with the 27th New York Infantry, and he did receive a pension for that service. His desertion, if one wishes to call it that, from the 9th Iowa Cavalry appears to have been ignored, as well it might have been. It was from a Little Rock, Arkansas hospital November 28, 1865, well after the end of the war.

Another three, John Adams, Emory A. Anderson, and John C. Franklin, were officially dishonorably discharged. It is assumed that the 14 dropped as deserters were also "dishonorably discharged" although their military files do not say so. The only other C-H-G soldier dishonorably discharged was Adonirana J. Rose who was previously discussed.

At least eight men were officially court-martialed. These included John Adams (who was a substitute and may, or may not, have been from the C-H-G area), Companies E and B, 14th New York Cavalry. Adams was charged with being drunk and with desertion. He was the most severely punished of all of the men. In addition to being dishonorably discharged he lost all pay and was sentenced to three years at hard labor. Emory A. Anderson was charged with desertion under fire and was dishonorably discharged. A severe penalty, but certainly not as severe as the one handed out to Adams whose charges of drunk and desertion cannot possibly be considered as bad as desertion under fire. The difference appears to be that Adams was a private and Anderson was a major. The other soldier dishonorably discharged for desertion was John C. Franklin, Companies A and E, 1st Michigan Cavalry. He also paid a fine. Franklin's was a strange case. He was in the hospital a lot and his records indicate he had "fits" of some sort. Due to previous honorable service in the 33rd Infantry he did receive a pension. His request in 1884 to have the dishonorable discharge removed from his records was denied.

Except for William Gray, the other men court-martialed were punished financially. Gray died during, or while awaiting, his court-martial. The charges against him were questionable as previously discussed. There is some evidence that George P. Goodale was also court-martialed, or at least was about to be court-martialed. His was another unique case, discussed earlier in this study, and further research is required to determine exactly what happened with respect to the desertion charges leveled against him.

Three of the deserters were with the 78th New York Infantry, which was apparently a totally disorganized regiment, that suffered numerous desertions. Most of the men from the 78th, who deserted, enlisted elsewhere, or eventually returned to the 78th. William Henry Harrison Keyes of C-H-G was one of these men. He deserted April 28, 1862, and returned in February of 1863. As indicated in the 1863 section above he was killed in action at Gettysburg.

In addition to Dodge and Higgins, six men, James H. Akin, Company F, 104th New York Infantry; Edward Bezant, Company B, 5th New York Cavalry; Henry Fetterley, Company I, 81st New York Infantry; John C. Franklin, Company A/E, 1st Michigan Infantry; Charles W. Poole, Company F, 33rd New York Infantry; and Edwin P. Poole, Company C, 104th New York Infantry all petitioned to have the desertion charges removed from their records in later years. Only Akin, Dodge, and Fetterley were successful. Charles W. Poole had his charge changed to AWOL. Bezant claimed he had received a disability discharge, but could not produce any papers. A third Poole brother, George M. (Company F, 33rd New York Infantry), was also charged with desertion as of April 1, 1863. He re-enlisted in Company B, 2nd New York Mounted Rifles and received an honorable discharge on August 10, 1865. Fetterley's charge was dropped years later when it was determined that he was charged with desertion as of August 7, 1865, and had been discharged August 4, 1865.

Ultimately 28 of the 45 C-H-G men charged with desertion, or their families, were determined eligible for a pension

February 1865

Daniel Orville Clark was injured in early February near Atlanta when a mule jumped on him. There was damage to his spine, lungs and side. Daniel was the son of Daniel and Betsey Clark and was born September 13, 1842, in Granger. He served with Company H, 136th New York Infantry and was with Sherman on his march to the sea. He marched in the Grand Review on May 24, 1865. In 1868 he married Mary Ellen Bradley, widow of Civil War soldier Nathan Bradley, who had died while a prisoner of war. Clark died March 22, 1930, probably in Fillmore, although one record says Short Tract.

February also marked the end of C-H-G casualties at Petersburg. Omar W, Fuller was born May 7, 1829, in Hamburg, Erie County to William H. Fuller and Mary W. Blackmer. He volunteered for Company F, 4th New York Heavy Artillery on September 4, 1862, and was severely wounded in the head February 18, 1865, at Petersburg when, as discussed earlier, a tree fell on him. The wound left him partially paralyzed. He was a resident of Granger and died September 26, 1900.

On February 23, 1865, Henry C. Hoadley died at Salisbury Prison, North Carolina. Hoadley was born in Oneida County. He married Laurinda Willey Eastman of Hume in 1858, and apparently was living in the Hume area. He was captured twice, first at Gettysburg on July 1, 1863. He was paroled September 29, 1863. He was captured again at Weldon Railroad August 18, 1864. This time he was not paroled and he died in prison.

The Petersburg death toll rang two more times in February. C-H-G man, Noble Bolton, discussed earlier, was captured October 30, 1864, at Petersburg and died of variola at a Richmond, Virginia prison February 25, 1865.

John Dorey was 28 years old when he volunteered for Company F, 19th New York Cavalry at Allen on August 30, 1864. He was born in Granger in 1836 to Deborah Dorey, who most likely was not married. (The name of his father is not known.) Deborah later married a Bartlett. Never married, John Dorey died of typhoid fever February 26, 1865, at Harpers Ferry, West Virginia.

March 1865

Even after Bolton died, and with only weeks left in the war, C-H-G men continued to suffer casualties at Petersburg. The next victim was Owen E. Hinkley, who would become a resident of Granger after the war. He was captured March 25. Hinkley was the son of Jaby and Mary Hinkley. He was born in 1835 and drafted July 21, 1863, into Company B,14th New York Heavy Artillery. He was paroled March 30, 1865, only five days after being captured, surly a sign of the times.

Stephen Draper was wounded again in March. He had already been wounded once and injured twice. This time, in hand to hand combat at White Post, Virginia, he received a scalp wound when hit in the head with a revolver on March 6, 1865.

The last man to die of disease in March of 1865 was Darius Martin Snider. Snyder was born March 14, 1842, in Allen to Edward Green Snyder and Mary Ann Curtis. He enlisted September 20, 1861, in Company E, 85th New York Infantry at Granger and died of remittent fever March 11, 1865, in New Bern, North Carolina. He is buried in New Bern.

First Division Hospital, Near Petersburg, Virginia, March 22, 1865

On March 22 James K. Kerns, or Kearns, died of an overdose of morphine at First Division Hospital. The Army claimed that the dose was self-administered and that therefore his widow, Lydia, was not entitled to a pension.

Kerns was a blacksmith in civilian life and was living with his wife and children in Mills Mill in 1860. Ironically he had been born in Virginia about 1814. He enlisted August 31, 1864, at Scipio, Cayuga County. He gave his age as 44, but the 1860 Federal census lists his age as 46. A relatively big man for the time, he was 5'8" tall with brown hair, a dark complexion, and dark eyes. Originally his cause of death was reported as "Cerebral Congestion." However, when Mrs. Kerns applied for a pension, additional information became available, including claims of drug use.

The surgeon's report on Kerns claimed that he was a habitual opium eater. Presumably some of his tent mates confirmed this, but their names were not included in the surgeon's report. Affidavits provided by two Hume doctors, A.B. Stewart and H.H. Lyman, stated that they had treated Kerns for 13 years and had never known him to use drugs. To emphasize their point, they specifically said that as his doctors they were in a position to know if he had been a habitual drug user. The tone of their affidavits makes clear that they did not believe the surgeon's report. Several other locals provided affidavits also stating that they had known Kerns for many years and that he had never used drugs. The Army surgeon, Brevet Lieutenant J.J. Woodward, claimed that Kerns had been under the influence of the morphine (poison) for several hours before he saw him and that it was too late to administer an emetic. The treatment therefore, consisted of putting his feet in hot water, his head in cold water and having him drink a half pint of very strong coffee. On the second day, he lapsed into a coma and died.

Doctor Woodward also addressed the source of the morphine. He claimed that Kerns told him his wife had sent it to him. He then goes on to minutely describe the bottle, which he claimed was found in Kerns' knapsack, including the fact that it had been sealed with the seal of the U.S.A. Medical Department. No explanation was provided as to how Mrs. Kerns could have gotten a bottle of morphine with the seal of the U.S.A. Medical Department on it.

The whole story, including the surgeon's report, seems concocted, but there also does not seem to be a reason for making up such a story. There is no evidence that Kerns had been sick or injured. If he had been, he might have visited the hospital for treatment and been given an overdose of morphine accidently. Everything else that followed would then make more sense. In particular the report, with its obvious weaknesses, especially the bottle explanation, could be viewed as covering up a mistake made by the surgeon. Frankly, that seems to be the most logical conclusion based on the information available. Another possible scenario is that Kerns had taken up using drugs, and they were being supplied by someone in the medical department. The story that he got the morphine from his wife in a Medical Department bottle doesn't seem plausible.

The fact that Kerns' wife did not receive a pension was a serious matter, and the surgeon's report, dated September 1869, was written as part of the investigation into her eligibility for a pension. She obviously did not have any income and was dependent upon her children for her support the rest of her life. The report was the sole reason she was determined ineligible.

White Post, Virginia, March 25, 1865

For those who believe that the end is the beginning, and the beginning the end, Rawson B. Hultz, son of Richard and Mandana Hultz, serves as a perfect example. Rawsom, or Ramson, (it is spelled both ways in different documents) volunteered July 9, 1861, just in time to participate in the first major battle of the war - 1st Bull Run. Now with the war drawing to a close, at the small hamlet of White Post, Virginia, in a minor engagement he was killed in action. He is believed to be buried in Pulteney, Steuben County, New York where he was born in 1841.

Fort Fisher, North Carolina, March 1865

John Townsend of Company H, 136th New York Infantry received his fourth and last wound of the war at Fort Fisher, North Carolina according to his records. Fort Fisher controlled access to Wilmington from the sea. It was located on Confederate Point Peninsula, bordered by the Atlantic Ocean and Cape Fear River. The first attempt to capture the fort in December of 1864 had failed, once again, due to inept leadership. In mid-January, under new leadership the fort was taken. This would appear to be the period when Townsend was wounded, if he was wounded at Fort Fisher. However, it does not appear that Townsend's regiment, the 136th, was at Fort Fisher in January. In fact, it appears that they were at Fayetteville, then moved north toward Averyboro, Bentonville, Goldsboro, and Raleigh. It does appear that Townsend was wounded in 1865. Exactly where may be in question. All of Townsend's wounds are discussed below.

The C-H-G area's most wounded man was John Townsend, Company H, 136th New York Infantry. He claimed four different wounds in four different battles. The last wound occurred at Fort Fisher, North Carolina where he suffered a gunshot wound to his right arm, and is discussed above. As previously stated, Townsend's pension was approved for rheumatism and other causes which made it unnecessary for the pension agency to determine the validity of the wounds he claimed. A review of the movements of his regiment shows that it was in the general areas where he claims he was wounded, and on the approximate dates of such wounds, except for Bull Run. Further, his muster cards show he was present for duty on all the dates he claims he was wounded, again except for Bull Run. When one considers that his first pension application was filed 26 years after the events, being off a date here or there does not seem exceptional. In fact, many men got the dates wrong. It is harder to accept his claim about Bull Run. That was a big and famous battle. It seems unlikely that one would claim he was wounded there if he hadn't even been there. Yet that is what Townsend claimed. It is not as if Townsend had to lie to get his pension. He was eligible for non-wound reasons and he had a minimum of two other wounds that were not under any question. Considering all of this, it seems reasonable to give Townsend the benefit of the doubt, and accept that he was wounded four times. He may have simply had the location wrong.

Townsend did fib a bit when he volunteered at Granger on September 1, 1862. He claimed he was 35 and born in Michigan. The 1860 census showed his age as 44 and that he was born in Vermont. He was certainly not unique in lying about his age. Numerous men did. Younger men claimed to be older, and older men claimed to be younger. The information about his state of birth may have been a misunderstanding, or a mistake, and was certainly not important. He was married in September of 1855 to Eliza J. Bates. Townsend died January 6, 1902.

Bentonville, North Carolina, March 19-21, 1865

Two famous generals clashed at Bentonville, William T. Sherman for the North and Joseph J. Johnston for the South. Bentonville was a major battle in Sherman's march north through the Carolinas, after his "March to the Sea" and capture of Savannah, Georgia. The battle raged from the 19th of March to the 21st, 1865. In the end, Johnston was finally defeated.

The Confederate forces did capture C-H-G soldier George W. Jones of Company D, 136th New York Infantry during this battle. Jones was born November 27, 1839, in Pike to John and Betsey Jones. He had been previously wounded at Resaca, Georgia. After his capture he was imprisoned at one of the Richmond, Virginia prisons, but was soon paroled. He married Ellen R. Van Dyke in Eagle, New York on November 27, 1867. Ellen had previously been married to Francis S. Lincoln, who was captured at Gettysburg and who died in prison on February 3, 1864. Jones died August 15, 1918 in Hume.

Gravelly Run, March 29 - 31, 1865

John P. Smith was hit in the cheek by a piece of shell on the 29th. The injury was so minor he didn't even require medical attention, or at least did not seek any. This was common, and many men later regretted their failure to seek medical attention for minor wounds. When they applied for their pensions, there was no documentation to support their claims of injury. This was important where minor injuries impacted their health as they aged.

Dinwiddie (Five Forks), Virginia, March 31 - April 7, 1865, April, 1865

General Robert E. Lee surrendered at Appomattox Court House April 9, 1865. Incredibly, in the period March 31 to April 7, 1865, twelve C-H-G men become casualties, and another was injured.

Daniel B. Hoes was injured in combat at Gravelly Run on March 31, 1865. An exploding shell blew the limb off a tree. The limb then fell on Hoes hurting his back and right shoulder. While the injury was fairly severe, Hoes recovered to be with his regiment at Appomattox Court House for Lee's surrender and to march in the Grand Review on May 23, 1865. Hoes was born in 1835 to Jesse and Deborah Hoes in Littlefield, New York. By 1890 he was living with his third wife Sarah Ada Powell in Granger.

April 1865

The casualties at Dinwiddie were Cassius C. Granger, Company B, 2nd New York Mounted Rifles and Jerome Woodworth, Co. B, 2nd NY Mounted Rifles.

Cassius C. Granger was born October 4, 1843, in Pike to Lyman and Lois Granger. In later years he was a resident of Hume. He volunteered for the 2nd Mounted Rifles at Pike February 13, 1864. He was wounded by gunshot to the groin on March 31. A Charter Member of Burnside G.A.R. Post 237, he died May 30, 1912, at Nunda.

Jerome Woodworth lost a hand in battle at Dinwiddie. His records are unclear where this occurred since he was also wounded at Petersburg in June of 1864. However, his military file shows him present for duty after his injuries at Petersburg (gunshot to both thighs), and it is unlikely he could have continued to serve if he had lost his hand earlier. He married his second wife, Lilly Armour on January 17, 1892, in Houghton. He died June 25, 1926, in Hemlock, Livingston County.

Five Forks and South Side Railroad, Virginia, April 1 & 2, 1865

Five Forks was literally the junction of five roads. This battle, and one at the South Side Railroad, effectively ended the long siege of Petersburg, and set the stage for the final confrontation at Appomattox Court House. These two battles brought the killing and maiming of C-H-G men in the battles in and around Petersburg to an end. At Five Forks, three C-H-G men were wounded, one was captured, and one was killed in action. At the South Side Railroad, three more were wounded.

The wounded at Five Forks were: George H. Kimball, Company C, 19th New York Cavalry; Sheldon Trall, Company F, 4th New York Heavy Artillery; and Frederick Zorns, Company B, 140th New York Infantry. George Dutton, Company C, 19th New York Cavalry, was captured and Ira Weaver, Company F, 4th New York Heavy Artillery, was killed in action

George H. Kimball was born December 29, 1835, in Centerville to Chester Kimball and Victoria Williams. He was wounded by gunshot to the right hip at Five Forks. He married Ann Eliza Veazey in Centerville on September 21, 1861. He died in Golden, Colorado June 7, 1903.

Sheldan Trall was born November 6, 1839, to Luman Trall and Mary Polly Short in Hume. On October 23, 1866, he married Camelia R. Allen Babcock. He was wounded in the left hip during the battle at Five Forks.

Frederick Zorn was born September 16, 1832, in Klein Mittling, Germany and emigrated to the United States in 1856. He received a gunshot wound to the lower leg at Five Forks. The doctors declared him totally disabled. He received treatment in three different District of Columbia hospitals, Armory, Douglas, and Harewood. His pension indicates that he lived in Fillmore after the war. A relative, John Zorns, lived in Fillmore and Granger. Frederick, never married and appears to have been a wanderer. He died February 24, 1916, in Angelica and is buried at Pine Grove in Fillmore.

George Washington Dutton was born May 27, 1836, in Oneida, New York to Horace Dutton and Katherine Coddington. He was captured at Five Forks March 31. A citizen of Centerville after the war, he died in Leroy, Genesee County, September 5, 1918.

While not the last C-H-G man to die in the war, the last C-H-G man killed in action was Ira Ramson Weaver. He died at Five Forks on April 7, 1865. Weaver was born in 1821 in Milton, Chittenden County, Vermont to William L. Weaver and Eunice Drury. On January 3, 1841, he was married to Cheney W. Smith in Granger. Prior to the war he was a farmer, according to his military records. The 1860 Federal Census lists him as a "Nereseyman." This is probably an incorrect spelling. It is the only time such an occupational title is used in the C-H-G census. He enlisted in Company F, 4th New York Heavy Artillery January 4, 1864, at Buffalo. His son, Jacob, also served. Ira was buried on the battlefield.

Lewis Amasa Berry was wounded by gunshot to the left thigh on April 2 at the South Side RR. Berry served with the 3rd Battery, 4th New York Heavy Artillery. He was born to Samuel W. and Hannah Berry August 6, 1835, in Granger. His brother Pembroke also served in the war.

Loomis H. Eldredge, Company F, 4th New York Heavy Artillery, was wounded April 2, 1865, at the South Side Railroad. He received gunshot wounds to both thighs. He was born in 1827 in Orleans County. He married Eliza Benson January 26,1853, in Granger and died March 27, 1872. It is certainly possible that his death was war related.

William Wesley Morse, Company D, 4th New York Heavy Artillery, was born in Hume on March

17, 1836, to David Morse and Henrietta Green. At the South Side Railroad he was hit by a shell which caused damage to his breast and right eye. William was married twice, first to Angeline Scott and then to Sarah Hovey. When he applied for his pension, he mentioned a possible third wife named Ellen. His family denied this, stating that he was old and confused. Ellen was merely an old girlfriend. He died May 28, 1905.

Alonzo M. Elmer was the last man from C-H-G to die in the war from combat. He was born June 9, 1833, in Hume to Joel Elmer and Mercy Russell. On March 3, 1860, he married Anna Clark in Hume. He volunteered at Hume on August 15, 1862, for the 19th New York Cavalry. He suffered a gunshot wound to his clavicle on April 2, 1865, at Five Forks, VA. He died May 14, 1865, of his wound, gangrene, and pneumonia at Point of Rocks, Maryland. He was originally buried at Point of Rocks. Eventually his body was shipped home and he now rests at Pine Grove Cemetery in Fillmore.

Like many men who died in the war, Elmer left personal effects. Army regulations provided that, if the effects were not administered within a short period after his death, the effects were to be disposed of by a Council of Administration. The proceeds from this disposition were to be credited to the United States until such time as such proceeds were claimed by a representative of the deceased. Elmer's effects included: one great coat, one pair of trousers, one pair of drawers, two shirts, and one pair of boots. Items such as knapsacks, haversacks, canteens, and shelter tents were considered government property, and turned over to the Quartermaster Department. A Court of Administration under Lieutenant H.E. Crane was convened at Point of Rocks, Virginia to dispose of the Elmer's effects. The total realized was $1.25, with the great coat bringing 50 cents and the boots 35 cents.

Seven more C-H-G men would die during 1865. Six died of diseases: Ferris E. Kendall died April 18 in Rushford of typhoid fever contracted in the service; Ralph Parker died April 28 of pneumonia at Ladies Home Hospital in New York City; George Coolidge, as previously mentioned, died May 10 of meningitis in Annapolis; Cyrus J. Hatch, Jr. died May 10 of small pox in Chapel Point, Maryland; John Barney died June 17 in Charleston from a "service related disease", Francis E. Fox died at home in Freedom, Cattaraugus County, on August 17 from chronic diarrhea contracted in the service.

Appomattox, April 5, 1865

The military and pension files of Alphonse J. Aldrich indicate that he was wounded on August 11, 1864, at New Town, Virginia while with Company F, 19th New York Cavalry. The 19th Cavalry was in New Town on the 11th, but there is no indication of a battle on that date. His records claim a gunshot wound to his thigh. The records also indicate another injury on April 8, 1865, at Appomattox. While riding his horse he was slammed into the pommel and suffered an injury to his testicles. During his service he rose from private to lieutenant. Aldrich was the son of Robb Benjamin Aldrich and Sarah Smith. He was born November 29, 1839, in Granger and enlisted in the 19th on August 13, 1862, at Oramel. On September 28, 1865, he married Mary Anna Beach in Mount Morris. He died in Canisteo, Steuben County, on March 28, 1913, and is buried there.

On April 8, 1865, Zenas Bradley, Company F, 104th New York Infantry, was injured in a train wreck at Painted Post, Steuben County. Bradley was returning to his regiment from leave and was riding on a cattle car. As the train passed over a bridge in Pained Post, the bridge gave way. This was Bradley's third injury of the war. According to his daughter, he attended Lincoln's funeral. His military records support that he was in Washington, DC at the time of the funeral.

Dyer's *Compendium of the War of the Rebellion, Part 3* provides the following information on the 188th New York Infantry:

> 188th Regiment Infantry Organized at Rochester, N. Y., and mustered in October 4-22, 1864. (Co. "A" organized as Co. "E," 183rrdNew York Infantry, and mustered in at Elmira, N. Y., September 24,1864.) Left State under orders to Join Army of the Potomac in the field October 13, 1864. Attached to 2nd Brigade, 1st Division, 5th Army Corps, Army of the Potomac, October, 1864, to July, 1865. SERVICE.-- Siege of Petersburg, Va., October 20, 1864, to April 2, 1865. Boydton Plank Road, Hatcher's Run, October 27-28, 1864. Warren's Raid on Weldon Railroad December 7-12. Dabney's Mills, Hatcher's Run, February 5-7. 1865. Hatcher's Run March 25. Appomattox Campaign March 28-April 9. Lewis Farm, near Gravelly Run, March 29. Junction of Boydton and Quaker Roads March 29. White Oak Road March 31. Five Forks April 1. Fall of Petersburg April 2. Pursuit of Lee April 3-9. Appomattox Court House April 9. Surrender of Lee and his Army. March to Washington, D.C., May 1-12. Grand Review May 23. Duty at Washington till July. Mustered out July 1, 1865. Regiment lost during service 9 Officers and 36 Enlisted men killed and mortally wounded and 53 Enlisted men by disease. Total 90.

At least nine men from the C-H-G area served with the 188th NY Infantry. They were: James Clute, William Dorey, Henry Dunning, Hiram Eells, David Hoes, John Lampman, Moses D. Luther, David H. Meyers, and John P. Smith. The 188th suffered few casualties. Three were wounded in action, one was injured, one died of disease and one other was sick.

Appomattox Court House, April 9, 1865

C-H-G soldiers were well represented at Lee's April 9 surrender. The regiments at Appomattox with multiple C-H-G men, included the 2nd New York Mounted Rifles, the 4th New York Heavy Artillery, the 5th New York Cavalry, the 19th New York Cavalry, the 64th New York Infantry, the 104th New York Infantry, and the 188th New York Infantry. The total number of C-H-G men who served in those regiments during the war was 361. Clearly, nowhere near that number were at Appomattox on April 9. Many men had been discharged by that date, and many others were dead or injured. Medal of Honor winner George E. Meach, a volunteer with Company I, 6th New York Cavalry, was in a DC hospital. On the other hand, other regiments with one or two C-H-G men were at Appomattox.

Around May 20 Stephen Draper was on his way from Warrenton, Virginia to Washington to march in the Grand Review. His horse stumbled and he injured his testicles. It was the third time Draper had been injured. He was also wounded twice.

James Bennett House, near Durham Station, North Carolina - April 26, 1865

The last major Southern army in the East, the Army of Tennessee under General Joseph E.

Johnston, surrendered April 26, even though Jefferson Davis had urged Johnston to continue the war. This was the same Johnston who had commanded the Southern forces at Williamsburg in May of 1862, when Willard Calkins became the first C-H-G soldier wounded in combat and captured. Several C-H-G men who had fought Johnston's army at Bentonville, NC were present at Bennett's House for the surrender. These included: John H. Boss, Jr., Co. E, 55th Ohio Infantry; William D. Harrington, Co. I, Jackson L. Wallace, and John Townsend, Co. H, 136th NY Infantry; Andrew Mearns, Jr., Co. A, 154th NY Infantry; and Augustus Sartar, Co. I, 147th PA Infantry. It is possible that others were also there.

The Grand Review, May 23-24, 1865

The grand review of Union troops was called "a benediction on the Civil War." It was a huge parade consisting primarily of the armies of Generals George Meade and William Sherman. It was also the first major step in demobilization for many of the troops. The review took two days. The Army of the Potomac under General Meade marched in review on May 23, and the Army of the West under General Sherman passed in review on the 24th. C-H-G men marched on both days. Of the regiments with multiple C-H-G men, at a minimum, the 4th New York Heavy Artillery, 19th New York Cavalry, 64th New York Infantry, 104th New York Infantry, and the 188th New York Infantry all marched with the Army of the Potomac on May 23. On the 24th at least the 136th New York Infantry and 154th New York Infantry marched with the Army of the West.

The 1865 toll on C-H-G soldiers was three killed in action, thirteen wounded, five injured, three captured, and thirteen dead of diseases.

As mentioned earlier, a total of 507 men who served in the war are clearly identified as from the C-H-G area. In addition, there were 73 men for whom there is some evidence that they lived at least part of their lives in the C-H-G area or had some other connection to the area. Of this total of 580, 311 individual men, or 54 percent, were either captured, killed, wounded, injured, or died of some disease during the war. If you omit those who were "only injured" the total is still 287, or 49 percent. Many of the men suffered multiple casualties. For instance, four of the 287 were wounded more than once, one four times. Thirty-five men were captured and later died of some disease. Twelve were both wounded and captured.

Saving the Union required a high price. Many C-H-G men, as well as many others, paid that price.

THE HOME FRONT AT WAR'S END

The state of New York conducted its own census in 1865. William R. Mills was the census enumerator for the Township of Hume and conducted the census during the period June 5 to June 30, 1865. The enumerator for Centerville Township was Franklin Williams and he completed the census during the period June 5 to June 24. In Granger, Washington Moses was the enumerator and he took the Granger Census during the period June 5 to June 28.

William R. Mills, age 47, obviously a very practical man, started the census count at his own home. He is the first person counted. Mills listed himself as a farmer. Franklin Williams, only 30 in 1865, shows his occupation as "none." He also lists his father as having no occupation. In 1860 he was listed as a merchant and his father as a gentleman. Washington Moses was 30 in 1865 and a farmer. He was also a prominent citizen. In later years he frequently provided affidavits for soldiers to assist them in obtaining their Civil War pensions.

Population

Not surprisingly, there was a decrease in the population for each of the three jurisdictions. Hume went from 2,142 in 1860 to 2,014 in 1865; Centerville from 1,403 to 1,190; and Granger from 1,281 to 1,064. The total population for the three jurisdictions was 4,302 compared to 4,826 in 1860. While the 524 decrease was close to the number of Civil War Volunteers, that is really only a coincidence, especially since many soldiers were home already, and many still in the service are listed in the census and were included in the population count, as well as in other counts, such as occupations.

Many other changes had occurred, most of no significance, but some of real substance. The 524 decrease in population works out to a three percent decrease in five years (probably only four years since the exodus most likely started in mid 1861), a significant decrease in a relatively short time period. Some of the decrease was almost certainly related to war time employment with people moving from the C-H-G area to more lucrative jobs in other locations. There may have even been some "How You Gonna Keep 'Em Down on the Farm, After They've Seen Paree?" It also may have been related somewhat to birth rates. With a lot of men in the service, the birth rates for 1862 to 1865 were probably less than in prior years.

Number of Occupations and Employed Workers

Along with the population, the total number of C-H-G occupations also decreased a little, although there was an increase in Centerville and a significant decrease in Granger. Part of this was due to the elimination of certain job titles that were really not appropriate, such as ladies and gentleman in Centerville in 1860. This may have reflected a better understanding by the enumerators of what should be in the census. Other 1860 occupations are not listed in 1865. This could mean any number of things including: that there was simply no one in the township performing those occupations, at the time of the census; the occupation was no longer a viable occupation in the area; the enumerator made a mistake; or the enumerator used another title for the occupation. Many new titles are listed. New titles might be a new name for an old occupation, or a new type of occupation altogether. See below for a discussion of the "lost" and "new" occupations.

The 1865 totals were 60 occupations in Hume, versus 66 in 1860; 32 in Centerville, versus 23 in 1860; and 17 in Granger, versus 38 in 1860. The total people employed changed very little overall, with 1318 employed in 1860, and 1373 employed in 1865. However, the percentage of the townships population employed in 1865 was significant when compared to the percentage of the population employed in 1860 - 32% in 1865, versus 27% in 1860. The same percentages for Hume were 31% for both years; percentages for Centerville were 23% in 1860, versus 33% in 1865; and for Granger 24% in 1860, versus 31% in 1865. While these figures are misleading, in that they compare employment to the population rather than the workforce. The fact was that more people, and a greater percentage of people, were employed in 1865 than were employed in 1860. This was good both for the individuals and for the local economy, and was almost certainly the result of the war.

Occupations

Farmers

All of these changes were clearly side events as farming continued to be the dominant occupation in the area. The 1860 Federal Census showed 215 farmers in Centerville, 265 in Hume, and 158 in Granger for a total of 638. In 1865 the respective figures for each jurisdiction were 342, 405, and 292 for a total of 1,039 and a supposed increase of 401. This does not, most likely, represent a significant increase, or maybe any increase, in the numbers of farmers in each township. It is more likely the result of two things; first, the enumerators did a better job and second, farm laborers were listed as farmers. The 1865 New York State Census lists only one farm laborer, in Centerville. In 1860 there were a total of 160; 15 in Centerville, 81 in Hume, and 64 in Granger.

Day laborers who worked for farmers may also have been listed as farmers in 1865. There are no day laborers listed in the 1865 New York State Census. There were 47 in the 1860 census; 39 in Hume and eight in Granger. Finally, no domestics were listed, whereas 78 were listed in 1860; 34 in Centerville, 35 in Hume, and nine in Granger. While domestics, farm laborers, and day laborers account for some of the difference in the number of farmers, it is most likely that, as mentioned earlier in discussing 1860 census data, the enumerators in 1860 failed to fill in the occupation column for a number of farmers. This probably happened where several farmers were listed one after the other, and the enumerator only filled in the occupation column for the first one. The disappearance, or significant reductions in the number of, day laborers, farm laborers, and domestics is interesting. These men, living on the margin, were certainly candidates for growth occupations, and better paying occupations, in C-H-G or in other areas.

School Teachers

Teaching was not a popular profession by 1865 and the number of teachers had decreased dramatically. In fact, there are no teachers listed for Granger, where there had been nine in 1860. For Hume there were only 19, versus 23 in 1860. Only Centerville showed an increase going from four to five. Not one of the five was one of the four teachers listed in 1860.

Of the 19 teachers in Hume, it appears that only five taught there in 1860. There may be more, since the first names of some 1865 teachers match first names from 1860. Some of the women may have married, and were teaching under their married names in 1865. If so, it is less than five. It is more likely, that once the women got married, they gave up their teaching jobs. One of the teachers, Mary W. Mix, wife of Leander Mix, was a music teacher.

Why no teachers are listed for Granger in 1865 is a mystery. There must have been some, unless schools were closed for some reason during the war. The 1870 Federal Census for Granger lists seven teachers, none of whom were Granger teachers in 1860. Two of the 1860 teachers are listed in the 1865 census under their 1860 names, but are no longer teachers - Hariette Miller and Mary Willard. Hariette is the wife of Civil War veteran and physician Myron Miller, as she was in 1860. There is no occupation listed for her. Mary is the wife of Samuel Willard, also a Civil War veteran. No occupation is listed for her, and she was probably at home tending to their almost four year old son Warren in 1865.

Physicians

The 1860 Federal Census distinguished between physicians and physicians-surgeons. The 1865 New York State Census does not make this distinction. A number of men listed as physician-surgeons in 1860 are simply listed as physicians in 1865. Unlike school teachers, many of the same physicians are listed in both 1860 and 1865. There was a slight decrease in number, with eleven physicians in the area in 1860 and only nine in 1865. Centerville still had one, Granger had three rather than four, and Hume had five rather than six.

Five of the physicians: Allie Mabie, David L. Barrows, and A.B. Stewart of Hume, and Charles D. Anderson and Reuben V. Smith of Granger, are listed in both the 1860 and the 1865 census. Five, or maybe six, physicians from 1860, William Smith and William Ferns of Granger, Daniel Shaver and H.H. Seymour of Hume, and Frederick Chang of Centerville are no longer in the area. William Smith had a distinguished Civil War career and eventually moved to California. It is likely that Hume physician Peter Hanks had also left the area.

Centerville had one physician in 1860, Frederick Chang, and one physician in 1865, Porter Hanks. There was a physician named Peter Hanks in Hume in 1860. It is difficult to tell if Peter and Porter are the same person. It does not appear so, which would mean that Peter had left the area by 1865 and Porter had taken his place, albeit in Centerville rather than Hume.

The five who had departed (in addition to Peter Hanks) were replaced by three new physicians, Julia A.P. Mills and H.H. Lyman of Hume Township and Myron Miller of Granger. Miller also had a distinguished Civil War career. Dr. H.H. Lyman was the first Lyman, but not the last to serve the area. There was a doctor named Lyman in Hume Township (Fillmore) for most of the next 100 years. (The Lymans were descended from Puritan stock.) Mills is certainly the first, and maybe the last, female physician in the area, to date. It is interesting to note, however, that even though a female physician was extremely rare, in 1866 Civil War doctor Mary Walker was awarded the Medal of Honor.

Dentists

In 1860 there were two dentists listed, Darwin Barrows and Myron Miller. No dentists are listed in the 1865 New York State Census. Barrows served with Company F, 4th New York Heavy Artillery and died in 1864 at Petersburg. Miller also served as staff with the 85th New York Infantry and returned home with his health permanently impaired. (He enlisted for three years, but only served eight months. His military file says he served as a hospital steward.) He is listed as a physician in the 1865 census. He lived until 1873 and probably died of war related problems.

Merchants

The number of men who called themselves merchants increased from ten in 1860 to twelve in 1865. Four of these men listed their occupations as merchants in both years. Of the six men who were no longer merchants in 1865, Milton Skiff of Hume had become a broker; Alanson Smith, also of Hume, had become a farmer; and Franklin Williams, of Centerville was the census enumerator, but had no occupation. The other two men, Richard Groves of Granger and Peter Cole of Centerville, are not listed in the 1865 census.

The new merchants in Hume were Edgar J. Snider, Albert Anderson, Isiah M. Burt, and Edson A. Hammond. In Granger the new merchant was George Ayrault. The new merchants in Centerville were Allen S. Thomson, David H. Brooks, and Milton M. Woods.

Ministers

In 1860 there were ten clergymen in the C-H-G area. In 1865 there were also ten. However, only three of the men from 1860 were still ministers in the C-H-G area in 1865. Except for Philo Woodworth in Centerville, the 1865 census does not list ministers by denomination. They are listed as clergyman. Philo was a Methodist minister. Overall, there were four clergymen in Hume, versus five in 1860; one in Centerville, compared to two in 1860; and five in Granger, versus three in 1860. John Trowbridge, a Baptist minister, whose son John died in the war, was still in Hume as was J. B. Sharp of the Universalist Church. Southworth Phinney, a Wesleyan minister, remained in Granger.

Manufacturers

The 1865 census lists six manufacturers. There were none in the 1860 census. However, the 1860 census did list two proprietors, William Mills and Joel Sherman. Mills is listed as a wool carder in 1865 and Sherman as a manufacturer. (Carding is where, usually, a machine is used for disentangling and arranging wool, cotton or other fibers.) All of the manufacturers are in Hume

Township. One, Nathan F. Sherman, is the son of Joel Sherman. Another, Nathan P. Eaton, like the Shermans, was originally from Connecticut. Since he also was a boarder with Sherman, he may have been a relative, almost surely worked for him, and was not in a separate manufacturing business. Solomon Dewey, age 56, from Madison County is the fourth man listed. It is possible that he was an independent manufacturer, although he lived next door to Sherman. Also listed is Sarah Hammond, age 22, a boarder with A.B. Smith. It is highly unlikely that she was a manufacturer in the same sense as the others, and it is more likely that she worked in one of the manufacturing plants. Thomas Hall, 54, is listed as a shingle manufacturer, whereas in the 1860 census he had been a shingle maker. Probably there was no practical difference. It is interesting, however, since Augustus Beardsley is listed as a house builder and there is certainly a relationship between house building and shingle making. Beardsley's home building business may have been the impetus for Chester Pool, age 66, to become a house painter, which is one of the new occupations in the 1865 census.

There is no indication in the census as to the type of manufacturing undertaken by these men, except for Thomas Hall. Sherman (and his son and boarder Eaton) was probably still in the stocking business, as he was in 1860, or something akin thereto. Mills, although not listed as a manufacturer, was certainly in the wool business as he had been in 1860. His occupational title probably should have been manufacturer.

In 1860 the census listed as an occupation factory operative. That title does not appear in the 1865 census. Based on occupations in the 1865 census the only people who can reasonably be identified as working in one of the factories (or in manufacturing) are Eliza Searl, age 21 and Ellen Searl, age 16, who are working in a knitting factory, and Catherine Fuller, age 42, who is working in a glove and mitten plant. Another possibility is Eugene M. Whitney, 36, of Hume. He listed himself as a pattern maker, an occupation that did not appear in the 1860 census.

George Meach, who was a factory operative for Joel Sherman in 1860, and who won the Medal of Honor in the war, was in a hospital in Washington, DC in June of 1865. Mary Hart, who also worked for Joel Sherman in 1860, is boarding with Sherman in 1865 and is now a book keeper, almost surely in Sherman's employ.

New/Lost/Unique 1865 Occupations

There were 21 occupations in which at least one person was employed in 1860, but in which no one was employed in 1865. Those occupations were: ambrotype artist, basket maker, day laborer, dentist, domestic, farrier, gardner, landlord, operative - furnace, operative - factory, publishers' agent, raftsman, sailor, seamstress, washer woman, watch repairer, and wheel wright. For at least three other occupations, a different title was used - hostelries became hotel keepers, proprietors became manufacturers, and physician-surgeons became merely physicians. Gentleman and lady were really titles and not occupations, and are not included as such in the 1865 census.

Day laborers, dentists, domestics, gentlemen, lady, operative-furnace, operative - factory, proprietor, and physician-surgeon, are all discussed elsewhere as appropriate in this study.

Ambrotype artist is discussed under the new 1865 occupational title, artist.

Basket making was not a lucrative occupation in 1860, and by 1865, for whatever reason, there were no basket makers listed in the 1865 census, versus three in 1860. Of those, Rufus Morse of Granger, age 48 in 1860, was enumerated as a farmer in Hume in 1865, and Benjamin Mach or Mack of Hume, age 60 in 1860, is not listed in 1865. The other 1860 basket maker, Miss L.L. Hamilton, 16 in 1860, does not appear under the name Hamilton.

The one hosteler in 1860 was George McElison(?), age 23, of Hume. By 1865 five-hotel-inn keepers were listed: Christopher Stewick, age 50; Hasell C. Fletcher, age 48; David W. Sweet, age 42; and Charles Ingram, age 45. All were hotel keepers in Hume. The inn keeper was Charles Tarrey, 47, in Centerville.

In 1860 there were seven landlords. In 1865 there were none, at least none enumerated as such. Two of the 1860 landlords, David Sweet and Charles Ingham, were reported as hotel keepers in 1865. Another, Thomas Dole, age 29 in 1865, was a grocer. Those not listed in the 1865 Census include: P.P. Foote, age 44 in 1860; A. Sanborn, 63 in 1860; F.J. Whithey, 23 in 1860; and Omar Olney, 38, in 1860.

Hariette Hunter of Wiscoy was the only watch repairer listed in the 1860 census. There are none in 1865, and Hariette is not included in the census, at least not as Hariette Hunter. She was 41 in 1860. R.B. Hill(s), who at 66 in 1860 was the only gardner, is not listed in the 1865 census.

The 1860 Federal Census for Hume lists Francis Palmer, age 34, as a publisher's agent. When he volunteered for service in 1861, the military listed his occupation as teacher. Palmer, the son of Humphrey Palmer and Sally Stacy, was born June 25, 1826, in Centerville and enlisted as a private in Company F of the 104th New York Infantry October 25, 1861, at Geneseo. He was wounded in the ankle at 1st Bull Run (Antietam) September 17, 1862. He was mustered out of the service as a first lieutenant on July 17, 1865. After the war he became a lawyer and moved to Alma, Michigan where he died August 16, 1915. He married twice, first to Amelia B. Vickery, whom he later divorced for desertion, and then to Frances S. Prichard Rockafellow. There are no publisher's agents listed in the 1865 census.

The title raftsman does not appear in the 1865 census. Boatman is listed in both censuses and some men who appeared as raftsmen in 1860 are listed as boatman in 1865. The terms are probably interchangeable. However, the total employed changed and most of the men changed. There were 36 raftsmen/boatmen in 1860. In 1865 there were 27 boatmen. Only three men were boatmen/ raftsmen in both 1860 and 1865. Two of the 1860 boatmen, Theron Foster and Charles Snell, were veterans and were engaged in farming in 1865. Theron served with Company D of the 4th New York Heavy Artillery. Born March 12, 1837, in Castile to Lewis Foster and Emma Ann Wheeler, he and his family, including his brother Adelbert, moved to the Hume area between 1850 and 1860 and became a life long resident. Theron is buried in Wiscoy. As discussed elsewhere in this study, Adelbert, born January 10, 1845, in Castile, served with the 21st New York Cavalry. Following the end of the war, the 21st was sent west to the Colorado Territory to perform guard duty for the

Overland Stage Coach Route. Adelbert was discharged July 7, 1866. Charles E. Snell was born August 16, 1833, in Manlius, New York and served with Company F of the 19th New York Cavalry. In 1860 he was living with the family of Alfred White of Hume. White also was a boatman on the canal in 1860. Willard E. Calkins, a raftsman in 1860, was also a farmer in 1865. Calkins, discussed elsewhere, served with Company F, 33rd New York Infantry.

It is somewhat surprising that no seamstresses are listed in 1865. Two, Lydia Dienar, age 30, and Fany Delay, age 45, were enumerated in 1860. Lydia Dienar was not listed in 1865. No occupation is shown for Fanny Delay in 1865. Nor is Nellie Huckly listed. In 1860, at age 49, she was enumerated as a washer woman.

Another surprise is that no wheelwrights are shown in the 1865 census. There were two in 1860. Harvey M. Howden, age 35 in 1860, was enumerated as a wagon maker in 1865, an occupation that is certainly related, if not actually the same. The other wheelwright in1860, Henry Griffith, age 35, was not listed in 1865. The military carried him as a deserter.

Occupations in which individuals were employed in 1865, but not in 1860, include: artist, "arcade" (most likely this was a place and not an occupation), bar keeper, boiler maker, book keeper, broker, cheese maker, glove and mitten maker, hewer of timber, hotel/inn keeper, home builder, house painter, jeweler, knitting factory worker, mail carrier, manufacturer, music teacher, overseer, pattern maker, railroad conductor, shingle manufacturer, spinner, stage driver, tanner, stone mason, surveyor, veterinary surgeon, and wool carder. Many of these have already been commented on, including: glove and mitten maker, hotel/inn keeper, house builder, house painter, knitting factory worker, manufacturer, music teacher, pattern maker, shingle manufacturer and wool carder. Others are standard type occupations, but some of the new ones do indicate the changing times in the area and deserve mention.

Whereas there were five ambrotype artists in 1860, none are listed as such in 1865. There were three artists, two of whom were not enumerated as artists in 1860. One was Sereno Health, age 25, of Hume, originally from Connecticut. Another is Edward Emory, 31, of Granger. He was born in Allegany County and was living with his mother Abigail. They may have been ambrotype artists or artists as one thinks of that term today. Of the five listed in 1860, Edmund Daggett, D.B. Granger, and Martin A. Brennan are not enumerated in the 1865 census. Edgar J. Snyder is listed as a merchant and is living with his wife Harriett and daughter Myra, age four. The last 1860 artist, George Washington Pitt, is still an artist according to the 1865 census. He eventually moved to Ottawa, Canada where he died April 28, 1921.

Sylvia Andrews, 26, of Centerville was employed in Arcade, Wyoming County. Her occupation is not stated, but it is not surprising that she was employed. All the information available indicates that she was a member of a talented and close family. She was the daughter of War of 1812 veteran Alanson Andrews, and sister of Civil War soldiers Andrew Andrews (who died January 27, 1863, of wounds received December 13, 1862, at Fredericksburg) and Elias Neilon Andrews (who was killed by guerillas December 15, 1862, near Aldie, Virginia).

Another new occupation in the area was bar keeper. In 1865 Civil War veteran Joel Bardwell, age 24, of Centerville held this position.

David Dicket, 47, and Azra M. Spencer, 19, were boiler makers. Dickey was born in Ireland. There were two employees in another new occupation, book keeper. The positions were held by Mary A. Hart, 27, (who was born in County Cork, Ireland as Mary Hickey, even though the 1865 census says she was born in England) and A.B. Smith, 65. Mary, almost surely, worked for manufacturer Joel Sherman, and Smith may have as well. Milton M. Skiff, age 54, a merchant in 1860, was a broker in 1865.

The most significant new occupation in 1865 was actually the creation of a new business, a cheese business in Centerville. The business was developed by Asa C. Hubbard, 47. His employees were his sons, Theodore, 20, and Dwight G., 19, and Clarinda Stacy, 31. Jason L. Moore, 31, of Centerville listed his occupation as jeweler. Jason was the son of Hiram and Mary A. Moore. Born in New York there is no occupation listed for him in 1860. He most likely was working for his father, a farmer.

Other new jobs reflected the changing economy in the area. This included two stage drivers, David L. Jones, 27, and John W. Jones, 23, both of Centerville. Both were sons of Martha Jones and were born in Wales. They worked out of Arcade. (It is possible Sylvia Andrews also worked for the stage company.) Frederick S. Butterfield, age 29, of Hume was the mail carrier. He and his wife Hannah were both born in Allegany County. It is surprising that no mail carrier is listed in the 1860 census. There was also a veterinarian surgeon, an occupation that a rural farm community finds hard to do without. The veterinarian surgeon was J.W. Sullivan, 36, who was born in Pennsylvania. Finally, there is a railroad conductor, H. W. Ingham of Hume.

Despite all of the above, the most interesting thing in the 1865 census is that five men are listed as unemployed. This may have been one of the first times that someone was listed as unemployed in a census. Three of the men had a right to be unemployed, Solomon Williams, 70, Reuben Ellis, 76, and a Veazey, age 67. The other two, however, were of prime working age - Franklin William, 30, and George M. Latham, 47. All five lived in Hume.

WINS AND LOSSES

Throughout the first half of the nineteenth century, the C-H-G area was a destination point for many people, both from other states and from abroad. The local communities were growing, and although poverty was widespread, a local economy was developing, fueled initially by timber and farming. However, other types of businesses were being created. The people had a better understanding of the world than one might suspect, and it would appear, based on the letters of the soldiers, that local education was important and effective. Families were very close and respectful of each other, at least those that provided Civil War soldiers. There were exceptions, but there always are. Religion was important, but the profession was not profitable, and clergymen tended not to stay in one place for extended periods. Again, there were exceptions. People were a lot more mobile than one might believe.

The war probably did not bring any changes that would not have occurred anyway, but without question it accelerated change. Long time residents, who may have stayed in the area another generation, moved on during, and/or after, the war. On the other hand, new people moved into the area. New businesses were born sooner. The war allowed some to prosper more than they would have otherwise. Exposure to, and knowledge of, other parts of the country were enhanced, at least sooner than might have happened in the normal course of events.

In the end, as one might expect, there were both winners and losers. Most important for the future of the country and the world, the country emerged from the war as a single nation. However, a generation of young men, from the North, from the South, and from C-H-G, were decimated.

THE C-H-G SOLDIERS

Following is an alphabetical listing of all Centerville - Hume - Granger Townships (C-H-G), Allegany County, New York, Civil War soldiers. Every soldier whose name appeared in a source document as from the C-H-G area is addressed. In some cases, it turns out, soldiers were not from the C-H-G area, despite the evidence of the source document. Where possible, the reason for these soldiers inclusion in the source document is explained. Source documents for names include: the 1865 NYS Census;1890 Federal Census Special Schedule for Civil War Soldiers and Sailors; *History of Allegany County 1879*; *Allegany and Its People*; 1865 Allegany County Town Clerk Register, 1910 Federal Census, *Civil War Veterans in and Around Allegany County, New York* by Calvin Matteson, and lists provided by local veteran's organizations.

For purposes of this study, a C-H-G soldier is someone who was born, died, or lived in the C-H-G area at some time during his life. Soldiers are given credit for being at Lee's surrender or Johnston surrender if their regiment was at Appomattox or Bennett's House, and their muster cards show that they were present for duty. Likewise they are given credit for marching in the Grand Review after the war if their regiment marched, and their muster cards show that they were present at the time of the march. For each soldier, military and biographical information are provided, if available, as follows:

Military Information. Last Name - First Name - Middle Name or Initial - Different Spellings of Last Name - Company and Regiment - Date and Place of Enlistment/Enlistment Period (Place of enlistment is what is listed in the military records. However, many times it is the same as the place of muster, and is likely wrong. In most cases it should be either Centerville, Hume or Granger.) - **Age at Enlistment** (per military files in most cases with explanations as appropriate) - **Characteristics - Date and Place of Muster** (in some cases the place where the regiment and company mustered is used) - **Bounty Received** (This is included to show that the soldier received a bounty. It is difficult to tell from the records reviewed whether the amounts reported in different documents are duplications or bounties awarded by different levels of government. Amounts may be overstated or understated, although I have tried to avoid overstating. In any case, the amount indicated should not be considered the exact amount awarded. It may be correct, but in most cases probably does not represent the exact amount awarded and/or received. At a town meeting in Granger on March 19, 1864, a measure was passed to pay a bonus of $300 to soldiers of the 85th and 104th Infantries who chose to reenlist.) - **Rank at Entrance and Completion of Service - Battles, Skirmishes in which the Soldier Participated** (There are no definitive military files listing battles and skirmishes in which Civil War soldiers participated. The information for each soldier in this study was obtained by comparing the present-absent muster cards and other information [hospital records, furloughs, etc.] for each soldier with the battle record for each soldier's regiment. If the soldier was present during the period his regiment engaged in a battle, a skirmish, etc., he received credit for participation. It is possible that this results in some soldiers receiving credit for battles in which they did not participate, and not receiving credit for some in which they did. Where it was unclear, I erred on the side of giving them credit for participating in the battle. Despite the uncertainty of the method used, I found that when comparing WIA, KIA, and POW information, with the battle records constructed using the method described, there was always a correct match. Nevertheless, the battles shown should not be considered a definitive list of every battle or skirmish in which the soldier may have participated. **Type of Discharge - Casualties** (The following designations, **KIA, WIA, INJ, POW** and **DD**, are used to define whether a soldier was a casualty. Soldiers who received a disability discharge for health reasons were not considered casualties. Information is provided for each type of casualty, when available. **Wounded in Action (WIA), How, When and Where - Injured (INJ), How, When and Where, - Prisoner of War (POW), Captured, When and Where, Imprisoned Where - Killed in Action (KIA), When and Where - Died of Disease (DD), What, When and Where.**

<u>**Personal Information.**</u> **Parents, Where Born - Siblings** (those known, there may be others) - **Born, When and Where - Pre War Occupation - Post War Occupation - Wife/Wives** (those known) - **Children** (those known) - **Died, When and Where - Buried Where**.

Additional Information (both military & personal.) - **Sources of Information**. Most source materials are self explanatory. The source "Matteson" refers to the book, *Civil War Veterans in and Around Allegany County, New York*, by Calvin Matteson.

<u>Abbey, Henry Lyman</u> - Co. B, 104th NY Infantry - 12/26/1861 at Geneseo, NY/3 yrs - 19 - 5'10", Light Complexion, Gray Eyes, Brown Hair - 2/26/1862 at Geneseo - $100 - Pvt, Pvt - Cedar Run, 2nd Bull Run, South Mountain, Antietam, Fredericksburg, Chancellorsville, Gettysburg - 7/1/1863 Honorable/Deceased - KIA, 7/1/63 at Gettysburg - Lyman and Alvira Abbey (Both B NY) - Fidelia, John - 4/2/1841 in Avon, Livingston Co., NY - Farmer - None (Deceased) - Never Married - None - July 1, 1863 at Gettysburg - INA -The 1865 NYS Census indicates that he also served with the Navy, but there is no record of such service. His Mother was likely previously married to a Merrill?. (Military and Pension Files, 1855 and 1865 NYS Censuses Hume, 1850, 1860 Fed. Censuses Hume, 1865 Allegany County Town Clerk Register, Allegany County Web Page Hume)

<u>Abbott, George W.</u> - Co. H, 19th NY Cavalry - 8/13/1862 at Portage, NY/3 yrs - 19 - 5'11", Light Complexion, Gray Eyes, Light Hair - 9/3/1862 at Portage Station - $100 - Pvt, Pvt - Deserted House - 1/30/1863 Honorable/Deceased - KIA, 1/30/1863 at Blackwater (Deserted House) VA - Charles (B-MA) & Lois Chapman (B-NY) Abbott - Louisa - 10/6/1836 in Granger - Farmer - None (Deceased) - Never Married - None - 9/30/1862 in Blackwater, VA - Hampton, VA. National Cemetery (originally buried Suffolk, VA) - Listed on Soldiers Monument in Granger. (Military & Pension Files - 1860 Fed. Census, 1865 NYS Census Granger, *Allegany & Its People*, *History of Allegany County 1879*, Granger American Legion, 1865 Allegany County Town Clerk Register Granger, Matteson, Roll of Honor Book)

<u>Adams, John</u> - According to the1865 Allegany County Town Clerk Register for Granger, a John Adams was a substitute for Henry Iserman of Granger who was drafted 7/4/1863 to served 3 years. Adams took his place and enlisted 8/15/1863 at Elmira in the 14th NY Cavalry. Adams pre-war occupation was shoemaker and he was 35 in 1863. He was born at Exeter in Otsego County.

There was a John Adams in the 14th Cavalry. However, he enlisted 1/12/1863, at NYC. He was 21 and his pre-war occupation was machinist. That Adams was eventually court-martialed, charged with desertion, and passing as an officer. He was convicted, sentenced to hard labor, and dishonorably discharged. It appears that the substitute John Adams was not the 14th Cavalry John Adams. The 1860 Federal Census shows a John Q. Adams, age 30, living in Mt Morris, Livingston County. His occupation was shoemaker. This John Adams may have served with the 136th NY Infantry, volunteering August 31, 1862. He was mustered September 25, 1862, and was declared a deserter June 18, 1863, when he failed to return from home leave. One could speculate, that while on leave he agreed to become a substitute for Iserman. The characteristics of the 136th Infantry Adams and the 14th Cavalry Adams are identical. The only differences are age and occupation. Like the 14th Cavalry Adams, the 136th Infantry Adams also deserted as outlined above.

Agar, John A. - Co. M, 4th NY Heavy Artillery - 12/26/1863 at Caneadea/3 yrs - 20 - 5'7", Light Complexion, Grey Eyes, Brown Hair - 12/26/1863 at Elmira - $300 - Pvt, Pvt - Wilderness, Spotsylvania - 9/26/1865 Honorable - WIA, gunshot to right hand at Spotsylvania, 5/16/1864, was in Satterlee G. H., Philadelphia, PA. - Absolom (B-England) & Mary Madison (B NY) Agar - Milton, Joseph, Mary - 8/26/1843 in Hume - Farmer - Farmer - Helen - Willie - INA - INA -Did not receive a pension - (Military Files - 1850, 1860 Fed. Censuses Hume,1865 NYS Census Hume, 1870 Fed. Census Caneadea, 1865 Allegany County Town Clerk Register Hume)

Akin, James Harvey. (Aikin) - Co. F, 104th NY Infantry - 2/2/1861 at Geneseo/3 yrs - 18 - 6', Light Complexion, Blue Eyes, Brown Hair - 2/26/1862 at Geneseo - No bounty - Pvt, Pvt - No battles - 9/1/1862 Honorable - Was not a casualty - William & Lucetta Akin (Both B NY) - Eugene, George - 1844/45 in Delaware Co., NY - Farmer - Farm Laborer - Ella O. Merwin, married 11/3/1866 in Portageville, NY - Homer W, Edna V - 1/15/1887 - Probably Bliss, NY - Died of consumption. Claimed it was service related. Caused by a cold caught at Geneseo in December of 1861. While he gave his age as 18 when he enlisted, based on the 1850 census he was more likely only 15. (Military & Pension Files, 1850, 1860, 1870 Fed. Censuses Centerville, 1890 Fed. Census Special Schedule Centerville)

Akin, Vernon Golitz (Aikin) - Unassigned, 4th NY Heavy Artillery - 12/23/63 at Hume/3 yrs - 21 - 5'9", Fair Complexion, Grey Eyes, Brown Hair - 12/23/63 at Elmira - $300 - Pvt, Pvt - No battles - 5/8/1865 Honorable - Was not a casualty - Charles & Mary Balcom Akin (Both B NY) - Harriet, Hellen- 5/31/1842 in Hume - Farmer - Farmer - Cornelia A. Smith, married 12/25/1862 in Hume - INA - 9/26/1885 in Genesee Falls - Grace Cemetery, Castile - He never joined his regiment. He was assigned as a clerk at post headquarters in Elmira for the entire war. (Military & Pension Files,1850, 1860 Fed. Censuses Hume - 1865 Allegany County Town Clerk Register Hume)

Aldrich, Alonzo Co. D, 4th NY Heavy Artillery - 12/26/63 at Granger/3 yrs - 27 - 5'10", Fair Complexion, Hazel Eyes, Dark Hair - 12/26/1863 at Elmira - $300 - Pvt, Pvt - Wilderness, Spotsylvania, North Anna River, Totopotomoy, Cold Harbor, siege of Petersburg, Weldon RR, Ream's Station, Peeble's Farm, Hatcher's Run, fall of Petersburg, Appomattox - 9/26/1865 Honorable - Was not a casualty - Amasa & Zeruatha Parker Aldrich (Both B NY) - Marilla, Linus P., Arvilla, Melissa -10/16/1836 in Granger - Farmer - Farmer/Highway Commissioner/Live Stock Dealer - Miranda Waite, married 5/20/1860 in New Hudson - Amasa & Charles - 2/12/1916 in

Granger - Short Tract, County Route 4 - Was present for Lee's surrender. Marched in Grand Review 5/23/1865. Grandfather Marmaduke Aldrich was a soldier in the War of 1812. (Military & Pension Files, 1890 Fed. Census Special Schedule Granger, 1850, 1910 Fed. Censuses Granger, 1865 NYS Census Granger, *Allegany & Its People*, Matteson, Granger American Legion)

Aldrich, Alphonso J. Co. F, 19th NY Cavalry - 8/13/1862 at Oramel/3 yrs - 22 - 6', Light Complexion, Blue Eyes, Brown Hair - 9/3/1862 at Portage Station - $100 - Pvt, 2nd. Lt - sicge of Suffolk, Wilderness, Todd's Tavern, Spotsylvania, North Anna River, Pamunkey, Totopotomoy, Cold Harbor, Trevillian Station, Charles County Court House, before Richmond & Petersburg, New Market, Dinwiddie Court House, Five Forks, Appomattox - 6/30/1865 Honorable - WIA, 8/11/1864, gunshot to lower right thigh, INJ, testicles injured 4/8/1865 by saddle pommel at Appomattox - Robb Benjamin & Sarah Smith Aldrich (Both B NY) - Myron B., Mary Jane - 11/29/1839 in Granger - Farmer - Farmer - Mary Anna Beach, married 9/28/1865 in Mt. Morris - Louella - 3/28/1913 in Canisteo - Canisteo (No headstone.) - Was present for Lee's surrender. Marched in Grand Review 5/23/1865. (Military & Pension Files, 1850,1860,1880 Fed. Censuses Granger, 1865 NYS Census Granger)

Allen, Earl Alfred Co. F, 4th NY Heavy Artillery - 12/28/1863 at Hume/3 yrs - 17 - 5/5", Fair Complexion, Blue Eyes, Brown Hair - 12/28/1863 at Elmira - $300 - Pvt, Pvt - Wilderness, Spotsylvania, North Anna River, Totopotomoy, Cold Harbor, siege of Petersburg, Weldon RR, Ream's Station, Peeble's Farm, Hatcher's Run, fall of Petersburg, Appomattox - 9/26/1865 Honorable - Was not a casualty - Milo & Betsey King Allen (Both B NY) - Martin, Cornelia, Milo - 1846 in Centerville - Farmer - Farmer - 1st Wife, Lydia M. Atherton, married 1/4/1867 in Oramel (died 8/21/1880), 2nd Mary M. Wheeler, married 6/7/1882 in Dansville - None Identified - 8/16/1921 in Dalton - Hunts Hollow - Present at Lee's surrender. Marched in Grand Review 5/23/65. (Military & Pension Files, 1850, 1870 Fed. Censuses Centerville, 1865 NYS Census, 1865 Allegany County Town Clerk Register Centerville)

Allen, Rennsalear Co. F, 104th NY Infantry - 2/5/1862 at Geneseo/3 yrs (Re-enlisted 2/27/1864 Mitchell's Station, VA.) - 18 - 5'6", Dark Complexion, Black Eyes, Dark Brown Hair - 2/26/1862 at Geneseo - No bounty - Pvt, Pvt - Cedar Creek, 2nd Bull Run, South Mountain, Antietam, Fredericksburg, Chancellorsville, Gettysburg, Bristoe's Station, Wilderness, Spotsylvania Court House, North Anna River, Pamunkey, Totopotomoy, Cold Harbor, Bethesda Church, Petersburg - 12/26/1864 Disability/Honorable - WIA, 6/18/1864 at Peterburg. Gunshot to face (fractured lower jaw) and right shoulder - Jonathan & Lana Robinson Allen (Both B NY) - None - 6/3/1845 in Granger or Cayuga County - Sawyer/Farmer - Farmer - Addie Arabella Townsend, married 10/17/1866 in Granger - Mattie J., George - 6/12/1892 in Jefferson, IA - Greene Co., IA. (Military & Pension Files, 1850 Fed. Census, Cayuga Co., NY, 1860 Fed. Census Granger, 1865 NYS Census Granger, 1870 Fed. Census Greene Co., IA, Granger American Legion, 1865 Allegany County Town Clerk Register Granger)

Anderson, Emory A. Co. B/F/S, 9th NY Cavalry - 9/23/1861 at Little Valley/3 yrs - 27 - INA - 10/3/1861 at Westfield, NY - No bounty - Captain, Major - siege of Yorktown, Freeman Ford, Culpeper, Rapidan, Brandy Station, Haymarket, Stafford Court House, Madison Court House,

Broad Run, Stevensburg, VA, Brandy Station - 12/20/1863 Dishonorable - Was not a casualty - INA - INA - 2/2/1834 - INA - Lawyer/Farmer - Melissa - Everett, Willie, Rosa - 4/12/1876 in probably Short Tract - Short Tract, County Route 4 (There is some question as to whether the Emory Anderson buried at Short Tract is the soldier Emory Anderson, mainly because the 1860 Warren County, PA Census has his wife as Lucretia and the 1870 Granger Censes has his wife as Melissa. There is correspondence in his military file that definitely ties the soldier Anderson to Warren Co., PA. However, a preponderance of the information available suggests that the Granger, NY and Warren County, PA Anderson's are the same person) - Was court-martialed and dismissed from service, due to desertion under fire on 10/11/1863 at Brandy Station, Stevensburg, VA. There were three charges at his court-martial. The first is strange. He was charged with absent without leave rather than desertion. This may be because he returned to his regiment at the end of the battle. The second charge was misbehavior before the enemy, and the third was conduct unbecoming an officer and a gentleman. He was found guilty on all three charges. Anderson had participated in a number battles up to that point, and had been promoted to Major only a few months before being dishonorably discharged. Elected Captain 10/31/1861, Promoted to Major 3/15/1863. (Military File, Granger American Legion, 1860 Fed. Census Sugar Grove, PA, 1870 Fed. Census Granger)

Andrews, Albert Co. D, 4th NY Heavy Artillery - 12/19/1863 at Caneadea/3 yrs - 24 - 5'7", Light Complexion, Blue Eyes, Black Hair - 12/19/1863 at Elmira - $300 - Pvt, Pvt - Wilderness, Spotsylvania, North Anna River, Totopotomoy, Cold Harbor, siege of Petersburg, Weldon RR, Ream's Station, Peeble's Farm, Hatcher's Run, fall of Petersburg, Appomattox- 9/26/1865 Honorable - Was not a casualty - Ansel & Charlotte Dresser Andrews (Both B NY) - Mary, Edson, Frances - 4/1/1839 in Owego - Laborer - Laborer - Lydia Manchester, married 7/24/1860 in Houghton - Addie, Edson, Arthur - 11/12/1908 at Hume - East Koy, Lamont Road - Was present for Lee's surrender. Marched in Grand Review 5/23/1865. (Military & Pension Files - 1860 Fed. Census Caneadea, 1880 Fed. Census Hume, 1865 Allegany County Town Clerk Register Caneadea, 1890 Fed. Census Special Schedule Granger)

Andrews, Andrew Judson Co. C, 104th NY Infantry - 10/9/1861 at Centerville/3 yrs - 26 - 5'6", Light Complexion, Blue Eyes, Auburn Hair, Scar over right eye - 2/26/1862 at Geneseo - No bounty - Sgt, 2nd Lt. - South Mountain, Antietam, Fredericksburg - 1/26/63 Honorable/Deceased - WIA,12/13/1862 at Fredericksburg, gunshot to lower leg, KIA, died at Douglas Hospital in DC 1/26/63 from amputation of wounded leg - Alanson (B-CT) & Mineva Fassett (B-VT) Andrews - Sara L., Amos, Elias M., Sylvia, S.L., Nancy, Charles P., Emma - 12/27/1834 in Centerville - Farmer - None (Deceased) - Never Married - None - 1/26/1863 in Washington, DC - Centerville Cemetery, Route 3, no headstone - A William B. Willey claimed that he was Andrews and applied for his pension. Willey said he had enlisted under the name Andrew Andrews and that his leg had not been amputated. His claim was rejected. Brother Elias also served during the war. (Military File & Willey Pension Application, 1850 Fed. Census Centerville, 1865 NYS Census Centerville, Centerville American Legion, Matteson, 1865 Allegany County Town Clerk Register Centerville)

Andrews, Elias Neilon Co. E, 5th NY Cavalry - 8/29/1861 at Centerville/3 yrs - 27 - 5'6", Light Complexion, Hazel Eyes, Brown Hair - 9/7/1861 at NYC - No bounty - Pvt, 3rd Sgt. - New

Market, Port Republic, Antietam, Aldie - 12/15/1862 Honorable/Deceased - KIA, Aldie, VA 12/15/62 - Alanson (B-CT) & Minerva Fassett (B-VT) Andrews - Andrew, Sara L., Amos, Elias M., Sylvia, S.L., Nancy, Charles P., Emma - 10/5/1836 at Rushford - Farmer - None (Deceased) - Never Married - None - 12/15/1862 at Aldie, VA - Centerville Cemetery, Route 3, no headstone - Brother Andrew also served. Was killed by guerillas while on a scouting party. Served as a Cavalry scout for General Windham. Mother Minerva applied for his pension, but the application was denied since Minerva was receiving her husband's Alanson's pension. He had served in the War of 1812. He received a land grand of 160 acres, but he sold the grant to a Goodien S. Gordon in 1855. (Military & Pension Files, Centerville American Legion, 1850 Fed. Census Centerville, 1865 NYS Census Centerville, Matterson, *History of Allegany County 1879*, 1865 Allegany Town Clerk Register Centerville)

Andrews, Richard At least one source document indicates that Richard Andrews served in the military during the Civil War. No evidence of such service has been located. Two Richard Andrews served in NYS regiments during the Civil War. Neither was from the C-H-G area. (Centerville American Legion)

Anstee, George Benjamin Co. E, 2nd NY Mounted Rifles - 9/10/1864 at Pike/1 yr - 22 - 5'8", Fair Complexion, Gray Eyes, Brown Hair - 9/10/1864 at Lockport - No bounty - Pvt, Pvt - Popular Springs Church, Pegram's Farm, Hatcher's Run, Weldon RR, Dinwiddie Court House, Five Forks, Appomattox - 5/28/1865 Honorable - Was not a casualty - Thomas & Susanna North Anstee (Both B England) - INA - 3/29/1841 in Buckinghamshire, England - Sailor on Great Lakes/Farmer - Farmer - Mary Haley, married 8/11/1862 in Toledo, OH - Elisabeth, Flora Gertrude, George May - 12/20/1917 in Hornell, NY - St. Anne Cemetery, Hornell - Was present at Lee's surrender. (Military & Pension Files, 1880 Fed. Census Centerville, 1890 Fed. Census Special Schedule Centerville)

Babcock, George Washington Co. F, 19th NY Cavalry - 8/9/1862 at Hume/3 yrs - 18 - 5'8", Dark Complexion, Black Eyes, Black Hair - 9/3/1862 at Portage Station - $150 - Pvt, Pvt - Deserted House, Manassas Junction, Bristoe's Station, Culpeper Court House, Wilderness, Todd's Tavern, Spotsylvania, North Anna River, Yellow Tavern, Pamunkey, Totopotomoy, Cold Harbor, Travillian Station - 6/15/1865 Honorable - Was not a casualty - William S. & Sarah Austin Babcock (Both B NY) - Sarah, Martin, Orlon, Celinda, Mary - 6/25/1844 in Centerville - Farmer - Farmer/Tannery Worker - Cevalla Lucy Wight, married 12/24/1866 in Centerville - Roy W., James C., Guy A., Elzer L., George C., Clarence E., Lucy A. - 3/17/1922 at Sunbright, TN - Sunbright - Brothers Martin and Orlon also served in the war. (Military & Pension Files, 1860 Fed. Census Centerville, 1870 Fed. Census Olean, Cattaraugus Co., 1865 NYS Census Centerville, *History of Allegany County 1879*, 1865 Allegany County Town Clerk Register Centerville)

Babcock, Martin Van Buren Co. F, 19th NY Cavalry - 8/11/1862 at Hume/3 yrs - 24 - 5'5", Dark Complexion, Black Eyes, Black Hair - 9/3/1862 at Portage Station - $40 - Pvt, Pvt - Deserted House, siege of Suffolk, Franklin, VA., Bristoe's Station, Culpeper Court House, Wilderness, Todd's Tavern, Spotsylvania, North Anna River, Yellow Tavern, Pamunkey, Totopotomoy, Cold Harbor - 5/31/1864 Honorable/Deceased - KIA, 5/31/1864 at Cold Harbor, shot through the head near Bottom's Ridge- William & Sarah Austin Babcock (Both B NY) - Sarah, Orlon, George, Celinda, Mary - 1/13/1838 in Rushford - Farmer - None (Deceased) - Cornelia R. Allen, married 8/16/1862 in Centerville - None - 5/31/1864 in Cold Harbor - Alger Cemetery, Hume, Route 19 - Brothers George and Orlon also served in the war. Military records say he was buried at Cold harbor National Cemetery. (Military & Pension Files, 1865 NYS Census Centerville, 1860 Fed. Census Centerville, Matteson, *History of Allegany County 1879*, 1865 Allegany County Town Clerk Register Centerville, *Roll of Honor*)

Babcock, Orlon Co. A, 108th NY Infantry - 7/21/1862 at Rochester/3 yrs - 21 - 5'11". Florid Complexion, Blue Eyes, Brown Hair - 8/18/1862 at Rochester - $100 - Pvt, Sgt - Fredericksburg, Hatcher's Run, fall of Petersburg, Farmville, Appomattox - INJ, 12/1863 at Mine Run, VA Exposure caused bronchitis, recovered at Bedloe Island Convalescent Camp, NY - William & Sarah Austin Babcock (Both B NY) - Sarah, Martin, George, Celinda, Mary - Farmer - Carpenter (Orlon's father was also a carpenter) - Phenic C. Jones, married 6/20/1867 in Portage - Martin, Jennie - 3/3/1887 in Skene, TN - Mt. Vernon Cemetery, Skene, TN - Brothers George and Martin also served in the war. Deserted 2/4/1863, captured at Centerville 9/26/63 and returned to duty. Was present at Lee's surrender. Marched in Grand Review 5/35/1865. (Military & Pension Files, 1865 NYS Census Centerville, 1865 Allegany County Town Clerk Register - Centerville, 1860 Fed. Census Centerville, 1870 Fed. Census - Wellsville)

Baker, Nelson P. At least one source document indicates that Baker served in the military during the Civil War. No evidence of such service has been located. A Nelson Baker did served with the 164th NY Infantry, but he was not from the C-H-G area. (Matteson)

Ball, Orestus Joseph Co. H, 19th NY Cavalry (Was detailed to 7th Independent Battery, Massachusetts Light Artillery from 1/3/1863 to 8/14/1863) - 8/11/1862 at Grove/3 yrs - 37 - 5'7", Light Complexion, Blue Eyes, Dark Hair - 9/3/1862 at Portage - $100 - Pvt, Pvt - INA - 8/20/1863 Disability/Honorable - Was not a casualty - Alanson & Sarah Wright (B Ireland) Ball - INA - 6/22/1825 in Derby, VT - Carpenter/Farmer - Laborer/Farmer - 1st Mercy, 2nd Amerlia Lobo Lyons, Married 6/1/1867 in Bloomfield, WI - 3 children by Mercy- 12/8/1893 at Downsville, WI - Arkansas Cemetery, Arkansas WI. - May have been married a third time. Went insane during service. Was assigned to St. Elizabeth's Hospital in DC Was eventually released to wife's custody. First name probably was Orasturd. Different documents list different places for his birth. Served also with Co. C, 194th NY Infantry, see below. (Military & Pension Files, 1865 NYS Census Hume, 1865 Allegany County Town Clerk Register - Hume, 1860 Fed. Census Orange Co., NY)

Ball, Orestus Joseph Co. C, 194th NY Infantry - 3/29/1865 at Hume/1 yr - 39 - 5'7", Light Complexion, Blue Eyes, Dark Hair - 4/7/1865 at Elmira - $400 - Pvt, Pvt - No battles - 5/3/1865 Honorable - Was not a casualty. Served also with 19th NY Cavalry, see above. Also see above for personal information and sources of information.

Bardwell, Joel William Co. E, 85th NY Infantry - 9/1/1861 at Cold Creek/3 yrs - 22 - 5'10", Light Complexion, Blue Eyes, Brown Hair - 10/25/1861 at Elmira - No bounty - Pvt, 3rd Sgt - defense of DC, siege of Yorktown, Williamsburg, Fair Oaks, before Richmond - 11/13/1862 Honorable -

POW, Captured 5/31/1862 at Fair Oaks, Prison: Libby at Richmond, paroled 9/21/1862 at Aikin's Island - Harrison & Anna Smith Bardwell (Both B NY) - Allen, Rhena (married David Haskell), Romain - 10/20/1839 in Granger - Day Laborer - Bar Keeper/Laborer / Hardware Store Worker - Nancy C. Andrews, married 6/28/1864 in Nunda - Anna M. - 11/16/1925 in Elmira - Hunts Hollow Cemetery - Spent six months in Libby Prison. Was sent to Stewart Mansion Hospital in Baltimore following his release from prison. His grandfather, Joel Bardwell was a skilled detective from Massachusetts and for years a deputy sheriff. His pension was originally $8 per month. It was increased to $24 per month in 1894. (Military & Pension Files, 1865 Allegany County Town Clerk Register, Centerville & Hume, 1850 Fed. Census - Grove, 1865 NYS Census Centerville, 1880 Fed. Census Hume, 1890 Fed. Census Special Schedule Hume, *Allegany & Its People*)

Barnard, Oliver Co. F, 19th NY Cavalry - 8/9/1862 at Hume/3 yrs - 18 - 5'4", Dark Complexion, Brown Eyes, Brown Hair - 9/3/1862 at Portage Station - $150 - Pvt, Pvt - Deserted House, siege of Suffolk, Franklin, VA., Manassas, Totopotomoy, Cold Harbor - 5/31/1864 Honorable/Deceased - KIA, 5/31/1864 at Cold Harbor - Charles & Martha Barnard (Both B NY) - Phebe, Susan - 1843/44 in Hume - Farmer - None (Deceased) - Never Married - None - 5/31/1864 in Cold Harbor, VA - Cold Harbor National Cemetery - He was originally buried on the battlefield. (Granger American Legion, 1865 Allegany County Town Clerk Register Hume, 1850 Fed. Census Hume, Allegany County Web Site, *History of Allegany County 1879*)

Barney, George W. Co. E, 85th NY Infantry - 9/1/1861 at Granger/3 yrs (Re-enlisted 1/1/1864 at Plymouth, NC) - 19 - 5'8", Dark Complexion, Black Eyes, Black Hair - 1010/1861 at Elmira - No bounty - Corp, Corp - defense of DC, siege of Yorktown, Williamsburg, Fair Oaks, before Richmond, Plymouth - 6/2/1865 Honorable - POW, Captured 4/20/1864 at Plymouth. Imprisoned at Andersonville, Charleston, Florence, SC & Wilmington, NC Escaped from prison 2/22/1865 - Zibra L. & Minerva Green Barney (Both B NY) - Ziba E., Harlan, John, Elvira - 1/20/1843 in Grove - Farm Laborer - Farmer/Town Clerk - Vicena Parker, married 8/8/1868 in Nunda - Allen S. & Maria P. - 11/24/1919 in Grove - Union Cemetery, Dalton - After escape was sent to Foster Hospital at New Berne, NC, then to hospital ship *Northern Light* for transfer to DeCamp Hospital, David's Island, NYC Harbor, and then to a hospital at Elmira, NY where he was discharged. Brother John also served in the war.(Military & Pension Files, *History of Allegany County 1879*, Matteson, 1860 & 1880 Fed. Censuses Grove, 1900 Fed Census - Granger)

Barney, John Co. E, 85th NY Infantry - 9/1/1861 at Granger/3 yrs (Re-enlisted 1/1/1864 at Plymouth, NC) - 18 - INA - 10/10/1861 at Elmira - $100 - Pvt, Pvt - defense of DC, Plymouth - 10/26/1864 Honorable/Deceased - POW 4/20/1864 at Plymouth, NC, DD Starved to death in prison,10/26/1864 at Charleston, SC - Zibra L. & Minerva Green Barney (Both B NY) - Ziba E., Harlan, George W., Elvira - 1/17/1845 in Grove - Farmer - None Deceased - Never Married - None - 10/26/1864 in Charleston, SC (POW) - Beaufort National Cemetery (Mass grave with a Marble Tablet on top which lists the men buried in the grave. John is listed as G. Barney.) Originally Potter's Field Cemetery (records indicate that John Barney died in Charleston 10/12/1864. Papers in brother George Barney's file also address the death of a Barney at Charleston Prison who died 110/12/1864. This Barney was buried at Potter's Field Cemetery and then re-buried at Beaufort National Cemetery. The re-buried soldier must be John.) - Brother

George also served in the war. John's file does not show date of death. However, papers in George's file say a Barney died 10/12/1864 at Charleston. Since George lived, those papers most likely apply to John. The 1860 Fed. Census shows John's age as 14, so he was likely only 15 or 16 when he entered the service. (Military File, *History of Allegany County 1879*, Matteson, Granger American Legion, 1860 Fed. Census Grove)

Barrows, Byron Co. F, 4th NY Heavy Artillery - 12/22/1863 at Hume/3 yrs - 24 - 5'4", Fair Complexion, Blue Eyes, Brown Hair - 12/22/1863 at Elmira - $300 - Pvt, Pvt - fall of Petersburg, Appomattox - 9/26/1865 Honorable - Was not a casualty - David (B MA) & Irena Parmily (B NY) Barrows - Darwin - 7/7/1839 in Freedom, Cattaraugus County - Blacksmith - Blacksmith - Cynthia J. - William - 3/3/1882 in Rochester, NY - Pine Grove Cemetery, Fillmore - His brother Darwin also served in the war. Deserted 12/20/1864, apparently from St. Mary's Hospital, Rochester. Returned 1/26/1865. His file indicates he suffered a sunstroke at Petersburg on 6/18/1864, which is probably why he was in the hospital. It also says he was carried off the battlefield by his son, which is incorrect. It may have been his brother Darwin who was at Petersburg, but not in June. It likely was Darwin, but Bryon must have suffered the sunstroke later than June, since Darwin was not in the service until August, 1864. Was at Lee's surrender. Marched in Grand Review 5/23/1864. (Military & Pension Files, 1850 Fed. Census Churchville, Monroe County, 1860 Fed. Census Great Valley, Cattaraugus County, 1870 Fed. Census Hume, 1865 NYS Census Hume, 1865 Allegany County Town Clerk Register Hume, Allegany County Web Site)

Barrows, Darwin Co. F, 4th NY Heavy Artillery - Drafted 8/24/1864 at Fillmore/1 yr - 33 - 5'7", Light Complexion, Blue Eyes, Brown Hair - 8/25/1864 at Elmira - $500 - Pvt, Pvt - Peeble's Farm, Peterburg - 10/4/1864 Honoarble/Deceased - KIA 10/4/1864 at Petersburg - David L. (B MA) & Irena Pamula (B NY) Barrows - Byron - 12/24/1831 in Freedom - Printer/Farmer - None Deceased - Never Married - None - 10//1864 in Petersburg - Poplar Grove National Cemetery, Petersburg - Died of gunshot through the body while on picket duty. 1860 Fed. Census has his age and occupation incorrect. (Military & Pension Files, Register of Men Drafted July 1863 to October, 1864, 1865 NYS Census Hume, Allegany County Web Site, 1850 Fed. Census Churchville, Monroe County, 1860 Fed. Census Fillmore)

Bartlett, Timothy Co. F, 189th NY Infantry - 7/20/1863 at Granger/1 yr - 19 - 5'5", Sandy Complexion, Grey Eyes, Sandy Hair - 9/14/1864 at Elmira - $100 - Pvt, Pvt - siege of Petersburg - 8/29/1865 Honorable - Was not a casualty - Timothy & Deborah Dorey (B England) Bartlett - Harriet E. (Drew), Gennie B. (Grover), half-brother John Dorey - 1844 or 45 in Allegany County - Farmer - Farmer - Never Married - None - 2-3/1895 - probably Union, Isabelle County, MI - Had malaria fever while in the service. Was in several hospitals, including City Point in VA, Columbia in DC, Harwood in DC, and Lincoln in DC. Fever may have caused an eye disease from which he eventually went blind. His father deserted the family in 1846, was reported dead in 1850. (Military & Pension Files, 1850, 1860 & 1870 Fed. Censuses Granger, 1865 NYS Census Granger)

Bates, William C. Co. K, 16th NY Cavalry - drafted 7/20/1863 at Buffalo/3 yrs - 30 - 5'11", Light Complexion, Hazel Eyes, Dark Hair - 9/22/1863 at NYC - $100 - Pvt, Corp - Dranesville, Culpeper - 8/17/1865 Honorable - Was not a casualty - Father, INA, Mary Bates (Both B VT) -

Clarissa A., Eliza, Charles W. - 1832/33 in Ira, VT - Farmer - Farmer/Teamster - Clarinda Reminton, married 1/24/1852 in Portage, NY - William, Sabria, Ida, Melva, Charley, Aaron E., Fannie E., Lizzie M. - 2/2/1908 - Weaver Settlement Cemetery, Granger - Was a deserter for one day, 4/13/1864. (Military & Pension Files, 1860, 1870, 1880 Fed. Censuses Granger, 1890 Fed. Census Special Schedule Granger, 1900 Fed. Census North Dansville)

Bean, Ebenezer Augustus Co. F, 19th NY Cavalry - 8/9/1862 at Centerville/3 yrs - 30 - 5'8", Light Complexion, Grey Eyes, Brown Hair - 9/3/1862 at Portage Station - $150 - Pvt, Pvt - Deserted Farm - 4/1/1864 Disability/Honorable - WIA, 1/30/1863 at Deserted House, gunshot, lost right thumb - Orison & Clarinda Van Buren Bean (Both B NY) - Adaline L., Ebenezer A., Elisha, Julia, Orison, Jay - 1844 in Centerville - Farmer - Farmer/Cheese Maker - 1st Flora A Stacy, married 3/12/1873 in Hume, 2nd Ollie G. Closson, married Knoxville, PA, divorced 11/23/1885, 3rd Abbie C. Knox, married 5/18/1890 in Hume - None - 8/25/1904 in Hume while visiting. Lived at Knoxville, Tioga County, PA. - Knoxville - Transferred to VRC 7/16/1863. (Military & Pension Files, 1865 Allegany Town Clerk Register Centerville, 1850, 1860, 1870 Fed. Censuses Centerville, Matteson, *History of Allegany County 1879*, 1865 NYS Census Centerville)

Bean, Willliam Co. I, 160th NY Infantry - 8/28/1862 at Allen/3 yrs - 38 - INA - 10/10/1862 at Auburn, NY - $100 - Pvt, Pvt - Gunboat Cotton, Fort Bisland, Port Hudson - 6/19/1864 Honorable/Deceased - POW, 10/31/1863, captured Opelousa, LA, Prison: not identified in records, Paroled 12/25/1863 at Stage Station, LA DD, 6/19/1864 of chronic dysentery at 12th Maine Infantry Hospital, Lake End, LA- Richard & Elizabeth Lime Bean (Both B England) - INA - 4/27/1820 in Sutton, England - Farmer/ Blacksmith - None Deceased - Polly Ann Davis, married 1861 - Bertha - 6/19/1864 in Lake End, LA - Chalmette National Cemetery, New Orleans (as Beam) - His widow Polly later married James Luckey. (Military & Pension Files, 1860 Fed. Census Allen, Granger American Legion 1865 Allegany Town Clerk Register, Allen, *Roll of Honor*)

Beardsley, Willis W. Co. D, 4th NY Heavy Artillery - 1/4/1864 at Hume/3 yrs - 43 - 5'5", Light Complexion, Blue Eyes, Black Hair - 1/4/1864 at Elmira - $300 - Pvt, Pvt - Petersburg, Appomattox - 9/26/1865 Honorable - Reuben (B CT) & Lidia Robinson Beardsley - Annette, Ortillas - 7/7/1820 in Hartwick, CT - Shoemaker - Shoemaker - Louise (Lovancha) Caner, married 12/31/1844 - Alphonzo, Clarissa A., Jennie, Mary, Reuben - 1/4/1876 in Hume - Pine Grove Cemetery, Fillmore - Was at Lee's surrender. Marched in Grand Review, 5/23/1865. Was sick in hospital most of 1864. (Military & Pension Files, 1865 Allegany County Clerk Register Hume, Allegany County Web Site, Fillmore American Legion, 1865 NYS Census Hume, 1850 Fed. Census Pike, 1870 Fed. Census - Hume)

Bemis, George W. (Bemus) Co. G, 78th NY Infantry - 12/3/1861 at Hume/3 yrs (Re-enlisted 12/26/1863 at Westchester, TN) - 30 - 5'7", Sandy Complexion, Blue Eyes, Sandy Hair - 12/11/1861 at Buffalo - $460 - Corp, Sgt - Cedar Mountain, Sulphur Springs, Groveton, 2nd Bull Run, Antietam, Chancellorsville, Gettysburg, Wauhatchie, Lookout Mountain, Mission Ridge, Rocky Face Ridge, Resaca, Kenesaw Mountain, Golgatha Church - 5/15/1865 Honorable - WIA, 5/3/1863 at Chancellorsville (slight wound not identified in records), INJ, slipped down a flight of stairs at a rice mill while foraging and injured testicles - Father INA, Alice (Both B VT) - possibly

Mary E. - 7/15/1831 in Hume - Mechanic/Carpenter - Carpenter - Emily A. Powers, married 1/13/1858 in Pike - Nettie, Eugene, George H., - 2/20/1906 in Pike - Pike Cemetery, Telegraph Road - Pension file claims he was a 2nd Lt. When discharged, Military File says Sergeant. The 78th was consolidated with the 102nd Infantry 12/1/1863, and Bemis served with both Cos. G and H, 102nd NY Infantry. (Military & Pension Files, *History of Allegany County 1879*, 1850, 1860, 1870 Fed. Censuses Pike)

Benchley, Edgar Arnold   Co. F, 189th NY Infantry - 8/30/1864 at Granger/1 yr - 27 - 5'9", Light Complexion, Black Eyes, Sandy Hair - 9/16/1864 at Elmira - $100 - Pvt, Pvt - Hatcher's Run, Quaker Road, Lewis Farm, Gravely Run, Five Forks, Appomattox - 5/30/1865 Honorable - Arnold & Eliza J. Benchley (Both B NY) - Solomon K., Mary A. - 1836/37 in Middlebury, NY - Farmer - Farmer - Jenette A. Chamberlain, married 3/28/1860 in Dale, NY - Summer, Eliza - Probably 5/20/1904 in Strickland, MI. - Lincoln Cemetery, Isabella County, MI. - Was at Lee's surrender. (Military & Pension Files, 1850,1860 Fed. Censuses Middlebury, NY, 1870 Fed. Census Granger, 1865 NYS Census Granger)

Benjamin, George W.   Co. E, 85th NY Infantry - 9/1/1861 at Granger/3 yrs (Re-enlisted 1/1/1864 at Plymouth, NC) - 23 - 5'11", Light Complexion, Blue Eyes, Dark Hair - 10/10/1861 at Elmira - $400 - Corp, Corp - defense of DC, siege of Yorktown, Williamsburg, Fair Oaks, before Richmond, Plymouth - 6/7/1865 Honorable - POW, 4/20/1864 at Plymouth, in Salisbury & Andersonville prisons. Paroled 2/22/1865 at Goldsboro, NC - Elias P. & Mary Anne Benjamin (Both B NY) - Abigail, Emily, Rebecca, Harriett A., William H. and Elmira C. (twins), Mary D. Elias - 4/25/1838 in Belfast - Farm Hand/Laborer - Farmer - Adaline Augustus Dean, married 9/20/1865 in Angelica - Willis Egbert & Merle Carleton - 8/13/1917 in Nickerson, KS - Nickerson, KS - As a result of his stay at Andersonville, Benjamin suffered from stomach, heart, kidney, and urinary problems the rest of his life. His pension file contains information that he was working on a farm at Short Tract at the time of his enlistment. (Military & Pension Files, *History of Allegany County 1879*, Matteson, 1850 Fed. Census Belfast, 1880 Fed. Census Friendship, 1900 Fed. Census Salt Creek, KS)

Bennett, Charles Chester   Co. E, 184th NY Infantry - 9/3/1864 at Granger/3 yrs - 5'6", Light Complexion, Grey Eyes, Brown Hair, Scar on back - 9/6/1864 at Elmira - $100 - Pvt, Pvt - Petersburg, Richmond - 6/29/1865 Honorable - Was not a casualty - Henry & Olive Pratt Bennett (Both B England) - Chauncey, Nathan - 7/22/1845 in Granger - Farmer - Farmer/Engineer Soap Factory - Mary E., married 1877 in Nebraska - Arthur - 3/17/1906 in Waterloo, IA - INA - His first name was most likely Charles, although he used Chester and signed his enlistment papers as Chester. (Military & Pension Files, *History of Allegany County 1879*, 1865 NYS Census Granger, 1865 Allegany County Town Clerk Register Granger, 1850, 1860, 1870 Fed. Censuses Granger, 1900 Fed. Census - Waterloo, IA)

Bennett, Charles William   Co. E, 85th NY Infantry - 9/1/1861 at Granger/3 yrs - 24 - 5'10", Light Complexion, Blue Eyes, Black Hair, 10/25/1861 at Elmira - None - Pvt, Pvt - defense of DC - 10/30/1863 Disability/Honorable - Was not a casualty - James & Frances Carter Bennett (Both B England) - Frederick Albert, George Carter, James Harrison - 8/24/1836 in Granger - Day Laborer

- Farm Laborer/Farmer - 1st Elizabeth Jane Dory, 2nd Cynthia A. Radcliff Levy - Ernest & Myron - 3/24/1915 in Fillmore - Short Tract - Was a musician in the service. Disability discharge was due to disease of the rectum caused by chronic diarrhea. Some source documents claim he was a POW, but that is not correct. Brothers Frederick, George, and James also served in the war. (Military & Pension Files, 1860, 1880, 1900, 1910 Fed. Censuses Granger, 1890 Fed. Census Special Schedule Granger, 1865 NYS Census Granger, Granger American Legion, Matteson, 1865 Allegany County Town Clerk Register Granger)

<u>Bennett, Frederick Albert</u> Co. A, 184th NY Infantry - 9/3/1864 at Granger/1 yr - 19 - 5'7", Fair Complexion, Blue Eyes, Brown Hair - 9/29/1864 at Elmira - $100 - Pvt, Pvt - Cedar Creek, Petersburg, Richmond - 6/29/1865 Honorable - Was not a casualty - James & Frances Carter Bennett (Both B England) Charles William, George Carter, James Harrison - 9/18/1846 in Granger - Farmer/Laborer - Farmer/Blacksmith/Overseer at Saw Mill/Wagon Maker - Mary A. Smith, married 12/24/1863 in Granger - Agnes, DeForest - 8/20/1925 in Granger - Short Tract - Brothers Charles William, George and James also served in the war. (Military & Pension Files, Matteson, Granger American Legion, 1865 Allegany County Town Clerk Register Granger, 1865 NYS Census Granger, 1860 1910 Fed. Censuses Granger, 1890 Fed. Census Special Schedule Granger)

<u>Bennett, George Carter</u> Co. A, 184th NY Infantry - 8/22/1864 at Granger/1 yr - 23 - 5'9", Light Complexion, Blue Eyes, Dark Hair - 9/29/1864 at Elmira - $100 - Pvt, Pvt - Cedar Creek, Petersburg, Richmond - 6/29/1865 Honorable - Was not a casualty - James & Frances Carter Bennett (Both B England) - Charles William, Frederick Albert, James Harrison - 6/8/1841 in Granger - Day Laborer - Farmer - 1st Lorinda M. Dorey, married 3/1/1862 in Fillmore, 2nd Eva Barnard, married 5/2/1910 in Attica, NY - None - 7/2/1917 probably in Nunda - Short Tract Cemetery - Brothers Charles William, Frederick Albert, and James Harrison all served in the war. (Military & Pension Files, 1865 Allegany County Town Clerk Register Granger, Granger American Legion, 1865 NYS Census Granger, 1860, 1910 Fed. Censuses Granger.)

<u>Bennett, Harrison</u> Actually James Harrison Bennett. Some source documents treat Harrison Bennett as a separate individual. See above. (1865 NYS Census Granger)

<u>Bennett, James Harrison</u> Co. E, 85th NY Infantry - 9/1/1861 at Granger/3 yrs (Re-enlisted 1/1/1864 at Plymouth, NC) -18 - 5'10", Light Complexion, Blue Eyes, Black Hair - 10/31/1861 at Elmira - None - Pvt, Pvt - defense of DC, siege of Yorktown, Williamsburg, Fair Oaks, before Richmond, Plymouth - 7/9/1864 Honorable/ Deceased - POW, 4/20/1864 at Plymouth, DD, 7/9/1864 of diarrhea at Andersonville - James & Frances A. Carter Bennett (Both B England) - Charles William, Frederick Albert, George Carter - 3/14/1844 in Granger - Farm Laborer - None Deceased - Never Married - None - 7/9/1864 in Andersonville Prison - Andersonville - Brothers Charles, Frederick, and George also served in the war, Known by his middle name Harrison (some source documents call him Harrison). Listed on Soldiers Monument in Granger. Originally buried at Andersonville Prison. (Military & Pension Files, *History of Allegany County 1879*, 1865 Allegany County Town Clerk Register Granger, Grange American Legion, Matteson, 1865 NYS Census Granger, *Allegany & Its People*, 1860 Fed Census Granger)

Bennett, Jesse   Co. F, 104th NY Infantry - 2/13/1862 at Granger/3 yrs - 18 - 5'9", Dark Complexion, Black Eyes, Black Hair - 2/26/1862 at Geneseo - $100 - Pvt, Pvt - Cedar Creek, 2nd Bull Run, South Mountain, Antietam, Fredericksburg, Chancellorsville, Gettysburg, Bristoe's Station, Wilderness, Spotsylvania Court House, North Anna River, Pamunkey, Totopotomoy, Cold Harbor, Bethesda Church, Petersburg, Weldon RR, 4/24/1865 Honorable - POW, captured 8/19/1864 at Weldon RR, paroled 2/24/1865 at Aikins Landing, Prisons: Libby & Belle Island at Richmond & Salsibury, NC - John & Sarah Marsh Bennett (Both B England) -Timothy, Rachael (Ayrault), Leah (Voss), Simeon, Mary, Henry, Thomas, Elizabeth (Collister), Samuel - 12/14/1844 in Granger - Farmer - Merchant/Manager - Carrie Snyder, married 11/5/1865 in Short Tract - Frances, Herbert, Cora, Maud - 7/16/1911 at Elgin, IL - McHenry, IL - Brothers Samuel and Simeon also served in the war. Was a prisoner for 6 months,   (Military & Pension Files, Granger American Legion, 1865 Allegany County Town Clerk Register Granger, 1865 NYS Census Granger, *History of Allegany County 1879*, *Allegany & Its People*, 1860, 1880 Fed. Censuses Granger, 1890 Fed. Census Special Schedule Granger)

Bennett, Robert   Co. H, 19th NY Cavalry - 8/13/1862 at Oramel/3 yrs - 23 - 5'4", Light Complexion, Hazel Eyes, Dark Hair - 9/3/1862 at Portage Station - $100 - Pvt, Pvt - Deserted House, siege of Suffolk, Cedar Mountain, 2nd Bull Run, South Mountain, Antietam, Fredericksburg, Chancellorsville, Gettysburg, Wilderness, Franklin, Manassas Junction, Bristoe's Station, Culpeper Court House, Rappahannock Station - 6/30/1865 Honorable - INJ, 6/30/1864 at Light House Point, VA. Was thrown from a mule and run over by the wagon the mule was pulling. Loss sight in one eye and partial sight in the other - Joseph (B England) & Eliza Jamison (B Ireland) Bennett - Betsey, Mary C. (Walbridge), Sarah J. (Wilcox), John J., Hugh,, Francis, Helen (Hussong) - 7/5/1839 in Granger - Miller - Miller/Farmer/Merchant/Partner, Wilson & Bennett Grist & Shingle Mills - Mary Jane McAllister, married 1/1/1866 in York - Mary, Lida J., Lena M., Flora, Ethel - 9/18/1899 in Moscow, PA. (Struck by a locomotive on D.L. & W RR) - Short Tract - Name appears on some records as Benet or Bennet. (Military & Pension Files, *Allegany & Its People*, 1865 Allegany County Town Clerk Register Granger, Matteson, Granger American Legion, 1865 NYS Census Granger, 1860, 1870 Fed. Censuses Granger, 1890 Fed. Census Special Schedule Granger)

Bennett, Samuel   Co. F, 104th NY Infantry - 2/13/1862 at Geneseo/3 yrs - 21 - 5'4", Dark Complexion, Black Eyes, Black Hair - 2/26/1862 at Albany - None - Pvt, Pvt - Cedar Creek, 2nd Bull Run, South Mountain, Antietam, Fredericksburg, Chancellorsville, Gettysburg - 4/21/1865 Honorable - Was not a casualty - John & Sarah Marsh Bennett (Both B Ireland) - Timothy, Rachael (Ayrault), Leah (Voss), Simeon, Mary, Henry, Thomas, Elizabeth (Collister), Jesse - 4/20/1840 in Granger - Teacher - Farmer - Carrie S. - Leah - 9/4/1879 in Washington, DC - INA - Transferred to 24th VRC, March 15, 1864. Brother's Jesse and Simeon also served in the war. Was in Soldier's Home in Milwaukee. Caught malaria on a march from Fredericksburg to Gettysburg in 1863. Was treated in several hospitals including Christ Church in Gettysburg and Judiciary Square Hospital in DC. Was determined insane prior to death. Was promoted to Corporal 3/7/1862 and Sergeant April, 1863. Reduced to the ranks 7/1/1863. (Military & Pension Files, Grange American

Legion, 1865 Allegany County Town Clerk Register Granger, 1865 NYS Census Granger, 1860, 1870 Fed. Censuses Granger)

Bennett, Samuel Co H, 24th Veterans Reserve Corps. Was transferred from the 104th NY Infantry to the VRC on March 15, 1864. He received an honorable discharge April 21, 1865. Was a sergeant, but was reduced to the ranks 1/24/1865. No reason in files. Also served with Co. F, 104th NY Infantry, see above. Also see above for personal information and sources of information.

Bennett, Simeon   Co. G, 19th NY Cavalry - 8/12/1862 at Granger/3 yrs - 34 - 5'6", Dark Complexion, Blue Eyes, Dark Hair - 9/3/1862 at Portage Station - $100 - Pvt, Corp - Deserted House, siege of Suffolk - 6/8/1865 Honorable - Was not a casualty - John & Sarah Marsh Bennett (Both B England) - Timothy, Rachael (Ayrault), Leah (Voss), Jesse, Mary, Henry, Thomas, Elizabeth (Collister), Samuel - 1827/28 in England - Farmer - Farmer - 1st Laura, 2nd Sarah Parsons, married12/25/1876 in Short Tract - Martha, Anson, Sarah, Lydia - 8/25/1894 in Short Tract - Short Tract - Was in hospital most of his enlistment. Suffered from enlarged heart & dilation of ventricle. May have been caused by a sun stroke he suffered in service, June, 1863. Brothers Jesse and Samuel also served in war. (Military & Pension Files, 1865 NYS Census Granger, *History of Allegany County 1879*, 1865 Allegany County Town Clerk Register Granger, Granger American Legion, Matteson, *Allegany & Its People*, 1860, 1870 Fed. Censuses Granger, 1890 Fed. Census Special Schedule Granger)

Bennett, Sylvester He was not from the C-H-G area. Originally served with Co. E, 107th NY Infantry and Co. C, 16th VRC. His re-enlistment in Co. C, 16th VRC was credited to Hume Township which paid the bounty of $500. (1865 Allegany Town Clerk Register Hume.)

Bentley, David Nortin   Co F, 4th NY Heavy Artillery - 9/28/1862/3 yrs - 18 - 5'7", Dark Complexion, Black Eyes, Black Hair - 10/2/1862 NYC - No bounty - Pvt, Pvt - Wilderness, Spotsylvania, North Anna River, Totopotomoy, Cold Harbor, Petersburg - 9/26/1865 Honorable - WIA, 6/18/1864 at Petersburg, gunshot to right breast - Father INA, Sarah Bentley (B ME) - Lucy, Sally, Judith - 1844/45 in Granger - Farm Laborer - Farmer - Eliza A. Stuart, married 6/20/1866 in Lawrence, MI - Mabel, George, Lillie M. - 2/23/1880 in Lawrence, MI - Lawrence, MI - Transferred to Co. B, 18th VRC 4/24/1865. Was in Campbell's G.H. in DC. Also served with Co. F, 33rd NY Infantry. Enlisted 7/4/1861. Mustered 7/6/1861 at Elmira for 2 years. Age 18. Spent entire enlistment in hospital. Received a disability discharge for miasmatic fever 5/27/1862 at Ladies Home Hospital in NYC. Father's name was probably Gideon. (Military & Pension Files, 1865 NYS Census Granger, Allegany County Town Clerk Register Granger, 1850, 1860 Fed. Censuses Granger, 1870 Fed. Census Lawrence, MI)

Bentley, John Melvin Co E, 85th NY Infantry - 9/1/1861 at Granger/3 yrs - 20 - 5'8", Sandy Complexion, Blue Eyes, Red Hair - 10/25/1861 at Elmira - No bounty - Pvt, Pvt - defense of DC - 10/15/1862 Honorable - Was not a casualty - Elisha & Rhoda Hortin Bentley (Both B NY) - Joseph - 9/27/1842 in Granger - Farmer - Farmer - Never Married - None - 9/26/1908 probably Granger - Granger? - Brother Joseph also served in the war. Dates used are from Bentley's military records. Many dates are different in his pension file. (Military & Pension Files, 1865 NYS Census

Granger, *History of Allegany County 1879*, Granger American Legion, Matteson, 1865 Allegany County Town Clerk Register Granger, 1860, 1900 Fed. Censuses Granger, 1890 Fed. Census Special Schedule Granger)

Bentley, Joseph Co. I, 18th NY Cavalry - 7/20/1863 at Buffalo/3 yrs - 24 - 5'7", Light Complexion, Blue Eyes, Red Hair - 12/2/1863 at Fort Columbus - No bounty - Pvt, Pvt - Red River Campaign - 6/10/1864 Honorable/Deceased - DD, 6/11/1864 at St. Louis Hospital, New Orleans of typhoid fever and chronic diarrhea - Elisha & Rhoda Hortin Bentley (Both B NY) - John Melvin - 1837/38 in Allegany County - Farmer - None Deceased - Never married - None - 6/11/1864 in New Orleans, LA - Chalmette National Cemetery, New Orleans. - Brother John Melvin also served in the war. Listed on Soldiers Monument in Granger. (Military & Pension Files, Granger American Legion, *Allegany & Its People*, 1860 Fed. Census Granger)

Bentley, Josh At least one source document indicates that Bentley served in the military during the war. No evidence of such service has been located. Josh may have been a nickname. No Josh Bentley served in any NYS Civil War regiment. (Matteson)

Bentley, William R. Co. F, 4th NY Heavy Artillery - 9/28/1862/3 yrs - 21 - 5'8", Light Complexion, Blue Eyes, Brown Hair - 10/2/1862, NYC - $25 - Pvt, Pvt - Wilderness, Spotsylvania, North Anna River, Totopotomoy, Cold Harbor, Petersburg - 6/18/1864, Honorable/Deceased - KIA, 6/18/1864 at Petersburg - Ira & Mary Bentley (Both B NY) - Philena, Jamette, Eleanor, Ira Jr., Charlotte - 1840 or 41 - Farmer - None (Deceased) - Never Married - None - 6/18/1864 in Petersburg - City Point National Cemetery, VA - Listed on Soldiers Monument in Short Tract. (Military Files, 1865 NYS Census Granger, 1865 Allegany County Town Clerk Register Granger, Granger American Legion, *Allegany & Its People*, 1860 Fed. Census Granger)

Benton, John L. Co. K/I, 5th NY Heavy Artillery - drafted 8/20/1864 at Watertown, NY/1 yr - 18 - INA - 9/3/1864 at Watertown - $100 - Pvt, Pvt - Five Forks, Petersburg, Appomattox - 6/24/1865 Honorable - Loren & Sarah Benton (Both B NY) - Thomas, Melissa, Dolly, Lucretia, Harriet, Charles - 1845 or 46 in Martinsburgh, Lewis County - Farmer - Minister - Eva I. - Anette, Glenn, Ray, Grace P., Earl C., Mable L. - 4/3/1919 in Gowanda, NY - Mount Pleasant Cemetery, Houghton - Census indicates his age was closer to 16 when he was drafted. (Military File, 1850 Fed. Census Martinsburg - 1880, 1900, 1910 Fed. Censuses Caneadea, Fillmore American Legion)

Berry, Lewis Amasa 3rd Battery, 4th NY Heavy Artillery - 9/11/1862 at Granger/3 yrs - 23 - 6', Dark Complexion, Brown Eyes, Dark Hair - 12/12/1862 - $100 - Pvt, Pvt - Petersburg, South Side Station - 6/26/1865 Honorable - WIA, gunshot to left thigh at South Side RR, 4/2/1865 - Samuel W. (B ME) & Mary Aldrich (B NY) Berry - Pembroke - 8/6/1835 in Granger - Farmer - Farmer - Jenette F. Fuller, married 11/25/1865 in Granger - Mary B. - 10/28/1917 in Bentonville, AR - Bentonville - Was discharged while still in Satterlee G.H. Philadelphia. Temporarily served with 3rd Independent Battery, NYLA. Brother Pembroke also served in the war. (Military & Pension Files, 1850, 1860 Fed. Censuses Granger, 1865 NYS Census Granger, 1900 Fed. Census Osage Twp, AR)

Berry, Pembroke   Co. F, 4th NY Heavy Artillery - 10/1/1862 at Granger/3 yrs - 20 - INA - 10/2/1862 NYC - $100 - Pvt, Pvt -No battles - 11/20/1862 Deceased/Honorable - DD, Typhoid fever at Fort Ethan Allen 11/20/1862 - Samuel W. (B ME) & Mary Aldrich (B NY) Berry - Lewis Amasa - 2/6/1843 in Granger - Farmer - None Deceased - Never Married - None - 11/20/1862 in Fort Ethan Allen - Arlington National Cemetery - Brother Lewis also served in the war, Listed on the Soldiers Monument in Granger. (Military File, *Allegany & Its People*, Matteson, 1850 Fed. Census Granger, 1865 NYS Census Granger)

Bezant, Edward (Bezent)   Co. B, 5th United States Artillery - 1/24/1863/3 yrs - 46 - 5'5", Florid Complexion, Blue Eyes, Light Hair - 1/24/1863 at Suffolk, VA - No bounty - Pvt, Pvt - No battles (at Ft. Hamilton, New York Harbor entire time) - 6/23/1863 Deserted - Was not a casualty - Edward & INA (Both B England) - Thomas, Ellen - 1816 Chautauqua Co. - Farmer/Shoemaker - Farmer/Shoemaker - 1st INA 2nd Louise Smith, married 7/20/1847 in Black Rock, NY - at least one daughter, probably Juliette - 5/23/1884 in Granger - Granger - 5th U.S. Artillery Enlistment Register says he was born at Champlain, NY. Per NYS Adjutant General Report, originally enlisted in 9th NY Cavalry 11/15/1862 as a private for nine months. Was unassigned. No further record. Louise did not receive a pension because Edward was carried as a deserter. 1865 NYS Census says he served with the 130th NY Infantry, but there is no record of such service. He also claimed that he served with the 9th NY Infantry prior to his service with the 5th U.S. Artillery. There is no record of that service. He most likely meant the 9th Cavalry or maybe he said Cavalry and the information was recorded incorrectly. (5th U.S. Artillery Enlistment Records, Pension Application, Granger American Legion, 1850 Fed. Census Attica [name spelled Beznt], 1865 NYS Census Granger, 1860, 1870 1880 Fed. Censuses Granger, 1890 Fed. Census Special Schedule Granger)

Billington, Joseph Benjamin   Co. F, 4th NY Heavy Artillery - 9/22/1862 at Amity/3 yrs - 32 - 5'4", Light Complexion, Blue Eyes, Dark Hair - 10/2/1862 at NYC - No bounty - Pvt. Pvt - Battles, probably none, served as a nurse in First Division Hospital - 9/26/1865 Honorable - Was not a casualty - Benjamin & Laura M. Billington (Both B NY) - Mary, Rachael, Elijah, Laura - 7/13/1830 at NY - Farmer - Lumber Worker/Carpenter - 1st Eliza Jacobs, married 1/11/1853 in Nunda, 2nd Phebe A. Wright, married 10/20/1868 in Portville - Children by Eliza: Runa, Clarence Arthur, Henry Stephen, Children by Phebe: Joseph Alfred, Minnie Elizabeth, Rolan Roy - 2/1/1899 in Olean - INA - Pension was based on rheumatism and disease of the kidneys. (Military & Pension Files, 1865 Allegany Town Clerk Register Amity, 1865 NYS Census Hume, 1850 Fed. Census Granger, 1870 Fed. Census Portville, Cattaraugus County)

Bingham, Carey Edward Co K, 4th NY Heavy Artillery - 12/23/1863 at Centerville/3 yrs - 24 - 5'8", Fair Complexion, Grey Eyes, Brown Hair - 1/5/1864 at Elmira - $600 - Pvt, Pvt - Wilderness, Spotsylvania, North Anna River, Totopotomoy, Cold Harbor, siege of Petersburg, Weldon RR - 8/10/1864 Honorable/Deceased - DD, 8/10/1864 of typhoid fever - Joseph (B VT) & Rumina Badger (B CT) Bingham - Austin, Cynthia L., Louisa L., Phidelia E. - 9/30/1837 in Centerville - Farmer - None Deceased - Julia M. Kimball, married 1/21/1862 in Genesee Falls - Flora - 8/10/1864 on hospital transport *Connecticut* (en route from City Point, VA to Alexandria, VA) - Alexandria, VA National Cemetery - (Military & Pension Files, 1865 NYS Census Centerville,

Bingham, Justin Jr. Co. F, 9th Iowa Cavalry - 10/26/1863 at McGregor, IA/3 yrs - 43 - 5'10",
Light Complexion, Hazel Eyes, Black Hair - 11/30/1863 at Davenport, IA - No bounty - Pvt, Pvt -
West Point, AR., Searcy, AR - 11/28/1865 Deserted - Was not a casualty - Father Justin, Mother
unknown - INA - 1808/09 in Windsor County, VT - Farmer - Farm Laborer - Malinda Moultrop,
married 1/10/1826 in Centerville - Napolean W., Thomas P., Kleber, Stella Ann - 4/3/1871 in
Centerville - Rogers Cemetery, Centerville (No headstone) - Deserted from Little Rock, AR
hospital 11/28/1865. Military age is clearly incorrect. The 1850 Census has his age as 41, and the
1870 has his age as 68. He was easily in his 50's when he enlisted. He had previously served with
the 27th NY Infantry. See below. His pension was based on his service with the 27th. The book,
Allegany & Its People indicates that Bingham, of Hume, was among the first to volunteer at a
meeting in Angelica. (Military & Pension Files, *Allegany & Its People*, *History of Allegany County
1879*, Matteson, 1870 Fed. Census Centerville, 1850 Fed. Census Walton, MI)

Bingham, Justin, Jr. Co. I, 27th NY Infantry - 5/13/1861 at Angelica/2 yrs - 43 - 5'10", Light
Complexion, Hazel Eyes, Black Hair - 5/21/1861 at Elmira - No bounty - Pvt, Pvt - 1st Bull Run -
3/18/1862 Disability/Honorable - WIA 7/21/1861 at 1st Bull Run, a rifle butt was slammed into his
ribs. The Doctor who treated him called him an old man. Served in Veterinary Surgeon's
Department and as Company Farrier. Also served with Co. F, 9th Iowa Cavalry, see above. Also
see above for personal and sources of information.

Bishop, J S. At least one source document indicates that Bishop served in the military during the
war. No evidence of such service has been located. The source document lists him as J.S. Bishop
which is how the name appears on his headstone. The 1870 Federal Census for Hume shows a
Jason S. Bishop. There is no Civil War military file for a Jason Bishop, nor for any Bishop with a
first name beginning with J. and a middle initial of S. (Matteson)

Blake, Daniel Webster   Co. D, 64th NY Infantry - 10/2/1861 at Rushford/3 yrs - 21 - 5'5", Light
Complexion, Blue Eyes, Light Hair - 10/5/1861 at Elmira - No bounty - Pvt, Pvt - siege of
Yorktown, Fair Oaks, Gaine's Mill, Savage Station, Malvern Hill, Antietam, Fredericksburg,
Chancellorsville, Gettysburg - Transferred 1/2/1864 to Co. D, Battery G, 1st NY Artillery - WIA,
7/2/1863 at Gettysburg gunshot to left leg - Father INA, Mother Mary Blake (Both B NH) - INA -
8/25/1840 in Geneva, NY - Farmer/Shoemaker - Carpenter/Shoemaker - 1st Sarah Van Dusen,
married late 1860's, 2nd Charlotte Ogden, married 3/1/1874 in Caneadea - Mabel - 7/24/1913 or
1915 in Caneadea - Pine Grove Cemetery, Fillmore - Burnside G.A.R. Post 237 Marker at Grave.
Was in St. Elizabeth's Hospital in DC from 1/6/1862 to 8/11/1862. Suffered a sunstroke at
Antietam which resulted in vertigo. His father, name unknown, died about two years after he was
born. Also served with 1st NY Light Artillery. See below. (Military & Pension File, 1865 NYS
Census Hume, 1850 Fed. Census Genesee Falls, 1900 Fed. Census Caneadea, Matteson, 1865
Allegany County Town Clerk Register Hume, Fillmore American Legion)

Blake, Daniel Webster   Battery G, 1st NY Light Artillery - 1/21/864 at Stevensburg, VA/3 yrs -
24 - 5'5", Light Complexion, Blue Eyes, Light Hair - $100 - Wilderness, Spotsylvania Court

House, assault on Salient, North Anna River, Pamunkey, Totopotomoy, Hanover Court House, Cold Harbor, Petersburg, Weldon RR, Deep Bottom - 10/4/1864 Honorable - Was not a casualty. Also served with 64th NY Infantry. See above. Also see above for personal and sources of information.

Blanchard, Donald Alonzo Co. F, 19th NY Cavalry - 8/9/1862 at Centerville/3 yrs - 20 - 5'8", Dark Complexion, Grey Eyes, Black Hair - 9/3/1862 at Portage Station - $100 - Pvt, Corp - Deserted House, siege of Suffolk, Franklin - 5/27/65 Honorable - Was not a casualty - Abel (B VT) & Harriet Thrall (B CT) Blanchard - Sophronia, Elsina, Ira, Harriett, Murray, Caroline, Anna - 11/30/1841 in Centerville - Carpenter/School Teacher - Carpenter & Joiner/Hardware Merchant - 1st Mary Elizabeth Batton, married 5/24/1868 in Adel, IA, 2nd H. Sue Worster, married 12/2/1887 in Adel, IA - Mary, Nellie C., Mable G. Ralph W., Anna B. - 6/24/1916 in Adel, IA - Adel, IA - Was a bugler during the war. Lost his fife at some point. (Military & Pension Files, *History of Allegany County 1879*, 1865 NYS Census Centerville, 1865 Allegany County Town Clerk Register Centerville, 1850 Fed. Census Centerville, 1870 Fed. Census Adel, IA)

Blanchard, John S. Co. F, 19th NY Cavalry - 8/9/1862 at Centerville/3 yrs - 20 - 5'7", Dark Complexion, Grey Eyes, Brown Hair - 9/3/1862 at Portage Station - $100 - Pvt, Pvt - Deserted House, siege of Suffolk, Franklin, Manassas Junction, Bristoe's Station, Culpeper Court House - 6/30/1865 Honorable - Was not a casualty - Barnes (B VT) & Rosaria Cleasby (B NH) Blanchard - Oland, Jane E., Julia Ann, John, Sarah Ann, Sophia - 1/12/1842 in Centerville - Farmer - Farmer - Mary A. - Frank A., Floyd J., Nellie M. - 2/17/1898 probably in Saginaw, MI - probably East Saginaw, MI - Marched in the Grand Review 5/23/1865. (Military & Pension Files, 1865 NYS Census Centerville, 1850, 1860 Fed. Censuses Centerville, 1870 Fed. Census Cortland - 1865 Allegany County Town Clerk Register Centerville, Matteson, *History of Allegany County 1879*)

Blossom, John S. Co. A, 47th NY Infantry - 3/1/1865 at Hume/3 yrs - 27 - 5'11", Light Complexion, Grey Eyes, Brown Hair - 3/1/1865 - $700 - Pvt, Pvt - No battles - 8/30/1865 Honorable - Enoch (B VT) & Betsey (B NY) Blossom - Daniel W., Mary M., Jane A., Betsey, Theodore E. - 1/12/1836 in Portage - Farmer - Farm Laborer - Never Married - None - 6/5/1905 - INA - Blossom was a substitute for Miles W. Doud of Hume. Sick 8/8/1865 in hospital at Raleigh, NC. In Soldiers Home, Milwaukee 1903/04. (1865 Allegany Town Clerk Register Hume, 1850 Fed. Census Portage, 1870 Fed. Census Hume)

Blowers, George Edgar Co. F, 4th NY Heavy Artillery - 1/12/1864 at Centerville/3 yrs - 5'5", Light Complexion, Blue Eyes, Light Hair - 1/12/1864 at Elmira - $300 - Pvt, Pvt - No battles with 4th Heavy Artillery, was detached to 6th Corps for entire service. Battles with 6th Corps unknown. - Was not a casualty - Jacob (B VT) & Mary Ann Pike (B NY) Blowers - Laura, Mary - 8/15/1849 in Pike - Farmer - Farmer/Night Watchman - 1st, Abigail S. Hayes, married 1/1/1873, 2nd Helen Hatch of Mortons Corner married 5/13/1898 in Gowanda, without first divorcing Abigail. He claimed Abigail was deceased. They separated in 1894. He was found guilty of bigamy in 1890. - Cora E., Carrie, Margritte, Edna - 12/4/1924 in Memorial Hospital, Buffalo - Forest Lawn Cemetery, Buffalo - Was really only 15 when he enlisted. Middle name may have been Edward. Lived in many places after the war including, Centerville, Arcade, Springville, East Aurora, and

Buffalo. Military file contains a pass he was issued 11/11/1864 to return to duty at Martinsburg, VA. (Military & Pension Files, 1865 NYS Census Centerville, 1865 Allegany County Town Clerk Register Centerville, 1850 Fed. Census Pike, 1860 Fed. Census Centerville, 1880 Fed. Census Yorkshire, NY)

Boardman, George W. At least one source document indicates that Boardman served in the military during the war. No evidence of such service has been located. A George W. Boardman did served with the 117th NY Regiment, but he was not from the C-H-G area. (Fillmore American Legion)

Boardman, James A. Co. G, 44th NY Infantry - 8/20/1861 at Albany (actually probably Hume)/3 yrs - INA - 9/30/1861 at Albany - No bounty - Pvt, Pvt - No battles - 4/28/1862 Honorable/ Deceased - DD, 4/28/1862 of typhoid fever at Annapolis Hospital - Samuel (B NH) and Lydia (B NY) Beard Boardman - INA - 1839/40 in North Adams, MA. - Lock Tender - None Deceased - Never married - None - 4/28/1862 in Annapolis - INA - Was probably a brother of George W. Boardman. (Military File, 1865 Allegany County Town Clerk Register Hume, Allegany County Web Site, 1860 Fed.Census Hume, 1850 Fed. Census - Adams, MA)

Bogardus, John Peter Co. H, 19th NY Cavalry - 8/7/1862 at Birdsall/3 yrs - 19 - INA - 9/3/1862 at Portage Station - $25 - Pvt, Pvt - No battles - 11/22/1862 Honorable/Deceased - DD, 11/22/1862 at Suffolk, VA of a "service related disease." - Ephraim & Catherine Kimpland Bogardus (Both B NY) - None - 7/5/1843 in Rose, Cayuga County - Farmer - None (Deceased) - Never Married - None - 11/22/1862 in Suffolk, VA- Hampton, VA National Cemetery - Was originally buried at Suffolk. (Military File, *History of Allegany County 1879*, Granger American Legion, 1865 Allegany County Town Clerk Register Birdsall, 1860 Fed. Census Birdsall, 1850 Fed. Census Allen, *Roll of Honor*)

Bolton The 1890 Federal Census, Special Schedule- Surviving Soldiers, Sailors and Marines, and Widows War of the Rebellion lists a "Nancy C., wife of a Bolton". No other information is provided, including Bolton's first name. The Special Schedule says that his record is unknown. This soldier has not been identified.

Bolton, Noble Co. E, 104th NY Infantry - 2/15/1862 at Geneseo/3 yrs - 40 - 5'6", Dark Complexion, Grey Eyes - Black Hair - 2/26/1862 - No bounty - Pvt, Pvt - No battles - 7/13/1862 Disability/Honorable - Was not a casualty - INA - INA - Probably about 1812 in Canada - Farm Laborer - None Deceased - 1st Laura (Died 9/1848), 2nd Nancy Electa Stowe - George, Louisa, Chauncey, Lydia Jane, Edgar, Denillow, Russell Frank (at least three others who died young) - 2/25/1865 in Richmond, VA- INA - His disability discharge (first enlistment) indicates that he was probably 50 when he was discharged. Sources cite three different places for his birth, Canada, Allegany County, and Aurelius, Cayuga County. Also served with Co. K, 111th NY Infantry. See below. (Military & Pension Files, 1890 Fed. Census Special Schedule Granger, 1865 Allegany County Town Clerk Register Hume, 1860 Fed. Census Hume)

Bolton, Noble Co. K, 111th NY Infantry - 7/21/1864 at Rome/3 yrs - 42 - 5'6", Dark Complexion,

Grey Eyes, Black Hair - 8/27/1864 at Rome - No bounty - Pvt, Pvt - Chaffin's Farm, New Market Heights, Petersburg - 2/25/1865 Honorable/Deceased - POW, captured 10/30/1864 at Richmond, Prison: Richmond - DD, 2/25/1865 of disease while in prison. Disease not listed in records. He was a substitute. Information in Pension Records say he received $1,000 payment for substituting, but who he substituted for is not listed. Some sources indicate that he transferred to the 4th NY Heavy Artillery. This is incorrect although some of his records may have been erroneously transferred to the 4th. Also served with 104th NY Infantry, see above. Also see above for personal information and sources of information.

Booth, Josiah E. Co. F, 85th NY Infantry - 8/26/1861 at Black Creek/3 yrs (re-enlisted 1/1/1864 at Plymouth) - 21 - 5'5", Dark Complexion, Grey Eyes, Brown Hair - 9/7/1861 at Elmira - $400 - Pvt, Pvt - defense of DC, siege of Yorktown, Williamsburg, Fair Oaks, before Richmond, Plymouth - 6/5/1865 Honorable - POW, Captured 4/20/1864 at Plymouth, NC, Prisons: Libby, Andersonville, paroled 2/24/2865 at Aiken's Landing - Alfred (B MA) & Cynthia Smith (B VT) Booth - Alfred S., Sydney S., Anna, Charles, Edwin S., Smith, Joseph - 5/17/1839 in Centerville - Farmer - Farmer/Waiter in D Room South - Mary Elizabeth Reminton, married 4/15/1876 in Evart, MI - Etta, Verne, May, others - 4/27/1913 at Grand Rapids, MI Soldiers Home - Fair Plains Cemetery, Grand Rapids, MI - Had many health problems at Andersonville including scurvy, dropsy, and brain fever. (Military & Pension Files, 1865 NYS Census Centerville, *History of Allegany County 1879*, 1865 Allegany County Town Clerk Register Centerville, 1850 Fed. Census Centerville, 1900, 1910 Fed. Censuses Grand Rapids, MI)

Boss, Ellis At least one source document indicates that Boss served in the military during the war. No evidence of such service has been located. The only Ellis Boss located in the C-H-G area from the Civil War time period died at the age of seven. No Ellis Boss served in any NYS Civil War regiment. (Matteson)

Boss, John H., Jr. Co. E, 55th Ohio Infantry - 10/11861 at Vermillon, OH/3 yrs (Re-enlisted 1/1/1864 at Lookout Valley, TN) - 23 - 5'8", Dark Complexion, Brown Eyes, Black Hair - January 25, 1862 at Norwalk, OH - No bounty - Pvt, 1st Lt - Moorefield, McDowell, Cross Keys, Cedar Mountain, 2nd Bull Run, Chancellorsville, Gettysburg, Wauhatchie, Orchards Knob, Tunnel Hill, Missionary Ridge, Rocky Face Ridge, Resaca, Dallas, Kenesaw, siege of Savannah, Bentonsville, Bennett's House - 7/11/1865 Honorable - Was not a casualty - John Henry (B RI) & Hannah (B MA) Boss - Stephen P. & Thomas W.E. - 11/19/1837 in Bolivar - Farmer/Student - Farmer - Esmina Ann married 2/13/1864 - Carrie & John - 6/19/1872 in Effingham County, IL - INA - Present at Johnston's surrender. Marched in Grand Review 5/24/1865. Brothers Stephen P. and Thomas W.E. also served in the war. Pension Index at National Archives has Esmina listed as his mother rather than his wife - Parents were married 6/3/1826 at New Bedford, MA. Promoted Sgt 12/31/61; 1st Sgt 8/1/62; QM Sgt 4/19/64; 1st Lt 9/2/64. Had typhoid fever while in service. Lived in Vermillion, OH after war. (Military & Pension Files, Granger American Legion, 1850 Fed. Census Allen, 1865 Allegany County Town Clerk Register Allen, 1860 Fed. Census Allen, 1870 Fed. Census Effingham County, IL)

Boss, Stephen Perry Co. F, 19th NY Cavalry - 9/1/1864 at Allen/1 yr - 36 - 5'8", Dark Complexion,

Blue Eyes, Dark Hair - 9/3/1864 at Elmira - $600 - Pvt, Pvt - Cedar Creek, Berryville, Gordonsville, Dinwiddie Court House, Five Forks, Appomattox - 6/30/1865 Honorable - Was not a casualty - John Henry (B RI) & Hannah (B MA) Boss - Thomas W.E., John H. - 8/21/1828 in New Bedford, MA - Farm Laborer - Farmer - Mary A.- Celia, Ophelia, Ellis - 5/11/1891- Short Tract, County Route 4 - Was at Lee's surrender. Marched in Grand Review 5/23/1865. Retained his pistol and sabre at discharge. Brothers Thomas W.E. Boss and John H. also served in the war. Parents were married 6/3/1826 in New Bedford, MA. (Military & Pension Files, Granger American Legion, *History of Allegany County 1879*, 1865 Allegany County Town Clerk Register Allen, 1860, 1870 Fed Censuses Allen)

Boss, Thomas William Eaton Co. F, 104th NY Infantry - 2/26/1862 at Short Tract/3 yrs - 18 - INA - 2/26/1862 Geneseo - No bounty - Pvt, Pvt - No battles - 3/29/1862 Honorable/Deceased - DD, 3/29/1862 of typhoid fever at Kalarama Hospital in DC - John Henry (B RI) & Hannah (B MA) Boss - Stephen P., John H. - 8/18/1845 in Bolivar - Farmer - None Deceased - Never married - None - 3/29/1862 in DC - Soldier's and Sailor's Home Cemetery of DC - Brothers Stephen P. & John H. also served in the war. Parents were married 6/3/1826 in New Bedford, MA. (Military & Pension Files, 1850, 1860 Fed. Censuses Allen, 1865 Allegany County Town Clerk Register Allen, *Roll of Honor*)

Botsford, Erwin Morgan Co. F, 19th NY Infantry - 9/3/1864 at Allen/1 yr - 20 - 5'10", Dark Complexion, Black Eyes, Dark Hair - 9/13/1864 at Elmira - $600 - Pvt. Pvt - No battles - 6/30/1865 Honorable - Was not a casualty - Reuben W. (B NY) & Ruth Morgan (B NH) Botsford - Edwin - 10/20/1843 (per pension, headstone says 1844) at Allen - Lumberman - Farmer - Cordelia M. Ackerman, married 4/5/1866 in Granger - Effie, Eddie- 12/23/1907 in Wiscoy - Pine Grove Cemetery, Fillmore - Burnside G.A.R. Post 237 Marker at grave. Marched in Grand Review 5/23/1865. (Military & Pension Files, Fillmore American Legion, *History of Allegany County 1879*, 1865 Allegany County Town Clerk Register Allen, 1850, 1860, 1870 Fed. Censuses Allen, 1880 Fed. Census Hume, Matteson)

Botsford, John M. Co. F, 19th NY Cavalry - 8/9/1862 at Portageville/3 yrs - 21 - 5'8", Dark Complexion, Brown Eyes, Dark Hair, 9/3/1862 at Portage Station - $100 - Pvt, Pvt - Deserted House, siege of Suffolk, Manassas Junction, Bristoe's Station, Culpeper Court House, Wilderness, Todd's Tavern, Spotsylvania, North Anna River, Yellow Tavern, Pamunkey, Totopotomoy, Cold Harbor, Trevillian Station, Charles County Court House, before Richmond & Petersburg - Was not a casualty - E. Harrison (B NY) & Lydia M. (B PA) Botsford - Lorenzo - 1840 or 41 in Granger - Farmer - Farmer - Susan C. Karnes, married 4/12/1866 in Vanango Co., PA - Lydia, Ezra, Blanche, Jennie, Maud, Maynine, Floyd - 3/22/1915 in East Hickory, PA - Pleasantville, PA - Marched in the Grand Review 5/23/1865. (Military & Pension Files, 1865 NYS Census Granger, 1865 Allegany County Town Clerk Register Granger, 1860 Fed. Census Granger, 1870 Fed. Census Vanango Co., PA)

Botsford, Lorenzo P. At least one source document indicates that Botsford served in the military during the war. No evidence of such service has been located. No Lorenzo Botsford served in any NYS Civil War regiment. (Matteson)

<u>Bowen, Azem F.</u>   Co. C, 19th NY Cavalry - 8/8/1862 at Arcade/3 yrs - 21 - 5'7", Dark Complexion, Blue Eyes, Dark Hair - 9/3/1862 at Portage Station - No bounty - Pvt, Pvt - Deserted House, siege of Suffolk, Franklin, Manassas Junction, Culpeper Court House, Trevillian Station, (one record says he was at the battle of Winchester (9/19/64) but his muster cards have him in a Philadelphia, PA hospital at that time) - 6/30/1865 Honorable - POW, captured 9/22/1863 at Manassas, Prisons: Libby & Belle Island, Richmond, paroled 11/16/1863 at City Point, VA, admitted Camp Parole, Annapolis hospital 11/18/63 - Elias & Lydia Wellington Bowen (Both B NY) -Mahaman, Alzina, Wellington, Lurana, Caleb, Jesse, Joseph, Lydia, Daniel, Judson - 2/1840 in East Otto, Cattaraugus County - Farmer - Farmer - Myra Squires, married 12/25/1863 in Franklinville - Ida May (Hogg), Newton Howard (Both adopted) - 10/24/1907 in Black Creek - Mount Prospect Cemetery, Franklinville - Was present for Lee's surrender. May have marched in Grand Review 5/23/1865. Charged with desertion 12/2/1863 from Annapolis hospital, arrested Anne Arundel Co., MD 1/1/64 (man who captured him earned $300). Admitted Division Hospital 6/28/1864, transferred to Philadelphia with open abscess on right hip. Paid $8.00 to keep his revolver when discharged. Charter Member of Burnside G.A.R. Post 237, Wiscoy. Had three brothers, not from the C-H-G area who also served during the war, Elias, Daniel, and Judson. (Military & Pension Files, 1890 Fed. Census Special Schedule Centerville, *Allegany & Its People*, 1850 Fed Census Otto [Name spelled Boin], 1880 Fed. Census Centerville)

<u>Bowen, Jermial.</u>   At least one source document indicates that a Jermial Bowen from C-H-G served in the military during the war. No evidence of such service has been located. The NYS Adjutant General Report on Civil War Soldiers does not list a Jermial Bowen. It does list a Jeremiah N. Bowen who served with Co. H, 118th NY Infantry, but he was not from the C-H-G area. There is a Jeremiah Bowen buried at Pine Grove Cemetery, Fillmore. There is a G.A.R. Post 237 marker at his grave, however this Jeremiah was born in 1801 and was surely too old to have served in the military during the Civil War. He likely was the father of Civil War soldier Samuel A. Bowen. The Civil War Jeremiah was only 21 in 1862 when he volunteered. (Matteson, Fillmore American Legion)

<u>Bowen, Samuel A.</u>   Co. H, 136th NY Infantry - 8/6/1862 at Orangeville/3 yrs - 20 - 5'9", Light Complexion, Blue Eyes, Auburn Hair - 9/25/1862 at Portage - No bounty - Pvt, Pvt - No battles - 3/7/1863 Disability Honorable - Was not a casualty - Jeremiah & Polly Bowen (Both B VT) -Allie - 8/6/1842 (headstone says 1846) in Orangeville - Farmer - Farmer - Mariam Akins, married 5/21/1866 in Angelica - Lawrence, Maud, David, Alman, Velney - 7/4/1927 (Headstone says 1930) in Fillmore - Pine Grove Cemetery, Fillmore - Burnside G.A.R. Marker at grave. Disability discharge due to typhoid fever and measles. (Military & Pension Files, Matteson, 1860 Fed. Census Orangeville, 1880 Fed. Census Caneadea)

<u>Bower, William Henry</u>   Co. I, 85th NY Infantry - 8/30/1862 at Ward/3 yrs -21 - 5'6", Light Complexion, Blue Eyes, Brown Hair - 9/12/1862 at Elmira - $100 - Pvt, Pvt - Franklin, Kingston, Whitehall, Goldsboro, Roanoke Island, Plymouth (no battle info for 1/1/64 to 4/64, was with Pioneer Corps) - 6/5/1865 Honorable - INJ, hurt hand crossing bridge at Pitts Landing, probably during raid on Roanoke Island, 8/1863 - POW, captured 4/20/1864 (one record says 5/6/64 at New Bern, actually was transferred to Co. A 5/6) at Plymouth, NC - Father INA (B PA) Mother

INA (B NY) - INA - 12/20/1840 in Alfred - Farmer - Farmer - 1st Mary E. (probably Eliza) Norton, married 6/20/1860 at Ward (Died 9/27/1903), 2nd Mary Bradley Streeter, married 10/9/1924 - Oscar, Homer, Clara, Ada - 3/15/1925 in Short Tract - Forest Hills Cemetery Belmont - Escaped from captivity when crossing a river on way to Andersonville Prison. Discharged from McDougal G.H., DC. His second wife, Mary Bradley Streeter claimed he had been shot in the right side, but there is no other evidence of such a wound. Mary's father Zenas, and brother Nathan Bradley were both Civil War soldiers. Zenas' father Benjamin was in the War of 1812. A nephew served in the Philippines, probably in the Spanish American War. (Military & Pension Files, Granger American Legion, 1860 Fed. Census Ward, 1910 Fed. Census Amity, 1920 Fed. Census Belmont)

Boyd, William H. Not from the C-H-G area. Served with Co. A, 19th NY Cavalry. His enlistment was credited to Hume Township which paid his enlistment bonus of $150. (1865 Allegany Town Clerk Register Hume.)

Boyington, Norton R. At least one source document lists a Norton R. Boyington of Hume as having served in the military during the Civil War. Actually his name was Roswell Norton Byington. See below. (1865 NYS Census Centerville)

Bradley, John Unassigned, 192nd NY Infantry. It is not certain Bradley was from the C-H-G area, although based on certain information, it is possible. He was a substitute for John Minard of Hume. Town Clerk has him born in Steuben County. He has not been positively identified in any census. (1865 Allegany County Town Clerk Register Hume)

Bradley, Nathan Charles Co. H, 19th NY Cavalry - 8/16/1862 at Oramel/3 yrs - 25 - INA - 9/3/1862 at Portage Station - No bounty - Sgt, Sgt - Deserted House, siege of Suffolk, Franklin, Manassas Junction - 3/9/1864 Honorable/Deceased - POW, captured 10/19/1863 at Manassas, Prison: Libby, Richmond, DD, 3/9/1864 at Libby Prison of diarrhea & pneumonia - Zenas (B VT) & Mary White (B Canada) Bradley - Sarah, Nancy, Mahalah, Martha Ann, Washington, Mary - 1836/37 in NY - INA - None deceased - Mary Ellen, married 7/4/1863 in Allen - No children - 3/9/1864 at Libby Prison, Richmond - Richmond, VA (Per Roll of Honor. Has first name as just M.) - His Father Zenas also served in the war. Father's pension said his son's name was Charles Nathan Bradley. Many records have first name as Nathan. Bradley took a one day leave in July of 1863 to visit the Irish Mission (which was part of the British Embassy at the time) in Washington, DC No information has been found to identify the purpose of his visit. (Military & Pension Files, Granger American Legion, 1850 Fed. Census - Belfast)

Bradley, Zenas Co F, 104th NY Infantry - 1/29/1862 at Allen/3 yrs, (reenlisted 9/2/1864 with Co. A/B, 16th VCR) - 44 -5'10", Light Complexion, Blue Eyes, Brown Hair - 2/26/1862 at Geneseo - No bounty - Pvt, Pvt - No battles - 10/4/1862 Honorable - INJ, 3 times, 7/3/1862 at Cattlett's Station, VA, bank collapsed when he was jumping a stream, landed on his equipment injuring his side; July,1862 at Cattletts Station, VA suffered a bad sunstroke; 5/4/1865 was returning to duty from a 10 day furlough (granted 4/27/1865), on a cow train when a bridge collapsed at Painted Post, Steuben County, hurt right leg and hip - Benjamin & Sally Bennett - INA - 10/14/1814 in St.

Alburn, VT - Mechanic/Wagon Maker - Farmer/Weaver - Mary White, married 7/16/1832 in Bethany, Genesee County - Sarah, Nancy, Mahalah, Martha, Washington, Mary, Charles Nathan - Killed 5/29/1880, tree he was cutting fell on him - Short Tract, County Route 4 - Son Charles Nathan also served in the war. Attended Lincoln's funeral. His father Benjamin served in the War of 1812. (Military & Pension Files, Granger American Legion, Matteson, 1865 Allegany County Town Clerk Register Allen, 1890 Fed. Census Special Schedule Granger, 1860 Fed. Census Allen, 1850 Fed. Census Belfast)

Bradshaw, James Co. I, 6th NY Cavalry - 10/22/1861 at Angelica/3 yrs - 44 - Sandy Complexion, Blue Eyes, Light Hair - 11/19/1861 at NYC - No bounty - Pvt, Pvt - Malvern Hill, Orange County Court House, Williamsburg, Hyattstown, South Mountain, Antietam - 10/28/1862 Honorable - Was not a casualty with the 6th Cavalry - INA - INA - 4/16/1817 in Northamptonshire, England - Adelia (Name may have been Arvilla Ardelia) Reynolds, married 1/15/1860 in Scio - INA - 2/14/1863 in camp near Falmouth, VA - Fairlawn Cemetery, Scio - Joined the regular Army 10/28/1862, see below. His records are not clear and it is difficult to determine if he participated in the last 4 battles mentioned. (Military & Pension Files, 2nd U.S. Cavalry Enlistment Register, 1865 Allegany County Town Clerk Register Hume, Allegany County Web Site Hume)

Bradshaw, James Co. F, 2nd United States Cavalry 10/28/1862 at Berlin, MD/Term of war - 45 - Sandy Complexion, Blue Eyes, Light Hair - 11/19/1861 at Berlin, MD - No bounty - Pvt, Pvt - Expedition to Richards & Ellis Ford's, Rappahannock River - 2/14/1863 Honorable/Deceased-DD, died 2/14/1863 of typhoid fever in a camp near Falmouth, VA - Probably Falmouth - Also served with Co I, 6th NY Cavalry. See above. Also see above for personal information and sources of information.

Brewster, Isaac H. Co. H, 114th NY Infantry - 8/11/1862 at Smithville/3 yrs - 18 - 5'10", Fair Complexion, Blue Eyes, Brown Hair - 8/14/1862 at Norwich - No Bounty - Pvt, Pvt - No battles - 5/1/1863 Honorable/Deceased - DD, 5/1/1863 of remittent fever at Brashear City, LA - Alfred B. (B NY) & Ruth (B CT) Brewster - Luceba C. - 1843 or 44 in Smithville, Chenago County - probably Farm Laborer - None Deceased - Never Married - None - 5/1/1863 in Brashear City, LA - Brashear City?, LA - Prior to the war he was probably working for his father, a farmer. (Military & Pension Files, 1860 Fed. Census Hume, 1865 NYS Census Hume)

Broadard, James D. (Broadhead/Brodard) Not from the C-H-G area. Originally served with Co. A, 120th NY Infantry. His enlistment was credited to Hume Township which paid his bonus of $500 when he reenlisted in Co C, 16th VRC. (1865 Allegany Town Clerk Register Hume, NYS Adjutant General Report 1903, 1850 Fed. Census Wawarsing, Ulster County)

Brockway, Isaiah D. Co. L, 14th NY Heavy Artillery - 12/17/1863 at Milo (Penn Yan)/3 yrs - 19 - 5'9", Light Complexion, Black Eyes, Black Hair - 1/8/1864 at Rochester - No bounty - Pvt, Pvt - Wilderness, Spotsylvania Court House, North Anna River, Pamunkey, Totopotomoy, Cold Harbor, Petersburg - 10/11/1864 Honorable/Deceased - DD, 10/11/1864 at US G.H. Alexandria, VA of tuberculosis - John Brockway & Lydia Davis Brockway (Both B NY) - Hannah, Talbert P., Ann - 1844 in Allegany, Cattaraugus County (Maybe an error, may have meant Allegany County)

- Farmer - None Deceased - Never Married - None - 10/11/1864 in Alexandria, VA - INA, however his pension records indicate that his mother paid to have his body shipped home, so it is likely he is buried in the Granger area - In applying for his pension, his mother Lydia claimed she was not married to John Broackway and that Isaiah was illegitimate. This does not appear likely since he is listed as Brockway in all the censuses and he listed John W. Brockway as next of kin when he was in the hospital. Further he was the youngest child of four per the 1850 Census. Maybe his parents were never married. This may have been some sort of ploy related to his pension. Pension was approved for his mother. It could also be that he was adopted or simply took Brockway's name. (Military & Pension Files, 1850, 1870 Fed. Censuses Granger, 1865 NYS Census Granger)

Brookins, Barney L.   Co. D, 58th NY National Guard (Militia) - 8/1864 at Fillmore/3 months - 18 - 6', Ruddy Complexion, Brown Eyes, Dark Hair - 9/10/1864 at Elmira - Pvt, Pvt - No battles - 12/2/1864 Honorable - Was not a casualty - Charles & Selesta Curtis Brookins (Both B NY) - George - 1845/46 in Granger in Fillmore - Robert H. & Bentman Lewis - 1/9/1935 in Detroit - (body shipped to Buffalo) - INA - He served less than 3 months, but was awarded a pension by an Act of Congress passed 2/8/1904 for deafness and catarrh. (Military & Pension Files, 1865 NYS Census Hume, 1850, 1860, 1870 Fed. Censuses Hume)

Brown, Edward At least one source document indicates that Brown served in the military during the war. No evidence of such service has been located. Many Edward Browns served in NYS Civil War regiments, but none in the NY 4th Hearvy Artillery. (1865 Allegany County Town Clerk Register Hume - says he served in 4th NY Heavy Artillery)

Brown, Elbert G.   Co. B, 8th NY Cavalry - 3/31/1865 at Rochester/1 yr - 24 - 5'7", Fair Complexion, Grey Eyes, Dark Hair - 3/31/1865 at Rochester - $100 - Pvt, Corp - Dinwiddie Court House, Five Forks, fall of Petersburg, Appomattox - 6/27/1865 Honorable - Was not a casualty - Chauncey & Lovinia A. Slusser (B NY) Brown - Lewis W., Chauncey, Warren - 1840 or 41 in Allegany County (likely Hume) - Farm Laborer - INA - INA - INA - INA - Church Street Cemetery Wiscoy - Promoted to 5th Corporal 5/25/1865. Was at Lee's surrender. Marched in Grand Review 5/23/1865. Brother Warren served in the war. His first name may have been Albert. Father died 9/26/1845; mother then married an Aaron Melville 10/1/1877. (Military File, No Pension, Fillmore American Legion, 1850, 1860 Fed. Censuses Hume)

Brown, Warren Major   Co. A, 19th NY Cavalry - 8/7/1862 at Pike/3 yrs - 19 - 5'11", Light Complexion, Blue Eyes, Light Hair - 9/3/1862 at Portage Station - $100 - Pvt, Pvt - Deserted House, siege of Suffolk, Manassas Junction, Bristoe's Station, Culpeper Court House, Wilderness, Todd's Tavern, Spotsylvania Court House, North Anna River, Yellow Tavern, Pamunkey, Totopotomoy, Cold Harbor, Trevillian Station, Charles County Court House, before Richmond & Petersburg - 6/30/1865 Honorable - Was not a casualty - Chauncey & Lovinia A. Slusser (B NY) Brown - Lewis W., Chauncey, Elbert - 2/12/1843 in Hume - Farm Laborer - None, was unable to work due to illness - Never married - None - 9/18/1872 in St. Joseph, MO - St. Joseph - Brother Elbert also served in the war. Was with Pioneer Corps 12/1862 to 5/1863. On extra duty with Adjutant 9/1863. Detached 6/24/1864 to U.S. Hospital, Cavalry Corps, Army of the Potomac, City

Point, VA as both a patient and a nurse. Came down with chronic bronchitis and consumption 6/27/1864 at Harrison's Landing. Father died 9/26/1845. Mother married an Aaron Melville 10/1/1877. (Military & Pension Files, 1865 NYS Census Hume, 1865 Allegany County Town Clerk Register Hume, Allegany County Web Site Hume, 1850 Fed. Census Hume)

Browne, Henry C. (Brown) Co. E, 5th NY Cavalry - 8/17/1861 at Cuba/3 yrs - 22 - 5'7", Dark Complexion, Brown Hair, Dark Grey Eyes - 8/31/1861 at NYC - $100 - Pvt, Sgt - New Market, Orange County Court House, 2nd Bull Run, Antietam, New Baltimore, Hanover, PA, Hay Market, Ellis Ford, Todd's Tavern, Wilderness, Cold Harbor, Malvern Hill, Ream's Station, Berryville, Mt Jackson - 9/3/1864 Honorable - POW, Captured 8/2/1862 at Orange County Court House, Prison, Richmond - paroled 10/1/1862 - Parents INA (B born NY) - INA - 8/29/1839 in Norfolk, St. Lawrence County - Apprentice Harness Maker - Harness Maker/Saddler/Town Clerk/Owner of Ingham House Hotel, Hume - 1st Melinda H. Price, married 4/11/1866, 2nd Ruthem F. Smith, married 11/23/1892 in Hume - Myrtle (Harding) - 6/7/1907 in Belfast - Pine Grove Cemetery, Fillmore - Reenlisted 3/28/1865 at Dunkirk with Co. F, 8th U.S. Vet. Cavalry, honorably discharged 3/29/1866. Had rheumatism and poor eyesight. Was a saddler during service. Name Browne is spelled with and without the *e* in different documents. Charter Member & First Commander of Burnside G.A.R. Post 237. Post 237 Marker at grave. (Military & Pension Files,1890 Fed. Census Special Schedule Hume, Fillmore American Legion, Matteson, *Allegany & Its People*, *History of Allegany County 1879*, 1860 Fed. Census Randolph, Cattaraugus County, 1880, 1900 Fed. Censuses Hume)

Brownell, William H. Co. C, 104th NY Infantry - 11/12/1861 at Geneseo/3 yrs (re-enlisted 1/3/1864) - 19 - 5'6", Light Complexion, Blue Eyes, Brown Hair - 2/26/1862 at Geneseo - $700 - Pvt, Pvt - Cedar Creek, 2nd Bull Run, South Mountain, Antietam, Fredericksburg, Chancellorsville, Gettysburg, Bristoe's Station, Petersburg, Hatcher's Run, Gravelly Run, Five Forks, Appomattox - 6/22/1865 Honorable - INJ, 9/14/1862 at Antietam, fell down a 12 embankment, hurt right knee, WIA, 9/16/1862 at Antietam, gunshot to head resulting in partial hearing loss - William & Phobe Youngs Brownell (Both B NY) - Armilla, Harriet, Isaac - 6/9/1841 in Castile - Farmer/Canal Driver - Carpenter/ Laborer - Adaline Hill, married 10/9/1865 in Mt. Morris - Charles H. & John T. - 5/4/1910 in Rochester - Mount Hope Cemetery, Rochester - Military file shows no formal discharge date, went on furlough 6/22/1865 and never returned. Did not stop him from getting a pension which says he was discharged 1/21/1865. Present at Lee's surrender. Marched in Grand Review 5/23/65. (Military & Pension Files, 1865 Allegany County Town Clerk Register Hume, 1865 NYS Census Hume, 1850 Fed. Census Leicester, Livingston County, 1880 Fed. Census Mt. Morris, Livingston County)

Buchanan, Edwin Co. F, 33rd NY Infantry - 7/4/1861 at Hume/2 yrs - 21 - 5'6", Light Complexion, Grey Eyes, Light Hair - 7/6/1861 at Elmira - No bounty - Pvt, Pvt - siege of Yorktown, Williamsburg, FT. Magruder, Gaine's Mill, Malvern Hill, 2nd Bull Run, South Mountain, Antietam, Fredericksburg - 6/2/1863 Honorable - Was not a casualty - John & Betsey Slusser (B NY) Buchanan - Lucy, Jane, Elizabeth - 5/10/1839 in Hume - Teacher - Cheese Maker - 1st Adaline Corey, married 1867 in Cattaraugus County, died 1868, 2nd Elizabeth O. Leach, married 1870 Lake Grove, WI, died 12/4/1904, 3rd Tabitha Elizabeth Timeley, married 11/22/1906, divorced

1/13/1910, 4th Martha Malinda Nipper, married 4/4/1911 - Willie S. - 7/31/1913 in Cleveland, TN - Cleveland, TN - Also served with the 2nd Mounted Rifles, see below. (Military & Pension Files, *History of Allegany County 1879*, 1865 NYS Census Hume, 1865 Allegany County Town Clerk Register Hume, 1850 Fed. Census Hume, 1880 Fed. Census Hebron, IL)

<u>Buchanan, Edwin</u> Co B, 2nd NY Mounted Rifles - 12/12/1863 at Hume 24 - 5'6", Light Complexion, Grey Eyes, Light Hair - 12/12/1865 at Ft Porter, Buffalo - $700 - Sgt, Sgt - Spotsylvania Court House, North Anna River, Pamunkey, Totopotomoy - Hanover Court House, Cold Harbor, Bethesda Church, siege of Petersburg, Weldon RR, Popular Springs Church, Pegram's Farm, Hatcher's Run - 8/10/165 Honorable - Sick in hospital 3/65 - 4/65. Also served with Co F, 33rd NY Infantry, see above. Also see above for personal information and sources of information.

<u>Buck, Franklin</u> Was not from the C-H-G area. Originally served with Co. D, 16th Maine Infantry. His re-enlistment in Co C, 16th VRC was credited to Hume Township which paid his re-enlistment bonus of $500. (1865 Allegany Town Clerk Register Hume)

<u>Buckbee, Charles</u> Co. E, 85th NY Infantry - 9/1/1861 at Granger/3 yrs (Re-enlisted 1/1/1864 at Plymouth, NC) - 21 - 5'7", Light Complexion, Blue Eyes, Brown Hair - 10/10/1861 at Elmira - $400 - Pvt, Pvt - defense of DC, siege of Yorktown, Williamsburg, Fair Oaks, before Richmond, Plymouth - 11/7/1864 Honorable/Deceased - POW, Captured 4/20/1864 at Plymouth, Prison: Andersonville - DD, 11/7/1864 at Andersonville of starvation - Edmund & Hannah Clark Buckbee (Both B NJ) - Mary & Martha -10/14/1841 in NY - Farm Laborer/Teamster - None Deceased - Never Married - None - 11/7/1864 at Florence, SC prison - INA - Parents married 12/31/1840 at Geneva. Last name spelling: 1850 Fed.Census, Buckley; 1860 Fed. Census Bgeby, (Bugsley in 1860 index) and elsewhere, Bugby. (Military & Pension Files, *History of Allegany County 1879*, Matteson, Granger American Legion - 1850, 1860 Fed. Censuses Portage)

<u>Buckingham, Maurice</u> Co C, 104th NY Infantry - 10/1861/3 yrs - 24 - 5'9", Light Complexion, Blue Eyes, Brown Hair - 2/26/1862 at Geneseo - No bounty - Pvt, Color Sergeant - Cedar Creek, 2nd Bull Run, South Mountain, Antietam, Fredericksburg, Chancellorsville, Gettysburg - 7/20/1863 Honorable/Deceased - WIA - 7/1/1863 at Gettysburg, severe gunshot wound to leg. Leg was amputated, KIA, died 7/20/1863 from leg wound and amputation (Some would say a broken heart, see below.) - INA - INA - 1836/37 in Livingston, England - Mechanic - None Deceased - Never Married - None - 7/20/1863 in Gettysburg - Gettysburg National Cemetery - Was called a "Noble boy" by his Commanding Officer, Originally buried in the Presbyterian Church Graveyard at Gettysburg. The sad story of his death appears in several books, including *Lincoln and the Human Interest Stories of The Gettysburg National Cemetery*. Probably arrived in the U.S. aboard the ship *Emerald Isle* on 2/6/1857. (Military File, 1865 NYS Census Centerville, Passenger Manifest of ship *Emerald Isle*)

<u>Bullock, Eber</u> Co. E, 85th NY Infantry - 9/1/1861 at Granger/3 yrs (re-enlisted 1/1/1864 at Plymouth, NC) - 20 - 5'9", Light Complexion, Blue Eyes, Dark Hair - 10/10/1861 at Elmira - No bounty - Pvt, Corp - defense of DC, siege of Yorktown, Williamsburg, Fair Oaks, before

Richmond, Plymouth - 9/24/1864 Honorable/Deceased - POW, captured at Plymouth, NC 4/20/1864, Prison Andersonville , DD, 9/23/1864 at Andersonville of diarrhea - David Bullock, Mother INA (Both B VT) - John, Sidney, Hannah, Adaline - 1840 or 41 in NY - Farm Laborer - None Deceased - Never Married - None - 9/23/1864 in Andersonville - Andersonville - Listed on Soldiers Monument in Granger. Brother John also served in the war. Parents were married at Allen in 1822 per pension file. (Military & Pension Files, 1850 Fed. Census Granger, *History of Allegany County 1879*, *Allegany & Its People*, Granger American Legion, Matteson, 1865 NYS Census Granger, 1865 Allegany County Town Clerk Register Granger, 1860 Fed. Census Portville, Cattaraugus County)

Bullock, John W. Co. A, 184th NY Infantry - 9/3/1864 at Granger/1 yr - 29 - 5'8", Light Complexion, Blue Eyes, Brown Hair - 9/29/1864 Elmira - $100 - Pvt, Pvt - Cedar Creek, Petersburg, Richmond - 6/29/1865 Honorable - Was not a casualty - David Bullock, Mother INA (Both B VT) - Eber, Sidney, Hannah, Adaline - 7/30/1835 in Granger - Mechanic/Farmer - Farmer/Drug Store Clerk - Harriet A. - Sidney & Emma - 3/26/1907 in Howard City, MI - Howard City, MI - Brother Eber also served in the war. Parents married at Allen in 1822. 1900 Census says he was born in 1838. This is inconsistent with his age at entrance into service. (Military & Pension Files, 1865 NYS Census Granger, 1865 Allegany County Town Clerk Register Granger, Granger American Legion, 1850, 1860 Fed. Censuses Granger, 1900 Fed. Census Reynolds, MI)

Burleson, Samuel T. Co. B, 2nd NY Mounted Rifles - 1/1/1864 at Allen/3 yrs - 35 - 5'7", Dark Complexion, Blue Eyes, Dark Hair - 1/12/1864 at Ft. Porter, Buffalo - $600 - Corp, Corp - Spotsylvania Court House, North Anna River, Pamunkey, Totopotomoy, Hanover Court House, Cold Harbor, Bethesda Church, siege of Petersburg - 6/18/1864 Honorable/Deceased - KIA, at Petersburg 6/18/1864 - probably Russell & Olive (B NY) Burleson - Chester, Andrew, William, at least 5 others - 1828 or 29 in Howard, Steuben County - Farmer - None Deceased - Mary M. Kirchbaum, married 2/28/1854 in Carson Town, PA - INA - 6/18/1864 in Petersburg - INA - Was originally reported as MIA. A note in his file indicates that he returned to his headquarters, but not his company, after the battle at Petersburg, but that is likely a mistake. He was never found. Wife's name is also spelled Crickbone or Creekvan in some documents. His wife was awarded his pension. (Military & Pension Files, 1865 Allegany County Town Clerk Register Allen, 1850 Fed. Census Wharton, PA, Granger American Legion)

Burroughs, Ira Hyde Co. F, 4th NY Heavy Artillery - 12/26/1863 at Centerville/3 yrs - 29 - 5'8", Fair Complexion, Grey Eyes, Brown Hair - 12/29/1863 at Elmira - $300 - Pvt. Pvt - Wilderness, Spotsylvania, North Anna River, Totopotomoy, Cold Harbor, siege of Petersburg, Weldon RR, Ream's Station - 12/15/1864 Honorable/Deceased - POW, captured 8/25/1864 at Ream's Station, Prison: Salisbury, NC, DD, 12/15/1864 at Salisbury, NC Prison of exposure & starvation - Rufus & Polly Hyde Burroughs - INA - 1833/34 in Cattaraugus County, Farmer - None Deceased - Martha E. Bridges, married 3/3/1855 in West Concord, Erie County - William Ira, Rufus Mark, Lucy Idelia - 12/15/1863 in Salisbury, NC Prison - Probably Salisbury National Cemetery - 1850 Census spells name Burrows. Lived in Centerville, apparently off and on, during the years 1859 to 1863. (Military & Pension Files, 1865 NYS Census Centerville, 1865 Allegany County Town

Clerk Register Centerville, 1850 Fed.. Census Mansfield, Cattaraugus County)

Butler, John Martin Co. D, 4th NY Heavy Artillery - 8/13/1862 at Rochester/3 yrs - 25 - 5'8", Sandy Complexion, Brown Eyes, Red Hair -8/13/1862 at Rochester - $50 - Pvt, Pvt - No battles - 11/9/1862 Deserted - ? & Elizabeth Martin (B NY) Butler - Henry M. & Mary E. - 1836/37 in Bethany, Genesee County - Farmer - Farmer - Pamela - B. W. - 6/9/1885 probably in Hume- Pine Grove Cemetery, Fillmore - As a result of his desertion he was not eligible for a pension. No further military information after 11/9/1862. Apparently the military did not try to find him. (Military File, 1865 Allegany County Town Clerk Register Hume, Fillmore American Legion, Allegany County Web Site Hume, 1850, 1870 Fed. Censuses Hume)

Butler, Seymour B. Co. F, 4th NY Heavy Artillery - 8/27/62 at Hume/3 yrs - 32 - 5'9", Light Complexion, Grey Eyes, Sandy Hair - 4/29/1862 - $50 - Pvt, Pvt - INA - 6/3/1865 Honorable - Was not a casualty - Daniel & Jerusha Berry Butler (Both B NY) - Charles, Julia A., Elvia (Gilman) - 10/30/1830 at Walton, Delaware County per 1865 NYS Census & Pension File - Farmer/Raftsman - Farmer - Hattie E. Shearman, married 10/8/1876 in Cheshire, MI - Elwyn S., Elbert A., Grace, Charlie J., Edith B., Low, George S.- 2/7/1909 in Allegan, MI of pneumonia - Allegan, MI - Allegany Town Clerk has his birth date as 10/23/1829 at Caneadea & his father's name as Samuel. May have been Daniel Samuel. A neighbor who did not attend the funeral said that 2/7/1909 was a cold and rainy day. (Military & Pension Files, 1865 NYS Census Hume, 1865 Allegany County Town Clerk Register Hume, 1850,1860 Fed. Censuses Hume, 1900 Fed. Census Allegan, MI)

Butterfield, Joseph Co. F, 19th NY Cavalry - 8/9/1862 at Centerville/3 yrs - 19 - 5'8", Light Complexion, Blue Eyes, Brown Hair - 9/3/1862 at Portage Station - $150 - Pvt, Corp - Deserted House, siege of Suffolk, Franklin, Manassas Junction, Bristoe's Station, Culpeper Court House, Wilderness, Todd's Tavern, Spotsylvania, North Anna River, Yellow Tavern, Pamunkey, Totopotomoy, Cold Harbor, Trevillian Station, Charles County Court House - before Richmond & Petersburg - New Market - Shepherdstown, Winchester, Fisher's Hill, New Market, Port Republic, Cedar Creek, Berryville, Gordonsville, Dinwiddie Court House, Five Forks, Appomattox - 6/30/1865 Honorable - Was not a casualty - John (B VT) & Amanda Johnson (B NY) Butterfield - Edwin, Richard, Sally, John, Polly Ann - 1841/42 in Centerville - Farmer - Farmer - Ellen - INA - 1/29/1927 in Vinton, IA - Vinton, IA - Kept his pistol and sabre when he left the service. Was present for Lee's surrender. Marched in the Grand Review 5/23/1865. (Military File, 1865 NYS Census Centerville, *History of Allegany County 1879*, 1865 Allegany County Town Clerk Register Centerville, 1850 Fed. Census Centerville, Matteson, 1870 Fed. Census Homer Township, IA)

Butterfield, Rozell Co. C, 104th NY Infantry - 2/4/1862 at Geneseo/3 yrs - 23 - 5'9", Light Complexion, Blue Eyes, Brown Hair - 2/26/1862 at Geneseo - No bounty - Pvt, Pvt - defense of DC - 6/8/1862 Disability/Honorable - Was not a casualty - Richard & Sarah Van Dresser Thurston Butterfield (Both B NY) - Frederick, Lorenzo, Amelia, William - 10/31/1838 in Hume - Farmer - Boatman/Stone Mason/Laborer - Amanda M. Babcock Putnam, married 4/22/1865 in Castile - Sarah Althea & Stephen V. - 3/18/1920 in Fillmore - Pine Grove Cemetery, Fillmore (No headstone) - Charter Member of Burnside G.A.R. Post 237. Mother was apparently previously

Reunion at Wiscoy 1890
Courtesy of Jeanne Mills Irwin and R. Craig Mills

Civil War veterans from Centerville, Hume and Granger Townships celebrate Decoration Day
May 30, 1897 in Fillmore, New York
Courtesy of Rare Books and Special Collections, University of Rochester

1st New York Dragoon (19th New York Cavalry)
Monument, Letchworth State Park
Portage, New York.
Author's Collection

William H. Bower
Company I, 85th New York Infantry
Source: *Northern Allegany Observer*

Willard Eddy Calkins
Company F, 33rd New York Infantry
(with wife Frances and grandson Alvin John
Aumick) Courtesy of Max J. Calkins

Joseph M. Chamberlain
Company I, 160th New York Infantry
Source: National Archives

Likely Chauncey Abrams Cronk
Company D, 4th New York Heavy Artillery
Courtesy of Gertrude Hall
Caneadea, New York Historian

Andrew and George N. Clark
(father and son)
Company E, 104th New York Infantry
Courtesy of Alfred Vasile

Perrie C. Soule
Company B, 18th New York Cavalry
Company I, 5th New York Cavalry
(note G.A.R rug) James Gleason Collection

William W. Gray
Company D, 1st New York Dragoons
(19th New York Cavalry)
New York State Military Museum
and Veteran's Research Center

Leonard Orlando Hackett
Company L, 4th New York Heavy Artillery
Courtesy of Thomas E. Van Buskirk

Leonard Orlando Hackett
Company L, 4th New York Heavy Artillery
Courtesy of Thomas E. Van Buskirk

John M. Hall
Company A, 1st New York Dragoons
(19th New York Cavalry)
New York State Military Museum
and Veteran's Research Center

Cyrus J. Hatch, Jr.
Company F, 1st New York Dragoons
(919th New York Cavalry)
New York State Military Museum
and Veteran's Research Center

Samuel P. Hyde
Company F, 4th New York Heavy Artillery
Courtesy of Ira N. Gelser

John A. Jones
Company E, 85th New York Infantry
Courtesy of Rondus Miller, Historian and Curator
Town of Hume Museum

George H. Kimball
Company G, 1st New York Dragoons
(19th New York Cavalry)
New York State Military Museum
and Veteran's Research Center

Harsey Sylvester Osborn
Company D, 4th New York Heavy Artillery
Source: National Archives

John S. Pitt's Fife and Drum Band, Granger
(All Civil War veterans)
Courtesy of Bernice Perry

Civil War monument in Short
Track Cemetery listing names of
some Granger Civil War volunteers
Author's Collection

Reunion of Civil War veterans, Declaration Day, May 30, 1905
in front of Fillmore Opera House
Courtesy of Allegany County Historian, Craig Braak

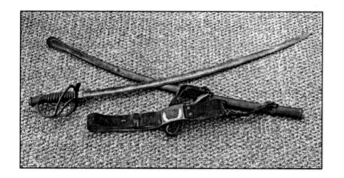

Sabre carried by Smith Dole
Company D, 1st New York Dragoons
(19th New York Cavalry)
Courtesy of R. Craig Mills and Jeanne Mills Irwin

Grave of Medal of Honor winner
George Ebenezer Meach
Company I, 6th New York Cavalry
Author's Collection

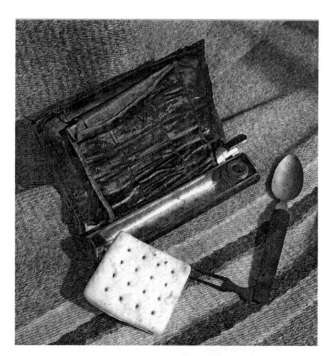

Letter writing kit, fork, spoon
and biscuit carried by Smith Dole
Company D, 1st New York Dragoons
(19th New York Cavalry) during the war
Courtesy of Jeanne Mills Irwin and R. Craig Mills

Clarence Lindon Cudebec
Company F, 1st New York Dragoons
(19th New York Cavalry)
Courtesy of Nunda Historical Society

Francis Palmer
Company C, 104th New York Infantry
New York State Military Museum
and Veteran's Research Center

John S. Pitt
Company F, 104th New York Infantry
Courtesy of Bernice Perry

Alonzo Smith Powell
Company B, 2nd New York Mounted Rifles
Courtesy of Jesse Roberts

Andrew Smith
Company E, 85th New York Infantry
Courtesy of Allegany County, New York, Historian
Craig Braak

Benjamin Swezy Snider
Company D, 64th New York Infantry
Source: National Archives

Judson Stickle
Company F, 1st New York Dragoons
(19th New York Cavalry)
New York State Military Museum
and Veteran's Research Center

George Stockweather
Company A, 1st New York Dragoons
(19th New York Cavalry)
Courtesy of Betty Stockman

Thomas James Thorp
Company E, 85th New York Infantry Staff
1st New York Dragoons, (19th New York Cavalry)
New York State Military Museum
and Veteran's Research Center

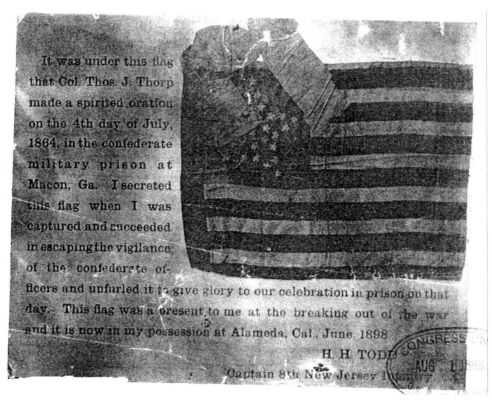

It was under this flag that Col. Thos. J. Thorp made a spirited oration on the 4th day of July, 1864, in the confederate military prison at Macon, Ga. I secreted this flag when I was captured and succeeded in escaping the vigilance of the confederate officers and unfurled it to give glory to our celebration in prison on that day. This flag was a present to me at the breaking out of the war and it is now in my possession at Alameda, Cal. June, 1898

H. H. TODD

Captain 8th New Jersey Infantry

Under this flag, Colonel Thomas James Thorp raised the morale of
his fellow POW's with a stirring speech on July 4, 1864
Source: National Archives

Union Ironclad ship *Cincinnati.* Barzillai B. Weeks of Hume served as
Master of Arms aboard the *Cincinnati* from November 1864 to July 1865
Courtesy of Naval Historical Center, Curator Branch, Photographic Section, Washington Naval Yard

Everett Van Nostrand
Companies A and I, 27th New York Infantry
Courtesy of Wilma Ikeler

Aaron Van Nostrand
Company F, 1st New York Dragoons
(19th New York Cavalry)
Courtesy of Jack and Ann Voss

Charles Van Nostrand
Company D, 1st Michigan Engineers
Courtesy of Wilma Ikeler

Ira R. Weaver
Company E, 4th New York Heavy Artillery
Courtesy of Ira L. Gelser

James H. Weaver
Company F, 1st New York Dragoons
(19th New York Cavalry)
New York State Military Museum
and Veteran's Research Center

Daniel Wight
Company E, 5th New York Cavalry
New York State Military Museum
and Veteran's Research Center

Edwin Wight
Company F, 1st New York Dragoons
(19th New York Cavalry)
New York State Military Museum
and Veteran's Research Center

James Williams
Company E, 1st New York Dragoons
(19th New York Cavalry)
Courtesy of Darlene Williams Mowers

married to a Thurston. Wife Amanda was previously married to Orrin D. Putnam. (1865 NYS Census Hume, 1890 Fed. Census Special Schedule Hume, *Allegany & Its People*, 1850, 1880, 1910 Fed. Censuses Hume)

Byington, Roswell Norton Co. E, 5th NY Cavalry - 8/29/1861 at Farmerville/3 yrs (Reenlisted 12/26/1863) - 21 - 5'8", Light Complexion, Blue Eyes, Sandy Hair - 9/7/1861 at NYC - $400 - Pvt, Sgt - New Market, Port Republic, Orange County Court House, Berryville, New Baltimore, Hanover, PA., Culpeper Court House, Hay Market, Ellis Ford, Cold Harbor, Dinwiddie Court House, Five Forks, Appomattox - others - 7/19/1865 Honorable - WIA, 6/30/1863 at Hanover, PA, wound not described, WIA, 6/3/1864 at Luiney's House (Cold Harbor), accidental gunshot wound to left calf - Richard (B VT) & Hester (B NY) Byington - Harriet - 5/1840 in Great Valley, Cattaraugus County - Farmer - Farmer - 1st Sophia A. Bixby, married 5/3/1868 (died 7/1/1870), 2nd Clara Freeman, married 12/31/1872, - Friend, Carrie, Mary, Charlie, - 8/15/1915 in Centerville - Centerville Cemetery, Route 3 - Was at Lee's surrender. Marched in Grand Review 5/23/1865. (Military & Pension Files, Medical Cards, 1890 Fed. Census Special Schedule Centerville, 1895 NYS Adjutant General Report Vol. 2, 1865 Allegany County Town Clerk Register Centerville, 1865 NYS Census Centerville, Centerville American Legion, 1850 Fed. Census Hume, 1880, 1900 Fed. Censuses Centerville)

Cain, Lewis Co. F, 4th NY Heavy Artillery - 9/11/1862 at Pike/3 yrs - 28 - INA, 9/12/1862 at NYC - $100 - Pvt, Corp - Peeble's Farm, Hatcher's Run, fall of Petersburg, Appomattox - 6/3/1865 Honorable - Was not a casualty - John & Cynthia Cain (Both B NY) - Cynthia, Yost - 3/28/1834 in Eagle - Farmer - Farmer - Chloe Goodrich, married 1858 in Hume - Albert L., Wead - 6/19/1915 in Pike - Pike Cemetery, Telegraph Road - Was at Lee's surrender. Marched in Grand Review 5/23/1865. Was in hospital from 5/64 to 8/64, probably with chronic diarrhea. Brother Yost also served in the war. Grandfather named Yost. (Military & Pension Files, 1865 NYS Census Hume, 1850 Fed. Census Eagle, 1880 Fed. Census Hume, 1890 Fed. Census Special Schedule Hume)

Cain, Yost Co. F, 104th NY Infantry - 1/11/1862 at Geneseo/3 yrs (Re-enlisted 1/3/1864) - 29 - 5'10", Light Complexion, Blue Eyes, Black Hair - 2/26/1862 at Geneseo - $100 - Pvt, Corp - Cedar Creek, 2nd Bull Run, Antietam, Fredericksburg, Chancellorsville, Gettysburg, Bristoe's Station, Mitchell's Station, Petersburg, Hatcher's Run, Gravelly Run, Five Forks, Appomattox - 7/7/1865 Honorable - WIA, 4/21/1864 at Mitchell's Station, gunshot to left foot - John & Cynthia Cain (Both B NY) - Cynthia, Lewis - 1832/33 in Wyoming County, Farmer/Day Laborer - Hose Factory - Sarah - Ida & Cynthia - 1884 - Alger Cemetery, Hume, State Route 19 - There was a dispute over whether he was wounded. Documents in file say both yes and no. However he was in Judiciary Square Hospital in DC. A Surgeon General statement, dated 5/5/1883, says at the time he was admitted to DeCamp G.H. at David's Island, NYC he had suffered a gunshot wound to his left foot. Promoted to Corp, 3/1/1862, to Sgt 9/1/1864. Named after his grandfather Yost. Brother Lewis also served in the war. (Military & Pension Files, Matteson, 1850 Fed. Census Eagle, 1860, 1870 Fed. Censuses Hume)

Caldwell, Addison H. Co. F, 19th NY Cavalry - 8/9/1862 at Hume, 3 yrs - 23 - 5'8", Light

Complexion, Blue Eyes, Brown Hair - 9/3/1862 at Portage Station - $150 - Pvt, Pvt - No battles - 11/5/1862 Honorable/Deceased - DD, 11/1/1862 of typhoid fever at Suffolk, VA. - James (B VT) & Betsey Frear (B NY) Caldwell - George, Andrew, Monroe, John - 3/15/1845 in Hume - Farmer - None Deceased - Never married - None - 11/5/1862 in Suffolk, VA. - Pine Grove Cemetery, Fillmore - Headstone has name as Edison and date of death as 11/4/1862. Lists age as 23 years, 7 months. If this is correct he was born in 1839 rather than 1845, as per the Allegany County Town Clerk for Hume. Burnside G.A.R. Post 237 Marker at grave. Cemetery records have date of death as 11/14. Probably date of burial. (Military Files, *History of Allegany County 1879*, Allegany County Web Site Hume, Fillmore American Legion, 1865 Allegany County Town Clerk Register Hume, 1860 Fed. Census Hume)

Caldwell, James At least one source document indicates that Caldwell served in the military during the war. No evidence of such service has been located. (Hume American Legion)

Calkins, Willard Eddy Co. F, 33rd NY Infantry - 5/13/1861 at Nunda/2 yrs - 25 - 5'10", Light Complexion, Blue Eyes, Brown Hair - 5/22/1861 at Elmira - No bounty - Pvt, Pvt - siege of Yorktown, Williamsburg, Malvern Hill, 2nd Bull Run, South Mountain, Antietam, Fredericksburg - 6/2/1863 Honorable - WIA, 5/5/1862 at Williamsburg, gunshot to right arm, POW, captured 5/5/1862 at Williamsburg, apparently released immediately. Sent to Baltimore Hospital for treatment of wound, INJ, 1/16/1863, in camp while cutting wood in the snow, slipped on a snow covered, downed tree, fell on the tree, and hurt his back - Hiram (B MA or possibly NY) & Rhoda (Polly) King (B RI) Calkins - James, Lorette, Hannah - 9/13/1835 in Hume - Raftsman - Farmer - Frances Ellen Smith, married 3/26/1865 in Castile - had 11 children, including Mary Frances, Almon H., Smith W. Wallace Heiman, Walter John, Martha Ellen, Rhoda Lucinda and Alice O. - 4/25/1914 in Hansen, ID - Twin Falls County, ID - His back injury led to kidney problems. 2nd Lt. Henry A. Hills reported that Calkins was the first man he had ever seen wounded. He said Calkins dropped "his gun when he saw the blood running from his sleeve." Calkins was a crusty guy. He chewed out the pension bureau on several occasions and in one letter called Teddy Roosevelt "Caesar." Calkins lived in at least 7 different states, NY, IL, IA, MO, KS, CO, & ID. (Military & Pension Files, 1865 NYS Census Hume, 1865 Allegany County Town Clerk Register Hume, Fillmore American Legion, 1860 Fed. Census Hume, 1910 Fed. Census Rock Creek, ID, discussions with great grandson Max Calkins)

Camp, Alonzo Co. D, 136th NY Infantry - 8/28/1862 at Pike/3 yrs - 18 - 6'1", Dark Complexion, Hazel Eyes, Black Hair - 9/25/1862 at Portage - No Bounty - Pvt, Pvt - Chancellorsville, Gettysburg, Orchard Knob, Tunnel Hill, Missionary Ridge, Resaca - 6/13/1865 Honorable - WIA, 7/2/1863 at Gettysburg, gunshot to right wrist, fractured radius & ulna of right forearm, WIA, 5/15/1864 at Resaca, gunshot to head - George (B NY) & Eliza (B VT) Camp - Henry, Griffin, Ann A., Lucy A. Seymour - 1843/44 in Yorkshire - Farmer - Cheese Factory - Lucy Vreeland married 9/6/1868 in Fillmore - INA - 6/16/1893 - Wiscoy - Was in both Totten G.H. in Louisville, KY and Satterlee G.H. in Philadelphia, PA. Originally enlisted in Co. C, 104th NY Infantry, apparently never served. Deserted 1/30/1862. Marched in the Grand Review 5/24/1865. Was a fine violin player prior to the wound to his wrist. Lived in Granger by 1891. (Military & Pension Files, 1890 Fed. Census Special Schedule Hume, Allegany County Web Site, Fillmore American Legion,

<u>Carter, George W.</u> Not from the C-H-G area. Hume Township received credit for his enlistment in Co. B, 194th NY Infantry when it paid his enlistment bonus of $450. (1865 Allegany County Town Clerk Register Hume)

<u>Cary, William H.</u> Co. I, 1st Wisconsin Infantry - 10/6/1861 at Larcade, WI/3 yrs - 21 - INA - 10/19/1861 at Milwaukee, WI - No bounty - Pvt, Pvt (Wagoner) - Granny White Pike, Perryville, Stone's River, Hoover's Gap. Chickamauga, siege of Chattanooga, Resaca, Dallas, New Hope Church, Allatoona Hills, Kenesaw, siege of Atlanta, Jonesboro - 10/13/1865 Honorable - Was not a casualty - David & Mary Cary (Both B Ireland) - Ellen, Mary Ann, Cynthia - 10/20/1840 in Fillmore - Farmer - Farmer - 1st INA, 2nd Lydia M. Wood married 9/16/1891 - Fred, Alice, William, Nina May - 5/20/1913 in St. Cloud, FL - St. Cloud, FL - Was detailed much of his service at Brigade, as a nurse, on an ambulance, as teamster etc. Lived in Fillmore until about 1882. Lived at Cheyenne County, NE until 1911 and then St. Cloud, FL First wife died 7/7/1885. (Military & Pension Files, 1865 NYS Census Hume, 1850 Fed. Census Hume, 1900 Fed. Census Sidney, NE)

<u>Caryl, Frank</u> Co. F, 4th NY Heavy Artillery - 8/22/1864 at Hume/1 yr - 18 - 5'7", Dark Complexion, Blue Eyes, Dark Hair - 9/1/1864 at Elmira - $500 - Pvt, Pvt - fall of Petersburg, Appomattox - 6/3/1865 Honorable - INJ, 11/16/1864 at Petersburg, while building a breastwork, another soldier dropped a log, causing several logs to fall on him injuring his back - William S. & Deney Wilcox Caryl (Both B VT) - Maryette, Julian, Frederick, Eugene. Loin, Willis, Horace, Roswell - 10/7 or 18/1846 in Senate, Cayuga County - Farmer - Farmer - Mary O'Neil, married 9/5/1880 in St. Joseph's Church in Buffalo, INA - 2/24/1915 in Wiscoy - Wiscoy - Marched in Grand Review 5/23/1865. Brothers Julian and Frederick also served during the war. Pension file says he died at Royal Oak, MI. Also says his mother was born in MA. (Military & Pension Files, 1865 NYS Census Hume, Matteson, 1860, 1910 Fed. Censuses Hume, *Allegany & Its People*, 1890 Fed Census Special Schedule Hume.)

<u>Caryl, Frederick W.</u> Co. F, 4th NY Heavy Artillery - 1/16/1864 at Genesee Falls/3 yrs - 23 - 6', Dark Complexion, Grey Eyes, Light Hair - 1/16/1864 at Lockport - $300 - Pvt, Pvt - Wilderness, Spotsylvania, North Anna River, Totopotomoy, Cold Harbor, siege of Petersburg, Weldon RR, Ream's Station, Peeble's Farm, Hatcher's Run, fall of Petersburg, Appomattox - 9/26/1865 Honorable - WIA, 6/18/1864 at Petersburg, gunshot to right elbow and shoulder - William S. & Deney Wilcox Caryl (Both B VT) - Maryette, Julian, Frank, Eugene, Loin, Willis, Horace, Roswell - 11/2/1840 in MA - Farmer - Farmer/Carpenter at a plumbing mill - Mary Jenette Gary, married 3/28/1869 in Hume - Demont & Jessie - 1/23/1911 in Wiscoy - Alger Cemetery, Hume, State Route 19 - Brothers Julian & Frank also served during the war. Was at Lee's surrender. Marched in Grand Review 5/23/1865. Charter Member of Burnside G.A.R. Post 237. 1865 NYS Census says parents were born in MA. (Military & Pension Files, 1890 Fed. Census Special Schedule Hume, 1860, 1880 1910 Fed. Censuses Hume, 1865 NYS Census Hume, Matteson, *Allegany & Its People*)

<u>Caryl, Julian</u> Co. C, 194th NY Infantry - 3/29/1865 at Hume/1 yr - 20 - 5'11", Fair Complexion,

Grey Eyes, Brown Hair - 4/7/1865 at Elmira - $450 - Pvt, Pvt - No battles - 5/3/1865 Honorable - Was not a casualty - William S. & Deney Wilcox Caryl (Both B VT) - Maryette, Frank, Frederick, Eugene, Loin, Willis, Horace, Roswell - 11/18/1846 at Senate, Cayuga County per Town Clerk (Pension says 11/7/1844) - Laborer - Boatman/Farmer - 1st. Sally Ann (Pratt?, died 1/17/1880 in Granger), 2nd Gertie Elizabeth Brinacombe, married 10/11/1884 in Granger - Cora Pratt, William S., Horace E, Densa F., Bertha - April,1923 - Elmer Cemetery, Rossburg, State Route19A - A soldier was only eligible for a pension after serving at least 90 days unless killed in action, wounded or injured, or contracted disease in service. Julian apparently had an infection of his left foot that made him eligible for a pension even though he served less than 90 days. Brothers Frank & Frederick also served during the war. 1870 and 1910 Censuses say parents born in VT, 1865 NYS Census says MA. Charter Member of Burnside G.A.R. Post 237. (Military & Pension Files, Fillmore American Legion, *Allegany & Its People*, Matteson, 1865 Allegany County Town Clerk Register Hume, *History of Allegany County 1879*, 1865 NYS Census Hume, 1870 Fed. Census Hume, 1880 Fed. Census Granger, 1860 Fed. Census, Vermont Township, IL [last name spelled Cary])

Caryl, William S. At least one source document indicates that Caryl served in the military during the war. No evidence of such service has been located. (Matteson, Fillmore American Legion)

Castleman, D. Clark Not from the C-H-G area. Hume Township received credit for his enlistment in Co. C, 194th NY Infantry by paying his enlistment bonus of $400. (Allegany County Town Clerk Register Hume, History of Allegany County 1879)

Chamberlain, Henry Walin. Co. D, 136th NY Infantry - 8/22/1862 at Eagle/3 yrs - 26 - 5'10", Dark Complexion, Black Eyes, Black Hair - 9/25/1862 at Portage - $50 - Pvt, Pvt - No battles - 4/15/1863 Disability/Honorable - Was not a casualty - Luther & Lucy Kendall Chamberlain (Both B NY) - Francis, Bannson, Caroline, Angeline, Milton, William, Holday, Carrol, Melonia, Horton - 10/31/1835 in China, Wyoming County - Farmer - Farmer - Mary Ann Welsh, married 2/28/1858 in Centerville, Martha, Adelbert - 12/4/1886 in Union Township, MI - Riverside Cemetery, Union Township, MI - Drafted into the 97th Infantry per the 1865 NYS Census, but never served with the 97th. There was a Henry B. Chamberlain in the 97th which may have created confusion when the records were established. Brothers William & Horton also served during the war. (Military & Pension Files, 1865 Allegany Town Clerk Register Centerville, 1865 NYS Census Centerville, 1850 Fed. Census Centerville, 1860 Fed. Census Eagle, 1870 Fed. Census Granger, 1910 Fed Census MI)

Chamberlain, Hiram At least one source document indicates that a Hiram Chamberlain served in the military during the war. No evidence of such service has been located. (Register of Draftees July 1863 to October, 1864 - Centerville)

Chamberlain, Horton Co D, 1st NY Veteran Cavalry - 9/23/1863 at Nunda/3 yrs - 18 - 5'8", Dark Complexion, Black Eyes, Black Hair - 10/10/1863 at Geneva - $100 - Snicker's Gap, New Market - 7/12/1864 Deceased/Honorable - POW, captured 5/15/1864 at New Market, VA, Prison: Andersonville, DD, 7/12/1864 at Andersonville of dysentery - Luther & Lucy Kendall Chamberlain

(Both B NY) - Francis, Bannson, Caroline, Angeline, Milton, William, Holday, Carrol, Melonia Henry - 1844 or 45 in China, Wyoming County - Farmer - None/Deceased - Never Married - None - admitted to Andersonville prison hospital 6/4/1864, died 7/12/1864 in Andersonville - Andersonville - Brothers Henry & William also served during the war. (Military File, 1865 NYC Census Granger, 1860 Fed. Census Centerville)

Chamberlain, Joseph Marion Co. I, 160th NY Infantry - 9/5/1862 at Allen/3 yrs 18 - 5'5", Light Complexion, Blue Eyes, Brown Hair - 11/21/1862 at Auburn - $100 - Pvt, Corp - Gunboat Cotton, assault on Port Hudson - 11/1/1865 Honorable - Was not a casualty - Robert Hubbert & Sarah Allerton Chamberlain (Both B NY) - Joanna, Stephen, Robert, Edwin, Adam, Sarah, George & Philip P. - 4/14/1846 in Belfast - Farmer - Farm Laborer - 1st Frances E. Simpson, married 3/31/1869 in Oramel (Frances was 14.), 2nd Belle Waits - James Roberts & Mary Edith - 8/1/1877 near Augustus, KY - maybe Augustus, KY or maybe Starksville, NY - Father Robert & brother Stephen also served during the war. Marched in the Grand Review 5/23/1865. Lived in Fillmore from 1869 to 1874. Not sure he ever divorced Frances. Was shot to death by a Stephen Waits for imposing on his daughter and marrying her without his permission. There was some question as to whether the Kentucky Joseph was the Fillmore Joseph, but an investigation by the U.S. Pension Bureau determined they were the same person. Pension says he is buried in KY, but Belle said his brother "Harvey" gave her $800 to let him take the body back to "Skateland," NY. The problem is that , as far as can be determined, Joseph did not have a brother Harvey. He did have a brother named Robert Hurlburt Chamberlain. If the Pension Bureau is right, then Belle was not telling the truth. There are indications that the Pension Bureau didn't really trust or believe Belle. His pension says that he was living in Fillmore in 1870, but he appears in the 1870 Census for Belfast. He may have been working in Belfast, and was there when the census was taken. (Military & Pension Files, 1850, 1860 Fed. Censuses Allen, 1865 Allegany County Town Clerk Register Allen, *Allegany & Its People*, 1870 Fed. Census Belfast)

Chamberlain, Robert Hurlburt Co. I, 160th NY Infantry - 9/6/1862 at Allen/3 yrs - 37 - 5'10", Dark Complexion, Black Eyes, Black Hair - 11/21/1862 at Auburn - $100 - Corp, Pvt - Gunboat Cotton, Bayou Teche, Camp Bisland - 5/23/1864 Disability/Honorable - Was not a casualty - David (death certificate lists Moses who was his brother) & Mary Kinney Chamberlain -Hepsabeth, Moses Van Campen (possibly the first white male born in Angelica), Elizabeth, Elisha, Prudence, Mary, David, Simon, Lucy, & Robert H. - 11/6/1824 in Belfast - Farmer - Farmer - 1st Sarah Allerton (died 6/22 1888), 2nd (Maybe) Cordova Young, 3rd Frances Caroline Faning, married 7/1/1890 in Fillmore - Joanna, Stephen, Robert, Edwin, Sarah, George, Joseph, & Philip P. - 2/15/1905 in Fillmore - Pine Grove Cemetery Fillmore - Military records state that " he showed good character while in the hospital", nevertheless he was reduced from corporal to private on 12/15/1864 while still in the hospital. Was discharged from Marine Hospital, LA. In a letter he wrote he said that, following the battle of Camp Bisland they were so tired they laid down to sleep in water which covered all but one shoulder and their heads. Sons Joseph & Stephen also served during the war, Burnside G.A.R. Post 237 Marker at grave. (Military & Pension Files, Matteson, 1865 Allegany County Town Clerk Register Allen, *Allegany & Its People*, 1890 Fed Census Special Schedule Allen, Fillmore American Legion, 1850, 1870 Fed. Censuses Allen)

Chamberlain, Stephen A. Co. G, 16th NY Cavalry - 7/30/1863 at Rochester/3 yrs - 18 - 5'6", Light Complexion, Blue Eyes, Brown Hair - 8/13/1863 at Plattsburgh - No bounty - Pvt, Pvt - No battles - 1/16/1864 Honorable/Deceased - DD, of typhoid fever at Brigade Hospital, Vienna, VA - Robert H. & Sarah Allerton Chamberlain (Both B NY) - Joanna, Stephen, Joseph, Edwin, Adam, Sarah, George & Philip P. - 1844 or 45 in Allegany County, Farmer - None Deceased - Never Married - None - 1/16/1864 in Vienna, VA - Arlington National Cemetery - Father Robert & brother Joseph also served during the war. He had extensive effects per military file. No indication of disposition. (Military & Pension Files, *Allegany & Its People*, 1850, 1860 Fed Census Allen)

Chamberlain, William Nelson Co C, 89th NY Infantry - 9/3/1861 at Mt. Morris/3 yrs (Reenlisted 1/14/1864) - 21 - 5'11", Dark Complexion, Grey Eyes, Brown Hair - 10/7/1861 at Elmira - No bounty - Pvt, Sgt - Camden, South Mountain, Antietam, Fredericksburg, Rappahannock, Nansemond River, Ware Church, Cold Harbor, Petersburg - 9/11/1865 Honorable - WIA, 9/17/1862 at Antietam (Sharpsburg, MD), slight gunshot wound (where not identified) - Luther & Lucy Kendall Chamberlain (Both B NY) - Francis, Bannson, Caroline, Angeline, Milton, Holday, Carrol, Melonia, Henry, Horton - 1/14/1840 (per Town Clerk), 2/29/1840 (per Pension) in China, Wyoming County - Laborer - Farmer - 1st Lorna S, Crane, married 12/24/1866 in Freedom (died 7/31/1874), 2nd Mary Faulkner, married 8/22/1877 in Wellsville - Nora, Tyrell, Bertie - 8/10/1917 in Dalton - Church Street Cemetery, Dalton - Was a hospital steward for a time during the war. In Ft. Monroe Hospital with debilitating diarrhea as of 9/17/1864. Had same problem in 1862 and was in 89th Regimental Hospital. His brothers Henry & Horton also served during the war. Lived in Granger during the 1870's. (Military & Pension Files, Medical Cards, 1865 NYS Census Granger, 1850 Fed. Census Centerville, 1870 Fed. Census Granger)

Chase, Andrew Actually Augustus Andrew Chase. See below. Listed as Andrew in Civil War soldiers section of 1865 NYS Census. (1865 NYS Census Centerville)

Chase, Augustus Andrew Co. D, 4th NY Heavy Artillery - 12/28/1863 at Hume/3 yrs - 18 - 5'8", Light Complexion, Blue Eyes, Brown Hair - 12/28/1863 - $300 - Pvt, Pvt - Wilderness, Spotsylvania - 5/19/1864 Honorable/Deceased - POW, captured 5/19/1864 at Spotsylvania, Prison Salisbury, NC - DD, Allegany County Town Clerk says he died at Salisbury. He was never found which was true for a lot of prisoners who died of disease at Salisbury. - Jacob M & Emeline Tucker Chase (Both B NY) - Sidney, Alice, Osland - 3/2/1846 in Castile - Laborer - None Deceased - Never Married - None - Actual date of death unknown. Date used, 5/19/1864, is the date he disappeared. Probably died at Salisbury, NC Prison - Probably Salisbury National Cemetery - Brother Sidney also served during the war. Two files for Augustus at National Archive. One shows him enlisting 5/30/1863 at Rochester. Deserted same day, nothing more. Based on his birth date he was too young in May, but he was still too young in December, although he gave his age as 18 at enlistment. His other military file provides basic enlistment information, plus that he was MIA at Spotsylvania. The information about Salisbury is contained in the Town Clerk's files. There is no pension file. (Military File, 1865 Allegany County Town Clerk Register Hume, Allegany County Web Site - 1865 NYS Census Centerville, 1860 Fed. Census New Hudson, Wyoming County Vital Records 1847 - 1851)

Chase, Elisha H. Co. G, 8th NY Cavalry - 3/20/1865 at Rochester/3 yrs - 22 - 5'6", Fair Complexion, Blue Eyes, Brown Hair - 3/20/1865 At Rochester - $300 - Pvt, Pvt - Dinwiddie Court House, Five Forks, Appomattox - No discharge date in file/probably mustered out with rest of regiment on 6/27/1865 Honorable - Was not a casualty - Elisha (B NY) & Martha Smith (B NJ) Chase - John, Lucinda - About 1840 in Portage - Tailor/Farmer - Laborer/Grocery Man - Melissa A. - Florence, Myra - INA - Pine Grove Cemetery, Fillmore - Brother John also served during the war. Was present at Lee's surrender. Marched in Grand Review 5/23/1865. (Military File, 1860 Fed. Census Hume, 1870 Fed. Census Burns, Fillmore American Legion, 1880 Fed. Census Hornell)

Chase, John Paul Co. F, 19th NY Cavalry - 8/13/1862 at Oramel/3 yrs - 22 - 5'9", Light Complexion, Grey Eyes, Black Hair - 9/3/1862 at Portage Station - $175 - Pvt, Pvt - No battles - 12/3/1862 Deceased/Honorable - DD, 12/3/1862 of typhoid fever & dysentery - Elisha (B NY) & Martha Smith (B NJ) Chase - Elisha & Lucinda - 10/14/1838 at Phelps, Ontario County, NY - Farmer - None Deceased - Never Married - None - 12/31/1862 in Suffolk, VA- Pine Grove Cemetery, Fillmore - Dr. William M. Smith of Granger recorded in his diary (later the book *Swamp Doctor*), that he embalmed Chase on Thursday, 12/4/1862. Brother Elisha also served during the war. Burnside G.A.R. Post 237 Marker at grave. (Military & Pension Files, 1865 Allegany Town Clerk Registers Oramel and Allen, Matteson, 1850 Fed. Census Allen)

Chase, Sidney M. Co. D, 4th NY Heavy Artillery - 1/12/1864 at Centerville/3 yrs - 20 - 5'10", Light Complexion, Blue Eyes, Brown Hair - 1/12/1864 at Elmira - $300 - Pvt, Pvt - Wilderness, Spotsylvania - 9/1/1864 Honorable/Deceased - POW, captured 5/19/1864 at Spotsylvania, Prison: Andersonville, DD, 9/1/1864 at Andersonville of starvation & exposure - Jacob M. & Emeline Tucker Chase (Both B NY) - Augustus, Alice, Osland - 1843/44 in Warsaw - Peddler - None deceased - Never Married - None - 9/1/1864 in Andersonville - Andersonville - His prison number was 10369. Brother Augustus also served during the war. Sister Alice Chase Thompson of Sheridan, MI received his pension. (Military & Pension Files, 1865 NYS Census Centerville, 1865 Allegany County Town Clerk Register Centerville , 1860 Fed. Census New Hudson)

Cheney, Herbert W. Co C, 19th NY Cavalry/Detached most of service to Co. G, 7th Independent Battery, Massachusetts Light Artillery, (also detached to Co. C, 136th NY Infantry) - 8/11/1862 at Eagle/3 yrs (Reenlisted 9/2/1864 at Eagle) - 20 - 5'9", Light Complexion, Dark Eyes, Light Hair - 9/3/1862 at Portage Station - $100 - Pvt, Pvt - Suffolk with 19th Cav, [battle information not available for MA, LA, nor 136th Inf.] - 6/21/1865 Disability/ Honorable - Was not a casualty - Simon & Mary Lewis Cheney (Both B NH) - INA -1/2/1842 in Freedom - Farmer - Farmer - Emily M. Chamberlain, married 10/19/1870 in Centerville - INA -5/8/1911 in Centerville - Centerville Cemetery, Route 3, no headstone - First disability discharge 10/30/1863 from Ladies Home Hospital, NYC. His doctor called him a man worn down. Second disability based on chronic diarrhea. 1860 census says father was born in MA. (Military & Pension Files, 1890 Fed. Census Special Schedule Centerville, Matteson, Centerville American Legion, 1850 Fed. Census Freedom, 1860 Fed. Census Eagle, 1870, 1880, 1910 Fed. Censuses Centerville)

Chillson, Daniel Co. F, 33rd NY Infantry - 5/13/1861 at Granger/2 yrs - 29 - 5'10", Dark

Complexion, Grey Eyes, Black Hair - 5/22/1861 at Elmira - No bounty - Pvt, Pvt - No battles - 4/21/1862 Honorable/Deceased - DD, 4/21/1862 at U.S.G.H. Mansion House, Alexandria, VA of inflamation of the bowels - William (B VT) & Margaret T. Passage (B NY) Chillson - Hannah, Devinia, Calvin - 1841/42 in Bennington, Wyoming County - Farm Laborer - None Deceased - Never Married - None - 4/21/1862 in Alexandria, VA - Alexandria National Cemetery - Listed on Soldiers Monument in Granger. Military files are under the name David Chillson. (Military & Pension Files, *Allegany & Its People*, Granger American Legion, Matteson, 1860 Fed. Census Granger, 1865 NYS Census Granger)

Clark, Andrew Co. E, 104th NY Infantry - 2/3/1862 at Geneseo/3 yrs - 41 - 5'11", Dark Complexion, Blue Eyes, Brown Hair - 2/26/1862 at Geneseo - No bounty - Pvt, Pvt - Cedar Creek, 2nd Bull Run, South Mountain, Antietam, Fredericksburg - 2/8/1864 Disability/Honorable - Was not a casualty - Cornelius & Catherine Pettengill Clark (Both B NY) - INA - 7/16/1821 in Elbridge, Onondaga County - Farmer - Laborer - Mary Colburn - George N., Mary A., C. Benjamin, Addison A., Oliver A. Frances A. - 10/1/1898 in Hume - Pine Grove Cemetery, Fillmore - Chronic diarrhea was basis for discharge. Transferred to 129th Co., 2nd. Battalion, VRC 8/1/1863. Son George also served during the war. (Military & Pension Files, Fillmore American Legion, 1865 Allegany County Town Clerk Register Hume, 1865 NYS Census Hume, 1860, 1870, 1880 Fed. Censuses Hume, 1890 Fed. Census Special Schedule Hume, descendant Wilfred Vasile)

Clark, Daniel J. Identified while researching military file for Daniel O. Clark. Appeared to be from C-H-G. Research showed he was from surrounding area, but apparently never lived in C-H-G.

Clark, Daniel Orville Co. H, 136th NY Infantry - 8/25/1862 at Genesee Falls/3 yrs - 20 - 5'9", Dark Complexion, Black Eyes, Black Hair - 9/25/1862 at Portage - No bounty - Pvt, Pvt - Chancellorsville, Gettysburg, Wauhatchie, Orchard Knob, Tunnel Hill, Missionary Ridge, others, was with Sherman on his march through Georgia - 6/13/1865 Honorable - INJ, February or March,1865 near Atlanta, mule jumped on him hurting spine and side - Daniel & Betsey Clark (Both B NY) - Henry, Helen, George, David - 9/13/1842 (1843 per headstone) in Granger - Probably a farm laborer working for his Father - Farmer - Mary Ellen? Bradley, married 8/6/1868 - Bruce, Merton, Bertha, Blanche, Ernest - 3/22/1930 in Fillmore - Short Tract Cemetery, County Route 4 - Military Index File lists him as David O. Clark. Became Brigade Corps Teamster in January, 1864. Present at surrender of Johnston Army. Marched in Grand Review 5/24/1865. Wife was previously married to Charles Nathan Bradley who died as a POW. (Military & Pension Files, Matteson, Granger American Legion, 1865 Allegany County Town Clerk Register Granger, *History of Allegany County 1879*, 1865 NYS Census Granger, 1860 Fed. Census Granger, 1870 Fed. Census Allen)

Clark, George Nathaniel Co. E, 104th NY Infantry - 2/3/1862 at Geneseo/3 yrs (Reenlisted 2/27/1864 at Mitchell's Station, Va.) - 19 - 5'5", Light Complexion, Blue Eyes, Dark Hair - 2/26/1862 at Geneseo - $400 - Pvt, 2nd Corp - Cedar Creek, 2nd Bull Run, South Mountain, Antietam, Fredericksburg, Chancellorsville, Gettysburg, Bristoe's Station, Wilderness, Spotsylvania Court House, North Anna River, Pamunkey, Totopotomoy, Cold Harbor, Bethesda Church, Petersburg, Weldon RR - 7/17/1865 Honorable - Was not a casualty - Andrew & Mary

Colburn Clark (Both B NY) - Mary A., C. Benjamin, Addison M., Oliver A., Frances A. -
1/10/1842 in Hume - Farm Laborer - Laborer - Mary Louise Close, married 10/17/1872 in
Northport, WI - Daisy Mae (Marvin), Lottie Effie, Anna A., Minnie Adell - 6/3/1887 in Hume -
Pine Grove Cemetery Fillmore - Was in Mt. Pleasant Hospital, DC and City Point Hospital, VA.
Had scarlet fever as a boy. Middle name was after his mother's father who was from Scotland.
Father Andrew also served during the war. (Military & Pension Files, Fillmore American Legion,
1865 Allegany County Town Clerk Register Hume, Matteson, 1865 NYS Census Hume, 1860
Fed. Census Hume, descendant Wilfred Vasile)

Clark, Hiram Co. L, 4th NY Heavy Artillery - 12/23/1863 at Hume/3 yrs - 18 - 5'6", Fair
Complexion, Grey Eyes, Light Hair - 12/23/1863 at Elmira - $300 - Pvt, Pvt - Wilderness,
Spotsylvania, North Anna River, Totopotomoy, Cold Harbor, siege of Petersburg, Weldon RR,
Peeble's Farm, Hatcher's Run, fall of Petersburg, Appomattox - 9/27/1865 Honorable - Was not a
casualty - Lyman & Elizabeth (Eunice) Haywood Clark (Both B NY) - Elizabeth, Ida, Milton -
11/7/1844 in Hume, Farmer - Farmer - 1st Cynthia D. Hamer married 7/3/1869 (Died 12/9/1872),
2nd Mary Jane Moore, married 10/25/1876 in Portageville - Roy & Ray (twins), Sarah Eunice,
2/20/1905 in Hume - Bates Cemetery, Centerville - Originally volunteered 5/3/63 or 6/21/63 at
Rochester. He apparently deserted. Per a 5/1/1888 notation in his military file, this desertion was
erased from his record. Present at Lee's surrender. Marched in Grand Review 5/23/1865. Charter
Member & Officer of Burnside G.A.R. Post 237. Grandparents, Silas & Sarah Clark were from
Massachusetts. (Military & Pension Files, 1890 Fed. Census Special Schedule Hume, *Allegany &
Its People*, 1865 Allegany County Town Clerk Register Hume, Centerville American Legion,
Matteson, 1865 NYS Census Hume, 1850, 1880 Fed. Censuses Hume)

Clark, Joel B. Co. F, 19th NY Cavalry - 9/1/1864 at Allen/1 yr - 31 - 5'10", Light Complexion,
Blue Eyes, Light Hair - 9/13/1864 at Elmira - $300 - Pvt, Pvt - No battles, 6/30/1865 Honorable -
Was not a casualty - Henry & Oliver Mariah Clark (Both B NY) - Amas, Clarsisa, Albert, Mary E.
- 2/20/1833 in Allen - Lumberman/Farmer - Farmer - Matilda Ann Harris, married 2/20/1860 in
Allen - Emerson A., Albert P., Lewis A., Orme C., Omer A., Ina D. - 5/9/1917 in Oramel - Short
Tract Cemetery - Retained his pistol & sabre at discharge. Marched in Grand Review 5/23/1865.
Town Clerk has birth as 11/17/1840. (Military & Pension Files, *History of Allegany County 1879*,
1890 Fed. Census Special Schedule Granger, 1850 Fed. Census Allen, 1865 Allegany County
Town Clerk Register Allen, 1880 Fed. Census Granger)

Clark, Simeon B. Co. B, 92nd NY Infantry - 9/23/1862 at Hermon/3 yrs - 40 - 5'5", Fair
Complexion, Auburn Hair, Hazel Eyes - 10/23/1862 at Albany - No bounty - Pvt, Pvt - No battles
- 6/1/1864 Disability/Honorable - INJ, 11/6/1862, right knee, caused by fall between two pieces of
timber while on a night march from Suffolk to Black Water, VA - INA - INA - per pension, 1820
in Roxbury, VT (1865 NYS Census says Oswego, Otsego County), - Chair Maker/Painter -
Farmer - Julie E. Minor (B1827/28) - Asher, Wait C. - 1896 - Pine Grove Cemetery, Fillmore -
Sick at New Bern, NC several months. Burnside G.A.R. Post 237 Marker at grave. (Military &
Pension Files, 1865 NYS Census Hume, Matteson, Fillmore American Legion, 1860, 1870 Fed.
Censuses Hume)

Claus, John W. Co. F, 5th NY Cavalry - 9/13/1861 at Hume/3 yrs - 19 - INA - 9/21/1861 at, probably, NYC - No bounty - Pvt, Pvt - New Market, Port Republic, Culpeper, Orange County Court House, 2nd Bull Run - 8/29/1862 Honorable/Deceased - KIA at 2nd Bull Run, 8/29/1862 - William & Lucinda (B NY) Klock Claus - Mary, Delphonia, Phidelia, Gertrude, Lucinda - 1/7/1842 in Hume - Farm Laborer - None Deceased - Never Married - None - 8/29/1862 in Bull Run, VA - Buried on battle field - Army carried him as John W. Closs. Worked for a William Couch before the war. (Military File, Allegany County Web Site, *History of Allegany County 1879*, 1865 Allegany County Town Clerk Register Hume, 1860 Fed. Census Hume)

Clement, Jacob Trunell (Clemont) Co. F, 19th NY Cavalry - 8/13/1862 at Portageville/3 yrs - 22 - 5'11", Light Complexion, Hazel Eyes - Brown Hair - 9/3/1862 at Portage Station - $100 - Pvt, Pvt - Deserted House, siege of Suffolk, Manassas Junction, Bristoe's Station, Culpeper Court House, Wilderness, Todd's Tavern, Spotsylvania, North Anna River, Yellow Tavern, Pamunkey, Totopotomoy, Cold Harbor, Trevillian Station, Charles County Court House, before Richmond & Petersburg, New Market, Shepherdstown, Winchester, Fisher's Hill, Port Republic, Cedar Creek, Berryville, Gordonsville, Dinwiddie Court House, Five Forks, Appomattox - 6/30/1865 Honorable - Was not a casualty - Cyrus (B NH) & Polly Herrick (B VT) Clement - Lorenzo, Lucia, Phidelia, Caroline - 1839 or 40 at Houghton - Farmer - Farmer - R. Electa Wilson, married 2/12/1873 in Caneadea - Mary, Ruth, Louise - 2/24/1910 in Houghton - Mount Pleasant Cemetery, Houghton - Present at Lee's surrender. Marched in Grand Review 5/23/1865. Retained his pistol and sabre at discharge. (Military & Pension Files, *History of Allegany County 1879*, Fillmore American Legion, 1860, 1900 Fed. Censuses Caneadea)

Close, John W. Actually John W. Claus. Some source documents have it as Close. (History of Allegany County 1879)

Clough, Clarence Melville Co. F, 5th NY Cavalry - 9/13/1861 at Hume/3 yrs - 19 - 5'10", Light Complexion, Blue Eyes, Brown Hair - 9/21/1861 at NYC - No bounty - Pvt, Pvt - No battles - 5/29/1862 Disability/Honorable - Was not a casualty - Asher & Emily Cough (Both B NY) - INA - 1841/42 in Nunda - Farmer - Saw Mill - Sarah Jane - Caroline, Herbert, Alta - 9/10/1916 in Muir, MI - INA - Discharged at Winchester, VA. Also served with 19th New York Cavalry, see below. 1860 Census has Melville as first name. (Military File, *History of Allegany County 1879*, 1870 Fed. Census Birdsall, 1850 Fed. Census Nunda, 1880, 1900 Fed. Census MI. Ionia County)

Clough, Clarence Melville Co. D, 19th NY Cavalry (1st NY Dragoons) - 8/17/1863 at Almond/3 yrs - 21 - 5'10", Light Complexion, Blue Eyes, Brown Hair - 8/29/1863 at Elmira - $100 - Wilderness, Todd's Tavern, Spotsylvania, North Anna River, Cold Harbor, Trevillian Station, Malvern Hill, Shepherdstown, Cedar Creek, Fisher's Hill, New Market, Dinwiddie Court House, Five Forks, Appomattox Court House - 6/30/1865 Honorable - Was not a casualty - Present at Lee's surrender. Marched in Grand Review 5/23/1865. Also served with Co. D, 19th NY Cavalry, see above. Also see above for personal information and sources of information.

Cluchey, William Co. D, 136th NY Infantry - 8/28/1862 at Pike/3 yrs - 21 - 5'10", Dark Complexion, Black Eyes, Black Hair, Scar at base of nose - 9/25/1862 at Portage - $100 - Pvt, Pvt

- Chancellorsville, Gettysburg, Wauhatchie, Orchard Knob, Tunnel Hill, Missionary Ridge, Resaca - 4/27/1865 Disability/Honorable - WIA, 5/15/1864 at Resaca, minnie ball to thigh - Lewis & Jane Clutchey (Both B Ireland) - Thomas, Mary A., George - Probably 1845/46 in Holley, Orleans County - Farmer - Laborer - Amelia E. Elmer, married 5/1867 in Hume - INA - 4/29/1909 - Ridgelawn Cemetery, Buffalo - 1860 Census has age as 14. Must have lied when he volunteered. Originally enlisted in Co. C, 104th NY Infantry on 12/15/1861 at Geneseo for 3 years. Gave age as 19, and said he was born in Portage. Deserted 3/20/1862. 104th file states that he reenlisted in 136th Infantry. Father Lewis also served during the war. Charter Member of Burnside G.A.R. Post 237. April 14, 1863 Muster Card has him under arrest in confinement in Alexandria, VA hospital. No other information. Muster card would have covered March, 1863. Muster card most likely wrong. Was sick in Alexandria Hospital from 10/1862 to 3/1863. As a result of wound, he was in Ashville, NC , Jeffersonville, IN, and Cleveland, OH hospitals. Got gangrene in one hospital. Discharged at Cleveland. 1870 and 1880 censuses spell name Cluchy. One record says parents were born in Canada. (Military & Pension Files, *Allegany & Its People*, 1860, 1870 Fed. Censuses Pike, 1880 Fed. Census Hume)

Clute, James Co. B, 188th NY Infantry - 9/16/1864 at Victor/1 yr - 22 - 6', Light Complexion, Blue Eyes, Light Hair - 10/7/1864 at Rochester - $100 - Pvt, Pvt - siege of Petersburg, Hatcher's Run, Weldon RR, Gravelly Run, Five Forks, Appomattox - 7/1/1865 Honorable - Was not a casualty - William (B NY) & Polly Stone Clute - Samuel, William H., Angelina M., 6/20/1842 or 43 in Springwater, Livingston County - Farmer - Farmer/Cemetery Sexton - 1st Hannah Havens , married 1867 in Grove, 2nd Bethania Melvinia Ranney, married 5/5/1869 in Wayland - Rosa Jane, Charles Henry, James Floyd, Dollie Irene (Mrs. Justus F. Pero) - 5/28/1919 in Fillmore - Pine Grove Cemetery, Fillmore - Present at Lee's surrender. Marched in Grand Review 5/23/1865. By 1860 his father was married to a Anna Maria. (Military & Pension Files, 1890 Fed. Census Special Schedule Hume, 1860, 1870 Fed. Censuses Grove, 1910 Fed. Census Hume)

Cole, George Henry Co. J, 4th NY Heavy Artillery - 12/26/1863 at Granger/3 yrs - 28 - 5'7", Fair Complexion, Blue Eyes, Brown Hair - 12/26/1863 at Elmira - $100 - Pvt, Pvt - Wilderness, Spotsylvania, North Anna River, Totopotomoy, Cold Harbor, siege of Peterburg, Weldon RR, Ream's Station - 9/26/1864 Honorable/Deceased - DD, 9/26/1864 at Lincoln Hospital, DC of chronic diarrhea - INA - INA - 1835 in Fair Haven, VT - Farm Laborer - None Deceased - Sarah Ann Worden, married 4/24/1856 in Granger - Lenora Annette & Samantha Adele - 9/26/1864 in Lincoln G. H., DC - Short Tract, County Route 4 - Listed on Soldiers Monument in Granger. (Military & Pension Files, Matteson, 1865 NYS Census Granger, Granger American Legion, 1865 Allegany County Town Clerk Register Granger, *Allegany & Its People*,1860 Fed. Census Granger)

Colegrove. 1890 Fed Census Special Schedule Hume lists only a last name. Lists wife as Ella. She claimed he served, but no records for a C-H-G Colegrove have been identified.

Collins, Michael Co E, 85th NY Infantry - 9/1/1861 at Granger/3 yrs - 40 - 5'6", Light Complexion, Blue Eyes, Black Hair - 10/16/1861 at Elmira - No bounty - Pvt, Pvt - defense of DC, siege of Yorktown, Williamsburg, before Richmond, Fair Oaks - 10/8/1862 Disability/Honorable - WIA, 6/1/1862 at Fair Oaks, shell wound to left hip - INA (Both B Ireland)

- INA - 1814/15 in Mallin Town, County Donegal, Ireland - Catherine Gallagher, married 1/12/1834 in Mallin, Ireland - John, Elizabeth, Margaret, William, Matilda, James, Michael, Mary - 12/17/1882 - Cottage Bridge Road Cemetery, Scio - Collins lived in Angelica before the war. Understated his age when he enlisted. 1850 Census has him as 35, making him 46 in 1861. (Military & Pension Files, 1865 Allegany County Town Clerk Register Angelica, Matteson, *History of Allegany County 1879*, 1850 Fed. Census Angelica, 1880 Fed. Census Hume)

Conron, Edward Co. C, 194th NY Infantry - 3/29/1865 at Hume/1 yr - 18 - 5'5", Fair Complexion, Blue Eyes, Brown Hair - 4/7/1865 at Elmira - $800 - Pvt, Pvt - No battles - 5/3/1865 Honorable - Was not a casualty - James & Ann Cunningham Conron (Both B Ireland) - Margarette, Mary A., Andrew J., Francis M.T. - 8/17/1847 in Ireland - Laborer - Moulder/State Gate Tender, City Water Works - Mary, married 1880 - Ann - INA - INA - Military records are under the name Edward Connor. Arrived in U.S. in 1852. (Military File, 1865 NYS Census Hume, 1865 Allegany County Town Clerk Register Hume, *History of Allegany County 1879*, Matteson, 1860 Fed. Census Hume, 1900, 1910 Fed. Censuses Skaneateles, Onondaga County)

Cook, Frank Marion Co. F, 4th NY Heavy Artillery - 8/27/1862 at Hume/3 yrs - 19 - 5'9", Light Complexion, Blue Eyes, Brown Hair - 8/29/1862 at NYC - $25 - Pvt, Pvt - Wilderness, Spotsylvania, North Anna River, Totopotomoy - Cold Harbor - siege of Petersburg - Weldon RR, Ream's Station - 2/11/1865 Honorable/Deceased - POW, captured 8/25/1864 at Reams Station, Prison: Richmond, VA, Salisbury, NC - DD, 2/11/1865 at Salisbury, NC of diarrhea - Nelson & Amalia Cook (Both B NY) - Mary M., Charles, Volney, John - 1842/43 in Allegany County - Laborer - None Deceased - Never Married - None - 2/11/1865 in Salisbury, NC - Probably Salisbury National Cemetery - Listed on Soldiers Monument in Granger. (Military File, 1865 NYS Census Granger, Matteson, 1865 Allegany County Town Clerk Register Granger, *Allegany & Its People*, 1860 Fed. Census Granger, *Roll of Honor*)

Cooley, Andrew W. Co. C, 104th NY Infantry - 10/30/1861 at Geneseo/3 yrs - 18 - 5'11", Light Complexion, Grey Eyes, Light Hair, Scar on right wrist - 2/26/1862 at Geneseo - No bounty - Pvt, Pvt - No battles - 5/16/1862 - Honorable/Deceased - DD, 5/16/1862 at Father's home in Hume on leave from disease acquired in service (specific disease not mentioned in files.) - Alfred (B NY) & Nancy Kingsley Cooley - Jerome, Albert, Orlando, Ellie - 7/7/1843 in Hume, Farmer - None Deceased - Never Married - None - 5/16/1862 in Hume - Elmer Cemetery Rossburg (No headstone) - Birth date of 5/1843 would make him 19 when he entered service. However the 1860 Census shows his age as 15, making him only 16 when he enlisted and not quite 17 when he was mustered. The Town Clerk Register lists Nancy Kingsley as his mother. Alfred's wife's name in the 1850 Census is Julie and in the1860 Census it is Emmanda. (Military File, 1865 NYS Census Hume, 1850, 1860 Fed. Censuses Hume, Allegany County Web Site, 1865 Allegany County Town Clerk Register Hume)

Coolidge, Augustus Eugene Co. A, 19th NY Infantry - 3/11865 at Hume/3 yrs 18 - 5'2", Fair Complexion, Grey Eyes, Brown Hair - 3/29/1865 at Elmira - $,100 - Pvt, Pvt - No battles - 5/3/1865 Honorable - Was not a casualty - Erasmus & Mary Elizabeth Curtis Coolidge (Both B NY) - Mary L., William W., George E. - 7/23/1848 in Hume - INA - INA INA - INA - Did not serve long enough to be eligible for a pension. Brother George also served during the war. (Military File, 1860 Fed. Census Hume, 1865 Allegany County Town Clerk Register Hume)

Coolidge, George Co. C, 104th NY Infantry - 8/11/1864 at Pike/3 yrs - 17 - 5'5", Fair Complexion, Hazel Eyes, Brown Hair - 8/24/1864 at Lockport - No bounty - Pvt, Pvt - Ream's Station - 5/11/1865 Honorable/Deceased - POW, captured 10/20/1864 at Ream's Station, Prison: Richmond, paroled 2/5/1865 at Coxes Wharf, DD, 5/10/1865 at Annapolis Hospital of meningitis - Erasmus & Mary Elizabeth Curtis Coolidge (Both B NY) - Augustus E., Mary L. William W. - 2/9/1847 in Hume - Farmer - None Deceased - Never Married - None - 5/11/1865 in Annapolis, MD - Annapolis National Cemetery (as Coolage) - Brother Augustus also served during the war. George was either drafted or about to be drafted, when he became a substitute for Eli Platt Sweet of Pike. Was carried as a deserter for a time until it was learned he was actually a POW. May have actually died 5/10/65. (Military File, 1865 Allegany County Town Clerk Register Hume, 1850 Fed. Census Hume)

Cooper, Harvey L. Co. F, 4th NY Heavy Artillery - 8/27/1862 at Hume/3 yrs - 22 - 5'7", Dark Complexion, Black Eyes, Black Hair - 8/29/1862 at NYC - $100 - Pvt, Pvt - Wilderness, Spotsylvania, North Anna River, Totopotomoy, Cold Harbor, siege of Petersburg, Weldon RR, Ream's Station - 5/29/1865 Honorable - POW, captured 8/25/1864 at Ream's Station, Prison, Richmond - paroled Vienna, VA 9/24/1864 - Joel & Ona Blair Cooper (Both B MA) - John E., Rosalie H., George F. Orin P., Jeremiah P. - 12/27/1845 in Hume, Farmer - Farmer - Rosan Morgan Helmer, married 9/27/1865 in Granger (Rosan had previously been married to a Clarkson Helmer who died in the war.) - Clara, Olivia, Orville H., Ruth, Clark E. Cora C. - 5/27/1892, possible Lake View , MI. INA - Was in Ralliston Hospital in Annapolis. Age when entering service not consistent with birth date. (Military & Pension Files, 1865 NYS Census Hume, 1865 Allegany County Town Clerk Register Hume, 1850 Fed. Census Hume, 1870 Fed. Census Caneadea)

Cowing, James Randolph Co. F, 4th NY Heavy Artillery - 12/21/1863 at Hume/3 yrs - 29 - 5'9", Fair Complexion, Blue Eyes, Light Hair - 12/29/1863 at Elmira - $300 - Pvt, Pvt - Wilderness, Spotsylvania, North Anna River, Totopotomoy, Cold Harbor, siege of Petersburg, Weldon RR, Ream's Station, Peeble's Farm, Hatcher's Run, fall of Peterburg, Appomattox - 6/5/1865 Honorable - Was not a casualty - Warren & Julia Nye Cowing (Both B NY) - Cornelia - 10/20/1835 in Hume - Farmer - Managed a Boarding House - Margarite Isted, married 7/2/1857 in Oramel - James, Frank, Clarence, Ned, Jennie - 2/28/1892 in Menomomie, WI - Menomomie, WI - Charged with desertion 1/7/1865, late reporting back from a furlough. Present at Lee's surrender. Marched in Grand Review 5/23/1865. Was in City Point, VA hospital and Columbia G.H. in DC with diaarhea. (Military & Pension Files, 1865 NYS Census Hume, 1865 Allegany County Town Clerk Register Hume, 1850 Fed. Census Hume, 1880 Fed. Census Menomomie, WI)

Cox, David M. Co. H, 19th NY Cavalry - 8/10/1862 at Birdsall/3 yrs - 18 - 5'8", Light Complexion, Blue Eyes, Dark Hair - 9/3/1862 at Portage Station - $100 - Pvt, Pvt - Deserted House, siege of Suffolk, Franklin, Manassas Junction, Bristoe's Station, Culpeper Court House, Wilderness, Todd's Tavern - 8/28/1864 Honorable - POW, captured 5/7/1864 at Todd's Tavern, Prison: Richmond, Andersonville, DD, 8/28/1864 at Andersonville of scorbutus - George &

Sussannal Cox (Both B England) - Sarah A. Clarinda A. - 9/18/1843 in Allen - Farmer - None Deceased - Never Married - None - 8/28/1864 in Andersonville - Andersonville - Was on detached duty for some time on reconnaissance. (Military & Pension Files, Granger American Legion, *History of Allegany County 1879*, 1850, 1860 Fed. Censuses Allen)

Crane, Ira Frank Co. B, 2nd NY Mounted Rifles - 12/18/1863 at Centerville/3 yrs - 21 - 5'8", Light Complexion, Blue Eyes, Light Hair - 1/12/1864 at Ft. Porter, Buffalo - $200 - Pvt, Pvt - Spotsylvania Court House, North Anna River, Pamunkey, Totopotomoy, Hanover Court House, Cold Harbor, Bethesda Church, siege of Petersburg, Popular Springs Church, Pegram's Farm - 6/26/1865 Honorable - POW, captured 9/30/1864 at Petersburg, VA Prison: Richmond, Paroled 3/2/1865 - Ira P. & Sally J. Pike Crane (Both B NY) - Janette, Esther - 11/26/1843 in Freedom - Farmer - Farmer - Jane Altoft, married 11/25/1867 in Portageville - William E., Ira P., Flora B. - 7/3/1919 at Buffalo G.H. - Caldwell Cemetery, Centerville - Received a 30 day furlough from Camp Parole following his parole. Middle name may have been Franklin, (Military & Pension Files, Matteson, 1890 Fed. Census Special Schedule Centerville, *History of Allegany County 1879*, Centerville American Legion, 1865 Allegany County Town Clerk Register Centerville, 1865 NYS Census Centerville, 1850 Fed. Census China, 1870 Fed. Census Centerville)

Crane, Ulysses Eugene Co. F, 19th NY Cavalry - 8/8/1862 at Hume/3 yrs - 22 - 5'6", Dark Complexion, Brown Eyes, Brown Hair - 9/3/1862 at Portage Station - $25 - Pvt, Pvt - No battles - 6/30/1865 Honorable - Was not a casualty - Lockhart Berry & Charity Eveline Sharp Crane (Both B NY) - Clark, Caroline, Roselle - 4/10/1839/40 in Freedom - Blacksmith - Blacksmith/Farmer/Art - 1st Margart M. Crotty, married 2/5/1860 in Fillmore, 2nd Harriet A. Crandall, married 1/5/1874 in Crandall, WI - Henry S., Almedal (married Fred Keiser) - 5/19/1923 at Vancouver, WA - Post Cemetery, Vancouver - Also served with VRC 32 Co. B, 2nd. Battalion. Had many marital problems. Big dispute over who he married, and when, and when divorced. Probably never divorced either wife. Was a good artist and sold a number of paintings, some at quite high prices for the period. He was named after his father's brother who once represented Cattaraugus in the State Legislature. (Military & Pension Files, 1865 NYS Census Granger, 1860 Fed. Census Freedom, *History of Allegany County 1879*, 1850 Fed. Census, Hume, 1865 Allegany County Town Clerk Register Caneadea, 1920 Fed. Census Vancouver, WA)

Crawford, Romanzo Co. F, 19th NY Cavalry - 8/9/1862 at Centerville/3 yrs - 23 - 5'8", Light Complexion, Blue Eyes, Brown Hair - 9/3/1862 at Portage Station - No bounty - Pvt, Pvt - Deserted House, siege of Suffolk - 5/13/1863 Disability/Honorable - INJ, 2/15/1863 near Suffolk, accidental self inflicted gunshot to left ankle while on picket duty - INA (Both B NY) - INA - 12/7/1839 or 40 in Oramel - Cooper - Day Laborer - Martha Jane Torrey, married 3/23/1861 in Centerville - James Henry, Alfred Leroy, Bird Adelbert, Charles Ellis, Alfred Lewellen, Frank Ellsworth, Homer Romanzo, Wallace Burdell - 10/31/1917 - Alger Cemetery, Hume, State Route 19 - Military questioned whether wound was self inflicted to get out of the service. (Military & Pension Files, 1890 Fed. Census Special Schedule Hume, Matteson, *History of Allegany County 1879*, 1900 Fed. Census Hume)

Crocker, John C. Co. K, 82nd Pennsylvania Infantry - 12/6/1864 at Williamsport, PA/1 yr - 18 -

5'11", Fair Complexion, Blue Eyes, Dark Hair - 12/6/1864 at Williamsport - No bounty - Pvt, Pvt - siege of Petersburg, Dabney's Mills, Hatcher's Run, fall of Petersburg, Appomattox - 7/3/1865 Disability/Honorable - Was not a casualty - Alfred Crocker (B NY) & Mary Wampole (B PA) Crocker - Lovinia, Winiford - 1/1/1834 in Ischau, Cattaraugus County - Laborer - Farmer - Phoeby Maria Shute - 10/25/1868 in Nunda - Susia, Lydia, Alta, Maggie - 8/7/1919 in Warsaw - Short Tract Cemetery, County Route 4 - Present at Lee's surrender. Corps Review 6/8/1865. Discharge due to chronic diarrhea. Was a substitute for a Hiram Cartwright, Harrison Township, Potter County, PA. (Military & Pension Files, Granger American Legion, 1860 Fed. Census West Sparta, Livingston County, 1910 Fed. Census Granger, 1890 Fed. Census Special Schedule Granger)

Cronk, Chauncey Abrams Co. D, 64th NY Infantry - 8/14/1862 at Rushford/3 yrs - 24 - 5'7", Light Complexion, Blue Eyes, Brown Hair, 10/16/1862 at Elmira - $110 - Pvt, Corp - Fredericksburg, Chancellorsville, Gettysburg, Bristoe, Wilderness, Spotsylvania, Cold Harbor, siege of Petersburg, Ream's Station, Hatcher's Run - 6/22/1865 Honorable - WIA, 5/12/1864 at Spotsylvania, charging enemy works (exact wound not described in files) - Daniel V. & Angeline Thayer Cronk (Both B NY) - Lester, Edward. Chester - 3/13/1838 in Victor - Farmer - Farmer - 1st Mary S. Butler, married 12/25/1868 in Hume, 2nd Olive M. Davis Wright, married 1/13/1904 in Fillmore - Etta, Edith Lenore, War, Winfield - 6/6/1917 in Houghton - Pine Grove Cemetery Fillmore - Brothers Edward, Chester, and Lester all served during the war. Burnside G.A.R. Post 237 Marker at grave. 1st wife Mary Butler was the great great granddaughter of Colonel Zebulon Butler. (Military & Pension Files, Medical Cards, Fillmore American Legion, Matteson, 1850 Fed. Census Centerville, 1870, 1900 Fed. Censuses Caneadea, descendant Sharon Myers)

Cronk, Chester Broughton Co. D, 64th NY Infantry - 8/14/1862 at Rushford/3 yrs - 22 - 5'7", Light Complexion, Blue Eyes, Brown Hair - 10/16 1862 at Elmira - $25 - Pvt, Pvt - Antietam, Fredericksburg, Chancellorsville, Gettysburg - 3/15/1864 Honorable - WIA, 7/2/1863 at Gettysburg, gunshot to right leg calf - Daniel & Angeline Thayer Cronk (Both B NY) - Chauncey, Edward, Lester - 3/30/1840 in Victor - Farmer - Farmer - 1st Marion Howden, married 3/18/1867, 2nd Lilian J. Houghton, married 12/25/1873 in Caneadea, 3rd Myra A. Dodge, married 8/14/1896 in Warsaw (Myra was previously married to C-H-G Civil War soldier Myron A. Dodge) - Angie, William, Herman, Milton, Marshall, Charles - 11/8/1904 in Fillmore - Pine Grove Cemetery Fillmore - Burnside G.A.R. Post 237 Marker at grave. Was incorrectly carried as a deserter for a time. Transferred to VRC 3/15/1864. (Military & Pension Files, Matteson, Fillmore American Legion, 1850 Fed. Census Centerville, 1870 Fed. Census Hume)

Cronk, Edward Belknap Co. F, 4th NY Heavy Artillery - 12/21/1863 at Caneadea/3 yrs - 20 - 5'3", Light Complexion, Blue Eyes, Light Hair - 12/21/1863 at Elmira - $300 - Pvt, Corp - Wilderness, Spotsylvania, North Anna River, Totopotomoy, Cold Harbor, siege of Petersburg, Weldon RR, Ream's Station, Peeble's Farm, Hatcher's Run, fall of Petersburg, Appomattox - 9/26/1865 Honorable - Was not a casualty - Daniel & Angeline Thayer Cronk (Both B NY) - Chauncey, Chester, Lester - 12/12/1843 in Centerville - Farmer - Bookkeeper - 1st Sarah A. Theraton (died 6/29/1882), 2nd Sara J. Brace Lorenz, married 10/19/1898 in Olean - Myrtle A., Phebe R., May Belle, John, Roscoe - 4/15/1909 in Duke Center, PA - Oramel - Brothers Chauncey, Edward and

Lester all served during the war. Some records have his first name as Edwin. Promoted Corporal 6/29/1882. Present at Lee's surrender. Marched in Grand Review 5/23/1865. (Military & Pension Files, 1865 Allegany Town Clerk Register Caneadea, 1850 Fed. Census Centerville, 1870 Fed. Census Caneadea)

Cronk, Lester Vernon Co. E, 194th NY Infantry - 4/11/1865 at Caneadea/1 yr - 19 - 5'5", Fair Complexion, Blue Eyes, Brown Hair - 4/22/1865 at Elmira - Pvt, Pvt - No battles - 5/3/1865 Honorable - Was not a casualty - Daniel & Angeline Thayer Cronk (Both B NY) - Chauncey, Chester, Edward - 1/3/1846 in Centerville - Farmer - Farmer - Jane - INA - 1920 - Pine Grove Cemetery, Fillmore - Brothers Chauncey, Edward & Chester also served during the war. (Military File, 1865 Allegany County Town Clerk Register Centerville, 1850 Fed. Census Centerville, 1870 Fed. Census Caneadea)

Crotty, John Henry Co. E, 85th NY Infantry - 9/1/1861 at Granger/3 yrs (Re-enlisted 1/1/1864 at Plymouth, NC) - 22 - 5'11". Light Complexion, Blue Eyes, Auburn Hair - 10/10/1861 at Elmira - No bounty - Pvt, Pvt - defense of DC, siege of Yorktown, Williamsburg, Fair Oaks, before Richmond, Plymouth - 6/7/1865 - POW, captured 4/20/1864 at Plymouth, Prisons: Andersonville, Florence, paroled 3/1/1865 at Wilmington, NC - John & Elizabeth Crotty (Both B Ireland) - INA - 1839 in Ireland - Farmer - Farmer - Frances M. Price, married 10/23/1867 in Oramel - Addie M. & George M. - 3/30/1918 in Granger - Pine Grove Cemetery, Fillmore - Pension based on rheumatism and hernia. (1890 Fed Census Special Schedule Granger, *History of Allegany County 1879*, Matteson, 1850 Fed. Census Allen, 1865 NYS Census Granger, 1865 Allegany County Town Clerk Register Granger, Granger American Legion, 1880, 1910 Fed. Censuses Granger)

Crowell, John Henry Co. C, 104th NY Infantry - 10/9/1861 at Geneseo/3 yrs - 27 - 5'9", Light Complexion, Blue Eyes, Brown Hair - 2/26/1862 at Geneseo - $400 - Pvt, Orderly Sgt - Cedar Creek, Fredericksburg, Chancellorsville, Gettysburg, Bristoe's Station, Spotsylvania, Cold Harbor, Bethesda Church, Petersburg, Weldon RR, Hatcher's Run, Gravelly Run, Five Forks, Appomattox - 7/17/1865 Honorable - POW, 8/19/1864 at Petersburg, Prison: Richmond, paroled Vienna, VA 710/8/1864, WIA, per pension claimed a gunshot wound above right knee at Fredericksburg, 12/13/1862. Could not have been serious as muster cards do not mention it and show him present at all times - Joseph & Elizabeth (Betsey) Higgins Crowell (Both B VT) - INA - 1831 in Allegany County - Farmer - Farmer - Jane Marilla Wildey, married 10/29/1859 in Centerville, Mary Odell, William D., Belinda M., Polly J., Inez, Seneca Odell - 6/21/1898 in Centerville - Rogers Cemetery, Centerville - Present at Lee's surrender. Marched in Grand Review, 5/23/1865. (Military & Pension Files, 1890 Fed. Census Special Schedule Centerville, Matterson, Centerville American Legion, 1865 NYS Census Centerville, 1850, 1880 Fed. Censuses - Centerville)

Crowell, Oliver Theodore Co. C, 104th NY Infantry - 11/9/1861 at Geneseo/3 yrs Re-enlisted Co. L, 1st Veteran Cavalry) - 18 - 5'8", Light Complexion, Grey Eyes, Light Hair, Two middle fingers on left hand grown together - 2/26/1862 at Geneseo - $100 - Pvt, Pvt - Cedar Creek, 2nd Bull Run, South Mountain, Antietam - 1/24/1863 Disability/Honorable - WIA, 9/17/1862 at Antietam, gunshot to left leg - Samuel & Lucy Wight Crowell (Both B NY) - Urana, William, Murray, Sylvester, Alfred - 5/5/1834 in Centerville - Farmer - Farmer - Rose Ann Moore, married

11/13/1875 in Hume - INA - 11/14/1905 in Rockford, IA - INA - Also served with 1st NY Veteran Cavalry. Enlisted 9/17/1863 for 3 years at Almond. Mustered 11/7/1863. Promoted to Corporal 12/29/1863, Sergeant 12/5/1864. Served as Orderly to Brigadier General Sullivan from 2/15/64 to May, 1864. At dismount camp 5/14 to July, 1864. Battles: Upperville, VA Kanawha Valley, WV, Mt. Jackson, WV. Discharged 7/20/1865, retained his arms at a cost of $13.00. (Military & Pension Files, 1865 NYS Census Centerville, 1890 Fed. Census Special Schedule Hume, 1865 Allegany Town Clerk Register Centerville, 1850 Fed. Census Centerville, 1880 Fed. Census Hume)

Cudebec, Clarence Lindon (Cuddebec) Co. F, 19th NY Cavalry - 8/13/1862 at Oramel/3 yrs 26 - 5'8", Light Complexion, Blue Eyes, Light Hair - 9/3/1862 at Portage Station - $100 - 6th Corp, 1st Sgt - Deserted House, siege of Suffolk, Franklin, Culpeper Court House, Wilderness, Todd's Tavern, Spotsylvania, North Anna River, Yellow Tavern, Pamunkey, Totopotomoy, Cold Harbor, Trevillian Station, Charles County Court House, before Richmond & Petersburg, Cedar Creek, Berryville, Gordonsville, New Market, Shepherdstown - 6/23/1865 Honorable - Was not a casualty - Elias & Polly Cudebec (Both B NY) - Harriet, Hellen, Orlando, Jemima, Waight F. - 9/11/1839 in Granger - Farmer - Farmer/Pension Attorney - 1st Abby G.(died 1/31/1876), 2nd Almeda A. Bennett, married 4/21/1877 - Clinton, Rosa, Marion, Lunetta , Floyd, Abby, Roy, Albert, Clyde, Almeda - 10/17/1904 in Nunda (fell from an Apple Tree) - INA - Marched in Grand Review 5/23/1865. Retained his sabre (cost $3.00) at discharge. Promoted Corporal 8/19/1862, Sgt 5/15/1863 Com Sgt 9/1/1863, 1st Sgt 5/5/1865, Was sick in both Emory and Carver hospitals in DC Suffered a sunstroke 7/30/64 at Lee's Pond (Petersburg). Brother Orlando also served during the war. (Military & Pension Files, History of Allegany County 1879, Granger American Legion, 1865 Allegany County Town Clerk Register Allen, 1850, 1870 Fed. Censuses Allen)

Cudebec, Orlando B. (Cuddebec) Co. K, 184th NY Infantry - 8/30/1864 at Granger/1 yr - 19 - 5'10", Light Complexion, Blue Eyes, Brown Hair - 9/20/1864 at Elmira - $100 - Pvt, Pvt - Bermuda Hundred, Petersburg, Richmond - 6/29/1865 Honorable - Was not a casualty - Elias & Polly Cudebec (Both B NY) - Harriet, Clarence, Hellen, Jemima, Waight F. - 5/20/1845 in Allen - Farmer - Farmer/Carpenter - Katherine Van Ess, married 4/2/1872 in Tyre, Seneca County - Bertha & Marian - 2/15/1913 in Rochester - Seneca Falls, Seneca County - Military spelled name Cuderbeck. Stationed at Harrison's Landing. Sick in camp January-February, 1865. Brother Clarence also served during the war. (Military & Pension Files, 1865 NYS Census Granger, 1865 Allegany County Town Clerk Register Granger, 1850 Fed. Census Allen, 1900 Fed. Census Seneca Falls)

Culver, William Henry Co. F, 104th NY Infantry - 2/13/1862 at Geneseo/3 yrs - 21 - 5'6". Fair Complexion, Blue Eyes, Light Hair - 2/26/1862 at Geneseo - No bounty - Pvt, Pvt - Cedar Creek, 2nd Bull Run, South Mountain, Antietam - 2/16/1863 Disability/Honorable - Was not a casualty - John & Mary Glover Culver (Both B NY) - George, Oliver, Effie? E. - 1/2/1841 in Victor - Farmer - Mill Engineer - Permelia Smith, married 8/9/1863 - George, Silas, Howard, Effie - 2/14/1914 in Doral, MI - Doral, MI - Some information in military file indicates he was a POW, when actually he was sick in Georgetown Union Hospital. Discharge due to chronic rheumatism. (Military & Pension Files, 1865 Allegany County Town Clerk Register Granger, 1855 NYS

Census Hume, 1900 Fed. Census Maple Valley Township, MI)

Curran, Dennis Was not from the C-H-G area. Originally with Co. D, 28th Massachusetts Infantry. His re-enlistment in Co. E, 16th VRC was credited to Hume Township which paid the re-enlistment bonus of $500. (1865 Allegany County Town Clerk Register Hume)

Curtis, George W. Co. A, 19th NY Cavalry - 8/7/1862 at Portage/3 yrs - 24 - 5'9", Light Complexion, Blue Eyes, Brown Hair - 9/3/1862 at Portage Station - $100 - Pvt, Sgt - Deserted House, siege of Suffolk, Franklin, Manassas Junction, Bristoe's Station, Culpeper Court House, Wilderness, Todd's Tavern, Spotsylvania, North Anna River, Pamunkey, Totopotomoy, Cold Harbor, Trevillian Station, Charles County Court House, before Petersburg & Richmond, Winchester, Fisher's Hill, New Market, Port Republic, Cedar Creek, Berryville, Gordonsville - 6/30/1865 Honorable at Clouds Mill, VA- Was not a casualty - Joseph & Adaline Reed Curtis (Both B NY) - Ebenezer B., Betsy Ann, Thomas J. - 3/22/1838 in Hume, Cooper - Traveling Salesman, Gravestones - Minerva M. Karns, married 8/26/1861 in Dansville - Homer G., Thomas J., Clara D., Sadie M., Grace E., Effie M., Joseph L. - 9/9/1904 in Creston, MT - INA - Marched in the Grand Review 5/23/1865. Promoted Corp 8/11/1863, Sgt 2/23/1865. Brother Thomas J. also served during the war. Charter Member of Burnside G.A.R. Post 237. His wife Minerva was the sister of Civil War soldier Palmer Karns. His grandfather James was born in CT. (Military & Pension Files, *History of Allegany County 1879*, *Allegany & Its People*, 1850 Fed. Census Hume, 1900 Fed Census Britton, SD)

Curtis, Thomas Jefferson Co. A, 104th NY Infantry - 10/1/1861 at Granger - 23 - 5'9", Light Complexion, Hazel Eyes, Light Hair - 2/26/1862 at Geneseo - No bounty - Pvt, 1st Sgt - Cedar Creek, 2nd Bull Run, South Mountain, Antietam, Chancellorsville, Gettysburg - 7/1/1863 Deceased/Honorable - WIA, 9/17/1862 at Antietam, gunshot to arm (In NYC Hosp.), KIA 7/1/1863 at Gettysburg - Joseph & Adaline Reed Curtis (Both B NY) - Ebenezer B., Betsy Ann, George W. - 1839 or 40 probably in Hume - Farmer/Cooper - None Deceased - Never Married - None - 7/1/1863 in Gettysburg - Gettysburg National Cemetery - Appointed Corp. 11/4/1861, 5th Sgt 4/24/1862, Sgt 7/4/1862, 1st Sgt 1/9/1863. Brother George W. also served during the war. Grandfather James was born in CT. (Military & Pension Files, 1865 NYS Census Hume, 1850 Fed. Census Centerville)

Daggert, John Co. G, 4th Michigan Cavalry - 8/9/1862 at Quincy, MI/3 yrs - 23 - 5'3", Light Complexion, Grey Eyes, Red Hair - 4/28/1862 at Detroit - $100 - Pvt, Pvt - Stanford, TN, Franklin, Stone River (Murfreesboro) - 4/11/1863 at Louisville, KY Disability/ Honorable - Was not a casualty - Halbridge (B MA) & Isabel Harriet (B NY) Daggert - George, Louisa, Lewis, Erastus, Mary - 4/1/1839 in Yorkshire - Farmer - Farmer - Never Married - None - 3/30/1914 in Freedom - Delevan - Had severe chronic diarrhea in service. Post war lived in many different locations. Lived in Centerville in the 1890's. (Military & Pension Files, 1890 Fed. Census Special Schedule Centerville, 1850 Fed. Census Yorkshire, 1880 Fed. Census Rock Falls, NE)

Daley, Ammon Co. D, 154th NY Infantry - 8/14/1862 at Freedom/3 yrs - 23 - 5'7", Dark Complexion, Blue Eyes, Brown Hair - 9/24/1862 at Jamestown - No bounty - Pvt, Pvt - No battles

- 3/18/1863 for epilepsy. Disability/Honorable - Was not a casualty - Alfred & Harriet Carr Daley (Both B NY) - Charles, William, Ephaim, Edwin, Hiram, Harriette - 9/17/1837 in Cattaraugus County per Town Clerk, (Pension records say 9/15/1835 or 36 in Waterloo, Seneca County. His father was born in Waterloo.) - Farmer - Farmer - Cynthia Jane Carr, married 5/5/1865 in Attica MI - Emma & Elmer - 3/16/1911 in Centerville - Centerville Cemetery, Route 3 - Spent almost entire service in hospital. Treated at Hammond G.H. Lookout Mountain, MD for epilepsy. 1910 Census & Civil War Index spells name Dailey. Also carried as Almon Daly, W. Darley, and Almond. Brothers Charles and William also served during the war. Census Bureau may have been confused and used his mother's last name as his wife's name. (Military & Pension Files, 1865 Allegany County Town Clerk Register Centerville, 1860, 1870, 1910 Federl Censuses Centerville)

Daley, Charles Seymour Co. F, 104th NY Infantry - 12/5/1861 at Eagle/3 yrs - 23 - 5'6", Dark Complexion, Black Eyes, Black Hair - 2/26/1862 at Geneseo - No bounty - Pvt, Sgt - No battles - 8/22/1862 at Falls Church, VA - Disability/Honorable (had necrosis of fibula, needed a cane to walk) - Was not a casualty - Alfred & Harriet Carr Daley (Both B NY) - Ammon, William, Ephraim, Edwin, Hiram Harriette - 4/22/1838 in Seneca County - Farmer/Teacher - Minister - Emma J. Cobb, married 1/1/1863 in Centerville - INA - 3/10/1899 in Sandusky - Sandusky - Promoted to Corp 1/15/1862 Sgt 3/7/1862. Name also spelled Dailey. Brothers Ammon and William also served during the war. (Military & Pension Files, 1865 Allegany County Town Clerk Register Centerville, 1860 Fed. Census Centerville, 1870 Fed. Census Cuba)

Daley, Roderick Was not from the C-H-G area. His re-enlistment in Co. E, 16th VRC was credited to Hume Township which paid the $500 re-enlistment bonus. Originally served with Cos. H/D, 116th Pennsylvania Infantry. (1865 Allegany County Town Clerk Register Hume)

Daley, William Henry Co F, 104th NY Infantry - 12/5/1861 at Geneseo/3 yrs - 19 - 5'7", Light Complexion, Blue Eyes, Brown Hair - 2/26/1862 at Geneseo - No bounty - Pvt, Pvt - No battles - 9/11/1862 Honorable/Deceased - DD, 9/11/1862 of typhoid fever - Alfred & Harriet Carr Daley (Both B NY) - Charles, Ammon, Ephaim, Edwin, Hiram, Harriette - 1/14/1842 in Seneca County per Town Clerk (Headstone says 4/15/1842) - Farmer - None Deceased - Never Married - None - 9/11/1862 in Alexandria, VA - Caldwell Cemetery, Centerville - Name also spelled Dailey. Brothers Ammon and Charles also served during the war. (Military File, Matteson, 1865 Allegany County Town Clerk Register Centerville, Centerville American Legion, 1865 NYS Census Centerville, 1850 Fed. Census Centerville)

Daniels, Charles Rice Co. F, 4th NY Heavy Artillery - 9/11/1862 at Caneadea/3 yrs - 36 - INA - 9/15/1862 at NYC - $100 - Pvt, Pvt - Wilderness, Spotsylvania, North Anna River, Totopotomoy, Cold Harbor, siege of Petersburg, Weldon RR, Ream's Station, Peeble's Farm, Hatcher's Run, fall of Petersburg, Appomattox - 6/3/1865 at Alexandria, VA Honorable - Was not a casualty - Timothy Spaulding (B VT) & Betsey Atherton (B NY) Daniels - Lucinda, Sally or Sarah, Mary Ann, Phoebe, William - 4/13/1826 in Caneadea - Farmer - Farmer - 1st Sarah I. (Died 1/1892), 2nd Mary Kennedy, married 7/23/1893 in Caneadea (Mary had been previously married to Henry Kennedy) - Sylvester, William, Frederick - 1/6/1898 - Pine Grove Cemetery Fillmore - Brother William also served during the war. Burnside G.A.R. Post 237 Marker at grave. Present at Lee's surrender. Marched in Grand Review 5/23/1865. (Military & Pension Files, 1865 Allegany County Town Clerk Register Caneadea, Matteson, 1850, 1860, 1870 Fed. Censuses Caneadea)

Daniels, Charles S. Co. F, 19th NY Cavalry - 8/9/1862 at Hume/3 yrs - 21 - 5'11", Light Complexion, Blue Eyes, Brown Hair - 9/3/1862 at Portage Station - $100 - Pvt, Corp - No battles - 3/31/1863 Disability/Honorable - Was not a casualty - INA -INA - 8/15/1840 in Stafford, Genesee County - Louisa - Walter - 6/6/1898 - Pine Grove Cemetery, Fillmore - Appointed Corp 8/19/1862. Birth date is questionable. Some source documents list a soldier S. Daniels. Only two S Daniels (Samuel & Stephen) are listed by the NYS Adjutant General as having served in NY State regiments during the war, and neither served with the 19th Cavalry. It is possible that the name was Charles S, maybe for Sylvester. (Military File, *History of Allegany County 1879*, Matteson, Allegany County Town Clerk Register Hume, NYS Adjutant General's Report 1895 Volume 6, 1860 Fed. Census Hume, 1870 Fed. Census Stafford)

Daniels, Sylvester At least one source list this man, who is buried in Pine Grove Cemetery in Fillmore as a Civil War soldier. The Sylvester Daniels buried in Pine Grove Cemetery was born in 1848 and died in 1866. There are no military files for a Sylvester Daniels, nor does the NYS Adjutant General Report identify a Sylvester Daniels. There was a Charles S. Daniels who served with the 19th NY Cavalry, but he gave his age as 21 when he enlisted in 1862. The Sylvester buried in Pine Grove Cemetery would have been only 14 in 1862. Further, the soldier Daniels lived until 1898, whereas Sylvester died in 1866. It is obvious they were two different people. (Fillmore American Legion. Matteson)

Daniels, William Curtis Co. F, 19th NY Cavalry - 8/2/1862 at Oramel/3 yrs - 18 - 5'8", Light Complexion, Hazel Eyes, Brown Hair - 9/3/1862 at Portage Station - No bounty - Pvt, Corp - Deserted House, siege of Suffolk, Franklin, Manassas Junction, Bristoe's Station, Culpeper Court House, Wilderness, Todd's Tavern, Spotsylvania, North Anna River, Yellow Tavern, Pamunkey, Totopotomoy, Cold Harbor, Trevillian Station, Charles County Court House, before Richmond & Petersburg, New Market, Shepherdstown, Winchester, Fisher's Hill, New Market, Port Republic - 9/26/1864 Honorable/Deceased - KIA, 9/26/1864 at Port Republic (killed by a minnie ball through the heart while on horseback) - Timothy Spaulding (B VT) & Betsey Atherton (B NY) Daniels - Charles R., Lucinda (Franklin), Sally or Sarah (Vreeland), Mary Ann (Place), Phoebe (Moore)- 1843 or 44 at Allen Township - Farmer - None Deceased - Never Married - None - 9/26/1864 Port Republic, VA. - INA - Bother Charles R. also served during the war. Promoted to Corp 11/1/1863. Sick in hospital 8/27/1864. (Military & Pension Files, Matteson, NYS Adjutant General Report 1895 Volume 6, 1850 Fed. Census Caneadea)

Davidson, Francis J. Co. D, 4th NY Heavy Artillery - 8/13/1862 at Rochester/3 yrs - 23 - 5'11", Dark Complexion, Blue Eyes, Light Hair - 8/13/1862 at Rochester - $25 - Pvt, Pvt - Wilderness, Spotsylvania, North Anna River, Totopotomoy, Ream's Station, Peeble's Farm, Hatcher's Run, fall of Petersburg, Appomattox - 6/3/1865 Honorable - Was not a Casualty - William & Anna Nesmith Davidson (Both B NH) - William E., John N., Thomas A., G.H., Francis Y., Albert, Jacob M., Hamilton E. - 3/17/1839 in Genesee Falls - Farmer - Farmer - Mary Elizabeth Merchant, married 8/17/1862 in Hume - Nellie B., Cora, Frank, William, Mary - 1901 - East Koy, Lamont

Road - Detailed as regiment mail carrier March and April 1865. July to August, 1864 sick at Brigade Hospital, 2nd Army Corps. Present at Lee's surrender. Marched in the Grand Review 5/23/1865. Brothers William & Thomas also served during the war. Charter Member and Commander of Burnside G.A.R. Post 237. (Military & Pension Files, *Allegany & Its People*, 1850, 1870 Fed. Censuses Genesee)

Davidson, Thomas Augustus Co. D, 4th NY Heavy Artillery - 8/1/1862 at Rochester/3 yrs - 28 - 5'10", Dark Complexion, Blue Eyes, Light Hair - 8/18/1862 at Rochester - $50 - Pvt, Pvt - Peeble's Farm, Hatcher's Run, fall of Petersburg, Appomattox - 6/3/1865 Honorable - Was not a casualty - William & Anna Nesmith Davidson (Both B NH) - William E., John N., G.H., Francis Y., Albert, Jacob M. Hamilton E. - 2/28/1844 in Concord, NH - Farmer/Cabinet Maker - Machinist/Cabinet Maker - 1st Julia E. Ross (Died 5/16/1871), 2nd. Jane Van Etten, (widow of Thomas Van Etten) married 2/25/1872 in Tuscarora - Wallace G. & Anna - 2/13/1875 in Wiscoy - Wiscoy - Present at Lee's surrender. Marched in Grand Review 5/23/1865. Was in Mt. Pleasant G.H. with chronic diarrhea for a while. Brothers Francis J. and William also served during the war. (Military & Pension Files, Allegany County Web Site, 1865 Allegany Town Clerk Register Hume, 1865 NYS Census Hume, Fillmore American Legion, Matteson, 1850 Fed. Census Genesee Falls, 1870 Fed. Census Hume)

Davidson, William E. Co. D, 4th NY Heavy Artillery - 9/13/1862 at Weschester County/3 yrs - 31 - 5'10", Light Complexion, Brown Eyes, Dark Hair - 9/13/1862 at NYC - No bounty - Pvt, Pvt - Wilderness, Spotsylvania, North Anna River, Totopotomoy, Cold Harbor, siege of Petersburg, Weldon RR, Ream's Station, Peeble's Farm, Hatcher's Run, fall of Petersburg, Appomattox - 6/3/1865 Honorable - Was not a casualty - William (B Windham, NH) & Anna Nesmith (B Derby, NH) Davidson - John N., Thomas A., G.H., Francis Y., Albert, Jacob M., Hamilton E. - 3/25/1831 in Windham, NH - Farmer - Farmer/RR Inspector/Carpenter - Lucy Jane Smith, married 3/2/1854 in Rossburg (Mixville) - Sarah, Wallace E., Annis - 3/30/1909 in Buffalo - East Koy, Lamont Road - Present at Lee's surrender. Marched in Grand Review 5/23/1865. Address at time of discharge was Wiscoy. Brothers Francis & Thomas also served during the war. (Military & Pension Files, 1865 NYS Census Hume, 1850 Fed. Census Genesee Falls, 1880 Fed. Census Buffalo)

Davies, Samuel At least one source lists this man as a Civil War soldier. No military files for a Samuel Davies from the C-H-G area have been located. (Matteson)

Davis, George Washington Co. E, 136th NY Infantry - 8/13/1862 at Allen/3 yrs - 29 - 5'9", Sandy Complexion, Grey Eyes, Light Hair - 9/25/1862 at Portage - $100 - Pvt, Pvt - Chancellorsville, Gettysburg, Wauhatchie, Orchard Knob (was detached as Brigade Teamster 1/1864, not sure of battles after that) County Clerk lists following battles, Rocky Face Ridge, Lookout Mountain, Missionary Ridge, Ringgold - 6/13/1865 Honorable - Was not a casualty - Seth (B MA) & Lovitha Rosetta Smith (B CT) Davis - Elijah, Isaac, Hiram H. Walter, Henry H. Seth P. - 1843 in Allen - Farmer - Farmer /Store Keeper - Sara Elizabeth Cox, married 10/28/1868 in Allen - Jennie, Everett, Nettie - 9/2/1904 in Allen - Route 15, Basswood Hill Cemetery, Allen - Also served as Company Cook. Marched in Grand Review 5/24/1865. Lived in Short Tract around 1895 per his pension. He moved a lot. Brother Henry also served during the war. County Clerk has birth date as

9/8/1833. The 1833 is probably a writing error. (Military & Pension Files, 1865 Allegany County Town Clerk Register Allen, 1850, 1900 Fed. Censuses Allen, Granger American Legion)

Davis, Henry Harrison Co. I, 160th NY Infantry - Drafted 1/14/1865 at Allen/3 yrs - 22 - 5'9", Light Complexion, Blue Eyes, Light Hair - 1/28/1865 at Elmira - $600 - Pvt, Pvt - No battles - 11/1/1865 at Savannah, GA Honorable - Was not a casualty - Seth H.(B MA) & Lovitha Rosetta Smith (B CT) Davis - Elijah, Isaac, George W. Hiram H. Walter, Seth P. - 8/8/1842 in Allen - Farmer - Farm Laborer - Mary D. Bray, married 1878 at Arcade - INA - 1/19/1920 in Bliss - Caldwell Cemetery, Centerville - Marched in the Grand Review 5/23/1865. Brother George W. also served during the war. (Military & Pension Files - 1865 Allegany County Town Clerk Register Allen, Matteson, Centerville American Legion, 1850 Fed. Census Allen, 1880 Fed.Census Arcade)

Davis, Stephen Sweet Co. D, 64th NY Infantry - 9/13/1861 at Rushford/3 yrs - 41 - 5', Dark Complexion, Blue Eyes, Black Hair - 9/24/1861 at Elmira - No bounty - Corp, Pvt - No battles - 3/3/1862 Disability/Honorable (Disability, Chronic Bronchitis) - Was not a casualty - Benjamin West & Lana Mosher Davis - INA - 3/27/1821 in Charleston, NH - Farmer - None, sick, unable to work - Maria H. Rice, married 5/20/1849 in Hume - Steve, Tim, Carrie B., Pauline, Rose Marion - 1/19/1864 in Caneadea - Lattice Bridge Cemetery, Caneadea - His wife Maria received his pension. His son Stephen tried to steal it from her. Maria is buried at Lattice Bridge Cemetery. Stephen & Maria were married at the home of B. M. Davis. (Military & Pension Files, 1850 Fed. Census Hume, Maria-1870 Fed. Census Caneadea, 1865 Allegany County Town Clerk Register Caneadea)

Davis, William L. Co. A, 104th NY Infantry - 10/1/1861 at Granger/3 yrs - 23 - 5'5", Light Complexion, Blue Eyes, Sandy Hair, Scar on left knee - 2/26/1862 at Geneseo - No bounty - Pvt, Pvt - Cedar Creek, 2nd Bull Run, South Mountain, Antietam, Fredericksburg, Chancellorsville, Gettysburg - 71/1863 Honorable/Deceased - KIA, 7/1/1863 at Gettysburg - Augusta & Lovina Davis (Both B NY) - Samuel, George - 1838 in Ontario County - Farmer - None Deceased - Never Married - None - 7/1/1863 in Gettysburg - Hunts Hollow Cemetery, Hunt (Military records say buried at Gettysburg, but no record of his burial at Gettysburg) - Listed on the Soldiers Monument in Granger. (Military & Pension Files, 1865 NYS Census Granger, *Allegany & Its People*, Matteson, Granger American Legion, 1850 Fed. Census, Candici)

Dill, Lewis Co. F, 4th NY Heavy Artillery - 8/11/1862 at Hume/3 yrs - 18 - 5'6", Medium Complexion, Blue Eyes, Brown Hair - 9/12/1862 at NYC - $50 - Pvt, Pvt - Wilderness, Spotsylvania, North Anna River, Totopotomoy, Cold Harbor, siege of Petersburg, Weldon RR, Ream's Station - 6/29/1865 Honorable - POW, captured 8/25/1864 at Ream's Station, Prison: Salisbury, NC - Philip & Elizabeth Griswould Lewis (Both B NY) - Maria, May E., Dermott - 4/27/1844 in Hume - Farm Laborer - Farmer - 1st Sarah Lydia Baker (died 4/4/1888), 2nd Mary - Edith and Charles - 3/19/1917 in Rossburg - Elmer Cemetery, Route 19A, Rossburg - Charter Member and Officer of Burnside G.A.R. Post 237. (Military & Pension Files, 1865 NYS Census Hume, 1890 Fed. Census Special Schedule Hume, Fillmore American Legion, *Allegany & Its People*, 1865 Allegany County Town Clerk Register Hume, 1850, 1880 1910 Fed. Censuses Hume)

Disbrow, Alonzo Almeron Co. F, 64th NY Infantry - 8/29/1862 at Napoli/3 yrs - 44 - 5'6", Light Complexion, Blue Eyes, Light Hair - 10/18/1862 at Elmira - No bounty - Pvt, Pvt - Antietam, Fredericksburg, Chancellorsville - 2/8/1864 Disability/Honorable - Was not a casualty - Maybe Russell (B VT) & probably Philander (B MA) Disbrow - INA- 1817 or 18 in Stafford, Genesee County - Farmer - Farmer - 1st Ellen Comption (Died 6/27/1857), 2nd Susan Jane Osborn, married October, 1857 (he left her for Elizabeth Pitt Mastin & eventually divorced her 6/10/1879), 3rd Elizabeth Pitt Mastin, married 10/28/1881 (Mastin was a grass widow. She claimed she thought her first husband Otis was dead when she married Disbrow. In fact, he had deserted her.) - Charles, Emily, Sarah A., George, Emma (married George Innes) - 10/2/1890 in Ulysses, PA - Ulysses, PA - Transferred to Invalid Corps 9/1/1863. His disability discharge said he was too old and feeble to perform duties. Disbrow, in a document in his pension file, reported that at the battle of Chancellorsville they had to walk through chest deep water. His military file contains the POW records of Charles Disbrow. Alonzo was not a POW. There was a major battle over who was his legal wife entitled to his pension, when he died. None of them received the pension. (Military & Pension Files, 1850 Federal Census, Stafford, Genesee Co., 1865 NYS Census Hume, 1860 Fed. Census, Farmville, Cattaraugus County, 1870 Fed Census Independence)

Dodge, Francis Gibbs Co. C, 104th NY Infantry - 10/21/1861 at Geneseo/3 yrs - 21 - 6'3", Light Complexion, Blue Eyes, Brown Hair - 2/26/1862 at Geneseo - No bounty - Pvt, Corp - No battles - 4/25/1862 Disability/Honorable - INJ, injured his hip when he fell in April, 1862 in DC - Francis W. (B MA) & Emily Scott (B NY) Dodge - William D. & Dallas W. - 9/26/1841 in Hume - Cooper/Farmer - Cooper - 1st Emily Huntington, married 6/1/1864 (died 6/20/1867), 2nd Ellen S. Smith, married 10/5/1869 in Oneida, MI - Stella, Robert, Ralph, Cecil, Glen, Clinton - 5/8/1910 in Manistique, MI - Manistique - Appointed Corporal 11/11/1861, reduced to private 3/5/1862. Enlisted in Co. B, 2nd NY Mounted Rifles (See below.) Was in Kalorama Hospital, DC with hip injury. Brother William also served during the war. (Military & Pension Files, 1865 NYS Census Centerville, 1865 Allegany County Town Clerk Register Centerville, *History of Allegany County 1879*, 1850 Fed. Census Charlton, MA, 1900 Fed. Census Hiawatha Township, MI)

Dodge, Francis Gibbs Co. B, 2nd NY Mounted Rifles - 12/17/1863 at Hume/3 yrs - 22 - 6'2", Light Complexion, Blue Eyes, Dark Hair - 1/12/1864 at Ft. Porter, Buffalo - $400 - R.M. L. Sgt, L.M. Sgt - Spotsylvania, North Anna River, Pamunkey, Totopotomoy, Hanover Court House, Cold Harbor, Bethesda Church, siege of Petersburg, Poplar Springs Church, Pegram's Farm, Hatcher's Run, Weldon RR, Dinwiddie Court House, Five Forks, Appomattox - 8/10/1865 Honorable - Was not a casualty. - Was present at Lee's surrender. Dodge also served with Co. C, 104th NY Infantry, see above. Also see above for personal information and sources of information.

Dodge, Myron Landon Co. F, 4th NY Heavy Artillery - 8/27/1962 at Hume/3 yrs - 32 - 5'9", Light Complexion, Blue Eyes, Brown Hair - 8/29/1862 at NYC - $50 - Pvt, Pvt - No battles - 1/22/1863 Deserted - Was not a casualty - Joseph (B MA) & Mary Chase (B CT) Dodge - INA - 7/25/1828 in Leroy - Moulder - Farmer/Machinist - Mary J. Curtis, married 1/1/1851 in Hume - Estella E. & Horace L. - 8/29/1903 in Stafford County (near Fredericksburg), VA - INA - Charge of desertion removed from his record 6/28/1890. January 22, 1863 established as his discharge date. (Military & Pension Files, 1865 Allegany County Town Clerk Register Hume, 1865 NYS Census Hume,

Dodge, William Decordus Co. F, 33rd NY Infantry - 5/13/1861 at Nunda/3 yrs - 19 - 5'7", Light Complexion, Grey Eyes, Light Brown Hair - 5/22/1861 at Elmira - No bounty - Pvt, Pvt - siege of Yorktown, Williamsburg, Ft. Magruder, Gaine's Mill, Malvern Hill, 2nd Bull Run, South Mountain, Antietam - 3/4/1863 Disability/Honorable at Baltimore - WIA, 9/17/1862 at Antietam, gunshot wound to left foot - Francis W. (B MA) & Emily T. Scott (B NY) Dodge - Francis G. & Dallas W. - 1/19/1843 in Hume - Farmer - Canal Worker/Oil Worker/Producer - Isadore Rawson, married 7/14/1870 in Caneadea - INA - 6/6/1923 at Boonville - Cemetery Road, Caneadea - Brother Francis also served during the war. Per hospital record, gunshot wound may have been self inflicted. Was in Mckine Mansion Hospital in Baltimore. Was a teamster in service. During January and February, 1862, he was detailed to the Pioneer Corps. (Military & Pension Files, 1850 Fed. Census Charlton Township, MA, 1880 Fed. Census Kendal, PA)

Dole, James K. Co. D, 19th NY Cavalry - 9/9/1864 at Genesee Falls/1 yr - 18 - 5'8", Light Complexion, Blue Eyes, Light Hair - 9/13/1864 at Lockport - $750 - Pvt, Pvt - Cedar Creek, Berryville, Gordonsville - 6/30/1865 Honorable - INJ, 12/20/1864 at Kearneytown, PA, injured testicles (on pommel when horse fell on him)- Summer (B VT) & Hannah Griffin (B NY) Dole - Smith, Mary - 7/31/1845 in Pike - Farmer/Boatman - Farm Laborer - Catherine (Kate) McNulty, married 11/13/1865 in Hume - INA - 1/19/1916 in Wiscoy - Wiscoy - Brother Smith also served during the war. Marched in the Grand Review 5/23/1865. Catherine divorced him 7/1/1878 due to his drinking. She then married a Moses Taylor who died in 1887. She remarried James 12/15/1897 in Cleveland. (Military & Pension Files, 1865 NYS Census Hume, Matteson, 1850 Fed. Census Pike, Fillmore American Legion, 1865 Allegany County Town Clerk Register Hume, 1870 Fed. Census Hume, 1900 Fed. Census Granger)

Dole, Smith Co. D, 19th NY Cavalry - 9/7/1864 at Pike/1 yr - 20 - 5'7", Fair Complexion, Hazel Eyes, Brown Hair - 9/7/1864 at Lockport - $500 - Pvt, Pvt - Cedar Creek, Berryville, Gordonsville - 6/30/1865 Honorable - INJ, sometime during period 12/19-28/1864, feet frozen while on picket duty at Gordonsville, VA - Summer (B VT) & Hannah Griffin (B NY) Dole - James, Mary - 8/12/1844 in Pike (Headstone says 1843.) - Farm Laborer - Farm Laborer - 1st Hannah J. Luther, 2nd Julie I. Hill - Julia J., Cora, Thomas R., Mary L. - Per headstone 1895 - Wiscoy - Marched in the Grand Review 5/23/1865. Charter Member and Officer of Burnside G.A.R. Post 237. Brother James also served during the war. (Military & Pension Files, 1890 Fed Census Special Schedule Hume, Matteson, 1865 Allegany County Town Clerk Register Hume, 1865 NYS Census Hume, *Allegany & Its People*, Fillmore American Legion, 1860 Fed. Census Genesee Falls, 1870, 1880 Fed. Censuses Hume)

Donahue, Patrick Donahue was not from the C-H-G area. He originally served with Co. E, 150th PA. Infantry. Hume received credit for his re-enlistment in Co. E, 16th VCR by paying the re-enlistment bonus of $500. (1865 Allegany County Town Clerk Register Hume)

Doolittle, Henry C. Co. K, 19th Ohio Infantry - 8/1/1861 at Janesville, OH - 21 - 5'9", Fair Complexion, Brown Eyes, Brown Hair - 8/28/1861 at Alliance, OH - No bounty - Pvt, Pvt -

possibly siege of Corinth and pursuit of Bragg's Army - 9/30/1864 Honorable at Columbus, OH - Was not a casualty - Alvan (B MA.) & Sarah Felch (B VT) Doolittle - INA - 6/25/1844 in Granger - Probably working for his father, a farmer - Merchant/Retail Grocer - Never Married - None - 3/27/1914 in Joplin, MO - INA - Spent entire service in the hospital. Based on the 1860 Census he was only 16 or 17 when he enlisted rather than the 21 he claimed. (Military & Pension Files, *Allegany & Its People*, 1890 Fed Census Special Schedule Hume, 1850, 1860 Fed. Censuses Granger, 1910 Fed. Census Shoal Creek, MO)

Dorey, Albert H. Co. A, 184th NY Infantry - 9/3/1864 at Granger/1 yr - 20 - 5'9", Light Complexion, Blue Eyes, Light Hair - 9/3/1864 at Elmira - $100 - Pvt, Pvt - No battles - 5/13/1865 Disability/Honorable - Was not a casualty - Darius & Rachael Dorsey Dorey (Both B England) - INA - 8/22/1844 in Granger - Farmer - Farmer - Ophelia - Minnie & Fran - 11/14/1921 in Allen - Short Tract - Sick in hospital almost his entire service. Likely 18 rather than 20 when he enlisted. No specific disability cited in his records. (Military File, *History of Allegany County 1879*, 1865 NYS Census Granger, Granger American Legion, 1865 Allegany County Town Clerk Register Granger, Matteson, 1860 Fed. Census Granger, 1870 Fed. Census Livonia, Livingston County, 1900 Fed. Census Allen)

Dorey, (Dory) John Co. F, 19th NY Cavalry - 8/30/1864 at Allen/1 yr - 28 - 5'9", Light Complexion, Blue Eyes, Light Hair - 9/3/1864 at Elmira - $600 - Pvt, Pvt - Cedar Creek, Berryville, Gordonsville - 2/26/1865 Honorable/Deceased - DD, 2/26/1865 at Harpers Ferry hospital of fever - Father unknown, Mother Deborah Dorey (who married a Bartlett) - Harriet E. Bartlett (Drew), Gennie B. Bartlett (Grover), Timothy Bartlett - 11/15/1835 in Granger - Farm Laborer - None Deceased - Never Married - None - 2/26/1865 in Harpers Ferry, WV - INA - Was working for a Ephraim Bullock in Granger in 1850. Worked for Reuben W. Botsford 11/14/1854 to 3/14/1857 and from 12/12/1859 to 5/7/1864. Was a half brother of Civil War soldier Timothy Bartlett. Harriett and Gennie were half-sisters. Dorey was most likely his mother's maiden name. She was likely never married to his father. (Military & Pension Files, 1865 Allegany County Town Clerk Register Allen, Granger American Legion, *History of Allegany County 1879*, 1850 Fed. Census Granger, 1860 Fed. Census Allen)

Dorey, Thomas Co. K, 184th NY Infantry - 8/31/1864 at Granger/1 yr - 21 - 5'9", Light Complexion, Blue Eyes, Light Hair - 9/30/1864 Elmira - $525 - Pvt, Pvt - Bermuda Hundred, Petersburg, Richmond - 6/29/1865 at City Point, VA Honorable - Was not a casualty - Robert (B England) & Sarah R. Hunt (B NY) Dorey - Isaac, Parmelia, William, Thomas, Jane, Huldah Ann, David L. - 4/28/1843 in Granger - Farmer - Day Laborer - Thallie L. Clark, married 4/21/1887 in Fabius, Onondaga County - Arthur, Ida, Ray, Frank, Bertha, Irene - 7/17/1913 in Dalton - INA - Was at Harrison's landing, VA from 9/16/64 to 10/31/64. Brother William also served during the war. (Military & Pension Files, 1850 Fed. Census Granger, 1865 Allegany County Town Clerk Register Granger, 1900 Fed. Census Nunda)

Dorey, William Co. I, 188th NY Infantry - 9/5/1864 at Leicester/1 yr - 26 - 5'7", Light Complexion, Blue Eyes, Dark Hair - 10/22/1864 at Rochester - $100 - Pvt, Pvt - siege of Petersburg, Hatcher's Run - 6/8/1865 Honorable - Was not a casualty - Robert (B England) &

Sarah R. Hunt (B NY) Dorey - Isaac, Parmelia, Thomas, Jane, Huldah Ann, David L. - 1837or 38 at Granger - Farm Hand - Farmer - Rhoda Ann - Willie - INA - INA - Brother Thomas also served during the war. (Military File, 1865 NYS Census Granger, 1850 Fed. Census Granger, 1860 Fed. Census Portage)

Dorman, Simeon T. Co. H, 109th NY Infantry - 8/11/1862 at Owego/1 yr - 21 - 5'9", Fair Complexion, Blue Eyes, Brown Hair - 8/12/1862 at Binghamton - No bounty - Pvt, Sgt - Railroad guard, defense of DC - 5/25/1863 Honorable - Was not a casualty - Tracy & Charity Dorman (Both B NY) - INA - !841or 42 at Sidney, NY - Carpenter - Carpenter - 1st Esther Ford (Died 1/1/1873), 2nd Katie Brundage, married 8/27/1883 - Lottie, Charles - 1/31/1899 - Until The Dawn Cemetery, Angelica - Enlisted 8/11/1864 at Owego for one year in Co. M, 50th NY Engineers. Was mustered 8/11/1864. Was sick in City Point, VA hospital entire enlistment. Honorably discharged 6/12/1865. (Military & Pension Files, 1890 Fed. Census Special Schedule Granger, 1892 NYS Census Hume, 1860 Fed. Census Owego, 1870 Fed. Census Bainbridge, Chenango County)

Doud, Eben At least one source document indicates that Eben Doud served in the military during the war. No evidence of such service has been located. (Matteson)

Dow, Orrin Marshall Co. C, 104th NY Infantry - 8/8/1861 at Centerville/3 yrs - 35 - 5'10", Light Complexion, Dark Blue Eyes, Auburn Hair - 2/26/1862 at Geneseo - No bounty - Pvt, Pvt - No battles - 5/27/1862 at Mt. Pleasant Hospital, DC, Disability/Honorable - Was not a casualty - Jacob & Elizabeth Conger Dow (Both B VT) - INA - 5/14/1826 in Leicester, VT (some records say 1829 but that is inconsistent with age in 1860 Census) - Farmer - Farmer - 1st Josephine Hewett (died 3/1855), 2nd Abbie R. Robbins, married 1/21/1869 in Rushford - Flora - 10/19/1907 in Centerville - Centerville Cemetery, Route 3 - Disability discharge the result of typhoid fever. Also served with Co. B, 2nd NY Mounted Rifles, see below. (Military & Pension Files, 1865 NYS Census Centerville, Matteson, *History of Allegany County 1879*, 1890 Fed. Census Special Schedule Centerville, Centerville American Legion, 1865 Allegany County Town Clerk Centerville, 1860, 1880 Fed. Censuses Centerville)

Dow, Orrin Marshall Co. B, 2nd NY Mounted Rifles - 12/12/1863 at Centerville/3 yrs - 37 - 5'10", Light Complexion, Dark Blue Eyes, Auburn Hair - 1/12/1864 at Ft. Porter, Buffalo - $700 - Pvt, Sgt - Cold Harbor, Bethesda Church, siege of Petersburg, Weldon RR, Hatcher's Run - 8/10/1865 at Petersburg, VA, Honorable - WIA, 6/6/1864 at Cold Harbor, gunshot above the heart - Some indication he spent time with the 2nd NY Cavalry, but no real records to support this. Some records say he was drafted, but this is doubtful since he had already served with the 104th for which he volunteered in 1861, see above. Also see above for personal information and for sources of information.

Dowing, Luther C. At least one source document lists Luther Dowing, buried in Wiscoy, as having served during the war. The person buried in Wiscoy is actually Luther C. Downing who died in 1849 and could not have served during the Civil War. There is a Burnside G.A.R. Post 237 Marker at Downing's grave, but it must have been moved there accidently. Dowing served with the Vermont militia in the War of 1812. (Fillmore American Legion)

Downey, David Smith Co. F, 4th NY Heavy Artillery - 8/29/1862 at Hume/3 yrs - 24 - 5'10", Dark Complexion, Blue Eyes, Black Hair - 9/12/1862 at NYC - $50 - Pvt, Pvt - No battles - 8/19/1863 Disability/Honorable - Was not a casualty - INA - INA - 3/1/1838 in Londonderry, Ireland - Potter - Farmer/Contractor - Ruby Ann Moore, married 3/14/1859 in Portage - Josephine, Leandis H., George A. Arabelle O., Sarah J., Guy D., Girtez - 1/1/1898 at Palouse City, WA - Palouse - Also served with 2nd NY Mounted Rifles, see below. May have served with Battery D, PA Volunteers. Disability discharge based on disease of heart & angina pectoris. Additional information may be available at Trinity Church, Palouse Mission, Spokane, WA (Military & Pension Files, 1865 NYS Census Hume, *History of Allegany County 1879*, 1865 Allegany County Town Clerk Register Hume, 1870 Fed. Census Alden Township, IA)

Downey, David Smith Co. B, 2nd NY Mounted Rifles - 12/14/1863 at Hume/3 yrs - 25 - 5'10", Light Complexion, Blue Eyes, Brown Hair - 1/12/1864 at Ft. Porter, Buffalo - $300 - Pvt, Pvt - Spotsylvania, North Anna River, Pamunkey, Totopotomoy, Hanover Court House, Cold Harbor, Bethesda Church, siege of Petersburg, Weldon RR, Hatcher's Run, Dinwiddie Court House, Five Forks, Appomattox - 8/10/1865 Honorable - Was not a casualty - Present at Lee's surrender. Also served with Co. F, 4th NY Heavy Artillery, see above. Also see above for personal information and sources of information.

Draper, Stephen Henry Co. B, 13th NY Infantry - 4/25/1861 at Dansville/2 yrs - 26 - 5'11", Light Complexion, Blue Eyes, Dark Hair - 5/14/1861 at Elmira - No bounty - Pvt, Corp - 1st Bull Run, siege of Yorktown, Hanover Court House, Malvern Hill, 2nd Bull Run, Fredericksburg, Ellis Ford, Chancellorsville, defense of DC, New Market, Gordonsville - 5/13/1863 Honorable - INJ, 7/1861 at Fort Corcoran, accidental bayonet to wrist; WIA, 8/30/1862 at 2nd Bull Run, gunshot to fore head - John & Susan Ralph Draper (Both B NY) - INA - 2/22/1836 at Gainesville - Carpenter/ Farm Laborer - Various/Day Laborer/ Merchant - Ellen Burke, married 3/26/1867 in Springwater, Livingston County (one record says 2/20/1867) - Frank - 8/12/1917 in Rossburg - Church Street Cemetery, Wiscoy (No headstone) - Promoted Corp 1/8/1862. Was a scout, sharpshooter, and guide. Also served with Co. K, 21st NY Cavalry, see below. Was in 24th Street Hospital, Philadelphia with gunshot wound. Only time in hospital. His death certificate was signed by fellow soldier and Doctor Perre C. Soule. His father died the year he was born and he was later adopted by the family of Ellery Gifford and moved to Springwater. By 1900 living apart from his wife. (Military & Pension Files, 1890 Fed. Census Granger, Fillmore American Legion, *Allegany & Its People*, 1860 Fed. Census Springwater, 1900, 1910 Fed. Censuses Granger)

Draper, Stephen Henry Co. K, 21st NY Cavalry - 1/5/1864 at Candici/3 yrs - 27 - 5'11', Light Complexion, Blue Eyes, Dark Hair - 1/5/1864 at Canandaigua - $60 - Pvt, 2nd Lt. - Hay Market, Hunter's raid on Lynchburg - 5/15/1865 Resigned/Honorable - INJ, 12/1864 at Smithfield, WV While trying to capture a Southern scout his horse bolted, ran into a tree and fell. Suffered laceration of thumb, right ear and a spinal injury, WIA, 3/6/1865 at White Post, VA, in hand to hand combat was struck by an army revolver and suffered scalp wounds to front and top of head, INJ, 5/1865 while on his way from Winchester, VA to DC for Grand Review, his horse stumbled and he fell over the cantle of a McClellan saddle and injured his testicles. Credited with running two locomotives out from behind enemy lines. Claimed secret service work, but no evidence of this found. On the other hand, his 21st Cavalry file indicates that he was on special duty at headquarters as of 12/9/1864 and that he was still absent on special duty as of April, 1865. Was at, but did not march in Grand Review. Also served with Co. B, 13th NY Infantry, see above. Also see above for personal information and sources of information.

Dresser, Henry Clay Co. A, 184th NY Infantry - 9/2/1864 at Granger/1 yr - 19 - 5'9", Light Complexion, Blue Eyes, Brown Hair - 9/3/1864 at Elmira - $100 - Pvt, Pvt - Cedar Creek, before Petersburg & Richmond - 6/29/1865 Honorable - Was not a casualty - Joel & Belinda A. Potter (Both B NY) - Harmon - 9/21/1844 in Granger (one record says Gainesville) - Farmer - Farmer/Carpet Dealer - Mary E. Campbell, married 11/6/1872 in Jefferson, IA - Ira, Joel, Gurden Charles, Hattie Alden - 11/30/1911 at Polk County, IA - Glendale Cemetery, Des Moines, IA - Like all recruits into the 184th, Dresser received a knapsack, haversack, canteen, cup, plate, knife, fork and spoon. One document says he was married at Boone County, IA. Last name was probably originally Van Dresser. (Military & Pension Files, 1865 Allegany Town Clerk Register Granger, Granger American Legion, *History of Allegany County 1879*, 1865 NYS Census Granger, 1850, 1860 Fed. Censuses Granger, 1900 Fed. Census Des Moines, IA, 1910 Fed. Census Bloomfield, IA)

Drew, Amos Frank Co. C, 104th NY Infantry - 12/30/1861 at Geneseo/3 yrs - 33 - 5'8", Light Complexion, Blue Eyes, Brown Hair - 2/26/1862 at Geneseo - No bounty - Pvt, Pvt - No battles - 1/13/1863 Disability/Honorable - INJ, June or July, 1862 at Catlett's Station, injured back (lumbar region) working on a bridge - Nathaniel (B NH) & Sally Nichols (B NY) Drew - Charles, Polly, James. Electa, John - 8/22/1825 in Warsaw - Laborer/Wagon Maker - Farmer - Hannah A. Drew (his cousin), married 6/14/1853 in Portage - George W., Charley F. - 10/16/1905 in Soldiers & Sailors Home, Grand Rapids, MI - Grand Rapids Soldiers and Sailors Home - Also served with 4th NY Heavy Artillery, see below. Disability discharge due to back injury. Lived in Fillmore 1860's, 70's. (Military & Pension Files, 1865 Allegany County Town Clerk Register Hume, 1865 NYS Census Hume, 1860, 1870 Fed. Censuses Hume, 1900 Fed. Census Union Township, MI)

Drew, Amos Frank Co. F, 4th NY Heavy Artillery - 12/23/1863 at Hume/3 yrs - 33 - 5'8", Light Complexion, Blue Eyes, Brown Hair - 1/5/1864 at Elmira - $300 - Pvt, Pvt - Wilderness, Spotsylvania, North Anna River, Totopotomoy, Cold Harbor, siege of Petersburg - 2/27/1865 Disability/Honorable - WIA, 6/18/1864 at Petersburg, gunshot to left thigh (caused paralysis, loss of sensation), INJ, 5/16/1864 at Spotsylvania, hearing affected by canon fire - Was in Emory Square Hospital with Spotsylvania wounds. Also served with 104th NY Infantry, see above. Also see above for personal information and sources of information.

Drew, Hiram Co. F, 4th NY Heavy Artillery - 12/23/1863 at Hume/3 yrs - 27 - 5'11", Dark Complexion, Black Eyes, Black Hair - 12/23/1863 at Elmira - $300 - Pvt, Pvt - Wilderness, Spotsylvania, North Anna River - 7/24/1864 Honorable/Deceased - POW, captured 3/25/1864 at North Anna River, Prison: Andersonville, DD, 7/24/1864 at Andersonville of typhoid fever - Hiram (B NH) & Anna Hopkins (B NY) Drew - John, Hannah, Anna, Julia Ann, Olive, Lycurgus, William, Matilda, Mary Jane - 1837 in Orangeville, Wyoming County - Laborer - None Deceased - Elizabeth A. Williams, married 4/13/1860 at Genesee Falls, Wyoming County - Probably William

Ira - 7/24/1864 at Andersonville - Andersonville (His headstone incorrectly lists the State as Indiana.) - Was never heard from after his capture. Wife finally heard of his death a long time later from the military. Was originally listed as MIA. Elizabeth later married Civil War Veteran John Harwood. Brothers John, Lycurgus, and William also served during the war. (Military & Pension Files, Allegany County Web Site, 1865 Allegany County Town Clerk Register Hume, 1850 Fed. Census Caneadea, 1860 Fed. Census Granger)

Drew, John Co. C, 104th NY Infantry - 12/30/1861 at Geneseo/3 yrs - 30 - 5'11", Light Complexion, Dark Blue Eyes, Brown Hair - 2/26/1862 at Geneseo - No bounty - Pvt, Pvt - Cedar Creek, 2nd Bull Run - 8/30/1862 Honorable/Deceased - KIA, 8/30/1862 at 2nd Bull Run - Hiram (B NH) & Anna Hopkins (B NY) Drew - John, Hannah, Hiram, Hannah, Anna Julia Ann, Olive Lycurgus, William, Matilda, Mary Jane - 9/1835 in Orangeville, Wyoming County - Laborer - None/Deceased - Never Married - None - 8/30/1862 at 2nd Bull Run - Arlington National Cemetery - Was originally buried on the battlefield at Manassas. Brothers Hiram, Lycurgus, and William also served during the war. (Military File, Allegany County Web Site, 1850 Fed. Census Caneadea)

Drew, Lycurgus D. Co. C/E, 85th NY Infantry - 9/1/1861 at Granger/3 yrs - 20 - 5'11", Light Complexion, Black Eyes, Brown Hair - 11/11/1861 at Elmira - No bounty - Pvt, Pvt - defense of DC, siege of Yorktown, Williamsburg, Fair Oaks, before Richmond - 12/1/1862 Disability/ Honorable - Was not a casualty - Hiram (B NH) & Anna Hopkins (B NY) Drew - John, Hannah, Hiram, Anna, Julia Ann, Olive, William, Matilda, Mary Jane - 1840 or 41 probably in Orangeville, Wyoming County - Farmer - INA - INA - INA - INA - INA - Was in convalescent hospital near Alexandria, VA. when discharged. Was in hospital at Harrison's Landing as of 8/15/1862 and at Blackwells Island (East River), NYC as of October, 1862. Brothers Hiram, John and William also served during the war. (Military File, *History of Allegany County 1879*, 1865 Allegany County Town Clerk Register Hume, Matteson, 1850 Fed. Census Caneadea)

Drew, William H. Co. C, 194th NY Infantry - 3/29/1865 at Hume/1 yr - 19 - 5'6", Dark Complexion, Black Eyes, Black Hair - 4/7/1865 at Elmira - $800 - Pvt, Pvt - No battles - 5/3/1865 Honorable - Was not a casualty - Hiram (B NH) & Anna Hopkins (B NY) Drew - John, Hannah, Hiram, Anna, Julia Ann, Olive, Lucurgus, Matilda, Mary Jane - 4/3/1846 in Caneadea - Laborer - Farmer - 1st Harriet A. Foster, married 4/3/1871 in New Haven Center, MI, 2nd Sarah - Erwin, Ira F., W. Eugene, Allen - 5/3/1931 in Watervliet, MI - INA - Brothers Hiram, John, and Lycurgus also served during the war. Had measles in service which affected his eyes, throat, and lungs. (Military & Pension Files, Book *History of Allegany County 1879*, 1850 Fed Census Caneadea, 1880 Fed Census, New Haven, MI, 1930 Fed Census Watervliet, MI)

Drury, Edwin S. Co. C, 4th Michigan Cavalry - 8/9/1862 at Comstock, MI/3 yrs - 28 - 5'7", Dark Complexion, Brown Eyes, Black Hair - 8/28/1862 at Detroit - $25 - Pvt, Corp - Stanford, TN, Franklin, Stone River, Middletown, Guy's Gap, Shelbyville, Chickamauga, McMinnville, Eastern & Georgia RR Raid, Cleveland, TN - 1/15/1864 Deceased/Honorable - WIA, 12/22/1863 at Cleveland, TN (exact wound not identified), KIA died 1/15/1864 at Cleveland, TN of wounds - Samuel & Hannah Burgers Drury (Both B England) - Eli - 1/1834 in Cayuga County, NY -

Farmer/Laborer - None Deceased - Never Married - None - 1/15/1864 in Cleveland, TN - Chattanooga National Cemetery - Promoted to Corporal 2/17/1863. His commander said of him, "The amiable comrade. A brave and patriotic soldier - never knew fear. He fell a martyr to the cause for which he so nobly fought." In 1860 he and his brother Eli were living with a Dr. Babcock, also born in NY, in Kalamazoo, MI. Parents were living in Granger. Listed on Soldiers Monument in Granger. Brother Eli also served during the war. (Military File, 1865 NYS Census Granger, *Allegany & Its People*, Granger American Legion, 1860 Fed. Census Kalamazoo, MI)

Drury, Eli Warren Co. E, 85th NY Infantry - 9/1/1861 at Granger/3 yrs - 23 - 6', Light Complexion, Black Eyes, Sandy Hair - 10/25/1861 at Elmira - No bounty - Pvt, Pvt - defense of DC, siege of Yorktown, Williamsburg, Fair Oaks, before Richmond - 12/1/1862 Disability/Honorable - Was not a casualty - Samuel & Hannah Burgers Drury (Both B England) - Edwin S. - 4/28/1838 (Pension says 9/11/38) in Geneseo - Farmer - Farmer - Grace Van Nostrand, married 3/10/1869 - William and Raymond - 4/22/1920 in Granger - Short Tract - Town Clerk says he was discharged as unfit for duty 9/1/1863, but military file almost surely correct on discharge date. Health report said he had a rupture of the rectum. Military File spells last name Drewry. Some documents have him as a Corporal, but nothing in Military File. Brother Edwin also served during the war. (Military & Pension Files, 1865 Allegany County Town Clerk Register Granger, Matteson, Granger American Legion, 1850, 1880, 1900, 1910 Fed. Censuses Granger, *History of Allegany County 1879*, 1890 Fed. Census Special Schedule Granger, 1865 NYS Census Granger)

Dudley, John L. Co. G, 19th NY Cavalry - 12/26/1863 at Angelica/3 yrs - 30 - 6', Dark Complexion, Black Eyes, Dark Hair - 12/26/1863 at Elmira - $100 - Pvt, Pvt - No battles - 7/19/1865 Disability/Honorable - INJ, 5/12/1864 at Spotsylvania, left knee joint - Elon (B CT) & Fanney L. (B RI) Dudley - Sara D., Horace E., George C., Charles H., Abigail E., Fanny C. - 9/1833 in Allegany County - Lumberman - Farmer - 1st Mary M. 2nd Artelissa - Archie, Fanny, George, Elon H., Lee J., Carl S. - 5/4/1919 in Granger - Short Tract - Was sick almost entire time in service. (Military File, 1890 Fed. Census Special Schedule Granger, Granger American Legion, Matteson, 1865 Allegany County Town Clerk Register Angelica, 1850, 1860 Fed. Censuses Angelica, 1870, 1880, 1900, 1910 Fed. Censuses Granger)

Dunning, Henry Co. D, 188th NY Infantry - 9/20/1864 at Avon/1 yr - 27 - 5'7", Dark Complexion, Black Eyes, Black Hair - 9/20/1864 at Rochester - $100 - Pvt, Pvt - siege of Petersburg, Hatcher's Run, Weldon RR, Gravelly Run, Five Forks, Appomattox - 7/1/1865 Honorable - Was not a casualty - Lewis & Flora Dunning (Both B VT) - Richard, Henry, Sara A., Joshua, Branson - 5/15/1837 in West Almond - Farmer - Farmer - Ann L. Easton, married 9/26/1860 in Phillips - Stephen L., Flora Lavilla, (died), Flora Lavilla, Jesse B. - 9/30/1917 in Hume - Pine Grove Cemetery, Fillmore - Burnside G.A.R. Post 237 Marker at grave. (Military & Pension Files, Fillmore American Legion, Matteson, 1890 Fed. Census Special Schedule Hume, 1850 Fed. Census West Almond, 1900 Fed. Census Hume)

Dutton, George Washington Co. C, 19th NY Cavalry - 8/16/1862 at Eagle/3 yrs - 25 - 5'9", Light Complexion, Blue Eyes, Brown Hair - 9/3/1862 at Portage Station - No bounty - Corp, Pvt - Deserted House, siege of Suffolk, Franklin, Manassas Junction, Bristoe's Station, Five Forks -

9/27/1865 Honorable - POW, captured 3/31/1865 at Five Forks, Prison not identified in files, released 4/30/1865 at Aikens Landing, VA - Horace & Katherine Coddington Dutton - INA - 5/27/1836 in Lee, Oneida County - Farmer - Farmer - Emma - Sarah, Sophia, Hattee - 9/5/1918 in Leroy - INA - Was sick in hospital at Rochester for quite a time. Contracted diarrhea at Manassas Junction. (Military & Pension Files, 1865 NYS Census Centerville, 1865 Allegany County Town Clerk Register Centerville, 1860, 1870 Fed. Censuses Eagle, Wyoming County)

Edmonds, John Co. D, 64th NY Infantry - 9/13/1861 at Rushford/3 yrs - 19 - INA - 9/24/61 at Elmira - No bounty - Pvt, Pvt - siege of Yorktown, Fair Oaks - 6/1/1862 Honorable/Deceased - KIA, 6/1/1862 at Fair Oaks - Rowland (B Wales) & Elizabeth Jones (B NY) Edmonds - Ervin, Catherine, Jane, John, Joseph, Elizabeth - 1/1840 - None listed in 1860, probably working for his father, a farmer - None Deceased - Never Married - None - 6/1/1862 in Fair Oaks - Fair Oaks? - At home sick on furlough 9/24/1861 to 2/1862. (Military File, 1865 NYS Census Centerville, 1865 Allegany County Town Clerk Register Centerville, 1850 Fed. Census Centerville)

Eells, Hiram Co. C, 188th NY Infantry - 9/3/1864 at Avon/1 yr - 5'8", Light Complexion, Blue Eyes, Brown Hair - 10/41864 at Rochester - No bounty - Pvt, Pvt - siege of Petersburg, Hatcher's Run, Weldon RR, Gravelly Run, Five Forks, Appomattox - 7/1/1865 Honorable, WIA, 10/27/1864 at 1st battle of Hatcher's Run, gunshot to jaw - Pitkin (B CT) & Isyphhena (B NY) Eells - Joseph, Eunice, Mary - 1845 in Steuben County - Pedlar - Farm Laborer - Nettie Whitbeck, married 9/18/1864 in Avoca, Steuben County - Frank W., Fred - 4/26/1921 at Granger (headstone says 1920) - Short Tract - Military Index has last name as Ellis. His commander called him a "good soldier." Present at Lee's surrender. Marched in Grand Review 5/23/1865. His father was born in France. (Military & Pension Files, Matteson, Granger American Legion, 1850 Fed. Census Wheeler, Steuben County 1880 Fed. Census Jerusalem, Yates, County1910, 1920 Fed. Census Granger)

Eldredge, Loomis (Eldridge) Co. F, 4th NY Heavy Artillery - 9/28/1862 at NYC/3 yrs - 35 - INA - 10/2/1862 at NYC - $100 - Pvt, Pvt - Wilderness, Spotsylvania, North Anna River, Totopotomoy, Cold Harbor, siege of Petersburg, Weldon RR, fall of Petersburg (South Side RR) - 6/8/1865 Honorable - WIA, 4/2/1865 at South Side RR, gunshot to both thighs - INA - possibly Milo, Henry, and Roswell - 1828 in Orleans County - Farmer - Farmer - Eliza A. Benson, married 1/26/1853 in Granger - Cora, Ada E., Edward E., Elsie L. - 3/27/1872 - INA - Marched in Grand Review 5/23/1865. Either had a sister named Cynthia or she was his first wife. (Military & Pension Files, 1865 NYS Census Granger, 1865 Allegany County Town Clerk Register Granger, Granger American Legion, 1850, 1860, 1870 Fed. Censuses Granger)

Eldredge, Mark Smith Co. F, 4th NY Heavy Artillery - 9/27/1862 at Hume/3 yrs - 23 - 5'8", Light Complexion, Black Eyes, Brown Hair - 10/2/1862 at NYC - No bounty - Pvt, Sgt - siege of Petersburg, Weldon RR, Ream's Station, fall of Petersburg, Appomattox - 9/26/1865 Honorable - Was not a casualty - Henry & Lucinda Smith Eldridge (Both B NY) - Lida, Willard, Lewis - 6/28/1839 in Livonia - Farmer - Farmer/Post Office - 1st Unknown, married 1861, 2nd Sarah, married 1866 (died 12/1913), 3rd Jennie G. Gleason, married 10/22/1918 in Los Angeles - INA - 5/12/1921 in Los Angeles - INA - Present at Lee's surrender. Marched in Grand Review

5/23/1865. Temporarily transferred to 3rd Independent Battery, NY Light Artillery, 4/27/1865 and returned 6/11/1864. Promoted to Corp 7/1864 and Sgt. 2/10/1864. 1/1865 on duty at regimental stables. His father owned farms in both Portage and Granger. (Military & Pension Files, 1865 Allegany County Town Clerk Register Granger, 1850 Fed. Census Granger, 1870 Fed. Census Bonus, IL., 1920 Fed. Census Los Angeles, CA)

Ellenwood, Laselle S. (Ellingwood) Co. D, 102nd NY Infantry - 10/2/1861 at Pike/3 yrs - 21 - 6'. Light Complexion, Grey Eyes, Brown Hair - 10/22/61 at Buffalo - No bounty - Pvt, Pvt - No battles - 6/22/1863 Disability/Honorable (per one muster card in file, Date on this card is probably wrong and it probably refers to his discharge from the 78th Infantry, see below.) - Was not a casualty - John F. & Adaline Spencer Ellingwood - Cora, Mary E., Fannie S. - 1/8/1840 in Conneaut, OH - Carpenter - None Deceased - Never Married - None - 9/28/1863 at a Rochester, NY hospital - Mt. Hope Cemetery, Rochester - Last name was probably Ellingwood. Files are a mess. Also served with the 78th NY Infantry, see below. He was never taken up on the rolls of the 102nd. (Military & Pension Files, Annual Report of NYS Adjutant General 1901 Volume 29, Allegany County Web Site Hume, 1860 Fed. Census Hume)

Ellenwood, Laselle S.(Ellingwood) Co. A/D 78th NY Infantry - 10/21/1861 at Pike or Buffalo/3 years - 25 - 6', Light Complexion, Grey Eyes, Brown Hair - 10/21/1861 at Buffalo - No bounty - Pvt, Pvt - Cedar Mountain, Sulfur Springs, Groveton, 2nd Bull Run, Antietam - 10/15/1862 Disability/Honorable - Was not a casualty - "Certificate of Discharge" shows he enlisted at Buffalo, 10/21/1861 and was discharged 10/25/1862. Had chronic diarrhea for 3 months, also typhoid fever. Was in hospital, possible at Frederick, MD, but also at Cliffburne Hospital, DC for 3 months. There is no mention in the 78th file about his enlistment in the 102nd, but clearly it is the same person. See above for 102nd information. Also see above for personal information and sources of information.

Ellis, Darwin Co. F, 19th NY Cavalry - 8/8/1862 at Centerville/3 yrs - 23 - 5'1", Light Complexion, Blue Eyes, Brown Hair - 9/3/1862 at Portage Station - $50 - Pvt, Pvt - Deserted House, siege of Suffolk, Manassas Junction, Bristoe's Station, Culpeper Court House, Wilderness, Todd's Tavern, Spotsylvania, North Anna River, Yellow Tavern - 5/16/1864 Honorable/Deceased - KIA, 5/16/1864 at Yellow Tavern, VA - David & Polly Woodward Ellis - Mary E. - 1/1839 in Centerville - Farmer - None Deceased - Never Married - None - 5/16/1864 in Hungary, VA - INA - Some reports indicate that he was wounded and died from his wounds within a day or two. Grandfather Reuben born in VT (Military & Pension Files, 1865 NYS Census Centerville, *History of Allegany County 1879*, Matteson, 1865 Allegany County Town Clerk Register Centerville, 1860 Fed. Census Centerville)

Ellis, James At least one source document indicates that James Ellis served in the military during the war. No evidence of such service has been located. (Register of Draftees July 1863 to October, 1864 Centerville)

Ellis, Richard D.or P. Co. G, 78th NY Infantry - 12/3/1861 at Centerville/3 yrs - 44 - 6'1", Dark Complexion, Hazel Eyes, Dark Hair - 10/11/1861 at Buffalo - No bounty - Pvt, Sgt - No battles -

5/24/1862 Deserted - Was not a casualty - INA - INA - 1817 or 18 in England - Farmer - Farmer - Mary Jane - Esther A., Elizabeth J., William P., Martha, Albert, May J. - INA - INA - Deserted from the Soldier's Retreat in DC. Apparently the military made little effort to locate him after he deserted, since he lived post war only about ten miles from where he lived prewar. (Military File, *History of Allegany County 1879*, Matteson, 1850, 1860 Fed. Censuses Freedom, 1870 Fed. Census Sardinia)

Ellsworth, Joseph Not from the C-H-G area. Served with Co. B, 1st NY Veteran Cavalry. Enlistment credited to Hume Township which paid his enlistment or enlistment bonus of $400. (1865 Allegany County Town Clerk Register Hume)

Elmer, Alonzo M. Co. F, 19th NY Cavalry - 8/15/1862/3 yrs - 5'8", Dark Complexion, Black Eyes, Black Hair - 9/3/1862 at Portage - $50 - Pvt, Pvt - Deserted House, siege of Suffolk, Franklin, Manassas Junction, Bristoe's Station, Culpeper Court House, Wilderness, Todd's Tavern, Spotsylvania, North Anna River, Yellow Tavern, Pamunkey, Totopotomoy, Cold Harbor, Trevillian, Charles County Court House, before Richmond & Petersburg, New Market, Shepherdstown, Winchester, Fisher's Hill, New Market, Port Republic, Cedar Creek, Berryville, Gordonsville, Dinwiddie Court House, Five Forks - WIA, 4/2/1865 at Five Forks, gunshot to left clavicle, KIA, died 5/14/1865 of gunshot wound and complications - Joel (B NY) & Mercy Russell (B MA) Elmer - Emery, America, Levi, George - 6/9/1833 in Hume - Farmer/Mason - None Deceased - Anna Clark, married 3/3/1860 in Hume - None - 5/14/1865 in Point of Rocks - Pine Grove Cemetery, Fillmore - Originally buried at Point of Rocks. His wife Anna requested that his body be shipped home and was told it would not be possible for at least a year. Brother George also served in the military during the war. (Military & Pension Files, Allegany County Web Site, 1865 NYS Census Hume, 1865 Allegany County Town Clerk Register Hume, 1860 Fed. Census Hume)

Elmer, George Co. F, 4th NY Heavy Artillery - 12/19/1863 at Hume/3 yrs - 41 - 6', Light Complexion, Blue Eyes, Brown Hair - 12/21/1863 at Elmira - $300 - Pvt, Pvt - Wilderness, Spotsylvania, North Anna River, Totopotomoy, Cold Harbor, siege of Petersburg, Weldon RR, Ream's Station - 5/31/1865 Honorable - Was not a casualty - Joel (B NY) & Marcy Russell (B MA) Elmer - Emery, America, Levi, Alonzo - 4/4/1823 in Hume - Mason/Weaver - Mason - 1st Caroline Brown, married 1/24/1844 in Centerville, 2nd Addie S., married 6/26/1900 in Milwaukee - Wilbur A., George F., Dora C. (had a total of 5 children) - 9/22/1905 in Lake Geneva, WI - INA - Brother Alonzo and son Wilbur also served during the war. Was in National Soldiers Home, Northwest Branch in 1904. (Military & Pension Files, 1865 NYS Census Hume, 1865 Allegany County Town Clerk Register Hume, 1850 Fed. Census Hume, 1900 Fed. Census Lake Geneva, WI)

Elmer, Wilbur A. Co. F, 4th NY Heavy Artillery - 9/9/1862 at Hume/3 yrs - 16 - INA - 9/11/1862 - $100 - Pvt, Pvt - Wilderness, Spotsylvania, North Anna River, fall of Petersburg, Appomattox - 6/3/1865 Honorable - Was not a casualty - George & Caroline Blackman Brown Elmer (Both B NY) - Charles A., George F., Lydia A., Della B., Dora, Nettie E. - 10/11/1844 in Hume - Probably working for his father, a mason - Stone-Brick Mason/Stone Cutter/Plasterer - Ellen Searl, married

2/12/1867 - Nellie - 3/13/1923 in Oramel - Riverside Cemetery, Belfast - Present at Lee's surrender. Marched in Grand Review 5/23/1865. Father George also served during the war. Had mumps & testicle disease in service. Wilbur's records are indexed under the name Wilber Elmore. He was so sick in the fall of 1862 and winter of 1863 that his father was told that if he wanted to see him alive, he should visit him at the Ft. Gaines, MD hospital. He did, and nursed Wilbur back to health. His father did not enter the service until 12/1863. (Military & Pension Files, 1865 NYS Census Hume, 1865 Allegany County Town Clerk Register Hume,1850, 1860 Fed. Censuses Hume, 1900 Fed Census Caneadea)

Elwood, William Co. G/I, 136th NY Infantry - 9/3/1862 at Granger/3 yrs - 22 - 5'10", Fair Complexion, Blue Eyes, Light Hair - 9/25/1862 at Portage - No bounty - Pvt, Pvt - Chancellorsville, Gettysburg, Wauhatchie, Orchard Knob, Tunnel Hill, Missionary Ridge, Resaca, New Hope Church, Pine Mountain, Golgotha, Kenesaw Mountain, Peach Tree Creek, siege and occupation of Atlanta - 9/25/1864 Honorable/Deceased - DD, 9/25/1864 at Atlanta of service related sickness (specific disease not listed in records) - Isaac & Elizabeth Buchanan Elwood - INA - 6/1840 in Sparta - Farm Laborer - None Deceased - Never Married - None - 9/25/1864 in Atlanta - Marietta National Cemetery, GA (Memorial headstone Church Street Cemetery, Dalton) - (Military File, 1865 NYS Census Granger, *History of Allegany County 1879*, 1865 Allegany County Town Clerk Register Granger, 1860 Fed. Census Granger, *Roll of Honor*)

Emory, Oscar Peter Co. C, 104th NY Infantry - 12/2/1861 at Granger/3 yrs - 21 - 5'9", Light Complexion, Blue Eyes, Dark Hair - 2/26/1862 at Geneseo - No bounty - Pvt, Pvt - No battles - 5/13/1862 Honorable/Deceased - Jonathan Sherwin (B NH) & Abigail Nourse (B VT) Emory - Edwin, George, Albert - 8/11/1838 in Granger - Farmer - None Deceased - Never Married - None - 5/13/1862 in Clermont Hospital, Alexandria, VA. - Arlington National Cemetery - Listed on Soldiers Monument in Granger Name spelled Emery and initials C.P. (Military & Pension Files, 1865 Allegany County Town Clerk Register Granger, Matteson, Book, *Allegany & Its People*, 1850 Fed. Census Granger)

Emmons John William Co. A, 19th NY Cavalry - 1/18/1864 at Grove/3 yrs - 18 - 5'4", Fair Complexion, Blue Eyes, Brown Hair - 1/18/1864 at Elmira - $400 - Pvt, Pvt - No battles - 2/28/1864 Honorable/Deceased - DD, 2/28/1864 at U.S. Post Hospital, Elmira of acute bronchitis - George W. (B NJ) & Loretta Coon (B NY) Emmons - Isaiah, Susan - 5/25/1845 in Fairfield, PA - Farmer - None Deceased - Never Married - None - 5/25/1845 in Fairfield, PA - Oakwood Cemetery, Nunda - Was actually only 16 when he volunteered. Listed on Soldiers Monument in Granger. (Military & Pension Files, Matteson, *Allegany & Its People*, Granger American Legion, 1860 Fed. Census Granger)

Emmons, Levi Co. F, 4th NY Heavy Artillery - 9/25/1862 at Hume/3 yrs - 37 - 5'11", Light Complexion, Black Eyes, Brown Hair - 10/2/1862 - $100 - Pvt, Pvt - Wilderness, Spotsylvania, North Anna River, Totopotomoy, Cold Harbor, siege of Petersburg, Weldon RR, Ream's Station, fall of Petersburg, Appomattox - 9/26/1865 Honorable - POW, captured 8/25/1864 at Ream's Station, Prison: Richmond, paroled Vienna, VA 10/8/1864 - John & Sylvia Meddler Emmons (Both B NY) - INA - 3/29/1823 - Blacksmith - Blacksmith/Farmer/Farm Worker - Elizabeth Ann

Babcock, married 3/23/1843 in Pike - Esther, Frank Leroy - 11/15/1899 in Fife Lake, MI - Fife Lake, MI - Spent some time in service detailed to Brigade Headquarters as a blacksmith. Present at Lee's surrender. Marched in Grand Review 5/23/1865. (Military & Pension Files, 1865 NYS Census Granger, 1865 Allegany County Town Clerk Register Granger, 1860 Fed. Census Granger, 1880 Fed. Census Otsego County)

Emons, H At least one source document indicates that H. Emons served in the military during the war. No evidence of this service has been identified. This most likely refers to one of the Emmons who did serve or someone else with a similar name. (Matteson)

Evans, David Co. M, 16th NY Cavalry - 9/9/1863 at Arcade/3 yrs - 18 - 5'6", Light Complexion, Blue Eyes, Dark Hair - 10/18/1863 at Staten Island - No bounty - Pvt, Pvt - Dranesville - 5/8/1864 Honorable/Deceased - DD, 5/8/1864 at Vienna, VA hospital of typhoid fever - Benjamin & Mary Morgan Evans (Both B Wales) - Ann - 4/1842 in Carmarthenshire, South Wales - Never Married - None - 5/8/1864 in Vienna, VA - Arlington National Cemetery - 1865 NYS Census says he died of battle wounds, no evidence of that in his files. Age at entrance and birth year are probably wrong. The 1860 Census has his age as 11, making him only 14 or 15 when he entered the service. (Military & Pension Files, 1865 NYS Census Centerville, 1860 Fed. Census Centerville)

Everett, James S., Jr. Not from the C-H-G area. Served with Co. D, 61st NY Infantry. Enlistment credited to Hume Township which paid his enlistment bonus of $400. (1865 Allegany County Town Clerk Register Hume)

Farman, Samuel Ara Co. F, 19th NY Infantry - 8/19/1862 at Hume/3 yrs - 26 - 5'11", Light Complexion, Blue Eyes, Light Hair - 9/3/1862 at Portage Station - $50 - 1st Lt, 1st Lt - Deserted House, siege of Suffolk - 7/30/1863 Resigned/Honorable - Was not a casualty - Burdock & Martha Dix Farman (Both B NY) - Elbert - 12/6/1835 in New Haven, Gratiot County - Clerk - Merchant/Dry Goods/Insurance Agent/Post Master - Sarah Andrina d'Autremont, married 4/19/1859 in Hume - Henry S. - 3/5/1912 in Portageville - Maple Grove Cemetery, Gainesville - Received 10 days leave 3/11/1863. May-June,1863 in Hampton, VA hospital. Suffered from varicose veins, chronic diarrhea, and hemorrhoids while in service. Wife was a descendant of French royalty. Her father had fled France with other royalists during the French Revolution. His brother Elbert was a substantial citizen. An attorney, he was Consul General in Egypt and a Judge of the Mixed Tribunals, International Court of Egypt. Originally moved to Fillmore in 1857. (Military & Pension Files, *Allegany & Its People*, 1865 Allegany County Town Clerk Register Hume, 1860, 1900 Fed. Censuses Hume, 1870 Fed. Census Wetherfield, 1910 Fed. Census Genesee Falls)

Fetterley, Henry (Fetely) Co. I, 81st NY Infantry - 12/21/1863 at Amesville/3 yrs - 21 - 5'6", Dark Complexion, Blue Eyes, Dark Hair - 12/28/1863 at Utica - $100 - Pvt, Pvt - Petersburg, Drury's Bluff, Richmond, Cold Harbor, Chaffin's Farm, New Marker Heights, Petersburg, Appomattox - 8/4/1865 Honorable - Was not a casualty - Darius & Sabrina Feterly (Both B NY) - Esther, Sally S. - 3/22/1842 in Jefferson County, NY - Farmer - Farmer - Dorcas McMurtry, married 4/2/1868 in Caneadea - Cora, Bruce - 2/20/1927 in Fillmore - Short Tract - Charged with desertion 8/7/

1865 at Williamsburg, VA. Charge later removed, since he had already been discharged. Present at Lee's surrender. (Military & Pension Files, Matteson, Granger American Legion, 1890 Fed. Census Special Schedule Granger, 1870 Fed. Census Allen, 1900, 1910 Fed. Censuses Granger)

Finch, Daniel Co. F, 4th NY Heavy Artillery - 12/19/1863 at Hume/3 yrs - 34 - 5'9", Fair Complexion, Blue Eyes, Black Hair - 12/19/1863 at Elmira - $300 - Pvt, Pvt - Wilderness, Spotsylvania, North Anna River - 9/22/1864 Honorable/Deceased- DD, 9/22/1864 at Willett's Point Hospital, NY Harbor of scorbutus - Enoch & Catherine Fox Finch (Both B NY) - Joseph, Celinda, Caroline - 4/14/1828 in Centerville - Farmer/Teamster - None Deceased - Never Married - None - Grant General Hospital, Willett's Point, NY - Cypress Hills National Cemetery, NY - Some question about the battles in which he participated, almost surely the Wilderness and Spotsylvania and probably North Anna River. (Military & Pension Files, Allegany County Web Site, 1840 Fed. Census Centerville, 1850 Fed. Census Franklinville)

Findley, Samuel (Findlay) (Findly) At least one source document indicates that Findley served in the military during the war. No evidence of such service has been located. (1865 NYS Census Centerville)

Fish, John C. Co. F, 4th NY Heavy Artillery - 8/9/1862 at Hume/3 yrs - 29 - 5'9", Light Complexion, Blue Eyes, Black Hair - 8/27/1862 at NYC - $50 - Pvt, Pvt - Wilderness, Spotsylvania, North Anna River, Totopotomoy, Cold Harbor, siege of Petersburg, Weldon RR, Ream's Station, Peeble's Farm, Hatcher's Run (Detached to Brigade Artillery, 2nd Corps, no information on battles.) - 6/3/1865 Honorable - Was not a casualty - Gurden & Eleanor Penuf Fish - INA - 4/18/1833 in Edingboro, PA - Moulder/Pattern Maker/Inventor - Machinist - Jane M. Jones, married 9/16/1854 in Chylerville, Livingston County - Emma J., L.J., Bettie, Grace - 5/26/1883 in Wiscoy - Wiscoy - Marched in Grand Review 5/23/1865. Slight chance his last name could have been Fisk. (Military & Pension Files, 1865 Allegany County Town Clerk Register Hume, Matteson, Fillmore American Legion, 1860 Fed. Census Hume, 1870 Fed. Census Geneseo, Livingston County)

Fisk, Coroden Co. D, 4th NY Heavy Artillery - 8/13/1862 at Rochester/3 yrs - 32 - 5'9", Florid Complexion, Blue Eyes, Black Hair - 8/13/1862 at Rochester - $50 - Pvt, Pvt - Peeble's Farm, Hatcher's Run, fall of Petersburg, Appomattox - 6/3/1865 Honorable - Was not a casualty - Jonathon & Fanny Streeter Fisk (Both B NY) - INA - 7/4/1830 in Freedom - Farmer - Farm Laborer/Farmer - Elizabeth Madison (1832-1905), married 4/9/1855 at her home in Caneadea - Fanny - 4/21/1897 in Wiscoy - Wiscoy - Present at Lee's surrender. Marched in Grand Review 5/23/1865. (Military & Pension Files, 1890 Fed. Census Special Schedule Hume, Allegany County Web Site, Matteson, Fillmore American Legion, 1865 Allegany County Town Clerk Register Hume, 1865 NYS Census Hume, 1860,1870, 880 Fed. Censuses Hume)

Fitch, Leander Chester Co. F, 4th NY Heavy Artillery - 9/11/1862 at Hume/3 yrs - 18 - 5'6", Light Complexion, Brown Eyes, Grey Hair - 9/22/1862 at NYC - $100 - Pvt, Pvt - Cold Harbor, siege of Petersburg, Weldon RR, Ream's Station, Deep Bottom - 6/9/1865 Honorable - INJ, 5/12/1864 at Spotsylvania, premature discharge of his rifle caused back injury and partial loss of hearing;

POW, captured at Ream's Station 8/25/1864, Prison: Libby (Richmond) and Salisbury, paroled 2/28/1865 at N.E. Ferry, NC - Seth & Caroline C. Keller Fitch (Both B NY) - John A., Clarissa, James S., Seth, William. - 2/11/1844/45 in Hume - Farm Laborer - Engineer - Minnie C. Detour, married 11/18/1868 in Wenonee, MI - Caroline L., Frank Alfred, Roy Edwin, Effie Adaline, Fannie B., Lena E.- 7/8/1924 - Alger Cemetery, Hume, Route 19 - When released from prison he weighed only 70 pounds, down from 150. He suffered from terrible diarrhea. His military file indicates he served with a Vermont artillery regiment prior to his enlistment in the 4th HA. However, there is no military file for any service in a Vermont regiment. He was transferred temporarily from the 4th to the 3rd Independent Battery, NY Light Artillery. Obituary says he was captured three times, but military file shows only one capture. (Military & Pension Files, 1865 Allegany County Town Clerk Register Hume, Matteson, 1865 NYS Census Hume, 1890 Fed. Census Special Schedule Hume, 1860 Fed. Census Hume, 1870 Fed. Census Au Sable, MI, family history provided by Richard Guy Fitch)

Flenagin, Ichabod Perkins (Flanagan) Co. F/A, 4th NY Heavy Artillery - 8/27/1862 at Hume/3 yrs (re-enlisted 8/3/1864) - 28 - INA - 8/29/1862 at NYC - $50 - Pvt, 2nd Lt - Wilderness, Spotsylvania, North Anna River, Cold Harbor, siege of Petersburg, Weldon RR, Ream's Station - 8/25/1864 Honorable/Deceased - KIA, 8/25/1864 at Reams Station - James (B PA) & Julia Ann Perkins (B NY) Flenagin - Margaret, Charles N. - 3/15/1844 in Hume - Maranda H. Nye, married 6/8/1858 - Julia A. - 8/25/1864 in Reams Station - Buried on battlefield - Appointed Commissary Sgt 7/1/1863. Maranda died 12/19/1915. (Military & Pension Files, 1890 Fed. Census Special Schedule Hume, Allegany County Web Site, 1865 Allegany County Town Clerk Register Hume, 1865 NYS Census Hume, 1850 Fed. Census Hume)

Flint, George W. Co. A, 104th NY Infantry - 12/4/1861 at Geneseo/3 yrs - 33 - 5'8", Light Complexion, Grey Eyes, Brown Hair - 2/26/1862 at Geneseo - No bounty - Pvt, Pvt - No battles - 1/9/1863 Disability/Honorable - Was not a casualty - INA - INA - 1828 in VT - Farmer - Farmer - Martha Alvord, married 2/10/1849 in Nunda - Marcus, George W., Martha, Ida M. - 10/25/1867 in Birdsall - INA - Disability due to lung disease from a cold he caught on picket duty at Catlett's Station. Was a musician in the service. (Military & Pension Files, Granger American Legion, 1860 Fed. Census Allen)

Foot/Foote, Gilbert At least one source document indicates that Foote served in the military during the war. No evidence of such service has been located. The 1865 NYS Census says he served (no regiment listed) and that he was hung for desertion. Goes onto say his friends (unidentified) say he simply fell asleep on guard duty and when he awoke wandered into enemy lines. No records have been found of a Gilbert Foote being hanged. The draft register entitled, Descriptive Book of Drafted Men 7/63 to 10/64 shows that a Gilbert Foote was drafted, but was rejected for service because of entropion of both eyes. (1865 NYS Census Centerville)

Foster, Adelbert Romain Co. D/G, 21st NY Cavalry - 10/10/1863 at Troy/3 yrs - 18 - 5'6", Light Complexion, Light Eyes, Dark Hair - 10/14/1863 at Troy - No bounty - Pvt, Pvt - Smithfield, New Market, Mt. Jackson, Snicker's Gap, Gordonsville, Shepherdstown, Point of Rocks, Berryville - 7/7/1866 at Denver, Colorado Territory, Honorable - Was not a casualty - Lewis & Emma Ann

Wheeler Foster (Both B NY) - Theron W., Mary - 1/8/1848 in Castile - Farmer/Genesee Valley Canal - Carpenter/Mason/Laborer - Florence J. Streeter, married 7/4/1871 in Pike - Myrtle A., Mildred E., Cora B., Rya S., Maude L. - 2/1/1941 in Perry (on a visit, lived in Pike) - Gainesville - Originally enlisted in Co. C, 104th NY Infantry. Claimed a friend dared him to enlist. Was found to be underage and was not taken up on the company rolls. May have still been too young when he enlisted in the 21st. Probably only 15. Claimed he shook hands with Lincoln. Brother Theron also served during the war. (Military & Pension Files, 1865 Allegany Town Clerk Register Hume, 1865 NYS Census Hume, 1850 Fed. Census Castile, 1860 Fed. Census Castile, 1900 Fed. Census Gainesville)

<u>Foster, Theron W.</u> Co. D, 4th NY Heavy Artillery - 8/13/1862 at Rochester/3 yrs - 25 - 6', Florid Complexion, Blue Eyes, Light Hair - 8/13/1862 at Rochester - $50 - Pvt, Pvt - Wilderness plus served as an ambulance driver and likely participated in numerous battles as such - 6/3/1865 Honorable - Was not a casualty - Lewis & Emma Ann Wheeler Foster (Both B NY) - Mary, Adelbert - 3/12/1837 in Castile - Farmer/Canal Boatman - Farmer/Stone Mason - Laura P. - Hiram, Emma - 2/16/1902 - Wiscoy - Brother Adelbert also served during the war. Service records say he was born in Greene or Genesee County. (Military & Pension Files, 1865 Allegany County Town Clerk Register Hume, Matteson, Fillmore American Legion, 1865 NYS Census Hume, 1850 Fed. Census Castile, 1860, 1870 Fed. Censuses Hume)

<u>Fox, Charles B.</u> Co F, 19th NY Cavalry - 12/9/1863 at Buffalo/3 yrs - 23 - 5'10", Light Complexion, Blue Eyes, Light Hair - 1/5/1864 at Elmira - $100 - Pvt, Pvt - Wilderness, Todd's Tavern, Spotsylvania - North Anna River, Yellow Tavern, Pamunkey, Cold Harbor, Gordonsville, Dinwiddie Court House, Five Forks - Appomattox - 6/30/1685 Honorable - Was not a casualty - Father INA, Hannah Fox (Both B NY) - INA - 5/19/1840 in Herkimer - Farmer/Laborer - Farmer/Laborer - Lettie S. White, married 2/26/1868 in Dalton - Eliza J., Stoddard - 11/1/1906 in Dalton - Union Cemetery Dalton - Present at Lee's surrender. Marched in Grand Review 5/23/1865. (Military & Pension Records, 1865 Allegany County Town Clerk Register Centerville, 1865 NYS Census Granger, 1860, 1870 Fed. Censuses Granger, 1900 Fed. Census Grove)

<u>Fox, Chauncey Joel</u> Co F, 19th NY Cavalry - 8/8/1862 at Centerville/3 yrs - 30 - 5'10", Dark Complexion, Dark Eyes, Brown Hair - 9/3/1862 at Portage Station - $150 - Pvt, Corp - Deserted House, siege of Suffolk, Franklin, Manassas Junction, Culpeper Court House, Wilderness, Todd's Tavern, Spotsylvania, North Anna River, Yellow Tavern, Pamunkey, Totopotomoy, Cold Harbor, Trevillian Station, Charles County Court House, before Richmond & Petersburg, New Market, Shepherdstown, Winchester, Fisher's Hill, New Market, Port Republic, Cedar Creek, Berryville, Gordonsville - 6/30/1865 Honorable - Was not a casualty - Willis (B CT) & Fanny Maria Crane (B NY) Fox - INA - 6/10/1832 in Freedom - Farmer/Mason - Farmer/Brick/Stone Mason - Mary Adelphia Cole, married 3/19/1869 in Centerville - None - 3/16/1917 in Omro, WI - Omro - Marched in Grand Review 5/23/1865. Probably died in Northern Hospital for the Insane at Omro. Divorced in 1894. A Mary Bennett was appointed his guardian when he was in the hospital. (Military & Pension Files, *History of Allegany County 1879*, Matteson, 1860 Fed. Census Freedom, 1870, 1880 Fed. Censuses Centerville)

Fox, Francis E. Co. F, 136th NY Infantry - 8/28/1862/3 yrs - 28 - 5'10", Fair Complexion, Blue Eyes, Black Hair - 9/25/1862 at Portage - $100 - Pvt, Pvt - Detached to Ambulance Corps. Was likely at many battles, but not necessarily as a combatant. Deserves credit, but not sure of battles - 7/11/1865 Honorable - Was not a casualty - Chauncey & Amanda Fox (Both B NY) - James M., George W., Harriet M., Sarah C. Matilda, Fidelia - 1834 in Centerville - Farmer - None Deceased - Tryphena Fox - None - 8/17/1865 in Freedom - probably Cadwell Cemetery, Centerville - His wife's father was the half brother of his father. Died of chronic diarrhea first contracted in the service 10/1863 at Bridgeport, TN (Military & Pension Files, 1865 NYS Census Centerville, 1850 Fed. Census Centerville)

Fox, Rodolph Co F, 4th NY Heavy Artillery - 1/13/1864 at Centerville/3 yrs - 40 - 6', Fair Complexion, Blue Eyes, Brown Hair - 1/16/1864 at Elmira - $300 - Pvt, Pvt - Wilderness, Spotsylvania, North Anna River, Totopotomoy, Cold Harbor, siege of Petersburg, Weldon RR, Ream's Station - 8/25/1864 Honorable/Deceased - POW, captured 8/25/1864 at Reams Station, Prison: Salisbury, NC - DD, 12/11/1864 at Salisbury, NC prison of debility - Joseph & Calinda Brooks Fox (Both B NY) - Dan B., John, Sarah - 6/13/1826 in Centerville - Mechanic/Carpenter - None Deceased - Lucy M. Hackett Youngs - Hiram - 12/11/1864 in Salisbury, NC prison - Probably Salisbury National Cemetery - Lucy was previously married to Civil War soldier David Youngs who also died in the war. She lost her pension because of "open and notorious adulterous cohabitation" with a Hiram Doty of Olean. She also had a son by a George King before living with Doty. (Military & Pension Files, 1865 NYS Census Hume, Allegany County Web Site, 1865 Allegany County Town Clerk Register Hume, 1860 Fed. Census Hume)

Franklin, Gurdin Jason Co E, 136th NY Infantry - 8/2/1862 at Allen/3 yrs - 25 - 5'4", Light Complexion, Grey Eyes, Brown Hair - 9/25/1862 at Portage - $25 - Pvt, Corp - Chancellorsville, Gettysburg, Wauhatchie, Orchard Knob, Tunnel Hill, Missionary Ridge, Resaca - 5/15/1864 Honorable/Deceased - KIA, 5/15/1864 at Resaca, GA - John & Betsey Miller Franklin (Both B NY) - Gurdin, Harriet, Sarah, Amarilla, Mary A., William M., Mortimer C., Spencer R., Julius & Julia E. (twins), Gertrude J. (twin sister) - 11/4/1837 in Brookfield - Farmer - None Deceased - Never Married - None - 5/15/1864 in Resaca, GA - Chattanooga National Cemetery (under initials J.G.) (Originally buried Resaca, Ga) (Memorial Headstone in Angelica) - Brother Julius also served during the war. Originally enlisted in the 130th NY Infantry. County Clerk has birthday as 10/14/1837. (Military & Pension Files, Allegany & Its People, 1865 Allegany County Town Clerk Register Allen, 1850, 1860 Fed. Censuses Allen)

Franklin, John Curdin Co, F, 33rd NY Infantry - 5/13/1861 at Nunda/2 yrs - 17 - 5'9", Fair Complexion, Blue Eyes, Light Hair - 7/6/1861 at Elmira - No bounty - Pvt, Pvt - siege of Yorktown, Williamsburg, Ft. Magruder, Gaine's Mills, Malvern Hill, 2nd Bull Run, South Mountain, Antietam, Fredericksburg - 6/2/1863 Honorable - POW, captured 5/4/1863 at Fredericksburg, Prison: Richmond, paroled at City Point, VA 5/15/1863 - Edward & Emily Higgins Franklin - INA - 8/25/1843 in Buffalo - Farmer - Farmer - 1st Sarah Waters, married 8/6/1864 in Philadelphia (Sarah was 16), 2nd Emma Dell Putnam, married 12/30/1877 - James Blain, Freddie Lee, Bessie, Willie Dell, Nellie Irene - 2/25/1908 in Jennings, LA - INA - Went home to Cold Creek on furlough 4/5/1862, and returned there after discharge. Also served with

Co. A, 1st Michigan Cavalry, see below. (Military & Pension Files, 1865 NYS Census Centerville, Granger American Legion, 1865 Allegany County Town Clerk Register Centerville)

Franklin, John Curdin Co, A/E 1st Michigan Cavalry - 11/21/1863 at Clinton, MI/3 yrs - 19 - 5'9", Fair Complexion, Blue Eyes, Light Hair - 11/26/1863 at Mt. Clemons, MI - No bounty - Pvt, Pvt - Richmond, Todd's Tavern, Wilderness - 8/20/1864 Dishonorable (for desertion) - INJ, horse fell on him at Battle of the Wilderness 5/6/1864. (He later claimed he had been dismounted before the Wilderness Battle and that the horse incident occurred at Ft. Stillman.) Injured leg and testicles. Was also in Summit G.H. with debility. Presumably deserted from hospital 8/20/1864. After Civil War, his regiment was sent west to fight Indians. One document says he was discharged 2/10/1866 at Salt Lake City. He denied this, and the 1865 NYS Census has him in Centerville in 1865. In 1884 his request that the discharge be made honorable was denied. Also served with Co. F, 33rd NY Infantry. Pension was awarded for honorable service in 33rd, see above. Also see above for personnel information and sources of information.

Franklin, Julius E. Co. A, 1st NY Light Artillery - 8/1/1862 at Brookfield/3 years - 29 - 5'6", Dark Complexion, Grey Eyes, Brown Hair - 8/13/1862 at Utica - $100 - Pvt, Corp - Primarily served in defense of Washington, DC, siege of Yorktown, Williamsburg, Fair Oaks - 6/28/1865 Honorable - Was not a casualty - John & Betsey Miller Franklin - Gurdin, Harriet, Sarah, Amarilla, Mary A., William M., Mortimer C., Spencer R., Julia E. (twin sister), Gurdin J. & Gertrude J. (twins) - 4/18/1833 in Brookfield - Farmer - Owned Cheese Factories - Delia B. Quinn, married 2/22/1881 in Belvidere - Earl Julius - 4/29/1898 in Fillmore - Pine Grove Cemetery, Fillmore - Promoted to Corp 10/3/1864. Head of a detail transporting 3 spies and 7 deserters to Harrisburg, PA from Chambersburg, PA in November, 1864. Detached service at Chambersburg July, 1864 to April, 1865. In Philadelphia G.H. 8/3/1863 - 10/24/1863. Was caught in a severe sleet storm while chasing deserters. Burnside G.A.R. Post 237 Marker at grave. Brother Gurdin J. also served during the war. (Military & Pension Files, *Allegany & Its People*, Fillmore American Legion, Matteson, 1890 Fed. Census Special Schedule Hume, 1850, 1870 Fed. Censuses Allen)

Fuller, Omar W. Co. F, 4th NY Heavy Artillery - 9/4/1862 at Granger/3 yrs - 32 - INA - 9/12/1862 at NYC - $200 - Pvt, Artificer - Wilderness, Spotsylvania, North Anna River, Totopotomoy, Cold Harbor, siege of Petersburg, Weldon RR, Ream's Station - 5/15/1865 Honorable - INJ, 6/7/1862 near Chain Bridge, DC, hurt back lifting heavy logs while building a bomb proof shelter, INJ, 2/15/1865 at Petersburg, a tree fell on him when he was in his tent, suffered a head injury causing some paralysis - William H. (B CT) & Mary W. Blackmer (B NY) Fuller - Frank, Oscar, Jennett - 5/7/1829 in Hamburg - Farmer/Carpenter - Farmer - Eliza G. Guptill (1832-1907) married 9/29/1852 in Angelica - Jeanette (Spohn) - 9/26/1900 - Pine Grove Cemetery Fillmore - Some records show him single when he entered service, but 1900 Census shows him married 48 years. (Military & Pension Files, 1890 Fed. Census Special Schedule Granger, Matteson, *Allegany & Its People*, 1865 NYS Census Granger, 1865 Allegany County Town Clerk Register Granger, 1860, 1880 Fed. Censuses Granger)

Fulton, James E. Co. G, 13th NY Infantry - 9/24/1861 at Dansville/3 yrs - 18 - 5'8", Light Complexion, Blue Eyes, Light Hair - 10/4/1861 at Dansville - No bounty - Pvt, Pvt - No battles -

5/14/1862 Disability/Honorable - Samuel & Harriett Fulton (Both B NY) - Elizabeth S., Nancy M., Stella A., Francis M., Ida C. - 1842/43 in West Almond - Farmer - Farmer - Harriet - Eve, stepchildren, Florence B. & Ziba E. Barney - INA - INA - Lived at Wiscoy at end of his service. Number of men from the town sent a letter to the pension bureau confirming his disability. Had typhoid fever in the service. Misreported as a deserter. The charge was removed from his records in 1887. (Military & Pension Files, 1865 NYS Census Hume, 1860, 1870 Fed. Censuses West Sparta)

Furbeck, Seymour H. Unassigned, 19th NY Cavalry - 8/11/1864 at Hume/1 yr - 39 - 5'7", Dark Complexion, Blue Eyes, Black Hair - 8/23/1864 at Elmira - $400 - Pvt, Pvt - No battles - 8/30/1864 Honorable/Deceased - DD, 8/31/1864 at Baltimore of typhoid fever & acute dysentery - INA - INA - 1824/25 in New Scotland - Tailor - None Deceased - Alvira L. Bun, married 8/8/1859 in Independence - None - 8/30/1864 in Baltimore - Loudon National Cemetery, Baltimore - Anna Seymour living with him per 1860 Census, may have been a sister. (Military & Pension Files, 1865 Allegany County Town Clerk Register Hume, 1860 Fed. Census Rushford)

Gallagher, Hugh Co. C/B, 44th NY Infantry - 8/27/1861 at Hume/3 yrs - 19 - INA - 8/30/1861 at Albany - No Bounty - Pvt, Corp - siege of Yorktown, Hanover Court House, Gaine's Mill, Malvern Hill, 2nd Bull Run, Chancellorsville, Gettysburg - 10/11/1864 Honorable - WIA, 7/1/1862 at Malvern Hill, gunshot to knee, POW, 8/30/862 at Manassas (2nd Bull Run), Prison: Richmond, paroled 9/4/1862 - John & INA Gallagher (Both B Ireland) - INA - 1842 in Ireland - Bridget Hurley, married 8/25/1866 - John & Bridget - 9/9/1870 in Wabasha, MN - INA - Promoted to Corp 12/4/1862. Was in hospitals in both Philadelphia & NYC with a tumor. (Military & Pension Files, 1865 Allegany County Town Clerk Register Hume, 1860 Fed. Census Hume, 1870 Fed. Census Wabasha County MN)

Gardner, Eli Co. C, 104th NY Infantry - 1/4/1862 at Geneseo/3 yrs - 22 - 6'2", Light Complexion, Blue Eyes, Brown Hair - 2/26/1862 at Geneseo - No bounty - Pvt, Corp - No battles - 4/24/1862 Disability/Honorable - Was not a casualty - Millard & Laura Wood Gardner (Both B CT) - INA - 1/7/1838 in Centerville - Farmer - Farm Laborer/Farmer - Huldah Evallena Chamberlain, married 1/7/1862 in Centerville - INA - 10/20/1921 in Centerville - Rogers Cemetery, Centerville - Suffered a ruptured hernia while in the service. (Military & Pension Files, 1890 Fed. Census Special Schedule Centerville, Matteson, 1865 NYS Census Hume, Centerville American Legion, 1860, 1880, 1910 Fed. Censuses Centerville.)

Gates, Jonathan At least one source document indicates that Gates served in the military during the war. No evidence of such service has been located. Register of Men Drafted shows that Jonathon Gates was drafted but transferred to 2nd class. Apparently never entered the service. (1865 NYS Census Centerville, Register of Men Drafted, July, 1863 to October, 1864.)

Gilbert, William R. Co. B, 2nd NY Mounted Rifles - 12/19/1863 at Centerville/3 yrs - 5'8", Light Complexion, Blue Eyes, Dark Hair - 1/12/1864 at Ft. Porter Buffalo -$800- Pvt, Pvt - Spotsylvania, North Anna River, Cold Harbor, siege of Petersburg - 9/17/1864 Deceased /Honorable - WIA, 6/18/1864 at Petersburg, shell fractured left femur, KIA, died 9/17/1864 while on leave at Centerville from wound suffered at Petersburg - Hiram & Anna Holcomb Gilbert (Both B NY) - Edmond, Mary, Julia C., Amy, David, Frances, Albert - 8/27/1846 in Yorkshire - Farmer - None Deceased - Never married - None - 9/17/1864 in Centerville - INA - Was in Armory Square Hospital, DC from 6/29 - 8/17/64. Granted a furlough from 8/17 to 10/16/1864 - Doctors could do no more. (Military & Pension Files, *History of Allegany County 1879*, 1865 Allegany County Town Clerk Register Centerville, Matteson, 1865 NYS Census Centerville, 1850 Fed. Census Centerville)

Gillett, Frederick A. Co. D, 4th NY Heavy Artillery - 8/13/1862 at Rochester/3 yrs - 18 - 5'9", Florid Complexion, Blue Eyes, Light Hair - 8/13/1862 at Rochester - $50 - Pvt, Pvt - No battles - 2/14/1863 Deceased/Honorable - DD, 2/14/1863 at Clermont G.H., Alexandria, VA of small pox - Edwin D. & Amy Bennett Gillett (Both B CT) - George J. - 11/25/1847 in Dryden - Farmer - None Deceased - Never Married - None - 2/14/1863 at Alexandria, VA - Arlington National Cemetery (as Gellett) - Was probably only 15 when he volunteered. Because he died of small pox, he was buried the same day he died. (Military & Pension Files, 1865 Allegany County Town Clerk Register Hume, Allegany County Web Site, 1860 Fed. Census Hume)

Gillett, William B. Co. H, 9th NY Heavy Artillery - 8/25/1862 at Rose/3 yrs - 28 - 5'7", Light Complexion, Blue Eyes, Red Hair - 8/25/1862 at Auburn - $100 - Pvt, Pvt - defense of DC - Pamunkey, Totopotomoy - Cold Harbor, Winchester, Cedar Creek, siege of Petersburg, Fort Fisher, fall of Petersburg, Appomattox - 7/6/1865 Honorable - Was not a casualty - Philo & Almira Gillett - Martha J., Oliver H., Mary E., Francis S. - 10/1833 in Bainbridge - Farmer - Farmer - Laura M. Stowell, married 2/2/1853 - Ellie, Martha Jane, Annie, William B., Frances, D.E. - 6/10/1908 - Pine Grove Cemetery, Fillmore - Was detailed as a teamster, 12/1863. Detached to City Point, VA August, 1864, probably to the hospital. Present at Lee's surrender. (Military & Pension Files, 1890 Fed. Census Special Schedule Hume, 1880, 1890 Fed. Censuses Hume, 1850, 1860 Fed Census Cortland)

Gloden, Lamont John Co. B, 2nd NY Mounted Rifles - 1/3/1864 at Allen/3 yrs - 18 - 5'6", Dark Complexion, Black Hair, Black Hair - 1/12/1864 at Ft. Porter, Buffalo - $800 - Pvt, Pvt - Spotsylvania, North Anna River, Pamunkey, Totopotomoy, Hanover Court House, Cold Harbor, siege of Petersburg, Popular Springs Church, Weldon RR, Hatcher's Run, Dinwiddie - 8/10/1865 Honorable - Was not a casualty - Lambert (B France) & Amelia (B NY) Gloden -Sarah, Munton - 6/12/1847 in Bethany - Farmer - Farmer/Saw Mill Worker - Isabelle (B Scotland) - William L., Ronabell, John L., Louis, Sarah, Viola - 4/13/1913 in Pisgah, MD - near Pisgah per Death Certificate - July, 1864 was on duty as a guard on an ammunition train. April, 1865 at dismount camp near City Point, VA. John may have been his first name. (Military File, *History of Allegany County 1879*, 1865 Allegany County Town Clerk Register Allen, Granger American Legion, 1850 Fed. Census Covington, 1860 Fed. Census Allen, 1870 Fed. Census Sheffield Township, PA, 1900 Fed. Census Hill Top, MD)

Goodale, George P. Co. E, 85th NY Infantry - 9/1/1861 at Granger - 17 - INA - 11/11/1861 at Elmira - No bounty - Pvt, Pvt - defense of DC, siege of Yorktown, Williamsburg -5/16/1862 Deserted - Was not a casualty - Elijah (B VT) & Mary (B NY) Goodale - Harriet A., Silas W.

Frederick W., Emma G. - INA - Printer - Probably 1st Josephine, 2nd Katherine - Probably Tom - INA - INA - Goodale charged with desertion from camp at Rofer's Church, VA 5/16/1862. Apparently returned to Angelica to work as a printer, the job he held when he "enlisted.." Father opposed his entering the service. Some question as to whether he understood he was enlisting. Some evidence that he may have thought that he was merely a personal clerk to Colonel Thorp. H.E. Purdy wrote a letter saying that Thorp had engaged in fraudulent conduct in enrolling Goodale. No court martial file. Post war probably in the newspaper business. Was possibly both a journalist and editor at the Detroit Free Press. It appears his only connection to C-H-G was his enlistment at Granger. (Military File, *History of Allegany County 1879*, Mattteson, 1850, 1860 Fed. Censuses Phelps, Ontario County, 1900 Fed. Census Detroit, MI, 1910 Fed Census Hamtramck, MI)

Goodrich, Albert Dan   Co. F, 19th NY Infantry - 8/14/1862 at Hume/3 yrs - 5'7", Light Complexion, Brown Eyes, Black Hair - 9/3/1862 at Portage Station - $150 - Pvt, Pvt - Deserted House, siege of Suffolk, Franklin, Manassas Junction, Bristoe's Station, Culpeper Court House, Wilderness, Todd's Tavern, Spotsylvania, North Anna River, Yellow Tavern, Pamunkey, Totopotomoy, Cold Harbor, Trevillian Station, Charles County Court House, before Richmond and Petersburg, New Market, Shepherdstown, Winchester, Fisher's Hill, New Market, Port Republic, Cedar Creek, Berryville, Gordonsville - 6/30/1865 Honorable - Was not a casualty - Ebenezer (B NY) & Alva Chloe Blossom (B VT) Goodrich - Willie - 11/4/1841 in Hume - Lucy E. Keyes, married 9/14/1865 in Centerville at her home - Floyd, John, Henry - 11/29/1905 in Eaton Hills, MI - Rose Hills Cemetery, Eaton Hills - Marched in Grand Review 5/23/1865. (Military & Pension Files, 1865 NYS Census Hume, 1865 Allegany County Town Clerk Register Hume, *History of Allegany County 1879*, 1860 Fed. Census Hume, 1880 Fed. Census Centerville)

Goodrich, Horace. At least one source document appears to indicate that he was from the C-H-G area. A detailed review of his records indicates that he was not from the area. Served with Cos. N/M, 85th NY Infantry. (*History of Allegany County 1879*)

Goodrich, John O. At least one source document appears to indicate that he was from the C-H-G area. A detailed review of his records indicates that he was not from the area. Served with Cos. D/G 85th NY Infantry. (*History of Allegany County 1879*)

Gordon (Jordan), John. Not from the C-H-G area. Served with Co. E, 54th NY Infantry. Hume Township received credit for his enlistment by paying the enlistment bonus of $500.(1865 Allegany County Town Clerk Register Hume)

Gorton, Jared A. Co. L/I, 4th Michigan Cavalry - 12/29/1863 at Corunna, MI/3 yrs - 32 - 5'11", Light Complexion, Grey Eyes, Dark Hair - 1/4/1864 - $300 - Pvt, Pvt - No battles - 8/15/1865 at Edgefield, TN Honorable - Was not a casualty - INA - Duly - 1833 in Brookfield - Farmer/Stage Driver - Farm Laborer - Olive C. Hubbard, married 5/25/1854 at Bellevue?, MI - Gilbert A., George W. (Both died very young.) - 11/8/1887 - INA - Transferred to Invalid Corps 2/1/1865. Spent entire service in a Nashville, TN hospital. Was detached to Nashville after enlistment to pick up horse equipment. Charter Member of Burnside G.A.R. Post 237. First name was probably Jeremiah. (Military & Pension Files, *Allegany & Its People*, 1870 Fed. Census Hume, 1860 Fed. Census Rochester.

Granger, Cassius C. Co. B, 2nd NY Mounted Rifles - 2/13/1864 at Pike/3 yrs - 20 - 5'3", Dark Complexion, Grey Eyes, Black Hair - 2/24/1864 at Lockport - $300 - Pvt, Pvt - Spotsylvania, North Anna River, Pamunkey, Totopotomoy, Hanover Court House, Cold Harbor, Bethesda Church, siege of Petersburg, Weldon RR, Popular Springs Church, Pegram's Farm, Hatcher's Run Dinwiddie, 7/11/1865 Honorable - WIA, gunshot wound to groin, 3/31/1865 at Dinwiddie Court House - Lyman & Louise Granger (Both B NY) - Sarah Ann, Mary L., Dewit - 10/4/1843 in Pike, Carpenter - Carpenter - Cornelia A. Burt, married 6/22/1869 in Wiscoy - Milton B., Lillian - 5/30/1912 in Nunda - Oakwood Cemetery, Nunda - Charter Member and Officer of Burnside G.A.R. Post 237. (Military & Pension Files, 1890 Fed. Census Special Schedule Hume, *Allegany & Its People*, 1850 Fed. Census Pike, 1900 Fed. Census Hume)

Granger, James M. Co. D, 4th NY Heavy Artillery - 8/13/1862 at Hume/3 yrs - 35 - 5'11", Florid Complexion, Blue Eyes, Light Hair - 8/13/1862 at Rochester - $100 - Pvt, Pvt - Wilderness, Spotsylvania, North Anna River, Totopotomoy, Cold Harbor, siege of Petersburg, Weldon RR, Ream's Station, Peeble's Farm, Hatcher's Run, fall of Petersburg, Appomattox - 6/3/1865 Honorable - Was not a casualty - Gurden & Nancy Flenagin Granger - INA - 5/29/1827 in Hume (Pike per military records) - Cooper - Farmer - Polly Jane Merchant, married 2/26/1854 in Wiscoy - Walter J., George - 1/16/1899 at Alma WI - Alma - Present at Lee's surrender. Marched in Grand Review 5/23/1865. (Military & Pension Files, 1865 Allegany County Town Clerk Register Hume, 1850, 1860 Fed. Censuses Hume, 1870 Fed. Census Alma, WI)

Granger, Peter V. Co. D, 3rd Michigan Infantry - 5/13/1861 at Grand Rapids, MI - 27 - INA - 6/10/1861 at Grand Rapids - No bounty - 1st Lt., 1st Lt. - defense of DC, Blackburn's Ford, 1st Bull Run, siege of Yorktown, Fair Oaks, Savage Station, Peach Orchard, Malvern Hill, Groveton, 2nd Bull Run, Chantilly - 9/20/1862 Resigned/Honorable - Was not a casualty - Gideon (B NY) & Mary (B PA) Granger - James, Margarett, Daniel, Albert, Elizabeth, Elison G. - 1833/34 in Allegany County - Carpenter - Carpenter - Juliette Sanborn, married 11/10/1857 in Saranac, MI - Helen, Mary - 10/13/1867 in Wiscoy - Wiscoy - Per a 2/9/1906 Notation, his appointment to 1st Lt became effective 5/13/1861. 1850 Fed. Census has his middle initial as S. Others have it as V. (Military & Pension Files, 1865 NYS Census Hume, Matteson, Allegany County Web Site, 1850 Fed. Census Hume)

Granger, Theodore P. At least one source document indicates that Granger served in the military during the war. No evidence of such service has been located. (Fillmore American Legion, Matteson)

Gray, William W. Co. D, 19th NY Cavalry - 8/20/1862 at Portage/3 yrs - 27 - 5'10", Light Complexion, Grey Eyes, Brown Hair - 9/3/1862 at Portage - No bounty - Pvt, Pvt - No battles - 7/30/1864 Deceased (was under arrest as a deserter) - DD, 7/30/1864 at Augur G.H, VA of chronic diarrhea - Ezra & Sophia Gray (Both B NY) - Alice. Sarah Jane, Willson L. - 1834 or 35 in Genesee - Farmer - None Deceased - Esther A., married in Perry - None - 7/30/1864 in Augur G.H., VA - Arlington National Cemetery - Charged with desertion as of 12/6/1863. Arrested 6/13/1864 at Castile. Was sick when regiment left Portage Station. He stayed there with orders to rejoin his regiment in 30 days or have a doctor's certificate of physical disability. Such a doctor's certificate is in the file. No evidence of a trial for desertion, but there were orders to discharge him as a deserter. Given the Doctor's letter of physical disability, not sure why he was charged with desertion. (Military File, Granger American Legion, 1850 Fed. Census Granger, 1860 Fed. Census Allen)

Green Henry Co. B, 76th NY Infantry - Drafted 7/14/1863 at Rochester/3 yrs - 36 - 5'10", Fair Complexion, Dark Eyes, Brown Hair - 7/14/1863 at Elmira - No bounty - Pvt, Pvt - Wilderness - 7/8/1865 Honorable - WIA, gunshot to left leg, below knee 5/6/1864 at the Wilderness - Eben & Caroline Green (Both B NY) - INA - 1826 or 27 in Saratoga County - Farm Laborer - Farmer - Never Married - None - INA - INA - Was drafted into the 76th Infantry. After his wound he was transferred to Co. A, 147th NY Infantry. Never served with that regiment. Spent rest of service in hospital. His age is never consistent in any two documents. (Military & Pension Files, 1865 Allegany County Town Clerk Register Hume, Matteson, 1850 Fed. Census Caneadea - 1860 Fed. Census Hume)

Green, Willard Walter Co. D, 4th NY Heavy Artillery - 12/22/1863 at Hume/3 yrs - 40 - 5'7", Light Complexion, Blue Eyes, Brown Hair - 12/22/1863 at Elmira - $300 - Pvt, Pvt - Wilderness, Spotsylvania, North Anna River, Cold Harbor, siege of Petersburg, Weldon RR, Ream's Station, Peeble's Farm, Hatcher's Run - 6/22/1865 Honorable - Was not a casualty - Silas & Sarah Caple Green - INA - 6/22/1816 in New Lisbon - Shoemaker - Farmer - Lovina Seaton, married 1/5/1852 in Hume - INA - 10/10/1893 - INA - Admitted to Mt. Pleasant Hospital, DC 4/30/1865, transferred to Philadelphia 5/29/1865. Transferred to VCR 4/15/1865. He was probably closer to 47 than 40 when he enlisted. (Military & Pension Files, 1865 Allegany County Town Clerk Register Hume, 1860 Fed. Census Hume, 1870 Fed. Census Caneadea)

Gregory, Emry Not from the C-H-G area. Served with Co. D, 118th NY Infantry. However, he lived almost his entire life at Chestertown and Horicon in Warren County. He moved to Wyoming County in 1903 and died there January 25, 1904. Never lived in Allegany County, but is buried in Caldwell Cemetery, Centerville. (Centerville American Legion, Matteson)

Griffith, Henry Co. F, 19th NY Infantry - 8/9/1862 at Hume/3 yrs - 38 - 5'8", Dark Complexion, Blue Eyes, Black Hair - 9/3/1862 at Portage Station - $50 - Pvt, Pvt - No battles - 9/13/1862 Deserted at Norfolk, VA with his gun, knapsack, haversack, and canteen - Was not a casualty - Nathan?/Mother INA - INA - 1824 in Rushford - Carriage Maker - INA - Deborah - Sarah, Francis, Charles, Flora S. - 1906 - INA - His 19th Cavalry file says he later served with the 4th NY Heavy Artillery, but no 4th Heavy Artillery file for him has been located. Further, the NYS Adjutant General Report does not show a Henry Griffith as having served with the 4th Heavy Artillery. (Military File, *History of Allegany County 1879*, 1860 Fed. Census Hume)

Griggs, Jasper Manly Co. C, 104th NY Infantry - 10/9/1861 at Pike/3 yrs - 19 - 5'9", Light Complexion, Brown Eyes, Brown Hair - 2/26/1862 at Geneseo - No bounty - Sgt, Captain - Cedar Creek, 2nd Bull Run, South Mountain, Antietam, Fredericksburg, Chancellorsville, Gettysburg, Bristoe's Station, Wilderness, Spotsylvania, North Anna River, Pamunkey, Totopotomoy, Cold Harbor, Bethesda Church, Petersburg, Weldon RR - 1/17/1864 Honorable - POW, captured 8/19/1864 at Weldon RR, Prison: Richmond, Salisbury, NC, Dansville, VA, paroled at Richmond 2/21/1865, WIA, 9/17/1862 at Antietam, slight wound, WIA, 12/18/1862 at Fredericksburg, gunshot to thigh, WIA, 7/1/1863 at Gettysburg, gunshot to both thighs - Philip (B VT) & Margrett Marvin (B NY) Griggs - Henrietta, Philip Monroe, Henry Marvin, Abigail Rebecca, Horace Benedict, Laura Louisa, Warner Marvin, Philo Mills - 1/4/1842 in Centerville - Teacher/Farmer - Lawyer/Carpenter - Maria Bronson, married 3/22/1869 in Detroit - INA - 5/8/1920 in Sugar Grove, PA - Alger Cemetery, Hume, Route 19 - Promoted 1st Lt. 5/2/1863, Captain 6/22/1864. Marched in Grand Review 5/23/1865. Despite his war record and wounds, it took a special Act of Congress to get him a pension. Separated from Margrett from 1872 to 1897. Divorced at Livingston County, IL in 1906. Started living together again in 1915. (Military & Pension Files, Matteson, 1850 Fed. Census Centerville, 1920 Fed. Census Sugar Grove, PA)

Grover, Charles Co. F, 19th NY Cavalry - 8/12/1862 at Fillmore/3 yrs - 37 - 5'5", Light Complexion, Blue Eyes, Auburn Hair - 9/3/1862 at Portage Station - $250 - Pvt, Pvt - No battles - 1/6/1863 Disability/Honorable - Was not a casualty - Aron & Hannah Stone Grover - INA - 5/28/1825 in Mitford - Farmer - Farm Laborer - Julia Ann - Edgar, Edwin, H.P., A.J., Mary, Julia - INA - INA - Disability discharge was for phthisis pulmonalis. (Military File, 1865 Allegany County Town Clerk Register Hume, 1860, 1870 Fed. Censuses Hume)

Grover, David Co. A, 84th Ohio Infantry - 5/27/1862 at Toledo, OH/3 months - 21 - 5'11", Fair Complexion, Blue Eyes, Light Hair - 8/18/1862 at Camp Chase, OH - No bounty - Pvt, Pvt - New Creek - 9/20/1862 at Camp Delaware, OH. Honorable - Was not a casualty - Leonard B. (B PA) & Abigail (B NY) Grover - INA - 10/13/1840 in Richfield, OH. Farmer - Farmer - 1st Maria M. Metcalf, married 2/7/1864, 2nd Jane S. Fleischer, married 7/7/1919 - Mitied - 9/3/1923 - INA - Lived in numerous places both before and after the war. 1st wife Maria was from Centerville (Military & Pension Files, 1865 Allegany County Town Clerk Register Centerville, 1865 NYS Census Centerville, 1850, 1860 Fed. Censuses Richfield, OH)

Groves, Richard David Co. E, 85th NY Infantry, 9/1/1861 at Granger/3 yrs - 21 - INA - INA - No bounty - Pvt, Pvt - defense of DC, siege of Yorktown, Williamsburg, Fair Oaks - 5/31/1862 Honorable/Deceased - KIA, 5/31/1862 at Fair Oaks - Richard & Olivia Groves (Both B England) - Mary Olivia, Rebecca, Grace Frances, Evangline Ann - 1841 in England - Probably working for his father, a merchant - None Deceased - Never Married - None - 5/31/1862 in Fair Oaks, VA - Pike - Was an orderly in the service. Dr. William M. Smith mentions Groves in his diary (book, *Swamp Doctor*), saying he attended his funeral 6/29/1862 at Pike. Listed on Soldiers Monument in Granger. Parents were married 4/30/1839 in Dorchester, Weymouth County, England. (Military & Pension Files, *History of Allegany County 1879*, Granger American Legion, Matteson, *Allegany & Its People*, 1860 Fed. Census Granger)

<u>Guernsey, Samuel Peter</u> Co. I, 4th NY Heavy Artillery - 12/2/1863 at Granger/3 yrs - 43 - 5'7", Dark Complexion, Grey Eyes, Black Hair - 12/26/1863 at Elmira - $300 - Pvt, Pvt - Wilderness, Spotsylvania, North Anna River, Totopotomoy, Cold Harbor, siege of Petersburg - Weldon RR - 5/25/1865 Honorable - Was not a casualty - John & Nancy Bolton Guernsey - INA - 2/11/1818 in Royalton - Farmer - Methodist Clergyman/Farmer - Mary A. White, married 8/14/1849 in Granger - Mary G. & Harriet - 5/15/1904 in Royalton - Mountain Ridge Cemetery, Royalton - On 8/27/1864 he was in Harewood G.H., DC with malaria. On leave 10/8 - 11/17/1864. Tried unsuccessfully to divorce his wife. Sued his wife over some property, but lost the case. In 1900 he was a widower and an inmate at the Masonic Home and School, Utica. (Military & Pension Files, 1865 NYS Census Granger, Granger American Legion, 1865 Allegany County Town Clerk Register Granger, 1850 Fed. Census Granger, 1870 Fed. Census Franklinville, 1900 Fed. Census Utica)

<u>Guptill, Joseph Nathaniel</u> Co. F, 4th NY Heavy Artillery - 9/11/1862 at Granger/3 yrs - 18 - 5'11", Light Complexion, Blue Eyes, Brown Hair - 10/2/1862 at NYC - $100 - Pvt, Pvt - Wilderness, Spotsylvania, North Anna River, Totopotomoy, Cold Harbor, siege of Petersburg, Weldon RR, Ream's Station, Appomattox - 6/3/1865 Honorable - WIA, about 6/17/1864 at Petersburg, slight gunshot wound to arm - William & Susan Ruth Fox Guptill (Both B MA) - Eliza, Matilda, Horace, Ellen - 5/28/1842 in Granger - Farmer - Farmer - Melissa J. Smith, married 9/9/1865 in Short Tract - Horace, Bessie D. - 7/11/1905 in Warsaw - Weaver Settlement Cemetery, Granger - Was detached to 2nd A.C. 9-10/1864. The bullet that wounded him lodged in his canteen. Present at Lee's surrender. 1/16/1863 at Fort Gaines, MD contracted measles, resulted in lung disease. 10/15/1862 at Fort Gaines, MD contracted piles due to over exertion from drilling and heavy lifting. When wounded he left his rifle on the field and went to the rear for treatment. Finding that the wound wasn't serious, and realizing he would have to pay for the rifle, at night he went back to the field and took a rifle from a dead soldier and returned to his company. Was attending Rushford Academy when the war started. (Military & Pension Files, 1865 NYS Census Granger, 1865 Allegany County Town Clerk Register Granger, Matteson, *Allegany & Its People*, 1890 Fed. Census Special Schedule Hume, 1850, 1880 Fed. Censuses Granger)

<u>Hackett, Leonard Orlando</u> Co. L, 4th NY Heavy Artillery - 8/22/1864 at Hume/1 yr - 25 - 5'5", Dark Complexion, Blue Eyes, Dark Hair - 9/1/1864 at Elmira - $500 - Pvt, Pvt - Peeble's Farm, Hatcher's Run, fall of Petersburg, Appomattox - 6/5/1865 Honorable - Was not a casualty - William H. (B PA) & Olive C. Berry (B NY) Hackett - Lucy H. - 10/13/1846 in Amity - Boatman - Farmer - Caroline Stickle, married 3/3/1871 in Belfast - Lorena - 1/18/1937 in Centerville - Bates Cemetery, Centerville - Present at Lee's surrender. Marched in Grand Review 5/23/1865. Age is wrong on enlistment papers. Government sent a flag for his funeral. Military files say he was born in Steuben County, not likely. Charter Member and Officer of Burnside G.A. R. Post 237. One record says he was Chaplain at time Post 237 was established. (Military & Pension Files, 1850 Fed. Census Amity, 1865 NYS Census Hume, Matteson, Centerville American Legion, 1880 Fed. Census Hume, 1890 Fed. Census Special Schedule Hume, 1865 Allegany County Town Clerk Register Hume, *Northern Allegany County Observer* newspaper)

<u>Haley, Patrick</u> Co. C, 104th NY Infantry - 2/3/1862 at Fillmore/3 yrs - 40 - 5'8", Dark Complexion,

Grey Eyes, Brown Hair - 2/26/1862 at Geneseo - No bounty - Pvt, Pvt - Cedar Creek, 2nd Bull Run, South Mountain, Antietam, Fredericksburg, Gettysburg, Bristoe's Station - 9/30/1864 Disability/Honorable - Was not a casualty - Patrick & Magret Connell Haley (Both B Ireland) - INA - Cork County, Ireland, probably around 1808 - Day Laborer - Farmer - Elizabeth (Betsey) Hickey McCarthy (Originally married to Daniel McCarthy) - John, Mary C., Margaret - 6/24/1882 in Fillmore - Holy Cross Cemetery, Fillmore - Military file is under the name Healey. Sick in Campbell Hospital, DC 4/20/1863 and 2/1/1864, the latter time with asthma. Campbell Hospital admission record lists his age as 54. Age at enlistment is clearly wrong. Hospital record says he was discharged 4/30/1864. (Military & Pension Files, 1865 Allegany County Town Clerk Register Hume, Allegany County Web Site, 1860 Fed. Census Hume, 1870 Fed. Census Allen)

Hall, John D. Co. E, 104th NY Infantry - 2/25/1862 at Geneseo/3 yrs - 36 - 5'10", Light Complexion, Grey Eyes, Light Hair - 2/26/1862 at Geneseo - No bounty - Pvt, Pvt - Cedar Creek, 2nd Bull Run, South Mountain, Antietam - 1/20/1863 Disability/Honorable - Was not a casualty - INA - INA - Circa 1812 in Ireland - Farmer - Laborer - 1st Jane, 2nd Nellie Hickey, married 5/8/1865 in Fillmore - John M., Margaret, Sarah, Matilda, George - 3/2/1889 in Fillmore - Holy Cross Cemetery, Fillmore - Was much older than the age he gave at enlistment. Age is 59 in 1870 Census. (Military & Pension File, 1865 NYS Census Hume, 1865 Allegany County Town Clerk Register Hume, Matteson, 1890 Fed. Census Special Schedule Hume, 1860 Fed. Census Granger, 1870 Fed. Census Hume)

Hall, John M. Co. A, 19th NY Cavalry - 8/4/1862 at Portageville/3 yrs - 20 - 5'5", Dark Complexion, Black Eyes, Brown Hair - 9/3/1862 at Portage Station - $100 - Pvt, Pvt - Manassas Junction, Bristoe's Station, Culpeper Court House, New Market, Shepherdstown - 6/30/1865 Honorable - Was not a casualty - John & Elizabeth Hall (Both B Ireland) - William - 10/14/1840 in Portage (he said 1838 at one point) - Farmer - Farmer/Clerk/Expressman - Elizabeth Ann Parr, married 4/10/1872 in Muskegon, MI - Michael - 5/24/1923 in Fresno, CA - Mt. View Cemetery, Fresno - Marched in Grand Review 5/23/1865. Was a Wagoner at end of service. February - May, 1863. Ambulance Corps driver, August, 1863. Teamster September, 1864 - May, 1865 Brigade Hospital Train. Brother William also served during the war. 1870 Census says he worked in a flousing? mill. (Military & Pension Files, 1865 NYS Census Granger, 1860 Fed. Census Granger, 1850 Fed. Census Portage, 1920 Fed. Census Fresno, 1870 Fed. Census Pontiac, MI)

Hall, Robert Co. F, 4th NY Heavy Artillery - 1/1/1864 at Genesee Falls/3 yrs - 28 - 5'5", Fair Complexion, Blue Eyes, Light Hair - 1/5/1864 at Lockport - $300 - Pvt, Pvt - Peeble's Farm - Hatcher's Run, fall of Petersburg, Appomattox - 9/26/1865 Honorable - Was not a casualty - Parents born in Ireland - INA - circa 1825 in Ireland - Farmer - Farmer - 1st Mary Greer, married Drumenure, County Armagh, Northern Ireland, 2nd Ellen Maloney, married 5/1/1858 in Portage (Apparently never divorced his first wife, however) - Ellen, Maggie, Robert, Bettie, Lincoln, Ellen, Anna, others - 5/5/1904 in Granger - Short Tract Cemetery - Present at Lee's surrender. Marched in Grand Review 5/23/1865. Probably arrived in U.S. in 1853. (Military & Pension Files, 1890 Fed. Census Special Schedule Granger, Granger American Legion, 1865 NYS Census Granger, 1860 Fed. Census Portage, 1870 Fed. Census Granger)

Hall, V.M. (Probably Hall, Virgil M.) Co. A, 13th NY Infantry - 5/21/1861 at Elmira/3 months - 27 - INA - 5/21/1861 at Elmira - No bounty - Pvt, Corp - defense of DC, occupation of Fairfax Court House, 1st Bull Run - 8/14/1861 Honorable - Was not a casualty - Charged with desertion 10/3/1861. Actually he had already been discharged, but since no official notice had been received by his regiment, he was charged. Charge was later removed. The 13th was mustered into service on May 14th for 3 months which is consistent with his discharge date. Left NY for Washington, DC 5/30/1861. Attached to Sherman's Brigade, McDowell's Army of Northeast Virginia June to August, 1861. Defense of DC till 6/3/1861. At Ft. Corcoran till 7/16/1861. Occupation of Fairfax Court House 7/17/1861. 1st Battle of Bull Run 7/21/1861. Regiment transferred to U.S. service 8/2/1861. No further information. Have been unable to locate him in other documents. No pension. (Matteson, NYS Adjutant General Report - Volume 19, 1899)

Hall, William C. Co. H/K, 136th NY Infantry - 8/31/1862 at Portage/3 yrs (Re-enlisted 9/1/1863 at Catlett's Station) - 26 - 5'8", Dark Complexion, Grey Eyes, Brown Hair - 9/25/1862 at Portage - No bounty - Sgt, 2nd Lt. - Chancellorsville, Gettysburg, Wauhatchie, Orchard Knob, Tunnel Hill, Missionary Ridge, Resaca - 5/24/1864 Honorable/Deceased - WIA, 5/15/1864 at Resaca, severe gunshot to foot, KIA died 5/27/1864 at Nashville, TN Hospital from tetanus caused by gunshot wound at Resaca. - John & Elizabeth Hall (Both B Ireland) - John M. - 1835 or 36 in either NY or Canada - Student - None Deceased - Helen C. Carpenter, married 3/30/1864 (while on 20 day leave granted 3/16/1864) - None - 5/27/1864 in Nashville, TN - INA (Body was shipped home to his wife.) - Promoted 1st Sgt 9/1/1863, 2nd Sgt 5/27/1864, Commissioned 2nd Lt 3/7/1863, 1st Lt 8/28/1863. Listed on Soldiers Monument in Granger. Before he died Hall wrote a letter of praise to the daughter of one of his men, George Worden, who was also killed at Resaca. Brother John M. also served during the war. (Military & Pension File, Granger American Legion, *Allegany & Its People*, 1850, 1860 Fed. Censuses Portage)

Hamlin, Alva Co. F, 19th NY Infantry - 8/11/1862 at Hume/3 yrs - 38 - 5'9", Light Complexion, Grey Eyes, Dark Hair - 9/3/1862 at Portage Station - $150 - Pvt, Pvt - Deserted House, siege of Suffolk - 2/12/1864 Honorable/Deceased - DD, died of small pox 2/12/1864 at Georgetown, DC - Alva & Elizabeth Cook Hamlin - INA - 12/19/1823 in Hume - Farmer - None Deceased - Perthena Maria Doud, married 10/11/1848 - None - 2/12/1864 in Georgetown - Alger Cemetery, Hume, Route 19 - May have been assigned Co. D, VRC. 7/4/1862 to 2/12/1864. Was transferred to Co. D, 1st Infantry VRC 10/28/1863. (Military & Pension Files, Matteson, Allegany County Web Site, 1865 Allegany Town Clerk Register Hume, 1890 Fed. Census Special Schedule Hume, *History of Allegany County 1879*, 1865 NYS Census Hume, 1860 Fed. Census Avon)

Hammond, Augustus At least one source document indicates that Hammond served in the military during the war. No evidence of such service has been located. (Fillmore American Legion)

Hammond, John Madison, Jr. Co. B, 44th NY Infantry - 8/19/1861 at Hume/3 yrs - 19 - INA - 8/30/1861 at Albany - No bounty - Pvt, Pvt - siege of Yorktown, Hanover Court House, Gaine's Mill, Winchester, Malvern Hill - WIA, 7/1/1862 at Malvern Hill, gunshot to bowels, KIA , died 7/2/1862 at Malvern Hill from 7/1/1862 gunshot wound - John M. & Elisa Ann Gillett Hammond (Both B NY) - Sarah Jane, Maryette, Jonas? D., Isadore S., Charles S. - 6/4/1842 in Hume -

Farmer - None Deceased - Never Married - None - 7/2/1862 at Malvern Hill - INA - His pension file appears to indicate that he was also captured on 7/1/1862 and actually died on 7/2 as a POW, no other info. Grandmother Susannah Gillett was born in CT. His great grandfather John Hammond was of Scotch descent and his grandfather Jonathon was a drummer in the War of 1812. (Military & Pension Files, 1865 NYS Census Hume, Allegany County Web Site, Matteson, *Allegany & Its People*, 1865 Allegany County Town Clerk Register Hume, 1850 Fed. Census Hume)

Hammond, Slyvanus/Sylvernus Not from the C-H-G area. Served originally with Co. D, 86th NY Infantry. Hume Township received credit for his re-enlistment in Co. C, 16th VRC on 8/13/1864 by paying the re-enlistment bonus of $500. (1865 Allegany County Town Clerk Register Hume)

Hanley, Patrick One source document list Hanley as a soldier. His name was actually Patrick Haley. See the Haley record above. (Matteson)

Harrington, William Delos Co. I, 136th NY Infantry - 8/9/1862 at Springwater/3 yrs - 21 - 5'10", Light Complexion, Blue Eyes, Light Hair - 9/25/1862 at Portage - $100 - Pvt, Pvt - Gettysburg Chancellorsville, Wauhatchie, Orchard Knob, Tunnel Hill, Missionary Ridge, Resaca, New Hope Church, occupation of Atlanta, Goldsboro, Bentonsville - 9/19/1865 at Elmira Honorable - WIA, 5/15/1865 at Resaca, gunshot to right side, (was also hurt when hit by a tree chopped down without warning, by another soldier) - Parents INA (Both B NY) - INA - 8/9/1842 in Geneseo - Farmer - Farm Labor - Cebelia F. Mapes, married 3/8/1866 in Dansville - William, Mattie B., Hascall B. - 11/22/1920 in Canaseraga - INA - Present at Johnston's surrender. Was in Division Hospital as of 3/34/1865. Does not appear to be from the C-H-G area. Matteson book has him from Granger. (Military & Pension Files, Matteson, 1870 Fed. Census Ossian, 1910 Fed. Census Canseraga.)

Harwood, George W. Co. B, 184th NY Infantry - 9/2/1864 at Clarksville/1 yr - 33 - 5'7", Light Complexion, Blue Eyes, Black Hair - 9/6/1864 at Elmira - $100 - Pvt, Pvt - Cedar Creek, before Richmond & Petersburg - Was not a casualty - Rufus & Rachael Harwood (Both B CT) - Holmer H., Sarah Ann, Palmer S. - 5/31/1831 in Angelica - Farmer - Farmer - Margarette A. Bixby, married 9/20/1852 in Allen - Margarette A., George A., Matilda E., Palmer S., Adeline C., Rufus H., John J., Nelly R., Samuel N. - 10/5/1920 in Allen - Until The Dawn Cemetery, Angelica - Had typhoid fever and chronic diarrhea, Harrison's Landing, Spring, 1865. (Military & Pension Files, Granger American Legion, 1850, 1870, 1910 Fed. Censuses Allen)

Harwood, John R. Co. I, 19th NY Cavalry - 8/9/1862 at Nunda/3 yrs - 46 - 6'1", Fair Complexion, Hazel Eyes, Grey Hair - 9/3/1862 at Portage Station - $100 - Pvt, Pvt - Deserted House, siege of Suffolk, Franklin - 10/5/1863 Disability/Honorable - Was not a casualty - INA - INA - 4/13/1810 in Thompson, CT - Farmer/Shoemaker/Constable - Farmer - 1st INA, 2nd Elizabeth A. Williams Drew, married 4/25/1865 in Granger - George, Andrew J., Susan (Ackermon), Catherine, Andrew, Joseph - 1/9/1894 - Pine Grove Cemetery, Fillmore - Was partly blind and deaf and had lost his desire when he was discharged. Hearing affected by being caught in rain and cold at Suffolk, VA in May of 1863. Burnside G.A.R. Post 237 Marker at grave. A cousin, Elijah Harwood, also served during the war. Likely in Jackson County, MI prison in 1850, lived in Monroe County. His second wife, Elizabeth, was the widow of Civil War soldier Hiram Drew who died in Andersonville. (Military & Pension Files, 1865 NYS Census Hume, Matteson, Fillmore and Granger American Legion Posts, NYS Adjutant General Report 1895 Volume 6, 1850 Fed. Census Jackson, MI, 1870 Fed. Census Hume)

Haskins, John Wesley Not from the C-H-G area. Originally served with Co. H, 16th Wisconsin Infantry. Hume Township received credit when he re-enlisted in Co F, 16th VRC by paying his re-enlistment bonus of $500. (1865 Allegany County Town Clerk Register Hume)

Hatch, Cyrus J. Co. F, 19th NY Cavalry - 9/13/1864 at Centerville/1 yr - 24 - 5'11", Fair Complexion, Blue Eyes, Light Hair - 9/27/1864 at Elmira - $100 - Pvt, Pvt - No battles - 5/10/1865 Honorable/Deceased - DD, 5/10/1865 at Cavalry Corps Hospital, Chapel Point, MD of small pox - Cyrus (B VT) & Phebe Brownell (B NY) Hatch - Orlando, Caroline - 10/14/1840 in Centerville - Farmer - None Deceased - Effie Y. Hotchkiss, married 1/10/1860 in Hume - Adelbert & Merton - 5/10/1865 in Chapel Point, MD - Chapel Point - Brother Orlando also served during the war. May also have served in Co. C for a time. Some time after Cyrus' death, Effie married a David Lewis. Cyrus' great grandson, Paul Hatch, was killed in action in 1945 at Bougainville during World War II. (Military & Pension Files, 1865 NYS Census Centerville, 1865 Allegany County Town Clerk Register Centerville, 1850 Fed. Census Centerville)

Hatch, Orlando F. Co. D, 4th NY Heavy Artillery - Drafted 12/28/1863 at Centerville/3 yrs - 28 - 5'6", Dark Complexion, Black Eyes, Black Hair - 12/28/1863 at Elmira - $600 - Pvt, Pvt - 5/25/1865 Honorable - Was not a casualty - Cyrus (B VT) & Phebe Brownell (B NY) Hatch - Cyrus, Caroline - 1835 in Centerville - Farmer - Farmer - Sarah Jane Conklin, married 5/1/1861 in Savannah, Wayne County - INA - 7/30/1886 in Gresham, OR - INA - Brother Cyrus also served during the war. Wife Sarah was previously married to a Alonzo Harlan. (Military & Pension Files, 1865 NYS Census Centerville, 1865 Allegany County Town Clerk Register Centerville, 1850 Fed. Census Centerville, 1870. Fed Census Ulster Township, IA)

Hawley, Asa Co. F/I 146th NY Infantry - 8/26/1862 at Rome/3 yrs - 40 - 6'3", Dark Complexion, Blue Eyes, Black Hair - 10/12/1862 at Rome - $100 - Pvt, Pvt - No battles - 5/11/1864 Deserted - Was not a casualty - INA - INA - 1821 or 22 in Vermont - Farmer - Farmer - Hariett - Jennie - INA - INA - Was sick in hospital. Received a furlough 4/21/1864 for 20 days, to expire 5/11/1864. Never returned. Apparently they never found him or didn't look. Appears in 1880 Census for Centerville as Asa Healee. 1860 Census has name spelled Heald. (Military File, Granger American Legion, 1860 Fed. Census Centerville, 1880 Fed. Census Centerville.)

Hawley, William Co. D, 19th NY Infantry - 9/7/1864 at Pike/1 yr - 18 - 5'9", Fair Complexion, Grey Eyes, Brown Hair - 9/7/1864 at Lockport - $100 - Pvt, Pvt - Cedar Creek, Berryville, Gordonsville, Dinwiddie Court House, Five Forks, Appomattox - 6/30/1865 Honorable - Was not a casualty - Nelson (B Wales) & Sally (B NY) Hawley - Wallace - 3/15/1846 in Rome, MI - Farmer - Teamster - 1st Mary D. Williams, married 3/15/1870, 2nd Lydia E. Wiles Hayes married

8/81885 - Elvira & Mary - 1/15/1928 in Bellevue, MI - Bellevue - Present at Lee's surrender. Marched in Grand Review 5/23/1865. Had a foot wound from chopping wood in 1871 and a knee injury in 1893. Grandparents: Levi (B CT) & Olive (B RI), 80 & 75 respectively in 1850. (Military & Pension Files, 1890 Fed. Census Special Schedule Centerville, 1850 Fed. Census Rome, MI, 1880 Fed. Census Centerville)

Henderson, Harry Not from the C-H-G area. His enlistment in Co. C, 194th NY Infantry was credited to Hume Township which paid his enlistment bonus of $775. May have been from Canada and first name may have been Henry. (*History of Allegany County 1879*, 1865 Allegany County Town Clerk Register Hume)

Hendricks/Hendricks, John Not from the C-H-G area. Originally served with Co. H, 68th PA Infantry and Co. B, 4th PA Infantry. Re-enlistment in Co. C, 16th VRC credited to Hume when the Township paid the re-enlistment bonus of $500. (Allegany County Town Clerk Register Hume)

Henretty, Francis (Henrietta) R. Co. D, 24th NY Cavalry - 12/18/1863 at Hume/3 yrs - 23 - 5'6", Light Complexion, Grey Eyes, Black Hair - 12/28/1863 at Auburn - $300 - Pvt, Pvt - Wilderness, Spotsylvania, North Anna River, Totopotomoy, Cold Harbor, Bethesda Church, Petersburg - 7/21/ 1865 at Rochester Honorable - WIA, 6/22/1864 minnie ball to left calf at Petersburg - Eugene Oren & Mary McCabe Henretty (Both B Ireland) - William, Catherine, Mary A., Oren, Mike, Margarette, Charles, Emogene - 1840 in Virginia - Canal Boatman - Laborer - Margaret Croel, married 9/12/1871 in Portageville - Mary- Frances - Cordelia - 4/4/1875 in East Pike - McCormack Street Cemetery, Portageville - Re-enlisted 1/23/1866 at Buffalo in Co. F, 25th U.S. Infantry. Discharged 5/1/1867 at Corinth, MS. Also served with VRC. Was incorrectly charged with being AWOL. Actually was in a hospital in Rochester due to wound at Petersburg. (Military & Pension Files, Allegany County Web Site, 1865 Allegany County Town Clerk Register Hume [spelled name Henrietta], 1860 Fed Census Gainesville [name spelled Henratta], 1870 Fed Census Genesee Falls [name spelled Henrietta])

Hicok, Samuel (Hickok) Co. D, 4th NY Heavy Artillery - 8/13/1862 at Rochester/3 yrs - 31 - 5'10", Florid Complexion, Light Eyes, Black Hair - 8/13/1862 at Rochester - $50 - Pvt, Pvt - Wilderness, Spotsylvania, North Anna River, Totopotomoy, Cold Harbor, siege of Petersburg, Weldon RR, Ream's Station, Peeble's Farm, Hatcher's Run, fall of Petersburg, Appomattox - 6/3/1865 at Alexandria, VA Honorable - Was not a casualty - Zacariah & ? Bliss Hickok - INA - 1831 in Hume - Carpenter/Sawyer - Carpenter - 1st Laura E. Runyan, 2nd Mary L. Burnell, married 8/1877 in Portage - Ida May, John, Elbert - 12/23/1913 in Soldiers Home in Bath - Lamont Road, East Koy - Said he contracted diarrhea at Fort Ethan Allen, VA (Military & Pension Files, 1865 Allegany County Town Clerk Hume, 1860 Federal Census Eagle, 1870 Fed. Census Buffalo)

Higby, Ephraim Bolivar (Higbee) Co. B, 104th NY Infantry - 10/15/1861 at Pike/3 yrs - 34 - 5'9", Dark Complexion, Blue Eyes, Sandy Hair - 2/26/1862 at Geneseo - No bounty - Pvt, Pvt - No battles - 6/13/1862 Disability/Honorable - Ira & Ruth Fuller Higbee - Ira W., Preston, Albert T., Martha H., - 12/11/1826 in Hume - Miller/Wheel Wright - Sawmill/ Worker/Lumberman/ Farmer/Laborer - Eleanor Merchant - Julia, Mary A., Albert, Frank Allison - 7/28/1901 in (probably) San Francisco - San Francisco? - Brother Ira also served during the war. Was In Mt. Pleasant Hospital in DC. Disability discharge caused by disease of lungs which he claimed he got at Could Mills, VA, and chronic rheumatism. (Military & Pension Files, 1865 Allegany County Town Clerk Register Hume, 1865 NYS Census Hume, 1855 NYS Census Hume, 1850 Fed. Census Hume, 1870 Fed. Census Alma, WI)

Higby, Ira W. (Higbee) Co. C, 104th NY Infantry - 12/26/1861 at Geneseo/3 yrs - 33 - 5'9", Sandy Complexion, Brown Eyes, Brown Hair - 2/26/1862 at Geneseo - No bounty - Pvt, Pvt - Cedar Creek, 2nd Bull Run, South Mountain, Antietam, Fredericksburg - 9/1/1863 Disability/Honorable - WIA, May, 1863 at Chancellorsville, neck wound - Ira & Ruth Fuller Higbee (Both B NY) - Ephraim, Preston, Albert T., Martha H. - 10/15/ 1828 in Hume - Wheel Wright/Miller - Miller - Mary J. Babcock, married 5/16/1849 in Wiscoy - Wallace?, Demming M., Sharon T., Thomas T. George A. William - 7/20/1877 in Red Cloud, NE - Red Cloud - Brother Ephraim also served. Was court-martialed for a minor offence, charged $5.00. In Carver G.H., DC, 3/14/1863. To NY G.H. 6/4/1863, transferred to DeCamp G.H., NY Harbor and then Bedloe Island, NY for convalescence. Transferred to VRC 9/1/1863. (Military & Pension Files, 1865 Allegany County Town Clerk Register Hume, 1855 NYS Census Hume, 1870 Fed. Census Dorr Center, MI)

Higgins, Leland Co. G, 78th NY Infantry - 11/3/1861 at Hume/3 yrs - 30 - INA - 3/5/1862 at Buffalo - No bounty - Pvt, Pvt - No battles - 4/29/1864 Deserted - Was not a casualty - Willard (B VT) & Jerusha (B CT) Higgins - Cornelia, Levina, Elizabeth - 1831 in New York - Probably working for his father, a farmer - Farm Laborer/Lumber Manufacturer - Lucy Means - Son Llewellan, Daughter Llanglan - INA - INA - The 78th was also known as the Eagle Brigade. Apparently not much of an effort was made to locate him after he deserted. (Military File, *History of Allegany County 1879*, 1850, 1860, 1870, 1880 Fed. Censuses Centerville)

Hildreth, Daniel Algeroy Co. F, 4th NY Heavy Artillery - 12/31/1863 at Genesee Falls/3 yrs - 32 - 6', Fair Complexion, Hazel Eyes, Brown Hair - 1/15/1864 at Lockport - $300 - Pvt, Pvt, Wilderness - WIA, 5/6/1864 at Wilderness, gunshot to right foot & shoulder - Lewis & Lucretia Kenyon Hildreth (Both B VT) - INA - 7/27/1831 in Camilius - Boatman - Tanner/Cooper/ Policeman - Catherine A. Sullivan, married 6/28/1873 in Cleveland - Ethel A., Algeroy John - 9/18/1884 at National Military Home, OH - INA - Was in Ladies Home Hospital, NYC as of 8/7/1864. Claimed on marriage certificate that Catherine was his first wife (and that his name was Daniel Algeroy). However both the 1860 and 1865 Census for Hume show him with a "wife" Alzada and children - Electa & Lucretia in 1860, and Linda & Franky in 1865. Ages in Census indicate that Lucretia and Linda are the same person. Alzada and Linda appear in the 1870 Hume Census. (Military & Pension Files, 1865 Allegany County Town Clerk Register Hume, 1865 NYS Census Hume, 1860 Fed. Census Hume. 1880 Fed. Census Cleveland, OH)

Hildreth, James Wilson - Co. F/H/M, 4th NY Heavy Artillery - 8/29/1862 at Hume/3 yrs (Re-enlisted 8/1/1864 at Alexandria, VA) - 5'9", Dark Complexion, Blue Eyes, Dark Hair - 8/29/1862 at NYC - $50 - Pvt, 2nd Lt. - Wilderness, Spotsylvania, North Anna River, Totopotomoy, Cold Harbor, siege of Petersburg, Weldon RR, Ream's Station - 1/20/1865 Honorable - WIA, 6/18/ 1864 at Petersburg, gunshot wound to right hand - Alanson & Mary Christy Hildreth (Both B VT)

- Joseph, George, Herbert, Mary, Axes - 8/29/1837 in Acton, VT - Farm Laborer - Farmer/ Dairyman - Caroline S. (Carrie) Hodge, married 4/4/1869 in Pike - Wilson J.- 1/21/1916 in Hume - Lamont Road, East Koy - Promoted to 2nd Lt 6/18/1864 for bravery at Petersburg. Was recommended for 1st Lt & Captain for his actions at Reams Station, but being ill with chronic diarrhea and stomach problems, was mustered out of service. Charter Member, Commander, and Officer of Burnside G.A.R. Post 237. Probably named after Grandfather Wilson Hildreth who was born in VT. (Military & Pension Files, *Allegany & Its People*, 1890 Fed. Census Special Schedule Hume,1865 NYS Census Hume, 1860, 1880, 1910 Fed. Censuses Hume)

Hildreth, Oscar Reed Co. D, 76th Pennsylvania Infantry - 10/10/1861 at Luzerne Co. PA./3 yrs - 24 - 5'8", Light Complexion, Blue Eyes, Light Hair - 10/16/1861 at Harrisburg, PA - $100 - Pvt, Corp - Secessionville, Pocataligo, Morris Island and Fort Wagner, before Petersburg & Richmond, Bermuda Hundred, Drury's Bluff, Cold Harbor, Chaffin's Farm - 11/28/1864 Disability/Honorable - Was not a casualty - Alonzo D. (B VT) & Sophia Wilkinson (B NY) Hildreth - Charles N., Cordelia R., William, Horace, Evander - 11/4/1836 in Putnam, VT - Engineer - Farmer - Anna M. Allen Hurlburt, married 9/18/1866 in Howard, Steuben County - Leverett George - 9/21/1913 in Britton, SD - Britton - Appointed Corporal 6/18/1862. Sick in Hilton Head Hospital 11/24/62 to 12/20/1862. January-February, 1863 sick in quarters. Anna was first married to Francis Hurlburt who died in the war. Charter Member of Burnside G.A.R. Post 237. Oscar was a distant cousin of James W. Hildreth. Disability discharge was related to RR injury initially from about 1858. Left leg became paralyzed and was basis of his pension. Was found unfit for duty. (Military & Pension Files, *Allegany & Its People*, 1850 Fed. Census Scio, 1880 Fed. Census Hume)

Hill, George V. Co. G, 44th NY Infantry - 8/20/1861 probably at Hume/3 yrs - 18 - 5'11", Fair Complexion, Grey Eyes, Brown Hair - 9/30/1861 at Albany - No bounty - Pvt, Pvt - siege of Yorktown, Hanover Court House, Gaine's Mills, Malvern Hill - 10/3/1862 Deserted - WIA, 5/27/1862 a shell exploded just above his head at Hanover Court House causing a flesh wound, WIA, 7/1/1862 fell over another soldier in a skirmish at Malvern Hill causing a rupture of the veins in his right leg - Franklin (Francis) (B CT) & Louise Galtia (B MA) Hill - Sarah, Julia, Hellen, Frederick - 3/1843 in Hornellsville - Laborer - Machinist - Carrie B. Scott, married 3/15/1879 in Jamestown - George, Linnie M. - 7/1/1893 - INA - Received a 20 day furlough 3/15/1879. Was given a furlough after Malvern Hill and didn't return. Pension request was denied due to desertion. Lived at Wiscoy at time of enlistment per pension application. (Military & Pension Files, 1865 Allegany County Town Clerk Register Hume, 1860 Fed. Census Hume)

Hill, (McHill), William Co. D, 50th NY Engineers - 9/10/1861 at Allegheny?/3 yrs - 30 - 5'6", Light Complexion, Blue Eyes, Brown Hair - 9/11/1861 at Elmira - No bounty - Pvt, Pvt - siege of Yorktown - 8/23/1862 at G.H., Philadelphia, Disability/Honorable - INJ, Injury to spine, paralysis left arm, leg and side - INA (Both B NY) - INA - INA - Painter - Painter - INA - INA - 2/9/1891- INA - Was injured in May, 1862 constructing a bridge across the Chickahominy River. Transported from Yorktown, VA to Philadelphia aboard the hospital steamer *State of Maine*. Disability discharge for nephritis. Military & Pension Index have name as McHill (Pension file has not been located.) Lived in Centerville around 1890. Probably lived in Cuba in 1870. (Military File, 1890 Fed. Census Special Schedule Centerville, 1880 Fed. Census Carrolton, Carded Medical

Records)

Hinkley, Owen E. Co. B, 14th NY Heavy Artillery - Drafted 7/21/1863 at Granger/3 yrs - 28 - 5'10", Light Complexion - 8/29/1863 at Rochester - $100 - Pvt, Pvt - Wilderness, Spotsylvania, North Anna River, Pamunkey, Totopotomoy, Cold Harbor, siege of Petersburg, Fort Steadman - 8/10/1865 Honorable - POW, captured 3/25, 1865 at Petersburg, Prison not listed. Paroled 3/30/1865 - Jaby (B VT) & Mary (B NY) Hinkley - Daniel, Esny R., Ann - 1844 or 45 in New York - Farmer - Farmer - Cornelia Adaline Hinman, married 9/24/1857 in Portage - Flora E., Edwin R., Archie J. - 4/12/1906 in Hunt - INA - In Emory Hospital, DC as of 8/1/1864, transferred from City Point, VA. March-April, 1864 on leave. July-December, 1864 sick in hospital. In Nunda 10/10/1864. Daily duty at Fort Richmond in the Ordnance Department. (Military & Pension Files, Register of Draftees 7/63 to 10/64, 1860 Fed. Census Granger, 1850 1880 Fed. Censuses Portage)

Hinman, Sherwood D. Co. D, 4th NY Heavy Artillery - 8/13/1862 at Rochester/3 yrs - 31 - 5'8", Florid Complexion, Blue Eyes, Black Hair - 8/13/1862 at Rochester - $100 - Pvt, Pvt - Regular duty regimental bugler, assume he participated in following battles: Wilderness, Spotsylvania, North Anna River, Totopotomoy, Cold Harbor, siege of Petersburg, Weldon RR, Ream's Station, Peeble's Farm, Hatcher's Run, fall of Petersburg, Appomattox - 6/3/1865 Honorable - Was not a casualty - H. & Margaret Hinman - INA - 2/8/1830 in Cairo, Green County - Farmer - Farmer - 1st Clarissa Randall, married 12/4/1850 in Portageville, 2nd Mary Elizabeth Snyder Foland, a widow, married 10/10/1877 in Oshkosh, WI - Frank M., Fred S., Hiram G. - 6/20/1905 in Cherokee, IA - Oak Hill Cemetery, Cherokee - Present at Lee's surrender. Marched in Grand Review 5/23/1865. All three of his sons became engineers. (Military & Pension Files, 1865 Allegany County Town Clerk Register Hume, 1860 Fed. Census Hume, 1870 Fed. Census Poysippe, WI)

Hoadley, Henry C. Co. C, 104th NY Infantry - 2/25/1862 at Geneseo/3 yrs - 34 - 5'4", Light Complexion, Grey Eyes, Brown Hair - 2/26/1862 at Geneseo - No bounty - Pvt, Pvt - Cedar Creek, 2nd Bull Run, South Mountain, Antietam, Fredericksburg, Chancellorsville, Gettysburg, Cold Harbor, Bethesda Church, Petersburg, Weldon RR - 2/23/1865 Honorable/Deceased - POW, captured 7/1/1863 at Gettysburg, Prison: Richmond, paroled 9/29/1863 at City Point, VA, POW, 8/19/1864 at Weldon RR, Prison: Richmond & Salisbury, NC, DD, 2/23/1865 at Salisbury - Probably Miles & Sally Hoadley - INA - 1827 or 28 in Oneida County - Boatman - None Deceased - Laurinda Willey Eastman, married 12/25/1858 - Adelia, Julia, George Henry - 2/23/1865 in Salisbury, NC - Probably Salisbury National Cemetery - The 1865 NYS Census says he hadn't been heard from in a year (at the time of the Census), but for some reason believed that he had been released and had died on his way home. An 1869 card in his military file says he died in prison. Was AWOL at one point and fined $8.00. After his initial capture and release he was in a hospital at Annapolis, then sent by steamer to NYC. Given a 15 day leave 10/31/1863. Was at DeCamp G.H., then at a convalescent camp (probably Bedloes Island), and then back to Annapolis. Back with his company by 6/6/1864. (Military & Pension Files, 1865 NYS Census Hume, Allegany County Web Site)

Hoes, Daniel B. Co. K, 188th NY Infantry - 9/20/1864 at Avon/1 yr - 29 - 5'11", Fair Complexion,

Blue Eyes, Light Hair - 10/15/1865 at Avon - $100 - Pvt, Sgt - Gravelly Run - 7/1/1865 Honorable - WIA, 3/31/1865 at Gravelly Run, a tree limb blown off by a shell fell on him, injured back and right shoulder - Jesse & Deborah Hoes (Both B NY) - INA - 1835 or 36 in Littlefield - Farm Laborer - Farmer - 1st Mary Campbell (Died 1/18/1872), 2nd Mary Ingalls (Died), 3rd Sarah Ada Powell, married 4/1/1882 - Elizabeth & Daniel - 11/8/1894 in Rossburg - Riverside Cemetery Belfast - Present at Lee's surrender. Marched in Grand Review 5/23/1865. Per military, 1865 address was Wiscoy. Appointed Corporal 1/12/1865, Sgt, 3/1/1865. Lived in Granger by at least 1890. (Military & Pension Files, 1890 Fed. Census Special Schedule Granger, 1850 Fed. Census Springwater, 1860 Fed. Census Livonia, 1870, 1880 Fed. Censuses Sparta)

Holbrook, James E. Co. E, 85th NY Infantry - 9/1/1861 at Granger/3 yrs (Re-enlisted 1/1/1864) - 21 - 5'5", Light Complexion, Blue Eyes, Brown Hair - 10/10/1861 at Elmira - $400 - Pvt, Pvt - defense of DC, siege of Yorktown, Williamsburg, Fair Oaks, before Richmond, Plymouth - 8/21/1864 Honorable/Deceased - POW, captured 4/20/1864 at Plymouth, Prison: Andersonville, DD, 8/21/1864 at Andersonville, of diarrhea. Horatio (B MA) & Mary Ann (Polly) (B NY) Holbrook - Sarah, Mary, Lewis, David, Anna (Hannah)? , Hester, Louisa, Frederick - 1840 in New York - Farmer - None Deceased - Never Married - None - 8/21/1864 in Andersonville Prison - Andersonville - Brother Lewis also served during the war. (Military File, Granger American Legion, *History of Allegany County 1879*, 1850 Fed. Census Granger, 1860 Fed. Census Portage)

Holbrook, Lewis James Co. E, 85th NY Infantry - 9/1/1861 at Angelica/3 yrs - 19 - INA - 11/11/1861 at Elmira - No bounty - Pvt, Pvt - defense of DC, siege of Yorktown - 4/23/1862 Honorable/Deceased - DD, 4/23/1862 of intermittent fever at Warwick, VA. - Horatio (B MA) & Mary Ann (Polly) (B NY) Holbrook - Sarah, Mary James, David, Anna (Hanah)?, Hester, Louisa, Frederick - 1841 or 42 in New York - None listed in 1860 Census - None Deceased - Never Married - None - 4/23/1862 in Warwick, VA - INA - Brother James E. also served during the war. (Military & Pension Files, Granger American Legion, 1850 Fed. Census Granger)

Holley, (Holly) Henry B. Co F, 4th NY Heavy Artillery - 12/31/1863 at Genesee Falls/3 yrs - 22 - 5'11", Fair Complexion, Blue Eyes, Brown Hair - 12/31/1863 at Lockport - $100 - Pvt, Pvt - Wilderness, Spotsylvania, North Anna River, Totopotomoy, Cold Harbor, siege of Petersburg, Weldon RR, Fall of Petersburg, Appomattox - 6/5/1865 Honorable - Was not a casualty - A.L. & Caroline Holley (Both B NY) - Rhoda, Leona - 5/9/1843 in Ceres, PA - Farmer - Farmer - Laura A. Van Dusen, married 7/25/1866 in Pike - Frederick, 6 others - 2/2/1913 in Portage - Probably Portage - Present at Lee's surrender. Marched in Grand Review 5/23/1865. (Military & Pension Files, 1865 NYS Census Granger, 1860 Fed Census Hume, 1910 Fed Census Portage)

Hopkins, Amos Co. C, 19th NY Cavalry - 9/13/1864 at Centerville/1 yr - 38 - 5'8", Fair Complexion, Blue Eyes, Brown Hair - 9/27/1864 at Elmira - $900 - Pvt, Pvt - Cedar Creek, Berryville, Gordonsville - 6/30/1865 Honorable - Was not a casualty - Clark & Phebe Morrill Hopkins - INA - 1/26/1826 in Centerville - Trader/Farmer - Farmer - Maria - Howard - 1888 in Houghton - INA - Got frostbite of right foot while on picket duty 12/23/1864 at Liberty Mills, VA. Marched in Grand Review 5/23/1865. (Military & Pension Files, 1865 NYS Census

Centerville, 1865 Allegany County Town Clerk Register Centerville, Matteson, *History of Allegany County 1879*, 1860, 1870 Fed. Censuses Centerville)

Hopkins, George Did not serve. Was listed in error in source document. Was seven in 1865. (1865 NYS Census Hume.)

Hopkins, Oliver Joseph Co. F, 19th NY Cavalry - 2/17/1865 at Hume/1 yr (3rd Enlistment - see below) - 26 - 5'10", Fair Complexion, Grey Eyes, Brown Hair - 2/20/1865 at Elmira - $700 - Pvt, Pvt - No battles - 6/30/1865 Honorable - Was not a casualty - John & Fancy Drew Hopkins - INA - 2/3/1838 in Stafford - Farmer - Farmer - 1st Matilda Drew, married Fillmore, separated 1863 (had an official bill of separation, but no divorce), divorced 7/8/1907, 2nd Melissa E. Derrick, married 9/8/1895 in New Haven Center, MI (apparently not a legal marriage), 3rd Emma Allen Lamphere, married November, 1908 at Tyrone, MI, 4th Ella Rice, married 9/12/1921 in Leslie, MI (deserted her 12/4/1921) - Fannie Alma, Jennie Ethel, Willie Warren, Amos Pearl, Henry Marsten, Rosa, Amos V., William M. - 4/15/1924 in Royal Oak, MI - New Haven Center Cemetery, Carson City, MI - Initially served with Co. C, 16th Michigan Infantry, discharged 2/10/1862, see below. His second enlistment was with Co. I, 1st Michigan Engineers & Mechanics, see below. Enrolled 8/1/1863 at New Haven for 3 yrs. Disability Discharge 1/14/1864 at Bridge Point. Was blind in left eye, almost blind in right. Probably participated in Grand Review 5/23/1865. Lived in Hume following his second enlistment (1864) per neighbor William Drew. (Military & Pension Files, 1865 Allegany County Town Clerk Register Hume, *History of Allegany County 1879*, 1840 Fed. Census Stafford, 1900 Fed. Census Chippewa, MI, 1910 Fed. Census Grand Rapids, MI)

Hopkins, Oliver Joseph Co. C, 16th Michigan Infantry - 8/1/1861 at Detroit/3 yrs - - 23 - 5'10", Fair Complexion, Grey Eyes, Brown Hair - 8/17/1861 at Detroit - No bounty - Pvt, Pvt - No battles - 2/24/1862 Disability/Honorable - Was not a casualty - Disability was for typhoid fever, which most likely caused a loss of sight in his left eye. Also served with 19th NY Cavalry, see above, and 1st Michigan Engineers and Mechanics, see below. See 19th Cavalry above for personal information and sources of information.

Hopkins, Oliver Joseph Co. I, 1st Michigan Engineers and Mechanics - 8/1/1863 at New Haven, MI/3 yrs - 25 - 5'10", Fair Complexion, Grey Eyes, Brown Hair - INA - No bounty - Pvt, Pvt - No battles - 1/14/1864 Disability/Honorable - Was not a casualty - Disability discharge was due to blindness in left eye and poor vision in right. Per an affidavit in his pension file from William Drew of Hume (who enlisted in the 194th Infantry in 1865), Hopkins lived near him and worked with him following his second enlistment. Also served with 19th NY Cavalry and 16th Michigan Infantry, see above. See 19th Cavalry entry for personal information and sources of information.

Horton, Sanford L. Co. F, 19th NY Infantry - 2/20/1865 at Hume/1 yr - 35 - 5'9", Dark Complexion, Blue Eyes, Black Hair - 2/20/1865 at Elmira - $700 - Pvt, Pvt - No battles - 7/1/1865 Honorable - Was not a casualty - John (B England) & Polly Randall (B VT) Horton - INA - 2/22/ 1830 in Ogden - Farmer - Farmer - 1st Susannah Fairwell, 2nd Cordelia, 3rd Maria W. Edgerton married 3/15 /1868 in Milwaukee - Victoria, James, John - 2/21/1910 in Fulton, WI - Fulton - Had intermittent fever while in service. Spent time in Finley Hospital in DC. Apparently never divorced

Susanna. (Military & Pension Files, *History of Allegany County 1879*, 1865 NYS Census Granger, 1865 Allegany County Town Clerk Register Hume, 1850 Fed. Census Hume, 1900 Fed. Census Bristol, WI)

Hotchkiss, George H. Co. G, 7th Michigan Infantry - 8/22/1861 at Monroe, MI/3 yrs (Re-enlisted 12/8/1863) - 20 - 5'8", Light Complexion, Blue Eyes, Light Hair - 8/22/1861 at Monroe, MI - No bounty - Pvt, Corp - siege of Yorktown, West Point, Fair Oaks, Peace Orchard, Savage Station, Malvern Hill, Antietam, Fredericksburg, Gettysburg, Bristoe's Station, Wilderness, Dabney's Mill, Hatcher's Run - fall of Petersburg, Appomattox - 7/5/1865 Honorable - WIA, 9/17/1862 at Antietam, gunshot to right arm, WIA, 5/6/1864 at Wilderness, gunshot wound to index finger, right hand - John (B VT) & Miranda King (B NY) Hotchkiss - Effie, Henry, Jerby, James, Marshall - 5/8/1841 in Centerville - Farmer - Farmer/Stone Mason - 1st Amanda Bennett, married Lewisburg, PA. (Died 1/8/1884), 2nd Ida Mae Johnson, married 3/8/1886 in Fillmore - Henry, James - 10/8/1924 in Franklinville - Caneadea - Present at Lee's surrender. Marched in Grand Review. Served in NYC during the draft riots of August and September, 1863. Brothers Henry & James also served during the war. (Military & Pension Files, Medical Card, 1865 NYS Fed. Census Centerville, 1850 Fed. Census Centerville, 1880 Fed. Census Rushford, 1920 Fed. Census Franklinville)

Hotchkiss, Henry L. Co. D, 64th NY Infantry - 9/18/1861 at Rushford/3 yrs - 18 - 5'10", Light Complexion, Blue Eyes, Light Hair - 9/24/1861 at Elmira - No bounty - Pvt, Pvt - siege of Yorktown, Fair Oaks, Gaines Mill, Savage Station, Malvern Hill, Wilderness, Spotsylvania - 5/20/1864 Honorable/Deceased - WIA, 5/12/1864 at Spotsylvania, gunshot to stomach when charging the enemy works, KIA, died 5/20/1864 at Harewood Hospital, DC of wounds received at Spotsylvania - John (B VT) & Miranda King (B NY) Hotchkiss - Effie, George, Jerby, James, Marshall - 1842 or 43 in Centerville - Farmer - None Deceased - Never Married - None - 5/20/1864 in Harewood Hospital, DC - Arlington National Cemetery - Brothers George & James also served during the war. His father died on 5/22/1864. (Military & Pension Files, 1865 NYS Census Centerville, 1865 Allegany County Town Clerk Register Centerville, 1850 Fed. Census Centerville, *Roll of Honor*)

Hotchkiss, James Co. A/E, 161st NY Infantry - 1/23/1864 at Hartwick/3 yrs - 18 - 5'5", Light Complexion, Blue Eyes, Light Hair - 1/23/1864 at Elmira - $300 - Pvt, Corp - Morganza, Mobile, siege of Fort Spanish, siege of Fort Blakely - 11/10/1865 Honorable - Was not a casualty - John (B VT) & Miranda King (B NY) Hotchkiss - Effie, George, Henry, Jerby, Marshall - 2/20/1846 in Centerville - Farmer - Farm Laborer/Farmer - Josephine M. Rich, married 2/16/1879 in Centerville - Frank, Florence, Floyd, Forest - 4/13/1925 at Allen - Caneadea - Brothers George and Henry also served. (Military & Pension Files, 1865 NYS Census Centerville, 1890 Fed. Census Special Schedule Centerville, 1865 Allegany County Town Clerk Centerville, 1850 Fed. Census Centerville, 1870 Fed. Census Hume)

Hubbard, Leander Co. F, 4th NY Heavy Artillery - 8/15/1862 at Hume/3 yrs - 42 - 5'10", Light Complexion, Blue Eyes, Brown Hair - 9/12/1862 at NYC - $100 - Pvt, Pvt - Wilderness, Spotsylvania, North Anna River, Totopotomoy, Cold Harbor, siege of Petersburg, Weldon RR,

Ream's Station - 5/22/1865 Honorable - Was not a casualty - Samuel & Abigail Carter Hubbard - INA - 11/19/1920 in Champion, Jefferson County - Farmer - Farmer - Susan Clark - Martha, Mary, Ward, Ellworth - 1879 in Kansas, probably Greenleaf, KS - INA - Was discharged from Lincoln Hospital in DC. Was also in City Point, VA hospital. (Military & Pension Files, 1865 NYS Census Hume, 1865 Allegany County Town Clerk Register Hume, 1860, 1870 Fed. Censuses Hume)

Hultz (Hulse), Rawson (Ranson) B. Co. F, 27th NY Infantry - 7/9/1861 at Elmira/2 yrs - 20 - INA - 7/15/1861 at Elmira - No bounty - Pvt, Pvt - Winchester, Cedar Mountain, Groveton, Antietam, 2nd Bull Run, Stafford Court House, Chancellorsville - 5/31/1863 Honorable - Was not a casualty during this enlistment - Richard & Mandana R. Ball Hultz (Both B NY) -Therese, Eugene, Flora A., Eva I., Kate A., Smith- 6/1841 in Pulteney - INA - None Deceased - Never Married - None - 3/22/1865 near White Post, VA - INA - 6/30/1862 to 2/28/1863 detached to Ambulance Service. Transferred to Ambulance Service 4/11/1863 for balance of term. Father also served during the war. Military File is under the name Ranson Hultz. Also served with the 21st NY Cavalry see below. Rawson and his father Richard were both at the battle of Antietam. Since he enlisted at Hume, it is likely that he was living at Hume with his parents in 1861, but not in 1860 census. (Military & Pension Files, 1865 Allegany County Town Clerk Register Hume, 1850 Fed. Census Pulteney)

Hultz (Hulse), Rawson (Ranson) B. Co. B, 21st NY Cavalry - 6/29/1863 at Elmira/3 yrs - 22 - INA - 8/28/1863 at Elmira - $50 - Pvt, Sgt - Smithfield, New Market, Mt. Jackson, Snicker's Gap, Gordonsville, Shepherdstown, Point of Rocks, Berryville - 3/22/1865 Honorable/Deceased - KIA, shot in head 3/22/1865 near White Post, VA., while on a scouting mission - Promoted to Sgt, 8/29/1863, to Sgt Major 1/1/1864, reduced to ranks (no reason cited) 2/24/1864, promoted to Sgt 3/1/1864. Father Richard served during the war. Also served with the 27th NY Infantry, see above. Also see above for personal information and sources of information.

Hultz, Richard (Hulse) Co. H, 50th NY Engineers - 8/22/1862 at Elmira (probably Hume)/3 yrs - 44 - 5'7", Dark Complexion, Blue Eyes, Dark Hair - 9/14/1862 at Elmira - No bounty - Pvt, Pvt, Antietam - 1/31/1863 Disability/Honorable - Was not a casualty - Richard & J. Hultz - INA - 1817 or 18 in Seneca County - Carpenter/Minister/Machinist - Horticulturist - Mandana R. Ball - Theresey, Rawson, Eugene, Flora A., Eva I., Kate A. Smith - 4/8/1883 - INA - In regimental Hospital at Alexandria 11/19/1862. Disability discharge result of rheumatism. Son Rawson also served during the war. Both were at the battle of Antietam. Richard was a musician during the war. (Military & Pension Files, 1850 Fed. Census Pulteney, 1860 Fed. Census Hume, 1870 Fed. Census Starkey, learned of Richard's service from Ransom's Pension File)

Huntington, Monroe Harrison Co. H, 9th NY Cavalry - 10/1/1861 at East Randolph/3 yrs - 22 - 5'9", Dark Complexion, Gray Eyes - Dark Hair - 10/7/1861 at Westfield - No bounty - Pvt, Pvt - defense of DC, siege of Yorktown, Williamsburg - 10/30/1862 Disability Discharge - Was not a casualty - Disability discharge was due to disease of the heart, which did not stop him from enlisting in the 13th NY Heavy Artillery. See below for 13th HA information. Also see below for personal information and sources of information.

Huntington, Monroe Harrison Co. B/C/E, 13th NY Heavy Artillery - 8/3/1863 at Salamanca/3 yrs - 22 - 5'9", Dark Complexion, Grey Eyes, Dark Hair - 8/29/1863 at Staten Island? - $200 - Pvt, 2nd Lt. - Fairfax Court House, Front Royal, Carter's Farm, Aldie - 8/24/1865 Honorable - Was not a casualty - Arnold (B NY) & Nancy Huntington - Lafayette, Maria, Emily - 8/4/1839 in Canaseraga - Farm Hand - Farm Laborer - Harriett Mapes, married 8/12/1867 in Belfast - Margarette - 9/23/1874 in Rushford of tuberculosis - INA - Transferred with Co. C to 6th Heavy Artillery on 7/18/1865 with balance of the 13th HA regiment. Most of the regiment had already been mustered out of service. Served with Co. K, 6th NY Heavy Artillery 7/18/1865 to 8/24/1865. One record says he was discharged 10/13/1862, but that is wrong and relates to his service with the 9th Cavalry. Another record says he was mustered 1/29/1865. Not sure what this date means, but it is not a muster date. He was detached in mid-1864 (July-August) to the 13th U.S. Colored Heavy Artillery where he served as a 1st Lt. On 10/18/1864 he was ordered to rejoin his company (presumably Co. C 13th NY Heavy Artillery) at Norfolk, VA While census shows him living in Rushford, per his pension he lived and worked most of the time in Centerville. Worked for Amos Hopkins for a number of years. Amos was married to Monroe's sister. (Military & Pension Files, 1865 Allegany County Town Clerk Register Centerville, 1850 Fed. Census Canewango, 1860 1870 Fed. Censuses Rushford)

Hurlburt, Riley A. Co. F, 5th NY Cavalry - 9/4/1861 at Pike/3 yrs - 29 - 5'6", Light Complexion, Black Eyes, Black Hair - 9/21/1861 at NYC - No bounty - Pvt, Pvt - No battles - 10/6/1862 Disability/Honorable - Was not a casualty - Brazilla & Lovina Hurlburt (Both B CT) - INA - 1832 (1833 per headstone) in Eagle - Farmer - Farm Laborer - Rosina Vanocker, married 12/28/1869 in Eagle - Carson & Earl - 6/21/1900 - Cadwell Cemetery, Centerville - One source document indicates that he also served with Co. F, 104th NY Infantry. There is no evidence of such service. No military file has been located and the NYS Adjutant General Report for the 104th does not list Hurlburt as having served with the regiment. His disability discharge was due to urinary problems and external hemorrhoids. (Military & Pension Files, Centerville American Legion, Matteson, 1850, 1860, 1870 Fed. Censuses Eagle)

Hussong, William Co. F, 104th NY Infantry - 1/23/1862 at Granger/3 yrs - 19 - 6'1", Light Complexion, Blue Eyes, Brown Hair - 2/26/1862 at Geneseo - No bounty - Pvt, Pvt - Cedar Creek, 2nd Bull Run, South Mountain, Antietam, Fredericksburg, Chancellorsville, Gettysburg - 7/4/1863 Honorable/Deceased - WIA, 9/17/1862 at Antietam, gunshot to ankle, WIA, 7/1/1863 at Gettysburg, slight gunshot to left leg, KIA, 7/4/1863 at Gettysburg - Christian (later John) & Dorie (maybe Dorothy) Lincner? Smith - William, Mary, Catherine, John - 9/18/1842 in Granger - Farmer - None Deceased - Never Married - None - 7/4/1863 at Gettysburg - Gettysburg per military records; not there per cemetery records - Listed on Soldiers Monument in Granger. (Military & Pension Files, Medical Cards, 1865 NYS Census Granger, Matteson, Granger American Legion, *Allegany & Its People*, 1865 Allegany County Town Clerk Register Granger, 1860 Fed. Census Granger)

Hyde, Samuel Plinn Co. F, 4th NY Heavy Artillery - 9/27/1862 at Hume/3 yrs - 44 - 5'6", Light Complexion, Blue Eyes, Brown Hair - 10/2/1862 at NYC - No bounty - Pvt, Artificer - Detached as Ambulance Driver almost entire service. Likely at, and maybe in, many battles, but no record -

9/26/1865 Honorable - Was not a casualty - Josephus & Sophia Mead Hyde - INA - June 18, 1818 in Vermont - Carpenter - Carpenter - Mary C. Weaver, married 12/20/1843 in Granger - Wallace - 12/24/1899 probably in Clear Lake, IA - Probably Clear Lake - Suffered sunstroke at Petersburg, VA July, 1864. Detached to 6th Corps Ambulance Dept. as of April, 1864. Was probably detached to Battery H, 1st Ohio Artillery, January to April 1865. Son Wallace also served during the war. Marched in Grand Review 5/23/1865. May have been at Lee's surrender. (Military & Pension Files, 1865 NYS Census Granger, 1865 Allegany County Town Clerk Register Granger, 1850 Fed. Census Granger, 1870 Fed. Census Mantorville, MN)

Hyde, Wallace William Co. F, 4th NY Heavy Artillery - 9/27/1862 at Hume/3 yrs - 17 - 5'5", Light Complexion, Brown Eyes, Light Hair - 10/2/1862 at NYC - $100 - Pvt, Pvt - Wilderness, Spotsylvania, North Anna River, Totopotomoy, Cold Harbor, siege of Petersburg, Peeble's Farm, Hatcher's Run, fall of Petersburg, Appomattox - 9/26/1865 Honorable - Was not a casualty - Samuel A. Plinn and Mary Catherine Weaver Hyde (Both B VT) - Eunice A, Sophia J. - 12/16/1846 in Granger - Carpenter - Farmer - Margaret Benson, married 7/29/1873 in Evansville, WI - Myrtle M., Samuel P., Mary C., Lammie R., Willie R. - 8/1/1920 in Clear Lake, IA - Probably Clear Lake - Served on detached duty July-August, 1864 with Batt B, 1st Rhode Island Artillery. May-June, 1864, was court-martialed for sleeping at his post. Pled guilty. Fined 3 months pay. Promoted to Waggoner 7/1/1865. Father Samuel also served during the war. Present at Lee's surrender. Marched in Grand Review 5/23/1865. (Military & Pension Files, 1865 NYS Census Granger, 1865 Allegany County Town Clerk Register Granger, 1850 Fed. Census Granger, 1870 Fed. Census Dodge County)

Ingham, Arthur Lycurgus Co H, 94th Illinois Infantry - 8/1/1862 at Bloomington, IL/3 yrs - 35 - 5'7", Light Complexion, Blue Eyes, Light Hair - 8/20/1862 at Bloomington - $100 - Pvt, Pvt - Prairie Grove, AR, siege of Vicksburg, Morgan's Ferry, Fort Morgan, Mobile Bay, AL, siege of Spanish Fort, siege and capture of Fort Blakely - 7/17/1865 Honorable - Was not a casualty - Chauncey (B NY) & Sarah Spaulding (B MA) Ingham - INA - 6/30/1831 in Hume - Farmer - Farmer/Erie RR Conductor-Brakeman - Annette A. Randle, married 9/24/1857 in Hume - Malcolm, Fanny E. (Smith) & Blanch S. (Mack) -11/11/ 1912 in Hornell - Hope Cemetery, Hornell - Had disease of the eyes caused by scurvy contracted at Brownsville, TX, the result of going without green vegetables from 12/63 through 8/64. Was diagnosed at Ft. Morgan, Mobile Point, AL. Promoted Corp. 1/21/1863. On furlough 10/27 to 12/27/1864 at Hume. (Military & Pension Files, 1865 NYS Census Hume, 1850 Fed. Census Hume, 1870 Fed. Census Binghamton, 1900 Fed. Census Hornell)

Ingham, Charles E. At least one source document indicates that Charles E. Ingham served in the military during the war. No evidence of such service has been located. (Matteson)

Ingham, Joseph N. Battery C, 1st Michigan Light Artillery - 12/13/1861 at Almont, MI/3 yrs - 39 - 5'10", Fair Complexion, Blue Eyes, Light Hair - 12/13/1861 at Detroit - No bounty - Pvt, Pvt - siege of Island No. 10, Mississippi River - 7/22/1862 Disability/Honorable - Was not a casualty - George C. & Sarah? Ingham (Both B NY) - INA - 1822 or 23 in Frankport - Butcher - Lock Tender/Laborer - 1st Lucinda Bemis Brown (Died 11/1890), 2nd Anna Elizabeth Knewthem Dolby, married 9/17/1864 in Rochester - None - 11/28/1894 - Pine Grove Cemetery, Fillmore - Had typhoid fever while in the service. Lucinda apparently ran off with another man while he was in the service. She and others claimed he abused her. She had 2 children from a previous marriage. Never divorced. Second wife was recognized by pension bureau as his common law wife and received his pension. (Military & Pension Files, 1865 NYS Census Hume, Fillmore American Legion, Matteson, 1860 Fed. Census Kalamazoo, MI, 1870, 1880 Fed. Censuses Hume)

Isted, Charles William Co, F, 4th NY Heavy Artillery - 9/9/1862 at Hume/3 yrs - 18 - 5'4", Light Complexion, Blue Eyes, Red Hair - 9/12/1864 at NYC - $100 - Pvt, Pvt - Wilderness, Spotsylvania, North Anna River, Totopotomoy, Cold Harbor, Peeble's Farm, Hatcher's Run, fall of Petersburg, Appomattox - 6/3/1865 Honorable - WIA, 6/2/1864 at Cold Harbor, gunshot to ring finger of left hand - Thomas & Henrietta Trumbell (Both B NY) Isted - John S.,Elizabeth J., Isabel - 4/8/1845 in Hume - Farmer - Farmer - 1st Rosa L. (Died 1887 or 88), 2nd Bessie Blodgett, married 7/1889 in Wheeler, WI - George, Frank, C.L. Artimea, Altie - 3/24/1914 in Spooner, MN - Hennepin County, MN - Received a 30 day furlough 8/4/1864. Brother John S. also served during the war. Present at Lee's surrender. Marched in Grand Review 5/23/1865. Charter Member of Burnside G.A.R. Post 237. (Military & Pension Files, 1865 Allegany County Town Clerk Register Hume, *Allegany & Its People*, 1850 Fed. Census Amity, 1850 Fed. Census Hume, 1900 Fed. Census Bayfield County, MI)

Isted, John Strickland Co. F, 4th NY Heavy Artillery - 9/8/1862 at Hume/3 yrs - 25 - INA - 9/12/1862 at NYC - $50 - Pvt, Pvt - No battles - 10/26/1862 Deserted - Was not a casualty - Thomas & Henrietta Trumbell Isted (Both B NY) - Charles W., Elizabeth J., Isabel - 8/13/1837 in Pittsford - Farmer - Laborer - Susan - Adopted daughter Minnie - INA - INA - Joined company 9/19/1862, deserted 10/26/1862 at Fort Gaines. Military Index spells name Istead. (Military File, 1865 Allegany County Town Clerk Register Hume, 1860, 1880 Fed Census Hume)

Johnson, John A. Co. B, 2nd NY Infantry - 10/15/1861 at Troy/3 yrs - 23 - INA - INA - $775 - Pvt, Pvt - No battles - 7/16/1862 Deserted - Was not a casualty - Richard & Abi Johnson (Both B NY) - Lucy Ann, Reuben A., James J., Melissa J - 1837 or 38 - INA - Laborer - Emma - Ida, Ada, Letta - 11/15/1896 - Pine Grove Cemetery, Fillmore - Was in hospital 6/29 to 7/15/1862. When released, did not return to regiment. Burnside G.A.R. Marker at Cemetery. The military information for this man may be incorrect. There is nothing in his file that ties him to the C-H-G area. However, head stone for a John Johnson at Pine Grove says he served in the 2nd Infantry. If so, the military information is correct. There are many John Johnsons who served. (Military File, Fillmore American Legion, Matteson, 1850 Fed. Census Centerville, 1880 Fed. Census Hume)

Johnson, John Not from the C-H-G area. His enlistment in Co. C, 194th NY Infantry was credited to Hume Township which paid his enlistment bonus of $775. (1865 Allegany County Town Clerk Register Hume.)

Johnson, Samuel MacArthur Co. D, 4th NY Heavy Artillery - 8/13/1862 at Rochester/3 yrs - 28 - 5'9", Florid Complexion, Blue Eyes, Light Hair - 8/13/1862 at Albany - No bounty - Pvt, Pvt - Wilderness, Spotsylvania, Peeble's Farm, Hatcher's Run, fall of Petersburg, Appomattox -

6/3/1865 Honorable - WIA, 5/19/1864 at Spotsylvania, minnie ball to abdomen (later deafness attributed to canon noise) - Woodbury & Matilda Foot Johnson (Both B NY) - Martha, Mary - 3/3/1839 in Wiscoy - Farm Laborer - Farmer - 1st Amanda M. Jacobs (died 6/29/1884), 2nd Julia J. Rease married 10/25/1887 at Wiscoy - Lillian - 10/25/1901 at Wiscoy - Pine Grove Cemetery, Fillmore - Charter Member & Officer of Burnside G.A.R. Post 237. Present at Lee's surrender. Marched in Grand Review 5/23/1865. (Military & Pension Files, 1860 Fed Census Granger, Matteson, 1890 Fed Census Special Schedule Hume, 1865 Allegany County Town Clerk Register Granger, *Allegany & Its People*, 1865 NYS Census Granger, Fillmore American Legion, 1880 Fed Census Granger)

Jones, George W. Co. E, 85th NY Infantry - 9/1/1861 at Granger/3 yrs (re-enlisted 1/1/1864) - 21 - 5'11", Light Complexion, Dark Eyes, Black Hair - 10/25/1861 at Elmira - No bounty - Pvt, Sgt - defense of DC, siege of Yorktown, Plymouth - 12/17/1864 Honorable/Deceased - POW, captured 4/20/1864 at Plymouth, NC, Prison: Andersonville, DD, 12/17/1864 on a transport from Andersonville to Port Royal Harbor, SC of starvation - William (B NY) & Phebe Alvira (B MA) Kinney Jones - Juba, Lettie H., Thomas K., Salina, Sidney M., Elsie H. - 7/13/1841 in Granger - Probably a farm laborer working for his father - None deceased - Never Married - None - 12/17/1864 on Southern medical transport on way to Port Royal Harbor, SC - Beauford National Cemetery - Promoted Corp. 11/7/1861, 5th Sgt 1/17/1863. This is not the same George W. Jones who served with the 136th NY Infantry. (Military & Pension Files, 1865 NYS Census Granger, *History of Allegany County 1879*, 1865 Allegany County Town Clerk Register Granger, *Allegany & Its People*, Matteson, Granger American Legion, 1850 1860 Fed. Censuses Granger)

Jones, George W. Co. D, 136th NY Infantry - 8/2/1862 at Pike/3 yrs - 22 - 5'7", Light Complexion, Hazel Eyes, Auburn Hair - 9/25/1862 at Portage - $100 - Pvt, Pvt - Chancellorsville, Gettysburg, Wauhatchie, Orchard Knob, Tunnel Hill, Missionary Ridge, Resaca, Goldsboro, Bentonville - 6/10/1865 Honorable - WIA, 5/15/1865 at Resaca, GA, slight gunshot wound to leg, POW, captured 3/19/1865 at Bentonor, NC, Prisons: Smithfield & Richmond. Paroled 4/2/1865 - John & Betsey Jones (Both B NY) - Sharlotte, John Jr. - 11/27/1839 in Pike - Farmer - Farmer - Ellen Van Dyke Lincoln, married 11/27/1866 in Eagle - None - 8/15/1918 in Hume - Alger Cemetery Hume, State Route 19 - Charter Member of Burnside G.A.R. Post 237. Wife Ellen was previously married to Civil War soldier Frances S. Lincoln. This is a different George W. Jones form the one who served with the 85th Infantry. (Military & Pension Files, 1890 Fed. Census Special Schedule Hume, Matteson, 1860 Fed. Census Pike, 1880 Fed. Census Hume)

Jones, John Azeza Co. E, 85th NY Infantry - 9/1/1861 at Granger/3 yrs (Re -enlisted 1/1/1864) - 21 - 5'9", Light Complexion, Blue Eyes, Dark Hair - 11/7/1861 at Elmira - $400 - Pvt, Sgt - defense of DC, Plymouth - 6/15/1865 Honorable - POW, captured 4/20/1864 at Plymouth , Prison: Andersonville, paroled 3/3/1865 - John & Margritt Reynolds Jones (Both B NY) - INA - 4/22/1843 in Allen - Farmer - Farmer/Veterinarian - Frances - John M. - 5/10/1841 - Family Cemetery, Jones Pond, State Road, Granger - Appointed Corp 11/7/1861. Sgt 1/17/1863. Spent a lot of time in hospital. 2/1862 Warwick, DC. Left sick at Lee's Mill 5/4/1862. In Philadelphia hospital July, 1862. Given a furlough to Granger after release from prison. Expired 5/7/1865, but Dr. Myron Miller, also a Civil War veteran, requested a 30 day extension due to continued debility.

Shook hands with President Lincoln per obit notice in *Northern Allegany County Observer*. (Military File, Pension not located, *History of Allegany County 1879*, 1865 NYS Census Granger, Matteson, Granger American Legion, 1860 Fed. Census Granger, 1870, 1920 Fed. Censuses Allen, 1865 Allegany County Town Clerk Register Granger, *Northern Allegany Observer* newspaper)

<u>Kaiser, Francis Joseph</u> Not from the C-H-G area. Served originally served Co. I, 139th Pennsylvania Infantry. Re enlistment in Co. F, 16th VRC credited to Hume which paid his re-enlistment bonus of $500. (1865 Allegany County Town Clerk Register Hume)

<u>Karns, Palmer R.</u> Co. A, 19th NY Cavlary - 8/31/1862 at Castile/3 yrs - 21 - 5'7", Light Complexion, Blue Eyes, Light Hair - 9/3/1862 at Portage Station - $100 - Pvt, Pvt - Deserted House, siege of Suffolk, Franklin, Manassas Junction, Bristoe's Station, Culpeper Court House, Wilderness, Todd's Tavern, Spotsylvania, North Anna River, Yellow Tavern, Pamunkey, Totopotomoy, Cold Harbor, Trevillian Station, Charles Court House, before Richmond & Petersburg, New Market, Shepherdstown, Winchester, Fisher's Hill, New Market, Port Republic, Cedar Creek, Berryville, Gordonsville, Dinwiddie, Appomattox - 6/30/1865 Honorable - INJ, injured right hip at Manassas Junction 8/15/1863 while loading freight - Daniel (B NJ) & Elizabeth (B PA) Karns - Martin S., Henry S. Aaron R., Minerva M., Lafayette C. Marlin D., Denis T. - 5/10/1840 in Dansville - Farmer - Farmer - 1st Lovina B. Wade, married 8/6/1862 in Castile, 2nd, Katy Taylor, married Newage Co., MI, 3rd Ellen, married 10/1910 in White Cloud, MI, May have had a 4th wife - Edith E., Lucius, Daniel P., Harvey D. - 9/28/1931 in Reed City, MI - INA - Charter Member of Burnside G.A.R. Post 237. 9/10/1863, left with horses at Manassas Junction. 8/7 to 12/31/1862, sick in quarters. Present at Lee's surrender. Marched in Grand Review 5/23/ 1865. (Military & Pension Files, *Allegany & Its People*, 1860 Fed. Census Burns, 1870 Fed. Census Charlevoix, MI)

<u>Keeber, Charles (Koeber)</u> Co. C, 1st Michigan Sharp Shooters - 3/8/1863 at Palmyra, MI/3 yrs - 44 - 5'5", Light Complexion - 3/31/1863 at Kalamazoo - No bounty - Pvt, Pvt - Petersburg - 6/22/ 1865 Honorable - POW, captured 6/17/1864 at Petersburg, Prison: Andersonville, paroled at Savannah 11/21/1864 - INA (Both B Germany) - INA - 1819 or 20 in Germany - Shoemaker - Shoemaker - 1st Mary J. 2nd Hannah? - INA - 7/19/1880 - Short Tract Cemetery, County Route 4 - Applied for a pension, but his application was not approved. Pension bureau said he had no medical conditions that could be attributed to his military service. Rather surprising since he was in Andersonville Prison. Claimed heart disease, dropsy, and rheumatism in application. (Military & Pension Files, Matteson, Granger American Legion, 1890 Fed. Census Special Schedule Granger, 1880 Fed. Census Hume)

<u>Keith, Joseph L.</u> Co. E, 85th NY Infantry - 9/1/1861 at Granger/3 yrs - 19 - INA - 10/10/1861 at Elmira - $100 - Corp, Corp - defense of DC, siege of Yorktown, Williamsburg, Fair Oaks, before Richmond, Plymouth - 2/25/1865 Honorable - POW, captured 5/31/1862 at Fair Oaks, paroled 9/13/1862 at Aiken's Landing; POW 4/20/1864 at Plymouth, Prisons: Andersonville, Charleston, Florence, SC - George E. & Nancy Keith (Both B NY) - Electa, Darius, Charles, Frances, Geroge - 10/23/1844 in PA - Farm Laborer - Oil Driller - 1st Ellen Farrington, 2nd Rosetta E. Edwards, married 8/8/1888 - INA - 2/23/1914 in Holgate, OH - Edwardsville, OH - Appointed Corporal

11/7/1861. (Military & Pension Files, *History of Allegany County 1879*, Matteson, 1860 Fed. Census Allen)

Kendall, Ezra Hiram Co. D, 64th NY Infantry - 9/14/1861 at Rushford/3 yrs - 25 - 5'9", Dark Complexion, Blue Eyes, Black Hair - 9/24/1861 at Elmira - No bounty - 3rd Sgt, 2nd Lt. - siege of Yorktown, Fair Oaks - 6/1/1862 Honorable/Deceased - KIA 6/1/1862 at Fair Oaks - Clark Rufus & Roxanna Gilman Kendall (Both B NY) - Ferris, Henry, Willis, Teresa, Flora - 1835 or 36 in Centerville - Farmer - None Deceased - Eliza Rachael Pratt, married 10/13/1859 in Centerville - Eliza Freemont - 6/1/1862 in Fair Oaks - Centerville Cemetery, Route 3 - Promoted to 2nd Lieutenant 2/28/1862. Brothers Ferris and Willis also served during the war. (Military & Pension Files, 1865 NYS Census Centerville, *History of Allegany County 1879*, Matteson, Centerville American Legion, 1865 Allegany County Town Clerk Centerville, 1860 Fed. Census Centerville)

Kendall, Ferris Enoch Co. F, 19th NY Cavalry - 8/9/1862 at Centerville/3 yrs - 5'7", Light Complexion, Blue Eyes, Brown Hair - 9/3/1862 at Portage Station - $250 - Pvt, Pvt - siege of Suffolk, Franklin, Bristoe's Station - 3/26/1865 Honorable/Deceased - POW, captured 10/25/1863 at Morrisville, VA Prison: Richmond, paroled Feb, 1865, DD died of typhoid fever 3/26/1865 at Centerville while on furlough - Clark Rufus & Roxanna Gilman Kendall (Both B NY) - Ezra, Henry, Willis, Teresa, Flora - 11/30/1837 in Centerville - Farmer - None Deceased - Never Married - None - 3/26/1865 in Centerville - Centerville Cemetery, Route 3 - Brothers Ezra and Willis also served during the war. (Military & Pension Files, 1865 NYS Census Centerville, *History of Allegany County 1879*, Matteson, Centerville American Legion, 1865 Allegany County Town Clerk Register Centerville, 1860 Fed. Census Centerville)

Kendall, Willis James Co. I, 27th NY Infantry - 5/13/1861 at Angelica/2 yrs - 20 - 6', Light Complexion, Blue Eyes, Dark Hair - 6/1/1861 at Elmira - No bounty - 1st Corp, 2nd Lt. - 1st Bull Run, Yorktown, Gaine's Mills, Malvern Hill, 2nd Bull Run, South Mountain, Antietam, Fredericksburg, Franklin - 5/31/1863 Honorable - Was not a casualty - Clark Rufus & Roxanna Gilman Kendall (Both B NY) - Ezra, Henry, Ferris, Teresa, Flora - 10/22/1840 in Centerville - Farmer - Farmer - Frances Amelia Barnum, married 3/30/1864 in Centerville - Fred E., Nellie R., Alice F., Eva L., Harry C., Frances B., Grace J., Blanche P. - 8/10/1918 Denver, CO - Riverside Cemetery, Denver - Sick in White House, VA hospital May/June 1862. Promoted 3rd Sgt 7/21/1861, 2nd Sgt 12/20/1861, 1st Sgt 9/28/1862, 2nd Lt 11/22/1862. (Military & Pension Files, 1865 NYS Census Centerville, *History of Allegany County 1879*, 1865 Allegany County Town Clerk Register Centerville, 1860 Fed. Census Centerville, 1880 Fed. Census Centerville)

Kerns, James K. (Kern-Kearns) Co. G, 111th NY Infantry - 8/31/1864 at Scipio/3 yrs - 44 - 5'8", Dark Complexion, Dark Eyes, Brown Hair - 8/31/1864 at Auburn - $300 - Pvt, Pvt - siege of Petersburg - 2/22/1865 Dishonorable - Was not a casualty - INA - INA - circa 1814 in Virginia (Understated his age at enlistment. 1860 Census shows age as 46, making him 50 when he joined) - Blacksmith - None Deceased - Lydia Smith, married 9/22/1841 in Pike - Frances, Frederick - 2/22/1865 in First Division Hospital near Petersburg - INA - Military claimed he died of a self administered dose of morphine. Said he was a "confirmed opium eater." This was vigorously denied by both his family and two doctors in Fillmore. Both doctors said they had known him for

13 years and would have known if he had been using opium. Many others said the same thing. There clearly was more to this than was discovered. Military claimed his wife had sent him the opium even though the bottle it was in was labeled U.S. Med. Dept. No one ever explained how she managed to get her hands on the bottle or the opium. (Military & Pension Files, Allegany County Web Site, 1860 Fed. Census Hume)

Keyes, William H. Harrison Co. G, 78th NY Infantry - 11/4/1861 at Centerville/3 yrs - 21 - 5'8", Dark Complexion, Dark Eyes, Dark Hair - 12/11/1861 at Buffalo - No bounty - Pvt, Pvt - Chancellorsville, Gettysburg - 7/15/1863 Honorable/Deceased - WIA, gunshot to side and back, 7/3/1863 at Gettysburg, KIA, died of wounds 7/15/1863 at Gettysburg - Thomas & Emeline Keyes (Both B VT) - Lucy Nelson - 1840 in NY - Probably working for his father, a farmer - None Deceased - Never Married - None - 7/15/1863 at Gettysburg - Gettysburg National Cemetery - Deserted 4/1/1863 at Camp Washington, Staten Island, NY. Returned 2/27/1863. While a deserter, he enlisted in Co. B, 154th NY Infantry at Portville on 8/11/1862. When reclaimed by the 78th on 2/27/62, he explained that he had deserted because the 78th was totally disorganized. There does appear to have been organizational problems in the 78th. Many men were transferred out of the 78th. His file showed him under arrest as of 4/10/1863. This notation was later canceled. No other charges mentioned. (Military & Pension Files, 1865 NYS Census Centerville, *History of Allegany County 1879*, Matteson,1860 Fed. Census Centerville)

Kimball, George Higgins Co. C, 19th NY Infantry - 9/13/1864 at Centerville/1 yr - 28 - 5'11", Fair Complexion, Blue Eyes, Dark Hair - 9/27/1864 at Elmira - $800 - Pvt, Pvt - Berryville, Gordonsville, Five Forks - 6/30/1865 Honorable - WIA, gunshot to right hip, 4/1/1865 at Five Forks - Chester (B VT) & Victoria Williams (B NY) Kimball - INA - 12/29/1835 or 36 in Centerville - Farmer - Farmer/Carpenter - Ann Eliza Veazey, married 9/24/1861 in Centerville - Mary Belle (MacGowan) - 6/7/1903 in Golden, CO - Golden - Purchased his revolver and sabre at discharge. Marched in the Grand Review 5/23/1865. (Military & Pension Files,1865 NYS Census Centerville, Matteson, 1865 Allegany County Town Clerk Register Centerville, 1850 Fed. Census Centerville, 1900 Fed. Census Golden)

King, Hiram Co. G, 15th NY Cavalry - 1/7/1864 at Franklinville/3 yrs - 34 - 5'6", Fair Complexion, Blue Eyes, Brown Hair - 1/7/1864 at Dunkirk - $300 - Pvt, Pvt - No battles - 7/19/1865 Honorable - Was not a casualty - Marlin & Damereas King (Both B NY) - INA - 12/6/1829 in Franklinville - Laborer - Farm Laborer - Lucy Ann Hitchcock, married 1/6/1865 or 66 - Vidette, Ransom Burdette - 10/10/1920 Silver Spring, Wyoming County - Possible Cadiz Street Cemetery, Franklinville - Was run over by an Army wagon in April of 1864 at Cumberland, MD. Suffered head, left shoulder, and lung injuries. Pension file says he lived in Hume in the 1890's and early 1900's. (Military & Pension Files, 1890 Fed. Census Special Schedule Centerville, 1860 Fed. Census Franklinville, 1900 Fed. Census Rushford)

King, Robert Wallace Co. F, 19th NY Cavalry - 8/11/1862 at Oramel/3 yrs - 24 - 5'9", Dark Complexion, Hazel Eyes, Brown Hair - 9/3/1862 at Portage Station - $100 - Pvt, Sgt - Deserted House, siege of Suffolk, Franklin, Manassas Junction, Bristoe's Station, Culpeper Court House, Wilderness, Todd's Tavern, Spotsylvania, North Anna River, Yellow Tavern, Pamunkey,

Totopotomoy, Cold Harbor, Trevillian Station, Charles County Court House, before Richmond and Petersburg, New Market, Shepherdstown, Winchester, Fisher's Hill, Port Republic, Cedar Creek, Berryville, Gordonsville, Dinwiddie, Five Forks, Appomattox - 6/30/1865 Honorable - Was not a casualty - Robert Kanada. & Susan King (Both B NY) - INA - 1/28/1838 in Allen - Farmer - Farmer - Frances Emily Smith, married 5/25/1871 in Belfast - Bertha, Catherine, Sarah - 5/4/1908 - INA - Promoted to Sgt 1/1/1865. Present at Lee's surrender. Marched in Grand Review 5/23/1865. County Clerk has middle name as Waller. (Military & Pension Files, *History of Allegany County 1879*, Matteson, 1865 Allegany County Town Clerk Register Allen, 1860, 1870 Fed. Censuses Allen)

King, William Morris Co. F, 19th NY Cavalry - 8/9/1862 at Hume/3 yrs - 32 - 5'7", Light Complexion, Blue Eyes, Brown Hair - 9/3/1862 at Portage Station - $150 - Sgt, Sgt - Deserted House - 5/15/1863 Disability/Honorable - WIA, 1/30/1863 at Deserted House, gunshot causing a compound fracture of both bones of lower left leg - Solomon & Catherine Snider King - INA - 4/24/1832 in Middletown, Orange County - Carriage Maker - Pedlar/Blacksmith - 1st Amy P. Buck, died 3/12/1872, 2nd Jennie Williams, married 1/13/1884 in Lincoln, NE - Marquis, Iria B., Marcy, Inis - 9/22/1899 in Centralia, WA - INA - Military records say he enlisted at Oramel. (Military & Pension Files, 1865 NYS Census Hume, 1865 Allegany County Town Clerk Register Hume - *History of Allegany County 1879)*

Kinney, John (Kenney-McKenney) E. Co. F, 19th NY Cavalry - 8/13/1862 at Hume/3 yrs - 22 - 5'7", Sandy Complexion, Blue Eyes - Auburn Hair - 9/3/1862 at Portage Station - $50 - Pvt, Pvt - Deserted House, siege of Suffolk, Manassas Junction - 3/12/1864 Disability/Honorable - INJ, Spring (probably April), 1863 at Suffolk, VA fractured ribs when gravel fell on him while he was assisting in building fortifications - INA (Both B Ireland) - INA - 1840 in Roscommon, Ireland - Farmer - Laborer - Bridget Gallagher, married 11/13/1866 in St Bonaventure Church, Allegany, Cattaraugus County - Mary Ann, John, Lizzie, Peter, Margaret, Susan - 7/17/1893 in Emlenton, PA - INA - Was at Judiciary Square Hospital in DC at time of discharge. (Military & Pension Files, 1865 Allegany County Town Clerk Register Hume, *History of Allegany County 1879*, 1870, 1880 Fed. Censuses Emlenton, PA)

Knowlton, William A. Co. F, 19th NY Cavalry - 8/8/1862 at Oramel/3 yrs - 41 - 5'8", Sandy Complexion, Blue Eyes, Brown Hair - 9/3/1862 at Portage Station - $100 - Pvt, Corp - Deserted House, siege of Suffolk, Franklin, Manassas Junction, Bristoe's Station. In November,1863 Knowlton was assigned to the Pioneer Corps, but may have participated in the following battles, Culpeper Court House, Wilderness, Todd's Tavern, Spotsylvania, North Anna River, Pamunkey, Totopotomoy, Cold Harbor, Trevillian Station, Charles County Court House, before Richmond & Petersburg, New Market, Shepherdstown, Cedar Creek, Berryville, Gordonsville, Dinwiddie, Five Forks, Appomattox - 6/30/1865 Honorable - Was not a casualty - Father INA Mother Esther Knowlton (Both B VT) - INA - 6/1821 in either Nunda or Mandon - Carpenter - Carpenter - Wing Ella - Wing Carie - Died 1907 - Centerville Cemetery, Route 3, no headstone - Promoted Corp. 10/29/1862. Kept both his pistol and sabre at discharge. (Military & Pension File, *History of Allegany County 1879*, Centerville American Legion, 1860, 1870, 1900 Fed. Censuses Belfast)

Kuhn, Andreas Not from the C-H-G area. Served originally with Co. G, 34th Missouri Infantry Co. Re-enlistment in VRC credited to Hume Township when it paid his re-enlistment bonus of $500. (Allegany County Town Clerk Register Hume)

Lafoy, Festus G. Co. C, 104th NY Infantry - 10/9/1861 at Geneseo/3 yrs - 21 - 5'8", Light Complexion, Blue Eyes, Dark Hair - 2/26/1862 at Geneseo - No bounty - Pvt, Pvt - Cedar Creek, 2nd Bull Run - 1/1/1863 Disability/Honorable - WIA, 8/30/1862 at 2nd Bull Run, gunshot to right shoulder and arm (fractured arm) - John & Martha Johnson Decker Lafoy (Both B NY) - Leonard, Relief, Louisa, Isaac, John, Addison, William Mary - 10/4/1842 in Castile - Boatman/Farmer - Boatman/Farmer - Harriett (Hattie) A. Bennett, married 12/2/1869 in Fillmore - Fred - 11/12/1917 in Portage - Pine Grove Cemetery, Fillmore - The Register of Drafted Men shows Lafoy as excused due to fractured right arm. He had completed his service by the time the draft was instituted. Brother John also served during the war. (Military & Pension Files, 1855 NYS Census Hume, Fillmore American Legion, Matteson, 1850, 1880 Fed. Censuses Hume, Registry of Drafted Men July, 1863 - October, 1864)

Lafoy, John Jr. Co. F, 33rd NY Infantry - 5/13/1861 at Nunda/2 yrs - 20 - INA - 5/22/1861 at Elmira - No bounty - Pvt, Pvt - Fredericksburg - 6/2/1863 Honorable - Was not a casualty - John & Martha Johnson Decker Lafoy (Both B NY) - Leonard, Relief, Louisa, Isaac, Festus, Addison, William, Mary - 1840/41 in Castile - Laborer - Laborer/Canal Watchman - 1st Susan Brownell, 2nd Emeline Huntington - William, John Jr. Arthur - INA - INA - Was a teamster in service. Deserted at Camp Griffin 11/15/1861, returned 9/1/1862, forfeited all back pay and allowances, plus one month's pay. Brother Festus also served during the war. (Military & Pension Files, 1865 NYS Census Hume, 1865 Allegany County Town Clerk Register Hume, 1855 NYS Census Hume, 1850 Fed. Census Mt Morris, 1870 Fed. Census Portageville)

Lampman, John Co. I, 188th NY Infantry - 9/26/1864 at Birdsall/1 yr - 44 - 5'4", Light Complexion, Blue Eyes, Gray Hair - 10/22/1864 at Rochester - $900 - Pvt, Pvt - siege of Petersburg, Hatcher's Run, Weldon RR, Gravelly Run, Five Forks - 7/1/1865 Honorable - Was not a casualty - Abraham & Elizabeth (Betsey) Koon Lampman (Both B NY) - Elizabeth, Jane E. - 9/4/1820 in Columbia County - Farm Laborer - Farmer - Martha E. Slocum, married 3/2/1889 Nunda - None - 4/10/1894 in Granger - INA - Present at Lee's surrender. Marched in Grand Review 5/23/1865. There is some evidence that Lampman was married before he married Martha, although the 1880 Census indicates his status as single. (Military & Pension Files, 1890 Fed. Census Special Schedule Granger, 1865 Allegany County Town Clerk Register Birdsall - 1850, 1880 Fed. Censuses Granger)

Laughlin, Michael (Loughlin) Co. F, 4th NY Heavy Artillery - 1/1/1864 at Genesee Falls/3 yrs - 34 - 5'10", Fair Complexion, Hazel Eyes, Auburn Hair - 1/1/1864 at Lockport - $300 - Pvt, Pvt - Wilderness, Spotsylvania, North Anna River - 10/31/1864 Disability/Honorable - WIA, 5/25/1864 at North Anna River, gunshot to right hand, lost first 2 fingers - Parents INA (Both B Ireland). - INA - 9/1822 in Tipperary, Ireland - Laborer/Farmer - Farmer - 1st Lucy S. Ralph, died 11/12/1885, 2nd Anna Lila Bailey, married 12/25/1889 in Hornell - None - 10/4/1915 in Rossburg - INA - Military records are under the name Michael Laughlin, 1890 Census shows his name as

McLaughlin or McLauflin. Arrived in the United States in 1849. (Military & Pension Files, 1890 Fed. Census Special Schedule Hume, 1850 Fed. Census Friendship, 1870 Fed. Census Granger, 1910 Fed. Census Hume)

Leach, Charles H. Co. C, 19th NY Cavalry - 8/7/1862 at Pike/3 yrs - 20 - 6', Light Complexion, Blue Eyes, Dark Hair - 9/3/1862 at Portage Station - No bounty - Pvt, Pvt - No battles - 1/1/1863 Deceased/Honorable - DD, 1/1/1863 at Suffolk, VA of typhoid fever - Charles (B MA) & Lois (B NY) Leach - Aseneth M., John D., Marett C., Lydia, Lucy - 1842 in Marathon, Cortland County - Farmer - None Deceased - Never Married - None - 1/1/1863 in Regimental Hospital, Suffolk, VA - Church Street Cemetery, Wiscoy, no headstone - Dr. William M. Smith (as recorded in his diary, book, *Swamp Doctor*) visited Leach on Thursday 12/30/1862. Was sick in Suffolk hospital as of 8/7/1862. Does not appear to be any connection to C-H-G, but carried on rolls of Hume American Legion. (Military & Pension Files, Hume American Legion, 1860 Fed. Census Pike, 1850 Fed. Census Palmer, MA)

Learn, Reuben Co. F, 19th NY Cavalry - 8/9/1862 at Centerville/3 yrs - 19 - 5'8", Dark Complexion, Grey Eyes, Brown Hair - 9/23/1862 at Portageville - $150 - Pvt, 1st Sgt - Deserted House, siege of Suffolk, Franklin, Manassas Junction, Bristoe's Station, Culpeper Court House, Cold Harbor, Trevillian Station, Charles County Court House, before Richmond & Petersburg, New Market, Shepherdstown, Winchester, Fisher's Hill, Port Republic, Cedar Creek, Berryville, Gordonsville, Dinwiddie, Five Forks, Appomattox - 6/30/1865 Honorable - Was not a casualty - Jacob & Catherine (Steel?) Learn - INA - 3/2/1844 in Hinsdale - Farmer - Farmer - Ellen Mathews, married 11/20/1866 in Otsego - INA - 4/22/1909 in Fife Lake, MI - INA - Was present at Lee's surrender. Marched in Grand Review 5/23/1865. Kept pistol and sabre at discharge. (Military & Pension Files, 1865 NYS Census Centerville, 1865 Allegany County Town Clerk Register Centerville, *History of Allegany County 1879*, Matteson, 1860 Fed. Census Centerville, 1850 Fed. Census Hinsdale, 1900 Fed. Census Fife Lake, MI)

Lee, Charles Co. D, 4th NY Heavy Artillery - 12/23/1863 at Hume/3 yrs - 29 - 5'9", Sandy Complexion, Blue Eyes, Brown Hair - 12/23/1863 at Elmira - $300 - Pvt, Pvt - Ream's Station, Peeble's Farm, Hatcher's Run, fall of Petersburg, Appomattox - 9/26/1865 Honorable - Was not a casualty - Andrew & Olive Wilcox Lee (Both B VT) - Reuben, Benjamin, Ebenezer, Hannah, Harriet, Cordelia, Mary Jane, William H. Sally Ann, Emma Jane, Diana, Augusta, Josephine - 12/1835 in Cayuga County - Boatman - Boatman - Margaret Levy, married 5/28/1857 at Tuscorara - Olive, Perry, Allen Jesse, Maggie, Charles, Lillie, Rosa, Sarah, Murta - 10 or 11/ 4/ 1884 - Mt. Morris - Present at Lee's surrender. Marched in Grand Review 5/23/1865. (Military & Pension Files, 1865 NYS Census Hume, Allegany County Web Site, 1865 Allegany County Town Clerk Register Hume, 1860, 1870 Fed. Censuses Granger)

Lee, Reuben H. Co. K/H, 19th NY Cavalry - 9/19/1864 at Genesee Falls/1 yr - 38 - 5'9", Fair Complexion, Blue Eyes, Brown Hair - 9/23/1864 at Lockport - $650 - Pvt, Pvt - Berryville, Gordonsville - 6/30/1865 Honorable - Was not a casualty - Reuben & Mary Nichols Lee - INA - 7/26/1826 in Sandgate, VT - Day Laborer - Farmer - Mary - Fanny, Levi, Albert - 1/16/1888 - Pine Grove Cemetery, Fillmore - Marched in Grand Review 5/23/1865. (Military & Pension Files,

1865 NYS Census Granger, Allegany County Web Site, 1865 Allegany County Town Clerk Register Hume, 1860 Fed. Census Hume)

Lee, Solomon Co. K, 19th NY Cavalry - 9/23/1864 at Genesee Falls/1 yr - 26 - 5'10", Fair Complexion, Blue Eyes, Brown Hair - 9/30/1864 at Lockport - $400 - Pvt, Pvt - Berryville, Gordonsville, Dinwiddie - 6/9/1865 Honorable - Was not a casualty - Reuben & Mary Kemp Lee - INA - 8/30/1839 in Milton, VT per Military File, County Clerk says Edinboro, , pension says Elbridge,) - Farmer - Farmer/Carpenter - 1st Caroline Spees, married Hunts Hollow about 1857/58 (she left him), 2nd Sarah Vestal, married 4/16/1912 at Washington County, VA - Henry, Stephen, Clarissa - 3/25/1923 - INA - Was with Sheridan's campaign in 1864. Marched in Grand Review 5/23/1865. Was in Mountain Branch Soldiers Home in 1914, Southern Branch in 1922. Per Pension, his father was a 2nd cousin of General Robert E. Lee. It is likely that Charles, Reuben and Solomon Lee were related, especially Reuben and Solomon. (Military & Pension File, 1865 NYS Census Granger, 1865 Allegany County Town Clerk Register Hume, 1860, 1870 Fed. Censuses Hume.)

Lemark, Woodman Not from the C-H-G area. Served originally with 116th Pennsylvania Infantry. Re-enlistment in Co. C, 16th VRC credited to Hume which paid the re-enlistment bonus of $500. (1865 Allegany County Town Clerk Register Hume)

Lincoln, Francis S. Co. C, 104th NY Infantry - 10/9/1981 at Geneseo/3 yrs - 26 - 5'5", Dark Complexion, Blue Eyes, Black Hair - 2/26/1862 at Geneseo - No bounty - Pvt, Sgt - Cedar Creek, 2nd Bull Run, South Mountain, Antietam, Fredericksburg, Chancellorsville, Gettysburg - 2/3/1864 Honorable/Deceased - POW, captured 7/1/1863 at Gettysburg, Prison: Richmond, VA, DD, 2/3/1864 at Richmond prison of pneumonia - INA - INA (Elijah?) - 1835 or 36 in Vermont - Farmer - None Deceased - Ellen Van Dyke, married June 10, 1856 - Florence - 2/3/1864 at Richmond (POW) - Richmond National Cemetery - Promoted to Corp 11/11/1862, to Sgt 5/1/1863. Widow Ellen married Civil War soldier George W. Jones in 1866. (Military & Pension Files, 1890 Fed. Census Special Schedule Hume, 1860 Fed. Census Eagle, *Roll of Honor*)

Lockwood, David Co. C, 136th NY Infantry - 8/31/1862 at Granger/3 yrs - 35 - 5'6", Light Complexion, Blue Eyes, Brown Hair - 9/25/1862 at Portage - No bounty - Pvt, Pvt - Chancellorsville, Gettysburg, Wauhatchie, Orchard Knob, Tunnel Hill, Missionary Ridge, Resaca - 5/15/1864 Honorable/Deceased - KIA, 5/15/1864 at Resaca - INA - Robert, Ira ?- 1826 or 27 in Allegany County - Farm Laborer - None Deceased - Mary Jane Utter, married 9/12/1848 in Nunda (Died 1/2/1859) - Ellen, William, Eugene - 5/15/1864 in Resaca, GA - Chattanooga National Cemetery - Was company cook. Listed on Soldiers Monument in Granger. Brothers (possibly) Robert & Ira also served during the war. (Military & Pension Files, 1865 NYS Census Granger, *Allegany & Its People*, Granger American Legion, *Roll of Honor*, Matteson, 1860 Fed. Census Granger)

Lockwood, Ira Wells Co. D, 4th NY Heavy Artillery - Drafted 12/24/1863 at Granger/3 yrs - 24 - 5'4", Fair Complexion, Blue Eyes, Brown Hair - 12/26/1863 at Elmira - $300 - Pvt, Pvt - Peeble's Farm, Hatcher's Run, fall of Petersburg, Appomattox (on detachment with 5th Artillery,

Wilderness, Spotsylvania, North Anna River, Pamunkey, Totopotomoy, Cold Harbor, Bethesda Church, siege of Petersburg, Weldon RR) - 9/26/1865 Honorable - Was not a casualty - Ira & Elizabeth Fulton Lockwood (Both B NY) - Robert, (maybe David) - 9/6/1837 in Grove, Allegany County (Ontario County per Census & Military Records) - Farm Laborer - Farmer - Amelia - David, George - INA - Pine Grove Cemetery, Fillmore (per cemetery records) - Present at Lee's surrender. Marched in Grand Review 5/23/1865. Detached to Battery D, 5th U.S. Artillery, May to August, 1864. The Register of Men Drafted says he paid commutation not to serve, but in fact he did serve. Brothers Robert & David? also served during the war. (Military & Pension Files, 1865 NYS Census Granger, Granger American Legion, 1865 Allegany County Town Clerk Register Granger, 1860 Fed. Census Granger, 1870 Fed. Census Ossian, Register of Men Drafted July, 1863 to October, 1864)

Lockwood, Robert W. Co F, 4th NY Heavy Artillery - 8/27/1862 at Granger/3 yrs - 21 - 5'4", Light Complexion, Blue Eyes, Brown Hair - 8/29/1862 at NYC - $100 - Pvt, Pvt - No battles - 11/16/ 1863 Deceased/Honorable - DD, 11/16/1863 at Fort Ethan Allen of typhoid fever - Ira & Elizabeth Fulton Lockwood (Both B NY) - Ira, (maybe David) - 11/20/1840 in Grove - Sawyer - None Deceased - Mary McDermott, married 4/27/1862 in Oakland - INA - 11/16/1863 at Fort Ethan Allen - Weavers Settlement Cemetery, Granger - Listed on Soldiers Monument in Granger. Brother Ira & David? also served during the war. (Military & Pension Files, Matteson, 1865 Allegany County Town Clerk Register Granger, Allegany County Web Site, 1860 Fed. Census Granger, Granger American Legion, *Allegany & Its People*)

Luckey, Samuel Benjamin Co. B, 184th NY Infantry - 9/3/1864 at Granger/1 yr - 18 - 5'8", Dark Complexion, Dark Eyes, Dark Hair - 9/29/1864 at Elmira - $100 - Pvt, Pvt - Cedar Creek, before Richmond & Petersburg - 6/29/1865 Honorable - Was not a casualty - James & Mary Watts Mills Luckey - INA - 11/14/1846 in Granger - Farmer - Farmer/Teamster/J.P. - 1st Anna A. Jones, married 11/24/1873 in Allen, (died 3/9/1874), 2nd Susan E. Robinson - Mary E. (married George Dorey), Hortence (Greenwald) & Glen Foster Luckey - 1/6/1928 in Granger (but apparently lived in Fillmore) - Short Tract Cemetery County Route 4 - Pension was awarded by an Act of Congress. (Military & Pension Files, 1890 Fed. Census Special Schedule Granger, Granger American Legion, Matteson, 1865 NYS Census Granger, 1865 Allegany County Town Clerk Register Granger, 1860, 1910 Fed. Censuses Granger)

Luther, Abinah At least one source document indicates that Luther served in the military during the war. No evidence of such service has been located. (Granger American Legion)

Luther, Frank Cashus Co. F, 19th NY Cavalry - 92/1864 at Allen/1 yr - 25 - 5'9", Light Complexion, Blue Eyes, Brown Hair - 9/3/1864 at Elmira - $700 - Pvt, Pvt - Winchester - 3/21/ 1865 Disability/Honorable - WIA, 9/19/1864 at Winchester, minnie ball to arm, serious injury - Ruphus & Mary Luther - INA - 6/5/1840 in Wurttemberg, Germany - Wagon Maker/Farmer - Farmer - Joanna Chamberlain - Mary A. (married Edmond W. Common of Fillmore), Frank - 9/14/1904 - Belfast - Was in both Patterson Park G. H., Baltimore and Chestnut Hill G.H. Philadelphia. Arrived in the U.S. in 1852. By 1886 he couldn't use his arm. Great grandson Adair Wells Common was killed in action in France on 1/1/1945. (Military & Pension Files, 1865

Allegany County Town Clerk Register Allen, *Allegany & Its People*, 1870 Fed.Census Allen, 1880 Fed. Census Oramel, 1900 Fed. Census Hume)

Luther, Moses D. Co. I, 188th NY Infantry - 9/6/1864 at Farmington/1 yr - 33 - 5'7", Dark Complexion, Blue Eyes, Brown Hair - 10/22/1864 at Rochester - $100 - Pvt, Pvt - siege of Petersburg, Hatcher's Run - 12/3/1864 Deceased/Honorable - DD, 12/3/1864 at 1st Division Hospital at City Point, VA of typhoid fever - Peter & Eliza Luther - INA - 1830/31 in Granger - Farmer - None Deceased - Rachael A. - Willis, Mary, Cary A., Oliver - 12/3/1864 in City Point, VA - Poplar Grove National Cemetery, Petersburg, VA - One military record says he was 23 when he joined. 1865 Census says he was 36 when he died. Originally buried at City Point. Listed on Soldiers Monument at Granger. Some documents claim that he was a POW. There is nothing in his military records to support this. (Military & Pension Files, 1865 NYS Census Granger, *Allegany & Its People*, 1850, 1860 Fed. Censuses Granger)

Mack, Enos Cook Co. C, 147th NY Infantry - Drafted 7/15/1863 at Hume/3 yrs - 29 - 5'11", Dark Complexion, Blue Eyes, Dark Brown Hair - 7/15/1863 at Elmira - $100 - Pvt, Pvt - No battles - 2/20/1864 Disability/Honorable - Was not a casualty - Moses & Polly Suel Mack - INA - 3/17/1834 in Gainesville - Shoemaker - Farm Laborer - Cynthia Romasser (born in Baden, Germany), married 6/29/1859 in Hermitage - Frederick, Frances - 11/27/1891 - INA - Admitted Armory Square Hospital 1/22/1864 (chronic rheumatism, external hemorrhoids, curvature of the spine). Register of Drafted Men has him already "in barracks" when he was drafted. He must have gone immediately when he was informed he had been drafted. (Military & Pension Files, 1865 Allegany County Town Clerk Register Hume, 1860 Fed. Census Sheldon, 1870 Fed. Census Hume, Register of Drafted Men July 15, 1863 to October, 1864)

Madison, Reuben Washington Co. I, 160th NY Infantry - 8/28/1862 at Caneadea/3 yrs - 39 - INA - 11/21/1862 at Auburn - $60 - Pvt, Pvt - Gunboat Cotton, Fort Bisland - 8/15/1863 Honorable/ Deceased - DD, 8/16/1863 at Regimental Hospital, Baton Rouge, LA of chronic dysentery - Reuben & Lucina (Sally?) Cummings Madison (Both B VT) - INA - 5/30/1822 in NY - Blacksmith - None Deceased - Sarah Ann Radley, married 5/6/1845 in Canandaigua - Lucretia, Theodora, Ida Estrella, Alta - 8/16/1863 in Baton Rouge, LA - Louisiana - Sarah died 2/18/1870. A Homer Peck became the guardian for the children. (Military & Pension Files, 1865 NYS Census Hume, 1865 Allegany County Town Clerk Register Caneadea, 1860 Fed. Census Hume)

Main, Edgar P. (Mayn) Co. B, 23rd NY Infantry - 5/16/1861 at Elmira/2 yrs - 20 - 5'9", Light Complexion, Blue Eyes, Light Hair - 5/16/1861 at Elmira - No bounty - Pvt, Pvt - Gainesville, Groveton, 2nd Bull Run, South Mountain, Fredericksburg - 5/22/1863 Honorable - Was not a casualty - Erastus (B CT) & Dorcas A. (B NY) Main - Lucian B., Alice A. John H. - 5/5/1840 in Clarksville - Farmer - Cooper/Farmer - 1st Almira (died 4/5/1882), 2nd Martha A. McClure, married 7/5/1893 in Friendship, 3rd Susie Estell Boyd, married 8/4/1916 in Bradford, PA - Alice, Arthur, Fanny, Nellie Bertha - 11/26/1927 in Kissimmee, FL - Mt. Hope Cemetery, Friendship - Also served with Co. D, 5th NY Heavy Artillery, see below. (Military & Pension Files, *History of Allegany County 1879*, Granger American Legion, 1890 Fed. Census Special Schedule Granger, 1850 Fed. Census - Friendship, 1880, 1910 Fed. Censuses Granger)

Main, Edgar P. (Mayn) Co D, 5th NY Heavy Artillery - 1/4/1864 at Friendship/3 yrs - 23 - 5'9",
Light Complexion, Blue Eyes, Light Hair - 1/4/1864 at Elmira - No bounty - Pvt, Corp - New
Market, Lynchburg, Cedar Creek, Berryville, Winchester, Fisher's Hill - 7/19/1865 Honorable -
Was not a casualty - Promoted Corp 8/19/1863. Also served with 23rd NY Infantry, see above.
Also see above for personal information and sources of information.

McCabe, Patrick (McCale-McCall) Co. A 76th NY Infantry - Drafted 7/14/1863 at Hume/ 3 yrs -
30 - INA - 8/7/1863 at Elmira - No bounty - Pvt, Pvt - Bristoe's Station - 12/28/1863
Honorable/Deceased - POW, captured 10/14/1863 at Bristoe's Station, Prison: Richmond, VA,
DD, 12/28/1863 at Richmond, VA prison of chronic diarrhea - INA - INA - 1832 or 33 in Ireland -
Farmer - None/Deceased - Mary - None - 12/28/1863 in Richmond, VA (POW) - Richmond, VA -
Military files are under the name McCabe, Register of Drafted Men spells name McKail, 1860
Census has it as McKale, Town Clerk has name as McCale, *Allegany & Its People* book has name
as McCall. Reported as a deserter 10/13/1863, army said he fell out during a march near
Warrenton, VA. Actually was a POW. Died at General Hospital #21 at Richmond. (Military File,
1865 Allegany County Town Clerk Register Hume, Allegany County Web Site, *Allegany & Its
People*, 1860 Fed. Census Hume, NYS Adjutant General Report 1901, Volume 29)

McDermott, James Co. D, 4th NY Heavy Artillery - 8/18/1862 at Rochester/3 yrs - 5'11", Dark
Complexion, Blue Eyes, Dark Hair - 9/1/1862 at Rochester - $100 - Pvt, Corp - Wilderness,
Spotsylvania, North Anna River, Totopotomoy, Cold Harbor, siege of Petersburg, Weldon RR,
Ream's Station, Peeble's Farm, Hatcher's Run, fall of Petersburg, Appomattox - 6/3/1865
Honorable - Was not a casualty - Michael & (Catherine Kelly?) McDermott (Both B Ireland) -
Martin, William, Jerome - 8/11/1831 in Ireland - Laborer/Farmer - INA - INA - INA - 11/19/1867
in Minnesota - Minnesota - Town Clerk Register says he was married at time of entry into the
service. No information on wife found. Could have been a seaman at one point. Allegany County
records say he died in Minnesota in 1867. Military File says he lived in Wiscoy at time of
discharge. Father Michael also served during the war. (Military File, 1865 Allegany County Town
Clerk Register Hume, Allegany County Web Site, 1860 Fed. Census Hume)

McDermott, Michael Co. F, 160th NY Infantry - 8/29/1862 at Angelica/3 yrs - 44 - INA - 11/21/
1862 at Auburn - No bounty - Pvt, Pvt - Gunboat Cotton - 7/28/1863 Honorable/Deceased - DD,
7/28/1863 at Baton Rouge, LA of chronic diarrhea - INA (Both B Ireland) - INA - 1817 in Ireland
- Farmer - None Deceased - 1st. INA, 2nd Catherine Kelly - James, Martin, William, Jerome -
7/28/1863 in Baton Rouge, LA - Baton Rouge National Cemetery - Sick at Brasher City? Hosp
April-May, 1863, New Orleans G.H. in June & Baton Rouge Hosp. in July. The Allegany County
Web Site says he served in the 136th Infantry. Actually no Michael McDermott (or any other
McDermott) served in the 136th. His pension records show clearly this is the right man. His son
Jerome was born in Hume. County also has him buried at Cottonwood, SC. He is buried under the
name Matthew McDermott. His surgeon called him Matthew in his reports which probably
accounts for the mistake, unless Matthew was his actual first or middle name. While he gave his
age as 44 when he enlisted, the 1860 Census shows his age as 49, making him at least 51 in 1862.
Another son Martin was blind and was awarded his father's pension after his stepmother died
1/20/1892. Likely both marriages were in Ireland as Catherine was also born there. Son James also

231

served during the war. (1860 Fed. Census Hume, Allegany County Web Site)

McElroy, Hugh Co. C, 104th NY Infantry - 12/3/1861 at Geneseo/3 yrs - 22 -5'7", Light Complexion, Grey Eyes, Brown Hair, slight bunch at front of right ear - 2/26/1862 at Geneseo - No bounty - Pvt, Pvt - Cedar Creek, Chancellorsville, Gettysburg, Bristoe's Station - 12/31/1864 Honorable - Was not a casualty - Thomas & Rose Galligher McElroy (Both B Ireland) - John - 12/25/1844 in Ireland (Service records say he was born at sea.) - Laborer - Laborer - Never Married - None - 12/3/1904 in Milwaukee, WI (Home for Disabled Volunteers) - Probably Milwaukee - Brother John also served during the war. Was in the Milwaukee Home by at least 1900. (Military & Pension Files, 1865 Allegany County Town Clerk Register Hume, 1860 Fed. Census Hume, 1900 Fed. Census Milwaukee)

McElroy, John Co. D, 4th NY Heavy Artillery - 12/18/1863 at Hume/3 yrs - 26 - 5'7", Light Complexion, Blue Eyes, Light Hair - 1/5/1864 at Elmira - $300 - Pvt, Pvt - defense of DC, Peebles Farm, Hatcher's Run - 6/16/1865 Honorable - INJ, April, 1864 at Hatcher's Run (per hospital records) accidental axe wound to right foot (2nd toe through phalanx) - Thomas & Rose Galligher McElroy (Both B Ireland) - Hugh - 9/30/1836 in Ireland - Laborer - Laborer/Farmer - 1st Mary Ann O'Brien (died 10/7/1885), 2nd Maria McNulty, married 5/9/1886 in St. Patrick's Church in Fillmore - Thomas, John Edward - 9/6/1900 - Holy Cross Cemetery, Fillmore (Headstone being repaired as of 2007) - Military records have the wound occurring at Hatcher's Run. Regiment was serving in defense of DC in April of 1863. Was initially in City Point, VA hospital. Some records also say he deserted from Lowell G.H. in Rhode Island on 7/6/1864. Other records show him "Present" in August. No further information. No evidence of any trial or punishment. Was also in a hospital March & April of 1865. Brother Hugh also served during the war. (Military & Pension Files, 1890 Fed. Census Hume, 1865, 1892 NYS Censuses Hume, 1860, 1880 Fed. Censuses Hume)

McHill, William See William Hill. (Military & pension files have name as McHill)

McIntyre, Edward Martin Not from C-H-G area. Hume Township received credit for his enlistment in Co. B, 194th NY Infantry when it paid his enlistment bonus of $500. - (1865 Allegany County Town Clerk Register Hume, NYS Adjutant General Report 1905, Volume 43)

McKinney, Archibald At least one source document indicates that Archibald McKinney served in the military during the war. No evidence of such service has been located. An Archibald McKinley did serve with Cos. D/C, 42nd NY Infantry, but his file shows no connection to the C-H-G area (he was from Long Island). There is a Burnside G.A.R. Post 237 Marker at his grave, but it must belong beside another grave unless he served in a non-NYS regiment. (Matteson, Fillmore American Legion)

McNulty, James E. Battalion B, 1st NY National Guard - 8/2/1864 at Rochester/100 days - 21 - INA - 8/2/1864 at Elmira - No bounty - Pvt, Sgt - No battles (never left NYS) - 11/22/1864 Honorable - Was not a casualty - INA - INA - 1842 or 43 - INA - INA - Mariah - INA - INA - INA -Promoted to Sgt 8/2/1864 - 1890 Census says he was in the Army for 3 years, 3 months and

20 days. May have served in another regiment. Info for the 1890 Census provided by his wife. He was deceased by 1890. No contemporary documentation that he was from C-H-G. His wife was remarried by 1890 and living in Hume. (Military File, 1890 Fed. Census Special Schedule Hume)

McWhorter, John At least one source document indicates that McWhorter served in the military during the war. No evidence of service has been located. Two John McWhorters served with NYS Civil War regiments, but their files do not show any connection to the C-H-G area. (Matteson, Fillmore American Legion)

Meabon, Edwin R. Co. E, 85th NY Infantry - 9/1/1861 at Granger/3 yrs (Re-enlisted 2/1/1865 in Co. B, 2nd U.S. Veteran Infantry, discharged 8/1/1866) - 21 - 5'6", Dark Complexion, Dark Hair, Dark Eyes - 10/10/1861 at Elmira - $100 - Pvt, Pvt - defense of DC, siege of Yorktown, Williamsburg, Fair Oaks, before Richmond, transferred to 2nd U.S. Artillery, Batteries B and L (7/16/ 1862 to 7/1/1864) for balance of service, no additional information on battles - 9/1/1864 Honorable - WIA, 5/31/1862 at Fair Oaks, gunshot to left leg and dislocation of left elbow - Amanda Meabon - Cyrus, Jare, Emily, Reuben, Alonzo - 1840 in Erie Co., PA - Farmer - Laborer - Mary K. Campbell, married 5/1/1872 at South West, PA - Horace Vernon, Guy L. - 10/18/1906 at Hospital for Insane, Spencer, WV - Probably Williamstown, WV. Letter in file from Thomas Thorp certifying that he enlisted Meabon and had known him for some time. Meabon must have been working in Granger in the early 60's. Maybe had worked there off and on for years. (Military & Pension Files, *History of Allegany County, 1879*, Matteson, 1850 Fed. Census Erie County, PA 1900 Fed. Census Warren Co., PA)

Meach, Arlington At least one source document indicates that Arlington served in the military during the war. In fact he died 1/6/1859 some two years before the war. His son George served. (Fillmore American Legion.)

Meach, George Ebenezer - Co. I, 6th NY Cavalry - 11/9/1861 at NYC/3 yrs (Re-enlisted 12/16/ 1863 at Culpeper, VA) - 21 - 5'8", Dark Complexion - Black Eyes, Black Hair - 11/19/1861 at Camp Scott, NYC - $400 - Pvt, Duty Sgt - Many, including Malvern Hill, Orange County Court House, Fredericksburg, Antietam Chancellorsville, Gettysburg, Wilderness, Todd's Tavern, North Anna River, Cold Harbor, Bethesda Church, Trevillian Station, before Petersburg, Berryville, Winchester, Cedar Creek - 8/16/1865 Honorable - Was not a casualty - Arlington (B MA) & Fanny Ayer (B NY) Meach - None apparently - 3/31/1844 or 45 - Factory Operative - Blacksmith - Never Married - None - 3/21/1873 in Meridian, MS - Pine Grove Cemetery, Fillmore - Meach won the Medal of Honor for capturing a enemy flag at the Battle of Winchester on 9/19/1864. The flag he captured is now at the Museum of the Confederacy at Richmond, VA. Was appointed Farrier/ Blacksmith May, 1864. Also served with Cos. F/I, 2nd NY Provisional Cavalry (6th & 15th Cavalries combined to form the 2nd). Was sick in DC hospital at end of war. Was only 16 or 17 when he volunteered. Father died 1/6/1859. Mother remarried her husband's brother George, creating confusion about who was the soldier George Meach's father. Also led some to believe that Reuben, the son of the elder George was the soldier George's brother. The soldier George was shot to death in Meriden, MS. (Military & Pension Files, Allegany County Web Site, 1865 Allegany County Town Clerk Register Hume, Matteson, 1850, 1860 Fed. Censuses Hume, 1865

Meach, Reuben Beardsley Co. D, 1st NY Veteran Cavalry - 10/10/1863 at Pike/3 yrs - 23 - 5'11",
Dark Complexion, Black Eyes, Black Hair - 10/10/1863 at Geneva - $100 - Pvt, Pvt - Snicker's
Gap, New Market, New Town, Piedmont, Liberty, Buford's Gap, Leetown, Kernstown,
Winchester, Cedar Creek, Berryville - 7/20/1865 Honorable - Was not a casualty - George &
Mariah Beardsley Meach - None - 11/1/1846 in Centerville - Farmer - Farmer - INA - INA - INA -
INA - Listed as Meech in the Military Files Index. His widowed father married the mother of
George Meach after George's father Arrington died. (Military File, 1865 NYS Census Hume, 1865
Allegany County Town Clerk Register Hume, 1850 Fed. Census Centerville, 1860 Fed. Census
Hume)

Mead, Ebenezer Not from the C-H-G area. Served with Co. B, 86th NY Infantry. Hume Township
was credited with his 8/12/1864 enlistment when it paid his enlistment bonus of $400. (1865
Allegany County Town Clerk Register Hume)

Mearns, Andrew, Jr. Co. A, 154th NY Infantry - 9/3/1864 at Freedom/1 yr - 44 - 5'5", Light
Complexion, Blue Eyes, Brown Hair - 9/3/1864 at Dunkirk - $400 - Pvt, Pvt - siege of Savannah,
Bentonsville, Goldsboro - Was not a casualty - Andrew & Mary Flagg Mearns (Both B Scotland) -
George, Agnus, Mary, William, Jane, Margaret, John - 9/5/1820 in Scotland - Farmer - Farmer/
Saw Mill Worker/Dealer, Wool & Meat - 1st Frances (Died 2/25/1878), 2nd Lydia C. Leach,
married 8/26/1878 in Hume - Mary, George - 11/19/1893 in Centerville - Rogers Cemetery,
Centerville - Suffered kidney problems at Savannah, GA 1/1/1865 and a sunstroke at Bowling
Green, VA 5/25/1865. Present at the surrender of General Johnston's army. Marched in Grand
Review 5/24/1865. Sunstroke may have been related to his participation in the Grand Review.
(Military & Pension Files, 1865 NYS Census Centerville, 1865 Allegany County Town Clerk
Register Centerville, Allegany County Web Site, Centerville American Legion, 1890 Fed. Census
Special Schedule Centerville, Matteson, 1850 Fed. Census Freedom, 1880 Fed. Census
Centerville)

Meier, Hans Jacob Not from the C-H-G area. Originally served with Co H. 74th PA. Infantry. Re-
enlistment in Co. E, 16th VRC was credited to Hume Township when it paid his re-enlistment
bonus of $500. (1865 Allegany County Town Clerk Register Hume)

Merchant, Marcus Dana Co. K, 19th NY Infantry - 9/16/1864 at Genesee Falls/1 yr - 19 - 5'4", Fair
Complexion, Blue Eyes, Brown Hair - 9/23/1864 at Lockport - $750 - Pvt, Pvt, Cedar Creek,
Berryville, Gordonsville, Dinwiddie, Five Forks - Appomattox - 6/30/1865 Honorable - Was not a
casualty - Orrin & Juliette Alverson Merchant (Both B NY) - Mary, William - 11/15/1845 in Hume
- Farmer - Farmer - Fanny - INA - INA - INA - Present at Lee's surrender. Marched in Grand
Review 5/23/1865. Kept his sabre at discharge at a cost of $3.00. Brother William also served
during the war. (Military File, 1865 NYS Census Hume, 1865 Allegany County Town Clerk
Register Hume, 1860 Fed. Census Hume, 1880 Fed. Census Alma, WI)

Merchant, William Whitney Co. F, 19th NY Cavalry - 8/8/1862 at Hume/3 yrs - 31 - INA -

9/3/1862 at Portage Station - $150 - Pvt, Pvt - Deserted House, siege of Suffolk, Franklin, Manassas Junction, Bristoe's Station, Culpeper Court House, Wilderness, Todd's Tavern, Spotsylvania, North Anna River, Yellow Tavern, Pamunkey, Fisher's Hill, New Market, Port Republic, Cedar Creek, Berryville, Gordonsville - 6/30/1865 Honorable - Was not a casualty - Orrin & Juliette Alverson Merchant (Both B NY) - Mary, Marcus - 3/29/1832 in Hume - Lawyer - his pension indicates that due to chronic bronchitis, he was unable to work post war - Madena R. Grover, married 9/29/1859 - William D., Juliette Etta, Sarah E. - 2/18/1870 in Alma, WI - INA - Marched in Grand Review 5/23/1865 - Was a bugler in service. Brother Marcus also served during the war. Military files are listed under Marchant. (Military & Pension Files, 1865 NYS Census Hume, 1865 Allegany County Town Clerk Register Hume, Allegany County Web Site, *History of Allegany County 1879*, 1860 Fed. Census Hume)

Meyers, David H. Co. B, 9th NY Cavalry - 11/10/1862 at Jamestown/9 months - 38 - 5'8", Dark Complexion, Blue Eyes, Black Hair - 2/11/1863 at Buffalo - No bounty - Pvt, Pvt - Stoneman's Raid, Haymarket, Gettysburg, Williamsport, Brandy Station- 12/18/1863 Honorable - Was not a casualty - Henry & Catherine Meyers (Both B PA.) - INA - 11/9/1822 in Almond per County Clerk, A note in his 188th Infantry file says he was born in Granger. The 1880 Fed. Census says PA (The most contemporary file, the 1865 Town Clerk Register is probably right.) - Farmer - Farmer - Louisa P. Parker, married 11/17/1846 in Nunda - Ira H., Hellen, William F., Edith P. - 12/11/1908 in Dalton - Weaver Settlement Cemetery, Granger - Also served with Co. G, 188th NY Infantry, see below. Was sick in Alexandria, VA regimental hospital as of 8/10/1863. Admitted to Lincoln G.H., DC 8/13/1863. Pension says he had intermittent fever and it resulted in a disease of the kidneys. Caught a cold at Weldon RR or Hatcher's Run in December of 1864, which resulted in deafness. (Military & Pension Files, 1890 Fed. Census Special Schedule Granger, 1865 Allegany County Town Clerk Register Granger, 1865 NYS Census Granger, 1860, 1880 Fed. Censuses Granger)

Meyers, David H. Co. G, 188th NY Infantry - 9/6/1864 at Farmington (Avon)/1 yr - 5'8", Dark Complexion, Blue Eyes, Black Hair - 10/4/1864 at Rochester - $100 - Pvt, Pvt - siege of Petersburg, Hatcher's Run, Weldon RR, Gravelly Run, Five Forks, Appomattox - 7/1/1865 Honorable - Was not a casualty - Present at Lee's surrender. Marched in Grand Review 5/23/1865. Apparently was originally rejected (for his second enlistment) due to curvature of the spine. Also served with the 9th NY Cavalry, see above. Also see above for personal information and sources of information.

Meyers, John P. Duplicate. See John P. Myers. (1865 NYS Census Hume)

Millard, John Bradford Co. D, 4th NY Heavy Artillery 8/13/1862 at Rochester/3 yrs - 26 - 5'11", Florid Complexion, Blue Eyes, Dark Hair - 8/13/1862 at Rochester - $100 - Pvt, Pvt - Wilderness, Spotsylvania, North Anna River, Totopotomoy, Cold Harbor, siege of Petersburg, Weldon RR, Ream's Station, Peeble's Farm, Hatcher's Run, fall of Petersburg, Appomattox - 6/3/1865 Honorable - Was not a casualty - Sherwood & Mary Bradford Millard - INA - 2/11/1836 in Canaan, CT - Farmer - Farmer - Jane Millard - Mattee J. - INA - INA - Present at Lee's surrender. Marched in Grand Review 5/23/1865. John and his wife Jane were probably related prior to their marriage. Her maiden name was apparently also Millard. (Military File, 1865 NYS Census Hume, 1865 Allegany County Town Clerk Hume, 1860 Fed. Census Canaan, CT)

Miller, Myron Cos. E/G/Staff, 85th NY Infantry - 9/1/1861 at Granger/3 yrs - 28 - INA - 11/7/1861 at Elmira - No bounty - Pvt, Hospital Steward - No battles - 4/8/1862 Honorable - Robert & Jane Doggett Miller - INA - 9/27/1832 in Andover - Dentist - Physician/Surgeon - Hariett - Mary, Lawrence - 6/6/1873 - Short Tract - Promoted Hospital Steward 11/7/1861. Some records treat Miller as a doctor during the war. According to his military file, he was a Hospital Steward. There was a Doctor Hiram C. Miller in the 85th that may have created some confusion. Myron Miller was a dentist prewar and a doctor post war. Dr. William M. Smith was very unimpressed with Dr. Hiram Miller who, Smith claimed, was not trusted by the men of the 85th. Dr. Hiram Miller eventually received a disability discharge. (Military File, 1865 NYS Census Granger, Matteson, *History of Allegany County 1879*, Granger American Legion, 1865 Allegany County Town Clerk Register Granger, 1860, 1870 Fed. Censuses Granger.)

Millspaugh, Frank Wrong first name. See Leander Millspaugh who was the Civil War soldier. Leander did have a son named Frank and it's likely Leander's middle name was Frank. Son Frank was 6 in 1860. See below. (Fillmore American Legion)

Millspaugh, Leander Co. D, 64th NY Infantry - 8/14/1862 at Rushford/3 yrs - 28 - 5'7", Sandy Complexion, Hazel Eyes, Brown Hair - 10/16/1862 at Elmira - $125 - Pvt, Pvt - Fredericksburg, Chancellorsville, Gettysburg - 12/15/1864 Disability/Honorable - WIA, gunshot to right elbow at Gettysburg, 7/2/1863 - Cornelius & Polly Estes Millspaugh (Both B NY) - INA - 8/1/1834 in Geneseo - Farmer - Farmer - 1st Charlotte Cronk (Died 3/9/1891), 2nd Hannah Moore Terry, married 6/12/1892 - Frank, Fred, D., Mary, Sarah, Ella M. - 2/3/1924 in Hornell - Pine Grove Cemetery Fillmore - His name was possibly Leander Frank Millspaugh. He had a son named Frank. (Military & Pension Files, Fillmore American Legion, 1865 Allegany County Town Clerk Register Caneadea, 1860 Fed. Census Centerville, 1910 Fed. Census Hume)

Minard, Ansel L. Cos. A/H/F, 4th NY Heavy Artillery - 9/7/1862 at Hume/3 yrs - 18 - INA - 9/13/1862 at NYC - $50 - Pvt, 1st Lt.-Wilderness, Spotsylvania, North Anna River, Totopotomoy, Cold Harbor, siege of Petersburg, Weldon RR, Ream's Station, Hatcher's Run, fall of Petersburg, Appomattox - 9/26/1865 Honorable - Was not a casualty - Luke Lincoln (B VT) & Esther Pride Minard (stepmother Laura) - Rosewell, Sarah, Mary - 10/4/1844 in Hume - Canal Boatman - Retail Grocer - Phebe B. Atherton , married 11/22/1864 in Caneadea - Bell - 9/1/1870 - Pine Grove Cemetery, Fillmore - promoted to 2nd Lt. 2/1/1865, 1st Lt. 5/31/1865. Present at Lee's surrender. Marched in the Grand Review 5/23/1865. Had a sunstroke while in the service. (Military & Pension Files, Allegany County Web Site, Matteson, 1865 NYS Census Hume, Fillmore American Legion, 1865 Allegany County Town Clerk Register Hume, 1860 Fed. Census Hume, 1870 Fed. Census Caneadea, 1865 Allegany County Town Clerk Register Caneadea.)

Moffet, Miles Not from the C-H-G area. Originally served with Co. E, 86th NY Infantry. Re-enlistment in Co. B, 16th VRC credited to Hume which paid his re-enlistment bonus of $500. (1865 Allegany County Town Clerk Register Hume.)

Moore, John Co. C, 19th NY Cavalry - 9/13/1864 at Centerville/1 yr - 19 - 5'8", Fair Complexion, Blue Eyes, Brown Hair - 9/27/1864 at Elmira - $900 - Pvt, Pvt - Cedar Creek, Berryville, Gordonsville - 6/30/1865 Honorable - Was not a casualty - Arel & Catherine Truman Moore (Both B NY) - Sidney, Lucy, Dennis - 1/19/1838 in Freedom - Farmer - Farmer - Never Married - None - 8/15/1895 in Brookings, SD - Probably Brookings - Military spelled name Moores. Brother Sydney also served during the war. Marched in the Grand Review 5/23/1865. (Military & Pension Files, 1865 NYS Census Centerville, 1865 Allegany County Town Clerk Register Centerville, Matteson, 1860 Fed. Census Freedom)

Moore, Sidney Co. D, 154th NY Infantry - 7/25/1862 at Freedom/3 yrs - 31 - 5'11", Light Complexion, Blue Eyes, Light Hair - 9/24/1862 at Jamestown - $100 - Pvt, Pvt - Chancellorsville, Gettysburg, Mission Ridge, Rocky Face Ridge, siege of Atlanta, occupation of Atlanta, siege of Savannah - 6/11/1865 Honorable - POW, captured 5/8/1864 at Rocky Face Ridge, Prison: not identified, escaped and returned to company 8/3/1864 - Arel & Catherine Truman Moore (Both B NY) - John, Lucy, Dennis - 9/6/1831 in Cattaraugus County - Farmer - Farmer - Sarah Findlay, married 4/26/1872 in Freedom - George, Sidney, Grace, Daniel, Flora, Elmer - 3/24/1891 - INA - Brother John also served during the war. Marched in Grand Review 5/24/1865. Was in hospital in Gettysburg for a while. (Military & Pension Files, 1865 NYS Census Centerville, 1890 Fed. Census Special Schedule Centerville, 1865 Allegany County Town Clerk Register Centerville, 1860 Fed. Census Freedom, 1880 Fed. Census Centerville)

Morgan, Leander At least one source document indicates that Leander served in the military during the war. However no evidence of such service has been located. (Matteson)

Morgan, Milton M. At least one source document indicates that Milton served in the military during the war. However, no evidence of such service has been located. (Fillmore American Legion)

Morgan, Samuel Harvey Co. B, 2nd NY Mounted Rifles - 12/14/1863 at Hume/3 yrs - 19 - 5/5", Light Complexion, Blue Eyes, Grey Hair - 1/12/1864 at Ft. Porter, Buffalo - $300 - Pvt, Corp - Spotsylvania, North Anna River, Pamunkey, Totopotomoy, Hanover Court House, Cold Harbor, Bethesda Church, siege of Petersburg, Weldon RR, Hatcher's Run - 8/10/1865 Honorable - Was not a casualty - Samuel & Clarissa S. Holt Morgan (Both B NY) - Ellen, half brother Willis Fox - 12/21/1843 in Pike - Farm Laborer - Farmer/Butcher/Wheat Market Operator - Frances A. Andrews, married 3/25/1866 in Caneadea - Berl H., Fred H., Jennie M. - 7/19/1913 in Mitchell, SD - Mitchell, S.D. - Samuel's mother Clarissa eventually married Abel Washburn whose first wife may have been Clarissa's first husband's sister. (Military & Pension Files, 1865 NYS Census Hume, 1865 Allegany County Town Clerk Register Hume, *History of Allegany County 1879*, 1860 Fed. Census Genesee Falls, 1900, 1910 Fed. Censuses Mitchell, SD)

Morris, Joseph Co. G, 23rd Kentucky Infantry - 9/27/1864 at Bowling Green, KY/1 yr - 20 - 5'6", Fair Complexion, Blue Eyes, Dark Hair - 10/2/1864 at Bowling Green - No bounty - Pvt, Pvt - Franklin, TN - 8/23/1865 Honorable - POW, captured 12/1/1864 at Franklin, (Nashville) TN, Prison: Andersonville, released 4/29/1865 - Father INA, Hannah Morris (B South Wales, England)

- Margaret - 1843 or 44 in South Wales, England - Wagon Maker - Wagon Maker/Lumber Merchant - Mercy Louise Holland, married 3/2/1876 in Lima, OH - George (may have been father's name) - 4/27/1903 in Lima, OH - Woodlawn Cemetery, Lima, OH - Was a prisoner for 5 months. His mother had 12 children. Came to U.S. at age 8. 1900 Census says he arrived 1861, but more likely it was 1851. After his father's death his mother married a John Roberts. Joseph was a substitute for a W.H. Roberts, quite possibly John's son. (Military & Pension Files, 1865 NYS Census Centerville, 1860 Fed. Census Centerville, 1900 Fed. Census Lima, OH)

Morse, Abel Green Co. D, 4th NY Heavy Artillery - 12/19/1863 at Hume/3 yrs - 31 - 5'11", Dark Complexion, Blue Eyes, Brown Hair - 12/21/1863 at Elmira - $300 - Pvt, Pvt - fall of Petersburg - Appomattox - 9/26/1865 Honorable - Was not a casualty - David & Harriet Green Wade Morse (Both B NY) - Benjamin T. Wade (from Harriet's first marriage), Mary Jane, Julia Ann, William Wesley, Philapena Dorlesca,, Harriet Ann, Ladorna Albertine - 8/18/1833 in Ontario County (Military files say Allegany Co.) - Laborer - Farmer - 1st Lucy L. (Died 2/15/1904 in Walker, IA), 2nd Mary E. Risdon, married 10/9/1907 in Cedar Rapids, IA - Lester D., Robert A., James H. - 3/13/1917 in Walker, IA - INA - Brother William also served during the war. Marched in Grand Review 5/23/1865. (Military & Pension Files, 1865 NYS Census Hume, 1865 Allegany County Town Clerk Register Hume, 1850 Fed. Census Hume, 1900 Fed. Census Grant, IA)

Morse, George Washington Co. F., 19th NY Cavalry - 8/9/1862 at Hume/3 yrs - 22 - 5'8", Dark Complexion, Grey Eyes, Black Hair - 9/3/1862 at Portage Station - $150 - Pvt, Pvt - Deserted House, siege of Suffolk, Franklin, Manassas Junction, Bristoe's, Station, Culpeper Court House, Wilderness, Todd's Tavern, Spotsylvania, North Anna River, Yellow Tavern, Pamunkey, Totopotomoy, Cold Harbor, Trevillian Station, Charles County Court House, before Richmond & Petersburg, New Market, Shepherdstown, Winchester - 4/3/1865 Disability/Honorable - WIA, gunshot to right foot (lost 2 toes) at Winchester, 9/19/1864 - Rufus (B NY) & Anna Tenyke (B CT) Morse - Isaac, Theodore, Rufus, Francis - 3/21/1839 per Town Clerk, in Granger per military file - Farm Laborer - Farmer - Martha Maria Wood, married 12/5/1860 - Betsey A.(Geravemberg), Estell S. (Carey) - 3/4/1901 - Mason Township, Arenac County, MI - Brothers Isaac & Theodore also served during the war. (Military & Pension Files, 1865 NYS Census Granger, *History of Allegany County 1879*, 1865 Allegany County Town Clerk Register Hume, 1860 Fed. Census Granger, 1900 Fed. Census Mason, MI)

Morse, Issac Lemuel Co. F, 4th NY Heavy Artillery - 12/21/1863 at Hume - 19 - 5'6", Dark Complexion, Grey Eyes, Black Hair - 12/23/1863 at Elmira - $300 - Pvt, Pvt - No battles - 7/12/1864 Honorable/Deceased - DD, 7/12/1864 at City Point, VA of typhoid fever - Rufus (B NY) & Anna Tenyke (B CT) Morse - George, Theodore, Rufus, Francis - 5/4/1846 in Caneadea - Boatman - None Deceased - Never Married - None - 7/12/1864 in City Point, VA - 6th Corps Section, City Point National Cemetery - Brothers George & Theodore also served during the war. Gave age as 19 at enlistment, was probably only 17. (Military & Pension Files, 1865 Allegany County Town Clerk Register Hume, Allegany County Web Site, 1860 Fed. Census Granger)

Morse, Theodore Co. F, 4th NY Heavy Artillery - 12/21/1863 at Hume/3 yrs - 18 - 5'5", Dark Complexion, Blue Eyes, Brown Hair - 12/23/1863 at Elmira - $300 - Pvt, Pvt - fall of Petersburg,

Appomattox - 9/26/1865 Honorable - Was not a casualty - Rufus (B NY) & Anna Tenyke (B CT) Morse - George, Isaac, Rufus, Francis - 6/30/1848 in Caneadea - Boatman - Farmer - Lucy M. Perkins Jarvis, married 4/18/1885 in Dayton Township, MI (her 2nd) - Ethel, Walter, Alice, Merton, Frank B. - 2/7/1910 in Wells Township, Tuscola County, MI - INA - Brothers George and Issac also served during the war. Gave his age as 18 at enlistment, was, at best, 15. Had typhoid fever while in service. Was in McDougall G.H., Fort Schuyler, NY. Also had severe diarrhea in November-December, 1864 at Petersburg. Present at Lee's surrender. Marched in Grand Review 5/23/1864. A memo in his file to his father written by a Reverend from the U.S. Christian Committee described Morse as an "unconverted Christian." (Military & Pension Files, 1865 NYS Census Hume, 1865 Allegany County Town Clerk Register Hume, 1860 Fed. Census Granger, 1880, 1900 Fed. Censuses Wells, MI)

Morse, William Wesley Co. D, 4th NY Heavy Artillery - 12/19/1863 at Hume/3 yrs - 27 - 5'9", Fair Complexion, Blue Eyes, Brown Hair - 12/21/1863 at Elmira - $300 - Pvt, Pvt - fall of Petersburg, Appomattox - 9/26/1865 Honorable - WIA, hit by a shell causing damage to breast and right eye 4/2/1865 at South Side RR, Peterburg - David & Harriet Green Morse (Both B NY) - Benjamin T. Wade (Harriet's son by first marriage), Mary Jane, Julia Ann, Philapena Dorlesca, Harriet Ann, Ladorna Albertine - 3/17/1836 in Hume - Laborer - Farmer - 1st Angeline Scott, married 2/6/1855 in Hume (separated before war-she died 6/26/1864), 2nd Sarah Hovey, married 4/9/1871 in Cono, Buchanan County, IA - Hellen, Mary, Eugene, Charles Wesley - 5/28/1905 - INA - Present at Lee's surrender. Marched in Grand Review 5/23/1865. He claimed a third marriage to an Ellen in one document. His family said it wasn't true, that he was confused by problems stemming from his injuries. They thought he may have been thinking of an old girlfriend or a daughter Hellen who died at age two. (Military & Pension Files, 1865 NYS Census Hume, 1865 Allegany County Town Clerk Register Hume, 1850 Fed. Census Hume, 1880 Fed. Census Linn, IA)

Moses, Charles At least one source document indicates that Moses served in the military during the war. No evidence of such service has been located. (Fillmore American Legion, Matteson)

Moses, Luther Co. E, 85th NY Infantry - 0/1/1861 at Granger/3 yrs (Re-enlisted 1/1/1864) - 29 - 6'2", Dark Complexion, Dark Eyes, Black Hair - 10/10/1861 at Elmira - $400 - Pvt, Pvt - Plymouth (also saw service with the Navy on a detached assignment) - 7/28/1864 Honorable/ Deceased - POW, captured 4/20/1864 at Plymouth, NC, Prison: Andersonville, DD, 7/28/1864 at Andersonville of diarrhea - Daniel & Phebe W. Beckworth Moses (Both B NY) - Frances, Ashbel, Washington, Aziza, Emeline - 10/28/1832 in Granger - Farm Laborer - None Deceased - Never Married - None - 7/28/1864 at Andersonville - Andersonville - Listed on Soldiers Monument in Granger. His brother Washington became a prominent local citizen and was a member of the legislative in 1882 and 1887. (Military File, 1865 NYS Census Granger, Granger American Legion, *Allegany & Its People*, Matteson, 1865 Allegany County Town Clerk Register Granger, *History of Allegany County 1879*, 1850, 1860 Fed. Censuses Granger)

Mosher, Edwin G. (George Madison) Co. E, 2nd NY Mounted Rifles - 12/23/1863 at Castile/3 yrs - 20 - 5'6", Light Complexion, Blue Eyes, Light Hair - 1/5/1864 at Ft. Porter, Buffalo - $400 - Pvt, Sgt - Poplar Springs Church, Pegram's Farm, Hatcher's Run, Weldon RR, Dinwiddie, Five Forks,

Appomattox - 8/10/1865 Honorable - Was not a casualty - William & Ann Louise Shaw Mosher (Both B NY) - Helen, Mary Jane, Ellen C., John H. Charles, Edward B., Henry R. - 2/1843 in Canadici, Ontario County - Carpenter/Joiner - Carpenter/Joiner/Weaver - 1st Ellen E., married 9/8/1862 (Ellen divorced him 7/8/1873 for desertion), 2nd Sarah A. Shoemaker, married 5/13/1873 before his divorce from Ellen was final. Sarah died 4/10/1888, 3rd Anna B. Pearst Trombley, married 9/8/1888 in Riga, MI (A brother though his first wife was a Nellie Rich form near Pike, but no other evidence of this. May have thought Ellen was Nellie.) - James, Hettie, Mark, Mary - 8/4/1901 in Riga, MI - INA - Present at Lee's surrender. Marched in Grand Review 5/23/1865. Mosher also served as George H. Mosher in Co. B, 104th NY Infantry from 12/2/1861 till 6/16/1862 when he deserted at Catlett's Station, VA. He used the name Edwin G. Mosher while in the Mounted Rifles. Made Wagoner 8/31/1864. Promoted to Sgt 11/1/1864. July 1865 was acting Sgt/Major. When he moved to Michigan after the war he used the name Edwin Watson. All the names caused problems when he applied for his pension since he had never used his correct name, George Madison Mosher, in the service, and he was using Edwin Watson when he applied for his pension. A sister said he had always pretended his middle name was Edwin. Retained his sabre and pistol at discharge. He died and was buried as Edwin Watson. He was charged with stealing $1100 by a E. Lovejoy, who put up wanted posters and offered $200 for his capture. The poster claimed that "perspiration starts on forehead at exercise or excitement." (Military & Pension Files, 1865 NYS Census Centerville, 1860 Fed. Census Genesee Falls, 1900 Fed. Census Whitehead, MI)

Moultrop, Gilbert Stephen Co. F, 4th NY Heavy Artillery - 9/21/1862 at Hume, 3 yrs - 25 - 5'10", Light Complexion, Blue Eyes, Black Hair - 10/2/1862 at NYC - $50 - Pvt, Pvt - Wilderness, Spotsylvania, North Anna River, Totopotomoy, Cold Harbor, Petersburg - 6/18/1864 Honorable/ Deceased - KIA, 6/18/1864 near Petersburg - Arila Riley & Susan Town Moultrop (Both B VT) - Lovinia - 6/20/1835 in Centerville - Farmer - None Deceased - Never Married - None - 6/18/1864 near Petersburg, VA - Rogers Cemetery, Centerville - Mother applied for his pension. The request was denied. She was unable to show that Gilbert had been the primary financial supporter of the family. (Military & Pension Files, 1865 NYS Census Centerville, 1865 Allegany County Town Clerk Register Centerville, Centerville American Legion, Matteson, Allegany County Web Site, 1850 Fed. Census Centerville)

Myers, Delos Co. F, 19th NY Cavalry - 8/9/1862 at Hume/1 yr - 28 - 5'6", Florid Complexion, Blue Eyes, Light Hair - 9/3/1862 at Portage Station - $50 - Pvt, Pvt - Suffolk, Wilderness, Todd's Tavern, Spotsylvania, North Anna River, Yellow Tavern, Pamunkey, Totopotomoy, Cold Harbor, Trevillian Station, Charles County Court House, before Richmond & Petersburg - 5/29/1865 Disability/Honorable - Was not a casualty - Eliphalet (Lifelet) & Nancy Robinson Myers - Eli C., Charlotte, Edmond, Harlen, John L., Noah, Sarah, Henry - 1833/34 in Cattaraugus County (Military records say Hume) - Farm Laborer - Farmer - Lydia - INA - 11/2/1871 - Alger Cemetery, Hume, Route 19 - Discharged for serious health problems, including enlargement of cervical, left parotid, and chronic diarrhea. Illnesses caused an early death. Was detached to Ambulance Corps for part of service. Also worked as a nurse. Was sick in Rochester, NY hospital from 8/5/1864 until discharge. Brothers Eli C., Edmond, John L., and Noah also served during the war. Eli and Edmond were not form the C-H-G area. (Military File,1865 NYS Census Hume, Allegany County Web Site, Matteson, 1860, 1870 Fed. Censuses Hume)

Myers, John L. Co. D, 154th NY Infantry - 8/9/1862 at Machias/3 yrs - 23 - 5'6", Light Complexion, Blue Eyes, Dark Hair - 9/24/1862 at Jamestown - $100 - Pvt, Pvt - No battles - 10/20/1862 Honorable/Deceased - DD, 10/19/1862 at G.H., Fairfax, VA of congestion of the brain (apoplexy) - Eliphalet & Nancy Robinson Myers - Eli C., Charlotte, Edmond, Noah L., Delos, Sarah, Henry - 1838/39 in Cattaraugus County - Farmer - None Deceased - Marian A. Pride, married 9/29/1859 in Elton - Wallace R., Helen P. - 10/19/1862 in Fairfax, VA - Arlington National Cemetery - By 1865 his wife Marian and two children were living in Hume. It is not clear that he ever lived in C-H-G. Brothers Eli C., Delos, Edmond, and Noah also served during the war. Eli and Edmond were not from the C-H-G area. (Military & Pension Files, wife1865 NYS Census Hume, 1860 Fed. Census Machias)

Myers, John Peck Co. C, 104th NY Infantry - 10/30/1861 at Hume/3 yrs - 18 - 5'9", Light Complexion, Dark Eyes, Brown Curly Hair - 2/26/1862 at Geneseo - No bounty - Pvt, Pvt - Cedar Creek, 2nd Bull Run, South Mountain, Antietam, Chancellorsville, Gettysburg - 6/20/1865 Honorable - WIA, gunshot to left ankle, 9/14/1862 at Antietam, POW, captured 7/1/1863 at Gettysburg, Prisons: Belle Island, Richmond, Andersonville, released 4/21/1865 at Vicksburg - William & Lucinda L. Burnell Myers (Both B NY) - Samuel B., George, Sarah, Peter, Anna, Ellen, Ermina, Fred - 7/1/1843 in Hume - Farmer - Farmer/Businessman/ Dry Goods Merchant/Produce Commission Merchant - Florence A. Beebe, married 9/28/1870 in Sandusky - Ethel & Ellen (adopted) - Disappeared 7/1/1895 on a business trip - INA - Wrote a letter to his wife dated 7/2/1895 and was never heard from again. Was a prominent businessman in Buffalo. Was deeply in debt at that time but, according to son-in-law James Wells, also a prominent Buffalo businessman, did not have any legal problems. Was a partner in the Buffalo firm, Myers, Woodward and Drake, Produce Commission Merchants. (Military & Pension Files, 1865 NYS Census Centerville, Allegany County Town Clerk Register Centerville, 1860 Fed. Census Hume, 1880 Fed. Census Erie County)

Myers, Noah Larkin Co. K, 147th NY Infantry - Drafted 7/14/1863 at Hume/3 yrs - 26 - 5'9", Dark Complexion, Blue Eyes, Brown Hair - 8/1863 at Elmira - $100 - Pvt, Pvt - Chancellorsville, Gettysburg, Wilderness - 8/7/1864 Honorable/Deceased - WIA, 5/5/1864 at Wilderness (He may not have been wounded, only captured. Information is not clear.), POW, captured 5/5/1864 at the Wilderness, Prison: Andersonville, DD, 8/7/1864 at Andersonville of dysentery (An 1899 document says he starved to death.) - Eliphalet (Lifelet) & Nancy Robinson Myers - Eli C., Charlotte, Edmond, Harlen, Delos, John L., Sarah, Henry - 1836 in Machias - Farm Laborer - None Deceased - Never Married - None - 8/7/1864 at Andersonville (POW) - Andersonville - Was in hospitals quite a bit during war. David's Island, NY Harbor10/29/1863 with rheumatism, Carver Hosp., DC 10/11/1863 with diarrhea, 10/8/1863 Division G.H. near Culpeper with dysentery. Deserted one day 10/17/1863. Brothers Eli C., Edmond, Delos, and John L. all served during the war. Eli and Edmond were not from the C-H-G area. Some documents claim he served with the 130th or 136th NY Infantry. A mix up with a Myer who did serve in the 136th. Pension bureau made a mess of handling the pension request submitted by his mother. (Military & Pension Files, Register of Men Drafted July, 1863 to October, 1864, 1865 Allegany County Town Clerk Register Hume, Allegany County Web Site, 1860 Fed. Census Hume)

Myers, Samuel Burrell Co. B, 154th Illinois Infantry - 2/14/1865 at Danville, IL/1 yr - 5'3", Fair Complexion, Hazel Eyes, Dark Hair - 2/14/1865 at Jacksonville, IL - $100 - Pvt, Pvt - No battles - 5/22/1865 Honorable - Was not a casualty - William & Lucinda Burnell Myers (Both B NY) - George, Sarah, Peter, Anna, John P., Ellen, Ermina, Fred - 6/30/1842 in Portageville - Farmer - Farmer/Gardner/Merchant - 1st Cornelia A. Davis (Divorced 4/16/1880), 2nd Mary E. Campbell, married 11/15/1880 (Died 2/22/1894), 3rd Mary Belle Cady, married 7/16/1895 in Franklinville - Frank A. - 9/14/1921 in Boulder, CO - Franklinville - Sick in Murfreesboro, TN hospital as of 4/29/1865. Brother John Peck also served during the war. (Military & Pension Files, 1865 NYS Census Centerville, 1855 NYS Census Hume (name spelled Meier), 1850 Fed. Census Hume (name spelled Mires) - 1900 Fed. Census Boulder, CO)

Neilan, Henry Patrick Co. F, 19th NY Cavalry - 8/9/1862 at Hume/3 yrs - 26 - 5'11", Dark Complexion, Brown Eyes, Black Hair - 9/3/1862 at Portage Station - $50 - Pvt, Orderly Sgt - Deserted House, siege of Suffolk, Franklin, Manassas Junction, Bristoe's Station, Culpeper Court House, Wilderness, Todd's Tavern - 6/30/1865 Honorable - WIA, gunshot to jaw 5/7/1864 at Todd's Tavern - James & Winifred Radigan Neilan (Both B Ireland) - Nicholas, William, James Jr., Mary, Sarah, Luke, Michael - 3/19/1835 in Oxford - Timber Hewer/Farmer - Timber Hewer/ Farmer - Ella E. Barry (Died 8/1885) - Frank B. - 3/18/1932 in Somerset, PA - Holy Cross Cemetery, Fillmore, no headstone - Transferred to 20th VRC,1/2/1865. Name was most likely Patrick Henry Neilan. Military files have Henry as first name. Promoted to Corp. 12/6/1862; Sgt 8/1/1863. Charter Member of Burnside G.A.R. Post 237. U.S. Government issued a flag when he was buried. (Military & Pension Files, 1865 NYS Census Hume, *History of Allegany County 1879*, *Allegany & Its People*, 1865 Allegany County Town Clerk Register Hume, 1855 NYS Census Hume, 1850 Fed. Census Hume, 1880 Fed. Census Granger)

Neilan, Nicholas H. At least one source document indicates that Nicholas, a brother of Henry Patrick, served in the military during the war. No evidence of such service has been located. (1865 NYS Census Hume - says he served with 4th NY Heavy Artillery)

Nickle, Joseph Not from the C-H-G area. Originally served with Co. A, 74th Pennsylvania Infantry. Hume received credit for his re-enlistment in Co. A, 16th VRC when it paid his re-enlistment bonus of $500. (Allegany County Town Clerk Register Hume)

Nutt, John C. Not from the C-H-G area. Originally served with Co. H, 11th New Jersey Infantry. Hume received credit for his re-enlistment in Co. F, 16th VRC when it paid his re-enlistment bonus of $500. (1865 Allegany County Town Clerk Register Hume)

Nye, Daniel Darwin Co. F, 4th NY Heavy Artillery - 9/8/1862 at Hume/3 yrs - 26 - 5'10", Light Complexion, Dark Eyes, Black Hair - 9/12/1862 at NYC - $100 - Pvt, Pvt - Detached to 6th Corps entire service, battles unknown - 6/3/1865 Honorable - Was not a casualty - Nelson & Abigail Mather Nye (Both B NY) - William L., Mary A., Dewitt C., Charles M. - 2/3/1836 in Hume - Shoemaker - Shoemaker - Anna Amelia Camp, married 3/6/1866 in Hume - Nellie, Nelson, Thomas, Robert, David - 11/3/1905 in Centerville, IA - Centerville, IA - Brother Dewitt C. also served during the war. (Military & Pension Files, 1865 NYS Census Hume, 1865 Allegany County

Town Clerk Register Hume, 1850 Fed. Census Hume, 1870 Fed. Census Nunda)

Nye, Dewitt Clinton Co. G, 4th NY Heavy Artillery - 9/8/1862 at Hume/3 yrs - 18 - 5'4", Light Complexion, Blue Eyes, Sandy Hair - 9/12/1862 at NYC - $50 - Pvt, Pvt - Wilderness, Spotsylvania, North Anna River, Totopotomoy, Cold Harbor, siege of Petersburg, Weldon RR, Ream's Station, Peeble's Farm, Hatcher's Run, fall of Petersburg, Appomattox - 6/3/1865 Honorable - Was not a casualty - Nelson & Abigail Mather Nye (Both B NY) - Daniel Darwin, William L., Mary A., Charles M. - 3/22/1846 in Hume - Shoemaker - Shoemaker - Isadora Stone - Mary S., Hallie R., Carrie S. - INA - INA - Brother Daniel Darwin also served during the war. May have been detailed for a short period to a Vermont Battalion. Present at Lee's surrender. Marched in Grand Review 5/23/1865. (1865 NYS Census Hume, 1865 Allegany County Town Clerk Register Hume, 1850 Fed. Census Hume, 1880 Fed. Census Caneadea)

Oakley, Andrew Jackson Co. F 4th NY Heavy Artillery - 8/29/1862 at Hume/3 yrs - 31 - 6', Light Complexion, Grey Eyes, Brown Hair - 9/11/1862 at NYC - $50 - Pvt, Pvt - siege of Petersburg, Weldon RR - 5/31/1865 Honorable - Was not a casualty - Nehemiah & Rhoda Bates Oakley (Both B NY) - Mary Ann, Henry H., Almina - 4/4/1831/32 in Wiscoy - Blacksmith - Blacksmith - Bridget McDermott, married 4/14/1858 in Wiscoy - Apparently no children - 4/20/1908 - Wiscoy - Charter Member & Officer of Burnside G.A.R. Post 237. Was detached to 3rd NY Light Artillery in early 1864 and may have participated in battles with that organization. Was on furlough 1/26/1865 - 2/23/1865. In Emory G.H., DC as of 4/6/1865 with acute diarrhea. (Military & Pension Files, 1890 Fed. Census Special Schedule Hume, 1865 Allegany County Town Clerk Register Hume, Matteson, 1865 NYS Census Hume, *Allegany & Its People*, Fillmore American Legion, 1850, 1870 Fed. Censuses Hume)

Osborn, Harsey Sylvester (Osborne) Co. D, 4th NY Heavy Artillery - 2/28/1863 at Centerville/3 yrs - 24 - 5'9", Fair Complexion, Grey Eyes, Brown Hair - 12/28/1863 at Elmira - $300 - Pvt, Pvt - Wilderness, Spotsylvania, North Anna River, Totopotomoy, Cold Harbor - 5/29/1865 Honorable - WIA, gunshot to left thigh, 6/1/1864 at Cold Harbor - Charles (B VT) & Sarah (probably Benjamin) (B NY) Osborne - Laura, Charles - 7/6/1839 in Centerville - Farmer - Farmer - Caroline A. Morse, married 7/5/1865 in Cuba - Fred - 1/2/1910 in Clinton, IA - Leon, IL - Was in Harwood G.H., DC with wound. Had his picture taken. He is holding a sign apparently indicating that he is the 15,000 soldier treated by the hospital. Picture probably taken close to 6/20/1864. Was on furlough from 6/20 to 8/5/1864. Sold his property to his granddaughter for $1.00 in 1907. (Military & Pension Files, 1865 NYS Census Centerville, 1890 Fed. Census Special Schedule Centerville, 1865 Allegany County Town Clerk Register Centerville, 1860 Fed. Census Centerville, 1892 NYS Census Hume, 1880 Fed. Census Whiteside County, IL)

Osborn, Harvey Blackman (Osburne) Co. F, 19th NY Cavalry - 8/15/1862 at Cold Creek (Hume)/3 yrs - 25 - 5'7", Fair Complexion, Grey Eyes, Sandy Hair - 9/3/1862 at Portage Station - $50 - Pvt, Pvt - No battles - 4/27/1863 at Ft. Monroe, VA Honorable - DD, died after leaving service, but records indicate he died from a "service related disease", unspecified, but he was in a hospital at Suffolk VA with a "lumbar abscess" - William & Emily Bours Osborn (Both B NY) - Harriet, Sarah - 2/1846 in Livonia - Farmer - None Deceased - Never Married - None - 9/21/1863 in

Centerville - Centerville Cemetery, Route 3 - Military records list him as both Henry and Harvey Osborn. Henry may have been a nickname. (Military File, 1865 NYS Census Centerville, *History of Allegany County 1879*, Centerville American Legion, 1865 Allegany County Town Clerk Register Centerville, 1860 Fed. Census Centerville)

Osborn, Henry L. See Osborn Harvey Blackman

Osborn, Jefferson (actual name Thomas Jefferson Osborn) Co. D, 64th NY Infantry - 9/13/1861 at Rushford/3 yrs - 23 - 5'9", Dark Complexion, Grey Eyes, Black Hair - 9/24/1861 at Elmira - No bounty - 2nd Sgt, 1st Sgt - siege of Yorktown, Fair Oaks - KIA, 6/1/1862 at Fair Oaks - Oramel (B NY) & Caroline (per Town Clerk) Osborn (1850 Census shows a Lydia Ann, B NY, age 35) - Sarah Ann, Perfina, Mary Jane - 1838 in Centerville - Farmer - None Deceased - Sara E. Hagg, married 12/28/1858 in Rushford - Myrta M. - 6/1/1862 at Fair Oaks, VA - Fair Oaks? - Assuming the Town Clerk is correct, his mother Caroline must have died before 1850. Since there are two young children named Farey living with the family in 1850, it is probable that Lydia Ann was previously married to a Farey and is not Jefferson's mother. (Military & Pension Files, 1865 NYS Census Centerville, Matteson, 1865 Allegany County Town Clerk Register Centerville, *History of Allegany County 1879*, 1850, 1860 Fed. Censuses Centerville)

Osman, Edward (Osmon) Co. D, 4th NY Heavy Artillery - 12/23/1863 at Hume/3 yrs - 37 - 5'6", Sandy Complexion, Grey Eyes, Ruddy Hair - 1/5/1864 at Elmira - $300 - Pvt, Pvt - Peeble's Farm, Hatcher's Run - 6/22/1865 Honorable - Was not a casualty - Edward & Elizabeth Osman (Both B England) - INA - 10/20/1826 in England - Farmer - Farmer - Sarah C. Billings, married 4/1/1846 in Glenville - Elmira, Jesse, Lucy, Ruth, Wooster, Charles, Hattie May, Eunice, Henry - 2/28/1899 in Woodville, Boone County, NE - INA - Was sick almost entire time in service. March - August 1864, November - December 1864, January - February 1865 treated at Columbia & Carver Hospitals, DC and David's Island Hospital, NY Harbor. Rheumatism & disease of the kidneys. (Military & Pension Files, 1865 NYS Census Hume, 1865 Allegany County Town Clerk Register Hume, 1860, 1870 Fed. Censuses Hume)

Palmer, Andrew Jackson Co. F, 4th NY Heavy Artillery - 8/22/1864 at Hume/1 yr - 25 - 5'5", Dark Complexion, Blue Eyes, Light Hair - 9/1/1864 at Elmira - $500 - Pvt, Pvt - Peeble's Farm, Hatcher's Run, Petersburg, Appomattox - 6/3/1865 Honorable - WIA, shell burst above his head 11/1/1864 at Petersburg, caused neurolgia (damage to his nervous system) - Ephraim & Jane Rail Palmer - INA - 10/15/1839 in Knoxville - Boatman/Lumberman - Boatman - Mariett A. Caryl, married 3/9/1860 in Portage - Suella, Azalia, Celestia, Eugene, Edith, Frank, Clara, Ira - 9/2/1898 - Wiscoy - Present at Lee's surrender. Marched in Grand Review 5/23/1865. (Military & Pension Files, 1865 NYS Census Hume, Fillmore American Legion, Matteson, 1865 Allegany County Town Clerk Register Hume)

Palmer, Flavel Ruthvan Co. C, 104th NY Infantry - 10/9/1861 at Geneseo/3 yrs - 29 - 5'8", Light Complexion, Blue Eyes, Light Hair - 2/28/1862 at Geneseo - No bounty - Pvt, Pvt - No battles - 9/25/1862 Disability/Honorable - INJ, a tree fell on him while on picket duty, 5/24/1862 near Warrenton, VA broke his left clavicle - William (B VT) & Eleanor Knickerbocker (B CT) Palmer -

Stephen, Silas W., Monroe, Jeremiah, Ada, Henry, Calvin, Ellen (Allerton), Laura, Emma - 12/15/1831 in Centerville - Writer of Prose & Verse - Farmer/Assessor/JP - 1st Cynthia Angeline Kellogg, married 8/5/1854 in Warsaw, (Died 3/31/1893), 2nd Salinda Mason Frye Whitney, married 3/30/1895 in Mt. Pleasant, MI (Died 3/24/1913), 3rd Jane Kate Phillips, married 3/2/1914 (also her 3rd marriage) - Florence Ellen, Cyrus Story - 12/11/1919 in Oramel - Oramel Cemetery, Caneadea Township (as Ruthena Palmer) - Military had Flavel as his first name. Named for his maternal grandfather. His paternal grandfather, Humphrey Palmer of Honiton, Devonshire, England, was driven from his estate for supporting the American colonies. The estate, which may have been rented, was later seized by the government. Flavel's sister Ellen was a noted Western poet, most famous for her work, "Poems of the Prairies." He was a student at Leland Academy in Vermont prior to the war. (Military & Pension Files, 1890 Fed. Census Special Schedule Centerville, *Allegany & Its People*, 1865 Allegany County Town Clerk Register Centerville, 1865 NYS Census Centerville, 1850, 1870 Fed. Censuses Centerville)

Palmer, Francis Co.'s C,E,F, Staff, 104th NY Infantry - 10/21/1861 at Geneseo/3 yrs (Re-enlisted 1/4/1864) - 35 - 5'7", Light Complexion, Dark Eyes, Brown Hair - 2/26/1862 - $100 - Pvt, 1st Lt. - Cedar Creek, 2nd Bull Run, South Mountain, Antietam, Wilderness, Spotsylvania, North Anna River, Pamunkey, Totopotomoy, Cold Harbor - 7/17/1865 Honorable - WIA, 9/17/1862 at Antietam, musket ball to left ankle - Humphery & Sally Stacey Palmer (Both B VT) - Marcellus, Marinda, Luke, Sammatha - 6/25/1826 in Centerville - Teacher - Teacher/Lawyer - 1st Amelia B. Vickery, married 5/25/1871 (he divorced her for desertion), 2nd Frances S. Prichard Rockafellow, married 2/3/1879 in Alma, MI - Emma, Blanche - 8/16/1915 in Alma, MI - Alma - His brother Marcellus also served during the war. Promoted Sgt 5/1/1864, QM Sgt 11/2/1864, 1st Sgt 3/23/1863, 5th Sgt 5/1/1862, 1st Lt 6/11/1865. On furlough as of 2/18/1864. (Military & Pension Files, 1865 NYS Census Hume, 1865 Allegany County Town Clerk Register Centerville, 1850 Fed. Census Centerville, 1910 Fed. Census Alma, MI)

Palmer, James Edgar Co. F, 85th NY Infantry - 9/1/1861 at Friendship/3 yrs - 22 - 5'5", Dark Complexion, Grey Eyes, Black Hair - 9/28/1861 at Elmira - No bounty - Pvt, Pvt - No battles - 4/7/1862 Disability/Honorable - Was not a casualty - Willet (B RI) & Mary (B NY) Palmer - Mary, Ada - 1839 (6/6/1841 per headstone) in Granger - Farmer - Carpenter - Nellie M. Strong, married 8/20/1871 in Friendship - Willet - 2/16/1915 in National Soldiers and Sailors Home, Hampton, VA - Mt. Hope Cemetery, Friendship - Palmer was left sick at Meridan Hill Hospital, DC 3/28/1862. One muster card has him as a deserter in May of 1862, but actually he had already been discharged. The Town Clerk said that James Palmer was a surgeon. The State Adjutant General said he was a private, which is correct. There was a John Palmer in the 85th who was a surgeon. He was from MA. (Military & Pension Files, 1865 Allegany County Town Clerk Register Granger, NYS Adjutant General Report 1901, Volume 30, 1850 Fed. Census Wirt)

Palmer, Marcellus Co. F, 4th NY Heavy Artillery - 8/20/1862 at Hume/3 yrs - 38 - 5'9", Light Complexion, Blue Eyes, Dark Hair - 9/29/1862 at Rushford - $50 - Pvt, Pvt - No battles - 1/22/1863 Disability/Honorable - Was not a casualty - Humphrey & Sally Stacey Palmer (Both B VT) - Francis, Marinda, Luke, Sammatha - 8/26/1824 in Centerville - Farmer - Farmer - Mary L. Gardner, married 2/22/1846 in Hume, Francelloct, Lodema, Luerer, Francis - 12/24/1915 in

Stanton, MI - INA - Lodeman & Luerer were twins. Discharged at Fort Ethan Allen. Brother Francis also served during the war. (Military & Pension Files, 1865 Allegany County Town Clerk Register Hume, 1850 Fed. Census Centerville, 1870 Fed. Census Day Township, MI)

Palmer, Ruthvan Flavel See Flavel Ruthvan Palmer. (1865 NYS Census Centerville has first and middle names reversed.)

Parker, Emerson Madison Co. F, 19th NY Cavalry - 8/13/1862 at Oramel/3 yrs - 23 - 5'8", Light Complexion, Blue Eyes, Brown Hair - 9/3/1862 at Portage Station - No bounty - Pvt, Pvt - Deserted House, siege of Suffolk, Manassas Junction, Bristoe's Station, Culpeper Court House, Wilderness, Todd's Tavern, Spotsylvania, North Anna River, Yellow Tavern, Pamunkey, Totopotomoy, Cold Harbor, Trevillian Station, Charles County Court House, before Richmond & Petersburg, New Market, Shepherdstown, Smithfield - 8/30/1864 Honorable/Deceased - KIA, 8/30/1864 at Smithfield - Ira & Polly Rosina Smith Parker (Both B NY) - Mary Ann, Erlindee, Jefferson, Ellen, Jasper N., Lindee - 11/24/1838 at Granger - Farm Laborer - None Deceased - Never Married - None - 8/30/1864 in Smithfield, VA - Weaver Settlement Cemetery, Granger - (Probably a memorial headstone) Promoted to Corp 5/31/1863, reduced to ranks 6/24/1864. Was in Emory G.H. in May, 1864 with intermittent fever. Brothers Erland and Jefferson also served during the war. Listed on Soldiers Monument in Granger. (Military File, 1865 NYS Census Granger, Matteson, *Allegany & Its People*, 1865 Allegany County Town Clerk Register Granger, *History of Allegany County 1879*, 1850, 1860 Fed. Censuses Granger.)

Parker, Erland S. Co. F, 19th NY Cavalry - 1/27/1864 at Burns/3 yrs - 28 - 5'8", Fair Complexion, Blue Eyes, Brown Hair - 1/27/1864 at Elmira - $300 - Pvt, Pvt - Wilderness - 12/3/1864 Disability /Honorable - WIA, gunshot to left hand (lost middle finger) at Wilderness 5/7/1864 - Ira & Polly Rosina Smith Parker (Both B NY) - Mary Ann, Emerson, Jefferson, Ellen, Jasper N., Lindee - 1835 in Allegany County - Boatman - INA - Never Married - None - 8/19/1892 - Weaver Settlement Cemetery, Granger - The 1850 Fed. Census shows Erland (Erlindee) as a female. The 1840 Fed. Census also tends to indicate that Erland was a female. 1880 Fed. Census shows Erland as a male in prison at Auburn, Cayuga County. Brothers Emerson and Jefferson also served during the war. Interestingly, while Erland's bothers Emerson and Jefferson are listed on the Soldier's Monument in Granger, Erland is not. Further on the headstone at Weavers Settlement Cemetery, Emerson and Jefferson are listed as the sons of Ira and Rosina. Erland is just listed. (Military & Pension Files, 1890 Fed. Census Special Schedule Granger, 1850 Fed. Census Granger, 1880 Fed. Census Auburn)

Parker, Jefferson Myron Co. E, 85th NY Infantry - 9/1/1861 at Granger/3 yrs - 24 - INA - 10/10/1861 at Elmira - No bounty - 1st Sgt, 1st Sgt - Defense of DC, siege of Yorktown, Williamsburg, Fair Oaks - 7/23/1862 Honorable/Deceased - POW, captured 5/31/1862 at Fair Oaks, Prison: Libby, Richmond, DD, 7/23/1862 (disease not identified) - Ira & Polly R. Smith Parker (Both B NY) - Mary Ann, Emerson, Erland, Ellen, Jasper N., Lindee - 9/24/1837 in Granger - Farm Laborer - None Deceased - Never Married - None - 7/23/1862 at Richmond, VA (POW) - Memorial Headstone at Weaver Settlement Cemetery, Granger (Probably a memorial headstone) - Listed on Soldiers Monument Granger. Brothers Emerson and Erland also served during the war. (Military File, 1865 NYS Census Granger, *Allegany & Its People*, *History of Allegany County 1879*, 1865 Allegany County Town Clerk Register Granger, Matteson, 1860 Fed. Census Granger)

Parker, Ralph Co. I, 6th NY Cavalry - 8/9/1862 at Caneadea/3 yrs - 32 - INA - 9/12/1862 at NYC - $300 - Pvt, Pvt - Snickerville, Spotsylvania, North Anna River, Yellow Tavern, Pamunkey, Fredericksburg, Chancellorsville, Bristoe's Station - 4/28/1865 Honorable/Deceased - WIA, 10/14/1863 at Bristoe's Station (nature of wound not described in file) DD, 4/28/1865 at Ladies Home Hospital, NYC of pneumonia - George (B NY) & Polly Cloos (B PA) Parker - Jackson, Lucy, Hellen - 4/1830 in Deerfield, PA - Farmer - None Deceased - Never Married - None - 4/28/1865 in NYC (5/10/1865 per Roll of Honor book.) - Pine Grove Cemetery, Fillmore (Was initially buried at Cypress Hills National Cemetery. Re-buried Pine Grove 2/27/1883.) Transferred to 145 Co. 2nd Battalion, VRC 12/7/1864. Re-enlisted as a Veteran Volunteer November - December 1863. January to June 1863 was regimental wagon master. Was in Jarvis Hosp. in Baltimore 7/9/1863 with a hernia. Promoted from ranks 10/1/1862. (Must have been reduced at some time since he is listed as a private at death.) Some records contradict each other. (Military File, Allegany County Web Site, Matteson, 1865 Allegany County Town Clerk Register Caneadea, 1860 Fed. Census Caneadea, Roll of Honor)

Parkes, Jackson Andrew (name was most likely Andrew Jackson Parks) Co. E, 85th NY Infantry - 9/1/1861 at Granger/3 yrs - 21 - 5'7", Light Complexion, Black Eyes, Dark Hair - 10/10/1861 at Elmira - No bounty - Pvt, Pvt - defense of DC, siege of Yorktown, Williamsburg, Fair Oaks - 1/31/1863 Disability/Honorable - Was not a casualty - William M. & Betsey Mathews Parks (Both B NY) - Nancy Ann, William M., Joel, Nancy E., John H., Hannah - 5/7/1840 in Nunda - Farmer - Farmer/Laborer - 1st Jennette K. Harwood (She was 16. Divorced 11/5/1873. She was convicted of adultery.), 2nd Mary A. Schenick, married 10/3/1886 in Perry - Milo E. - 11/22/1907 in Perry - Perry - Military Index has name as Jackson Parker. Military file as Jackson Parkes. His disability discharge was due to a hernia which he acquired prior to enlistment. Most documents have him as Parks. Was married in Perry as Andrew Parkes. (Military & Pension Files, 1865 Allegany County Town Clerk Register Granger, Matteson, *History of Allegany County 1879*, NYS Adjutant General Report 1901, Volume 30, 1850 Fed. Census Granger, 1900 Fed. Census Perry)

Parks, Andrew Jackson See Jackson Andrew Parkes. Actually Andrew Jackson Parks may be the correct name. (1865 NYS Census Granger.)

Parks, John See John H. Pasko. (*Allegany & Its People*.)

Parks, William H. Co. F, 5th NY Cavalry - 8/30/1861 at Oramel/3 yrs - 42 - 5'8", Light Complexion, Blue Eyes, Brown Hair - 9/21/1861 at NYC - $50 - Corp, Corp - No battles - 4/30/1862 Disability/Honorable - INJ, 1/1/1862 at Poolesville, was thrown from his horse, injured his back and raptured his left groin when horse fell on him - INA - INA - 1819 or 20 in Bradford, PA - Farmer - Pedlar/Drayman - 1st Mary?, 2nd Eliza A. Jackson, married 6/24/1877 in Bloomfield, MI - Seely?, Elizabeth?, Lilly, Anna, Etha - 5/29/1887 in Pontiac, MI - Pontiac - Disability discharge due to chronic bronchitis. Not sure of his connection to C-H-G. Matteson book has him from Granger. (Military & Pension Files, Matteson, 1860 Fed. Census Caneadea, 1870 Fed. Census Pontiac, MI)

Parsons, Walter Scott Co. E, 85th NY Infantry - 9/1/1861 at Granger/3 yrs (Re-enlisted 1/1/1864) - 18 - 5'5", Light Complexion, Blue Eyes, Brown Hair - 11/22/1861 at Elmira - $400 - Pvt, Pvt - defense of DC, siege of Yorktown, Plymouth - 6/27/1865 Honorable - POW, captured 4/20/1864 at Plymouth, Prison: Richmond, paroled 3/3/1865 at NE Ferry, NC - William & Dorey Ditawire Parsons - (Both B England) - Ann P., Emma, Eli, Franklin, Adalise - 7/27/1844 in Granger - Farmer - Farmer - 1st Anna Thayer Welsh, married 5/1/1867 in Stevens Point, WI, divorced 3/31/1884, 2nd Cecelia Everson Welsh, married 5/7/1884 in Almond, WI (her first husband had also been in the war) - Lizzie, Delwork, Everett, Emily, Lottie - 12/5/1920 in National Soldiers Home, WI - Probably Plover, WI - Was in Ft. Monroe Hospital following parole, then to Parole Camp in MD, and then to NYC for discharge. (Military & Pension Files, 1865 NYS Census Granger, *History of Allegany County 1879*, Matteson, 1865 Allegany County Town Clerk Register Granger, 1860 Fed. Census Granger, 1900 Fed. Census Plover, WI)

Pasco, John Henry (Pasko) (John Parks) Co. F, 85th NY Infantry - 8/26/1861 at Black Creek/3 yrs - 19 - 5'8", Dark Complexion, Black Eyes, Brown Hair - 7/7/1861 at Elmira - No bounty - Pvt, Pvt - defense of DC, siege of Yorktown, Williamsburg, Fair Oaks - 10/28/1863 Disability/Honorable - Was not a casualty - William & Elizabeth Pasco (Both B England) - Azan, Edwin, Mary, William, Daniel, Jeremiah - 12/15/1841 in Allegany County - Farmer - Farmer - Mary Craig, married 10/21/1891 in Groton, SD (She was 18, he was 50) - Ethel, Laura, Caroline D. - 12/29/1931 at Owosso, MI - Hill Crest Cemetery, Owosso, MI - Pasco is listed as John Parks on the Soldiers Monument in Granger. The NYS Adjutant General Report 1901, Volume 30 carries him as Parks, but indicates "Also borne as Pasko". He was also carried as John H. Parks by the 85th. His signature could be interpreted as Parks, unless one looks closely. But it is odd that Granger men from his company did not know his correct name. Even though there is no indication that he ever lived in Granger, he and his parents did live close by. Disability discharge was based on chronic hepatitis and an enlarged spleen. Also served with Co. F, 8th U.S. Veteran Infantry 4/5/1865 to 4/4/1866. (Military & Pension Files, *Allegany & Its People*, NYS Adjutant General Report 1901, Volume 30, 1860 Fed. Census New Hudson, 1900 Fed. Census MI Owosso)

Paul, William H. Not from the C-H-G area. His enlistment in Co. F, 1st NY Cavalry was credited to Hume Township when it paid his enlistment bonus of $400. (1865 Allegany County Town Clerk Register Hume)

Peck, Oren Co. D, 4th NY Heavy Artillery - 8/13/1862 at Rochester/3 yrs - 35 - 5'11", Florid Complexion, Blue Eyes, Black Hair - 8/13/1862 at Rochester - $100 - Pvt, Pvt - Cold Harbor, siege of Petersburg, Weldon RR, Ream's Station, Peeble's Farm, Hatcher's Run, fall of Petersburg - Appomattox - 6/3/1865 Honorable - Was not a casualty - Daniel (B RI) & Thursey Cooley (B CT) Peck - Tompkins, Crissta, Charlotte, Gilbert - 4/27/1827 in Hume - Day Laborer - Hotel Keeper - Emily J. Kingsley, married 1/29/1854 - Belle Rose (married Menzer J. Doud) - 1893 - Church Street Wiscoy - Present at Lee's surrender. Marched in Grand Review 5/23/1865. Had a hernia and smallpox while in the service. Charter Member of Burnside G.A.R. Post 237, proprietor of Pecks Hotel in Wiscoy after the war. (Military & Pension Files, 1890 Fed. Census Special Schedule Hume, *Allegany & Its People*, Allegany County Web Site, 1865 NYS Census Hume, Fillmore American Legion, 1865 Allegany County Town Clerk Register Hume, Matteson, 1850, 1880 Fed. Censuses Hume)

Pendergast, Thomas Co. F, 19th NY Cavalry - 8/9/1862 at Hume/3 yrs - 22 - INA - 9/3/1862 at Portage Station - $50 - Pvt, Corp - Deserted House, siege of Suffolk, Franklin, Manassas Junction - 10/17/1863 Honorable/Deceased - KIA, Manassas Junction (Centerville, VA) on 10/17/1863 - Patrick & Mary Pendergast (Both B Ireland) - INA - 1839 or 40 at Ireland - Farm Laborer - None Deceased - Never Married - None - 10/17/1863 at Centerville, VA (KIA) - On the battlefield. In 1865 men buried at Manassas battlefield were disinterred and moved to the Rose Garden section of Arlington National Cemetery. In most cases, they were re-buried with headstones marked "Unknown". - Promoted Corporal 1/1/1863. (Military & Pension Files, 1865 NYS Census Hume, Allegany County Web Site, Book *History of Allegany County 1879*, 1860 Fed. Census Hume)

Perkins, Elisha Ogilvie Co. C, 104 NY Infantry - 11/20/1861 at Geneseo/3 yrs - 32 - 5'6", Dark Complexion, Dark Eyes, Black Hair - 2/26/1862 at Geneseo - No bounty - Pvt, Pvt - No battles - 10/15/1862 Disability/Honorable - INJ, was sick with "fistula in ano" and was sent to the hospital on a flat bed train car. It was raining and he was left on the train for hours without being able to move, causing a serious injury to his spine, 8/1862 at Falls Church, VA - Elisha & Mary Orswell Perkins - INA - 5/29/1829 in Barnard, VT - Laborer/Farmer - Farmer - 1st Clarissa Haskins (Died 2/17/ 1869), 2nd Caroline (Carrie) Lucinda Humphrey Watrous, married 10/14/1871 in Allegan, MI (a divorcee) - Julia, Frank T. Charles T. Robert L. - 1/4/1900 in Allegan - Allegan - Disability discharge due to spinal problems. (Military & Pension Files, 1865 NYS Census Centerville, 1865 Allegany County Town Clerk Register Centerville, 1860 Fed. Census Centerville)

Perkins, John R. Not from the C-H-G area. Originally served with Co. I, 16th Massachusetts Infantry. His re-enlistment in Co. F, 16th VRC was credited to Hume Township when it paid his re-enlistment bonus of $500. (1865 Allegany County Town Clerk Register Hume)

Perry, Ebenezer B. Co. C, 194th NY Infantry - 3/29/1865 at Hume/1 yr - 19 - 5'7", Fair Complexion, Hazel Eyes, Brown Hair, had tattoo "E.B. Perry" on left arm - 3/29/1865 at Geneseo - $800 - Pvt, Pvt - No battles - 5/3/1865 Honorable - Was not a casualty - Peter (B Canada) & Roxey Smith (B NH) Perry - Jane A., Albert, Peter, Jr. - 8/12/1845 in Mt. Morris - Laborer - Boatman/RR Engineer/Odd Job Laborer - Elizabeth Palmer, married 5/8/1865 - None - 9/4/1926 in Wiscoy - Wiscoy - Originally enlisted in Co. F, 104th NY Infantry 1/3/1862. Was discharged for being underage. Had claimed he was 18, was 16. (Military & Pension Files, 1890 Fed. Census Special Schedule Hume, 1865 NYS Census Hume, Matteson, *History of Allegany County 1879*, 1865 Allegany County Town Clerk Register Hume, Fillmore American Legion, 1850 Fed. Census Mt. Morris, 1900 Fed. Census Hume)

Peterson, Peter C. Not from the C-H-G area. Originally served with Co. F, 15th New Jersey Infantry. His re-enlistment in Co. F, 16th VRC was credited to Hume Township which paid his re-enlistment bonus of $500. (1865 Allegany County Town Clerk Register Hume.)

Pettee, Nelson A. Co. A, 19th NY Cavalry 8/7/1862 at Pike/3 yrs - 28 - 5'11", Light Complexion, Blue Eyes, Dark Hair, ankylosis of joints of fingers on right hand - 9/3/1862 at Portage Station - No bounty - Pvt, Pvt - Deserted House, siege of Suffolk - 8/28/1863 Disability/Honorable - Was not a casualty - Ebenezer (B MA) & Sally Whitney (B NH) Pettee - Joshua, William H. - 9/14/1834 in Pike - Day Laborer/Farmer - Farmer/Carpenter/Contractor/Builder - 1st Catherine Olin (Died 7/26/1867 at Mills Mills), 2nd Julia Burnell (Died 5/10/1887 at Denver, CO.), 3rd Clara M. Dodge Kinsley, married 11/6/1889 in Wiscoy - Frank A., Julie (Lulu) E. (Yorks), William, also adopted Fred Van Dyke - 6/27/1909 in Wiscoy - Wiscoy - Accidently shot right hand 11/1/1862 at Suffolk. Lost 3rd finger. Pension board claimed this was not in the line of duty, and maybe not even while he was in the service. A. Dr. Kneeland claimed he shot his finger off to get out of the service. Nevertheless, he still received his pension. *Allegany & Its People* says he enlisted in Co. A, 150th NY Infantry. No evidence to support this. Charter Member and Officer of Burnside G.A.R. Post 237. (Military & Pension Files, 1890 Fed.Census Special Schedule Hume, *Allegany & Its People*, Fillmore American Legion, 1860 Fed. Census Pike, 1880 Fed. Census Hume)

Pettys, Edwin Jacob Co. F, 4th NY Heavy Artillery - 12/23/1863 at Hume/3 yrs - 36 - 5'5", Light Complexion, Blue Eyes, Brown Hair - 1/4/1863 at Elmira - $300 - Pvt, Pvt - Ream's Station, Peeble's Farm, Hatcher's Run (Detached to 6th Corps for quite a time and may have participated in battles there.) - 9/26/1865 Honorable - Was not a casualty - Jacob & Hepsibiah Sallesley Pettys - INA - 9/17/1827 in Easton, Washington County - Farmer - Farmer - Mary Crowell, married in Hume - Minnie, Emma, Elbert E. - 3/20/1907 in MI - INA - Military files spell last name Petteys. Marched in Grand Review 5/23/1865. (Military & Pension Files, Allegany County Web Site, 1865 NYS Census Hume, 1860 Fed. Census Hume)

Phillips, Andrew A. At least one source document indicates that Phillips served in the military during the war. No evidence of such service has been located. (1865 NYS Census Hume, Matteson, Fillmore American Legion)

Phipps, William Dunn Co. H, 19th NY Cavalry - 8/13/1862 at Short Tract/3 yrs - 29 - 5'8", Dark Complexion, Blue Eyes, Dark Hair - 9/3/1862 at Portage Station - $100 - Pvt, Pvt - Deserted House, siege of Suffolk, Franklin, Manassas Junction, Bristoe's Station, Culpeper, New Market, Shepherdstown, Winchester, Fisher's Hill, New Market, Port Republic, Cedar Creek, Berryville, Gordonsville, Dinwiddie, Five Forks, Appomattox - 6/30/1865 Honorable - Was not a casualty - Joseph & Mary Houser Phipps (Both B PA) - Jonathan, Sarah, Henry - 7/17/1833 in Nunrey? (Nunda?), NY - Farmer - Farmer - Sophia J. Walbridge, married 6/12/1866 in Allen - Jesse M., Fred L., Roy R., Verna A. - 2/17/1900 in Short Tract - Short Tract - Sick in DC hospital July and August 1864. Had malaria fever November 1862. Marched in the Grand Review 5/23/1865. (Military & Pension Files, 1890 Fed. Census Special Schedule Granger, 1865 Allegany County Town Clerk Register Granger, 1865 NYS Census Granger, Granger American Legion, Matteson, *History of Allegany County 1879*, 1860, 1870 Fed. Censuses Granger)

Pierson, Egbert Benson Co. F, 4th NY Heavy Artillery - 8/29/1862/3 yrs - 29 - 5'5", Dark

Complexion, Dark Eyes, Black Hair - 9/12/1862 at NYC - $50 - Pvt, Corp - Wilderness, Spotsylvania, North Anna River, Totopotomoy, Cold Harbor, siege of Petersburg, Weldon RR - 8/20/1864 Honorable/Deceased - DD, 8/20/1864 at City Point, VA of enteritis - George (Jesse) & Hannah Slusser Pierson (Both B NY) - Lucinda B., Mary L., James, Everett - 1/1/1832 in Avon - Farmer - None Deceased - Minerva Cain, married 6/15/1859 in Nunda - INA - 8/20/1864 in City Point, VA. - City Point National Cemetery - Question as to whether his father's name was George or Jessie. Both names appear in different documents. (Military & Pension Files, 1865 Allegany County Town Clerk Register Hume, 1855 NYS Census Hume, 1860 Fed Census Hume, *Roll of Honor*)

Pitt, George Washington Co. E, 85th NY Infantry - 9/1/1861 at Granger/3 yrs (Re-enlisted 1/1/1864)- 24 - 6'3", Fair Complexion, Bluish Grey Eyes, Brown Hair - 10/25/1861 at Elmira - No bounty - Pvt, 2nd LT. - defense of DC, siege of Yorktown, Williamsburg, Fair Oaks, before Richmond, Plymouth - 3/24/1865 Honorable - WIA, gunshot to left foot and knee at Fair Oaks, 5/31/1862, POW, captured 4/20/1864 at Plymouth, NC, Prison: Darrien, GA. escaped 2/15/1865 - William & Elizabeth Vincent Pitt (Both B England) - Jane (Whitcomb), Eliza (Fletcher), Mary, Anna, Emma, William H., Elizabeth (Disbrow), James, John S. - 4/20/1835 in Granger - Farmer/Ambrotype Artist - Artist/Watchmaker/Jeweler - Mary Lena Grant, married 5/18/1869 at Wellsville - Mamie Vincent, Maude Victoria - 4/28/1921 in Victoria Hospital, London, Canada - Woodland Cemetery, London, Canada - Promoted to Sgt 10/10/1861, 1st Sgt 11/1/1862, 2nd Lt 1/17/1863. He was detached to the Balloon Corps May, June, 1862. The fact that he was an artist, apparently both drawing and an early photographer, may be the reason he was detached to the Balloon Corps. He started out in the jewelry business as a traveling salesman for H. Davis & Co. of NYC. One of his daughters married into the wealthy Darch family of London, Canada. He is buried in the Darch family plot. He was a Founding Member of London's Hannibal Hamlin G.A.R. Post 652 and a member of the Independent Order of Foresters. His brother John also served during the war. (Military & Pension Files, 1865 NYS Census Granger, *History of Allegany County 1879*, Matteson, Granger American Legion, 1865 Allegany County Town Clerk Register Granger, *Allegany & Its People*, 1860 Fed. Census Granger, 1870 Fed. Census Cuba, Letter from Thomas Brooks of Gravenhurst, Canada)

Pitt, John Samuel Co. F, 104th NY Infantry - 1/29/1861 at Granger/3 yrs (re-enlisted 2/27/1864) - 19 - 5'11", Dark Complexion, Blue Eyes, Brown Hair - 2/26/1862 at Geneseo - No bounty - Musician - Musician - Cedar Creek, 2nd Bull Run, South Mountain, Antietam, Fredericksburg, Chancellorsville, Gettysburg, Bristoe's Station, Wilderness, Spotsylvania, North Anna River, Pamunkey, Totopotomoy, Cold Harbor, Bethesda Church, Petersburg, Weldon RR, Gravelly Run, Five Forks, Appomattox, (One document says he participated in 43 battles and skirmishes.) - 7/17/1865 Honorable - WIA, He damaged his knee when he tripped on something and fell down a bank into the river charging the enemy lines 5/23/1864 at North Anna River, VA. Some muster cards indicate that he was a POW, captured 8/9/1863 at Rappahannock. Prison: not listed, exchanged 2/24/1864, 1865. Other muster cards indicate he was present with his regiment during the August - January period - William & Elizabeth Vincent Pitt (Both B England) - Jane (Whitcomb), Eliza (Fletcher), Mary, Anna, Emma, William H., Elizabeth (Disbrow), James, George W. - 10/1/8142 in Granger, Farmer - Framer/Bridge Builder, I & St. Louis RR - Lucinda

Jane "Jennie" Drake Ralston, married 1/19/1869 in Granger - INA - 10/21/1929 in Fillmore - Short Tract - Present at Lee's surrender. Marched in Grand Review 5/23/1865. Father William was a Science Professor, brother William was also a teacher. Brother George served during the war. (Military & Pension Files, 1890 Fed. Census Special Schedule Granger, *Allegany & Its People*, 1865 Allegany County Town Clerk Register Granger, 1865 NYS Census Granger, *History of Allegany County 1879*, Granger American Legion, 1860, 1910 Fed. Censuses Granger)

Platt, Nathan Co. E, 85th NY Infantry - 9/1/1861 at Angelica/3 yrs - 24 - 5'8", Light Complexion, Blue Eyes, Red Hair - 12/2/1861 at Elmira - No bounty - 2nd Lt., 2nd Lt. - defense of DC, Fair Oaks, before Richmond - 7/29/1862 Honorable - Was not a casualty - Joseph & Alvira Platt (Both B CT) - Frances H., Margaret, Caroline A., Eliza, Nancy C. - 1836/37 in NYS - Probably working for father, a merchant - Dry Goods Merchant - Myra Ella Porter, married 10/31/1878 in Muskegon, MI - Ella, Richard, 5/13/1895 in Chicago, IL or Muskegon, MI - INA - He received an early discharge by "Order of the President." No reason cited for early out. Was on detached service recruiting in January, February, and March 1862. He was a widower by 1880. (Military & Pension Files, Matteson, Granger American Legion, 1850 Fed. Census Granger, 1860 Fed. Census Angelica, 1880 Fed. Census Muskegon, MI)

Plumb, Marion C. Co. D, 154th NY Infantry - 8/26/1862 at Franklinville/3 yrs - 28 - 5'5", Light Complexion, Blue Eyes, Light Hair - 9/24/1862 at Jamestown - No bounty - Pvt, Pvt - No battles - 11/24/1862 Honorable/Deceased - DD, 11/24/1862 at Findley Hospital, DC of pneumonia - Father INA, Elizabeth Plumb (B VT) - INA - 1833 or 34 in Allegany County - Farmer - None Deceased - Sara, married 1/26/1860 - Roman - 11/24/1862 in Findley Hospital, DC - Soldier's and Sailors Home Cemetery, DC - Sarah was born in Wales. (Military & Pension Files, 1865 NYS Census Centerville, 1850 Fed. Census Hume, 1860 Fed. Census Rushford, *Roll of Honor*)

Poole, Charles Wesley (Pool) Co. F, 33rd NY Infantry - 5/13/1861 at Nunda/2 yrs - 19 - 6', Light Complexion - 5/22/1861 at Elmira - No bounty - Pvt, Pvt - South Mountain, Antietam, Fredericksburg - 6/2/1863 Honorable - Was not a casualty - Charles & Emily Childs Poole (Both B MA) Edwin, David, George, Margrette - 8/2/1838 in Buffalo (Some records say 2/6/1837) - Watch Repairer - Blacksmith/Jeweler - Never Married - None - 8/3/1911 in Bath Soldiers and Sailors Home - Bath National Cemetery - He deserted 9/28/1861 at Fort Ethan Allen, returned 9/1/1862 and forfeited all back pay and allowance, plus one months pay. Charge of desertion was changed to AWOL in 1887. He suffered a sunstroke while in service. Brothers Edwin and George also served during the war. (Military & Pension Files, 1865 NYS Census Hume, 1890 Fed. Census Special Schedule Hume, 1865 Allegany County Town Clerk Register Hume, 1850, 1880 Fed. Censuses Hume)

Poole, Edwin Chester Co. C, 104th NY Infantry - 10/21/1861 at Geneseo/3 yrs - 31 - 5'10', Dark Complexion, Dark Brown Eyes, Black Hair - 2/26/1862 at Geneseo - No bounty - Pvt, Pvt - No battles - 6/18/1863 Deserted - Was not a casualty - Chester & Emily Childs Poole (Both B MA) - David, George, Margrette, Charles - 8/21/1830 in Pike - Blacksmith/Mechanic - Blacksmith - 1st Mary, 2nd Harriet - Augusta, Hattie - 1/7/1916 - Church Street Cemetery Wiscoy - He spent part of his time as Brigade armorer. He had debilitas and sciatica. He was in Alexandria, VA hospital, then a hospital steamer to NY, and then Ft. Wood Hospital, Bedloes Island. He deserted from Ft. Wood Hospital. In 1889 he petitioned to have desertion charge removed. Petition was denied. 1890 Fed. Census Special Schedule says he suffered from a gun shot wound. There is no other evidence of such a wound. Brothers George & Charles also served during the war. (Military & Pension Files, 1890 Fed. Census Special Schedule Hume, 1865 Allegany County Town Clerk Register Hume, Fillmore American Legion, 1855 NYS Census Hume, 1860, 1870, 1910 Fed. Censuses Hume)

Poole, George Morel Co. F, 33rd NY Infantry - 7/4/1861 at Elmira/2 yrs - 18 - 5'9", Light Complexion, Black Eyes, Black Hair - 7/6/1861 at Elmira - No bounty - Pvt, Pvt - siege of Yorktown, Williamsburg, Ft. Magruder, Gaine's Mill, Malvern Hill, 2nd Bull Run, South Mountain, Antietam, Fredericksburg, - 6/2/1863 Honorable - Was not a casualty - Chester & Emily Childs Poole (Both B MA) - Edwin, David, Margrette, Charles - 1844 in Pike - Painter - INA - INA - INA - 1/1/1881 in Angelica - Church Street Cemetery Wiscoy - Also served with 2nd NY Mounted Rifles, see below. He deserted 1/2/1863 at White Oak Church, Falmouth, VA and returned 4/1/1863. At his death he was an inmate in the County House. Brothers Edwin and Charles also served during the war. (Military File, 1865 NYS Census Hume, Fillmore American Legion, Matteson, *History of Allegany County 1879*, Allegany County Web Site, 1865 Allegany County Town Clerk Register Hume, 1850, 1860 Fed. Censuses Hume, 1880 Fed. Census Angelica)

Poole, George Morel Co. B, 2nd NY Mounted Rifles - 12/12/1863 at Hume/3 yrs - 20 5'9", Light Complexion, Black Eyes, Black Hair - 1/2/1864 at Fort Porter, Buffalo - $700 - Pvt, Corp - Spotsylvania, North Anna River, Pamunkey, Totopotomoy, Hanover Court House, Cold Harbor, Bethesda Church, siege of Petersburg, Weldon RR, Hatcher's Run, Dinwiddie, Five Forks, Appomattox - 8/10/1865 - Was not a casualty. Promoted Corporal 9/1/1864. Sick in McDougal Hospital July to September 1864. Present at Lee's surrender. Brothers Edwin and Charles also served during the war. Also served with 33rd NY Infantry, see above. Also see above for personal information and sources of information.

Powell, Alonzo Smith Co. B, 2nd NY Mounted Rifles - 1/4/1864 at Centerville/3 yrs - 22 - 5'5", Light Complexion, Blue Eyes, Light Hair - 1/4/1864 at Ft. Porter, Buffalo - $50 - Pvt, Corp - Spotsylvania, North Anna River, Pamunkey, Totopotomoy, Cold Harbor, Weldon RR, Pegram's Farm, Hatcher's Run, Weldon RR, Dinwiddie, Five Forks, Appomattox - 8/10/1865 Honorable - Israel & Ruth Davis Powell (Both B NY) - Byron, Caroline, Henry, Alvah - 1841 or 43 in China - Farmer - Farmer/Laborer - Rosalette (1849 -1949) - INA - 1935 per Headstone - Caldwell Cemetery, Centerville - Present at Lee's surrender. Was in Camp Hospital with diarrhea, June, July, August 1864. (Military File (Pension file lost at V.A.), 1865 NYS Census Centerville, *History of Allegany County 1879*, Matteson, Centerville American Legion, 1865 Allegany County Town Clerk Register Centerville, 1860 Fed. Census Centerville, 1910 Fed. Census Eagle)

Powell, Byron M. At least one source document indicates that Byron served in the military during the war. No evidence of such service has been located. A Myron B. Powell served with Co. L, 2nd NY Mounted Rifles, but the information in his file shows no connection to the C-H-G area.

Pratt, Eugene M. Co. F, 5th NY Cavalry - 9/18/1861 at China/3 yrs (Re-enlisted 2/20/1864) - 21 - 5'8", Light Complexion, Grey Eyes, Brown Hair - 9/21/1861 at NYC - $100 - Pvt, Duty Sgt - New Market, Port Republic, Orange County Court House, Aldie, New Baltimore, Hanover, PA, Hagerstown, Gettysburg, Culpeper Court House, Hay Market, Ellis Ford, skirmish on Rapidan, North Anna River, Pamunkey, Totopotomoy, Cold Harbor, Ream's Station, Berryville, Dinwiddie, Five Forks, Appomattox - 7/19/1865 Honorable - POW, captured 8/2/1862 at Orange County Court House, Prison: Richmond, paroled, WIA, 3/4/1864 at Ellis Ford suffered 8 flesh wounds. Was hit by 3 musket balls and 5 buck shot wounds, primarily to left thigh and leg. Was in Armory Square Hosp, DC for treatment , POW, captured 9/1/1864 at Berryville, Prison: Richmond, paroled Varina, VA 9/24/1864 - Otis (B VT) & Mary (B MA) Pratt - Orsemus, Rosina - 1/1844 in Eagle - Farmer - Farmer - Mary A. Battles, married 10/6/1870 in Castile - Fred E., Edith L.- 11/30/1903 in Wiscoy - East Koy Cemetery, Lamont Road - Present at Lee's surrender. Marched in Grand Review 5/23/ 1865. (Military & Pension Files, 1890 Fed. Census Special Schedule Hume, Fillmore American Legion, 1860 Fed. Census Wethersfield, 1880 Fed. Census - Granger, 1900 Fed. Census Hume)

Preston, Henry N. Co. D/I, 14th NY Heavy Artillery - 9/12/1863 at Dansville/3 yrs - 24 - INA - 9/12/1863 at Rochester - No bounty - Pvt, Corp - Wilderness, Spotsylvania - WIA, 5/12/1864 at Spotsylvania, gunshot to right thigh - Henry N. & Louisa B. Preston (Both B Ireland) - INA - 1838 in Fowlerville, Wyoming County - Farmer - Farmer - 1st Carrie Hay, 2nd Adell Kinney, married 9/5/1863 - Frank, William, Janice, Frederick, Emery, Clarence - 1902 per Headstone - Holy Cross Cemetery, Fillmore - Deserted Sept. to Dec.1863, fined $25.00. Served with 14th Co. 2nd Battalion, VRC, from 8/26/1865 to 9/16/1865. Lived in both Hume Township and Fillmore after war per Pension. Burnside G.A.R. Post 237 Marker at grave. (Military & Pension Files, Matteson, 1860 Fed. Census Ossian, 1880,1900 Fed. Censuses Allen)

Prior, David (Pryor) Co. D, 64th NY Infantry 9/13/1861 at Rushford/3 yrs - 22 - 5'9", Dark Complexion, Blue Eyes, Dark Hair - 9/24/1861 at Elmira - No bounty - Pvt, Color Corp - siege of Yorktown, Fair Oaks, Gaines Mill, Savage Station, Malvern Hill, Antietam, Fredericksburg, Chancellorsville, Gettysburg, Wilderness, Spotsylvania, North Anna River, Pamunkey, Totopotomoy, Cold Harbor, Petersburg, Reams Station - 12/21/1864 Honorable/Deceased- WIA, 6/1/1862 at Fair Oaks, gunshot wound to head, WIA, 6/22/1864, gunshot to head at Petersburg, POW, captured 8/25/1864 at Reams Station, Prison: Salisbury, DD, 12/21/1864 at Salisbury, NC prison of diarrhea - Ormand (B NY) & Cynthia Elis Cultan Prior - Elisha, A. & Mary A. - 3/5/1841 in Shawneetown, IL - Miller - None Deceased - Never Married - None - 12/21/1864 in Salisbury, NC Prison (POW) - Probably Salisbury National Cemetery - Half brother Elisha also served during the war. Military file says he was born at Farmerville, Cattaraugus County, IL is correct. (Military File, Medical Card File, 1865 NYS Census Hume, *History of Allegany County 1879*, Matteson, 1850 Fed. Census Wash. Twp, PA, 1860 Fed. Census - Farmerville, 1865 Allegany County Town Clerk Register Caneadea)

Prior, Elisha Co. D, 64th NY Infantry - 1011/1862 at Rushford/3 yrs - 18 - 5'4", Dark Complexion,

Hazel Eyes, Brown Hair - 10/19/1862 at Elmira - No bounty - Pvt, Pvt - siege of Yorktown, Fair Oaks, Gaine's Mill, Savage Station, Chancellorsville, Gettysburg, Bristoe's Run - 7/24/1863 Disability/Honorable (but died of service related diseases in 1864)- POW, captured 6/30/1862 at Savage Station, Prison: Richmond, paroled at City Point, VA 8/3/1862, DD, 4/5/1864 at Caneadea after discharge for several service acquired medical problems: inflammatory rheumatism, hepatitis, & scrofula diathesis - Ormand (B NY) & Elizabeth Berry Wold (B PA) Prior - David A. Mary A. - 2/11/1844 or 45 in Clarion County, PA - Farmer - None Deceased - Never Married - None - 4/5/1864 in Caneadea - Caneadea - Was probably underage when he volunteered. Half brother David also served during the war. (Military & Pension Files, 1865 NYS Census Hume, *History of Allegany County 1879*, Matteson, 1850 Fed. Census, Wash Twp, PA, 1865 Allegany County Town Clerk Register Caneadea, 1860 Fed. Census Farmerville)

Purdy, Augustus F. Co. F, 4th NY Heavy Artillery - 9/11/1862 at Centerville/3 yrs - 38 - 5'9", Light Complexion, Blue Eyes, Light Hair - 9/15/1862 at NYC - No bounty - Pvt, Pvt - Wilderness, Spotsylvania, North Anna River, Totopotomoy, Cold Harbor, siege of Petersburg, Weldon RR, Ream's Station, Hatcher's Run, also served with 2nd Army Corps as a stretcher bearer - 6/3/1865 Honorable - Was not a casualty - INA - INA - 6/24/1823 in Elbridge - Farmer - Farmer - 1st Mary Jane Horton (died 10/9/1855), 2nd Celia Amanda Butler, married 3/18/1856 in Caneadea - Mary, Jane, Elbert A., Ellen, Frank, Fred - 12/13/1909 in Fillmore - Pine Grove Cemetery, Fillmore - Marched in Grand Review 5/23/1865. (Military & Pension Files, 1890 Fed. Census Special Schedule Hume, 1865 NYS Census Hume, Fillmore American Legion, Matteson, 1860, 1870 Fed. Censuses Hume)

Quinn, Patrick Co. C, 194th NY Infantry - Drafted 1864 per Town Clerk at Hume/1 yr - 24 - 5'7", Fair Complexion, Black Eyes, Black Hair - 3/29/1865 at Elmira - $800 - Pvt, Pvt - No battles - 5/3/1865 Honorable - Was not a casualty - James & Bridget Clark Quinn (Both B Ireland) - Thomas, Mary, Bridget, Ann, James, William, Ellen - 1840 or 41 in Ireland - Lock Tender/Farmer - Laborer - INA - INA - INA - INA - 1890 Special Schedule says he served with Co. A, 49th NY Infantry from 8/25/1861 to 6/16/1866. No documents found to support that information. (1890 Fed. Census Special Schedule Centerville, 1865 Allegany County Town Clerk Register Hume, *History of Allegany County 1879*, 1860 Fed. Censuses Hume)

Randall, Abijah Co. E, 19th NY Cavalry - 8/4/1862 at Wellsville/3 yrs - 24 - 5'9", Light Complexion, Blue Eyes, Brown Hair - 9/3/1862 at Portage Station - No bounty - Pvt, Pvt - Jamison Forest & Jackson, NC - 11/11/1862 Honorable - Was not a casualty - Orville (B NY) & Betsey Jones Randall - Rosilla, Nancy, Harrison, Amanda, Elias - 11/3/1837 in Hume - Farmer - INA - Mary Buchanan, married 4/1866 - None - 12/9/1916 in Soldiers Home, Orting, WA - INA - Was discharged from the 19th on 11/11/1862 to allow enlistment in Battery H, 4th U.S. Artillery, see below. Brother Elias also served during the war. One muster card spells name Randle. Was divorced by 1880. (Military & Pension Files, 4th U.S. Artillery Enlistment Register, 1865 Allegany County Town Clerk Register Alma, 1850 Fed. Census Angelica, 1860 Fed. Census Alma, 1880 Fed. Census Alma, 1910 Fed. Census Tacoma, WA)

Randall, Abijah Co. C, 4th U.S. Artillery - 11/11/1862 at Suffolk, VA/Balance of 3 yrs - 25 - 5'9",

Sallow Complexion, Grey Eyes, Brown Hair - 11/11/1862 at Suffolk - No bounty - Pvt, Pvt - Stone River, Chickamauga, defense of DC - 8/11/1865 near Richmond - Was not a casualty - Also served with Co. E, 19th NY Cavalry, see above. Also see above for personal information and sources of information.

Randall, Elias Co. K, 160th NY Infantry - 8/29/1862 at Alma/3 yrs - 20 - 5'7", Dark Complexion, Hazel Eyes, Brown Hair - 11/21/1862 at Auburn - $100 - Pvt, Pvt - Gunboat Cotton, Port Hudson, Sabine Cross Roads - 11/1/1865 Honorable - Was not a casualty - Orville(B NY) & Betsey Jones Randall - Rosilla, Nancy, Harrison, Abijah, Amanda - 1/21/1842 in Hume - Farmer - Farm Laborer - Alice A. - Ernest B., Vernon A., Stephen J., Silas A., Pearl?, Virginia? - 5/22/1929 in Palo Alto, CA - Grand Army Plot, Alta Mesa Cemetery, Palo Alto - Marched in Grand Review 5/24, 1865. March - April, 1863 hospital at Brasher, LA, September - October 1863 St. Louis hospital, New Orleans, LA, July - August, 1864 hospital at Baton Rouge, LA. Received a 50 day furlough 9/27/1864. Went home to NY. Also listed as Elias Randel. Brother Abijah also served during the war. (Military File, 1865 Allegany County Town Clerk Register Alma, 1860, 1870 Fed. Censuses, Alma, 1910 Fed. Census Tacoma, WA, 1920 Fed. Census Paso Robles, CA, 5/23/1929 *Palo Alto Times* article)

Randall, George W. Co. E, 85th NY Infantry - 9/1/1861 at Granger/3 yrs - 44 - 5'8", Light Complexion, Blue Eyes, Brown Hair - 10/25/1861 at Elmira - No bounty - Pvt, Pvt - No battles - 1/24/1863 Disability/Honorable - Was not a casualty - INA (B CT) - INA - circa 1802 in Stafford County - Maria Sophia Hyde , married 4/19/1827 in Freedom - Mariah, Clarissa, Gabrilla, Hubert, Andulsia - 6/7/1881 in Savannah Hill, IL on a visit - INA - Was detached as a recruiter for most of his military service. Gave age as 44 when he entered service. Was more likely 58 or 59, 1850 Census has age as 48. When he entered hospital in 1865, gave age as 65. Was in both Douglas G.H. and Harwood G.H., DC Disability discharge was for infirmities due to old age and diarrhea. Was in Warwich Hospital, DC in 1862 with diarrhea. (Military & Pension Files, *History of Allegany County 1879*, Granger American Legion, Matteson, 1850 Fed. Census Portage, 1870 Fed. Census Lima, 1880 Fed. Census Poysippe, WI)

Randle, John At least one source document indicates that John Randle served in the military during the war. No evidence of such service has been located. It is possible the name was Randall. (1890 Federal Census Special Schedule Granger)

Ratchford, David (Rochford) Co. I, 108th Illinois Infantry - 8/15/1862 at Peoria, IL/3 yrs - 29 - 5'10", Dark Complexion, Blue Grey Eyes, Black Hair, Initials tattooed on right forearm - 8/28/ 1862 at Peoria, IL - $100 - Corp, Sgt - Chickasaw Bayou, assault and capture Ft. Hinman, AK, Port Gibson, Champion's Hill, Guntown, MS, Memphis, siege of Spanish Fort, siege & capture of Ft. Blakely - 8/5/1865 Honorable - Was not a casualty - Both born Ireland - INA - 1843/44 in Ireland - Farm Laborer/Lumber Worker/ Railroad Worker - Laborer - Never Married - None - 9/5/1913 in Soldiers & Sailors Home, Quincy, IL - INA - Name was most likely Rochford. Appears to have arrived in U.S. 5/7/1855 aboard the *Albert Gallitin*. Promoted to 5th Sgt 11/1/1862, to 2nd Sgt 9/14/1863. Claimed he injured a leg jumping over a ditch while his regiment was retreating at Gun Town, MS. Had varicose veins in both legs. Lived in many places. Lived in

Hume Township in late 1870's, in the 1880's, and early 1890's. Was listed in the 1890 Census Special Schedule. (Military & Pension Files, 1890 Fed. Census Special Schedule Hume, 1900, 1910 Fed. Censuses Riverside, IL)

Rearwin, Nelson Preston At least one source document indicates that Rearwin served in the military during the war. No evidence of such service has been located. Actually there most likely was no such person. The name comes from a family headstone and probably represents at least two different people. (Matteson)

Rearwin, William Co. K, 26th NY Cavalry - 2/2/1865 at Buffalo/1 yr - 21 - 5'7", Light Complexion, Grey Eyes, Brown Hair - 2/22/1865 at Buffalo - $100 - Pvt, Pvt - No battles (never left NY) - 6/29/1865 Honorable - Was not a casualty - William & Catherine Croll Rearwin (Both B Germany (Prussia)) - INA - 7/20/1844 in Greenbush, Albany County - Cooper - Farmer - Susan Preston, married 1869 - Wilbur D., Fred, Ed - 3/12/1926 of arteriosclerosis - Pine Grove Cemetery, Fillmore - Gave age as 21 at enlistment, was more likely 17. Kept his sabre and sabre belt at a cost of $3.00. Moved to Fillmore in 1875. Burnside G.A.R. Post 237 Marker at grave. 1890 Special Schedule says he served with Co. K, 1st NY Cavalry. No military records for a Rearwin in the 1st Cavalry have been located. (Military & Pension Files, 1880, 1900, 1910 Fed. Censuses Hume, 1890 Fed. Census Special Schedule Hume, Fillmore American Legion)

Redmond, Frank J. At least one source document indicated that Frank Redmond served in the military during the war. No evidence of such service has been located. (Fillmore American Legion)

Relya, Charles Edwin (Relyea, Relyen) Co. F, 179th NY Infantry - 4/21/1864 at Warsaw/3 yrs - 20 - 5'7", Light Complexion, Blue Eyes, Sandy Hair - 5/25/1864 at Elmira - $100 - Pvt, Pvt - Cold Harbor, Petersburg - 10/31/1864 Honorable/Deceased - POW, captured mid-1864 at Petersburg, Prison: Andersonville, DD, 10/31/at Andersonville of chronic diarrhea - Michael & Chloe A. Alcott Relya - John, Lucinda, Henry H., Sally, George M., Alfred D. - 1843 or 44 in Lee - Farmer - None Deceased - Never Married - None - 10/31/1864 at Andersonville (POW) - Andersonville - Entered Andersonville hospital on 10/11/1864. May have been wounded before he was captured. Military spelled name Relyea. While a source document identifies him as from the C-H-G area, it doesn't appear that he ever lived there. His brother Henry lived in Hume and he may have lived with him at some time. Brother George M. also served during the war. (Military & Pension Files, *Allegany & Its People*, 1850 Fed. Census Lee Township, Oneida County)

Relya, George M. (Relyea, Relyen) Co. F, 179th NY Infantry - 4/21/1864 at Warsaw/3 yrs - 18 - 5'8", Light Complexion, Blue Eyes, Light Hair - 4/21/1864 at Elmira - $100 - Pvt, Pvt - Cold Harbor, Petersburg, Weldon RR, Hatcher's Run, Appomattox - 6/8/1865 Honorable - Was not a casualty - Michael & Chloe A. Alcott Relya - John, Lucinda, Henry H., Sally, Charles Edwin, Alfred D.- 1845/46 in Lee - Farmer - Tinsmith - Catherine - INA - INA - INA - Present at Lee's surrender. Marched in Grand Review 5/23/1865. Military spelled name Relyea. July-August 1864, absent sick. Brother Charles Edwin also served during the war. Brother Henry, a lawyer, lived in Hume. (Military File [Pension file is lost], *Allegany & Its People*, 1850 Fed. Census Lee Township, 1870 Fed. Census Hume)

Reniff, William J. Not from the C-H-G area. Served with Co. B/C, 194th NY Infantry. His enlistment was credited to Hume Township which paid his enlistment bonus of $500. (1865 Allegany County Town Clerk Register Hume)

Reynolds, Oren Simeon Co. E, 85th NY Infantry - 9/1/1861 at Granger/3 yrs (Re-enlisted 1/1/1864) - 18 - 10/10/1861 at Elmira - $400 - Pvt, Pvt - defense of DC, siege of Yorktown, Plymouth - 8/25/1864 Honorable/Deceased - POW, captured 4/20/1864 at Plymouth, NC, Prison: Andersonville, DD, 8/25/1864 at Andersonville Prison of diarrhea - George Azeza & Mary Elizabeth Thorp Reynolds (Both B NY) - Cora E. (Shields) & Nettie D. (Snow) - 12/4/1843 in Granger - Cooper - None Deceased - Never Married - None - 8/25/1864 at Andersonville (POW) - Andersonville - Was a musician. One document says that he starved to death at Andersonville. (Military & Pension Files, 1865 NYS Census Granger, Matterson, *History of Allegany County 1879*, Granger American Legion, 1865 Allegany County Town Clerk Register Granger, 1860 Fed. Census Granger)

Rhodes, Elijah Co. F, 19th NY Cavalry - 8/15/1862 at Hume/3 yrs - 38 - 6'1", Sandy Complexion, Blue Eyes, Brown Hair - 9/3/1862 at Portage Station - $50 - Pvt, Pvt - Deserted House, siege of Suffolk, Franklin - 6/30/1865 Honorable - Was not a casualty - Jeremiah & Mary King Rhodes (Both B NY) - Mary Ann, William, Clarinda - 4/30/1834 in Hume - Farmer - Farmer - Mary Ann Horton, married 10/2/1848 in Centerville - Loretta, Henry, Willard, William - 2/20/1905 in Potter County, PA - Probably Ford Cemetery, Allegheny Township, PA - Marched in Grand Review 5/23/1865. (Military & Pension Files, 1865 NYS Census Hume, *History of Allegany County 1879*, 1865 Allegany County Town Clerk Register Hume, 1860, 1870 Fed. Censuses Hume)

Rice, Harvey Walter Co. E, 1st NY Veteran Cavalry - Drafted 10/18/1864 at Caneadea/1 yr - 24 - 5'9", Dark Complexion, Blue Eyes, Brown Hair - 10/21/1864 at Elmira - $800 - Pvt, Pvt - No battles - 7/20/1865 Honorable - Was not a casualty - Stephen (B VT) & Eunice Gaylord (B NY) Rice - Candace (Clark), James, Garritt S. - 5/26/1840 in Caneadea - Farmer - Farmer - Lydia C. Butler, married 1/1/1866 in Rushford, Edwin E. (Adopted) and Mary - 7/28/1921 in Fillmore - Pine Grove Cemetery, Fillmore - County Clerk says he was drafted 8/13/1864. Register of Men Drafted says he paid commutation not to serve. Kept his sabre when mustered out. Grandfather was Eber Rice of Vermont. Burnside G.A.R. Post 237 Marker at grave. (Military & Pension Files, 1890 Fed. Census Special Schedule Hume, 1865 Allegany County Town Clerk Register Hume, 1865 NYS Census Hume, Fillmore American Legion, Matteson, *Allegany & Its People*, 1850 Fed. Census Caneadea, 1880 Fed. Census Hume, Register of Men Drafted July, 1863 to October, 1864)

Rich, William Henry Co. C, 104th NY Infantry - 10/9/1861 at Geneseo/3 yrs - 28 - 5'9", Sandy Complexion, Blue Eyes, Brown Hair - 2/26/1862 at Geneseo - No bounty - Pvt, Pvt - Cedar Creek, 2nd Bull Run, South Mountain, Antietam, Fredericksburg, Chancellorsville, Gettysburg - 10/25/1864 Honorable - WIA, gunshot to both thighs, 7/1/1863 at Gettysburg - Sylvester (B NY) & Phidelia Boden Rich - Esther, Sally, George, Amelia, Albert, Mary - 1835 in Centerville - Farmer - Farmer - Mary L. Edwards, married 11/14/1865 in Little Genesee - INA - 2/4/1898 in Limona, FL - INA - Some records say he had a hip wound at Gettysburg. Father may have married twice,1850 Census shows a Laura as his wife. (Military & Pension Files, 1865 NYS Census

Centerville, 1865 Allegany County Town Clerk Register Centerville, 1850 Fed.Census Centerville)

Ricketts, Frank (Rickets) Co. E, 85th NY Infantry - 9/1/1861 at Granger/3 yrs - 21 - 5'8", Light Complexion, Blue Eyes, Dark Hair - 10/31/1861 at Elmira - No bounty - Pvt, Pvt - No battles - 11/7/1861 Deserted - Was not a casualty - File says he deserted 11/7/1861. No other information. No action taken on desertion by the military. Age at enlistment was actually about 18. He also served with Co. A, 184th NY Infantry, see below. Also see below personal information and sources of information.

Ricketts, Frank (Rickets) Co. A, 184th NY Infantry - 8/30/1864 at Granger/1 yr - 21 - 5'8", Light Complexion, Blue Eyes, Dark Hair - 9/3/1864 at Elmira - $100 - Pvt, Corp - Cedar Creek, before Richmond and Petersburg - 6/29/1865 Honorable - Was not a casualty - Richard & Grace Mayer Ricketts (Both B England) per death certificate in pension file/Samuel and Mary A. Brewer Ricketts per *Allegany & Its People*, book is correct - Emma, Charlotte (Parker), Isabelle (Framingham), George, Richard, Fred per *Allegany & Its People* - 5/6/1843 in Dorchester, England - Farmer - Farmer - Catherine Closser, married 1/1/1867 in Grove - Rose M., Samuel F., Ethel L. - 7/10/1915 in Houghton - Hunts Hollow Cemetery, Hunt, NY - Appointed Corporal 12/13/1864. Richard Ricketts was likely Frank's grandfather. The Passenger List for the ship *General Victoria* which arrive from London at the Port of New York on 9/20/1843 lists the following: Richard Ricketts 60, Annes? 55, James 16, Heron? 19, Samuel 21, Mary Jane 22 with infant. (Military & Pension Files, *History of Allegany County 1879*, *Allegany & Its People*, 1865 Allegany County Town Clerk Register Granger, 1860, 1880 Fed. Censuses Granger)

Roach, Frank K. See Charles Rotch. (Granger American Legion)

Robbins, Hiram O. Co. F, 33rd NY Infantry - 5/13/1861 at Nunda/2 yrs - 33 - INA - 5/22/1861 at Elmira - No bounty - Pvt. Pvt - No battles - 6/3/1863 Honorable - Was not a casualty - Asa & Louise C. Dow Robbins (Both B VT) - Abigail, Maria, Marion, Byron, Wilson, Wilmot, Lorna, Emma, Vernon, Aaron - 4/2/1828 in Vermont - Farmer - Farmer - INA - INA - 4/6/1892 in Bradford, PA - INA - Spent almost entire service in hospital. Was sick at New York, Annapolis, DC, Hagerstown, MD, Sharpsburg, MD and Antietam. Brothers Wilson and Wilmot also served during the war. (Military File [Pension File is lost], 1865 NYS Census Centerville, 1865 Allegany County Town Clerk Register Centerville, 1860 Fed. Census Centerville)

Robbins, Wilmot E. Co. F, 85th NY Infantry - 8/26/1861 at Black Creek/3 yrs - 18 - INA - 9/7/1861 at Elmira - No bounty - Pvt, Pvt - No battles - 12/20/1861 Honorable/Deceased - DD, 12/20/1861 at Centerville on furlough of congestion of the lungs caused by measles - Asa & Louisa C. Dow Robbins (Both B VT) - Abigail, Maria, Marion, Byron, Hiram, Wilson, Lorna, Emma, Vernon, Aaron - 1842 in Centerville - Chopped and sold Wood - None Deceased - Never Married - None - 12/20/1861 in Centerville on furlough - Centerville Cemetery, Route 3 - Was buried in his uniform with his furlough and other military papers. Brothers Hiram and Wilson also served during the war.(Military & Pension Files, 1865 NYS Census Centerville, *History of Allegany County 1879*, 1865 Allegany County Town Clerk Register Centerville, 1850 Fed. Census Centerville)

Robbins, Wilson C. Co. C, 104th NY Infantry - 10/21/1861 at Geneseo/3 yrs - 21 - 5'6", Light Complexion, Hazel Eyes, Brown Hair - 2/26/1862 at Geneseo - $300 - Pvt, Pvt - No battles - 6/23/1862 Disability/Honorable - Was not a casualty - Asa & Louisa C. Dow Robbins (Both B VT) - Hiram, Abigail, Maria, Marion, Byron, Wilmot, Lorna, Emma, Vernon, Aaron - 9/10/1841 in Centerville - Farmer - Farmer/Coal Dealer - 1st Mary Metcalf, married 7/3/1867 (Died 10/26/1895), 2nd Sara Berry Houghton, married 8/9/1904 in Caneadea - Nellie - 6/4/1930 in Houghton - Rushford - Was in Alexandria G.H., Columbia College Hospital, and Mt. Pleasant Hospital, DC. Also served with the 2nd NY Mounted Rifles, see below. Brothers Hiram and Wilmot also served during the war. Disability discharge due to general debility caused by typhoid fever. (Military & Pension Files, 1865 NYS Census Centerville, 1865 Allegany County Town Clerk Register Centerville, 1850, 1880 Fed. Censuses Centerville)

Robbins, Wilson C. Co. B, 2nd NY Mounted Rifles - 12/18/1863 at Centerville/3 yrs - 22 - 5'6', Light Complexion, Hazel Eyes, Brown Hair - 1/12/1864 at Ft. Porter, Buffalo - No bounty - Pvt, 2nd Sgt. - Spotsylvania, North Anna River, Pamunkey, Totopotomoy, Hanover Court House, Cold Harbor, Bethesda Church, siege of Petersburg, Dinwiddie, Five Forks - Appomattox - 8/10/1865 Honorable - WIA, gunshot to left knee 6/18/1864 at Petersburg - Was in Baltimore G.H., but apparently no treatment was required for wound. Promoted to Sgt 9/1/1864. Present at Lee's surrender. Also served with 104th Infantry, see above. Also see above for personal information and sources of information.

Robinson, Almond Duane Co K/F, 8th NY Cavalry - 8/18/1862 at Rochester/3 yrs - 25 - 6', Fair Complexion, Blue Eyes, Brown Hair - 9/29/1862 at Rochester - $100 - Corp, Pvt - Antietam, Shepherdstown, Fredericksburg, Wilderness - 5/18/1865 Honorable - POW, captured by guerrillas while on picket duty 3/4/1863 at Dumfries, VA (Union Church), Prison: not listed and probably none, paroled 3/18/1863, INJ, 5/3/1864 at Stephensburg, VA, was on picket duty and was riding to report that the South had opened fire on the line. His horse stumbled, threw him and landed on him, pommel hit his shoulder. Suffered fractured humerus and some paralysis of left arm - INA - INA - 1837 in Lodi, Seneca County - Mechanic - Liveryman - Clara Louise Scott, married 2/20/1860 in Caledonia - John O. - 2/26/1880 in Hume - Pine Grove Cemetery Fillmore - Reduced to private 1/29/1863 for neglect of duty. Was in Patterson Park G.H. Baltimore and Mower G.H. Philadelphia with injuries. Received a 15 day furlough 10/31/1863. Pension says he lived in Hume as a boy, moving to Caledonia about 1857. Military Index under A. Duane Robinson. (Military & Pension Files, Allegany County Web Site, Annual Report of NYS Adjutant General 1894, Volume 2, 1860 Fed. Census Caledonia, 1870 Fed. Census Tidioute, PA)

Robinson, Gardner E. Co. I, 160th NY Infantry - 8/28/1862 at Caneadea/3 yrs - 26 - 6', Dark Complexion, Black Eyes, Black Hair - 11/21/1862 at Auburn - No bounty - Pvt, Corp - Gunboat Cotton - 6/19/1863 Disability/Honorable - WIA, 1/13/1863 at battle of Gunboat Cotton, lost right eye and damaged left (gun cap hit him in the eyes) - Esquire & Betsey Potter Robinson (Both B NY) - INA - 6/3/1836 in Hume - Canal Boatman - Boatman/Farmer - 1st Lois Ann Morse (Died 4/1/1880), 2nd Augusta Delia Catlin - Delia, Theodore, Albert, Bertha, Ira G., Sherman - 2/22/1913 - Pine Grove Cemetery, Fillmore - Promoted to Corporal 1/29/1862. First wife Lois died in Insane Asylum at Machias. (Military & Pension Files, 1890 Fed. Census Special Schedule Hume, 1865 NYS Census Hume, 1860 Fed. Census Granger, 1870, 1910 Fed. Censuses Hume,

Roblee, Hewitt At least one source document indicates that Roblee served in the military during the war. No evidence of such service has been located, nor has any evidence of anyone by that name been located. (Centerville American Legion)

Rogers, Marshall James Co. C/D/F/Staff, 104th NY Infantry - 10/9/1861 at Geneseo/3 yrs - 23 - 5'11", Dark Complexion, Blue Eyes, Brown Hair - 2/26/1862 at Geneseo - No bounty - Pvt, Capt - Cedar Creek, 2nd Bull Run, South Mountain, Gettysburg, Wilderness, Spotsylvania, North Anna River, Pamunkey, Totopotomoy, Cold Harbor, Bethesda Church, Petersburg, Weldon RR - 7/14/1865 Resigned/Honorable - WIA, 9/14/1862 at South Mountain (type of wound not described), POW, captured 8/19/1864 at Weldon RR, Prisons: Libby at Richmond, Salisbury, NC, Dansville, VA, paroled 2/23/1865 at Aiken's Landing - Nathaniel & Lucretia Rogers (Both B MA) - INA - 1839 (per headstone) in Wyoming County - Blacksmith - Farmer - Elizabeth Hayes, married in Greene, Chenango County - None - 8/23/1870 in Franklinville - Mount Prospect Cemetery, Franklinville - Sent to Annapolis G. H. following parole. Given a furlough 3/6/1865. Promoted Corporal 11/11/1861, Sgt 12/15/1862, 1st Lt. 11/8/1863, Captain 5/25/1865. Sick with diarrhea 2/2/1864. (Military & Pension Files, Medical Cards, 1865 NYS Census Centerville, 1850, 1870 Fed. Censuses Franklinville)

Rose, Adonirana Judson Co. E, 104th NY Infantry - 10/2/1861 at Geneseo/3 yrs - 27 - 5'8", Light Complexion, Blue Eyes, Brown Hair - 10/21/1861 at Geneseo - No bounty - Pvt, 2nd Lt. - Cedar Creek, 2nd Bull Run, South Mountain, Antietam, Fredericksburg, Chancellorsville, Gettysburg - 10/24/1863 Dishonorable - POW, captured 7/1/1863 at Gettysburg, Prison: None, paroled (He negotiated his own parole.) - Uriah (B RI) & Sarah Patch (B VT) Rose - Delos, Samuel, Malissa, Elisa Ann - 5/1834 in Hume - Farmer - Carpenter/Joiner - Susan M. - Fred, Lolla, Gilbert - INA - INA - The Military refused to recognize the parole that Rose had negotiated and ordered him to perform certain duties. Rose, who believed he had given his word to honor the condition of his parole refused to perform the duties. He was court-martialed and dishonorably discharged. The court martial was really about honor versus duty. Both sides seem to recognize this. The Army ordered Rose to do duty that was, in effect, ceremonial. Rose believed his word (honor) forbade his doing even that. A classic case of the military's need to maintain discipline versus an individual's sense of his personal honor. Promoted to Sgt 10/11/1861, Sgt Major 5/1/1862, 2nd Lt. 9/16/1862. Sick in Keedesville, VA hospital 9/16/1862. Maternal Grandmother Mary Patch born in Canada. (Military File, 1865 Allegany County Town Clerk Register Hume, 1850 Fed. Census Hume, 1880 Fed. Census Perry)

Ross, Mahlon L. At least one source document indicates that Mahlon served in the military during the war. No evidence of such service has been located. (Fillmore American Legion, Matteson)

Rotch, Charles R. Co. E, 85th NY Infantry - 9/1/1861 at Granger/3 yrs - 22 - INA - 11/29/1861 at Elmira - No bounty - Pvt, Pvt - defense of DC, siege of Yorktown, Williamsburg, Fair Oaks, before Richmond, Plymouth - 6/11/1864 Honorable/Deceased - POW, captured 4/20/1864 at Plymouth, NC, Prison: Andersonville, DD, 6/11/1864 at Andersonville of diarrhea/starvation -

Chester or Charles Edward (B NY) & Lucia (B CT) Rotch - Jackson, Martin - 7/18/1838 in Allen - Farmer - None Deceased - Never Married - None - 6/11/1864 at Andersonville (POW) - Andersonville - (Military File, *History of Allegany County 1879*, 1865 Allegany County Town Clerk Register Allen, Matteson, 1850, 1860 Fed. Censuses Allen, *Roll of Honor*)

Sabin, David Not from the C-H-G area. His enlistment in Co. H, 148th NY Infantry was credited to Granger Township which most likely paid his enlistment bonus. No amount listed.(Allegany County Town Clerk Register Granger)

Sartar, Augustus (Sattyr) Co. R, 17th NY Infantry - 5/20/1861 at Warsaw/2 yrs - 20 - 5'10", Light Complexion - 5/24/1861 at NYC - $100 - Pvt, Pvt - 2nd Bull Run, Antietam, Shepherdstown, Sharpsburg, Fredericksburg, Chancellorsville - 6/2/1863 Honorable - Was not a casualty - Jacob & Catherine Sattyr (Both B Germany) - Jacob, Henry - 1841 in Germany - INA (Living with a druggist, maybe working for him) - Farmer - Margaraetha Schimpf, married 2/15/1866 in Warsaw - Jennie (Dunker), Henry A, Katie E. - 3/12/1885 in Centerville - Bates Cemetery, Centerville - Military Index and file spell name Satyr. Pension file is under Sattyr. Census Index for 1860 spells name Saltyn. Wife was also born in Germany. He apparently came to U.S. in 1851. Also served with Co. I, 147th Pennsylvania Infantry, see below. While carrying wood at Big Shanty, GA in August of 1864, he slipped and fell down an embankment with the wood on top of him. Slight internal injury to right side. Census taker spelled father's name Sartous in 1860. (Military & Pension Files, 1890 Fed. Census Special Schedule Centerville, 1860 Fed. Census Warsaw, 1880 Fed. Census Centerville, Parents in 1860 Fed. Census, Orangeville)

Sartar, Augustus (Sattyr) Co. I, 147th Pennsylvania Infantry - 8/8/1863 at Philadelphia/3 yrs - 22 - 5'10", Light Complexion - 8/8/1863 at Philadelphia - $400 - Pvt, Pvt - Lookout Mountain, Missionary Ridge, Ringgold Gap, Taylor's Ridge, Rocky Face Ridge, Resaca, New Hope Church, Dallas, Allatoona, Golgotha Church, Kolb's Farm, Kenesaw Mountain, siege of Atlanta, siege of Savannah, Bentonsville, Raleigh, Bennett's House - 7/15/1865 Honorable - Was not a casualty - Present at surrender of General Johnston and his army. Marched in Grand Review 5/24/1865. Promoted to Corporal 5/1/1864; reduced to ranks 10/18/1864, probably for being a straggler. Index spells name Satyr, file is labeled Satter. Was in hospitals in Chattanooga, Nashville and Louisville. Also served with 17th NY Infantry, see above. Also see above for personal information and sources of information.

Scott, Edwin F. Co. C/D, 12th NY Cavalry -11/11/1862 at Cuba/3 yrs - 24 - 5'6", Light Complexion, Blue Eyes, Light Hair - 3/31/1863 at Camp Washington - $100 - Com Sgt - QM Sgt - Tarboro, Whiting, Weldon RR, Goldsboro, Faisson's Station, Bennett's House - 7/19/1865 Honorable - Was not a casualty - David (B NY) & Lodensky Butterfield (B MA) Scott - Caroline & Emma - 11/1837 in Cuba - Farmer - Farmer - Lola M. Stebbins, married 6/2/1862 in Rushford - Lucy Lynn, Eugene H. - 4/9/1905 - Alger Cemetery, Hume, Route 19 - Present at the surrender of General Johnston and his army. Promoted Quarter Master Sgt 6/1/ 1864. (Military & Pension Files, 1890 Fed. Census Special Schedule Hume, Matteson, 1850 Fed. Census Cuba, 1900 Fed. Census Hume)

Scott, Martin V.B.(probably Van Buren) Co. E, 85th NY Infantry - 9/1/1861 at Granger/3 yrs (Re-enlisted 1/1/1864 at Plymouth, NC) - 18 - 5'9", Light Complexion, Blue Eyes, Sandy Hair - 11/7/1861 at Elmira - $400 - Pvt, Corp - defense of DC, siege of Yorktown, Williamsburg, Fair Oaks, before Richmond, Plymouth - Unknown Honorable/Deceased - POW, captured 4/20/1864 at Plymouth, Prison: Florence, SC , DD, Florence, SC, no date, of probably scrofula - Worstell (B NH) & Martha (B NY) Scott - Chester, Walter, Filinda, Lucy - 1843 - Farm Hand - None Deceased - Never Married - None - Florence, SC (POW) - Probably Florence National Cemetery - Promoted to Corporal 11/1/1862. Absent sick as of 8/15/1862. His only connection to C-H-G appears to be his enlistment at Granger. (Military File, Matteson, Granger American Legion, *History of Allegany County 1879*, 1850, 1860 Fed. Censuses Friendship)

Sears, John Co. H, 136th NY Infantry - 8/16/1864/3 yrs - 46 - 6'2", Dark Complexion, Blue Eyes, Brown Hair - 8/17/1864 at Elmira - $500 - Pvt, Pvt - No battles - 5/27/1865 Disability/Honorable - Was not a casualty - Father INA, Catana "Polly" Huff Sears - Probably Abigail, William W. Inea - 7/12/1816 in Caneadea - Farmer - Farmer/Farm Laborer - Susan J. (Roba) - Herman, Juliana, Diana, Polly (Cate), Phebe, Jasper, Susan - INA - INA - His discharge said he was not fit mentally or physically to be a soldier. He was denied a pension on the grounds that all of his physical problems existed prior to his service. (Military & Pension Files, 1865 NYS Census Hume, 1865 Allegany County Town Clerk Register Hume, 1850, 1860, 1880 Fed. Censuses Caneadea)

Seekins, Josiah Beardsley Co K, 184th NY Infantry - 9/3/1864 at Granger/1 yr - 36 - 5'7", Light Complexion, Blue Eyes, Black Hair - 9/29/1864 Elmira - $100 - Pvt, Pvt - Petersburg, Richmond - 6/29/1865 Honorable - Was not a casualty - Thomas (B VT) & Philena Mathews (B CT) Seekins - INA - 8/12/1830 in Geneseo - Farmer - Farmer - Sarah Ann Smith, married 1/3/1856 in Granger - Lorenzo, Lela V. - 11/8/1914 in Dryden - Green Hills Cemetery, Dryden - Marriage document says Seekins was from Walker, Kent County, MI. (Military & Pension Files, 1865 NYS Census Granger, 1865 Allegany County Town Clerk Register Granger,1860, 1880 Fed. Censuses Granger)

Severance, Hugh M. At least one source document indicates that Severance served in the military during the war. No evidence of such service has been located. No Hugh Severance served in a NYS regiment during the war. (Fillmore American Legion, Matteson)

Shafer, George Washington (Schaffer) Co. F, 4th NY Heavy Artillery - 9/28/1862 at Granger/3 yrs - 26 - 5'11", Light Complexion, Light Eyes, Brown Hair - 10/2/1862 at NYC - $100 - Pvt, Pvt - Peeble's Farm, Hatcher's Run, fall of Petersburg, Appomattox - 9/26/1865 Honorable - Was not a casualty - Samuel & Nancy Campbell Shafer - INA - October 1834 in Geneseo - Carpenter/Farmer - Carpenter/Joiner - Almira Whalen Dunn (She was previously married to Caleb Dunn.), married 10/14/1855 Livonia - George A., Ida M., Delmont, (Almira had a daughter Julia by her first husband) - 6/13/1893 in Valley Springs, SD - INA - Present at Lee's surrender. Marched in Grand Review 5/23/1865. (Military & Pension Files, 1865 NYS Census Granger, 1865 Allegany County Town Clerk Register Granger, Granger American Legion, 1860 Fed. Census Granger, 1870 Fed. Census Hume)

Sheppard, George H. (Shepard) Co. F, 19th NY Cavalry - 8/7/1862 at Hume/3 yrs - 5'7", Dark Complexion, Brown Eyes, Brown Hair - 9/3/1862 at Portage Station - $150 - Pvt, Pvt - Deserted

House, siege of Suffolk - 5/25/1863 Disability/Honorable - Was not a casualty - Disability discharge was due to chronic diarrhea. Was actually 19 at enlistment rather than 21. Also served with Co. F, 4th NY Heavy Artillery, see below. Also see below for personal information and sources of information.

Sheppard, George H. (Shepard) Co. F, 4th NY Heavy Artillery - 12/26/1863 at Granger/3 yrs - 21 - 5'9", Dark Complexion, Black Eyes, Black Hair - 12/30/1863 at Elmira - $60 - Pvt, Pvt - Wilderness - 11/25/1864 Honorable/Deceased - POW, captured 5/6/1864 at the Wilderness, Prison: Florence, SC, DD 11/25/1864 of fever and chronic diarrhea at Florence, SC - Henry & Mary W. Blackman Sheppard - INA - 11/24/1842 in Granger - Saw Miller/Farmer - None Deceased - Never Married - None - 11/25/1864 in Florence, SC (POW) - Probably Florence National Cemetery - Also served with Co. F, 19th NY Cavalry, see above. Listed on Soldiers Monument in Granger. He filed for a pension after his first enlistment and then abandoned it when he enlisted in the 4th HA. (Military & Pension Files, 1865 Allegany County Town Clerk Register Granger, *Allegany & Its People*, *History of Allegany County 1879*, Matteson, Granger American Legion, 1860 Fed. Census Granger)

Shoots, John Lawrence Co. F, 19th NY Cavalry - 8/9/1862 at Hume/3 yrs - 28 - INA - 9/3/1862 at Portage Station - $150 - Pvt, Pvt - No battles - 4/18/1863 Honorable/Deceased - DD, 4/18/1863 of remittent fever at Hampton, VA hospital - John & Elizabeth Somers Shoots - INA - 2/18/1834 in Montgomery County - Farm Laborer - None Deceased - Never Married - None - 4/18/1863 at Hampton, VA - Hampton National Cemetery - Was working for an Edmund Skiff in Hume in 1860. (Military File, *History of Allegany County 1879*, Allegany County Web Site, 1865 Allegany County Town Clerk Hume, 1860 Fed. Census Hume, *Roll of Honor*)

Sibbald, George (Sibald) Co. E, 85th NY Infantry - 9/1/1861 at Granger/3 yrs (Reenlisted 1/1/1864 at Plymouth, NC) - 18 - 5'11", Dark Complexion, Blue Eyes, Light Hair - 11/10/1861 at Elmira - No bounty - Pvt, Pvt - defense of DC, siege of Yorktown, Williamsburg, Fair Oaks, before Richmond, Plymouth - 12/25/1864 Honorable/Deceased - POW, captured 4/20/1864 at Plymouth, NC, Prison: Savannah/Charleston, paroled 12/10/1864 at Charleston (another document says 11/30/1864 which is probably correct, since still another document has him reporting to Division Hospital in Annapolis on 12/14/1864), DD, 12/25/1864 at Division Hospital, Annapolis of diarrhea - William (B Scotland) & Sara Eaton (B NY) Sibbald - William H., Ann - 11/30/1846 in Oswegatchee, St. Lawrence County - Farmer - None Deceased - Never Married - None - 12/25/1864 in Annapolis, MD - Annapolis National Cemetery - Had a promissory note for $80.00 at time of death. The debt was collected by the Council of Administration and made a part of his effects. Was actually only 15 when he volunteered and 18 when he died. Brother William also served during the war. (Military File, *History of Allegany County 1879*, Matteson, *Allegany & Its People*, Granger American Legion, 1865 Allegany County Town Clerk Register Granger, 1860 Fed. Census, Granger)

Sibbald, William Henry (Sibald) Co. F, 19th NY Infantry - 8/13/1862 at Granger/3 yrs - 19 - 5'8", Fair Complexion, Hazel Eyes, Dark Hair - 9/3/1862 at Portage Station - No bounty - Pvt, Pvt - Deserted House, siege of Suffolk - 1/8/1864 Disability/Honorable - WIA, 4/13/1863 at Suffolk, gunshot to abdomen and thigh by Sharp Shooters - William (B Scotland) & Sarah Eaton (B NY)

Sibbald - George, Ann - 10/11/1842 in Oswegatchee, St. Lawrence County - Farmer - Farmer - Emily Alice Millen, married 12/24/1873 in King City, MO - Minnie A., Lena, Grace, George Clyde - 11/4/1904 in King City - INA - Brother George also served during the war. (Military & Pension Files, Matteson, 1865 Allegany County Town Clerk Register Granger, 1860 Fed. Census Granger, 1880 Fed. Census Jackson County, MO)

Skiff, George Vernon Co F/Staff, 12th NY Infantry - 9/20/1862 at Hume/3 yrs - 26 - INA - 9/23/1862 at Albany - No bounty - Assistant Surgeon - Surgeon - Richmond, Gaine's Mill, Malvern Hill, 2nd Bull Run, Antietam, Shepherdstown, Sharpsburg, Fredericksburg, Ellis Ford, Chancellorsville - 5/17/1863 Honorable Was not a casualty - Micajah & Mary P. Hopkins Skiff (Both B NY) - Albert, Samuel, Edwina - 3/11/1836 in Pike - Physician - Physician - INA - INA - 1890 - INA - Accidently shot himself in the hand about 4/1/1865 near Burlington, WV. 12th Infantry was transferred as Companies E & F to the 5th NY Infantry 6/2/1864. Lived in NYC, Manhattan after the war. While the Skiff family was tied closely to the Hume area, George Skiff's only relationship to C-H-G appears to have been his enlistment at Hume. It is likely that he never married. The town of Pike was part of Hume township at one point. (Military & Pension Files, 1865 Allegany County Town Clerk Register Hume, 1850. Fed Census Pike, 1860 Fed. Census Perry, 1880 Fed. Census Manhattan)

Skiff, John Milton Co. E, 3rd Iowa Infantry - 5/22/1861 at Nevada (more likely Newton), IA/3 yrs - 21 - INA - 5/29/1861 - No bounty - Corp, Corp - Utica, MO - Kirkville, action against guerrillas in North Central Missouri, Shelbiana, Fonda, Shiloh, TN - 4/6/1862 Honorable/Deceased - KIA, 4/6/1862 at Shiloh - Joseph & Lidia Fitch Skiff (Both B NY) - Stephen M., Chester F., Joshua, Clarissa L., Vira (Morrow) Harvey J., Lucina (Cochran), Addie (Thomas) - 5/26/1840 in Hume - Teacher - None Deceased - Never Married - None - 4/6/1862 in Shiloh, TN - Shiloh National Cemetery (Originally buried on the battlefield. Memorial Headstone at Pine Grove Cemetery, Fillmore.) - Brother Stephen M. also served during the war. (Military File, Allegany County Web Site, Matteson, Fillmore American Legion, *Allegany & Its People*, 1865 Allegany County Town Clerk Hume, 1860 Fed Census Hume, *Roll of Honor*)

Skiff, Stephen Morse Co. A, 19th NY Cavalry - 8/7/1862 at Pike/3 yrs - INA - 9/3/1862 at Portage Station - $50 - Corp, Corp - Franklin - 6/17/1863 Honorable/Deceased - KIA, 6/17/1863 at Franklin while on picket duty - Joseph & Lidia Fitch Skiff (Both B NY) - John M., Chester F., Joshua, Clarissa L., Vira (Morrow) Harvey J., Lucina (Cochran), Addie (Thomas) - 4/1/1842 in Hume - Farmer - None Deceased - Never Married - None - 6/17/1863 near Franklin, VA - Hampton National Cemetery (Originally buried at Suffolk, VA) - Brother John also served during the war. Memorial headstone at Pine Grave Cemetery, Fillmore. Burnside G.A.R. Post 237 Marker at grave. (Military File, Book *History of Allegany County 1879*, Allegany County Web Site, Matteson, *Allegany & Its People*, 1865 Allegany County Town Clerk Register Hume, Fillmore American Legion, 1850 Fed. Census Hume, *Roll of Honor*)

Slade, George At least one source document indicates that Slade served in the military (131st NY Infantry) during the war. No evidence of such service has been located. A George O. Slade did serve during World War I. He is buried at Short Tract. A. George H. Slade served during the Civil War in the 89th Infantry, but he was not from the C-H-G area. (Matteson)

Smith, Altorney/Alturnia C. Co. H, 136th NY Infantry - 8/30/1862 at Genesee Falls/3 yrs - 18 - 5'5", Dark Complexion, Black Eyes, Brown Hair - 9/25/1862 at Portage - No bounty - Pvt, Pvt - Chancellorsville, Gettysburg, Orchard Knob, Tunnel Hill, Missionary Ridge, Resaca - 5/30/1864 Honorable/Deceased - WIA 5/15/1864 at Resaca, DD, 5/30/1864 at Nashville, TN G.H. Death caused by the administration of chloroform to amputate a wounded finger - Possibly Joel & Phoebe de Porter Smith (Both B NY) - Vernon, Delvin, Jane (only if parents are Joel & Phoebe)- 1843/44 in Canada - Farmer - None Deceased - Never Married - None - 5/30/1864 in Nashville, TN - Nashville National Cemetery - Several source documents identify a soldier named Altorney Smith. The Granger Town Clerk said he served with the 136th Infantry. The Granger American Legion said he served with the 85th Infantry. No Altorney Smith served in either regiment. A Alturnia Smith served with the 136th Infantry. Altorney is listed on the Soldiers Monument in Granger. Assuming he was Joel's son, his name was most likely Alturnia or Alternus. Alturnia's hospital records indicate his closest relative was a W.W. Smith of Nunda. The *History of Allegany County 1879* lists a Joel M.W. Smith. The 1860 Census shows Joel's son as Alternus Smith, age 14, making him 16, rather than 18, at time of enlistment. Assuming his father is Joel M.W., he served in the same company and regiment as his father, and was mustered the same day. Again, assuming he is the son of Joel, his brother Vernon also served during the war. Records in Canada say that Alturnia was an 18-year-old Canadian born farmer. The Carded Medical files for Alturnia Smith shows that he had just recovered from pneumonia when he was wounded. Since his lungs were still weak, the doctor did not want to administer chloroform (per the doctor), but Smith insisted. (Military File, 1865 Allegany Town Clerk Register Granger, Granger American Legion, Book *Allegany & Its People*, Matteson, *History of Allegany County 1879*, Canadian Tom Brooks)

Smith, Andrew Washington Co. E, 85th NY Infantry - 9/1/1861 at Granger/3 yrs - 23 - 5'10", Dark Complexion, Blue Eyes, Black Hair - 12/2/1861 at Elmira - No bounty - 1st Lt., 1st Lt. - No battles - 4/3/1862 Resigned/Honorable - Was not a casualty - Reuben (B MA) & Orpha E. Van Blarcom (B NJ) Smith - William, Melissa - 7/10/1838 - Lain Redlands, CA - INA - Brother Dr. William M. Smith also served during the war. Received his commission 10/9/1861. (Military & Pension Files, *History of Allegany County 1879*, 1865 Allegany County Town Clerk Register Granger, Matteson, Granger American Legion, 1850, 1880 Fed. Censuses Granger)

Smith, Assil At least one source document indicates that Assil Smith served in the military during the war. No evidence of such service has been located. There was an Asil Smith living in Granger in 1870. He was 38. No Assil Smith served in any NYS Civil War regiment. (1890 Fed Census Special Schedule Granger)

Smith, Daniel K. Co. A, 194th NY Infantry - 3/10/1865 at Hume/3 yrs - 41 - 5'11", Fair Complexion, Grey Eyes, Brown Hair - 3/29/1865 at Elmira - $300 - Pvt, Pvt - No battles - 5/3/1865 Honorable - Was not a casualty - INA, INA - 1823 or 24 in Schuyler County - Farmer - INA - INA - INA - INA - INA - It is possible that Daniel K. Smith was not from the C-H-G area and that his enlistment was credited to Hume Township because the Township paid his enlistment bonus. However the Town Clerk Register does not include his name. (*History of Allegany County 1879*)

Smith, George Washington Co. D, 19th NY Cavalry - 9/13/1864 at Genesee Falls/1 yr - 24 - 5'7",

Dark Complexion, Black Eyes, Black Hair - 9/23/1864 at Lockport - $350 - Pvt, Pvt - Cedar Creek, Berryville, Gordonsville - 6/30/1865 Honorable - John Alexander & Lucinda Wilcox Smith (Both B NY) - Martha, Frances - 2/6/1840 in Elbridge - Farm Laborer - Laborer - 1st Almira Orcelia Oakley, married 12/22/1861 in Wiscoy, deserted family 3/1898 because, according to George, Almira was unchaste and immoral, divorced 9/25/1907, 2nd Martha Ann Galloway, married 8/10/1911 in Central Lake, MI - Henry Dewane, Arthur, Dewit, Willard, Jerome, Mabel, John, Lucinda, George, Erwin, Hara, Hazel - 2/19/1919 in Central Lake, MI - INA - Marched in the Grand Review 5/23/1865. Father John A. also served in the same regiment. Wife Almira was born in Jordan, NY. (Military & Pension Files, 1865 NYS Census Hume, 1865 Allegany County Town Clerk Register Hume, 1890 Fed. Census Special Schedule Hume,1860, 1880 Fed. Censuses Hume)

Smith, Henry W. Co. I, 19th NY Cavalry - 8/27/1864 at Angelica/1 yr - 21 - 5'6", Dark Complexion, Blue Eyes, Brown Hair - 9/6/1864 at Elmira - $100 - Pvt, Pvt - Gordonsville - 6/30/1865 Honorable - Was not a casualty - Henry & Margaret Smith (Both B Germany) - Mary, Phillip, Margaret, John, Barbary - 7/7/1843 in Grove - Farmer - Shoemaker - Sara Ann Rapp, married 1/21/1875 in Geneseo, IL - Emma S., Herbert Wesley, Vernon Albert, Alma Helena - 11/6/1915 in Geneseo, IL - INA - Retained Colt revolver and sabre at discharge. Marched in Grand Review 5/23/1865. Was at Harper's Ferry 9/12/1864. Not sure of his connection to C-H-G. Matteson Book has him enlisting at Granger. (Military & Pension Files, Matteson, 1850 Fed. Census Grove, 1900, 1910 Fed. Censuses Geneseo, IL)

Smith, Horatio Augustus Co. B, 44th NY Infantry - 8/19/1861 at Hume/3 yrs - 24 - INA - 10/19/1861 at Albany - No bounty - Pvt, Pvt - siege of Yorktown, Hanover Court House, Gaine's Mill, Malvern Hill, 2nd Bull Run - 8/30/1862 Honorable/Deceased - WIA, gunshot to left arm at Hanover Court House, 5/27/1862, KIA, 8/30/1862 at 2nd Bull Run - Watson & Betsey Miller Smith - Cornelia - 1836 or 37 in PA, - INA - None Deceased - Never Married - None - 8/30/1862 at Bull Run - INA - Parents did not apply for his pension, (Military File, Medical Cards, 1865 Allegany County Town Clerk Register Hume, Allegany County Web Site, 1850 Fed. Census Hume)

Smith, Joel M.W. Co. H, 136th NY Infantry - 9/1/1862 at Granger/3 yrs - 40 - 5'10", Fair Complexion, Blue Eyes, Light Hair - 9/25/1862 at Portage - No bounty - Pvt, Pvt - No battles - 4/16/1863 Disability/Honorable - Was not a casualty - INA - INA - 1821 or 22 in Orangeville - Farmer - Farmer/Laborer - 1st Phoebe de Porter (Divorced 10/23/1869), 2nd Sarah A. Durkee, (widow), married in Millbrook, MI - Alternus, Vernon, Delvin, Jane - 6/20/1895 in Soldiers Home, MI - Kent County, MI - Was a musician in the service. Son Vernon also served during the war. His son Alternus may have also served. See Alturnus Smith above. Disability discharge due to a disease of the knee joint. Was in Stafford, VA G.H. (Military & Pension Files, *History of Allegany County 1879*, Matteson, 1865 Allegany County Town Clerk Register Granger, 1860 Fed. Census Granger, 1870 Fed. Census Millbrook, MI, 1880 Fed. Census Walker, MI)

Smith, John Alexander Co. K, 19th NY Infantry - 9/20/1864 at Genesee Falls/1 yr - 44 - 5'5, Fair Complexion, Blue Eyes, Brown Hair - 9/23/1864 at Lockport - $400 - Pvt, Pvt - Gordonsville - 6/30/1865 Honorable - Was not a casualty - John & Rhoda Bates Smith (Both B NY) - INA -

2/6/1818 in White Creek - Farmer/Hotel Keeper/Lumberman - Farmer - 1st Lucinda Wilcox (Died 3/23/1877 in Hume), 2nd Adelphia Rose, married 7/23/1877 in Caneadea, (she was about 17, he was 57) - George W. Martha J., Frances Ellen, Emile?, L.A., Martha - 9/26/1906 in Wiscoy - Elmer Cemetery, Wiscoy - Son George W. also served during the war. Marched in Grand Review 5/23/1865. (Military & Pension Files, 1865 NYS Census Hume, 1890 Fed. Census Special Schedule Hume, 1865 Allegany County Town Clerk Register Hume, 1860, 1880 Fed. Censuses Hume)

Smith, John P. Co. I, 188th NY Infantry - 9/5/1864 at Avon/1 yr - 36 - 5'7", Light Complexion, Grey Eyes, Dark Hair - 10/22/1864 at Rochester - No bounty - Pvt, Pvt - siege of Petersburg, Hatcher's Run, Weldon RR, Gravelly Run, Five Forks - 7/1/1865 Honorable - INJ, 12/15/1864 at Weldon RR, Was helping to dismantle tracks and pile up the track ties to burn them when one fell off stack and hit him, causing back and kidney problems, WIA, piece of shell cap went through his cheek and into his mouth 3/29/1865 at Gravelly run. He spit it out - Jacob & Catherine Smith? - INA - 1827 or 28 in Monroe or Cayuga County - Farmer - Farmer - Rosette Parkes, married 1/9/1853 in Granger - Romelia, Polly, Alvia, Sheridan - 3/26/1901 - INA - Present at Lee's surrender. Marched in Grand Review 5/23/1865. Was Company cook. Paid $2.15 to keep arms and equipment (knapsack and ½ tent shelter) at discharge. Was in Rochester with a 20 day furlough as of 6/19/1865. Discharged at Rochester. Was known as a big drinker in his younger years. (Military & Pension Files, 1890 Fed. Census Special Schedule Granger, 1865 NYS Census Granger, 1860, 1870 Fed. Censuses Granger)

Smith, Manning Hardy Co. F 4th NY Heavy Artillery - 9/1/1862 at Hume/3 yrs - 33 - 5'6", Light Complexion - 9/12/1862 at NYC - $100 - Pvt, Pvt - fall of Petersburg, Appomattox - 6/16/1865 Honorable - Was not a casualty - Darling & Mary Luther Smith (Both B NY) - INA - 3/10/1839 in Granger - Farm Laborer - Laborer/Farmer - Laura Billington, married 9/22/1853 in Nunda - Laurence, Loren, Elsworth - 8/9/1885 in Hume - Church Street Cemetery, Wiscoy - Marched in Grand Review 5/23/1865. Sick in Finley G.H., DC as of 4/30/1864 with diarrhea; In Philadelphia G.H. much of 1864, diarrhea. (Military & Pension Files, Fillmore American Legion, 1865 NYS Census Granger, 1865 Allegany County Town Clerk Register Granger, Matteson, 1850 Fed. Census Granger, 1880 Fed. Census Hume)

Smith, Norman J. Co. C, 136th NY Infantry - 8/11/1862 at Livornia/3 yrs - 24 - 5'10', Light Complexion, Blue Eyes, Light Hair - 9/25/1862 at Portage - No bounty - Pvt, Pvt - No battles - 12/4/1862 Honorable/Deceased - DD, 12/4/1862 at Carver Hospital, DC of chronic diarrhea - Henry & Sarah Smith (Both B NY) - Chauncey, William, Hiram, Sarah, Jane, Samuel - 1837 or 38 in NY - Farmer - None Deceased - Never Married - None - 12/4/1862 in DC - Soldier's and Sailors Home Cemetery DC - Listed on Soldiers Monument in Granger. The military returned a number of personal effects to his father. (Military File, Matteson, *Allegany & Its People*, 1850 Fed. Census Granger)

Smith, Robert Not from the C-H-G area. Originally served with Co. D, 107th NY Infantry. Re-enlistment in Co. C, 16th VRC was credited to Hume Township which paid his re-enlistment bonus of $500. (1865 Allegany County Town Clerk Register Hume)

Smith, Samuel J. Co. F, 19th NY Cavalry - 8/11/1862 at Hume/3 yrs - 41 - INA - 9/3/1862 at Portage Station - $150 - Pvt, Corp - Deserted House, siege of Suffolk, Franklin, Manassas Junction, Bristoe's Station, Culpeper, Wilderness, Todd's Tavern, Spotsylvania, North Anna River, Yellow Tavern, Pamunkey, Totopotomoy, Cold Harbor, Trevillian Station, Charles County Court House - before Richmond & Petersburg - New Market - Shepherdstown, Winchester, Fisher's Hill, Port Republic, Cedar Creek, Berryville, Gordonsville - 6/30/1865 Honorable - Was not a casualty - Ebenezer & Sarah Clark Smith - INA - 1/1/1821 in Sheldon, VT - Farm Laborer/Cooper - Farm Laborer/Cooper - 1st Mariah Benton, (died 2/18/1984), 2nd Mary M. Blanchard, married 5/13/1895 in Eagle - Cynthia M. (Long), Samuel James, Caroline A. (Gould) - INA - INA - Marched in Grand Review 5/23/1865. (Military & Pension Files, 1865 NYS Census Hume, 1865 Allegany County Town Clerk Register Hume, *History of Allegany County 1879*, 1860, 1870 Fed. Censuses Hume)

Smith, Varius Quintilius Co. E, 85th NY Infantry - 9/1/1861 at Granger/3 yrs (Re-enlisted 1/1/1864)- 24 - 5'4", Dark Complexion, Grey Eyes, Brown Hair - 10/10/1861 at Elmira - $100 - Pvt, Pvt - defense of DC, siege of Yorktown, Williamsburg, Fair Oaks, before Richmond, Plymouth - 4/21/1865 Honorable - POW, captured 4/20/1865 at Plymouth, NC, Prison: Andersonville, Charleston, SC, Florence, SC, Paroled 3/1/1865 at North East Bridge - John, Jr. & Susannah Upham Smith (Both B MA) - Myron, William, Nancy (Bennett), Largius F., Claudius, Sardius, Sevius, Clarinda (Cox) - 2/9/1837 in Portage - Farmer - Farmer - 1st Mary Redmond, married 5/1/1871 in Short Tract (Died 6/25/1882), 2nd Mary A. Whitbeck (per *Allegany & Its People*) 2nd (per pension file), Lucy A. Scott (widow), married 6/20/1899 in Allen - Bertha S. (Lyon), Ida L. (Jerman) - 8/25/1913 in Granger - Short Tract - Was a surgeons orderly for a while. Served as a nurse most of 1862, 1863, and 1864. Lived on Short Tract Road per 1900 Census. Served as Justice of the Peace for 20 years. (Military & Pension Files, *History of Allegany County 1879*, *Allegany & Its People*, Matteson, 1865 Allegany County Town Clerk Register Allen, Granger American Legion, 1865 NYS Census Allen - 1850, 1870, 1900 Fed. Censuses Allen)

Smith, Vernon Patrick Co. B, 64th NY Infantry - 8/13/1864 at Granger/1 yr - 18 - 5'5", Dark Complexion, Brown Eyes, Brown Hair - 8/19/1864 at Elmira - No bounty - Pvt, Pvt - No battles - 6/27/1865 Honorable - Was not a casualty - Joel M.W. & Phebe Smith (Both B NY) - Alternus, Delvin, Jane - 1843 or 44 in Livingston County - Laborer - INA - INA - INA - INA - INA - Was a substitute. Admitted Emory G.H., DC 5/11/1865 from City Point hospital with measles. Also in Lincoln G.H. as of 10/29/1864. Furloughed for 30 days as of 1/5/1865. Was late returning and charged as a deserter. Arrested 4/1/1865 "on the cars" (RR Cars), and treated as a straggler until discharge. Father Joel M.W. Smith also served during the war. Brother Alternus may also have served. See Alturnus Smith above. (Military File, 1865 Allegany County Town Clerk Register Granger, 1860 Fed. Census Granger)

Smith, William Mervale Co. E/Staff, 85th NY Infantry - 10/29/1861 at Granger/3 yrs - 35 - INA - 10/29/1861 at Elmira - No bounty - 1st Lt, 1st Lt - defense of DC, siege of Yorktown, Williamsburg, Fair Oaks - 6/17/1863 Resigned/Honorable - Was not a casualty - Reuben (B MA) & Orpha E. Blarcom (B NJ) Smith - Mellissa E., Andrew - 7/18/1825 in Patterson, NJ - Physician - Physician/Orange Farmer - 1st Adaline M. Weeks (Died 3/21/1855 in Granger), 2nd Emma J. Spinks (Died 9/18/1859 in Granger), 3rd. Frances A. Lyon, married 7/16/1863 in Pike - Frank -

1/18/1902 in Redlands, CA - INA - Brother Andrew also served during the war. Both his father and his brother (after the war) were physicians. Also served as a surgeon with the 103rd NY Infantry. Was commissioned 1/7/1862. March 1863 absent for a medical board exam in DC Detached to DC from the field, March 1 and April 8-9, 1863. Granted 15 days of leave 6/13/1862. Was also detached to Suffolk, VA for a period. After his service, wrote a paper on the siege and capture of Plymouth, NC. In 2001, the book *Swamp Doctor* was published. The book is the diary Smith kept during his military service. (Military & Pension Files, Allegany County Town Clerk Register Granger, *Allegany & Its People*, Granger American Legion, *Swamp Doctor* edited by Thomas P. Lowry, M.D., 1850, 1860 Fed. Censuses Granger, 1900 Fed. Census Redlands)

Smith, William Silas Co. E, 85th NY Infantry - 9/1/1861 at Granger/3 yrs (Re-enlisted 1/1/1864) - 28 - 5'8", Light Complexion, Blue Eyes, Light Hair - 11/10/1861 at Elmira - $400 - Pvt, Pvt - defense of DC, siege of Yorktown, Williamsburg, Fair Oaks, before Richmond, Plymouth - 12/20/1864 Honorable/Deceased - POW, captured 4/20/1864 at Plymouth Prison: Charleston, Florence, SC, DD, on or about 12/20/1864 at Florence, SC (disease not listed) - Darling & Elmira Barney Smith - INA - 4/29/1832 in Granger - Ellen E. Havens, married 6/14/1854 (Died 10/27/ 1860) - Henry, Eugene, Herman (His father Darling became the children's legal guardian.) - On or about 12/20/1864 in Florence, SC prison - Probably Short Tract Cemetery - Was an ambulance driver. Left sick at Suffolk, VA 12/5/1862. Appointed Wagoner 6/1/1862. Moved from Charleston prison to Florence about 12/13/1864. (Military & Pension Files, *History of Allegany County 1879*, Matteson, 1860 Fed. Census Granger)

Snell, Charles E. Co. F, 19th NY Cavalry - 8/11/1862 at Hume/3 yrs - 25 - 5'8", Light Complexion, Blue Eyes, Brown Hair - 9/3/1862 at Portage Station - $250 - Pvt, Pvt - Deserted House, siege of Suffolk, Franklin - 6/30/1865 Honorable - Was not a casualty - INA (Both B England) - INA - 8/16/1833 in Manlius - Farmer/Canal Boatman - Farmer - 1st Wethy Wilson (Died 1/1/1877), 2nd Elizabeth Wilson, married 7/14/1893 in Caneadea - Myron, Mary (Jennings) - 11/9/1908 in Belfast - Fillmore - Marched in Grand Review 5/23/1865. Was Brigade Teamster as of October, 1863. After war, lived in Black Creek until 1867, Fillmore until July, 1908 then Belfast. (Military & Pension Files, *History of Allegany County 1879*, 1860, 1880 Fed. Censuses Hume)

Snider, Benjamin Swezy (Snyder) Co. D, 64th NY Infantry - 10/10/1861 at Rushford/3 yrs (Re-enlisted 12/21/1863) - 43 - 5'6", Dark Complexion, Blue Eyes, Brown Hair - 10/10/1861 at Elmira - No bounty - Pvt, Pvt - siege of Yorktown, Malvern Hill, Chancellorsville - 11/14/1864 Honorable - WIA, slight wound to side of face from a fall (one record says gunshot), 5/3/1863 at Chancellorsville, POW, captured 5/4/1863 at US Ford, VA, Prison: Libby at Richmond, paroled at City Point, VA 5/31/1863 - Benjamin S. & Charity Green Snyder - INA - 6/14/1821 in Rushford (1865 Census says Ontario County) - Farmer - Farmer/Evangelist - 1st Priscilla B. Very (Died 1879), 2nd Hannah Webster, married 1882 in barn by an African minister - Lucy Addie, Julia M. (Jennie), Charity, Sophia - 6/30/1896 in Belfast - INA - Brother Edward Green Snider also served during the war. Early 1862 was in Ft. Monroe hospital. Was AWOL 10/62 to 2/1863. Arrested 7/6/1863, released 7/20/1863, no reason provided. Was in several hospitals. The military did have him examined to determine if he should be sent to the lunatic asylum. There is a claim that he convinced General Grant to give him a pass through the lines so that he could convince the

Southern soldiers to surrender by using the "Sword of the Spirit" rather than the "Sword Of Arms." To get the pass, he told Grant that his commanding officer had agreed with his effort. Snider was mentally disturbed much of his life. After his military service he was in and out of mental institutions. He billed himself as a "National Evangelist" and announced that he would speak at various locations. Was eventually declared insane, but later released. His daughter Lucy A. was investigated for fraud. (Military & Pension Files, 1865 NYS Census Hume, 1865 Allegany County Town Clerk Register Hume, 1850 Fed. Census Granger, *Allegany & Its People*, Matteson, 1870 Fed. Census Hume)

Snider, Charles William (Snyder) Co. F, 104th NY Infantry - 2/12/1862 at Royalton/3 yrs - 18 - 5'7", Dark Complexion, Blue Eyes, Brown Hair - 2/26/1862 at Geneseo - $100 - Pvt, Pvt - Cedar Creek, 2nd Bull Run, South Mountain, Antietam, Fredericksburg, Chancellorsville, Gettysburg - 6/27/1865 Honorable - POW, captured 7/1/1863 at Gettysburg, Prison: Americus and Andersonville, released 4/15/1865 at Vicksburg - Edward Green (B NY) & Mary Ann Curtis Snider - Darius, Sarah - 11/9/1843 in Granger - Farmer - Farmer/Ran Cheese Factory - 1st Francis A. Rowley, married 4/11/1871 in Fillmore, 2nd Melissa - Lida M. (Williams), Lora O. Darius R., Elizabeth H. (Campbell) - 1/6/1930 in Hastings Upon Hudson - Pine Grove Cemetery, Fillmore - Brother Darius and Father Edward Green Snider also served during the war. Was a cook for his Captain at least part of his service. (Military & Pension Files, 1865 NYS Census Granger, Granger American Legion, 1865 Allegany County Town Clerk Register Granger, 1860 Fed. Census Portage, 1850 Fed. Census Granger, 1880 Fed. Census Nunda)

Snider, Darius Martin (Snyder) Co. E, 85th NY Infantry - 10/20/1861 at Granger/3 yrs (Re-enlisted 1/1/1864 at Plymouth, NC) - 19 - INA - 10/30/1861 at Elmira - $300 - Pvt, Pvt - defense of DC, siege of Yorktown, Williamsburg, Fair Oaks, before Richmond, Plymouth - 3/11/1865 Honorable/Deceased - DD, 3/11/1865 at New Bern, NC Hospital of remittent fever - Edward Green (B NY) & Mary Ann Curtis Snider - Charles, Sarah - 1/14/1842 in Allen - Farm Laborer - None Deceased - Never Married - None - 3/11/1865 in New Bern, NC (POW?) - New Bern National Cemetery (as Darins Snyder) - Brother Charles and Father Edward Green Snider also served during the war. Listed on the Soldiers Monument in Granger. 1865 NYS Census says he died escaping. There is no information in his military or pension file which supports that. (Military & Pension Files, 1865 NYS Census Granger, Matteson, Granger American Legion, 1865 Allegany County Town Clerk Register Granger, *History of Allegany County 1879*, *Allegany & Its People*, 1850 Fed. Census Granger, 1860 Fed. Census Portage, *Roll of Honor*)

Snider, Edward Green (Snyder) Co. H, 19th NY Cavalry - 8/13/1862 at Portage/3 yrs - 43 - 5'8", Light Complexion - 9/3/1862 at Portage Station - No bounty - Pvt, Pvt - Deserted House, siege of Suffolk, Franklin, Manassas Junction, Bristoe's Station, Culpeper, Wilderness, Todd's Tavern, Spotsylvania, North Anna River, Yellow Tavern, Pamunkey, Totopotomoy, Cold Harbor, Trevillian Station, Charles County Court House, before Richmond & Petersburg - 12/31/1865 (per 1890 Special Schedule), Regiment mustered out 6/30/1865 Honorable - Was not a casualty - Benjamin S. & Charity Green Snider (Both B NY) - Benjamin - 5/2/1819 in Goram - Artist - Farmer/Cheese Factory/Laborer - 1st Mary Ann Curtis, married 2/14/1841 (Died 4/25/1847), 2nd Harriet Bennett, married 12/31/1850 (Died 10/5/1851), 3rd Maria A. Price (widow), married 12/5/1852 at Portage - Charles W., Darius Martin, Sarah - 5/4/1883 - Pine Grove Cemetery,

Fillmore - Also served with 238th Co., 1st Battalion, VRC. Transferred to VRC 10/10/1864. March - April 1864 on special duty at Battalion Dismount Camp as a saddler. July 1864 to April 1865 sick in DC hospital. Suffered a sunstroke, 6/1/1864 at Trevillian Station. 12/1863 had dropsy at Culpeper. Was in hospital at Camp Stoneman 8/18/-8/20/1864, no reason cited. AWOL 2/16/1865, overstayed 10 day furlough. Probably worked for his son Charles at Cheese Factory post war. Burnside G.A.R. Post 237 Marker at grave. Sons Charles and Darius and brother Benjamin also served during the war. (Military & Pension Files, 1890 Fed. Census Special Schedule Granger, 1865 NYS Census Granger, Granger American Legion, Matteson, *History of Allegany County 1879*, 1865 Allegany County Town Clerk Register Granger, 1850, 1880 Fed. Censuses Granger)

Snider, Edwin (Snyder) This is likely Edward G. Snider. (Matteson)

Snider, Harmon Emmons (Snyder) Co. D, 4th NY Heavy Artillery - 12/26/1863 at Granger/3 yrs - 23 - 5'9", Dark Complexion, Blue Eyes, Brown Hair - 1/12/1864 at Elmira - $300 - Pvt, Pvt - No battles - 5/13/1865 Honorable - Was not a casualty - John T. & Rachael Emmons Snyder (Both B NY) - Laura, John Lewis, Catherine, Horatio Emerson, Martin William - 1/5/1840 (1841 per headstone) in Hume - Farmer - Farmer - 1st Harriet E. Wallace 9/5/1865 in Nunda (she later married Welcome Hall) - Charles E., Martin W., Ellen, Clarence E. Jesse - 3/7/1874 in Granger - Short Tract Cemetery County Route 4 - Was in hospital entire service with a hernia on his right side. First at City Point, VA and then Armory Square, DC. Brothers Horatio Emerson (twin), John Lewis, and Martin William also served during the war. (Military & Pension Files, 1890 Fed. Census Special Schedule Granger, Granger American Legion, 1865 Allegany County Town Clerk Register Granger, *Allegany and Its People*, 1865 NYS Census Granger - 1850 Fed. Census Hume, 1870 Fed. Census Granger)

Snider, Horatio Emerson (Snyder) Co. D, 4th NY Heavy Artillery - 12/30/1863 at Angelica/3 yrs - 23 - 5'8", Dark Complexion, Blue Eyes, Brown Hair - 12/20/1863 at Elmira - $300 - Pvt, Pvt - Wilderness, Spotsylvania, North Anna River, Totopotomoy, Cold Harbor, siege of Petersburg, Weldon RR, Ream's Station, Peeble's Farm, Hatcher's Run, fall of Petersburg, Appomattox - 9/26/1865 Honorable - Was not a casualty - John T. & Rachael Emmons Snyder (Both B NY) - Harmon Emmons, Laura, John Lewis, Catherine, Martin William - 1/5/1840 in Hume - Farmer - Farmer - Mary Maria Bennett, married 11/26/1881 in Allen - Oscar, Kittie May, Dollie, Paul E. - 9/12/1923 - Short Tract - Present at Lee's surrender. Marched in Grand Review 5/23/1865. Brother's Harmon Emmons (twin), John Lewis, and Martin William also served during the war. Moved to Michigan after war. (Military & Pension Files, Matteson, 1865 Allegany County Town Clerk Register Angelica, *Allegany & Its People*, 1850 Fed. Census Hume, 1870 Fed. Census Allen, 1880 Fed. Census Marilla, MI)

Snider, John Lewis (Snyder) Co. I/A, 19th NY Cavalry - 8/5/1862 at Portage/3 yrs - 20 - INA - 9/3/1862 at Portage Station - No bounty - Pvt, Corp - Deserted House, siege of Suffolk - 7/13/1865 Honorable - Was not a casualty - John T. & Rachael Emmons Snyder (Both B NY) - Laura, Martin William, Catherine, Horatio Emmons, Harmon Emerson - 1842 (headstone says 1837) in PA (Death certificate says Fillmore, but sisters Laura & Catherine, born on either side of him, were both born in PA) - INA - Farmer - 1st Mary C. Wallace (Died 1/29/1872), 2nd Annette (Nettie) Roseltha Wallace, Mary's sister (later married William O'Leary), married 8/22/1872 -

William M. - 4/14/1903 (1902 per headstone) - Short Tract Cemetery- May-June, 1863 sick in G.H., Ft. Monroe, VA, 8/6/1863 transferred to Invalid Corps (19th VRC). (Military & Pension Files, 1865 NYS Census Granger, Book *Allegany & Its People*, 1850 Fed. Census Hume, 1880 Fed.Census Angelica - NYS Adjutant General Report 1895 Volume 6)

Snider, Martin William (Snyder) Co. G, 19th NY Cavalry - 8/4/1862 at Allen/3 yrs - 19 - INA - 9/3/1862 at Portage Station - $100 - Pvt, Pvt - Deserted House, siege of Suffolk, Franklin, Manassas Junction, Bristoe's Station, Culpeper, Wilderness, Todd's Tavern, Spotsylvania, North Anna River, Yellow Tavern, Pamunkey, Totopotomoy, Cold Harbor, Trevillian Station, Charles County Court House, before Richmond & Petersburg, New Market, Shepherdstown - 8/25/1864 Honorable/Deceased - KIA, 8/25/1864 at Shepherdstown - John T. & Rachael Emmons Snyder (Both B NY) - Laura, John Lewis, Catherine, Harmon Emmons, Horatio Emerson - 1/8/1842 in Hume - Farm Laborer - None Deceased - Never Married - None - 8/25/1864 in Shepherdstown, WV - Short Tract - Listed on Soldiers Monument in Granger. January, February 1864 on detached service with reconnoitering party. (Military File, 1865 NYS Census Granger, *Allegany & Its People*, Matteson, 1865 Allegany County Town Clerk Register Granger, 1860 Fed. Census Granger, Granger American Legion.)

Somers, William F. At least one source document indicates that Somers served in the military during the war. No evidence of such service has been located. No William Somer(s) served in any NYS Civil War regiment. (Fillmore American Legion)

Soule, George W. (Sowle) Co. F, 4th New York Heavy Artillery - 8/27/1862 at Hume/3 yrs - 24 - 5'9", Light Complexion, Blue Eyes, Brown Hair - 8/29/1862 at NYC - $50 - Pvt - Wagoner - Wilderness, Spotsylvania, North Anna River, Totopotomoy, Cold Harbor, siege of Petersburg, Weldon RR, Ream's Station, Peeble's Farm, Hatcher's Run, fall of Petersburg - Appomattox - 6/3/1865 Honorable - Was not a casualty - Aaron Crain & Almira Bushnell Soule (Both B NY) - Gideon Wilbur, June C., Harriet E., Jackson F., Michael P. - 11/16/1837 in Warsaw - Farmer - Saw Mill Worker - 1st Catherine F. Clark, married 2/3/1861 in Fillmore, 2nd Anna H. Allen, married 5/1/1880 in Wiscoy - Virginia, Claude A., Anna M., Maud A., Roy L. - 1921 in Bliss - Pine Grove Cemetery, Fillmore - Present at Lee's surrender. Marched in Grand Review 5/23/1865. (Military & Pension Files, 1865 NYS Census Hume, Matteson, Fillmore American Legion, 1850 Fed. Census Caneadea, 1880 Fed. Census Pike)

Soule, Perrie (Peter) Clement Co. B, 18th NY Infantry - 9/1/1861 at Albany/2 yrs - 18 - 5'8", Fair Complexion, Grey Eyes, Light Hair - 9/1/1861 at Albany - No bounty - Pvt, Pvt - 1st Bull Run, Springfield, siege of Yorktown, Richmond, Gaine's Mill, Malvern Hill, South Mountain, Antietam, Fredericksburg, Franklin Crossing, Bank's Ford - 5/28/1863 Honorable - Was not a casualty while with the 18th Cavalry per military file. His records at the University of Rochester indicate that he was wounded in at least one battle and maybe in two - Absalom & Sara Clement Soule - Martha Jane, Charles Woster, Nelson, Sarah Ann, Catherine, Julia, Lucy Drucillo, Absolom Regraff, Lewis Hatfierd, Emeline Amelia, Malissa - 9/16/1844 in Palmyra - Farmer - Physician - 1st Clara E. Barber, 2nd Ada A., married 1898, she was 17 - Harold, Robert, Fred E., Ada, Lena M., Frank P., Mabel C., Varnie L. - 7/24/1924 in Rochester - INA - Served at one time as a mounted scout for General Sheridan. His Mother, according to the book, *Allegany & Its People*, was a lineal descendent of Pope's Clement XIII and XIV. The book also notes that his Mother was with a group of Quaker women who met with President Lincoln in 1862 to urge the immediate emancipation of all slaves. The book claims Soule participated in 170 battles and skirmishes. Charter Member & Officer of Burnside G.A.R. Post 237 and also served as Senior Vice Commander of the State G.A.R. Personal records are at the University of Rochester Library. Access at www,library.rochester.edu/rbk/soule.stm, or by visiting the University. When he enlisted he gave his age as 18, but was actually still 16. Also served with Co I, 5th NY Cavalry (see below). His son Frank P. served in the military during the Spanish-American War. (Military File [Pension File is apparently lost.], 1890 Fed. Census Special Schedule Hume, *Allegany & Its People*, 1900 Fed. Census Hume, 1860 Fed. Census Watervliet. University of Rochester Library)

Soule, Perrie Clement Co. I, 5th NY Cavalry - 1/14/1864 at Windsor/3 yrs - 18 per military file (probably 22) - 5'8", Fair Complexion, Grey Eyes, Light Hair - 1/14/1864 at Oswego - $400 - Pvt, C Sgt - Parker's House, Todd's Tavern, Wilderness, Spotsylvania, North Anna River Pamunkey, Totopotomoy, Hanover Court House, Cold Harbor, Gaine's Mill, Salem Church, Bethesda Church, Malvern Hill, South Side RR, Roanoke Bridge, Ream's Station, before Petersburg, Kernstown, Winchester, Fisher's Hill, New Market, Port Republic, Cedar Creek, Mount Jackson - 7/19/1865 Honorable - WIA, 11/22/1864 at Mount Jackson badly wounded by gunshot; 2 to left thigh, 1 to left hand, 1 to right leg, 2 to left leg, 2 to right arm, one to his abdomen - Promoted to Sgt 11/1/1864. Also served with Co. B, 18th NY Infantry, see above. Also see above for personal information and sources of information.

Sowersby, William W. Co. F, 5th NY Cavalry - 9/19/1861 at Hume/3 yrs (Re-enlisted 12/26/1863)- 20 - 5'9", Light Complexion, Blue Eyes, Light Hair - 9/21/1861 at NYC - $400 - Pvt, Sgt - New Market, Port Republic, Orange County Court House, 2nd Bull Run, Antietam, New Baltimore, Hanover Court House, Hagerstown, Gettysburg, Culpeper, Hay Market, Ellis Ford, Todd's Tavern, Wilderness, Cold Harbor, Ream's Station, Berryville, Cedar Creek, Dinwiddie, Five Forks, Appomattox - 7/19/1865 Honorable - Was not a casualty - George (B England) & Pauline Kenyon (B MI) Sowersby - Wilbur, William, Charles, Esther Ann, Alice - 8/4/1842 in Hume - Farmer - Farmer - Matilda Baxter, married 2/19/1867 - Donald J., Mary, George - 1/19/1899 in Town of New Hudson - Bellville Cemetery, New Hudson Township - Present at Lee's surrender. Marched in the Grand Review 5/23/ 1865. On furlough 2/4-20/1865. Promoted to Corp. 1/5/1863. (Military & Pension Files, 1865 NYS Census Hume, 1865 Allegany County Town Clerk Register Hume, *History of Allegany County 1879*, 1850 Fed. Census Hume, 1870 Fed. Census Rushford)

Spease, Henry Whitney (Speas) Co. H, 19th NY Cavalry - 9/22/1864 at Genesee Falls/1 yr - 23 - 5'10", Light Complexion, Blue Eyes, Brown Hair - 9/23/1864 at Lockport - $400 - Pvt, Pvt - No battles - 6/30/1865 Honorable - Was not a casualty - Isaac & Nancy Cary Spease (Both B NY) - A. Jackson, Gertrude A., Almina E., Caroline C., Frances H. -8/13/1841 in Portageville - Farmer - Farm Laborer - Cordelia A. Olee, married 1/13/1862 in Fillmore - None - 10/24/1898 in Portageville - Portageville, East Koy Road - Marched in Grand Review 5/23/1865. Deserted 10/6/1864, at Barracks 1, Elmira. Arrested 10/6/1864 at Big Flats, NY. Court-martialed, fined $10.00. Town Clerk spelled name Spear. (Military & Pension Files, 1865 Allegany County Town Clerk Register Hume, 1850 Fed. Census Genesee, 1860 Fed. Census Hume, 1880 Fed. Census

Granger)

Spencer, Anson Hinman Co. F, 19th NY Cavalry - 8/13/1862 at Hume/3 yrs - 32 - INA - 9/3/1862 at Portage Station - $100 - Pvt, Pvt - No battles - 1/5/1863 Honorable/Deceased - DD, 1/5/1863 at Suffolk, VA of fever - William & Hannah Edmonds Spencer (Both B VT) - INA - 1829 or 30 in Pike - Carpenter - None Deceased - Never Married - None - 1/5/1863 in Suffolk, VA - Hampton, VA National Cemetery (as O.H. Spencer) - Originally buried at Suffolk. Per his diary, Dr. William M. Smith visited Spencer on 12/30/1862. (Military File. *History of Allegany County 1879*, Allegany County Web Site, 1860 Fed. Census Pike, *Roll of Honor*, *Swamp Doctor* edited by Thomas P. Lowry, M.D)

Standard, Silas E. (Stannard) Co. D, 4th NY Heavy Artillery - 12/4/1863 at Caneadea/3 yrs - 43 - 5'6", Fair Complexion, Light Eyes, Light Hair - 12/21/1863 at Elmira - $300 - Pvt, Pvt - Wilderness, Spotsylvania, North Anna River, Totopotomoy, Cold Harbor, siege of Petersburg, Weldon RR - 11/2/1864 Honorable/Deceased- DD, 11/2/1864 at Caneadea while on furlough, of dropsy - Probably Grinnel & Betsey Stanard - INA - 1822/23 in Castile - Lumberman/Farmer - None Deceased - Catherine Spees, married 5/12/1843 in Portage - Mary, Adaline, Emma, Henry, Evaline, Sarah, Cora C. - 11/2/1864 in Caneadea - East Koy, Lamont Road - Name is spelled Stanard in pension file. (Military & Pension Files, Matteson, 1865 Allegany County Town Clerk Register Caneadea, 1860 Fed. Census Hume)

Standish, Gideon B. Co. E, 85th NY Infantry - 9/1/1861 at Granger/3 years 18 - 5'11", Light Complexion, Blue Eyes, Light Hair - 11/25/1861 at Elmira - No bounty - Pvt, Pvt - defense of DC, siege of Yorktown - 11/27/1863 Disability/ Honorable - Was not a casualty - Ira (B VT) & Laura Beman (B CT) Standish - J.H., Elizabeth C., Orin N., Miron N., Hiram C. - 10/1843 in South Bristol - Blacksmith - Blacksmith - Ruth E. Bowhall, married 12/23/1877 in Rochester - William H. (adopted, born in Canada) - 1912 - INA - Disability discharge due to atrophy of left lung. Reported as a deserter 9/4/1862. Rejoined company 5/20/1863. Was actually in hospital in Newport News, VA as of 5/27/1862, moved to hospital steamer *Fulton* 6/10/1862 to be transferred to NYC. Charge of desertion removed from his record 5/26/1888. Went home to Cold Creek 6/15/1862. At the time he was under the impression he was dying. In November he was admitted to a hospital in Detroit. Brothers Myron M. and Orin also served during the war. (Military & Pension Files, 1865 Allegany County Town Clerk Register Hume, 1850 Fed. Census Naples, 1900 Fed. Census Siuslaw, OR)

Standish, Myron (Miron) M. Co. D, 64th NY Infantry 10/2/1861 at Rushford/3 yrs - 24 - 5'11", Dark Complexion, Blue Eyes, Brown Hair - 10/19/1861 at Elmira - No bounty - Corp, Pvt - siege of Yorktown, Fair Oaks - 6/3/1862 Honorable/Deceased - WIA, gunshot to abdomen, 6/1/1862 at Fair Oaks, KIA, died 6/3/1862 of battle wounds at White House, VA - Ira (B VT) & Laura Beman (B CT) Standish - J.H., Elizabeth C., Orin N., Gideon B., Hiram C. - 11/17/1837 in South Bristol (County Clerk says Hume) - Gunsmith - None Deceased - Eunice M. Isted, married 8/18/1860 - Frederick C. - 6/3/1862 in White House, VA - INA - Some documents spell the first name Mirum. (Military & Pension Files, 1865 NYS Census Hume, Allegany County Web Site, 1865 Allegany County Town Clerk Register Hume, *History of Allegany County 1879*, 1850 Fed. Census Naples)

Standish, Orin Nelson Co. D, 64th NY Infantry - 10/5/1861 at Rushford/3 yrs - 27 - 6'1", Sandy Complexion, Blue Eyes, Sandy Hair - 10/1861 at Elmira - No bounty - Pvt, Pvt - siege of Yorktown, Fair Oaks - 8/9/1862 Disability/Honorable - WIA, gunshot to left hand (lost index finger) 6/1/1862 at Fair Oaks - Ira (B VT) & Laura Beman (B CT) Standish - J.H., Elizabeth C., Gideon B., Myron M., Hiram C. - 5/8/1834 in South Bristol - Harness Maker - Salesman - Charlotte - INA - 8/5/1897 - Dayton National Cemetery - Was in Portsmouth, VA hospital and Philadelphia G.H. with wound. Was mistakenly charged with desertion. (Military & Pension Files, 1865 Allegany County Town Clerk Register Hume, 1860 Fed. Census Hume)

Stanley, Henry At least one source document indicates that Stanley served in the military during the war. No evidence of such service has been located. Wife claimed she never heard from after his enlistment. No census cites found. No Henry Stanley served in any NYS Civil War regiment. (1890 Fed Census Special Schedule Centerville.)

Stannard, Grinwold At least one source document indicates that Grinwold served in the military during the war. No evidence of such service has been located. No Grinwold Stannard served in any NYS Civil War regiment. (Fillmore American Legion, Matteson)

Steih, Daniel (Stich, Steh) Co. F, 9th NY Heavy Artillery - 2/22/1864 at Groveland/3 yrs - 20 - 5'7", Dark Complexion, Grey Eyes, Dark Hair - 2/25/1864 at Canandaigua - $300 - .Pvt, Pvt - North Anna River, Pamunkey, Totopotomoy, Cold Harbor, siege of Petersburg, Weldon RR, Monocacy, Winchester, Fishers Hill, Cedar Creek - 6/6/1865 Disability/Honorable - WIA, gunshot to right leg at Cedar Creek, probably 10/19/1864 - Godfrey(Christian) & Catherine Steih (Both B Germany) - Christian?, Jacob - 11/7/1844 in Bavaria, Germany - Farmer - Farmer - Catherine Husson, married 12/11/? in East Granger - Elizabeth (Lizzie) and Mary - 2/2/1920 - Union Cemetery, Dalton - Came to U.S. in 1854. Was in Patterson Park, Baltimore hospital. Listed his father's name as Gregory. Confusion in records regarding name of father, probably Godfrey. (Military & Pension Files, 1860, 1870, 1880 Fed. Censuses Grove, Granger American Legion, NYS Adjutant General Report)

Steward, Lanson Alanson Co. D, 4th NY Heavy Artillery - 12/26/1863 at Granger/3 yrs - 33 - 5'7", Dark Complexion, Black Eyes, Brown Hair - 12/26/1863 at Elmira - $300 - Pvt, Pvt - Wilderness, Spotsylvania, North Anna River, Totopotomoy, Cold Harbor, siege of Petersburg, Weldon RR, Ream's Station, Peeble's Farm, Hatcher's Run, fall of Petersburg, Appomattox - 9/26/1865 Honorable - Was not a casualty - Horace & Marinda Dart Steward (Both B CT) - INA - 3/24/1832 in Belfast - Lumberman/Farm Laborer - Mill Worker - Esther Hogeboom, married 10/29/1857 in Belfast - Horace, Matthias, Eleanor Kegia, Rosa Bella - 1/4/1913 in Ischua - Fitch Cemetery, Ischua - Had a total of ten children. (Military & Pension Files, 1865 Allegany County Town Clerk Register Granger, 1880, 1910 Fed. Censuses Ischua)

Stewart/Steward, John T. Co. D, 4th NY Heavy Artillery - 12/2/1863 at Granger/3 yrs - 36 - 5'2", Dark Complexion, Hazel Eyes, Dark Hair - 12/26/1863 at Elmira - $300 - Pvt, Pvt - Wilderness, Spotsylvania, North Anna River, Totopotomoy, Cold Harbor, Peeble's Farm, Hatcher's Run, fall of Petersburg, Appomattox - 9/26/1865 Honorable - Was not a casualty - INA (Both B NY) - INA - circa 1830 in PA - Lumberman - Grocer - Hariette - Maryette, Angeline G., Frances, Clarissa,

Emma T., Frank, Wesley - 10/26/1905 in Ischua - Clover Leaf Road Cemetery, Black Creek (last name spelled Steward) - Present at Lee's surrender. Marched in Grand Review 5/23/1865. Was in Alexandria G.H. July 2, 1864 with chronic diarrhea. (Military & Pension Files, 1865 Allegany County Town Clerk Register Granger, 1860 Fed. Census Granger, 1880 Fed. Census New Hudson)

Stickle, John Murray Co. F, 19th NY Cavalry - 8/12/1862 at Hume/3 yrs - 23 - 5'9", Light Complexion, Grey Eyes, Dark Hair - 9/3/1862 at Portage Station - $150 - Pvt.,1st Corp - Deserted House, siege of Suffolk, Franklin, Manassas Junction, Bristoe's Station, Culpeper, Wilderness, Todd's Tavern, Spotsylvania, North Anna River, Yellow Tavern, Pamunkey, Totopotomoy, Cold Harbor, Trevillian Station - 7/4/1864 Honorable/Deceased - WIA, 6/12/1864 at Trevillian Station, wound unspecified, POW, captured 6/12/1864 at Trevillian Station, Prison: not listed , KIA, died of wounds 7/4/1864 at Gordonsville (Dansville), VA - Morris (B NY) & Susannah Wight Stickle - Samuel? - 10/16/1838 in Centerville - Farm Laborer - None Deceased - Never Married - None - 7/4/1864 in Gordonsville (Dansville), VA - Gordonsville, VA - Promoted to Corporal 9/1863. (Military File, 1865 NYS Census Centerville, 1890 Fed. Census Special Schedule Centerville, 1865 Allegany County Town Clerk Register Hume, Allegany County Web Site, Matteson, *History of Allegany County 1879*, 1850 Fed. Census Centerville, 1860 Fed. Census Hume)

Stickle, Judson Co. F, 19th NY Cavalry - 8/11/1862 at Centerville - 18 - 5'10", Light Complexion, Grey Eyes, Brown Hair - 9/3/1862 at Portage Station - $400 - Pvt, Pvt - Deserted House, siege of Suffolk, Franklin, Manassas Junction, Bristoe's Station, Culpeper, Wilderness, Todd's Tavern, Spotsylvania, North Anna River, Yellow Tavern, Pamunkey, Totopotomoy, Cold Harbor, Trevillian Station, Charles County Court House, before Richmond & Petersburg - 6/18/1865 Honorable - Was not a casualty - Chilon & Mabel Norton Stickle (Both B VT) - Jason M., Betsy M., Hulda E. Leland, Caroline, Erwin - Caroline - 6/22/1844 in Centerville - Farmer - Farmer - Loretta B. Lyon, married 10/22/1866 in Hume - Chilon J.- Howard (Howard's son William was killed in a plane crash in World War II) - 11/12/1929 in Fillmore - Bates Cemetery, Centerville - January - February, 1864 on picket duty. September - October, 1863 left at Manassas Junction with horses. Charter Member of Burnside G.A.R. Post 237. (Military & Pension Files, 1865 NYS Census Centerville, *History of Allegany County 1879*, *Allegany & Its People*, 1865 Allegany County Town Clerk Register Centerville, Matteson, Centerville American Legion, 1850, 1880, 1900, 1910 Fed. Censuses Centerville)

Stockweather, George Co. F, 19th NY Cavalry - 12/16/1863 at Buffalo/3 yrs - 5'7", Light Complexion, Blue Eyes, Sandy Hair - $300 - 1/5/1864 at Elmira - Wilderness, Todd's Tavern, Spotsylvania, North Anna River, Yellow Tavern, Pamunkey, Totopotomoy, Cold Harbor, Trevillian Station - 6/30/1865 Honorable - WIA, gunshot to face, 6/12/1864 at Trevillian Station, ball entered left cheek, existed behind lower part of left ear. Deaf in left ear and left side of jaw did not function, POW, captured 6/12/1864 at Trevillian Station, Prison; Richmond, Paroled 9/26/1864 at Varina, VA - George (B NY) & Mahittable Wells (B ME) Stockweather - INA - 4/15/1847 (or 46) in Granger, Farmer - Farmer - Mary A. Vincent, married 9/29/1870 in Allen - Albion Grant, Adelbert, May - 5/5/1936 in Hunt, Short Tract - Was probably only 16 when he volunteered. Was in Annapolis hospital. Returned to duty 12/22/1864. Sent to Remount Camp in MD. May have marched in Grand Review 5/23/1865. (Military & Pension Files, Matteson, 1860

Fed. Census Angelica, 1880 Fed. Census Granger)

Stone, Joseph Sr. At least one source document indicates that Joseph, Sr. served in the military during the war. No evidence of such service has been located. There is a Burnside G.A.R. Post 237 Marker at the grave, which is probably misplaced and may be the cause of confusion about Joseph's service. A number of Joseph Stones served in NYS regiments during the war. To date none has been identified as being from the C-H-G area. (Fillmore American Legion)

Stone, Silas Wyman Co. D, 4th NY Heavy Artillery - 8/13/1862 at Rochester/3 yrs - 29 -5'7", Dark Complexion, Blue Eyes, Dark Hair - 8/13/1862 at Rochester - $100 - Pvt, Pvt - fall of Petersburg, Appomattox - 6/3/1865 Honorable - Was not a casualty - Thomas & Nancy Babcock Stone - INA - 8/21/1833 in North (East?) Essex, PA - Carpenter/Farmer - Carpenter - Julia L. Colgrove, married 11/20/1861 in Pike - Lonnie, Alonzo - 1/6/1875 in North East, PA - North East, PA - Present at Lee's surrender. Marched in Grand Review 5/23/1865. Sick at DC, March - December 1864. Received a furlough 7/20/1864. 8/7/1863 diagnosed with lung disease at Fort Ethan Allen. Moved to Pennsylvania after the war. (Military & Pension Files, 1865 Allegany County Town Clerk Register Hume, Allegany County Web Site, Matteson, 1860 Fed. Census Hume, 1870 Fed. Census Erie County, PA)

Sutter, Samuel Jacob Not from the C-H-G area. Served with Co. K, 8th NY Cavalry. His enlistment in the 8th Cavalry was credited to Hume Township, which paid his enlistment bonus of $800. The Town Clerk had him serving with the 19th Cavalry as did the NYS Adjutant General Report. The Adjutant General also has him serving with the 8th Cavalry. Adjutant General information for the Sutter in the 19th is exactly the same as for the Sutter in the 8th. There is, however, no military file for a Sutter in the 19th Cavalry. Someone simply made a mistake. (1865 Allegany County Town Clerk Register Hume, NYS Adjutant General Report 1895 Volume 6, NYS Adjutant General Report 1894 Volume 2)

Taber, Albert Owen Co. E, 85th NY Infantry - 0/1/1861 at Granger/3 yrs - 28 - INA - 10/10/1861 at Elmira - No bounty - Pvt, Sgt - defense of DC, siege of Yorktown - 10/28/1862 Honorable/ Deceased, DD, 10/28/1862 at Regimental Hospital, Suffolk, VA of remittent gastric fever - Record (B NY) & Sally (B NJ) Tabor - Louisa, Clark W. - 1832 or 33 in NY - Farmer - None Deceased - Never Married - None - 10/28/1862 in Suffolk, VA - INA (Possibly in Hampton National Cemetery.) Appointed Sgt 11/7/1861. Taber death is mentioned in Dr. William M. Smith diary, (*Swamp Doctor*). Smith mentions that Taber was an Orderly and "a most excellent young man". Was left sick at Lee's Mill, 5/4/1862. (Military File, *History of Allegany County 1879*, Matteson, 1850 Fed. Census Portage, *Swamp Doctor*, *Roll of Honor*)

Tadder, David E. (Tedder) (Teder) Co. A, 104 NY Infantry - 12/4/1861 at Granger/3 yrs - 24 - 6', Light Complexion, Blue Eyes, Light Hair - 2/26/1862 at Geneseo - No bounty - Pvt, Pvt - Cedar Creek, 2nd Bull Run, South Mountain, Antietam, Fredericksburg - 2/5/1863 Disability/Honorable - WIA, gunshot wound to head12/13/1862 at Fredericksburg - James (B VT) and ?(B Germany) Tadder - Mary (married Alonzo Gillette) - 1836 or 37 in Livingston County - Farmer - Farmer - Charlotte M. Aldrich, married 2/28/1863 in Oakland - William Graham (Adopted B1861), Carrie Head (B 1872, living with them) - 5/27/1884 in Dalton - Church Street Cemetery Dalton,

Livingston County - Was in St. Elizabeth's Hospital, DC for treatment. The ball that injured him entered left side of face and exited his neck. Lost his left eye, was deaf in left ear, had paralysis of left side of face, injured his tongue and had problems turning his head. (Military & Pension Files, Matteson, *History of Allegany County 1879*, Granger American Legion, 1870, 1880 Fed. Censuses Granger, 1860 Fed. Census Portage)

Taylor, Randall Co. C, 19th NY Cavalry - 9/13/1864 at Centerville/1 yr - 34 - 6', Fair Complexion, Blue Eyes, Sandy Hair - 9/27/1864 at Elmira - $150 - Pvt, Pvt - Cedar Creek, Berryville, Gordonsville - 6/30/1865 Honorable - Was not a casualty - Stephen & Electa Taylor (Both B NY) - Wilson, Ralph, Cynthia Bethanee? - 1830 in Centerville - Farmer - Farmer - Mary Jane Hawkins, married 1/28/1858 in Hume - Ella - INA (Disappeared in 1875 and was never heard from again) - INA - He was eventually declared dead and his wife Mary received his pension. Purchased his revolver for $8.00 when discharged. (Military & Pension Files, 1865 NYS Census Centerville, *History of Allegany County 1879*, Matteson, 1865 Allegany County Town Clerk Register Centerville, 1860, 1870 Fed. Censuses Centerville)

Thatcher, Edward Edgar Co. C, 194th NY Infantry - 3/29/1865 at Hume/3 yrs - 22 - 5'5", Fair Complexion, Blue Eyes, Brown Hair - 4/7/1865 at Elmira - $500 - Pvt, Pvt - No battles - 5/3/1865 Honorable - Was not a casualty - James & Harriet Mason Thatcher - INA - 9/1842 in Allegany County - Farmer - Farm Laborer - Melvina - None - INA - INA - Also served with Co. C, 27th Michigan Infantry from 9/1862 to 12/1863. Military Index for 27th has name as Tachter, but the file cannot be located at the National Archives. Claimed injury to left shoulder and gunshot wound to right leg at Lookout Mountain. Pension application was not approved. Based on the 1865 Town Clerk Register, it appears that Thatcher was not from the C-H-G area. The Register states that Hume received credit for his enlistment, presumably for paying the re-enlistment bonus. (Military & Pension Files, 1865 Allegany County Town Clerk Register Hume, Book *History of Allegany County 1879*, 1880 Fed Census Juniata Township, MI, 1865 Allegany County Town Clerk Register Caneadea, 1900 Fed Census Thetford Township, MI)

Thorp, Alexander Kelsey Co. F, 19th NY Cavalry - 8/19/1862 at Granger/3 yrs - 35 - INA - 9/3/1862 at Portage Station - No bounty - 2nd Lt., Capt. - Deserted House, siege of Suffolk, Franklin, Manassas Junction, Bristoe's Station, Culpeper, Wilderness, Todd's Tavern, Spotsylvania, North Anna River, Yellow Tavern, Pamunkey, Totopotomoy, Cold Harbor, Trevillian Station, Charles County Court House, before Richmond & Petersburg, New Market, Shepherdstown, Winchester - KIA, 9/19/1864 at Winchester - Montgomery (B CT) & Bethiah (Bertha) Jones (B Canada) Thorp - Simon M. Harriet, Thomas, Eliza, Emily, Anna - 6/21/1828 at Amherst - Wagon Maker - None Deceased - 1st Mary E. Stewart, married 2/16/1851 (Died 11/30/1856), 2nd Harriet A. Swain, married 4/29/1858 - Sarah, John, Mary E. - 9/19/1864 in Winchester, VA (one document says he died 9/26 of wounds) - Short Tract Cemetery, County Route 4 - Promoted to Captain 12/22/1862. Brother Thomas also served during the war. His brother Simon M. was murdered in Lawrence, Kansas during the infamous Quantrell raid on Lawrence. 8/31/1863 telegram in his file advising him of his brother's death and the terminal illness of his father. (Military & Pension Files, 1865 NYS Census Granger, Matteson, 1850, 1860 Federal Censuses Granger, Granger American Legion, 1865 Allegany County Town Clerk Register Granger)

Thorp, Thomas James Co. E/Staff, 85th NY Infantry - 9/1/1861 at Granger/3 yrs - 24 - 5'10", Dark Complexion, Dark Eyes, Dark Hair - 12/21/1861 at Elmira - No bounty - Capt., Lt. Col. - defense of DC, siege of Yorktown, Williamsburg, Fair Oaks, before Richmond - 8/26/1862 Honorable - WIA, gunshot to left thigh and below left knee 5/31/1861 at Fair Oaks - Montgomery (B CT) & Bethiah (Bertha) Jones (B Canada) Thorp - Simon M. Harriet, Alexander, Eliza, Emily, Anna - May, 1837 - INA [likely was in law school] - Lawyer - Mandan C. Major, married 9/6/1862 (or more likely 1861) in Portage in the "hollow square" of his regiment. (Regiment would not have been in Portage in 1862.) - Montgomery S., Bessie M. - 7/25/1915 in Corvallis, OR Cyrstal Lake Cemetery, Corvallis, OR - Brother Alexander also served during the war. Promoted to Captain 10/9/1861. Helped to organize the 85th Regiment and probably did organize Company E. His military files for the 85th are under the name Thorpe. Was home on leave 8/1/1862. His brother Simon M. was murdered in Lawrence, Kansas during the infamous Quantrell raid on Lawrence. Also served as staff with the 19th NY Cavalry, see below. Dr. William M. Smith mentions Thorp a number of times in his diary (book *Swamp Doctor*), and does not speak highly of him. He did mention that he ran into Thorp and his wife in Norfolk, VA on Friday, 4/3/1863 when they both were attending the theater. (Military and Pension Files, *History of Allegany County 1879*, Matteson, 1865 Allegany County Town Clerk Register Granger, 1850 Fed. Census Granger, 1870 Fed. Census Wexford, MI, 1910 Fed. Census Crovallis, OR, *Swamp Doctor*)

Thorp, Thomas James Staff, 19th NY Cavalry - 8/27/1862 at Washington, DC - 25 - 5'10", Dark Complexion, Dark Eyes, Dark Hair - 8/27/1862 at DC - No bounty - Lt. Col., Colonel - Todd's Tavern, Trevillian Station - 6/30/1865 Honorable - POW, captured 6/11/1864 at Trevillian Station, Prisons: Richmond, Macon, Charleston, Paroled at N.E. Ferry, NC 3/1/1865 - received 30 day furlough following his release. 8/27/1862 promoted to Lt. Colonel, to Colonel on 3/1/1865 (this promotion was made retroactive to 12/24/1864 on 7/8/1889), to Brevet Brigadier General 10/14/1865 (Brevet is an honorary rank, but was awarded for "gallant and meritorious service). In editing Dr. William Smith's diary (book *Swamp Doctor*), Dr. Thomas Lowery notes that Thorp tried to escape from prison several times and would have made it once, had it not been for bloodhounds. He also notes that Colonel Alfred Gibbs considered Thorp one of the best officers in the service. Lowery does have Thorp in prison until the end of the war, which is incorrect. Thorp was at home on leave when the war ended. See above for 85th Infantry information. Also see above for personal information and sources of information.

Thurston, William Wallace Co. C, 104th NY Infantry - 9/22/1861 at Geneseo/3 yrs (Re-enlisted 1/3/1864) - 21 - 5'8", Dark Complexion, Blue Eyes, Black Hair, Scar over right eye - 2/26/1862 at Geneseo - $400 - Pvt, Sgt - Cedar Creek, 2nd Bull Run, South Mountain, Fredericksburg, Antietam, Chancellorsville, Gettysburg, Bristoe's Station, Wilderness, Spotsylvania, North Anna River, Pamunkey, Totopotomoy, Cold Harbor, Bethesda Church, Petersburg, Weldon RR - 6/10/1865 Honorable - POW, captured at Petersburg 8/18/1864, Prisons: Libby & Belle, Richmond, VA, Salisbury, NC , Paroled N.E. Ferry NC 3/1/1865 - Thomas & Nancy Van Dresser Thurston (Both B NY) - Esau - 1/16/1841 or 42 - Farmer - Farmer - Emma L. Skiff, married 3/7/1876 (died 10/2/ 1885) - None - 1/15/1903 in his home - Pine Grove Cemetery, Fillmore - Charter Member of Burnside G.A.R. Post 237. Post Market at grave. Usually went by his middle name Wallace. Appointed Corp 4/16/1864, Sgt 7/27/1864. Got bone fever while in prison at Salisbury. (Military & Pension Files, 1865 Allegany County Town Clerk Register Hume, Matteson,

Tibbitts, George Henry Allen Co. E, 85th NY Infantry - 9/1/1861 at Granger/3 yrs (Re-enlisted 1/1/1864) - 21 - 5'8", Dark Complexion, Blue Eyes, Brown Hair - 10/10/1861 at Elmira - $400 - Sgt, Sgt - defense of DC, siege of Yorktown, Williamsburg, Plymouth - 8/1/1865 Honorable - POW, captured 4/20/1864 at Plymouth, NC, Prison: Florence, SC Andersonville, paroled N.E. Ferry, NC 2/27/1865 - Charles & Mary Tibbitts (Both B MA) - Charles, Clarinda, Alvira, Sophia, William H. - 6/12/1840 in Perry - Laborer/Artist - Paper Hanger/Attendant, Electric Substation/ RR Brakeman - Frances J. Bertholf, married 7/24/1865 in Whiteford - Effie, Ruel, Gail, Sherman M., Ada O., Bruce J., Charles H., Naomi, Agnes H. -12/8/1929 in Detroit - INA - Appointed 5th Sgt 11/7/1861, 4th Sgt 11/1/1862, 3rd Sgt 1/17/1863, Sgt 1/1/1864. Absent sick as of July 5, 1862. Detached to the Balloon Corps 5/1/1862. Apparently also served three months in 1861 with Co. K, 14th Ohio Infantry under the name Henry Allen. Father married to a Hannah in 1860. (Military & Pension Files, *History of Allegany County 1879*, Matteson, 1850 Fed. Census Nunda, 1860 Fed. Census Lucas County, OH, 1870 Fed. Census Oregon Township, OH)

Tooley, William L, Battery D, 1st NY Light Artillery 8/29/1862 at Antwerp/3 yrs - 23 - 5'9", Dark Complexion, Blue Eyes, Black Hair - 9/8/1862 at Albany - $25 - Pvt, Pvt - Chancellorsville - 7/20/1865 Disability/Honorable - WIA, gunshot to lower cheek and jaw (slight), 5/3/1863 at Chancellorsville - Israel & Mary Ann Tooley - Lewis, Alvin, Dexter, Lucy M., Sarah E. Betty P. - 1839 in Antwerp - Farmer - Clergyman/Baker - 1st Lydia Clark, married circa 1870 (Died 1879), 2nd Emma J. Brewer Deuel (widow) - William, Robert, Clarence, Delbert - 1/2/1907 in Portageville - Pine Grove Cemetery, Fillmore - Transferred to Co. D, 12th VRC. 8/13/1863 sick in Albany hospital. Transferred to Co. 44, 2nd Battalion, VRC 11/1/1863. On detached service at U.S. Post Hospital, Albany as of 3/10/1864. Transferred to 138th Co., 2nd Battalion, VRC, 10/27/1864. Transferred to Co. L, 12th VRC 6/16/1865. Burnside G.A.R. Post 237 Marker at grave. (Military & Pension Files, Matteson, Fillmore American Legion, 1850 Fed. Census Antwerp, 1870 Fed. Census Granger)

Townsend, John Co. H, 136th NY Infantry - 9/1/1862 Granger/3 yrs - 35 - 5'4", Fair Complexion, Blue Eyes, Brown Hair - 9/25/1862 Portage - No bounty - Pvt, Pvt - Chancellorsville Gettysburg, Lookout Mountain, Resaca, New Hope Church, Kenesaw, siege of Atlanta, occupation of Atlanta, Goldsboro, Bentonsville, Bennett's House. 6/13/1865 Honorable - WIA, gunshot above left knee (date and place not certain - maybe Chancellorsville. He claimed 2nd Bull Run), WIA, gunshot below left knee, 7/2/1863 at Gettysburg, WIA, 8/63 at Lookout Mountain, gunshot right hip on picket duty (ball never removed), WIA, early 1865 gunshot to right arm (date & place not certain, maybe Goldsboro. He claimed Fort Fisher.) - INA - INA - 1825 or 26 in Michigan - Farm Laborer - Farmer - Eliza J. Bates, married 9/1855 - Lettie, Viola - 7/6/1902 - Probably Hunt - Detached to Ordnance Department 3/28/1863 to 3/24/1864. Present at the surrender of General Johnston and his army. Marched in Grand Review 5/25/1865. Gunshot wounds not accepted for pension purposes because of lack of medical records, even though medical evidence for some of the wounds was available. The Pension Board did not contradict the wound claims. Pension awarded for rheumatism and other disabilities. (Military & Pension Files, Matteson, *History of Allegany County 1879*, Granger American Legion, 1865 Allegany County Town Clerk Register Granger,

1860 Fed. Census Granger, 1870 Fed. Census Portage)

Trall, George Co. C, 104th NY Infantry - 11/9/1861 at Geneseo/3 yrs - 21 - 5'9", Dark Complexion, Brown Eyes, Brown Hair - 2/26/1862 at Geneseo - No bounty - Pvt, Pvt - No battles - 8/4/1862 Disability/Honorable - Was not a casualty - Luman (B CT) & Mary Potter Short (B NY) Trall - Abel, Spencer, Sheldon, Almira, Sarah - 6/23/1842 in Hume - Farmer - Laborer - 1st Mary A. Nye (Died 12/1879), 2nd Alice Miller Peters (widow), married 10/12/1884 - Cora A., Edmon, Lillie M., Minnie - 3/11/1920 in Soldiers Home, Bath - Bath National Cemetery - Also served with Co. C, 194th NY Infantry, see below. Disability was for phthisis and an umbilical hernia. Sick in hospital as of 7/5/1862, lost 120 days of duty. A 5/19/1903 note in his file says that the discharge date of 8/4/1862 is correct. Age when he volunteered is incorrect, was only 19. Charter member of Burnside G.A.R. Post 237. Brothers Sheldon and Spencer also served during the war. George and his 2nd wife Alice had a real fight over his pension. She accused him of desertion, cruelty, and an affair. He denied all, and accused her of an affair. The Pension Board sided with Alice, and awarded her his pension. Also served with 194th NY Infantry, see below. (Military & Pension Files, 1865 Allegany County Town Clerk Register Hume, 1890 Fed. Census Special Schedule Hume, *Allegany & Its People*, *History of Allegany County 1879*, 1860, 1880 Fed. Censuses Hume)

Trall, George Co. C, 194th NY Infantry - 3/29/1865/1 yr - 22 - 5'9", Dark Complexion, Brown Eyes, Brown Hair - 4/7/1865 at Elmira - $400 - Pvt, 1st Sgt - No battles - 5/3/1865 Honorable - Was not a casualty - Promoted to Sgt 4/8/1865. Brothers Sheldon & Spencer also served during the war. Also served with Co. C, 104th NY Infantry, see above. Also see above for personal information and sources of information.

Trall, Sheldon T. Co. F, 4th NY Heavy Artillery - 8/1/1862 at Hume/3 yrs - 21 - 5'10", Light Complexion - 8/29/1862 at NYC - $100 - Pvt, Sgt - Wilderness, Spotsylvania, North Anna River, Totopotomoy, Cold Harbor, siege of Petersburg, Weldon RR, Ream's Station, Peeble's Farm, Hatcher's Run, fall of Petersburg, Five Forks, Appomattox - 6/3/1865 Honorable - WIA, gunshot to left hip 4/1/1865 at Five Forks - Luman (B CT) & Mary Polly Short (B NY) Trall - Abel, George, Spencer, Almira, Sarah - 11/6/1839 in Hume - Farmer - Farmer - Cornelia R. Allen Babcock, married 10/23/1866 in East Pike - Charles R. - 2/18/1897 in Hume - Alger Cemeter Hume, Route 19 - Promoted to Sgt 8/1/1864, 1st Sgt 1/1/1865. Suffered a sunstroke 5/6/1865 near Richmond. Charter Member of Burnside G.A.R. Post 237. Present at Lee's surrender. Marched in Grand Review 5/23/1865. Brothers George and Spencer also served during the war. (Military & Pension Files, 1865 NYS Census Hume, Matteson, 1865 Allegany Town Clerk Register Hume, *Allegany & Its People*, 1860, 1880 Fed. Censuses Hume)

Trall, Spencer Co. F, 4th NY Heavy Artillery - 8/7/1862 at Hume/3 yrs - 26 - 5'10", Light Complexion, Grey Eyes, Black Hair - 8/29/1862 at NYC - $50 - Pvt, Corp - fall of Petersburg, Appomattox - 6/3/1865 Honorable - Was not a casualty - Luman (B CT) & Mary Polly short (B NY) Trall - Abel George Sheldon, Almira, Sarah - 1/5/1836 in Hume - Farmer - Laborer - Celinda Irene Tabor, married 7/27/1856 - Fred, Frank, Mary, Ada May - 12/4/1918 in Pike - Pike Cemetery, Telegraph Road - Promoted to Corporal 1/1/1865. Brothers George and Sheldon also served during the war. Was on detached service and probably participated in more battles.

Detached to Battery C, 1st Rhode Island, March to April, 1865, to 2nd Artillery Brigade, 6th Corps 4/27/1864 to 6/11/1864. Extra duty with Engineers at Fort Ethan Allen July - August, 1863. November 24,1862 started a 10 day furlough. January - February 1865 on leave. July - October 1864 sick in hospital, probably City Point, VA. Was present at Lee's surrender. Marched in Grand Review 5/23/1865. (Military & Pension Files, 1865 Allegany County Town Clerk Register Hume, 1850 Fed. Census Hume, 1870 Fed. Census Pike)

Trowbridge, John S. Co. E, 5th NY Cavalry - 8/28/1861 at East Rushford/3 yrs - 24 - INA - 9/21/1861 at NYC - $100 - Sgt, Sgt - New Market, Port Republic, Orange County Court House, Berryville, Aldie, New Baltimore, Hanover, PA - 7/6/1863 Honorable/Deceased - POW, captured 8/2/1862 at Orange County Court House, Prison: Richmond, paroled 9/13/1862, WIA, 6/30/1863 at Hanover, PA, gunshot to leg requiring amputation, KIA, died of wounds & amputation 7/6/1863 at Hanover, PA - John (B Lower Canada) & Anna Swain or Swin Trowbridge - Jane, Harrison, Mary, Edward, William, Eliza - 1836 or 37 in NY - Baptist minister - None Deceased - Never Married - None - 7/6/1863 at Hanover, PA - Pine Grove Cemetery, Fillmore - His father John was also a minister and was married at least twice. The soldier John's mother, Anna, died 1/11/1842. His father's wife in the 1850 Census is Frances, in the 1860 Census it's Lydia. A copy of his will, in the pension file, leaves everything to his father. Burnside G.A.R. Post 237 Marker at grave. (Military & Pension Files, *History of Allegany County 1879*, Allegany County Web Site, Matteson, Fillmore American Legion, 1860 Fed. Census Amity)

Truax, Josiah Not from the C-H-G area. Originally served with Cos. A/D, 23rd NY Infantry. Hume Township was credited with his re-enlistment in Co. C, 18th VRC when it paid his re-enlistment bonus of $500. (1865 Allegany County Town Clerk Register Hume)

Underhill, Edward Co. E, 85th NY Infantry - 9/1/1861 at Angelica/3 yrs (Re-enlisted 1/1/1864) - 18 - 5'4", Dark Complexion, Grey Eyes, Black Hair - 10/10/1861 at Elmira - $300 - Pvt, Pvt - defense of DC, siege of Yorktown, Williamsburg, Fair Oaks, before Richmond, Plymouth - 7/21/1865 Honorable - POW, captured 4/20/1864 at Plymouth, NC, Prison: Charleston, SC, Andersonville, Florence, SC, paroled 2/26/1865 - Jessie & Emeline Sophronia Underhill (Both B NY) - Foster, Carman, Amanda, Emory, William John, Janet - 4/15/1843 in Allen - Farm Laborer - INA - Never Married - None - 11/3/1879 - INA - Early 1863 served as hostler and waiter to a Major King. Detached as teamster at New Berne May - June 1863. August lost his cap, pouch, and cartridge belt and had to pay $1.47 to the government. Given a 30 day furlough 3/21/1865 from Camp Parole, MD. Contracted measles at Elmira. Eventually died of measles and lung disease. Lived in Orlin, MI after war. (Military & Pension File, 1850, 1860 Fed. Censuses Allen, 1865 Allegany County Town Clerk Register Allen, Granger American Legion, *History of Allegany County 1879*, Family - 1870 Fed. Census Millgrove, IN)

Underhill, George Titus Co. H, 19th NY Cavalry - 8/5/1862 at Oramel/3 yrs (Re-enlisted 2/13/1864) - 19 - 5'4", Dark Complexion, Blue Eyes, Brown Hair - 9/3/1862 at Portage Station - $100 - Pvt, Pvt - Deserted House, siege of Suffolk, Franklin, Manassas Junction, Culpeper, Wilderness, Todd's Tavern, Spotsylvania, North Anna River, Yellow Tavern, Pamunkey, Totopotomoy, Cold Harbor, Trevillian Station - 6/30/1865 Honorable - WIA, gunshot (minnie ball) to left leg 6/2/1864 at Trevillian Station - Livingston & Etta (Esther) Underhill (Both B NY) -

Mary, Phebe, Harriet A., Jane Amy, James W., Charlotte E., Charles A. - 3/20/1846 in Allen (some sources say Angelica) - Farmer - Farmer - Jane Simpson (Divorced 1880) - Eunice, Flora, Carrie - 1909 - INA - The Granger American Legion lists the last name Underhill with no first name as a Granger Civil War soldier. There are other Underhills who served, including James and Jesse, but George appears to be the Granger soldier since he listed Phebe Cox of Short Tract as his nearest relative when he was in Mt. Pleasant Hospital in DC with his gunshot wound. Gave his age as 19 when he volunteered, actually he was 16. Sick with dysentery 9/18-22/1862. Per County Clerk, lived in Short Tract after the war. His brother James W. could be the no first name Underhill listed by the Granger Legion. Brother Jesse's pension documents show him living in Michigan and Minnesota post war, thus, he was not likely to have been involved with post war veterans' groups in Granger. (An assumption here is that Granger Legion Civil War listings are based on old GAR Post listings.) (Military & Pension Files, 1865 Allegany County Town Clerk Register Allen, Granger American Legion, *History of Allegany County 1879*, 1850 Fed. Census Allen, 1870 Fed. Census Courtland, MI)

Vallance, Robert Co. F, 19th NY Cavalry - 8/8/1862 at Centerville/3 yrs - 32 - INA -9/3/1862 at Portage Station - $250 - Pvt, Pvt - No battles - 12/3/1862 Honorable/Deceased- DD, 12/3/1862 at Regimental Hospital, Suffolk, VA of remittent fever - Alexander & Margrit Hamilton Vallance (Both B Scotland) - INA - 8/1829 in Scotland - Farmer - None, Deceased - Margaret Van Dercar, married 4/5/1855 in Eagle - Margaret & Alexander - 12/3/1862 in Suffolk, VA - Hampton, VA National Cemetery (as Valance. Originally buried at Suffolk) - Pension went to children. Pension Bureau found mother to be immoral because she had deserted the children. Grandfather Alexander was appointed guardian. (Military & Pension Files, 1865 NYS Census Centerville, *History of Allegany County 1879*, 1865 Allegany County Town Clerk Register Centerville, Matteson, 1860 Fed. Census Centerville)

Van Akin, Ralph R. (Van Aikin) Co. C, 104th NY infantry - 11/9/1861 at Geneseo/3 yrs - 19 - 5'7", Ruddy Complexion, Dark Grey Eyes, Brown Hair - 2/26/1862 at Geneseo - No bounty - Pvt, Pvt - Cedar Creek, 2nd Bull Run, South Mountain, Antietam, Fredericksburg (Maybe more. Assigned to Corps headquarters 3/27/1863. Cannot determine if he participated in more battles.) - 11/9/1864 Honorable - Was not a casualty - Levi & Caroline Van Akin (Both B NY) - Charlotte, Triphena?, Levi, Earnest - 10/20/1843 in Hume - Blacksmith - INA - INA - INA - INA - INA - The original detail order to Corps headquarters is in his military file. (Military file, 1865 Allegany County Town Clerk Register Hume, 1850 Fed. Census Hume)

Van Antwerp, Milton M. Co. E, 85th NY Infantry - 9/1/1861 at Granger /3 yrs - 28 - 5'7", Light Complexion, Blue Eyes, Brown Hair - 10/25/1861 at Elmira - No bounty - Pvt, Corp - Defense of DC, siege of Yorktown - 10/14/1862 Disability/Honorable - Was not a casualty - INA - Probably Amos/maybe James, Mother INA - INA - 1832 or 33 in Tioga County - Shoe Maker - INA - Julia A. Reynolds (divorcee) , married 6/14/1855 in Short Tract - Platt - 1878 in Missouri apparently - INA - Was sick with typhoid fever at Yorktown. Disability discharge was for general debility and nervousness. Julia applied for pension, but was denied. Milton left Julia after the war and moved west. No further information. (Military & Pension Files, 1890 Fed. Census Special Schedule Granger, Matteson, *History of Allegany County 1879,* Granger American Legion, 1850 Fed. Census Portage)

Van Brunt, Irwin Co. F, 33rd NY Infantry - 5/13/1861 at Elmira/2 yrs - 18 - INA - 5/22/1861 at Elmira - No bounty - Pvt, Pvt - No battles - 10/16/1861 Honorable/Deceased - DD, 10/16/1861 at Fort Ethan Allen of service related disease (file does not specifically identify disease), David (B NY) & Harriet Johnson Van Brunt - Jane - 1842 in Centerville - Domestic - None Deceased - Never Married - None - 10/16/1861 in Fort Ethan Allen - Soldier's and Sailor's Home Cemetery DC - Working for farmer James W. Fisk in 1860. Mother was deceased by 1850. (Military File, 1865 NYS Census Centerville, 1865 Allegany County Town Clerk Register Centerville, 1850, 1860 Fed. Censuses Centerville)

Van Buren, Sylvester 24th Independent Battery, NY Light Artillery - 2/15/1864 at Mount Morris/3 yrs - 22 - 6', Dark Complexion, Grey Eyes, Black Hair - 2/16/1864 at Canandaigua - No bounty - Pvt, Pvt - Plymouth, NC - 7/20/1865 Honorable - POW, captured 4/20/1864 at Plymouth, Prisons: Richmond, Charleston, Escaped 4/9/1865 - Martin & Catherine Peckens Van Buren (Both B Ireland) - Alfred L. Angeline, Charles, De Leon, William, John, Martin Jr. - 8/1839 per headstone 1837 per 1900 Census in Otsego - Boatman - Wood Cutter/Laborer/Farmer - 1st Ann Rector, married 1858/59 (separated 1860/61, never divorced), 2nd Elizabeth Behn (Buhan), married 10/22/1866 in Syracuse - None - 5/6/1902 in Hume - Pine Grove Cemetery, Fillmore - 24th Independent Battery transferred to 3rd NY Artillery as Battery L, 3/8/1865. Burnside G.A.R. Post 237 Marker at grave. He was convicted of counterfeiting and sent to prison, which was the reason for the separation from Ann. Elizabeth was determined eligible for his pension (as a common law wife of 21 years [lived together 21 years after Ann's death]). She died before receiving any money. (Military & Pension Files, 1890 Fed. Census Special Schedule Hume, Matteson, 1850 Fed. Census Albion, 1900 Fed. Census Hume)

Van Dresser, Alfred Philip Co. C, 104th NY Infantry - 10/21/1861 at Geneseo/3 yrs - 20 - 5'7", Light Complexion, Blue Eyes, Brown Hair - 2/26/1862 at Geneseo - No bounty - Pvt, Captain - Cedar Creek, 2nd Bull Run, Fredericksburg, Chancellorsville - 5/14/1864 Disability/Honorable - Was not a casualty - Jeremiah & Phebe Ann Slocum Van Dresser (Both B NY) - Almon B., Amanda, Charles, Emma - 6/22/1841 in Hume - Farmer - Farmer/Librarian/Book Keeper - Elida Huntington, married 8/31/1868 in Church of the Atonement, NYC - Frederick H., William T. Alfred P. May B. - 6/13/1914 in Memphis, TN - Elmwood Cemetery, Memphis - Promoted to Sgt 11/11/1861, Com Sgt 3/15/1862, 1st Lt 10/8/1862, Captain 2/5/1863. Received a 10 day furlough 12/23/1863. Disability discharge due to typhoid fever and diarrhea. Some records indicate he also had malaria fever. Was sick in Seminary Hospital in Georgetown. Honorary member of James Daley Post, Veterans of Foreign Wars at Hastings on Hudson. Brothers Almon B. and Charles also served during the war. (Military & Pension Files, 1865 NYS Census Centerville, 1865 Allegany County Town Clerk Register Centerville, 1850 Fed. Census Hume, 1900 Fed. Census Memphis)

Van Dresser, Almon Benton Co. C, 104th NY Infantry - 10/21/1861 at Geneseo/3 yrs - 19 - 5'8", Ruddy Complexion, Blue Eyes, Brown Hair, Mole on side of neck, small star "picked" on arm - 2/26/1862 at Geneseo - No bounty - Pvt, Pvt - Cedar Creek - 2/17/1863 Disability/Honorable - Was not a casualty - Jeremiah & Phebe Ann Slocum Van Dresser (Both B NY) - Alfred P., Amanda, Charles, Emma - 11/10/1842 in Hume - Farmer - Farmer/Fireman on RR/Yard Engineer - Emma R. Harris, married 6/23/1866 in Cuba - Ray H., Lena M., Almon J., Mabel E., 2 others -

8/1/1910 in Oil City, PA - Grove Hill Cemetery - Appears on 1863-64 Register of Draftees, but was already in and out of the service. Disability discharge due to heart disease. Brothers Alfred and Charles also served during the war. (Military & Pension Files, 1865 NYS Census Centerville, 1865 Allegany County Town Clerk Register Centerville, 1850 Fed. Census Hume, 1900 Fed. Census Oil City, PA)

Van Dresser, Charles Dudley Co. B, 2nd NY Mounted Rifles - 12/9/1863 at Centerville/3 yrs - 18 - 5'5', Light Complexion, Blue Eyes, Dark Hair - 1/12/1864 at Ft. Porter, Buffalo - $300 - Pvt, Pvt - Spotsylvania, North Anna River, Pamunkey, Totopotomoy, Hanover Court House, Cold Harbor, Bethesda Church, siege of Petersburg, Weldon RR, Popular Springs Church, Pegram's Farm - 8/10 /1865 Honorable - POW, captured 9/30/1864 at Pegram's Farm, Prisons: Libby at Richmond & Salisbury, NC, paroled 3/2/1865 - Jeremiah & Phebe Ann Slocum Van Dresser (Both B NY) - Alfred P., Almon B., Amanda, Emma - 10/13/1846 or 47 at Hume - Farmer - Farmer/Hotel Keeper - 1st Mary E. Butler, married 10/2/1868 (Died 4/10/1885 at Hume), 2nd Rose Elizabeth (Libbie) Buchanan (widow) , married 5/12/1886 in Buffalo - Mary & Pearl - 3/8/1909 in Hume - Pine Grove Cemetery, Fillmore - Charter Member of Burnside G.A.R. Post 237. Burnside Post 237 Marker at grave. (Military & Pension Files, *History of Allegany County 1879, Allegany & Its People*, 1890 Fed. Census Special Schedule Hume, 1865 Allegany County Town Clerk Register Centerville, Fillmore American Legion, Matteson, 1865 NYS Census Centerville, 1850, 1880, 1900 Fed. Censuses Hume, 1860 Fed. Census Centerville)

Van Duzen, George Co. B, 2nd NY Mounted Rifles - 1/25/1864 at Freedom/3 yrs - 34 - 6'2", Light Complexion, Grey Eyes, Black Hair - 1/25/1864 at Dunkirk - No bounty- Pvt, Pvt - No battles - 3/6/1865 Disability/Honorable -Was not a casualty - Henry & Eliza Walker (B NY) Van Dosen - Chauncey, Manda M. - 6/10/1831 in Centerville - Farmer - Farmer - 1st Emily Johnson (Died 12/18/1887), 2nd Florence R. Bartlett McMillan (widow), married 10/9/1890 in East Jordan, MI - Ellen, Henry, Nellie, Della, twins - Guy & Glen - INA - INA - Military index has him listed as George Van Dulen. Pension file index has him as Van Dosen. Was in Carver General Hospital with chronic dyspepsia. (Military & Pension File, 1865 NYS Census Centerville, 1865 Allegany County Town Clerk Register Centerville, 1850 Fed. Census Centerville, 1870 Fed. Census Oshtemo, MI)

Van Guilder, David S. Co. D, 4th NY Heavy Artillery - 12/26/1863 at Granger/3 yrs - 36 - 5'11", Dark Complexion, Blue Eyes, Black Hair - 12/26/1863 at Elmira - $300 - Pvt, Artificer - Wilderness, Spotsylvania, North Anna River, Totopotomoy, Cold Harbor, siege of Petersburg, Weldon RR, Ream's Station, Peeble's Farm, Hatcher's Run, fall of Petersburg, Appomattox 9/26/1865 Honorable - Was not a casualty - Elisha (B CT) & Waita (B NY) Van Guilder, INA - 2/17/1828 in Skaneateles - Farmer - Farmer - 1st Alma J. Clark, married 1/7/1862 (Died 8/30/1877), 2nd Carrie E. Johnson, (widow), married 11/12/1880 - Burt V. - 8/8/1903 in Fillmore - Short Tract - Present at Lee's surrender. Marched in Grand Review 5/23/1865. (Military & Pension files, 1865 NYS Census Granger, Matteson, 1865 Allegany County Town Clerk Register Granger, Granger American Legion, 1860, 1880 Fed. Censuses Granger)

Van Lone, William S. Not from the C-H-G area. His enlistment in Co E/I, 8th NY Cavalry was credited to Hume Township which paid his enlistment bonus of $400. (1865 Allegany County Town Clerk Register Hume)

<u>Van Name, Byron</u> Co. F, 19th NY Cavalry - 8/9/1862 at Centerville/3 yrs - 22 - 5'10", Light Complexion, Grey Eyes, Brown Hair - 9/3/1862 at Portage Station - $500 - Pvt, Pvt - Deserted House, siege of Suffolk, Franklin, Manassas Junction, Bristoe's Station, Culpeper, Wilderness, Todd's Tavern, Spotsylvania, North Anna River, Yellow Tavern, Pamunkey, Totopotomoy, Cold Harbor, Trevillian Station, Charles County Court House, before Richmond and Petersburg, New Market, Shepherdstown, Winchester, Fisher's Hill, New Market, Port Republic, Cedar Creek, Berryville, Gordonsville, Five Forks, Dinwiddie, Appomattox - 6/10/1865 Honorable - Was not a casualty - Henry & Maria Van Name (Both B NY) - Benjamin, Richard, Harriet, William - 11/1837 in Ashford - Farmer - Farmer - Emeline - Julia, Nellie, Willis, Mary - 1922 - Poponque Cemetery Rushford - Present at Lee's surrender. Marched in Grand Review 5/23/1865. 12/62 to 2/63 detached to Pioneer Corps, March - May 1863 with Pontoon Corps, August - September 1864 a teamster, December 64 - February 65 company cook, March - April 1865 at Remount Camp, Chapel Point, MD. May 1865 officer's attendant. Brother Richard also served during the war. Military file is under the name Vanamy. Grandfather was named Benjamin Van Name (B NY). (Military & Pension Files, 1865 NYS Census Centerville, *History of Allegany County 1879*, Matteson, 1865 Allegany County Town Clerk Register Centerville, 1850, 1860, 1870 Fed. Censuses Centerville)

<u>Van Name, Richard</u> Co. C, 19th NY Cavalry - 9/13/1864 at Centerville/1 yr - 19 - 5'9", Fair Complexion, Blue Eyes, Brown Hair - 9/27/1864 at Elmira - $500 - Pvt, Pvt - Cedar Creek, Berryville, Gordonsville - 6/30/1865 Honorable - INJ, hurt spine near lumbar region (when and where not noted in file) - Henry & Maria Van Name (Both B NY) - Benjamin, Byron, Harriet, William - 4/12/1844 in Centerville - Farmer - Farmer - 1st INA, 2nd Anna, married 1888 - Ruth (from 1st wife) - 1922 - Centerville Cemetery, Route 3 - Brother Byron also served during the war. Both brothers died in 1922. Military Index spells name Vanama. Grandfather was Benjamin Van Name. (Military File [Pension file lost], 1865 NYS Census Centerville, 1865 Allegany County Town Clerk Register Centerville, Centerville American Legion, Matteson, 1890 Fed. Census Special Schedule Centerville, *History of Allegany County 1879*, 1850, 1880, 1910 Fed. Censuses Centerville)

<u>Van Nostrand, Aaron</u> Co. F, 19th NY Cavalry - 8/13/1862 at Granger/3 yrs - 37 - INA - 9/3/1862 at Portage Station - No bounty - Pvt, Sgt - No battles - 11/19/1862 Honorable/Deceased - DD, 11/19/1862 at Suffolk, VA hospital of remittent fever - Isaac & Grace Hatch Van Nostrand (Both born CT) - Luzon, Lewis, Sidney, William, Mary (Jones), Anna (Fuller), Rebecca (Smith), Lucinda (Smith), Aaron, Polly Jane, Sidney - 5/30/1825 in Granger - Carpenter/Farmer - None Deceased - Almira Chapman, married 4/28/1852 in West Sparta (Almira was the daughter of his father's second wife, Maria Chapman.) - Nellie, Florence, Lena May - 11/19/1862 in Suffolk, VA - Short Tract Cemetery, County Route 4 - Listed on Soldiers Monument in Granger. Promoted to Sgt 8/19/1862. Brother Isaac also served during the war. (Military & Pension Files, 1890 Fed. Census Special Schedule Granger, 1865 Allegany County Town Clerk Register Granger, 1865 NYS Census Granger, *Allegany & Its People*, Granger American Legion, Matteson, *History of Allegany County 1879*, 1850, 1860 Fed. Censuses Granger. Descendant Robert Van Nostrand)

<u>Van Nostrand, Charles</u> Co. D, 1st Michigan Engineers - 9/9/1861 at Grand Rapids/3 yrs - 24 - 5'5", Light Complexion, Blue Eyes, Brown Hair - 10/29/1861 at Detroit - $100 - Pvt, Sgt - Mills

Springs, siege of Corinth. Primary duty was engineering work, especially repairing track and building block houses on the Nashville & Chattanooga RR, Nashville & Northwestern RR, Tennessee & Alabama RR and Memphis & Charleston RR in TN, AL, & KY. Also build RR bridges and repaired roads. - 10/31/1864 Honorable - Was not a casualty - Luzon & Harriet Gilchrist Van Nostrand (Both B NY) - William, Everett, Ellen, Eunice, Elmira, Martha - 8/28/1837 in Short Tract - Farmer - Farmer/ Carpenter - 1st INA, 2nd Jemina St. John - Walter R. - 8/13/1921 - Short Tract Cemetery, County Route 4- Promoted to Corp 4/1/1863, to Sgt 2/3/1864. Married to Jemima 10 years in 1900. Brother Everett also served during the war. (Military & Pension Files, Granger American Legion, Matteson, 1850 Fed. Census Granger, 1860 Fed. Census Allen, 1900, 1910 Fed. Censuses Nunda. Descendant Robert Van Nostrand)

Van Nostrand, Everett Co. A/I, 27th NY Infantry - 5/13/1861 at Angelica/2 yrs - 21 - INA - 5/21/1861 at Elmira - $100 - Pvt, Sgt - 1st Bull Run, Yorktown, Gaine's Mill, Malvern Hill, 2nd Bull Run, South Mountain, Antietam, Fredericksburg, Franklin's Crossing - 5/31/1863 Honorable - Was not a casualty - Luzon & Harriet Gilchrist Van Nostrand (Both B NY) - William, Charles, Ellen, Eunice, Elmira, Martha - 1/15/1840 in Granger - Farmer - Druggist - Prudence M. Smith, married 11/10/1869 in Wellsville - None - 1/24/1935 in Wellsville - Woodlawn Cemetery, Wellsville - was a nurse and attendant at regimental hospital during the war. Had measles while in the military. *History of Allegany County 1879* lists him as Everett Van Ostrand of Wellsville, which is incorrect. Government provided a burial flag for his funeral. Brother Charles also served during the war. (Military & Pension Files, *History of Allegany County 1879*, Granger American Legion, 1850 Fed. Census Granger, 1860 Fed. Census Allen, 1900 Fed. Census Wellsville, NYS Adjutant General Report, Descendant Robert Van Nostrand)

Van Nostrand, Isaac N. Co. F, 19th NY Cavalry 8/13/1862 at Oramel/3 yrs - 28 - 5'11", Dark Complexion, Black Eyes, Black Hair - 9/3/1862 at Portage Station - No bounty - Pvt, 2nd Corp - No battles - 5/31/1863 Disability/Honorable - DD, 8/25/1863 at Granger following discharge of remittent fever and chronic diarrhea - Isaac & Grace Hatch Van Nostrand (Both born CT) - Luzon, Lewis, Sidney, William, Mary (Jones), Anner (Fuller), Rebecca (Smith), Lucinda (Smith), Aaron, Polly Jane, Sidney - 2/10/1834 in Granger - Farmer - None Deceased - Almira T. Townsend, married 12/26/1858 in Granger - Agnes M. - 8/25/1863 in Granger - Short Tract Cemetery County Route 4 - Listed on Soldiers Monument in Granger. Brother Aaron also served during the war. Father was married twice, second wife Maria Chapman. (Military & Pension Files, 1865 NYS Census Granger, *History of Allegany County 1879*, Granger American Legion, *Allegany & Its People*, Matteson, 1865 Allegany County Town Clerk Register Granger, 1860 Fed. Census Granger. Descendant Robert Van Nostrand)

Van Nostrand, William At least one source document indicates that William served in the military during the war. There were at least two William Van Nostrands, one a son of Isaac Senior and the other a son of Luzon. No evidence of service for either has been located. No William Van Nostrand served in any NY Civil War regiment. (Matteson.)

Vaughn, Amos Pratt Co. F, 19th NY Cavalry - 8/13/1862 at Granger/3 yrs - 32 - 5'10", Dark Complexion, Dark Eyes, Black Hair - 9/3/1862 at Portage Station - $100 - Pvt, Pvt - Deserted House, siege of Suffolk - 3/11/1864 Disability/Honorable - Was not a casualty - Daniel & Alice

Crane Vaughn - Stewart - 1/6/1830 in Henrietta - Farmer - Farmer - Mary A. Sanderson, married 7/4/1853 in Granger - Daniel, Alice, Stewart - 9/19/1898 in Eldred, PA - Eldred - Brother Stewart also served during the war. Sick in Hampton, VA hospital with chronic hepatitis and diarrhea. His commanding officer was not fond of him. Put a letter in his file which in part said he "had never been good for anything." (Military & Pension Files, 1865 NYS Census Granger, *History of Allegany County 1879*, Grange American Legion, 1865 Allegany County Town Clerk Register Granger, 1860 Fed. Census Granger, 1870 Fed. Census Eldred, PA)

Vaughn, Stewart Austin Co. F, 19th NY Cavalry - 8/13/1862 at Portageville/3 yrs - 42 - 5'10", Light Complexion - No bounty - Pvt, Pvt - Deserted House, siege of Suffolk, Franklin, Charlottesville - 6/19/1865 Honorable - Was not a casualty - Daniel & Alice Vaughn - Amos - 7/25/1820 at Pittsford - Farmer - Farmer - 1st Malinda Welton (Died 1850 at Granger), 2nd Mary Elizabeth Hunt, married 8/22/1851 in China - Belle (Hakes), Nellie (McCullough), Charles Stewart, William W., Herman Floyd - INA - INA - January - February 1864 on detached duty with reconnaissance party. February 20, 1864 on a raid at Charlottesville, VA, his horse fell on him as he was crossing a ditch and he hurt his leg. Was in White House, VA Hospital with typhoid fever 6/11/1864, transferred to Lincoln G.H. 6/16 and then to Willetts Point, NY 6/22. May also have had consumption. January - February, 1865 in Buffalo hospital. 4/1/1865 at dismount camp. Brother Amos also served during the war. (Military & Pension Files, 1865 NYS Census Granger, *History of Allegany County 1879*, Granger American Legion, 1865 Allegany County Town Clerk Register Granger, 1860 Fed. Census Granger, 1870 Fed. Census Eldred, PA)

Veazey, Lewis Cass Co. C, 104th NY Infantry - 10/11/1861 at Centerville/3 yrs - 44 - 5'10", Dark Complexion, Blue Eyes, Dark Hair - 2/26/1862 at Geneseo - No bounty - Pvt, Pvt - No battles - 3/18/1863 Disability/Honorable - Was not a casualty - Jeremiah (B NH) & Abigail Clark Veazey - Emily - 5/21/1811 in Brentwood, NH - Farmer - Farmer/Mail Carrier/Constable - Sarah Ann Warner, married 11/21/1837 in Centerville - Strong Warner, Daniel, Ann Eliza (Kimball), Emily (Wing) - 7/21/1873 - Centerville Cemetery, Route 3 - Was 49 at enlistment rather than 44. Son Strong Warner also served during the war. Disability discharge was for diarrhea and rheumatism. (Military File, 1865 NYS Census Centerville, 1865 Allegany County Town Clerk Register Centerville, 1850, 1870 Fed. Censuses Centerville)

Veazel, Strong Warner Co. C, 104th NY Infantry - 10/21/1861 at Geneseo/3 yrs - 18 - 5'10", Light Complexion, Blue Eyes, Brown Hair - 2/26/1862 at Geneseo - No bounty - Pvt, Pvt - Cedar Creek, 2nd Bull Run, South Mountain, Antietam, Fredericksburg, Chancellorsville, Gettysburg - 7/4/1863 Honorable/Deceased - WIA, gunshot to left leg at Gettysburg, 7/1/1863, KIA, died of gunshot wounds 7/4/1863 - Lewis Cass (B NH) & Sarah Ann Warner (B NY) Veazey - Daniel, Ann Eliza (Kimball), Emily (Wing) - 7/9/1845 in Centerville - Farm Laborer - None Deceased - Never Married - None - 7/4/1863 at Gettysburg - Gettysburg National Cemetery - Left leg was amputated in an effort to save his life. Father Lewis Cass also served during the war. Mother awarded Strong's pension. (Military & Pension Files, 1865 NYS Census Centerville, 1865 Allegany County Town Clerk Register Centerville, 1850 Fed. Census Centerville)

Vosbough, Henry (Vosbourgh) (Vosburgh) Co. B, 2nd NY Mounted Rifles - 12/14/1863 at Pike/3 yrs - 33 - 5'6", Dark Complexion, Blue Eyes, Dark Hair - 1/12/1864 at Ft. Porter, Buffalo - No bounty - Pvt, Pvt - Spotsylvania, North Anna River, Pamunkey, Totopotomoy, Hanover Court House, Cold Harbor, Bethesda Church, siege of Petersburg - 9/23/1864 Honorable/Deceased - DD, 9/23/1864 at Emory Hospital, DC of Diarrhea - INA - INA - 1830 in Pike - Farmer - None Deceased - Julia Ann Morse, married 12/28/1856 in Livonia - Julius Henry, Harriette Elizabeth - 9/23/1864 in DC - Arlington National Cemetery (listed as Bosburg in Index, Bosburgh on headstone) - Wife Julia applied for his pension, but then married a Rollin Dain. Reapplied after Dain died. (Military & Pension Files, 1865 NYS Census Hume, 1860 Fed. Census Pike, *Roll of Honor*)

Vreeland, James Isaiah Co. C, 5th NY Cavalry - 8/26/1864 at Angelica/1 yr - 20 - 5'8", Light Complexion, Blue Eyes, Light Hair - 9/9/1864 at Elmira - $100 - Pvt, Pvt - Mount Jackson, Dinwiddie, Five Forks, Appomattox - 6/13/1865 Honorable - Was not a casualty - Isaac & Olive Vreeland (Both B NY) - Mary, Frances, Weltey- 1844 in Centerville - Farmer - Day Laborer - Helen Woodard, married 8/8/1865 - Lucius S., 3 others - 12/11/1902 - Fairlawn Cemetery, Scio - Present at Lee's surrender. Marched in Grand Review 5/23/1865. Paid $2.00 for a lost Remington revolver and $1.60 for lost haversack & canteen. (Military & Pension Files, 1865 Allegany County Town Clerk Register Angelica, 1860 Fed. Census Bolivar, 1900 Fed. Census Scio)

Vreeland, John Jr. At least one source document indicates that Vreeland served in the military during the war. No evidence of such service has been located. Four John Vreelands served in NY Civil War regiments. None of them had any connection to C-H-G. (Matteson)

Wait, Theodore B. Co. F, 4th NY Heavy Artillery - 11/18/1861 at NYC/3 yrs - 24 - 5'9", Light Complexion, Blue Eyes, Auburn Hair - 11/18/1861 at NYC - $100 - Pvt, Pvt - Wilderness, Spotsylvania, North Anna River, Totopotomoy, Cold Harbor, siege of Petersburg, Weldon RR - 12/24/1864 Honorable - Was not a casualty - William & Mary Ann Neely Wait (Both B NY) - None - 12/4/1836 in Wiscoy - Farmer - Farm Laborer - Was married, INA, wife left him for another man - None - 9/6/1923 in Bath, NY - INA - Was divorced in 1880. While in the military built a stone house and kitchen on extra duty. (Military & Pension Files, 1865 NYS Census Hume, 1865 Allegany County Town Clerk Register Hume, 1850, 1860, 1870 Fed. Censuses Hume)

Walker, Marshall E. Co. D, 47th NY Infantry - 2/28/1865 at Angelica/3 yrs - 20 - 5'9", Fair Complexion, Grey Eyes, Dark Hair - 2/28/1865 at Elmira - No bounty - Pvt, Pvt - No battles - 6/27/1865 Honorable - Was not a casualty - George Lysander & Martha Franklin Walker (Both B NY) - Frank - 10/24/1844 in Allen - Farmer - Farmer - Hattie Pitt, married 9/24/1864 in Belfast - Dexter M., Minnie A., Mattie E., Clyde L. - 9/22/1926 - Short Tract Cemetery County Route 4 - One card in his file says he was a substitute for Lewis Peck of Hume, another card say for Mitchele S. Blain. It must have been the latter since Edwin Washburn's file indicates he was a substitute for Lewis Peck. Was sick in hospital March - June 1865. Another card says he was discharged 12/31/1863 in order to reenlist as a veteran volunteer. That is incorrect. He did originally enlist 9/1862 in Co. I, 160th NY Infantry. However, his father got him out of the service quickly, since he was underage, and his father had not given his consent for Marshall to enlist. Grandparents were Erastus and Betsy Porte Walker. (Military & Pension Files, Matteson, *Allegany & Its People*, Granger American Legion, 1850, 1860 Fed. Censuses Allen, 1870 Fed. Census Granger)

Wallace, Jackson L. Co H, 136th NY Infantry - 8/26/1862 at Portage/3 yrs - 19 - 5'9", Fair Complexion, Blue Eyes, Black Hair - 9/25/1862 at Portage - No bounty - Pvt, Corp - Chancellorsville, Gettysburg, Wauhatchie, Orchard Knob, Tunnel Hill, Missionary Ridge, Resca, Goldsboro, Bentonsville, Bennett's House - 6/13/1865 Honorable - WIA, gunshot in side (lumbar region) at Resaca, 5/15/1864 - William (B NY) & Harriet (B PA) Wallace (1850 Census says Both B NY) - Mary, James, David, William, Harriet, Ardella Ida - 1/13/1843 in Charleroi, PA (1850 Fed. Census says NY) - Farmer - Farm Laborer - Ellen Texas Gibbs, married 10/25/1866 in Portage - Georgia May - 12/7/1926 in Livonia - INA - Promoted to Corporal 12/17/1863. In Cumberland G.H., Nashville with wound. Given a furlough 8/3/1864 and then sent to Jefferson G.H., Jeffersonville, in hospital as of 9/21/1864. From there he was sent to Bridgeport, AL field hospital. By March of 1865 he was back with his regiment. Present at surrender of General Johnston. Marched in the Grand Review 5/24/1865. Brothers James and William also served during the war. (Military & Pension Files, Granger American Legion, *Allegany & Its People*, Matteson, 1850 Fed. Census Grove, 1860 Fed. Census Granger.)

Wallace, James Co. E, 85th NY Infantry - 9/1/1861 at Short Tract/3 yrs - 21 - INA - 10/10/1861 at Elmira - No Bounty - Pvt. Sgt - defense of DC, siege of Yorktown, Fair Oaks, before Richmond, (most likely other battles with the 1st Pennsylvania Light Artillery, INA) - 12/18/1863 from the 85th (final discharge date 6/27/1865) - Was not a casualty - William (B NY) & Harriet (B PA) Wallace (1850 Fed. Census says both B NY) - Jackson L., Mary, David, William, Harriet, Ardella Ida - 11/26/1840 in Tioga Co., PA (1850 Fed Census says NY) - Farmer - Carpenter - Sadie C. Laundsburg, married 1867 in Blossburg, PA - Lillie, C.A., Rita, Nora - 5/26/1915 at Hood River County, OR - Knights of Pitheus Cemetery, Hood River, OR - Left sick at Lee's Mill 5/14/1862. Detached to Battery H, 1st Pennsylvania Light Artillery 8/18/1862. Reenlisted in 1st 12/18/1863, discharged from 1st 6/27/1865. Brothers Jackson and William also served during the war. (Military & Pension Files, Matteson, Granger American Legion, *History of Allegany County 1879*, 1850 Fed. Census Grove, 1910 Fed .Census Hood River, OR)

Wallace, William Co. F, 104th NY Infantry - 1/29/1862 at Geneseo/3 yrs - 18 - 5'10", Light Complexion, Blue Eyes, Brown Hair - 2/26/1862 at Geneseo - $100 - Pvt, Pvt - Cedar Creek, 2nd Bull Run, South Mountain, Antietam, Fredericksburg, Chancellorsville, Gettysburg - 2/17/1864 Honorable/Deceased - POW, captured 7/1/1863 at Gettysburg, Prison: Libby at Richmond, DD, 2/17/1864 at Libby prison of bronchitis - William (B NY) & Harriett (B PA) Wallace - Jackson, James, Mary, David, Harriet, Ardella, Ida - 1842 or 43 in Allegany County - Farmer - None Deceased - Never Married - None - 2/17/1864 in Libby Prison, Richmond, VA (POW) - Richmond, VA National Cemetery - Listed on Soldiers Monument in Granger. Was actually only 16 when he volunteered, 1860 Census shows age as 14. Brothers Jackson and James also served during the war. Mother Harriet received his pension. Father William deserted his wife and family around 1861 or 62, came back in mid-60's, and then deserted again. Despite large family, only William Jr. really helped his mother. A couple of local men informed the pension bureau that William Sr. was a drunkard. Some documents say William Sr. served. No real evidence of such service has been found. (Military & Pension Files, 1860 Fed. Census Granger, 1850 Fed. Census Grove, Granger American Legion, *Allegany & Its People*, Matteson)

Wallace, William Sr. At least one source document indicates that William Sr. served in the military during the war. No evidence of such service has been located. He did disappear (deserted his wife and family) during the early 60's, and again in the mid to late 60's apparently for good, creating some belief that he was in the service. Many William Wallaces served in NY Civil War regiments. No evidence to connect any of them to C-H-G. (Granger American Legion)

Warn, Chandler W. Co. D, 4th NY Heavy Artillery - 8/13/1862 at Rochester/3 yrs - 18 - 5'7", Florid Complexion, Hazel Eyes, Black Hair - 8/13/1862 at Rochester - $50 - Pvt, Pvt - Peeble's Farm, Hatcher's Run, fall of Petersburg - 9/7/1862 Honorable/Deceased - Died accidently, drowned in the Potomac River - David H. & Clarissa A. Robbins Warn (Both B NY) - Charles, Cynthia, Anna - 2/28/1844 in Hume - Farmer - None Deceased - Never Married - None - 9/7/1862 in DC - Body never recovered. Memorial Headstone East Koy Road, Portageville. - Drown near Chain Bridge. Military said he did not die in the line of duty and would not approve a pension. His Commander, Captain Engall, said he died 9/6 and that he died in the line of duty. (Military & Pension Files, 1865 NYS Census Hume, Allegany County Web Site, 1865 Allegany County Town Clerk Register Hume, 1850 Fed. Census Hume)

Warner, William Wells Co. D, 136th NY Infantry - 8/28/1862 at Pike/3 yrs - 18 - 5'5", Light Complexion, Grey Eyes, Brown Hair - 9/25/1862 at Portage - No bounty - Pvt, Pvt - Chancellorsville, Gettysburg, Wauhatchie - 3/4/1864 Disability/Honorable - DD, 5/1/1864, shortly after discharge of chronic dysentery - Edward & Cornelia Lamberson Warner (Both B NY) - Lucius S., Cornelia Henrietta, Mary Ruth - 1843 or 44 in Centerville - Farmer - None Deceased - Never Married - None - 5/1/1864 in Centerville - Centerville - Was an ambulance driver in the service. Entered Nashville hospital sick on 11/7/1863, sent to Evansville, IN (Military & Pension Files, 1865 NYS Census Centerville, 1850 Fed. Census Centerville)

Washburn, Abel (Washborne) At least one source document indicates that Abel served in the military during the war. No evidence of such service has been located. An Abel S. Washbond did serve with the 118th NY Infantry. There is no information which connects him to the C-H-G. area (Fillmore American Legion)

Washburn Edwin M. Co. C, 47th NY Infantry - 3/1/1865 at Hume/1 yr - 5'5", Fair Complexion, Blue Eyes, Brown Hair - 3/1/1865 at INA - $400 - Pvt, Pvt - Goldsboro, Bennett's House - 8/30/1865 Honorable - Was not a casualty - Abel S. & Philanca Morgan Washburn (Both B NY) - Lucretia, Theodore, Huldah, Oliver, George - 8/3/1846 in Hume - Farmer - Farmer/Saw Mill Worker - Margaret A. Durkee, married 10/9/1866 in Gainesville - Rose B., Emma A., Clarence A., Leon E. - 5/25/1921 in Caneadea - Cemetery Street Cemetery, Caneadea - Was a substitute for Edwin Peck of Hume. Was paid a sufficient consideration on 2/25/1865 for being a substitute. Present at surrender of General Johnston and his army. Brothers Oliver and Theodore also served during the war. (Military & Pension Files, 1890 Fed. Census Special Schedule Centerville, 1865 NYS Census Hume, 1865 Allegany County Town Clerk Register Hume, 1850 Fed. Census Hume, 1860 Fed. Census Genesee Falls, 1870 Fed. Census Caneadea)

Washburn, Oliver R. Co. A, 19th NY Cavalry - 8/4/1862 at Genesee Falls/3 yrs - 18 - INA - 9/3/1862 at Portage Station - No bounty - Pvt, Pvt - Deserted House - 1/30/1863 Honorable/ Deceased - KIA, 1/30/1863 at Deserted House - Abel S. & Philanca Morgan Washburn (Both B

NY) - Lucretia, Edwin, Theodore, Huldah, George - 1844 in NYS - Farm Laborer - None Deceased - Never Married - None - 1/30/1863 at Deserted House, VA - Pine Grove Cemetery, Fillmore - Burnside G.A.R. Post 237 Marker at grave. Brothers Edwin and Theodore also served during the war. (Military File, Matteson, 1865 NYS Census Hume, 1865 Allegany County Town Clerk Register Hume, 1850 Fed. Census Hume)

Washburn, Theodore Co. A, 19th NY Cavalry - 12/31/1863 at Hornell/2 yrs - 20 - 5'7", Light Complexion, Blue Eyes, Light Hair - 12/31/1863 at Elmira - No bounty - Pvt, Pvt - No battles - 10/13/1865 Disability/Honorable - Was not a casualty - Abel S. & Philanca Morgan Washburn (Both B NY) - Lucretia, Edwin, Oliver, Huldah, George - 5/14/1841 in Geneseo - Farmer - None, Invalid - Never Married - None - 2/20/1873 in Caneadea of consumption - Pine Grove Cemetery Fillmore - Disability discharge due to tubercular disease of right lung. Was in Ira Harris G.H., Albany. Military records are under Washborne. Burnside G.A.R. Post 237 Marker at grave. Never served with his company. Detailed as Provost Guard soon after his muster. Brothers Edwin and Oliver also served during the war. (Military & Pension Files, 1865 Allegany County Town Clerk Register Hume, Matteson, 1865 NYS Census Hume, Fillmore American Legion, Allegany County Web Site, 1850 Fed. Census Hume, 1860 Fed. Census Genesee Falls, 1870 Fed. Census Caneadea)

Watson, Albert P. Co. F, 33rd NY Infantry - 5/13/1861 at Nunda/2 yrs - 32 - 5'6", Light Complexion, Blue Eyes, Grey Hair - 5/22/1861 at Elmira - No bounty - Pvt, Pvt - Fredericksburg, Chancellorsville - 6/2/1863 Honorable - WIA, gunshot through right ankle 5/3/1863 at Chancellorsville, POW, captured 5/3/1863 at Chancellorsville, Prison: None, paroled at Fredericksburg 5/16/1863 - INA (Both B NY) - INA - 1830 or 31 in Ulster County (New Baltimore), Laborer/Baker - Stone Cutter/Farmer - 1st Clarissa Guild (Died 3/21/1869 in Centerville), 2nd Amelia P. Pratt, married 9/12/1869 in Caneadea - Stella, Harry, Jesse P., Elva M., Nettie B., Albert L., Allison, Lucia, Lillie, Mary, John - 11/4/1902 in Pike - Pike Cemetery, Telegraph Road - Also served with Co. B, 2nd NY Mounted Rifles, see below. (Military & Pension Files, 1865 NYS Census Hume, 1860, 1900 Fed. Census Eagle)

Watson, Albert P. Co. B, 2nd NY Mounted Rifles - 1/5/1864 at Eagle/2 yrs - 33 - 5'6", Light Complexion, Blue Eyes, Grey Hair - 1/12/1864 at Ft. Porter, Buffalo - No bounty - Pvt, Sgt - Spotsylvania, North Anna River, Pamunkey, Totopotomoy, Hanover Court House, Cold Harbor, Bethesda Church, siege of Petersburg - 8/10/1865 Honorable - POW, captured 10/14/1864 at Petersburg, Prison: Richmond, paroled 2/15/1865 - was originally reported as a deserter and was reduced in rank 12/6/1864 for being AWOL. Not sure the desertion was ever erased from his record, or that his rank was restored. Did get his pension, but that may have been based on service with the 33rd Infantry. Received a furlough after his release from prison. Also served with Co. F, 33rd NY Infantry, see above. Also see above for personal information and sources of information.

Weaver, Ira Ransom Co. F, 4th NY Heavy Artillery - 1/4/1864 at Buffalo/3 yrs - 43 - 5'11", Dark Complexion, Grey Eyes, Black Hair - 1/12/1864 at Buffalo - $300 - Pvt, Pvt - Southside RR - 4/2/1865 Honorable/Deceased - KIA, 4/2/1865 at Southside RR - William L. & Eunice Drury Weaver - INA - January 14, 1822 in Milton, VT - Farmer/Nereseyman? - None Deceased - Cheney White Smith, married 1/3/1841 at Granger - Hiram, William, Edwin R., Harriet B., Elisha - Jacob - 4/2/1865 at Southside RR VA - Buried on battlefield (Memorable Headstone in Weaver

Settlement Cemetery, Granger) - Listed on Soldiers Monument in Granger. Was 43 years 3 months and 15 days old at time of death. Son Jacob also served during the war. Had very bad diarrhea in service. In White House, VA and Mt. Pleasant, DC hospitals. (Military & Pension Files, 1865 NYS Census Granger, 1865 Allegany County Town Clerk Register Granger, Granger American Legion, *Allegany & Its People*, 1850 Fed. Census Granger, Great grandson Ira L. Gelser)

Weaver, Jacob, Darling Co. I, 27th NY Infantry - 5/13/1861 at Angelica/2 yrs - 19 - INA - 5/21/1861 at Elmira - No bounty - Pvt, Pvt - 1st Bull Run, Yorktown, Gaine's Mill, Malvern Hill, 2nd Bull Run, South Mountain, Antietam, Fredericksburg, Franklin's Crossing - 5/31/1863 Honorable - Was not a casualty - Ira Ransom (B VT) & Cheney White Smith (B NY) Weaver - Hiram, William, Edwin R. Harriet B. Elisha - 7/27/1842 in Granger - Farmer - None Deceased - Never Married - None - 9/21/1864 at Andersonville (POW) - Andersonville (Memorial Headstone in Weaver Settlement Cemetery, Granger) - Also served with Co. D, 1st NY Veteran Cavalry, see below. Was sick in quarters when mustered. Father Ira also served during the war. (Military File, 1865 NYS Census Granger, Granger American Legion, *Allegany & Its People*, 1850 Fed. Census Granger, *Roll of Honor*)

Weaver, Jacob Darling Co. D, 1st NY Veteran Cavalry 8/28/1863 at Nunda/3 yrs - 21 - INA - 10/10/1863 at Geneva - $400 - Pvt, Pvt - Snicker's Gap - 9/21/1864 (per Military File) Honorable/ Deceased - POW, captured 3/4/1864 at Snickers Gap, Prison: Andersonville, DD, 9/21/1864 at Andersonville of scorbutus and diarrhea - Andersonville - Listed on Soldiers Monument in Granger. Two J. Weavers in *Roll of Honor*, one dying 9/21/1864 and the other 10/ 5/1864 at Andersonville Prison. Both were with the 1st Veteran Cavalry. Likely the same person. Also served with Co. I, 27th NY Infantry, see above. Also see above for personal information and sources of information.

Weaver, James Henry Co. F, 19th NY Cavalry - 8/9/1862 at Centerville/3 yrs - 27 - INA - 9/3/1862 at Portage Station - $50 - Pvt, Corp - Deserted House, siege of Suffolk, Manassas Junction, Bristoe's Station, Culpeper, Wilderness, Todd's Tavern, Spotsylvania, North Anna River, Pamunkey, Totopotomoy, Cold Harbor, Trevillian Station, Charles County Court House, before Richmond & Petersburg, New Market, Shepherdstown, Winchester, Fisher's Hill, New Market, Port Republic, Cedar Creek, Berryville, Gordonsville, Dinwiddie, Five Forks, Appomattox - 6/30/ 1865 Honorable - Was not a casualty - William & Rachael Lyon Weaver (Both B NY) - Joseph, J.L., Lorenzo, Milton - 1834 in Centerville - Probably a farm hand working for his father - Farm Hand - Huldah E. Stickles, married 7/2/1866 - None - 11/7/1866 in Water Cure Establishment, Dansville of liver disease - Bates Cemetery, Centerville - Present at Lee's surrender. Marched in Grand Review 5/23/1865. Had malaria December, 1862, was in Suffolk, VA hospital January - February 1864 on detached service with reconnoitering party. Promoted to Corp 1/1/1865. Retained his carbine and sabre at discharge. Brother Milton also served during the war. (Military & Pension Files, 1865 Allegany County Town Clerk Register Centerville, *History of Allegany County 1879*, Matteson, 1865 NYS Census Centerville, 1850, 1860 Fed. Census Centerville, Centerville American Legion)

Weaver, L.B. At least one source document indicates that a L.B. Weaver served in the military during the war. No evidence of such service has been located. The only possible L.B. Weaver located in the Census is a Lucian B. Weaver of Centerville, but no evidence of service for a Lucian B. Weaver has been located. No Weaver with given names beginning with L.B. served in any NY Civil War regiment. Several with a first name beginning with L. served, but no connection to the C-H-G area for any of these men has been identified. (Matteson)

Weaver, M.D. At least one source document indicates that a M.D. Weaver served in the military during the war. No evidence of such service has been located. No M.D. Weaver has been located in the Census. No Weaver with given names beginning with M.D. served in any NY Civil War regiment. Several with a first name beginning with M. served, but no connection to the C-H-G area for any of these men has been identified. (Matteson)

Weaver, Milton S. Co. A, 11th Illinois Infantry - 4/19/1861 at Cairo, IL/3 yrs - 21 - 5'4", Light Complexion, Gray Eyes, Brown Hair - 7/30/1861 at Freeport, IL - No bounty - Pvt, Pvt - No battles - 9/20/1861 Honorable/Deceased - DD, 9/20/1861 at Birds Point, MO hospital of typhoid fever - William & Rachael Lyon Weaver (Both B NY) - James, Joseph, J. L., Lorenzo - 1840 in Allegany County - Farmer - None Deceased - Never Married - None - 9/20/1861 in Bird's Point, MO - Freeport, IL - Brother James Henry also served during the war. (Military File, 1865 NYS Census Centerville, 1850, 1860 Fed. Censuses Centerville)

Weaver, William Unassigned (Co. B), 9th NY Cavalry - 11/10/1862 at Jamestown/9 months - 34 - INA - 11/11/1862 at Jamestown - No bounty - Pvt, Pvt - No battles - 2/3/1863 Honorable - Was not a casualty - William L. (B VT) & Eunice S. Dewey (B NY) Weaver - None - 1/27/1828 in Westford, VT - Farmer - Farmer/Granger Supervisor (4 yrs)/1880-86 keeper of the County Almshouse/ 1886-92 Superintendent of the Poor - Esther Parker - Everett I. - INA - INA - Was suppose to serve 9 months, served less than 3. The military surgeon who examined him found him "unfit for service." Was suppose to be assigned to Co. B, but apparently never reported due to discharge. No military record found, only Adjutant General Report. Grandparents William & Nancy Weaver. (Adjutant General Report 1894 Volume 3, 1865 Allegany County Town Clerk Register Granger, *Allegany & Its People*, 1860, 1870 Fed. Censuses Granger)

Weeks, Barzillai R. U.S. Navy Ships: *USS Tawah, USS Great Western, USS Cincinnati, USS Kittatinny, USS Potomac, USS W.G. Anderson.* - 9/1/1864 at Erie/1 yr - 27 - INA - 9/13/1864 - No bounty - Landsman, Master at Arms - Johnson Mills (probably others) - 9/13/1865 Honorable - Was not a casualty - Father, INA, Mother Ann - Brother William - 1826 or 27 in NYS - Farmer - INA - Charlotte A. Buck, married 12/18/1859 in Hermitage, Wyoming County - Fred, Mariette, Hattie, William, Frank - 11/23/1893 in Hume - Probably Nunda - *USS Tawah* was lost at the battle of Johnson Mills. (Military & Pension Files, 1890 Fed. Census Special Schedule Hume, 1892 NYS Census Hume, 1860 Fed. Census Geneseo.)

Weingartner, Felix Co. G, 116th NY Infantry - 7/29/1862 at Buffalo/3 yrs - 20 - 5'3", Light Complexion, Blue Eyes, Light Hair - 9/3/1862 at Buffalo - $100 - Pvt, Pvt - Port Hudson, Plain Stores, Sabine Cross Roads, Snicker's Gap, Winchester, Fisher's Hill, Cedar Creek - 5/18/1865 Disability/Honorable - WIA, gunshot to left thigh, 5/27/1863 at Port Hudson, LA - John & Kathaine Peterhaus - Had a brother named or called Albert who lived in Buffalo - 12/13/1834 in Switzerland - Farm Laborer - Farm Laborer - Never Married - None - 12/7/1918 in Soldiers Home in Bath -Bath National Cemetery (as Winegardner)- Was in Baton Rouge, LA hospital with gunshot wound. Was in and out of the Bath Soldiers Home over the years. Weinigartner in military index. Lived in Hume many years. His real name was Phillip Heimgartner. Claimed military misspelled it at his enlistment. (Military & Pension Files, 1880 Fed. Census (as Philip Winegardner) 1890 Fed. Census Special Schedule Centerville)

Wells, George Washington Co. F, 5th NY Cavalry - 9/2/1861 at Pike/3 yrs - 21 -INA - 9/21/1861 at NYC - No bounty - Pvt, Pvt - New Market, Port Republic, Orange County Court House, 2nd Bull Run, Antietam, New Baltimore, Hanover, PA, Gettysburg, Hagerstown, Ream's Station, Berryville - 9/21/1864 Honorable - POW, captured 7/6/1863 at Hagerstown, Prison: Richmond, paroled early September 1864, - Nathaniel M. & Polly Wright Wells (Both B NY) - Ann G. (Phillips), Miles W., George M., Joshua, Mary A., William H., Arminia L. (Daine), Henry C., Nathaniel M., Julia L., Lydia - 12/16/1840 in Pike - Probably a farm laborer for his father - Carpenter - 1st Minerva Button, married 1859 (died 1863), 2nd Flora Λ. Daine, married 3/15/1866 in Gainesville - Flora, Clifford A., Cora S., 2 others - 2/15/1908 in Farmington, MN - Covent House Cemetery, Farmington - Brothers Miles and William also served during the war. May have been a deserter in May and June of 1863, but was never court-martialed. Also thought to be a deserter when he was a POW. (Military & Pension Files, 1865 Allegany County Town Clerk Register Hume, 1850, 1860 Fed. Census Hume, 1900 Fed Census Dakota County)

Wells, Miles W. Co. F, 5th NY Cavalry - 8/25/1861 at Pike/3yrs - 23 - 6', Light Complexion, Dark Eyes, Black Hair - 9/21/1861 at NYC - No bounty - Pvt, Sgt - New Market, Port Republic, Orange County Court House, 2nd Bull Run, Antietam, Aldie, New Baltimore, Hanover, PA, Gettysburg, Hagerstown, Culpeper, Hay Market, Ellis Ford, Todd's Tavern, Wilderness, Cold Harbor, Ream's Station, Berryville - 9/21/1864 Honorable - Was not a casualty - Nathaniel M. & Polly Wright Wells (Both B NY) - Ann G. (Phillips), Miles W., George M., Joshua, Mary A., William H., Arminia L. (Daine), Henry C., Nathaniel M., Julia L., Lydia. - 10/1/1838 in Pike - Farmer - Farmer - Eliza Babbitt, married 10/17/1865 in Pike - INA - 2/14/1914 in Hume - Lamont Road, East Koy - Promoted to Corporal at enlistment, to Sgt 6/20/1862. Had chronic diarrhea and piles at Warrenton, VA 8/25/1862. Brothers George W. and William also served. (Military & Pension Files, 1890 Fed. Census Special Schedule Hume, Matteson, 1865 Allegany County Town Clerk Register Hume, 1850, 1910 Fed. Censuses Hume)

Wells, William Harrison Co. F, 5th NY Cavalry - 10/23/1861 at Pike/3 yrs - 19 - 5'9", Light Complexion, Dark Blue Eyes, Brown Hair - 10/28/1861 at Staten Island - No bounty - Pvt, Pvt - New Market, Port Republic, Orange County Court House, 2nd Bull Run, Antietam, Aldie, Hanover, PA, Gettysburg, Hagerstown, Culpeper, Hay Market - 2/15/1864 Honorable/Deceased - POW, captured 2/13/1863 at New Baltimore, Prison: Richmond, paroled 3/18/1863 at City Point, VA, POW, captured 1/22/1864 at Ellis Ford, Prison: Andersonville, DD, possibly 2/15/1864 at Andersonville of scorbutus or 2/8/1864 at Richmond in Howard's Grove Hospital - INA - Nathaniel M. & Polly Wright Wells (Both B NY) - Ann G. (Phillips), Miles W., George M., Joshua, Mary A., William H., Arminia L. (Daine), Henry C., Nathaniel M., Julia L., Lydia - 2/4/1842 in Pike - Farmer - None Deceased - Never Married - None - 2/15/1864 in Andersonville (POW) - Andersonville - Was on picket duty when captured at Ellis Ford. Brothers George and Miles also served during the war. (Military File, 1865 NYS Census Hume, Allegany County Web

<u>Welstead, James F.</u> Co. I, 136th NY Infantry - 8/30/1862 at Nunda/3 yrs - 18 - 5'5", Dark Complexion, Brown Eyes, Black Hair - 9/25/1862 at Portage - No bounty - Pvt, Pvt - No battles - 2/4/1863 Disability/Honorable - Was not a casualty - John & Margaret Wilcox Welstead (Both B England) - Betsey, John, William, Jane (Ralf), Thomas, Daniel - 2/20/1844 in Granger - Farmer - Laborer - 1st Hattie Clubine, married 9/23/1866 (Died 4/13/1873), 2nd Clara Geralthine Cleveland, married 12/17/1876 in Platteville, NE - Ernest, Myrtle, Agnes Edna, James A., Thomas B., Daniel W., Baby, died immediately, William E., Ida Victoria, 2/7/1940 in Cedar Bluffs, NE - Ridge Cemetery, Fremont, NE - Disability discharge due to chronic diarrhea. November - December 1862 sick in Fairfax, VA hospital. Had no middle name, but used initial *E.* primarily to avoid confusion with his brother John. Brother John H. also served during the war. 1850 Census says Father John born in England, Mother Margaret in NY. (Military & Pension Files, *Allegany & Its People*, 1860 Fed. Census Granger, 1880 Fed. Census Dodge, NE, 1865 Allegany County Town Clerk Register Granger.

<u>Welstead, John H.</u> Battery F, 1st Illinois Light Artillery - 11/27/1861 at Elkhorn, IL/3 yrs - 25 - 5'5" - 2/20/1862 at Springfield, IL - $100 - Pvt, Artificer - siege of Corinth, siege of Vicksburg, siege of Jackson, Trenton, GA Tunnel Hill, Missionary Ridge, Resaca, Dallas, New Hope Church, Allatoona Hills, Kenesaw Mountain, Atlanta, Jonesboro - 1/4/1865 Honorable - Was not a casualty - John & Margaret Wilcox Welstead (Both B England) - Betsey, William, Jane (Ralf), Thomas, James, Daniel - 9/1836 in Granger - Laborer - Farmer/Carpenter - 1st Harriet Stamer (Divorced 9/18/1876 at Carroll County, IL), 2nd Jane Hutton, married 3/4/1878 in Wahoo, IL (Died 2/22/1899) - Jessie, Maud M., Claud R. - 12/2/1905 in Dixon, IL - Oakland Cemetery, Dixon, IL - Appointed Artificer 1/1/1863. Brother James also served during the war. Moved to IL about 1860. After war moved to Nebraska. 1900 Census says parents born in England. 1850 Census says John born England, Margaret born NY, probably correct. (Military & Pension Files, *Allegany & Its People*, 1850 Fed. Census Granger, 1870 Fed. Census Bennington, IA, 1900 Fed. Census Dixon IL)

<u>Westbrook, George W.</u> Co. A, 104th NY Infantry - 11/29/1861 at Geneseo/3 yrs - 20 - 5'11", Light Complexion, Blue Eyes, Brown Hair, Scar on right leg - 2/26/1862 at Geneseo - No bounty - Pvt, Pvt - Cedar Creek, 2nd Bull Run, South Mountain, Antietam - 12/9/1862 Disability/ Honorable - WIA, gunshot to head at Antietam, 9/17/1862 - S.E. (B VT) & Mary (B England) Westbrook - Elizabeth - 10/21/1841 or 42 in Perry or Castile - Farmer - Laborer/Hotel Owner - Estella P. Nichols, married 12/24/1860 in Castile - George, Josephine, Hattie, Laura, Blanch, Blossom, Kittie - 7/13/1917 in Soldiers Home, Bath - Warsaw - Disability discharge due to hypertrophy of heart. Had typhoid fever while in service. Owned a hotel in Hunt, which he built, but lost it due to poor management. Had a running battle with his wife over who left who. He moved out in 1889. Son George was killed in the Spanish American War. (Military & Pension Files, 1865 NYS Census Hume, 1860 Fed. Census Castile, 1850. Fed Census Perry, 1870 Fed. Census Portage, 1910 Fed. Census Sheldon)

<u>Whaley, W.A. Marcus</u> Co. C, 104th NY Infantry - 10,1861 at INA/3 yrs - 23 - 6'1", Dark Complexion, Brown Eyes, Black Hair - 2/26/1862 at Geneseo - No bounty - Pvt, Pvt - defense of

DC - 6/26/1862 Honorable/Deceased - DD, 6/26/1862 at regimental hospital, Weaversville, VA of typhoid fever - Charles & Angeline Whaley (Both B NY) - Amelia - July 20, 1838 in Michigan (Allegany County per military) - Farmer - None Deceased - Never Married - None - 6/26/1862 in Weaversville, VA - Per military records, Catlett's Station, VA Headstone at Rogers cemetery, Centerville - A letter in his military file to his mother from a comrade states, "We buried him in the open field under a wide spreading butternut tree between Catlett's Station (a rail road depot) & Weaversville about ½ mile from either place. The grave is about 20 rods from the road - - we put up a headboard inscribed on it, 'W.A. Whaley, Co. C, 104th N.Y.S. V. died in camp at Catlett's Station, VA June 26, 62." - (Military & Pension Files, Matteson, 1865 NYS Census Centerville, 1860 Fed. Census Centerville, 1850 Fed. Census Pike)

White, C. H. At least one source document indicates that White served in the military during the war. No evidence of such service has been located. There is a Charles White in the 1860 Granger Federal Census. No C.H. White served in any NY Civil War regiment. Many Whites with a first name beginning with C. served. (Matteson)

Whitney, Edwin Merchant Co. D, 4th NY Heavy Artillery - 8/13/1862 at Rochester/3 yrs - 35 - 5'11", Florid Complexion, Blue Eyes, Light Hair - 8/13/1862 at Rochester - $100 - Pvt, Pvt - Spent entire service with, first his regiment's band, and then with the 2nd Army Corps Band - 6/3/1865 Honorable - Was not a casualty - William & Lydia Merchant Whitney (Both B NY) - William - 9/19/1827 in Warsaw - Moulder/Machinist - Pattern Maker - Laura A. Pride, married 9/25/1849 in Otsego County - Morris P., Jennie C. (married Thomas H. Culver) - 2/2/1875 in Wiscoy of chronic diarrhea and rheumatism, both acquired in service according to pension application of wife - Wiscoy - Brother William also served during the war. Marched in Grand Review 5/23/1865. (Military & Pension Files, Allegany County Web Site, 1865 Allegany County Town Clerk Register Hume, 1890 Fed. Census Special Schedule Hume, 1865 NYS Census Hume, 1860, 1870 Fed. Censuses Hume)

Whitney, W. George Confusion over name. See entry for William Graves Whitney. (Matteson)

Whitney, William Graves Co. D, 4th NY Heavy Artillery - 8/13/1862 at Portageville/3 yrs - 22 - 5'9", Florid Complexion, Blue Eyes, Light Hair - 8/13/1861 at Rochester - $50 - Pvt, Sgt - No battles - 6/15/1865 Honorable - Was not a casualty - William G. & Lydia Merchant Whitney (Both B NY) - Edwin - 5/19/1837 in Warsaw - Machinist - Engine Builder/Machinist - Sylvia Jennie Baker, married 1/25/1868 in Portageville - William C., Mary J., Angie W. - 3/3/1899 in Cuba - Wiscoy - Brother Edwin also served during the war. Promoted to Sgt 9/1/1862. , Was detached from his regiment and spent almost his entire service at Hart Island, NY taking care of conscripts. Sick at Ricker's Island, winter 1863/64 with rheumatism. Charter Member of Burnside G.A.R. Post 237. (Military & Pension Files, 1890 Fed Census Special Schedule Hume, Fillmore American Legion, 1865 NYS Census Hume, *Allegany & Its People*, 1865 Allegany County Town Clerk Register Hume, Matteson, 1860, 1870 Fed. Censuses Hume)

Whittle, William C. Co. E, 85th NY Infantry - 9/1/1861 at Granger/3 yrs (Re-enlisted 1/1/1864) - 27 (Military File says 45, a mistake)- INA - 10/10/1861 at Elmira - $100 - Pvt, Pvt - Defence of

DC, siege of Yorktown, Williamsburg, Fair Oaks, before Richmond, Plymouth - 9/25/1864 Honorable/Deceased - POW, captured 4/20/1864 at Plymouth, NC, Prison: Andersonville, DD, 9/25/1864 at Andersonville of scorbutus - Robert & Dinah Sophia Whittle (Both B England) - Thomas, George, Elizabeth, Mary Ann, Christine H., Caroline - 1838 in Allegany County - Farm Laborer - None Deceased - Never Married - None - 9/25/1864 in Andersonville (POW) - Andersonville - Listed on Soldiers Monument in Granger. (Granger American Legion, Matteson, *History of Allegany County 1879*, *Allegany & Its People*, 1850 Fed. Census Granger, 1860 Fed. Census Dover, IL)

Wicks, Peter M. (Weeks) Co. I, 160th NY Infantry - 8/28/1862 at Allen/3 yrs - 38 - 5'9", Dark Complexion, Grey Eyes, Dark Hair - 11/21/1862 at Auburn - $50 - Pvt, Pvt - No battles - 12/28/1862 Disability/Honorable - Was not a casualty - Benjamin & Emeline Wicks (Both B NY) - INA - 3/1/1824 in NYC - Farmer/Blacksmith - Blacksmith - 1st Harriet W., 2nd Nancy Quay?, married 1897, George M. Syrillan?, Clarissa E., Chester A., Mary - 1910 - INA - Disability discharge due to epilepsy. Discharged at Fort Wood General Hospital. (Military & Pension Files, 1865 NYS Census Granger, 1865 Allegany County Town Clerk Register Allen, NYS Adjutant General Report Volume 40, 1860, 1870 Fed. Censuses Tompkins County, 1900 Fed. Census Grove)

Wiederight, John Co. F, 104th NY Infantry - 12/24/1861at Granger/3 yrs - 23 - 5'11", Light Complexion, Blue Eyes, Brown Hair - 2/26/1862 at Geneseo - No bounty - Pvt, Corp - Cedar Mountain, 2nd Bull Run, South Mountain, Antietam, Fredericksburg, Chancellorsville, Gettysburg - 1/24/1865 Honorable - WIA, gunshot to right foot at Gettysburg 7/3/1863, lost second toe - David & Elizabeth Boss Wiederight (Both B Germany) - Catherine, Jane, Amelia, Mary, Alanta, George - 5/1833 or 35 in Grove - Shoemaker - Shoemaker/Farmer/Grocer - Susan C. Saylor, married 4/29/1865 - Herbert L., Mary E.- 10/4/1904 in Granger - Short Tract - Deserted 9/18/1862, returned 11/9/1862. Appointed Corp 3/7/1862, reduced to ranks 9/18/1862 for being AWOL. Transferred to Co D., 10th VRC 12/26/1863. (Military & Pension Files, 1890 Fed. Census Special Schedule Granger, Matteson, 1865 NYS Census Granger, Granger American Legion, 1860, 1900 Fed. Censuses Granger)

Wight, Daniel Co. F, 5th NY Cavalry - 9/12/1861 at Centerville/3 yrs (Re-enlisted 2/11/1864) - 21 - 5'7", Light Complexion, Blue Eyes, Dark Hair - 9/21/1861 at NYC - $100 - Pvt, Pvt - New Market, Port Republic, Orange County Court House, Antietam, Aldie, New Baltimore, Hanover, PA. Gettysburg, Todd's Tavern, Wilderness, Cold Harbor, Ream's Station - 7/20/1864 Honorable/ Deceased - WIA, Ream's Station 6/30/1864, POW, captured 6/30/1864 at Ream's Station, Prison: Salisbury, NC or Richmond, KIA Ream's Station (6/30/1864 - Died 7/20/1864 at "Rebel Hospital, Columbia, SC" per pension file. Military file says at or near Richmond - Benjamin & Jerusha Lyon Wright (Both B NY) - Marvin, Edwin, Clinton, Orissa, Emory, Melinda, Wesley - 1/15/1841 in Centrville - Farmer - None Deceased - Never Married - None - Date of death is an estimate. Pension record says 7/25/1864. Military records say both July and August, 1864 - Columbia, SC (Maybe buried at Florence National Cemetery) - Detached as Orderly to General Franklin's 9/10/1863 and to General Sykes August,1863. November - February, 1863 detached to NY for recruiting purposes. Missing on General Wilson's raid 6/29/1864. Brothers Edwin and

Marvin also served during the war. (Military & Pension Files, *History of Allegany County 1879*, Matteson, 1865 Allegany County Town Clerk Register Centerville, 1865 NYS Census Centerville, 1850 Fed. Census Centerville)

Wight, Edwin Co. F, 19th NY Cavalry - 8/9/1862 at Hume/3 yrs - 18 - 5'10", Dark Complexion, Brown Eyes, Black Hair - 9/3/1862 at Portage Station - $150 - Pvt, Pvt - Deserted House, Franklin, Manassas Junction - 10/17/1864 Honorable/Deceased - KIA, 10/17/1864 at Manassas Junction (Centerville, VA) - Benjamin & Jerusha Lyon Wight (Both B NY) - Daniel, Marvin, Clinton, Orissa, Emory, Melinda, Wesley - 1/28/1844 in Centerville - Farmer - None Deceased - Never Married - None - 10/17/1864 in Centerville, VA - Arlington National Cemetery - Detailed to Ambulance Corps January - February 1863. (Military File, *History of Allegany County 1879*, 1865 Allegany County Town Clerk Register Centerville, 1850 Fed. Census Centerville)

Wight, Marvin Co. F, 5th NY Cavalry - 9/12/1861 at Centerville/3 yrs - 22 - 5'9", Light Complexion, Blue Eyes, Light Hair - 9/21/1861 at NYC - $100 - Pvt, 2nd Sgt - New Market, Port Republic, Orange County Court House, 2nd Bull Run, Antietam, Aldie, New Baltimore, Hanover, PA, Hagerstown, Gettysburg, Hay Market, Ream's Station, Berryville - 9/21/1864 Honorable - POW, captured 10/29/1863 at Hay Market, VA, Prison: Belle Island, Richmond, paroled 3/7/1864 at City Point, VA - Benjamin & Jerusha Wight (Both B NY) - Daniel, Edwin, Clinton, Orissa, Emory, Melinda, Wesley - 7/11/1839 in Centerville - Carpenter/Farmer - Carpenter & Joiner/ Tanner/Pattern Maker - Louise Bracken, married 10/17/1866 in Columbus PA - Nellie - 4/16/1929 in Corry, PA - INA - Brothers Daniel & Edwin also served during the war. Appointed Corp. 4/6/1862, QM Sgt 1/5/1863. (Military & Pension Files, 1865 NYS Census Centerville, *History of Allegany County 1879*, Matteson, 1865 Allegany County Town Clerk Register Centerville, 1850 Fed. Census Centerville, 1870 Fed. Census Columbus Boro)

Wight, Wilbur S. Co. C, 19th NY Cavalry - 9/13/1864 at Centerville/1 yr - 19 - 5'9", Fair Complexion, Blue Eyes, Brown Hair - 9/24/1864 at Elmira - $600 - Pvt, Pvt - Cedar Creek, Berryville, Gordonsville, Dinwiddie, Five Forks, Appomattox - 6/30/1865 Honorable - Was not a casualty - James & Aurelia Hall Wight (Both B NY) - Abby Jane, Cevalla - 1844 in Irondequoit - Farmer in Knox County, TN - Knox County, TN - Purchased his revolver and sabre for $11.00 at discharge. Present at Lee's surrender. Marched in Grand Review 5/23/1865. (Military & Pension Files, 1865 NYS Census Centerville, *History of Allegany County 1879*, Matteson, 1865 Allegany County Town Clerk Register Centerville, 1860 Fed. Census Centerville, 1870 Fed. Census Knoxville, TN)

Wilday, Sylvester (Wilde) Co. D, 19th NY Cavalry - 9/9/1864 at Genesee Falls/1 yr - 37- 5'8", Fair Complexion, Blue Eyes, Brown Hair - 9/13/1864 at Lockport - $400 - Pvt, Pvt - No battles - 1/11/ 1865 Honorable/Deceased - DD, 1/11/1865 at Jarvis Hospital, Baltimore of pneumonia - INA - INA - 4/27/1826 in Schoharie County - Roxana Lee, married 8/13/1848 in Portage - Leonard D., Diadama, Franklin M., William H., Martin D. - 1/11/1865 in Baltimore - Loudon National Cemetery, Baltimore - *Allegany & Its People* says he served with 104th Infantry. No evidence to support that has been located. Military says he was born at Burns. County Clerk says Schoharie. (Military & Pension Files, 1890 Fed. Census Special Schedule Hume, Allegany County Web Page,

1865 Allegany County Town Clerk Register Hume, 1865 NYS Census Hume, 1850 Fed. Census Granger, *Allegany & Its People*)

<u>Willard, Frederick</u> Co. I, 160th NY Infantry - 8/29/1862 at Caneadea/3 yrs - 43 - INA - $50 - Sgt, Sgt - Gunboat Cotton, Fort Bisland, assault on Port Hudson, Sabine Cross Roads - 10/14/1864 Honorable/Deceased - DD, 10/14/1864 at McKenis Mansion, Baltimore of typhoid fever - Marcus & Lydia Abby Willard - INA - 8/13/1818 in Charleston, NH - Millwright - None Deceased - Rachael E. Washburn, married 2/4/1841 - Summer Clary, Mary, Charles, William, Lydia, Ellory, Ida, Ephraim, Franklin - 10/14/1864 in Baltimore - Pine Grove Cemetery, Fillmore - Burnside G.A.R. Post 237 Marker at grave. Originally buried in Baltimore 10/16/1864. Body later taken back to Fillmore by friends. (Military & Pension Files, Allegany County Web Site, Matteson, Fillmore American Legion, 1865 Allegany County Town Clerk Register Caneadea, 1860 Fed. Census Granger)

<u>Willard, Samuel</u> Co. G, 136th NY Infantry - 8/9/1862 at Geneseo/3 yrs - 26 - 5'9", Light Complexion, Blue Eyes, Dark Hair - 9/25/1862 at Portage - $100 - Pvt, Pvt - Chancellorsville, Gettysburg, siege & occupation of Atlanta - 6/6/1865 Honorable - WIA, 7/2/1863 at Gettysburg (wound not described) - Alvanious (B NH) & Lydia (B MA) Willard - INA - 3/30/1836 in Portage - Farmer - Miller, Day Laborer - Eunice Bennett, married 3/8/1860 at Short Tract - Warren, Hattie, Lizzie H., Ernest Delbert - 10/10/1915 at Springfield, IA - INA - AWOL, 5/13/1863 at Stafford, VA Sick with intermittent fever at least five times. In hospitals in Frederick, MD, Louisville, KY, Chattanooga, TN, and Madison, IN. (Military & Pension Files, Medical Cards, 1865 NYS Census Granger, 1865 Allegany County Town Clerk Register Granger, 1850 Fed. Census Genesee, 1900 Fed .Census Brown Twp, IA. 1910 Fed. Census Waterloo, IA)

<u>Williams, Charles R.</u> Co. E, 85th NY Infantry - 9/1/1861 at Granger/3 yrs (Re-enlisted 1/1/1864) - 18 - INA - 10/20/1861 at Elmira - No bounty - Pvt, Pvt - INA except for Plymouth - 8/20/1864 Honorable/Deceased - POW, captured 4/20/1864 at Plymouth, Prison: Andersonville, DD 8/20/ 1864 at Andersonville of dysentery - Charles R. & Marion Electa Curtis Williams (Both B NY) - Washington A., Mary Adelia, Cloe A., Ella - 5/1/1843 per Town Clerk - Probably working for his father, a farmer - None Deceased - Never Married - None - 8/20/1864 at Andersonville (POW) - Andersonville - Listed on Soldiers Monument in Granger. Birth date in county clerk records is consistent with age at enlistment, but not consistent with ages in 1850 and 1860 censuses. Per those censuses, he would have been only 15 in 1861. Likely lied about his age and his birth date. Possibility that the soldier Williams is a different person than the census Williams, but not likely. Middle initial is also different. However the soldier's middle initial, *R,* is the same as the middle initial of the census Williams' father. His middle initial was probably *L.* (Military File, *History of Allegany County 1879*, Granger American Legion, Matteson, *Allegany & Its People*, 1865 Allegany County Town Clerk Register Granger, 1850, 1860 Fed. Censuses Portage.)

<u>Williams, David Wilbur</u> Co. E, 2nd NY Heavy Artillery - 9/21/1861 at Utica/3 yrs - 25 - 5'9", Light Complexion, Blue Eyes, Dark Hair - 10/2/1861 at Staten Island - No bounty - Pvt, Corp - 2nd Bull Run, defense of DC - Transferred to VRC 5/1864 - N/A (see below) - INJ, injured back & left testicle in an accident, late November early December 1863 - William J. & Jane Jones Williams

(Both B Wales, England) - Guy - 10/17/1836 in Floyd - Farmer/Porter - Farmer - Minnie Owens, married 9/27/1861 at Freedom - Maggie E., Minnie J. - 3/28/1914 at Centerville - Freedom - Also served with VRC, see below. Was accidently injured while erecting a log cabin for his company near Alexandria, VA. He fell astride a hewn log. Main job was company cook. (Military & Pension Files, 1865 NYS Census Centerville, 1890 Fed. Census Special Schedule Centerville, 1880, 1900 Fed. Censuses Centerville)

Williams, David Wilbur Unassigned, VRC - 5/1864 at Alexandria, VA - 27 - 5'9", Light Complexion, Blue Eyes, Dark Hair - N/A - No bounty - Pvt, Pvt - No battles - 8/31/1864 Disability /Honorable - Was not a casualty with the VRC - Disability discharge was due to injured back and testicles. VRC file is under the name Wilbure Williams. Initially served with 2nd Infantry, see above. Also see above for personal information and for sources of information.

Williams, James Co. E, 19th NY Cavalry - 9/1864 at Centerville/1 yr - 22 - 5'7", Fair Complexion, Blue Eyes, Brown Hair - 9/13/1864 at Elmira - $400 - Pvt, Pvt - Records unclear, probably Cedar Creek, Berryville, Gordonsville - 6/30/1865 Honorable - Was not a casualty - William J. & Sarah Williams (both B Wales) - Eliza (maybe Eleanor), Thomas, Ann, Mary, Samuel - 8/6/1842 in South Wales - Farmer/Carpenter - Farmer - 1st Theresa Kendall, married 3/10/1866, divorced (presumably) 4/10/1872. She went west with her brother Willis and was never heard from again. Rumor was she died in an insane asylum. 2nd Catherine (Kate) Williams, married 9/24/1872 (Died 12/10/1876), 3rd Hannah Jane Jones, married 3/27/1877 in Freedom - Flora, Thomas J., Fred D., Sara Jane - 5/23/1927 in Farmersville - Freedom - During March - April 1865 he was at Remount Camp. Marched in Grand Review 5/23/1865. One record said he came to U.S. at age 6. Manifest for the ship *Hyperion* which arrived at the port of New York on 6/30/1849, shows the following passengers: William Williams 35, Sarah 42, Eleanor 13, Thomas 12, Ann 3, Mary Ann Infant, Mary Murphy 30, Mary Murphy 18, Michael Claron 25, and James Williams 6. (Military & Pension Files, 1865 NYS Census Centerville, 1890 Fed. Census Special Schedule Centerville, 1865 Allegany County Town Clerk Register Centerville, 1850, 1880 Fed. Censuses Centerville)

Wilson, James Co. C, 26th NY Infantry - 8/13/1861 at Rochester/3 yrs - 22 - INA - 9/5/1861 at Rochester - No bounty - Pvt, Pvt - Cedar Mountain, Groveton, 2nd Bull Run, Antietam, Fredericksburg, Chancellorsville - 5/28/1863 (some records say 6/21/1863) Honorable - WIA, gunshot to right arm, 9/17/1862 at Antietam - Andrew & Elizabeth McConnell Wilson (Both B Scotland) - INA - 2/20/1843 in Clarendon - Laborer/Teamster - Mason - Mary L. Raymond, married 12/21/1870 in Columbia Farm, Venango County, PA - Andrew, William, Clara, Robert, John, Raymond - 11/18/1923 in Belmont - Forest Hills Cemetery, Belmont - Promoted to corporal 1/1/1862; reduced to ranks 2/28/1863 (no reason provided). Was in DC hospital with Antietam wound. Rejoined company 12/5/1862. (Military & Pension Files, 1890 Fed. Census Special Schedule, Centerville, 1860 Fed. Census Rochester, 1900 Fed. Census Rushford)

Wilson, Marvin - Co. F, 33rd NY Infantry -8/22/1862 at Nunda/3 yrs - 54 - 5'11", Dark Complexion, Blue Eyes, Brown Hair - 9/11/1862 at Albany - $25 - Pvt, Sgt - siege of Yorktown, Williamsburg, Ft. Magruder, Gaine's Mill, Malvern Hill, 2nd Bull Run, South Mountain, Antietam, Fredericksburg - 6/2/1863 Disability/Honorable - POW, captured 5/3/1863 at Fredericksburg, paroled 5/16/1863 (some records indicate that he was also wounded at Fredericksburg) - INA - INA - 1807 in Litchfiled, CT - Farmer - Farmer - 1st Polly I., 2nd Catherine M. Christopher, married 9/8/1867 in Brooks Grove - INA - 6/10/1885 in Nunda - Church Street Cemetery Dalton - Disability discharge due to old age, general debility. (Military & Pension Files, 1860 Fed. Census Belfast, 1870 Fed. Census Nunda, 1890. Fed Census Special Schedule Granger)

<u>Wolsey, William J. (Woolsey)</u>   Co. F, 19th NY Cavalry - 8/8/1862 at Oramel/3 yrs - 23 - INA - 9/3/1862 at Portage Station - $100 - Pvt, Sgt - Deserted House, siege of Suffolk, Franklin, Manassas Junction, Bristoe's Station, Culpeper, Wilderness, Todd's Tavern, Spotsylvania, North Anna River, Yellow Tavern, Pamunkey, Totopotomoy, Cold Harbor, Trevillian Station, Charles County Court House, before Richmond & Petersburg, New Market, Shepherdstown, Winchester, Fisher's Hill, New Market, Cedar Creek, Berryville, Dinwiddie, Five Forks, Appomattox - 6/30/1865 Honorable - WIA, gunshot to abdomen and upper right arm at Berryville, 8/24/1864 - William David & Esther Drew Wolsey (Both B NY) - Spence, Fred, Frank - 11/23/1840 in Weschester County - Clerk - Hotel Clerk - Never Married - None - 11/5/1883 at Warren, PA - Warren - Promoted Corporal 6/1/1863, Sgt 2/1/1864, Q.M. Sgt 1/20/1865. Present at Lee's surrender. Marched in Grand Review 5/23/1865. Was in Field Hospital, Fredericksburg, Patterson Hospital, Baltimore, and Chestnut Hill Hospital, Philadelphia. Language in *History of Allegany County 1879* appears to tie him to the C-H-G area. However, a review of his records indicates that, while he lived in the surrounding areas (Oramel, Portage Station), he apparently never lived in the C-H-G area. (Military & Pension Files, *History of Allegany County 1879*, 1850 Fed. Census NYC, 1880 Fed. Census Eldred. PA,1865 Allegany County Town Clerk Register Caneadea)

<u>Wood, Emery M.</u> Co. C, 104th NY Infantry - 11/13/1861 at Geneseo/3 yrs - 20 - 5'7", Dark Complexion, Dark Brown Eyes, Black Hair - 2/26/1862 at Geneseo - No bounty - Pvt, Pvt - Cedar Creek, 2nd Bull Run, South Mountain, Antietam - 10/3/1862 Honorable/Deceased - DD, 10/3/1862 at Physicians Mills Hospital, MD of a service related disease (exact disease not in files) - Elisha & Aurelia Palmer Wood (Both B NY) - Ashford S., Marion, Ella F., Lucy - 1840 or 41 in Centerville - Farmer - None Deceased - Never Married - None - 10/3/1862 in Physician's Hospital, MD - Rogers Cemetery Centerville - Sick on furlough in Centerville, 2/20/1862 to July. (Military File, 1865 NYS Census Centerville, Matteson, Centerville American Legion, 1865 Allegany County Town Clerk Register Centerville, 1860 Fed. Census Centerville)

<u>Woodworth, Jerome B.</u> Co. B, 2nd NY Mounted Rifles - 12/7/1863 at Pike/3 yrs - 17 - 5'9", Light Complexion, Blue Eyes, Light Hair - 1/12/1864 at Ft. Porter, Buffalo - No bounty - Pvt, Pvt - Spotsylvania, North Anna River, Pamunkey, Totopotomoy, Hanover Court House, Cold Harbor, Bethesda Church, siege of Petersburg, Popular Springs Church, Pegram's Farm, Hatcher's Run, Weldon RR, Dinwiddie - 8/10/1865 Honorable - WIA, gunshot to thigh 6/16/1864 at Petersburg, (apparently was not serious), WIA, 3/31/1865? at Dinwiddie, lost hand? - Washburn & Caroline Woodworth (Both B VT) - Joseph M., Eleanor - 5/15/1846 in Pike - Farmer - Farmer - 1st Ida (Died 12/31/1871), 2nd Lily Armour, married 1/7/1892 in Houghton - Clifford, Norma M. - 6/25/1926 in Hemlock - Richmond Center Cemetery, Town of Richmond, Ontario County - Was in several National Soldiers Homes including Tennessee, Ohio and Virginia. Brother Joseph also served during the war. For thigh wound was sent to Annapolis G.H. Was in Mt. Pleasant G.H. DC

8/24/1864 with chronic rheumatism. Was in City Point following hand loss. Some records indicate he lost his hand at Petersburg, but that does not seem possible since he was recorded as being present for duty at a number of battles in which his regiment engaged subsequent to Petersburg, and there is an entry about being wounded at Dinwiddie. (Military & Pension File, 1865 NYS Census Centerville, 1850 Fed. Census Pike, 1900 Fed. Census Ontario County, 1910 Fed. Census Tioga County PA)

Woodworth, Joseph Milton Co. A, 154th NY Infantry - 7/28/1862 at Carlton/3 yrs - 26 - 5'10", Light Complexion, Grey Eyes, Light Hair - 9/24/1862 at Jamestown - No bounty - Pvt, Pvt - Chancellorsville, Gettysburg, Rocky Ridge, Resaca, occupation of Atlanta - 6/11/1865 Honorable - Was not a casualty - Washburn & Caroline Woodworth (Both B VT) - Jerome B., Eleanor - 2/24/1834 in Wetherfield - Lumberman - Farmer - 1st Eliza A. Hendee (Died 12/18/1869), 2nd Ellen or Nellie E. Mosier (a divorcee), married 12/16/1873 in Pike - INA - 9/14/1916 in Soldiers & Sailors Home, Bath - Bath National Cemetery - Brother Jerome also served during the war. Was assigned as Brigade Teamster as of 7/3/1864 and remained there for the rest of the war. Marched in Grand Review 5/24/1865. Wife Helen claimed half of his pension. Claimed he had deserted her. Others claimed she deserted him. Her request was not approved. (Military & Pension Files, 1865 NYS Census Centerville, 1850 Fed. Census Pike, 1910 Fed. Census Centerville)

Worden, George Thomas Co. H, 136th NY Infantry - 8/29/1862 at Portage/3 yrs - 40 - 5'9", Light Complexion, Blue Eyes, Brown Hair - 9/25/1862 at Portage - No bounty Pvt, Pvt - Chancellorsville, Gettysburg, Wauhatchie, Orchard Knob, Tunnel Hill, Missionary Ridge, Resaca - 5/16/1864 Honorable/Deceased - WIA, gunshot to bowels, 5/15/1864 at Resaca, GA, KIA, died 5/16 in Atlanta Hospital of 5/15 wounds - Thomas & Rebecca Worden (Both B NH) - James P. - 1822 in Granger - Farmer - None Deceased - Mary C. Anderson, married 11/27/1850 in Leroy - Mary E., George E. - 5/16/1864 in Atlanta, GA- Chattanooga National Cemetery (as Wordin) - Listed on Soldiers Monument in Granger. Name is spelled Warden. Detailed as Provost Guard 4/9/1863 to 5/19/1863; 6/27/1863 to 1/15/1864. (Military & Pension Files, Medical Cards, 1865 Allegany County Town Clerk Register Granger, *Allegany & Its People*, 1860 Fed. Census Granger)

Wright, Aaron H. (Wight) Co. I, 27th NY Infantry - 5/13/1861 at Angelica?/2 yrs - 28 - 5'11", Dark Complexion, Black Eyes, Black Hair - 5/21/1861 at Elmira - No bounty - Pvt, Pvt - 1st Bull Run, Yorktown, Gaine's Mill, Malvern Hill, 2nd Bull Run, South Mountain, Antietam, Fredericksburg, Franklin's Crossing - 5/31/1863 Honorable - Was not a casualty - Lowell (B MA) & Catherine (B NY) Wright - Alfred, Joel, Lewis, Mary A. - Circa 1833 in Allegany County - Blacksmith - Blacksmith - Julia Ann - George Edward & Catherine Genette - INA - INA - Was company cook. November - December, 1861 AWOL. Returned January 1862. Also served with Co. F, 4th NY Heavy Artillery, see below. (Military File, 1865 Allegany County Town Clerk Register Hume, 1850, 1860, 1870 Fed. Censuses Rushford)

Wright, Aaron H. (Wight) Co. F, 4th NY Heavy Artillery - 12/19/1863 at Hume/3 yrs - 32 - 5'11", Dark Complexion, Black Eyes, Black Hair - 12/19/1863 at Elmira - $300 - Pvt, Pvt - INA, was detached to 6th Corps for entire enlistment - 9/26/1865 Honorable - Was not a casualty - Probably marched in Grand Review 5/23/1865. Sick in hospital July to December 1864. Also served with Co. I, 27th NY Infantry, see above. Also see above for personal information and sources for information.

Wright, Lewis L. Co. D, 64th NY Infantry - 8/15/1862 at Rushford/3 yrs - 28 - 5'7", Light Complexion, Hazel Eyes, Brown Hair - 10/16/1861 at Elmira - $25 - Pvt, Pvt - Fredericksburg, Chancellorsville - 2/10/1864 Disability/Honorable -INJ, ruptured abdomen 5/1/1863 at Chancellorsville - Daniel & Julia B. Wright (Both B CT) - INA - 10/27/1835 or 36 in Rushford - Boatman/Blacksmith/Laborer - Blacksmith - 1st Charlotte Frances Carpenter (Died 1877), 2nd Julia E. Baker Green married 12/1/1878 in East Rushford - Hershel S., Mary S., Marella, Edna A., Fred - 2/28/1912 in Hunt - Pine Grove Cemetery, Fillmore - Burnside G.A. R. Post 237 Marker at grave. Was late returning from a 30 day furlough (9/22/63 to 10/10/63). Returned 10/25/1863. In Fairfax Hospital with urinary problems as of 6/19/1863. Disability discharge due to sunstroke (at Fairfax Court House 6/15/1863) and hernia problems. File said he received both government and state bounties. (Military & Pension Files, 1890 Fed. Census Special Schedule Hume, Fillmore American Legion, Matteson, 1870 Fed. Census Granger, 1910 Fed. Census Hume.)

Yager, John H. Co. F, 19th NY Cavalry - 9/3/1864 at Allen/1 yr - 18 - 5'6", Light Complexion, Blue Eyes, Light Hair - 9/13/1864 at Elmira - $600 - Pvt. Pvt - Dinwiddie, Five Forks, Appomattox - 6/30/1865 Honorable - Was not a casualty - William & Martha Yager (Both B NY) - Mary, Albert, Archibald - 6/1/1846 in Vienna - Lumberman - Farm Laborer - Helen Frances Seaver, married 10/13/1867 (Died 1924) - Bertha Lillian, Walter Emons, John Paul, Daniel Seaver, Ferrie William - 9/13/1918 in Hume - Pine Grove Cemetery, Fillmore - Present at Lee's surrender. Marched in Grand Review 5/23/1865. Burnside G.A. R. Post 237 Marker at grave. Retained his pistol and sabre at discharge for $11.00. (Military & Pension Files, *History of Allegany County 1879*, Matteson, 1865 Allegany County Town Clerk Register Allen, 1860 Fed. Census Allen, 1910 Fed. Census Hume, Fillmore American Legion)

Youngs, David Co. C, 104th NY Infantry - 10/9/1861 at Geneseo/3 yrs - 32 - 5'7", Dark Complexion, Blue Eyes, Brown Hair, Face pitted due to small pox - 2/26/1862 at Geneseo - No bounty - Pvt, Pvt - No battles - 4/19/1862 Honorable/Deceased - DD, 4/19/1862 at Mt. Pleasant Hospital, DC of pneumonia - Peter (B NY) & Polly Wood (B MA) Youngs - Amos- 8/19/1829 in Williamstown - Farmer - None Deceased - Lucy W. or M. Hackett, married 7/3/1856 in Amity - Charlotte Rebecca and Florence Isabel - 4/19/1862 in Washington, DC - Military Asylum Cemetery, DC. Promoted Corporal 11/11/1861, reduced to ranks 4/1/1862, no reason cited. Lucy later married soldier Rodolph Fox of Hume who died as a POW at Salisbury Prison, NC on 12/11/1864. Her brother Leonard Hackett also served during the war. Leonard apparently worked for David's father Peter for several years. (Military & Pension Files, 1855, 1865 NYS Censuses Hume, Allegany County Web Site, 1865 Allegany County Town Clerk Register Hume, 1860 Fed. Census Hume)

Youngs, William M. Co. A, 104th NY Infantry - 11/2/1861 at Geneseo/3 yrs - 33 - 5'9", Light Complexion, Blue Eyes, Brown Hair - 2/26/1862 at Geneseo - No bounty - Pvt, Pvt - Cedar Creek, 2nd Bull Run, Antietam - 11/1/1864 Honorable - WIA, gunshot at Antietam 9/14/1862, not described, must have been a slight wound - Simeon (B VT) & ? (B RI) Youngs - INA - 1/27/1829 in Castile - Farmer - Farmer - Saphronia Greene, married 9/10/1846 in Granger - William, Edith, Caryl, Edwin - 3/16/1912 in Pike - Pike Cemetery, Telegraph road - Transferred to Co. E, 9th VRC 10/1/1863. Was in convalescent camp, Alexandria, VA much of 1863, and various hospitals for most of latter half of 1864. Was sick with diarrhea. (Military & Pension Files, Medical Cards, 1865 NYS Census Granger, 1890 Fed. Census Special Schedule Granger, 1850, 1880 Fed. Censuses Granger)

Zorn, Frederick Co. B, 140th NY Infantry - 8/25/1862 at Rochester/3 yrs - 30 - 5'6", Light Complexion, Blue Eyes, Dark Hair - 9/13/1862 at Rochester - $100 - Pvt, Pvt - Fredericksburg, Chancellorsville, Gettysburg, Wilderness, North Anna River, Pamunkey, Totopotomoy, Cold Harbor, siege of Petersburg, Weldon RR, Peeble's Farm, Hatcher's Run, Five Forks - 1/24/1866 Disability/Honorable - WIA, 4/1/1865 at Five Forks, gunshot to lower leg - INA, INA (relative John Zorn lived in Fillmore) - 9/16/1832 in Klein Mittling, Germany - Farmer - INA - Never Married - None - 2/24/1916 in Angelica - Pine Grove Cemetery, Fillmore - His injury was serious. His doctors declared him totally disabled for both military and civilian activities. Was in Armory Square, Douglas General, and Harewood hospitals in DC. According to his pension, he lived in Fillmore after the war. Burnside G.A.R. Post 237 Marker at grave. (Military & Pension Files, Matteson, Fillmore American Legion, 1900, 1901 Fed. Censuses Caneadea.

Addendum

Just as this study was being completed, another source document listing Civil War volunteers from the Town of Centerville was discovered. The document, a pamphlet entitled, "Centerville, NY - Diamond Centennial 175 Years 1808 - 1983 July 15-17, 1983" contains the names of 96 men who, according to the pamphlet, volunteered for the Civil War at Centerville. It was prepared by Centerville historians Lois Fiegl and Elizabeth Popp. The only information provided is the names.

Seventy of the 96 men listed are already included in the information contained in this study. Following is information regarding the other 26. Some of these 26 are included in the above information, but are listed here for clarification purposes. The pamphlet may spell their names differently or there may be other distinctions. Of the 26, only two appear to be soldiers who lived at least part of their lives in Centerville Township and who were not previously included in the study. Most of the others lived in non-C-H-G Allegany County townships or townships in other counties which directly border Centerville. It is possible that by the time of the Diamond Centennial, descendants of these men lived in the Centerville area and added their names to the list that was being compiled for the pamphlet, or they were included for some other reason. The 26 names were checked only against New York Civil War regiments. While it is possible, it is not likely, that any of them served with non-NYS regiments. Data for these men is not included in the summary information for this study.

Amos, Thomas - The only Thomas Amos who served in a NY Civil War regiment enlisted at Perry, NY. He was born, most likely, in London, Canada. He served with Company H, 179th New York Infantry. There is a Thomas Amos in the 1870 Federal Census for Centerville, but he was 49 in 1870, whereas the soldier Amos was only 18 in 1864. No other Census lists a Thomas Amos in Allegany County. There is a 14 year old Thomas Amos listed in the 1860 Census at West Farms, Westchester County. He is the right age, but he was born in NY whereas the soldier Amos was born in Canada.

Anderson, Charles - There is no Charles Anderson listed as living in Centerville in any Federal Census 1790 to 1930. A Charles Anderson did enlist in the 64th NY Infantry at Rochester on September 13, 1864, and his enlistment was credited to Congressional District 28. Many men enlisted in (or were credited to) the 64th at Rushford, NY, Centerville's next door neighbor. It is likely the Anderson who enlisted at Rochester was credited to the 64th and that he is the Anderson referred to in the pamphlet. Anderson deserted nine days after his enlistment, September 22nd, at Halifax, Pennsylvania. He was born in Canada..

Babcock, Cornelius - Cornelius served with Company G, 64th NY Infantry. He enlisted October 18, 1861, at Wellsville and was mustered October 19 at Elmira. He was born in Broome County. There is no evidence that indicates he ever lived in Centerville. However, many Babcocks have lived in Centerville over the years. Cornelius' pension file indicates he lived in Steuben County after the war.

Bills, Richard - A Richard Bills served with both the 4th NY Heavy Artillery and the 118th NY

Infantry. He is the only Richard Bills listed by the NYS Adjutant General Report as having served in a NY regiment during the Civil War. He was killed in battle in 1864. His family lived in Saratoga and Warren Counties post war. There is no Richard Bills in Centerville in any Federal Census from 1790 to 1930. Bills' wife Almira applied for his pension, and there was a Richard Bills with a wife Almira living in Saratoga County in 1860.

Burlingame, Albert - Albert Burlingame served with Company F, 19th NY Cavalry (1st NY Dragoons). He was born in Caneadea and lived his entire life in Belfast. He enlisted August 13, 1862, at Portageville. There is no evidence that he ever lived in Centerville. He is the only Albert Burlingame listed by the NYS Adjutant General as having served in a NY regiment.

Crawford, Malachi - Malachi Crawford served with Company F, 19th NY Cavalry (1st NY Dragoons). He enlisted August 11, 1862, at Portageville, just two days before Albert Burlingame per their military records. Crawford, like Burlingame, was from Belfast. There is no information that shows that he ever lived in Centerville. It is likely that he was a brother of Romanzo Crawford who did enlist at Centerville August 9,1862, and was mustered at Portageville August 19, 1862 according to his military file. The 19th Cavalry (in August 1862, the 19th was still the 130th NY Infantry) was mustered at Portage September 2, 1862. It is likely that Burlingame and Romanzo and Malachi were all mustered September 2 at Portage. Crawford is buried in Riverside Cemetery, Belfast.

Davis, Silas - Co. G, 64th NY Infantry - 9/14/1861 at Wellsville/3 yrs - 24 - 5'4", Dark Complexion, Grey Eyes, Brown Hair - 10/5/1861 at Elmira - No bounty - Pvt, Pvt - Siege of Yorktown, Fair Oaks - June 1, 1862, Deceased - KIA Fair Oaks - James (B VT) & Almira H. (B NH) Davis was from Steuben County. Davis' mother Almira applied for his pension. In 1860 a Silas Davis, age 22 (consistent with the soldier Davis' age), was living in Willing, Allegany County with his parents James and Almira. There is no evidence that he ever lived in Centerville. There was a Silas Davis living in Centerville in 1860. He was 17, which is not consistent with the age of the soldier Silas Davis.

Ellis, Damon - There is no military record for a Damon Ellis, nor does a Damon Ellis appear in any Census for Centerville. It is possible that he served under a name other than Damon. A Darwin Ellis from Centerville served with Company F, 19th NY Cavalry. His information is included in "The C-H-G Soldiers" section above.

Elmer, Henry - A Henry Elmer did serve with both Company C, 104th NY Infantry and Company B, 2nd NY Mounted Rifles. He enlisted in the Mounted Rifles at Rushford, however there is no evidence that indicates he ever lived in Centerville Township. He did live in Rushford for a short time.

Gould, Adelbert E. - An Adelbert E. Gould did serve with Company E, 5th NY Cavalry. He enlisted August 28, 1861, at Rushford. There is no information that indicates that he ever lived in Centerville. The 5th Cavalry Adelbert Gould is the only Adelbert Gould listed as having served in a NY regiment by the NYS Adjutant General.

Kendall, George H. - There is no George <u>H.</u> Kendall listed in the Civil War military index for New York. A George Kendall did serve with Company I, 111th NY Infantry, but there is no indication in his files that he was from the Centerville area. The same is true for a George Kendall, who served with Company H, 47th NY Infantry. Further, there is no George Kendall listed in any census (1790-1930) for Allegany County, except for a George Kendall, born in 1914, living in Bolivar in 1930.

Lamb, Reuben (Palmer) - The only Reuben Lamb who served with a NY regiment served with Company E, 9th NY Heavy Artillery. There is no evidence in his files or in any census that connects him to Centerville. The 9th Heavy Artillery Lamb is the only Reuben Lamb listed by the NY Adjutant General Reports as having served in a NY Civil War regiment. He was from Wayne County.

Merville, Sperry A. - Merville served with Company C, 19th NY Cavalry. He was from Eagle in Wyoming County, adjacent to Centerville. He died in the war and there is no evidence that he ever lived in Centerville.

Metcalf, Lyman B. - Metcalf served with Company D, 64th NY Infantry enlisting September 13, 1861, at Rushford. He also served with Company B, 2nd NY Mounted Rifles. There is no evidence that he ever lived in Centerville. The 64th Infantry and 2nd Mounted Rifles Metcalf is the only Lyman B. Metcalf listed by the NYS Adjutant General as having served with a NY Civil War regiment. He did live, and is buried, at Rushford.

Morris, John - Morris served with Co. I, 64th NY Infantry. Middle initial was likely *T* although some documents have it as *P* and others as *W*. Both of his children had a middle initial of *T*. Morris was from the Town of Allegany in Cattaraugus County. There is no evidence that he ever lived in Allegany County. He died June 4, 1872.

Morrison, Jeremiah R. - There is only one Jeremiah Morrison listed by the NYS Adjutant General. He enlisted October 7, 1863, in Company B, 2nd NY Mounted Rifles at Pike, or at least was credited to Pike. He had previously served with Company F, 33rd NY Infantry. He was born in Ireland and was killed in action at Cold Harbor June 6, 1864. There is no evidence that he ever lived in Centerville.

Morse, Sidney - There is no evidence that a Sidney Morse from the Centerville area served in the Civil War. However, there is a Sidney <u>Moore</u> from Centerville who served, and his information is included in "The C-H-G Soldiers" section above. The only Sidney Morse in a census for Allegany County (1790 - 1930) lived in Friendship in 1900. He was born in 1832. Two different Sidney Morses served in NYS regiments during the Civil War. One, from Syracuse, served with the 101 NY Infantry. The other, from Warwick, served with the 56th NY Infantry.

Palmer, Rudy - There is no Rudy or Rudolph Palmer who served in any NY Civil War regiment. Further, no Rudy or Rudolph appears in any Centerville Census. A Flavel Ruthvan Palmer from Centerville did serve during the war. It is possible he was called Rudy. Ruthvan's information is contained in "The C-H-G Soldiers" section above.

Roberts, John E. - There are several John E. Roberts listed in the NYS Adjutant General Report of Civil War Soldiers. However, a John H. Roberts served with Co. D, 64th NY Infantry, and information in his pension file indicates that he was a brother of Robert and Owen Roberts who both served with Co. D, 64th NY Infantry. Therefore, since Robert and Owen are also listed in the pamphlet, John H. is most likely the Roberts referred to in that pamphlet. A John Roberts from Centerville appears in the "Register of Draftees for Centerville 7/1863 to October, 1864." According to the Register that John Roberts, a farmer, was 33 and was born in Oneida County. He was accepted for service, but paid commutation.

While John H. Roberts' age when he enlisted in 1861 is listed as 33, census data indicate that he was most likely 31. The 1870 Census shows his age as 41 at the time of that census. There was a John Roberts, age 20, living in Centerville according to the 1850 Census. This was most likely the John Roberts drafted in 1863 who paid commutation. That John Roberts was born in NY, and may have been John W. Roberts.

Roberts, Owen W. - Owen Roberts was born in Oneida County and was living with his parents in 1850 and 1860 in Freedom, Cattaraugus County. He served with Co. D, 64th NY Infantry and died of consumption at Fort California, VA in 1862. He was a brother of John H. and Robert Roberts, both of whom also served with Co. D. There is no evidence that he ever lived in Centerville.

Roberts, Robert - Robert Roberts served with Co. D, 64th NY Infantry and Co. H, 9th NY Cavalry. Roberts was from Cattaraugus County, but also lived in Centerville at least in 1860 according to the 1860 Census. His brothers Owen and John H. also served with Co. D, 64th NY Infantry.

Roberts, age 35, volunteered for three years at Rushford on October 3, 1861. A prewar farmer, he was born in Wales and was 5'10" with blue eyes, brown hair and a dark complexion. He was mustered October 5, 1861, at Elmira. At the battle of Fair Oaks, June 1, 1862 he was severely wounded by gunshot to the right arm, thigh, and scrotum. His right testicle was damaged and his left was removed. He was treated at the U.S.A. General Hospital in Philadelphia, from which he may have deserted for a short time in July of 1862. Some records indicate he was on leave at that time. The charge of desertion was later removed. He received a disability discharge November 1, 1862.

His pension file indicates that he lived in Sandusky and Freedom post war. While the file does not mention a marriage, both the 1860 and 1870 Censuses show that he was married. He was, most likely, married in 1856, since the 1860 Census shows a three year old daughter Harriett. His wife's name was Margaret. His children included Harriett, Willis, Mary, Owen, Katie and Carrie (twins). (Diamond Centennial Pamphlet, Military & Pension Files, 1850, 1860, 1870 Federal Censuses, Cattaraugus County Records.)

His parents were most likely Hugh and Elizabeth Roberts, both born in Wales. His siblings, besides John H. and Owen, were probably Hugh, Benjamin, Jane Ann, and Elizabeth, and maybe others.

VanDusen, Charles - Charles Van Duzen served with Co. D, 64th NY Infantry. He was killed in action at Spotsylvania Court House May 12, 1864. Van Duzen was born in Freedom. He did live in Centerville and is listed in the Centerville 1860 Census working for Charles Torry. His name is spelled Vandeuser in the 1860 Census (Vndeuser in the Census Index). He is living with his parents in 1850, and his name is spelled Van Duzen (Van Deezen in the index.)

Van Duzen enlisted October 1, 1861, for three years at Rushford. He was mustered October 5, 1861, at Elmira. He was 5'11" with gray eyes, light brown hair, and had a fair complexion. Van Duzen received a $100 bonus for enlisting. It eventually was paid to his parents. On December 13, 1862, he was wounded at the battle of Fredericksburg and on December 17 he was admitted to Campbell General Hospital in Washington, DC. While still recovering, Van Duzen received a 30 day leave on January 12, 1863. Released from the hospital, he returned to his regiment August 11, 1863. On May 12, 1864, he was killed by canister shot through the head while charging the Spotsylvania Court House.

He was the son of John B. and Gertrude Van Duzen and was never married. His siblings included Ophelia, Lavancha, Julia A., Catherine, Sarah J., and Joel M. (Diamond Centennial Pamphlet, Military & Pension Files, 1850, 1860 Federal Censuses, Cattaraugus County Records.)

VanDuser, Charles - This is most likely Charles Van Duzen. The name was spelled many different ways. A Charles E. Van Deuser did serve as Staff with the 133rd NY Infantry. However, he was from Ulster County.

Veazey, Richard - There is no Richard Veazey listed as having served in any NY Civil War regiment. Further, no Richard Veazey appears in any Centerville Census. It may be that he served under a name other than Richard.

Warner, Lucius - There is no Lucius Warner listed as having served in any NY Civil War regiment. There is a Lucius Warner, age 8, listed in the 1850 Centerville Census. He is living with his parents Elwood? and Cornelia Warner. It may be that he served under a name other than Lucius.

Williams, Morris - A Morris Williams enlisted September 13, 1861, in Company D, 64th NY Infantry at Rushford. There is no evidence that he ever lived in the Centerville area. He is listed in both the 1850 and 1860 Federal Censuses living with his parents at Freedom, Cattaraugus County. He died March 6, 1862, of "fever" at Camp California, VA.

Sources

Books

Ackerman, F.M.	*Recollections of F.M. Ackerman, Co. I, 6th NY Cavalry Annual Reports of the New York State Adjutant's General Office*
Allegany County, NY	*History of Allegany County, New York 1806 - 1879*
Boston Publishing Co., Editors	*Above and Beyond A History of the Medal of Honor from the Civil War to Vietnam*
Beaudey, Louis N.	*Historic Records of the Fifth New York Cavalry"*
Bonnell, John C. Jr.	*Sabres in the Shenandoah*
Chamlee, Roy Z., Jr.	*Lincoln's Assassins*
Cole, James M. & Frampton, Rev. Roy E.	*Lincoln and the Human Interest Stories of The Gettysburg National Cemetery*
Davis, William C.	*The Battle of New Market*
Dyer, Frederick H.	*A Compendium of the War of the Rebellion*
Eicher, David J.	*Civil War Battlefields*
Evans, Charles M.	*War of the Aeronauts*
Faust, Patricia L. Ed.	*Historical Times Illustrated Encyclopedia of the Civil War*
Geer, Walter	*Campaigns of the Civil War*
Gelbert, Doug	*Civil War Sites, Memorials, Museums and Library Collections*
Hall, Hillman Allyn	*History of the Sixth New York Cavalry*
Hastings, Earl C., Jr. & David	*A Pitiless Rain - The Battle of Williamsburg 1862*
Hayden, F. Stansbury	*Military Ballooning during the Early Civil War*
Hewett, Janet B. Ed.	*The Roster of Union Soldiers 1861 - 1865*
Holberton, William B.	*Homeward Bound*
Jacob, Kathryn A.	*Testament to Union Civil War Monuments in Washington, D.C.*
Kirk, Hyland Clare	*Heavy Guns and Light - A History of the 4th New York Heavy Artillery*
Longacre, Edward G.	*Lincoln's Cavalrymen*
Lowry, Thomas P. M.D., Ed.	*Swamp Doctor The Diary of a Union Surgeon in the Virginia & North Carolina Marshes*
Matteson, Calvin	*Civil War Veterans in and Around Allegany County, New York*
Merrill, Georgia Drew	*Allegany & Its People - A Centennial Memorial History*
Mitchell, Joseph B.	*The Badge of Gallantry*
Musicant, Ivan	*Divided Waters*
Phisterer, Frederick	*Campaigns of the Civil War*
Steers, Edward Jr.	*Blood on the Moon - The Assassination of Abraham Lincoln*

Records

Library of Congress	Regimental Histories/Ackerman Letter
National Archives	Civil War Military Records
National Archives	Civil War Pension Files
National Archives	Civil War Carded Military Files
National Archives	Register of Men Drafted, July 1863 to October 1864
U.S. Army Military History Institute	Photographic Records
NYS Archives, Albany, NY	1865 Allegany County Town Clerk's Reports
Library and Archives of Canada, Ottawa	Canadian Civil War Soldiers
Museum of the Confederacy, Richmond	Meach Flag

Census Records

1810, 1820, 1830, 1840, 1850, 1860, 1870, 1880, 1900, 1910, 1920, 1930 US. Federal Census'
1855, 1865, 1875, 1892 NYS Census' - Centerville, Hume, Granger Townships, Allegany County, NY

Newspapers

Northern Allegany County Observer
The Angelica Reporter

Reports
Committee on Veterans Affairs, United States Senate - Medal of Honor Recipients 1863 - 1978

Diaries/Journals

The transcribed journal entries of Private Chauncey A. Cronk - Transcribed and written by Douglas J. Mergler

Libraries

Wide Awake Club Library, Fillmore, NY
Cuba Public Library

Historical Societies

Belfast, NY Historical Society
Cuba, NY Historical Society
Fillmore, NY Historical Society

Index

Farman, Samuel A., 46, 193
Fetterley, Henry, 110, 112, 193
Fillore, Millard, 4
Finch, Daniel, 66, 80, 194
Findley, Samuel, 194
Fish, John C., 80, 194
Fisk, Coroden, 80, 194
Fitch, Leander C., 80, 82, 194
Five Forks, 116
Flenagin, Ichabod P., 66, 80, 97, 98, 195
Flint, George W., 34, 72, 195
Foote, Gilbert, 63, 195
Foreign Born C-H-G Soldiers, 69
Fort Fisher, NC, 114
Foster, Adelbert R., 78, 79, 195
Foster, Theron W., 79, 80, 126, 196
Fox, Charles B., 46, 196
Fox, Chauncey J., 46, 196
Fox, Francis E., 86, 118, 197
Fox, Rodolph, 66, 80, 97, 197
Franklin, Gurdin J., 66, 83, 86, 197
Franklin, John C., 16, 19, 48, 73, 78, 111, 112, 197
    198
Franklin, Julius E., 198
Franklin Square, 13, 14
Franklin, TN, 107
Fredericksburg, VA, 39
Fuller, Omar W., 30, 80, 94, 112, 198
Fulton, James E., 198
Furbeck, Seymour H., 199

Gallagher, Hugh, 24, 31, 34, 35, 50, 199
Gardner, Eli, 34, 199
Gates, Jonathan, 199
Gettysburg, PA, 50
Gilbert, William R., 66, 90, 91, 92, 93, 94, 199
Gillett, Frederick A., 43, 80, 200
Gillett, William B., 200
Gloden, Lamont J., 92, 200
Goodale, George P. 71, 111, 200
Goodrich, Albert D., 46, 201
Goodrich, Horace, 201
Goodrich, John O., 201
Gordon, John, 201
Gordonsville, VA, 108
Gorten, Jared A., 19, 201
Gould, Adelbert, 308
Grand Review, The, 120
Granger, Cassius C., 92, 116, 202
Granger, James M., 80, 202
Granger, Peter V., 19, 202
Granger, Theodore P., 202

Granger Civil War Monument, 90
Grant, Ulysses S., 15, 21,55, 58, 64, 73, 75, 87, 108
Gravelly Run, VA, 116
Gray, William W., 46, 66, 111, 202
Green, Henry, 73, 74, 203
Green, Willard W., 80, 203
Greenhow, Rose O. 11
Gregory, Emory, 203
Griffith, Henry, 46, 111, 203
Griggs, Jasper M., 34, 36, 39, 50, 67, 96, 204
Grover, Charles, 46, 204
Grover, David, 19, 204
Groves, Richard D., 9, 24, 25, 26, 71, 90, 204
Guernsey, Samuel P., 80, 205
Guptill, Joseph N., 80, 90, 205

Hackett, Leonard O., 80, 205
Haley, Patrick, 34, 205
Hall, John D., 34, 206
Hall, John M., 46, 206
Hall, Robert , 80, 206
Hall, V.M., 207
Hall, William C., 66, 84, 86, 90, 207
Hamlin, Alva, 46, 66, 207
Hammond, Augustus, 207
Hammond, John M. Jr., 24, 31, 207
Hammond, Sylvanus, 208
Hanley, Patrick, 208
Hanover Court House, VA, 23
Harrington, William D., 84, 120, 208
Hart, Mary, 6, 125
Harwood, George W., 208
Harwood, John R., 46, 208
Haskins, John W., 209
Hatch, Cyrus J. Jr., 46, 118, 209
Hatch, Orlando F., 80, 209
Hatcher's Run, VA, 69, 106
Hayes, Rutherford B., 103
Hay Market, VA, 64
Hawley, Asa, 111, 209
Hawley, William, 46, 209
Heavy Artillery, 4th New York, 2, 20, 79
Henderson, Harry, 210
Hendricks, John, 210
Henretty, Francis R., 94, 210
Hickok, Samuel L., 80, 210
Higby, Ephraim B., 34, 210
Higby, Ira W., 34, 48, 49, 211
Higgins, Leland, 111,112, 211
Hildreth, Daniel A., 67, 73, 74, 80, 211
Hildreth, James W., 80, 94, 211
Hildreth, Oscar R., 19, 212

ABOUT THE AUTHOR

Robert N. Colombo was born and reared in Fillmore, Hume Township, New York. He holds degrees in history and government from the University of Buffalo. He is a retired Senior Executive Service Member of the U.S. Department of Labor, a veteran of the U.S. Air Force (including fourteen months in Saudi Arabia), and was a Peace Corps volunteer (Columbia, South America). He devoted six years to the research for this book.

Made in the USA